# UNDERSTANDING RESEARCH IN CLINICAL AND COUNSELING PSYCHOLOGY

# UNDERSTANDING RESEARCH IN CLINICAL AND COUNSELING PSYCHOLOGY

Edited by

**Jay C. Thomas**
**Michel Hersen**
*Pacific University*

**LEA**

2003

LAWRENCE ERLBAUM ASSOCIATES, PUBLISHERS
Mahwah, New Jersey                                    London

*Senior Acquisitions Editor:* Susan Milmoe
*Editorial Assistant:* Kristen Depken
*Cover Design:* Kathryn Houghtaling Lacey
*Production Editor:* Marianna Vertullo
*Full-Service Compositor:* TechBooks
*Text and Cover Printer:* Sheridan Books

This book was typeset in 10/12 pt. Times, Italic, and Bold.
The heads were typeset in Helvetica Bold, and Helvetica Bold Italic.

Lawrence Erlbaum Associates, Inc., Publishers
10 Industrial Avenue
Mahwah, New Jersey 07430


**Library of Congress Cataloging-in-Publication Data**

Understanding research in clinical and counseling psychology / edited by Jay C. Thomas
and Michel Hersen.
    p.   cm.
Includes bibliographical references and indexes.
ISBN 0-8058-3671-3 (pbk. : alk. paper)
1. Clinical psychology—Research.   2. Counseling—Research.   3. Psychotherapy—
Research.   I. Thomas, Jay C., 1951–   II. Hersen, Michel.

RC467 .U53   2002
616.89′.0072—dc21                                                        2002026377

# Contents

# Preface

The development of *Understanding Research in Clinical and Counseling Psychology* is the result of our experiences teaching and working with students in professional psychology over many years. Although virtually all graduate programs require a course on research, the basis for that requirement is often shrouded in mystery for many students. Students enter their graduate training with the admirable ambition of learning skills important for assisting clients to make changes. Although they understand that practice may be somehow loosely based on research findings, the connection is not clear and the value of psychological research not readily apparent. In this book, we introduce students to research as an indispensable tool for practice.

This is a collaborative text. We invited authors we know to be experts in both psychological research and practice to contribute chapters in their particular areas of expertise. This approach has the advantage of each subject being presented by authors who are experienced in applying the concepts and who are enthusiastic about how the information can help both practitioners and researchers to advance knowledge and practice in psychology. The information may at times be complex, but it is never only of interest in the "ivory tower." The book reflects the concerns of the real world.

The book is divided into four parts. Part I (Foundations) contains four chapters that form the basis for understanding the material in the rest of the book. Part II (Research Strategies) consists of five chapters covering the most important research strategies in clinical and counseling psychology. Each of these chapters includes an illustration and analysis of a study, explaining the important decision points encountered by the researcher and how the results can be used to inform practice. Part III (Practice), a short section, comprises three chapters on issues related to actually planning, conducting, and interpreting research. Finally, Part IV (Special Problems) includes four chapters. The first of these addresses one of the most important controversies in mental health research today: the distinction between "gold standard" efficacy studies and more realistic effectiveness stud-ies. This nicely sets the stage for the next, which discusses how a psychologist can operate an empirically oriented practice and actually conduct research. The remaining two chapters focus on how to perform research with children and the elderly, respectively.

Overall, the book gives students what they need and want to know while staying at a size appropriate for a semester long course. Many individuals have contributed to bringing this book to fruition. First and foremost are the authors who agreed to share their expertise and experiences with us. Second are Carole Londerée, Kay Waldron, Alex Duncan, and Angelina Marchand, who provided technical expertise. Finally, but hardly least of all, are our many friends at Lawrence Erlbaum Associates, who understood the inherent value of this project.

Jay Thomas
Portland, Oregon

Michel Hersen
Forest Grove, Oregon

# I

# Research Foundations

# 1

# Introduction: Science in the Service of Practice

Jay C. Thomas
Johan Rosqvist
*Pacific University, Portland, Oregon*

Today, psychologists are called on to help solve an ever wider range of personal and social problems. It has been recognized that a large proportion of the population can benefit from psychotherapeutic services. Current estimates of the prevalence of mental disorders indicate that they are common and serious. Sexton, Whiston, Bleuer, and Walz (1997) cited evidence that up to one in five American adults suffers from a diagnosable mental disorder. The provision of psychotherapy services is a multibillion dollar industry (Sexton et al., 1997). In addition, clinical and counseling psychologists are asked to intervene in prevention efforts in situations involving individuals and/or families, prisons, schools, and, along with industrial and organizational psychologists, in the work setting.

When so many people trust the advice and assistance of psychologists and counselors, it is important that professionals rely upon a foundation of knowledge that is known to be valuable. Many students in clinical and counseling psychology wonder about the relevance of a research courses and of research in general pertaining to their chosen profession. These students often primarily value the role of the psychologist as helper and expect to spend their careers helping clients in dealing with important issues. Their ambition is very worthy, but we argue that effective helping can occur only when the best techniques are used, and that it is only through scientific research so that we can determine what is "best."

We illustrate this fundamental point through a brief history of treatment for obsessive-compulsive disorder (OCD) in which a client, "Sue," received the assistance she needed from an empirically based treatment.

## THE CASE OF SUE

Sue, a 28-year-old married woman, engaged in a broad range of avoidant and compulsive behaviors (Rosqvist, Thomas, Egan, Willis & Haney, in press). For example, she executed extensive checking rituals—hundreds of times per day—that were aimed at relieving obsessive fears that she, by her thoughts or actions, would be responsible for the death of other people (e.g., her 1-year-old child, her husband, other people that she cared for, and sometimes even strangers). She was intensely afraid of dying herself. She also avoided many social situations because of her thoughts, images and impulses.

As a result of these OCD symptoms and resultant avoidant behavior, Sue was left practically unable to properly care for herself and her child. In addition, she was grossly impaired in her ability to perform daily household chores, such as grocery shopping, cleaning, and cooking. Her husband performed many of these activities for her, as she felt unable to touch many of the requisite objects, like pots and pans, food products, cleaning equipment, and so on.

Additionally, Sue was unable to derive enjoyment from listening to music or watching television because she associated certain words, people, and noises, with death, dying, and particular fears. She also attributed losing several jobs to these obsessions, compulsions, and avoidance. Sue reported feeling very depressed due to the constricted nature of her life that was consumed with guarding against excessive and irrational fears of death.

Sue eventually became a prisoner of her own thoughts, and was unable do anything without horrendous fears and guilt. For all intents and purposes, she was severely disabled by her OCD symptoms, and her obsessions, compulsions, and avoidance directly impacted her child and husband.

Her fears were so strong, in fact, that she eventually became uncertain that her obsessions and compulsions were irrational, or excessive and unreasonable. She strongly doubted the assertion that her fears would not come true, even though she had little, if any, rational proof of her beliefs. She was unsuccessful in dismissing almost none of her obsessive images, impulses, thoughts, or beliefs. She had very little relief from the varied intrusions, and she reported spending almost every waking hour on some sort of obsessive compulsive behavior. She felt disabled by her fears and doubts, and felt that she had very little control over them.

Obviously, Sue was living a very low quality of life. Over the course of some years, she was treated by several mental health practitioners and participated in many interventions, including: medication of various kinds, psychodynamic, interpersonal, supportive, humanistic, and cognitive-behavioral therapies (individually and in groups), as both an inpatient and outpatient. Sue made little progress and was considered for high-risk, neurological surgery. As a last-ditch effort, a special home-based therapy emphasizing exposure and response prevention (ERP) along with cognitive restructuring was devised. This treatment approach was chosen because the components had the strongest research basis and empirical support. Within a few months, her obsessive and compulsive symptoms remitted and she was eventually sufficiently free of them to return to work and a normal family life. Thus, when research based treatment was applied, Sue, who was considered "treatment refractory," was effectively helped to regain her quality of life.

## The Role of Research in Treatments for Obsessive-Compulsive Disorder

OCD has a long history. For example, Shakespeare described the guilt-ridden character of Lady Macbeth as obsessing and hand-washing. Other, very early descriptions of people with obsessional beliefs and compulsive behaviors also exist, such as those having intrusive thoughts about blasphemy or sexuality. Such people were frequently thought (both by sufferer and onlooker) to be possessed, and they were typically "treated" with exorcisms or other forms of torture.

Obsessions and compulsions were first described in the psychiatric literature in 1838, and throughout the early 1900s, it received attention from such pioneers as Janet and Freud; however, OCD remained virtually an intractable condition, and such patients were frequently labeled as psychotic and little true progress was thought possible. That was until the mid-1960s, when Victor Meyer (1966) first described the successful treatment of OCD by ERP.

Since Meyer's pivotal work, the behavioral and cognitive treatment of OCD has been vastly developed and refined. Now, it is generally accepted that 70% to 83% of patients can make significant improvement with specifically designed techniques (Foa, Franklin, & Kozak, 1998). Also, patients who still, initially, prove refractory to the current standard behavioral treatment, can make significant improvement with some additional modifications. OCD does not appear to be an incurable condition any longer.

This change has only been made possible by the systematic and deliberate assessment and treatment selection for such patients. That is, interventions for OCD, even in its most extreme forms, have been scientifically derived, tested, refined, retested, and supported. Without such a deliberate approach to developing an effective intervention for OCD, it would possibly still remain intractable (as it still mostly was just 35 years ago).

The empirical basis of science forms the basis of effective practice, such as what has made OCD amenable to treatment. This empirical basis is embodied in the *scientific method*, which involves the systematic and deliberate gathering and evaluating of empirical data, and generating and testing hypotheses based upon general psychological knowledge and theory, in order to answer questions that are answerable and "critical."

Answers derived should be proposed in such a manner so that they are available to fellow scientists to methodically repeat. In other words, *science*, and *professional effectiveness* can be thought of as the observation, identification, description, empirical investigation, and theoretical explanation of natural phenomena.

Ideally, conclusions are based upon observation and critical analyses, and not upon personal opinions (i.e., biases) or authority. This method is committed to empirical accountability, and in this fashion it forms the basis for many professional regulatory bodies. It remains open to new findings that can be empirically evaluated to determine their merit, just as the professional is expected to incorporate new findings into how he or she determines a prudent course of action.

Consider, for example, how the treatment of obsessions has developed over time. Thought-stopping is a behavioral technique that has been used for many years to treat unwanted, intrusive thoughts. In essence, the technique calls for the patient to shout "STOP," or make other drastic responses to the intrusions (e.g., clapping hands loudly, or snapping a heavy rubber-band worn on her or his wrist) to extinguish the thoughts through a punishment paradigm. It has since been determined that thought-suppression strategies for obsessive intrusions may have a paradoxical effect (i.e., reinforcing the importance of the obsession) rather than the intended outcome (reference). Since then, it has been established, through empirical evaluation and support, that alternative, cognitive approaches (e.g., challenging the content of cognitive distortions)—like correcting overestimates of probability and responsibility—are more effective in reducing not only the frequency of intrusions, but also the degree to which they distress the patient.

An alternative to thought-stopping, exposure-by-loop tape, has been systematically evaluated and its effectiveness has been scientifically supported. In this technique, the patient is exposed to endless streams of "bad" words, phrases, or music. As patient's obsessions frequently center on the death of loved ones, they may develop substantial lists of words that are anxiety producing (e.g., Satan, cribdeath, "SIDS," devil, casket, coffin, cancer). These intrusive thoughts, images, and impulses are conceptualized as aversive stimuli, as described by Rachman (see Emmelkamp, 1982). Such distortions and intrusions are now treated systematically by exposure-by-loop-tape (and pictures) so that the patient can habituate to the disturbing images, messages, and words. This procedure effectively reduces emotional reactivity to such intrusions, and lowers overall daily distress levels. Reducing this kind of reactivity appears to allow patients to more effectively engage ERP (van Oppen & Arntz, 1994; van Oppen, & Emmelkamp, 2000; Wilson, & Chambless, 1999).

The point of this OCD example is that over time, more and more effective methods of treatment have been developed by putting each new technique to empirical testing and refining it based on the results. In addition, the research effort has uncovered unexpected findings, such as the paradoxical effect of thought suppression. Traditional *thought-stopping* is in essence a method of thought suppression, whereby the individual by aversive conditioning attempts to suppress unwanted thoughts, images, or impulses. However, systematic analyses have revealed that efforts at suppressing thoughts (or the like), in most people, lead to an increased incidence of the undesired thoughts. It is much like the phenomenon of trying to not think about white bears when instructed to not think about them; it is virtually impossible! What has been supported as effective in reducing unwanted thoughts, whether about white bears, the man behind the curtain, or germs and death, is exposure by loop-tape. This method does not attempt to remove the offending thought, but rather "burns it out" through overexposure.

In light of this experience, it is prudent for the professional to incorporate these techniques into treating intrusive thoughts. Although a therapist may be very familiar with thought-stopping, it is reasonable to expect that the scientifically supported techniques will be given a higher value in the complete treatment package. This follows the expectations of many managed care companies, and it also adheres to the ethical necessity to provide the very best and most appropriate treatment possible for any given clinical presentation. To do anything less would do a great disservice to the patient, as well as put the professional into possible jeopardy for providing substandard care.

In these days of professional accountability and liability for our "product," it has become necessary to be able to clearly demonstrate that what we do is prudent given the circumstances of any particular case. Most licensing boards and regulatory bodies will no longer accept arbitrary, individual decisions on process, but rather dictates and expects that a supported rationale is utilized in the assessment and treatment process.

With this in mind, it has become increasingly necessary, if not crucial, that the professional engage in a systematic method to assessment and treatment selection in order to create the most effective interventions possible (given current technology and methodology). Today the empirical basis of science forms the basis of effective practice. This empirical basis is embodied in the scientific method, which involves the systematic and deliberate gathering and evaluating of empirical data, and generating and testing hypotheses based on general psychological knowledge and theory, in order to answer questions that are answerable and "critical."

Answers derived should be proposed in such a manner that they are available to fellow scientists to repeat methodologically. In other words, science, and professional effectiveness, can be thought of as the observation, identification, description, experimental investigation, and theoretical explanation of natural phenomenon.

Conclusions (or the currently most effective hypotheses) are based on observation and critical analyses, and not upon personal opinions (i.e., biases) or authority. This method is committed to empirical accountability, and in this fashion it forms the basis for many professional regulatory bodies. It remains open to new findings that can be empirically evaluated to determine their merit, just as the professional is expected to incorporate new findings into how they determine a prudent course of action.

## SCIENTIFIC METHOD AND THOUGHT

Early in the 20th century the great statistician, Karl Pearson, was embroiled in a heated debate over the economic effects of alcoholism on families. Typical of scientific battles of the day, the issue was played out in the media with innuendoes, mischaracterizations, and, most important, spirited defense of pre-established positions. Pearson, frustrated by lack of attention to the central issue, issued a challenge that we believe serves as the foundation for any applied science. *Pearson's challenge* was worded in the obscure language of his day, and has been updated by Stigler (1999) as "If a serious question has been raised, whether it be in science or society, then it is not enough to merely assert an answer. Evidence must be provided and that evidence should be accompanied by an assessment of its own reliability" (p. 1).

Pearson went on to state that adversaries should place their "statistics on the table" for all to see. Allusions to unpublished data or ill-defined calculations were not to be allowed. The issue should be answered by the data at hand with everyone free to propose their own interpretations and analyses. These interpretations were to be winnowed out by the informed application of standards of scientific thought and method. This required clear and open communication of methods, data, and results.

The classic scientific method involves the objective, systematic, and deliberate gathering and evaluating of empirical data, and generating and testing hypotheses based on general psychological knowledge and theory, in order to answer questions that are answerable and "critical." Answers derived should be proposed in such a manner that they are available to fellow scientists to methodologically repeat. Conclusions are based on observation and critical analyses, and not upon personal opinions (i.e., biases) or authority. This method is committed to empirical accountability. It is open to new findings that can be empirically evaluated to determine their merit. Findings are used to modify theories to account for discrepancies between theory and data. Results are communicated in detail to fellow scientists.

We accept the general outline of the scientific method just described. It has had its critics who object to one or another of the components. We explore each component in somewhat more detail and address some of the more common objections.

### Objective, Systematic, and Deliberate Gathering of Data

All research involves the collection of data. Such data may be self-report, surveys, tests, or other psychological instruments, physiological, interview, or a host of other sources. The most common approach is to design a data collection procedure and actually collect purposely data for a particular study. It is possible to perform archival studies, in which data that might bear on an issue are pulled from files or other archival sources, even though the information was not originally collected for that purpose. In either case the idea is to obtain information that is as free of the investigator's expectations, values, and preferences, as well as other sorts of bias. Originally it was expected that data could be obtained that was completely free of bias and atheoretical. That has not proven to be possible, yet objectivity in data gathering as well as analysis and interpretation remains as the goal for the scientist. No other aspiration has proven as effective (Cook, 1991; Kimble, 1989).

### Generating and Testing Hypotheses

Hypotheses are part of everyday life in psychological practice. A treatment plan, for example, contains implicit or explicit hypotheses that a particular intervention will result in an improvement in a client's condition. In the case of Sue, the hypothesis was that home based ERP would reduce her OCD symptoms to the point where she would no longer be a candidate for neurosurgery. Many research hypotheses are more complex than that one, but they serve an important purpose in meeting Pearson's Challenge. They specify what data are relevant and predict in advance what the data will show. Hypotheses are derived from theories and it is a poor theory that fails to allow us to make relevant predictions. Thus, by comparing our predictions against the obtained data, we put theories to the test.

Theories are used to summarize what is known and to predict new relationships between variables and, thus, form the basis for both research and practice. John Campbell (1990) provided an overall definition of theory as "... a collection of assertions, both verbal and symbolic, that identifies what variables are important for what reasons, specifies how they are interrelated and why, and identifies the conditions under which they should be related or not related" (p. 65). Campbell went on to specify the many roles which a theory may play:

> Theories tell us that certain facts among the accumulated knowledge are important, and others are not.
> Theories can give old data new interpretations and new meaning . . .
> Theories identify important new issues and prescribe the most critical
> research questions that need to be answered to maximize understanding of the issue.
> Theories provide a means by which new research data can be interpreted and coded for future use.
> Theories provide a means for identifying and defining applied problems.
> Theories provide a means for prescribing or evaluating solutions to applied problems.
> Theories provide a means for responding to new problems that have no previously identified solution strategy (Campbell, 1990, p. 65).

From abstract theories we generate generalizations, and from generalizations, specific hypotheses (Kluger & Tikochinsky, 2001). A useful theory allows for generalizations beyond what was previously known and often into surprising new domains. For example, Eysenck's (1997, cited in Kluger & Tikochinsky, 2001) arousal theory of extroversion predicts that extroverts will not only prefer social activities, but also other arousing activities, such as engaging in crimes such as burglary.

Karl Popper (1959), one of the most influential philosophers of science, has maintained that it is not possible to confirm a theory; all we can do is disconfirm it. If our theory is "All ravens are black" (this is a classic example dating back to the ancient Greeks), all we can say in the way of confirmation is that we have not observed a non-black one. However, observing a single non-black raven is sufficient to disprove the theory. The problem is compounded by the fact that the other day the author (Jay Thomas), observed a raven, or what he thought was a raven, and in the bright sunlight its feathers had a dark blue, iridescent sheen. Thomas concludes that the theory, "All ravens are black" is disproven. But, two issues remain. Is a "blue iridescent sheen" over a basically black bird what we mean by a non-black raven? Second, how do we know it was a raven? Although Thomas reports seeing such a raven, Johan Rosqvist retorts that Thomas is no means a competent ornithologist, his description cannot be trusted, and consequently, the theory has not been disproven. Before we can put a theory to a convincing test, we must be very careful to specify what we are looking for.

This level of attention to detail has been rare in psychology. It is sometimes noted that few theories have ever been completely rejected on the basis of the research evidence (Mahrer, 1988). There are two major reasons for this conclusion. One is the naive confusion of null hypothesis significance testing (NHST) from inferential statistics with theory testing; or as Meehl (1997) preferred to call it, theory appraisal. NHST is a tool for the researcher to use, just as a carpenter may use a hammer for joining boards. But, it is not the only tool, nor even the optimal one. NHST has many problems (as described by Thomas and Selthon, chap. 9, this volume) and the method itself has little to do with theory testing (Meehl, 1997).

The second reason why psychology has so often failed to reject theories is because of the problem of *auxiliary theories* (Lakatos, cited in Serlin & Lapsley, 1993; Meehl, 1997). Auxiliary theories are not part of the content of a theory, but are present when we try to put the theory in action, that is, to test it. The problem with auxiliary theories is that the validity of one or more auxiliary theories may impact the results of a study so that it is not possible to determine whether the results bear on the original theory. In the case of Sue, we had a hypothesis that home based ERP would change her OCD symptoms. This hypothesis was derived from ERP theory in response to the failure of ERP to have any effect in its usual clinic-based administration. One auxiliary theory related to Sue's treatment was that ERP therapy was competently conducted. Had the therapy failed, we would be more inclined to suspect a problem in implementation rather than a problem in the theory itself. Auxiliary theories reside in almost every aspect of research, from instrumentation to design and analysis. Later, when we examine the hallmarks of "Gold Standard" clinical research in chapter 11, it is seen that the standard has been designed to minimize the ability of auxiliary theories to influence our conclusions.

## Replication

Replication is critical for science. A given finding may be the result of many factors besides the effects specified by theory or the researcher. Random chance is a common culprit, others include unusual features of a study's design, biased sampling or observation, inconclusive statistical analyses, and even the researcher's hopes and dreams. The most famous instance in recent years is that of "cold fusion." *Cold fusion* was the supposed fusion of two atomic nuclei at much lower temperatures than previously thought possible. If such a thing were possible, the world would have been vastly changed by the availability of abundant, inexpensive, and nonpolluting power. Such a development would have had unimaginable benefits. There was one problem. The effect could not be obtained in other laboratories (Park, 2000). Not only did other labs find it impossible to duplicate the energy release predicted by cold fusion, but other labs could not observe the expected by-products of fusion, such as lethal doses of nuclear radiation. Cold fusion today is stone-cold dead.

Science relies on two types of replication. *Exact replication* involves repeating the original study in every detail to see if the same result is obtained. This is what the replicators of cold fusion set out to do, but were hampered by the failure of the original "discoverers" to provide sufficient detail about the experiment. Cold fusion as a research topic lasted a bit longer because of this, but met its demise in spite of its originators obstructionism. Psychology has not done well by exact replication. Journals prefer to publish original findings and are rarely interested in exact replications. This has led to an emphasis on *conceptual replications*, testing the same or a similar hypothesis, but using different measures or conditions. The idea seems to be that if the effect is large enough, it will be observed again. The problem is that when the effect is not replicated, we do not know why. It could be the original finding was spurious or it could be the changes in the research design were sufficient to mask or eliminate it; or the replication may have lacked sufficient power to detect the effect.

The limitations of conceptual replications are illustrated in a current controversy on the value of a recently introduced, psychotherapy technique, eye movement and desensitization and reprocessing (EMDR). The original developer of EMDR, Francine Shapiro, and proponents of the method have reported substantial success with this technique. However, other researchers have failed to obtain positive results. Shapiro (1999) argued that the failed replications have been characterized by inadequate treatment fidelity. In other words, the studies did not properly implement the technique, so the failure to replicate results is not surprising. Rosen (1999), meanwhile, contended that the issue of treatment fidelity is a "red herring," which distracts the reader from a negative evaluation of the theory and permits its perpetuation. This is an example of an auxiliary theory in action. On one hand, EMDR theory is protected by the supposedly inept implementation of EMDR practice, while on the other hand, if there is anything to the theory, it should work in spite of imperfect fidelity. We take no position on the issue except to note three things. First, this controversy would not exist if exact replication were attempted. Second, although claims of inadequate treatment fidelity may well be a legitimate issue, this general tactic is one that is often abused and its employment has been a "red flag" throughout history (cf. Park, 2000; Shermer, 2001). Third, conscientious researchers examine their own findings from many angles to ensure that they have eliminated as many competing explanations as possible. This may mean running studies two, three, or more times with slight modifications to determine for themselves how robust the findings are.

We cannot replicate many natural phenomena; natural catastrophes and the horrors of war are two examples. We can still fulfill the replication requirement in two ways. First, we can attempt to collaborate observations by multiple observers. Bahrick, Parker, Fivush, and Levitt (1998) examined the impact of varying levels of stress on young children's memories for Hurricane Andrew. Children between the ages of 3 and 4 were interviewed a few months after the hurricane about what happened during the storm. The interviews were recorded and scored for several facets of memory. By having two raters score each transcript, and comparing their scoring, Bahrick et al. (1998) demonstrated that similar scores would be derived by different raters. This represents a replication within the study. Bahrich et al. (1998) also provided detailed information about how the data were collected and the nature of the analyses they carried out. This makes it possible for other researchers to attempt to replicate the results after some other disaster. We would expect that the impact of hurricanes, tornadoes, floods, and the like to be comparable and other researchers could replicate the results following another disaster. Thus, although exact replication is impossible in these cases, conceptual replication is possible and should be expected to establish the validity of any important finding from such circumstances.

### Findings are Used to Modify Theories

Good theories account for past results. They also predict new results beyond what other theories are capable of predicting. Unfortunately, sometimes the data do not support the theory. This may be due to some of the reasons already presented, but it may be that the theory is actually wrong in some respects. We expect our theories to be wrong in at least some respects. That is why we test them. Still, many researchers, particularly those just beginning their careers, will often conclude that *they* have failed when the data do not come out as expected. If the idea was sound in the first place and the study has been conducted as well as possible, then the failure of a prediction is an opportunity to learn more and create a even better understanding of behavior. Petroski (1985), a noted structural engineer, made the case that without failure, engineering would not advance. That the Roman aqueducts have stood for hundreds of years is instructive, but the collapse of a newly built bridge can be even more so. Applied psychology is like engineering in this respect; we must learn from failure. It is the rare theory that does not change over time to accommodate new findings. The modified theory should be making different predictions than the old one and, thus, needs to be tested again. Critics of theory testing may be correct in stating that often theories do not die out from lack of empirical support, but these critics forget that theories evolve. Perhaps the most memorable statement to this effect is that of Drew Westin (1998), writing on the scientific legacy of Sigmond Freud. Freud's critics largely lambast his theory as it stood in the early 1920s although the theory had changed substantially by the time Freud died in 1939, even though since then "he has been slow to undertake further revisions" (p. 333).

## Clear and Open Communication of Methods, Data, and Results

Pearson's Challenge means nothing if it is not answered. Research must include the dissemination of results so that others can study, evaluate, and contest or use them. In the cold fusion debacle, what irreparably damaged the researcher's reputations in the scientific community was not that they made an error—that could, and should, happen in cutting-edge research—but they refused to divulge details of their procedure, thus making it difficult to replicate and evaluate the phenomenon (Park, 2000). There are norms in science for effectively communicating information. The *Publication Manual of the American Psychological Association* (APA, 2001) provided guidelines for what information should be included in research reports. In addition to following these guidelines, researchers are expected to make copies of their data available to others on request. Of course, care must be taken to ensure that all participant identifying information has been removed so there is no possible breach of confidentiality (cf. Miller, chap.10, this volume).

## CAUSALITY

Clinical and counseling psychology seem to get by with a straightforward theory of causality. Interventions, such as psychotherapy, are implemented because it is assumed that the intervention causes change in the clients. Similarly, life events are often expected to cause changes in people, which may later lead them to become clients (Kessler, 1997). But, it is a big leap from believing that there is a causal relationship to developing a convincing demonstration that the relationship actually exists in a causal fashion.

The nature of causality and the proof of causality has been a favorite topic of philosophers for centuries. The most widely employed analysis comes from the 19th-century philosopher, John Stuart Mill. Mill's formulation (cited in Shadish, Cook, & Campbell, 2002) consisted of three tests: (1) the cause must precede the effect in time, (2) the cause and effect must co-vary, and (3) there must be no other plausible explanations for the effect other than the presumed cause.

## Cause Must Precede the Effect

This is the least controversial of Mill's tests. Lacking a time machine, no one has ever figured out how to change an event after it has happened. It is very unlikely that a researcher would make the error of attributing the status of cause to something that occurred after the observed effect. However, comparable errors are sometimes made in cross-sectional studies in which two variables are measured at the same time. We may have a theory that self-esteem has a causal influence on school performance, but measure both at the same time and no causal conclusions can be drawn. Sometimes a study will be retrospective in nature; people are asked to remember their condition prior to a given event, for example, how much alcohol they consumed a day prior to the onset of some disease or an accident. Unfortunately, circumstances after the event has occurred may influence memory (Aikin & West, 1990), so the timing of the variables is now reversed, the effect (disease or accident) now precedes the presumed cause (amount of alcohol consumed) and no causal conclusions can be drawn.

## Cause and Effect Must Covary

In a simple world, this test would specify that when the cause is present, the effect must be present and when the cause is absent, the effect is absent. Unfortunately, we do not live in such a simple world. Take a dog to a park and throw a stick. That action is sufficient to cause the dog to run. But, dogs run for other reasons (for example, a squirrel digging in the dirt nearby). Throwing the stick is not a necessary cause for the dog to run. *Sufficient causes* are those, which by themselves, may cause the effect, but do not have to consistently result in the effect. For example, a well-trained guide dog on duty when the stick is thrown will probably not run. *Necessary causes* must be present for the effect to occur, but they do not have to be sufficient. Driving too fast may be a necessary cause for a speeding ticket, but most drivers have exceeded the speed limit on occasions without getting cited. As if this is not confusing enough, consider the case of schizophrenia. Schizophrenia is thought to have a genetic basis, yet a family background cannot be found in all schizophrenics, indicating that there are other causal factors (Farone, M. T. Tsuang, & D. W. Tsuang, 1999). Many people appear to have at least some of the genes related to schizophrenia, but show no symptoms. Thus, a family background of schizophrenia can be considered a risk factor for schizophrenia. If present, schizophrenia is more likely than if the family background is not present. Risk factors may or may not have a causal relationship with an event; they may simply be correlated with it.

"Correlation does not prove causation" is a statement every aspiring psychologist should learn. The statement says that Mill's second criterion is a necessary, but not sufficient, reason to attribute causality. A study may find a negative correlation between depression and self-esteem such that people with lower self-esteem are found to report higher levels of depression. The temptation is to conclude that people are depressed because they have low self-esteem (and that by raising self-esteem, depression will be reduced). This temptation must be resisted because nothing in the data lends support to a causal inference. Seligman, Reivich, Jaycox, and Gillham (1995) cogently argued that there may be a third factor that causes both low self-esteem and depression. Seligman and his colleagues have gone so far as to argue that ill-advised attempts to raise self-esteem in the general population may have set up many people for a propensity toward depression. So, we must be very careful in not assuming that a correlational relationship implies a causal relationship.

Sometimes a third variable influences the causal relationship between two others. It has often been noted that even the best psychological interventions fail to help some people. Prochaska and DiClemente (Prochaska, 1999) postulated that clients may have differential readiness to change. Some may have never considered making changes in their lives or do not wish to do so. Such clients are unlikely to benefit from interventions designed to create change, whereas clients who are motivated to change may well benefit from those therapies. What is variously called *stage of change* or *readiness to change*, if supported by further research, could be a moderator of the causal impact of psychotherapy on a client's outcome.

Mill's second test gets even more complicated when we consider the possibility of *reciprocal causation*. Sometimes two or more factors cause each other. A basic tenet of economics lies in the relationship between supply and demand. If a desirable good is in short supply, demand increases. As demand increases, producers ramp up production until it eventually satiates demand, which then falls. Thus, supply and demand are reciprocally related. Psychology does not have as well-defined examples, but there are probably many cases of reciprocal causation. Lewinsohn's (1974) behavioral theory of depression, for example, postulates that lack of reinforcement leads to a depressed mood, which leads to less activity, which, in turn, leads to less reinforcement. A study that examines these factors at only two points in time will miss this reciprocal relationship.

The statement, "correlation does not prove causation," does contribute its share of mischief to the field due to a misunderstanding of the meaning of *correlation*. Correlation in this sense refers to the co-occurrence of two or more variables. It does not refer to the set of statistics known as coefficients of correlation. No statistic or statistical procedure indicates or rules out causation. Our ability to infer causation depends on the study design, not the statistical analysis of data. Some analytic methods have been developed to facilitate the investigation of causation, but the conclusions regarding possible causal relationships depends on how, where, when, and under what conditions the data were gathered.

### There Must be No Other Plausible Explanations for the Effect Other than the Presumed Cause

Mill's third requirement is the one that causes the most problems for researchers and, except for effectiveness research, most study designs have been developed with it in mind. Sherlock Holmes once told Dr. Watson that "... when you have eliminated the impossible, whatever remains, *however improbable*, must be the truth" (Doyle, 1890/1986, p. 139). But, if Holmes cannot eliminate the alternatives as being impossible, then he cannot deduce the answer. There are innumerable alternative causes of an observed effect in psychological research. Consider a study comparing two different treatments for OCD. Sampling may be faulty; assigning people to different treatments in a biased manner eliminates our ability to say that one treatment caused greater change than another. Failure to control conditions may influence the results; for example, if people in one treatment have a friendly, warm, empathic therapist while those in another treatment have a cold, distant therapist, we cannot determine if any observed effect was due to differences in the treatment or differences in the therapists.

The key in Mill's third criterion is to rule out *plausible* alternative explanations. It takes a great deal of expense and trouble to control outside factors that might contaminate results. Therefore, we expend most of our budget and effort in controlling those that offer the most compelling alternative explanations. Space aliens could abduct the members of one of our study's treatment groups and subject them to some strange "cure," but this possibility is considered so improbable that no one ever controls for the effects of alien abduction. Outside the bizarre, deciding which alternatives are plausible requires an understanding of the rationale underlying research design and the phenomenon under study. As a consumer of research, you need to pay close attention to the Methods section of research articles because that is where you will find how the researchers chose to control what they believed were the most plausible alternative explanations, the Results section because more control is exerted there, and the Discussion section because that is where researchers often confess to any remaining limitations of the study.

## SCIENCE IN THE SERVICE OF PRACTICE

Influential clinicians recognized a few years ago that it was desirable to carefully examine and enumerate those treatments that could be described as having been shown to have an efficacious effect on client outcomes (Seligman, 1998a). This led to an ambitious effort by the Society for Clinical Psychology (Division 12 of the American Psychological Association) to do exactly that. The findings, first published in 1995 (Division 12 Task Force (APA), 1995), were controversial in that many popular methods in long use did not make the list. How can this be? Usually, it was not so much a consequence of documented treatment failures as a paucity of outcome research on these treatments (Seligman, 1998b). It could not be determined that those treatments are effective because adequate studies have not been conducted. The Division 12 effort continues; updates are periodically posted on the Society for Clinical Psychology's Web page, http://www.apa.org/divisions/div12/homepage.shtml. It is important for clinical and counseling psychologists to develop the knowledge and skills to interpret the results of this program, if not to contribute to it, because the results have shaped practice and will do so to an even greater extent in the coming years.

Because of stories like Sue's, clinical and counseling psychologists have an interest and responsibility in demonstrating that their interventions are effective and to use the scientific method in advancing practice. Managed care also has a legitimate interest in verifying that the services it pays for are effective and clients and their families are also concerned that treatments result in real change (Newman & Tejada, 1996). Still, some clinicians/therapists ask "What difference does it make if our clients feel better after therapy? Do we really need to fuss around with all this research stuff if its secondary to feeling better?" These questions were actually raised by a graduate student in the senior author's, Research Methods class. In spite of the author's own apoplexy in response to the question, these are legitimate and proper issues to raise. They deserve an answer. If "feeling better" is the objective of the work with a client, then how are other outcomes relevant, as assessed on standardized measures? If the outcomes employed in outcome studies are not relevant, then the studies themselves are a poor foundation for practice. If progress in treatment, ethics, concerns of leading thinkers, demands of third party payers, and social imperative are not enough basis for relying on research, there is still one more excellent reason that justifies an emphasis on research based practice. For most of history, people with psychological disorders were stigmatized and denied the same rights and dignity as others (Stefan, 2001). This treatment was considered justified because such people were considered to be weak, having flawed characters, being unreliable, and, worse, unchangeable. Social and legal opinion has changed over the past 20 years or so, but those changes can only be sustained by continual rigorous demonstrations that personal change is possible, and that people with disorders are not fated to a low quality of life. That is the lesson of Sue's OCD. A few years ago she would undoubtedly be institutionalized, probably for the rest of her life. Today, with effective, empirically based treatment, she is back to work and has a normal homelife. She is indistinguishable from any other member of "normal" society. She "feels better" too.

We subtitled this chapter, Science in the Service of Practice, because, although it is possible to pursue science for its own sake, we expect that most readers of this volume will be mostly interested in learning about clinical or counseling practice. Science can make for a stronger, more effective practice. So far we have concentrated on the scientific investigation of treatment effects. Research impacts practice in many other ways: causes of disorders, validation of measures, cultural effects, human development, even practitioners' acceptance of treatment innovations (e.g., Addis & Krasnow, 2000), to name a few. The history of science shows that there have been few scientific findings that have not had some effect on practical affairs, but when science is purposely employed to advance practice, it can be an exceptionally powerful method. Applied science differs a bit from so-called "pure" science in that some issues appear, which are not the concern of the pure scientist. For example, the distinction between "efficacy" and "effectiveness" studies (see Truax & Thomas, chap. 11, this volume) does not surface in the laboratory. In efficacy studies, we are concerned about showing a causal relationship between a treatment and an outcome. Effectiveness studies are not designed to show causality, but are concerned with the conditions under which an established causal relationship can be generalized.

## The Local Clinical Scientist

One model of practice that encourages the incorporation of the scientific method into the provision of services is the Local Clinical Scientist (Stricker & Trierweiler, 1995). This model applies to psychological science in two ways: (1) approaching the local situation in a scientific way (i.e., gathering and evaluating data, and generating and testing hypotheses based on general psychological knowledge and theory), and (2) systematically questioning how local variables impact the validity of generalizing such knowledge to the local situation. Local is contrasted with universal or general in four ways: (1) local as a particular application of general science; (2) local culture consists of persons, objects and events in context, including the way that people speak about and understand events in their lives (i.e., in the local perspective, science itself is a local culture that practitioners bring into the open systems of their clients' local cultures); (3) local as unique (i.e., some aspects of what the practitioner observes will fall outside the domain of available science, like a local phenomenon that has not yet been adequately studied because it is not [yet] accessible to the methods of scientific inquiry); and (4) space–time local (i.e., not just the physical and temporal properties of the object of inquiry, but also to the specific space–time context of the act of judgment).

The effective local clinical scientist knows the research in the areas in which he or she works and utilizes the scientific method in their practice. Table 1.1 illustrates how the phases of clinical practice and scientific investigation have common elements and how the scientific approach can be incorporated into practice.

## Skepticism, Cynicism, and the Conservative Nature of Science

One of the authors, Jay C. Thomas, teaches a course in statistics. After going over one assignment with the class (reading Huff's, 1954, *How to Lie With Statistics*), one student commented that he was now more cynical than ever when it comes to reading research reports. To become *cynical* is to doubt the sincerity of one's fellows, to assume that all actions are performed solely on the basis of self interest, and to trust anyone's reports is naive. Developing cynicism in students is hardly a desirable outcome of studying research and statistical methods, particularly because it is hard to believe that a cynical clinician will be very successful in practice. We do hope that students become skeptical, doubting assertions until evidence is submitted to substantiate the claims. To be skeptical is to be "not easily persuaded or convinced; doubting; questioning" (Guralnik et al.,1978, p. 1334). Effective clinicians do not believe everything they hear or read. They ask for, and evaluate, the evidence based on their understanding of the principles and methods of science. This is especially necessary in the age of the Internet and World Wide Web. Today, information can be disseminated at a fantastic pace. It is not all good information and cannot be relied on by a professional until it is vetted and proven to be reliable.

To be a skeptic is not the same as being a pugilist. Although some scientists on opposite sides of a theoretical controversy go at one another with ferocity of heavyweight boxers fighting for the world championship, such ferocity is not necessary. Skepticism demands that we examine the evidence, but when we find it weak or otherwise unpersuasive, we can declare our distrust of the evidence, usually without distrusting or disrespecting those who reported it. In fact, Shadish et al. (2002) go so far as to state, "the ratio of trust to skepticism in any given study is more like 99% trust to 1% skepticism than the opposite" (p. 29). They continue with asserting that "thoroughgoing skepticism" is impossible in science. We assert that the issue revolves around who should be trusted, what should be trusted, and in what circumstance.

TABLE 1.1
Incorporating Research Knowledge Into Practice

| Client Phase | Practice Issue | Scientific Method | Scientific Issue |
|---|---|---|---|
| 1. Intake | • What brought the client here?<br>• What is troubling the client?<br>• What are the client's strengths, weaknesses, resources?<br>• What is salient about client's background and history?<br>• What's relevant about client's background and history for presenting problem?<br>• What are the client's expectations about your services?<br>• What is client's stage of change?<br>• Who is the client? | 1. Observe | • Attend to subject expectancies, experimenter expectancies, demand characteristics.<br>• Utilize multiple sources of information to maximize reliability and validity.<br>• Ask questions in a way that elicits useful information.<br>• Obtain information in as objective and value free a manner as possible.<br>• Obtain assessment information that may help clarify client's situation. |
| 2. Develop diagnosis | • What makes this client similar to other clients?<br>• What makes this client unique?<br>• What parts of the client's presentation are credible? What parts need further checking?<br>• What hasn't the client told you?<br>• Evaluate the client on case conceptualization factors:<br>1. Learning & modeling<br>2. Life events<br>3. Genetics & temperament<br>4. Physiological factors affecting psychological factors<br>5. Drugs affecting physiological factors<br>6. Sociocultural factors | 2. Develop hypotheses | • Do client's symptoms or complaints match diagnostic criteria?<br>• What about symptoms that overlap with other diagnoses?<br>• What are the base rates?<br>• What is the co-morbidity rate?<br>• What additional information do you need?<br>• What is the evidential basis for your conclusions on the conceptualization factors? |

(Continued)

TABLE 1.1
(Continued)

| Client Phase | Practice Issue | Scientific Method | Scientific Issue |
|---|---|---|---|
| 3. Develop treatment plan | • What priorities make sense for this client? <br> • What is apt to work for this client given the resources? <br> • What will client agree to? <br> • What are you and the client comfortable trying? <br> • How can you monitor progress? | 2. Develop hypotheses | • What is known to work with clients similar to this one? <br> • What is known to *not* work with similar clients? <br> • If no "standard of care," what methods can be said to have the best chance of being effective? <br> • Develop plan for data collection as part of ongoing treatment. <br> • Ensure clear operational definitions of goal attainment, behaviors, and results. <br> • Behavioral specificity is preferred over vague statements. |
| 4. Implement treatment plan | • How is client reacting to treatment? <br> • Is client complying with treatment assignments? <br> • Is therapist adhering to the treatment plan? <br> • Are therapist and client maintaining a satisfactory alliance? <br> • Is client making progress toward goals? | 1. Observe <br> 3. Test hypotheses <br> 4. Observe results <br> 5. Revise hypotheses <br> 6. Test new hypotheses | • Is client attending sessions? <br> • Is client showing change? <br> • Is change consistent with what was expected? <br> • Has new information surfaced that would change the hypotheses? <br> • Are there trends that might indicate that a change in treatment plan is needed? |
| 5. Verify results | • Did client meet goals? <br> • Do other clients meet goals? | 4. Observe results <br> 5. Revise hypotheses <br> 6. Test new hypotheses <br> 7. Disseminate results | • How can you perform an unbiased assessment of your own work? <br> • Can you demonstrate a causal relationship between treatment and change? <br> • How can you modify your practice based on results? <br> • Would these results be of interest to others? |

Huff (1954) used actual examples from the media to demonstrate many tricks that will lead a reader to draw a conclusion the data do not support. This is the book that the student believed made him a cynic, but it should have turned him into a skeptic. At the end of the book, Huff provides five questions, which the alert and skeptical reader can use to determine whether a statistic, a study full of statistics, or an author can be trusted. Huff's questions are now given.

*"Who Says So?"*   The nonspecialist in a field has no idea who has a track record of doing excellent work, so they often look for an institutional or professional affiliation for guidance. Being associated with famous institution affords an author with an "OK name," whether or not it is deserved. Several years ago, a physician wrote a book on sex that became a best seller. The good doctor claimed to be a psychiatrist and to have received his medical education at Harvard. Neither proved to be true. In general, watch out for the researcher or institution who has a vested interest in proving a point. Much of the evidence in favor of psychopharmacological remedies originates with the companies who produce the medications. This concerns us.

*"How Does He (She) Know?"*   Ask where the data came from, how large the sample size was, and how it was obtained. Very large and very small samples can be misleading and a biased sample should always be considered misleading until proven otherwise.

*"What's Missing?"*   Pearson's Challenge demands that evidence be provided with an assessment of its own reliability. For statistics, that means confidence intervals, standard errors, or effect sizes. It also means defining one's terms. If an "average" is reported, ask which kind. Means, medians, and modes are impacted by different factors and a cheat will report the one that best states his or her case. In examining research reports in general, ask how well the design of the study matches up with the principles covered in this book.

*"Did Somebody Change the Subject?"*   Suppose a researcher surveys clients about their satisfaction with therapy and rapport with their clinician, finds a relationship between the two variables, and reports greater rapport leads to better treatment outcomes. Notice the change from "satisfaction" to "outcome." The two are by no means synonymous. This is a case of switching the subject. The clinical literature is replete with examples. Other forms of changing the subject include using far different definitions of terms than the audience expects and either not providing that information or burying it so the reader tends to skip over it. Kovar (2000) documented one such switch in the case of teenage smoking. President Clinton, a cabinet secretary, and the Director of the Food and Drug Administration all cited that 4 million American

adolescents smoke, the implications being that $\frac{1}{5}$ of the country's youth were regular and probably addicted smokers. The data came from a well-conducted national survey sponsored by a large government agency and the statistics were not in doubt. What was in doubt was the definition of being a "regular" smoker. The 4 million figure was an extrapolation from the percentage in the survey, which stated that they had smoked even a single puff of a cigarette at any time within the past 30 days. That definition included regular smokers but also a good many who may never become "hooked."

**"Does it Make Sense?"**    Huff (1954) reminded us that sometimes a "finding" makes no sense and the explanation is there is no intrinsic reason for it to do so. As an example, he cited a physician's statistics on the number of prostrate cancer cases expected in this country each year. It came out to 1.1 prostrates per man, a spurious figure! A few years ago, a method was devised, which supposedly allowed autistic children to communicate with parents, teachers, and therapists (McBurney, 1996). *Facilitated Communication* involved having a specially trained teacher hold the autistic child's hand, and the child held a marking device over a board on which the letters of the alphabet were printed. Wonderful results were reported. Children who found it impossible to communicate even simple requests were creating complex messages even beyond what would be expected of other children their age. Too good to be true? It was. Sensible? It was not. Skepticism may have seemed cruel in denying the communicative abilities of these children, but even crueler was the discovery that the communication unconsciously sprang from the facilitator, not the child.

The most difficult aspect of being a skeptic is being a fair skeptic. If a study supports what we already believe, we are much less likely to subject it to the same scrutiny as a study in which the results are contrary to our preferences. Corrigan (2001) recently illustrated this in *The Behavior Therapist*, the newsletter of the Association for Advancement of Behavior Therapy (AABT). There are some psychotherapies for which behavior therapists have a natural affinity and other therapies that they view with some suspicion, a case in point being EMDR. Corrigan (2001) found after a fairly simple and brief literature search that there appears to be as much empirical support for EMDR as there is for the preferred therapies. Corrigan did not attempt to compare results nor to examine the quality of the studies. His goal was simply to point out that without going to that effort, there is no more *a priori* reason to reject EMDR than there was to accept the others. We can only add that the best strategy is to redouble one's efforts in double checking results when the results fit one's previously established preferences.

Science is conservative due to its need for skepticism and evidence. There are always new ideas and techniques that fall outside the domain of science. Some fall into what Shermer (2001) called the "borderlands of science," not quite scientific, although potentially so. Often however the latest fads fail to have much of a lasting impact on science and practice just as 10-year-old clothing fashions have little influence on the current mode of dress. It takes time to weed out what is of lasting value when it comes to the cutting edge. This means that there are potentially helpful interventions that the local clinical scientist does not employ and this does represent a cost of ethical practice. There is, however, an even greater cost to clients, payers, the profession, and society at large if skepticism and the rigorous inspection of evidence are abandoned and every fad is adopted on the flimsiest of support (Dunnette, 1966). There are tremendous demands from clients and the market to give in to instant gratification, but that is not what a professional does. Be skeptical; ask questions; generate answers.

## REFERENCES

Addis, M. E., & Krasnow, A. D. (2000). A national survey of practicing psychologists' attitudes toward psychotherapy treatment manuals. *Journal of Consulting and Clinical Psychology, 68,* 331–339.

Aiken, L. S., & West, S. G. (1990). Invalidity of true experiments: Self report pretest biases. *Evaluation Review, 14,* 374–390.

American Psychological Association (2001). *Publication manual of the American Psychological Association* (5th ed.). Washington, DC: Author.

Bahrick, L. E., Parker, J. F., Fivush, R., & Levitt, M. (1998). The effects of stress on young children's memory for a natural disaster. *Journal of Experimental Psychology: Applied, 4,* 308–331.

Campbell, J. T. (1990). The role of theory in industrial and organizational psychology. In M. D. Dunnette & L. M. Hough (Eds.), *Handbook of industrial and organizational psychology* (2nd ed., Vol. 1, pp. 39–74). Palo Alto, CA: Consulting Psychologists Press.

Cook, T. D. (1991). Postpositivist criticisms, reform associations, and uncertainties about social research. In D.S. Anderson & B.J. Biddle (Eds.), *Knowledge for policy: Improving education through research* (pp. 43–59). London: The Falmer Press.

Corrigan, P. (2001). Getting ahead of the data: A threat to some behavior therapies. *The Behavior Therapist, 24*(9), 189–193.

Division 12 Task Force (APA). (1995). Training in and dissemination of empirically validated psychological treatments: Report and recommendations. *The Clincial Psychologist, 48,* 3–23.

Doyle, A. C. (1986). The sign of four. In *Sherlock Holmes: The complete novels and stories* (Vol. 1, pp. 1–105). New York: Bantoam Books. (Original work published 1890).

Dunnette, M. D. (1966). Fads, fashions, and folderol in psychology. *American Psychologist, 21,* 343–352.

Emmelkamp, P. M. G. (1982). *Phobic and obsessive-compulsive disorders: Theory, research, and practice.* New York: Plenum Press.

Farone, S. V., Tsuang, M. T., & Tsuang, D. W. (1999). *Genetics of mental disorders.* New York: Guilford Press.

Foa, E. B., Franklin, M. E., & Kozak, M. J. (1998). Psychosocial treatments for obsessive-compulsive disorder: Literature review. In R. P. Winson, M. M. Antony, S. Rachman, & M. A. Richter (Eds.), *Obsessive-compulsive disorder: Theory, research, and treatment* (pp. 258–276). New York: Guilford Press.

Guralnik, D. B. et al. (1978). *Webster's new world dictionary of the American language* (2nd college ed.). Cleveland, OH: William Collins & World Publishing Company.

Huff, D. (1954). *How to lie with statistics*. New York: Norton.

Kessler, R. (1997). The effects of stressful life events on depression. *Annual Review of Psychology, 48,* 191–214.

Kimble, G. A. (1989). Psychology from the standpoint of a generalist. *American Psychologist, 44,* 491–499.

Kluger, A. N., & Tikochinsky, J. (2001). The error of accepting the "theoretical" null hypothesis: The rise, fall, and resurrection of common sense hypotheses in psychology. *Psychological Bulletin, 127,* 408–423.

Kovar, M. G. (2000), Four million adolescents smoke: Or do they? *Chance, 13*(2), 10–14.

Lewinsohn, P. M. (1974). A behavioral approach to depression. In R. M. Friedman & M. M. Katz (Eds.), *The psychology of depression: Contemporary theory and research* (pp. 157–185). New York: Wiley.

Mahrer, A. R. (1988). Discovery oriented psychotherapy research: Rationale, aims, and methods. *American Psychologist, 43,* 694–702.

McBurney, D. H. (1996). *How to think like a psychologist: Critical thinking in psychology.* Upper Saddle River, NJ: Prentice-Hall.

Meehl, P. (1997). The problem is epistemology, not statistics: Replace significance tests with confidence intervals and quantify accuracy of risky numerical predictions. In L. L Harlow, S. A. Mulaik, & J. H. Steiger (Eds.), *What if there were no significance tests?* (pp. 393–425). Mahwah, NJ: Lawrence Erlbaum Associates.

Meyer, V. (1966). Modification of expectations in cases with obsessional rituals. *Behavior Research and Therapy, 4,* 273–280.

Newman, F. L., & Tejada, M. J. (1996). The need for research that is designed to support decisions in the delivery of mental health services. *American Psychologist, 51,* 1040–1049.

Park, R. (2000). *Voodoo science: The road from foolishness to fraud.* New York: Oxford University Press.

Petroski, H. (1985). *To engineer is human: The role of failure in successful design.* New York: St. Martin's Press.

Popper, K. (1959). *The logic of scientific discovery.* New York: Basic Books.

Prochaska, J. O. (1999). How do people change and how can we change to help many more people change? In M. A. Hubble, B. L. Duncan, & S. D. Miller (Eds.), *The heart and soul of change: What works in therapy* (pp. 227–255). Washington, DC: American Psychological Association.

Rosen, G. M. (1999). Treatment fidelity and research on Eye Movement Desensitization and Reprocessing (EMDR). *Journal of Anxiety Disorders, 13,* 173–184.

Rosqvist, J., Thomas, J. C., Egan, D., Willis, B. C., & Haney, B. J. (in press). Home-based cognitive-behavioral therapy successfully treats severe, chronic and refractroy obsessive-compulsive disorder: A single case analysis. *Clinical Case Studies.*

Seligman, M. E. P. (1998a). Foreword. In P. E. Nathan & J. M Gorman (Eds.), *A guide to treatments that work* (pp. v–xiv). New York: Oxford University Press.

Seligman, M. E. P. (1998b). Afterword. In P. E. Nathan & J. M Gorman (Eds.) *A guide to treatments that work* (pp. 568–572). New York: Oxford University Press.

Seligman, M. E. P, Reivich, K., Jaycox, L., & Gillham, J. (1995). *The optimistic child.* Boston: Houghton Mifflin Co.

Serlin, R. C., & Lapsley, D. K. (1993). Rational appraisal of psychological research and the good-enough principle. In G. Keren & C. Lewis (Eds.), *A handbook for data analysis in the behavioral sciences: Methodological issues* (pp. 199–228). Mahwah, NJ: Lawrence Erlbaum Associates.

Sexton, T. L., Whiston, S. C., Bleuer, J. C., & Walz, G. R. (1997). *Integrating outcome research into counseling practice and training.* Alexandria, VA: American Counseling Association.

Shadish, W., Cook, T. D., & Campbell, D. T. (2002). *Experimental and quasi-experimental designs for generalized causal inference.* Boston: Houghton Mifflin Company.

Shapiro, F. (1999). Eye Movement Desensitization and Reprocessing (EMDR) and the anxiety disorders: Clinical and research implications of an integrated psychotherapy treatment. *Journal of Anxiety Disorders, 13,* 35–67.

Shermer, M. (2001). *The borderlands of science.* New York: Oxford University Press.

Stefan, S. (2001). *Unequal rights: Discrimination against people with mental disabilities and the Americans with Disabilities Act.* Washington, DC: American Psychological Association.

Stigler, S. M. (1999). *Statistics on the table: The history of statistical concepts and methods.* Cambridge, MA: Harvard University Press.

Stricker, G., & Trierweiler, S. J. (1995). The local clinical scientist: A bridge between science and practice. *American Psychologist, 50,* 995–1002.

Van Oppen, P., & Arntz, A. (1994). Cognitive therapy for obsessive-compulsive disorder. *Behaviour Therapy and Research, 32,* 273–280.

Van Oppen, P., & Emmelkamp, P. M. G. (2000). Issues in cognitive treatment of obsessive-compulsive disorder. In W. K. Goodman, M. V. Rudorfer, & J. D. Maser (Eds.), *Obsessive-compulsive disorder: Contemporary issues in treatment* (pp. 117–132). Mahwah, NJ: Lawrence Erlbaum Associates.

Westin, D. (1998). The scientific legacy of Sigmund Freud: Toward a psychodynamically informed psychological science. *Psychological Bulletin, 124,* 333–371.

Wilson, K. A., & Chambless, D. L. (1999). Inflated perceptions of responsibility and obsessive-compulsive symptoms. *Behaviour Therapy and Research, 37,* 325–335.

# Understanding Measurement

Warren W. Tryon
David Bernstein
*Fordham University*

The history of science is a history of measurement in that measurement quality sets an upper bound on science quality. Just as a test cannot consistently be more valid than it is reliable, research findings cannot be more solid than the measurements on which they are based. The main purpose of this chapter is to help investigators in clinical and counseling research better understand fundamental measurement issues so that they can improve the quality of their research. The first major section entitled the Fundamentals of Measurement Theory reviews basic concepts in measurement theory, including measurement error, classical reliability theory, reliability coefficients, standard error of measurement, parallel tests, domain sampling, coefficient alpha, and alternatives to alpha. The principle of aggregation is introduced and leads to the development of a scale for determining the number of repeated measurements needed to achieve a predetermined level of reliability. This is analogous to designing a study so that it has a predetermined level of statistical power. The next section discusses the impact of reliability on validity. Increasing the former predictably increases the latter. The next major section, entitled Developing Operational Definitions, discusses both the univariate and multivariate case. The following section entitled, Methods of Collecting Data, covers interviews, questionnaires, behavioral observation, psychological tests, and instruments. A subsequent section discusses how instruments can and have driven the construction of scientific theory. Reasons are given for why instruments can make such contributions. The next section, entitled *Types of Psychological Scales*, covers nominal, ordinal, interval, and ratio scales. The importance of measurement units is raised and considered in further detail in a subsequent fifth section, entitled Units of Measure. Measurement units in psychology are discussed. An example is presented showing how the absence of units can lead to measurement that is highly reliable and valid but inaccurate. A method for evaluating the reliability of instruments is presented. The following section, entitled Reliability of Measurement: Generalizability Theory, extends the material on reliability presented in the Fundamentals of Measurement Theory section to present an introduction to and overview of generalizability theory. The *Validity of Measurements* section reviews construct, convergent, discriminant, content, and criterion-related validity. The issue of phantom measurement is discussed. The final section, entitled Measuring Outcomes, discusses the evaluation of change and the unreliability of change scores, among other topics.

## FUNDAMENTALS OF MEASUREMENT THEORY

Whenever we measure something, we do so with a certain degree of imprecision. This imprecision is known as "measurement error." Reliability is the extent to which tests are free from measurement error (Lord & Novick, 1968; Nunnally, 1978). The less the measurement error, the more reliable the test. To take a simple example from the physical sciences, if we were to take multiple measurements of the length of a table using a ruler, we would find that these measurements would vary by fractions of an inch; such variation is due to measurement error. Another way to think about measurement error is in terms of the repeatability of a measurement, either repeatability over time or across alternative forms of the same instrument. If the same test or alternative forms of a test are given repeatedly to the same person, we wish the scores to be as nearly identical as possible. For example, if I.Q. scores were to change markedly over a short interval of time (e.g., a few weeks or months), they would be unusable, because the unreliability of the test would make it impossible to estimate the trait being measured (i.e., intelligence) in a sufficiently precise manner.

There are two kinds of measurement error: random error and systematic error. In *random error*, the test scores of individuals are affected in idiosyncratic ways. Sources of random error include testing conditions (e.g., the temperature or amount of noise in the room when the test is given), the physical or mental state of the subjects when taking the test, the subjects' level of motivation, the way in which subjects' interpret items, and so forth. While random error affects the test scores of different individuals in different ways, systematic error affects the scores of all individuals equally, or affects scores differentially for different groups. If systematic error affects all observations equally, it is typically not much of a problem, because only the mean of the distribution of scores would be affected, and not the variance of the scores. This would leave the correlation between the test and other measures unchanged. But if systematic error affects scores differentially for different groups, it can bias results, by raising the scores of individuals in some groups, and lowering the scores of individuals in other groups. For example, systematic error might raise the scores of all males who take a test, while lowering the scores of all females.

Measurement error affects the measurements that are made in the physical sciences as well as in the social sciences. Measurements of blood pressure, temperature, and so forth contain some error. However, theories of measurement error have been developed largely within in the social sciences, and particularly within the field of psychology. This is probably because psychologists are interested in measuring phenomena for which there are no clear physical sequelae. Some of the key concepts of classical reliability theory were formulated 100 years ago by Charles Spearman, a psychologist who also made seminal contributions to the development of factor analysis and the study of general intelligence (Nunnally, 1978). By the 1960s, classical reliability theory (also known as "classical test theory") had assumed its present form. Two major alternatives to classical reliability theory have been developed since then: generalizability theory and item response theory. Although all three have important uses, classical reliability theory remains the most widely used by clinicians and is adequate for many purposes. It also has the advantage of being fairly easy to understand. In this chapter, we discuss both classical reliability theory and generalizability theory, but not item response theory, the latter being a very large topic in itself (Hambleton, Swaminathan, & Rogers, 1991; Suen, 1990).

Given the attention that reliability has received in psychology, one might conclude that it is the most important topic in psychological measurement. In fact, this is not the case. The validity of a test is more important than its reliability (Suen, 1990). Validity concerns the question of whether a test measures the thing that it purports to measure. Reliability can be seen as a prerequisite for validity. The reason for this is that the validity of a test is established by correlating the test with other measures. In the context of test validation, these correlation coefficients are known as *validity coefficients* (Nunnally, 1978). Random error attenuates the correlations between tests. Thus, tests with poor reliability produce low correlations with other tests. In other words, reliability places a ceiling on a test's validity. This gives rise to the old psychometric adage, "reliability is the upper limit of validity." If reliability is merely a precondition for validity, why has so much attention been devoted to it? The reason is probably because it is possible to develop elegant mathematical models for reliability, whereas establishing the validity of a test is a somewhat murkier matter.

## Classical Reliability Theory

*Classical reliability theory* deals only with random error. It assumes that systematic error has been controlled through uniform testing conditions (Suen, 1990). The fundamental equation of classical reliability theory is the following:

$$X = t + e$$

This equation states that the test score of any individual $(X)$ can be decomposed into two parts: a true score, $t$, and an error score, $e$ (Lord & Novick, 1968; Nunnally, 1978). The *true score* is the score that the person would have received, if we could measure the attribute in question perfectly; that is, without any error. The *error score* reflects the contribution of random error to the person's observed score. In other words, the error score is simply the difference between the observed score and the true score, $e = x - t$. This fundamental equation is a tautology. It is definitional and cannot be proven (Lord & Novick, 1968).

What are some of the properties of observed scores, true scores, and error scores? First, for any given person, the true score is assumed to be a constant, whereas the error score and observed score are assumed to be "random variables" (Lord & Novick, 1968). If you give a test repeatedly, or alternative forms of the same test, the person's true score presumably will not change. It remains constant. In other words, so long as the trait being measured is invariant, the true score for that trait should remain the same. However, the observed score will change because the amount of random error will presumably vary from administration to administration. Thus, the error score and observed score are random variables, in the sense that they can take on a variety of different values. Second, over repeated administrations of a test, the mean error score is presumably zero, $M(e) = 0$ (Lord & Novick, 1968). On any given administration of a test, the error score can either raise or lower the observed score, relative to the true score. However, over many administrations, error scores tend to average out. In the example of multiple measurements of the length of a table, some measurements would overestimate the table's true length, whereas others would underestimate it. In the long run, however, these errors of measurement presumably average out to zero. We refer to this later as the principle of aggregation. This is the rationale for combining multiple items to form a test. The items' respective errors tend to balance each other out, producing a scale that is more reliable than the separate items that constitute it. Third, over repeated administrations of a test, true and error scores are presumably uncorrelated with each other, $r_{te} = 0$ (Lord & Novick, 1968). This is known as the "assumption of independence." Because measurement error is presumed to be random, it is uncorrelated with anything else. For this reason, the random error component of test scores is thought to be entirely uncorrelated with the true score component. Similarly, in classical reliability theory, the error scores of two different tests, $X_1$ and $X_2$, are assumed to be uncorrelated with each other, $r_{e1,e2} = 0$, and the error score for each test is assumed to be uncorrelated with the other test's true score, $r_{e1,t2} = 0$ and $r_{e2,t1} = 0$.

What are true scores? They have been defined in different ways (Lord & Novick, 1968, Nunnally, 1978). True scores are sometimes thought of in Platonic terms. That is, true scores are thought to have an underlying reality that we can only perceive indirectly. Recall Plato's famous analogy of the cave. The person inside the cave can only see the shadows cast by passing objects outside the cave. In Platonic terms, the true scores are the objects themselves, which cannot be seen directly. The observed scores are the shadows that the objects cast. An alternative view is that the true score is the average score that the person would obtain from infinitely many repeated measurements (Lord & Novick, 1968). In the example of multiple measurements of the length of a table, the true score would be the $M$ of the measurements, if we were to take an infinite number of them. Thus, the true score can be defined as the $M$ value of the observed scores over an infinite number of measurements, $t = M(x)$. As a practical matter, we cannot make an infinite number of measurements. However, if we were to make a very large number of measurements, the $M$ would usually give us a good approximation of the person's true score.

### Reliability Coefficient and Index

Having defined true and error scores, and discussed some of their properties, we can use these concepts to define reliability (Lord & Novick, 1968). From the fundamental equation of classical test theory, it follows that:

$$\sigma_x^2 = \sigma_t^2 + \sigma_e^2$$

If a test is given to a group of individuals, the variance of the observed scores can be decomposed into two parts, true score variance and error. If reliability is the degree to which a test is free from measurement error, reliability can be defined as the proportion of a test's observed score variance that consists of true score variance:

$$r_{11} = \frac{\sigma_t^2}{\sigma_x^2}$$

$r_{11}$ is referred to as the "reliability coefficient." Another way to think about the reliability coefficient is as the proportion of variance that observed scores and true scores share with each other:

$$r_{11} = r_{xt}^2$$

Recall that when correlation coefficients are squared, they describe the proportion of variance that two variables share in common. The *reliability coefficient* is therefore the squared correlation between observed scores and true scores. A related quantity is the *reliability index*. It is simply the square root of the reliability coefficient:

$$r_{xt} = \sqrt{r_{xt}^2}$$

In other words, the reliability index is the Pearson correlation between observed scores and true scores.

## Standard Error of Measurement

The standard error of the measurement is defined as the average amount that observed scores would be expected to deviate from true scores because of random error (Lord & Novick, 1968; Nunnally, 1978). In the example of taking repeated measurements of the length of a table, the standard error of the measurement is the average amount that the measurements of the table's length (i.e., the observed scores) deviate from the table's true length. In other words, in the distribution of repeated measurements of a table's length, the standard error of the measurement is the standard deviation of this distribution. As we noted earlier, the *M* of the distribution of repeated measures would be equal to the table's true length if we had an infinite number of measurements. Thus, the standard error of the measurement is an index of measurement error. If there is relatively little random error in a test, the standard error of the measurement will be small. Therefore, on average, observed scores will deviate little from the true scores. The standard error of the measurement can be used to set confidence intervals that estimate the range within which a person's true score on a test is likely to fall (Lord & Novick, 1968; Nunnally, 1978).

The standard error of the measurement can be derived mathematically in the following way (Lord & Novick, 1968; Nunnally, 1978). If the reliability coefficient, $r_{11}$, is the proportion of true score variance in a test, it follows that the proportion of error variance in a test is $1 - r_{11}$, or equivalently, $1 - r_{xt}^2$. For example, if $r_{11} = .91$, $1 - .91 = .09$. That is, 91% of the observed score variance is true score variance,

$$S_e = S_x \sqrt{1 - r_{xx}^2}$$

and 9% is error variance. When the square root of this proportion is multiplied by the standard deviation, the result is the standard error of the measurement. In the above example, if the standard deviation of the observed scores is equal to 15, the standard error of the measurement is equal to $15\sqrt{(1 - .91)} = 4.5$.

Thus, on average, observed scores on the test would be likely to fall 4.5 points away from true scores.

## Model of Parallel Tests

We defined the reliability coefficient in terms of the relationship between observed scores and true scores. However, because true scores are ideal quantities, we do not have direct access to them. Therefore, we can only estimate a test's reliability. One way of doing this involves the model of parallel tests. *Parallel tests* are defined as tests that have the same true score and equal observed score variances (Lord & Novick, 1968). If $X_1$ and $X_2$ are parallel tests, $t_1 = t_2$ and variance $(x_1)$ = variance $(x_2)$. In other words, parallel tests measure exactly the same thing in the same scale, and measure it with equal precision. Although we will not demonstrate it here, it can be shown that if we have two parallel tests, we can estimate their reliability in a straightforward way:

$$r_{11} = r_{x_1 x_2}$$

The reliability coefficient is equal to the correlation between two parallel tests (Lord & Novick, 1968). If two tests measure the same thing in the same scale, and they are entirely free from measurement error, their intercorrelation should be perfect, $r_{11} = 1.0$. Any random error will lower this correlation. The model of parallel tests has played a central role in classical reliability theory. However, as a practical matter of establishing reliability, it has its limitations. For one thing, it is not always possible to develop parallel tests. Moreover, demonstrating that two tests are parallel can be difficult. An alternative way of estimating reliability, and one that is more widely used in practice, is by computing a statistic known as *Cronbach's alpha* (Nunnally, 1978). Alpha is a measure of the internal consistency of items on a test, a measure of the extent to which the items "hang together." To understand the concept behind alpha, we need to introduce another theoretical model, known as the *domain sampling model*.

## Domain Sampling Model

The domain sampling model is based on the idea that the items on a test can be thought of as a random sample taken from an infinitely large domain of possible items (Nunnally, 1978). For example, the items on a depression test, such as the Beck Depression Inventory (Beck & Steer, 1987), can be thought of as a random sample taken from an infinitely large domain of depression items. Domain, universe, and population are synonymous terms for this infinitely large set of items (Nunnally, 1978). The true score for an individual would be the $M$ of their responses to all of the items in the domain (Nunnally, 1978). Their observed score on any given test would typically be higher or lower than their true score, due to chance variation in the random sampling of items from the domain. In other words, because all items contain some measurement error, random samples of these items would deviate from the true score for the domain (Nunnally, 1978). Of course, in reality, tests are not made up of random samples of items. They are composed by the test's author, who has presumably written items that he or she believes are the best examples of the domain. However, in most circumstances, the domain sampling model is a reasonable approximation of reality that enables us to develop various reliability estimates, such as alpha.

If we imagine an infinitely large domain of items, we can imagine an infinitely large matrix containing the intercorrelations among the items. The average correlation in the matrix, $M$ ($r_{ij}$), indicates the extent to which the items in the matrix share in a "common core," the extent to which they "hang together" (Nunnally, 1978). The intercorrelations of individual pairs of items will vary from the $M$ correlation due to measurement error. In others words, some items will share in the common core to a greater extent than other items. If we make the assumption that all of items in the matrix share equally in the common core, and that the matrix is infinitely large, it can be demonstrated that:

$$r_{1t} = \sqrt{\bar{r}_{ij}}$$

The reliability of an item (e.g., item 1)—the correlation of an item with its true score—is a function of the average intercorrelation among all the items in an infinitely large domain (Nunnally, 1978). The more highly intercorrelated the items in the domain, the more they share in the common core, the greater the reliability. It is easy to extend this logic from the sampling of individual items to tests consisting of many items. Thus, using the domain sampling model, we can conceive of reliability as the extent to which the items in a domain hang together, or how internally consistent they are. Of course, in reality, we cannot compute this quantity for the entire domain, because it is infinitely large. However, we can estimate it by using a sample of the items from the domain, namely, the items on a particular test. Assuming that items on a test are representative of the domain as a whole, we can use the mean intercorrelation of the items on a test, $M(r_{ij})$, to estimate the same quantity for the domain as a whole. This is the conceptual basis of Cronbach's alpha. Alpha provides an estimate of a test's reliability by determining the degree of relatedness or internal consistency among its items (Nunnally, 1978).

## Coefficient Alpha

The formula for coefficient alpha is the following (Nunnally, 1978):

$$r_{kk} = \alpha = \frac{k}{k-1} \left( 1 - \frac{\sum \sigma_i^2}{\sigma_y^2} \right)$$

In this formula, $k$ refers to the number of items on the test, Variance ($i$) refers to the variances of the individual items, and Variance ($y$) refers to the overall variance of the test. It is evident from the aforementioned formula that the size of alpha is partially dependent on the number of items on the test (because $k/k-1$ approaches 1 as $k$, the number of items increases). All other things being equal, the greater the number of items, the higher the value of alpha. This leads to the old adage that "a long test is a good test." If a test's reliability is poor, adding more items can raise it. The Spearman-Brown "prophesy" formula can be used to determine the factor by which the length of the test would need to be increased in order to achieve a desired level of reliability (see upcoming text; Nunnally, 1978). Of course, longer tests also take more time to complete, so considerations of reliability and convenience need to be balanced in deciding the optimal length for a test.

Although it is not obvious from the formula just displayed, the size of alpha is also dependent on the average intercorrelation among the items on the test (this quantity is "hidden" in the denominator of the formula, variance [$y$]). As we have already discussed, the average intercorrelation among the items is a measure of internal consistency, the degree to which the items hang together or share in a "common core." If all the items on a test are perfectly intercorrelated, alpha is equal to 1. When there is no internal consistency among the test items, alpha is equal to zero. By convention, alpha coefficients of .8 or greater are considered to represent good to excellent reliability. However, tests with reliabilities of .7 or even .6 may still contain enough true score variance to be usable (Nunnally, 1978).

## Alternatives to Alpha

Coefficient alpha is by far the most widely used measure of reliability, both because of its comprehensibility and ease of computation. However, alternative measures, such as split-half reliability and test–retest reliability, are sometimes used as well (Nunnally, 1978). Split-half reliability is easy to compute, and for that reason was popular in the era before computers. The method is to divide the items on a test into two equal groups (e.g., evenly numbered items and odd numbered items), then compute the Pearson correlation between the two halves of the test. The Spearman-Brown formula (see upcoming text) can then be used to "prophesize" the reliability of the full-length test. The split-half reliability is actually a special case of coefficient alpha. In fact, alpha is equal to the $M$ of all possible split-half reliabilities of a test (Nunnally, 1978). The split-half reliability is rarely used today.

The test–retest reliability involves administering a test on two separate occasions, usually 1 to 2 weeks apart, then computing the Pearson correlation between the two test administrations (Nunnally, 1978). The same test can be administered on two occasions, or alternative forms of a test can be given, if practice effects are a concern. The test–retest method estimates reliability using the parallel-test model. The assumption is that true scores for the test are the same on the two testing occasions, $t_1 = t_2$, and that the observed variances are equal as well, variance $(x_1)$ = variance $(x_2)$. Reliability can therefore be estimated simply by correlating the scores on the two testing occasions. The drawback to the test–retest approach is that it the trait being measured by the test may have changed with the passage of time; if this is the case, the assumption of identical true scores on the two testing occasions has been violated. Moreover, some tests are designed to measure mental or emotional states rather than traits. State-tests are highly sensitive to fluctuations that may occur over very brief time intervals, such as days, hours, or even minutes, and therefore would not be expected to show a high degree of test–retest reliability. Despite these limitations, test–retest reliability is an important alternative to coefficient alpha, because it corresponds to a definition of reliability as the repeatability or stability of a measurement. As seen, alpha defines reliability as the internal consistency of a measurement, rather than its repeatability. For this reason, coefficient alpha and test–retest reliability can be thought of as complementary approaches to estimating reliability. In general, values of alpha will be higher than for test–retest reliability, because the passage of time will attenuate test–retest coefficients (Nunnally, 1978). As a practical matter, many investigators report both statistics, coefficient alpha and test–retest reliability, in their research reports.

## *K* SCALE

Recall the first equation that maintained that every score or measurement ($X$) can be thought of as a true score ($t$) plus error ($e$). The principle of aggregation mentioned holds that when repeated measurements are combined (summed or averaged), the random error components tend to cancel one another, whereas the constant true score component is maintained. Hence, aggregate scores have smaller error components than do single scores.

Some phenomena can be reliably measured with a few items, whereas other phenomena require many items to be reliably measured. Said differently, some variables have small error terms, whereas others may have very large error terms. Such variables may require many repeated measurements before their error term reduces to an acceptable level.

It occurred to one of us (Warren Tryon) that the number of repeated measurements (test items) necessary to achieve a predetermined level of reliability may be a characteristic property of the concept being measured. It is necessary to learn more about the Spearman-Brown formula before this point can be developed further.

The Generalized Spearman-Brown formula can be used to calculate how reliable a test will be if its length is doubled ($K = 2$), tripled ($K = 3$), or halved ($K = .5$) ) (Anastasi, 1988, p. 121; Gullikson, 1950, p. 78) if one knows the reliability of the original test, called the *unit test*, and the number of items in that test. Most clinicians are interested in increasing test reliability by lengthening a test. Other clinicians desire a short form and can use the generalized Spearman-Brown formula to estimate how reliable their test will be if it is 90% as long ($K = .9$), 80% as long ($K = .8$) etcetera. $r_a$ is used now to symbolize the reliability of the longer aggregated (or shorter) test, $r_u$ equals the reliability of the initial test, also called the unit test, and $K$ is the number of units long the proposed test is compared to the unit test. The initial test is called the unit test because it is thought of as a basic entity or unit that will be multiplied to get a longer test or divided to get a shorter test. The generalized Spearman-Brown formula is as follows:

$$r_a = \frac{K r_u}{1 + (K - 1) r_u}$$

For example, if a test with a reliability coefficient of .6 is made three times as long, its reliability will become $(3)(.6) \div (1 + (3 - 1)(.6) = 1.8 \div 1 + 1.2 = .82$ when rounded.

The Spearman-Brown formula can be applied to measurements other than psychological tests. Epstein (1979, 1980, 1983) demonstrated that this formula can be used to predict reliability increases when ratings are repeated and aggregated over time. Averages of repeated measurements, including self-ratings, ratings of others, and behavioral observations are more repeatable, stable, and therefore more reliable than are single observations. We begin with one pre and one post measurements for every participant, which allow us to calculate test–retest reliability. Perhaps the reliability of such measurements is a very low and unacceptable .15. Getting 7 ratings each time would increase repeated measurements by a factor of $K = 7$ resulting in a predicted reliability of $7(.15) \div 1 + (7 - 1).15 = 1.05 \div 1.9 = .55$, which is rather better than .15 but still not good.

The question naturally arises: How many repeated measurements are required to reach a prescribed reliability level? The next formula answers this question. Suppose we want to know how many repeated measurements are required to obtain a reliability coefficient of .80. This equation solves the Spearman-Brown formula for $K$ (Gullikson, 1950, p. 83). The quantities involved have the same definitions as already given.

$$K = \frac{(1 - r_u)r_a}{(1 - r_a)r_u}$$

Increasing reliability from .55 to .80 requires us to lengthen the 7-measure aggregate by a factor of $K = (1 - .55).80 \div (1 - .80).55 = 3.27$. Hence $7 \times 3.27 = 22.89$ or 23 repeated measurements. Put another way, the average of 23 ratings is expected to correlate .80 with the average of another 23 ratings provided what is rated remains the same. Ratings could be repeated by a single rater or could stem from multiple raters as long as they were trained to rate in the same way.

Alternatively, we could have asked how many repeated measurements are necessary when the test–retest reliability of a single measurement (unit test of length = 1) are necessary. We find the answer to be $K = (1 - .15).80 \div (1 - .80).15 = 22.67$, which rounded gives 23 repeated measurements. The same answer is found either way.

Now we come to the concept of $K$ scale. The just cited formula shows that it is always possible, in principle, to achieve any degree of reliability except for perfect reliability, which requires an infinitely long test. If we select an arbitrary level of reliability such as .80, then it is always possible to determine the number of repeated measurements (items) needed to achieve the stated level of reliability. Certain information can be reliably obtained with one question; one's phone number or date of birth are examples. But psychological traits and behaviors require repeated measurements to achieve the same degree of reliability. Some traits and behaviors require more repeated measurements than others. Calculating the number of repeated measurements required to achieve an arbitrary level of reliability such as .80 yields a value of $K$ for each trait and/or behavior so evaluated. Rank ordering the resulting values of $K$ produces a $K$ scale. Recall that measurement error is what attenuates reliability and that aggregating repeated measurements reduces measurement error. $K$ can therefore be understood as a way to index the previously unknown size of the error term associated with the true score component of measurements. The $K$ scale therefore orders traits and behaviors by an important characteristic property of measurement.

The $K$ scale has both theoretical and practical applications. Its theoretical application is to demonstrate that construct existence is not an all-or-nothing proposition but rather a matter of degree. Constructs with high $K$ values have what might be called a virtual existence at low levels of aggregation in that they cannot be reliably measured with one, two, or even a few repeated measurements because their measurement errors are so large that they swamp the true score values. Only with enough repeated measurements to reduce the error terms to an acceptable level can adequate reliability be obtained. Only then can one reasonably expect to find the empirical evidence that is theoretically associated with the construct. In other words, only at some reasonable level of reliability does the construct have empirical existence. It would be a mistake to reject a construct when the only empirical studies of it are based on so few repeated measurements that empirical support cannot be obtained. A direct analogy can be made to statistical power. Experiments with low statistical power frequently fail to yield empirical support because they had little chance of doing so. It is a mistake in these situations to conclude that no effect exists. The $K$ scale indirectly quantifies the size of the error term associated with true scores and emphasizes the need to aggregate repeated measurements in order to obtain adequate reliability and consequently allow for a proper empirical test of the construct in question.

The practical application of the $K$ scale is that it informs investigators about the number of repeated measurements needed to obtain a specified degree of reliability; empirical existence. The value of .80 was chosen as a compromise between small measurement error and many repeated measurements. Any other value could be chosen but .80 is a useful compromise in the same way that 80% power is a useful recommendation. Investigators should therefore obtain sufficient repeated measurements to obtain a reliability coefficient of .80 before proceeding to test hypotheses related to these variables.

## IMPACT OF RELIABILITY ON VALIDITY

It is generally understood that reliability places an upper bound on validity. Validity coefficients cannot consistently be larger than the square root of reliability coefficients (Gulliksen, 1950, p. 97). It is less well recognized that increases in reliability coefficients lead to increases in validity coefficients. If a test has a (unit) reliability coefficient of $r_u$ and a validity coefficient of $r_{vu}$ then increasing the test length by a factor of $K$ will increase the validity coefficient to $r_{va}$ as follows (cf. Gulliksen, 1950, p. 89):

$$r_{va} = \frac{r_{vu}\sqrt{K}}{\sqrt{1 + (K - 1)r_u}}$$

For example, if we assume that the 7-measure aggregate with the reliability coefficient of .55 presented had a validity coefficient of .2, then by extending the number of repeated measurements by a factor of 3.27 would increase the validity coefficient to .24. Notice that the increase in validity due to increased repeated measures is much more modest than the increase in reliability.

Investigators may wish to know how much longer they must make a test in order to achieve the desired validity. Gulliksen (1950, p. 93) provides the following formula where $r_{va}$ is the validity coefficient chosen for the aggregated test, $r_{vu}$ is the validity coefficient for the shorter unit test and $r_u$ is the reliability coefficient for the unit test.

$$K = \frac{r_{va}^2(1 - r_u)}{r_{vu}^2 - r_u r_{va}^2}$$

There are limits to which validity coefficients can be increased by augmenting reliability coefficients. The maximum reliability coefficient that can be obtained using an infinitely long test ($r_{\infty l}$) from a test with a (unit) reliability coefficient of $r_u$ and a unit validity coefficient of $r_{vu}$ is given below (Gulliksen, 1950, p. 95). For example, the maximum possible validity that can be obtained by increasing the length of unit test with the reliability coefficient of .55 and validity coefficient of .20 is .2697.

$$r_\infty = \frac{r_{vu}}{\sqrt{r_u}}$$

## DEVELOPING OPERATIONAL DEFINITIONS

Definitions give meaning. We specify meaning when we define a word. We distinguish positive from negative instances to what the word refers. Operational definitions equate meaning with measurement in that they define concepts and constructs in terms of the procedures used to measure them. Different measurement procedures mean different things. A corollary implication of the assertion that operational definition confers meaning is to intimately connect measurement with theory. An adequate test of theory requires adequate measurement of the concepts and constructs entailed by the theory. Otherwise, research is either partial or trivial to the extent that it measures only part or none of what the theory intended to study.

### Univariate Definitions

*Operational definitions* frequently specify the psychological test used to quantify the construct in question. A univariate operational definition entails a single test. For example, it is sometimes said that "intelligence is what intelligence tests measure," meaning that the intelligence test operationalizes the definition of intelligence. The test items and manual that govern test administration are part of the operational definition because they structure the collection and scoring of the obtained behavioral sample. Similarly, one can say that "depression is what depression tests measure," and that "anxiety is what anxiety tests measure," referring again to both the test items, the way in which the test is administered (e.g., paper and pencil vs. interview format), and the test instructions. In a real sense, measurement defines what we mean when we discuss some topic. Certainly, it is what our research means when we use such tests to evaluate theoretically driven hypotheses. If intelligence tests do not really measure intelligence, anxiety tests do not really measure anxiety, and depression tests do not really measure depression, etcetera, then we should change them until they do. Only when tests properly measure what we intend them to measure is it possible to adequately test hypotheses about these constructs. Said otherwise, test construction is about construct definition! Investigators are encouraged to refine and develop tests until they reflect their underlying constructs.

## Multivariate Definitions

Structural Equation Modeling (SEM) entails a measurement component and a structural component. The measurement component uses two or more indicators to measure an underlying latent construct. This multidimensional approach to operational definition uses the common variance shared by the multiple indicators to operationally define latent constructs. For example, an indicator of social support from family and an indicator of social support from peers might be used to define the construct of social support. Alternatively, an indicator of perceived social support and an indicator of rated ("actual") social support might be used to define the construct of social support. The common variance shared by the first pair of indicators is not identical to the common variance shared by the second pair of indicators, which means that these two *multivariate* operational definitions of social support are not the same.

More indicators are, by definition, more comprehensive in that more facets of the construct are being tapped. The hidden cost is that the shared, common, variance decreases as more indicators are used. It is not unlike identifying common meeting times as the number of participants increases. Fewer times that all participants can meet occur as the number of participants increases. Range (variance) restriction attenuates (reduces) correlation coefficients, including validity coefficients. Only by increasing sample size can one counter the effects of using many indicators and this entails its own set of problems.

## METHODS OF COLLECTING DATA

Various methods are available for collecting data. We address interviews, questionnaires, psychological tests, behavioral observation, and instruments. Each of these methods of collecting data has advantages and disadvantages.

### Interviews

Interviews can be unstructured, semistructured, or structured (Sattler & Mash, 1998). *Unstructured interviews* allow the interviewer to choose the topics that will be covered, the number of questions to be asked, the way each question shall be posed, the order in which questions shall be posed, and what shall be recorded—if anything. Open or closed questions can be used. Leading questions may or may not be used. Each subject might be interviewed in a different way with regard to each of the aforementioned matters. If subjects in different groups such as clients meeting certain diagnostic criteria and control subjects are interviewed differently, any differences found could be due to these methodological differences rather than substantive differences. Reliability and validity coefficients are unavailable for unstructured interviews. Unstructured interviews should generally be avoided in all but purely exploratory research because the methodological inconsistencies in combination with the absence of psychometric properties can be used to explain any differences the clinician wishes to interpret as meaningful.

*Semistructured interviews* orient the interviewer to topics that should be covered during the interview and provide specific questions that can be asked. They do not govern follow-up questions nor do they regulate what is recorded. Appendix F of Sattler and Mash (1998, pp. 917–1027) provides many semi-structured questions covering a wide variety of child and family issues. The psychometric properties of unstructured interviews are assumed rather than demonstrated.

*Structured interviews* specify the questions to be asked, the order in which they are to be presented, and the responses that can be recorded (Segal, 1997). Research and clinical demands for reliable interview data largely motivated the development of structured interviews. The Schedule for Affective Disorders and Schizophrenia (SADS; Endicott & Spitzer, 1978), the Diagnostic Interview Schedule (DIS; Robins, Helzer, Croughan, & Ratcliff, 1981), the Structured Clinical Interview for DSM-IV (SCID; First, Spitzer, Gibbon, & Williams, 1995), the Structured Interview for DSM-IV Personality (SIDP-IV; Pfohl, Blum, & Zimmerman, 1995), and the International Personality Disorder Examination (PIDE; Loranger et al., 1994) are examples of structured interviews for adults. The Child and Adolescent Psychiatric Assessment (CAPA; Angold, Cox, Rutter, & Simonoff, 1996), Child Adolescent Schedule (CAS; Hodges, 1997), Diagnostic Interview for Children and

Adolescents-Revised (DICA-R; Reich, 1996), and Schedule for Affective Disorders & Schizophrenia for School-Age Children (K-SADS-IVR; Ambrosini & Dixon, 1996) are examples of structured interviews for children and adolescents. Psychometric properties, reliability and validity coefficients, are generally available for structured interviews and they typically meet accepted psychometric standards.

## Questionnaires

Questionnaires come in many formats and are designed for many purposes. Their great diversity defines easy description. Information requested ranges from objective data such as name, sex, address, and birth date to open-ended prompts, where the respondent writes what they wish. Questionnaires are typically constructed by an investigator for a specific study and are generally not used again without revision by the same or other investigators. The psychometric properties of most questionnaires are typically not unreported; probably because they are not known. Questionnaires are taken as face valid, meaning that it is simply assumed that they measure what they purport to measure. There is no way to know if respondents would fill them out the same way twice. The more detailed the questionnaire, the less likely respondents are to complete them in exactly the same way on two occasions, and the less reliable they probably are.

## Behavioral Observation

Direct observation of behavior requires one to first define what to observe. Behavioral categories are defined in terms of observable characteristics. Inferences should be minimized. Observers typically tally the frequency with which each behavioral category occurs. Training is generally required to enable observers to consistently categorize behaviors. Consistency across observers is taken as evidence of measurement reliability. Informed consent of those being observed is required.

The validity of behavioral observation has frequently been assumed rather than demonstrated. Behavioral samples vary with regard to setting. Children are frequently observed in playrooms housed in a clinic or laboratory run with the intention of generalizing the results to school and home. Is one to expect generalization entirely on the basis of personality traits? Is the situation at home or school sufficiently similar to the observational setting in enough critical ways to warrant generalization from one to the other? It is best to sample behavior directly from the situations to which one intends to generalize. This means observing at home if one intends to generalize to home and observing at school if one intends to generalize to school. Cost and logistic factors complicate such efforts.

Behavioral samples vary with regard to duration. Sometimes investigators generalize from a short, 20-minute observation period to all other waking hours from the recent past through the indefinite future. Other investigators observe behavior for many hours prior to generalizing the results. Behavioral sample size is important, in that, all other things being equal, it is safer to generalize from larger than smaller samples. The duration of observations should be directly proportional to behavioral variability; longer observation periods are needed to properly characterize more variable behavior.

## Psychological Tests

Anastasi (1988) stated that "A psychological test is essentially an objective and standardized measure of a sample of behavior" (p. 23). Tests of intelligence, achievement, and personality contain standardized stimuli. The subject's behavior is recorded and the test manual provides instructions for scoring (quantifying) the subject's behavior and provides norms for interpreting test results. Evidence of test reliability and validity are also presented in the manual to facilitate the interpretation of test results. A wide variety of objective and projective psychological tests are available from publishers. More tests are in the public domain and can either be obtained from the journals in which they were published or they can be obtained directly from the author. Professional ethics now require clinicians to use tests of acceptable reliability and validity. Tests that have been standardized on one group of people are sometimes used on groups of different race, ethnicity, and age, which calls the validity of the obtained results into question. Administering tests to Hispanics that have only been standardized on Whites is a case in point. Additional normative data are needed in these cases.

## Instruments

Operational definitions frequently entail instruments. The operational definition of body weight might be to place people on a (brand name, model, and manufacturer) scale. A wide variety of instruments is available for psychological research. For example, depressed people take longer to process information and to respond to stimuli. One operational definition of depression severity is to record the time it takes the patient to count from zero to 25 or some other number. Self-concept can be measured by the time taken to endorse self-referent adjectives (Marcus & Wurf, 1987; Markus, Crane, Bernstein, & Siladi, 1982; Mueller, Thompson, & Dugan, 1986). The time taken to answer personality test items is systematically related to personality characteristics (Holden, Fekken, & Cotton, 1991; Holden, Woermke, & Fekken, 1993; Popham & Holden, 1990). Activity level is part of the inclusion and/or exclusion criteria of 48 Diagnostic and Statistical Manual of Mental

Disorders (4th ed.; DSM-IV) disorders (Tryon, 2002). Activity level can be quantified by many devices based on various technologies. Many methods have been used to measure physical activity (Bouten, Westerterp, Verduin, & Janssen, 1994; Freedson, 1991; LaPorte, Montoye, & Caspersen, 1985; Melanson, Jr., & Freedson, 1996; Meijer, Westerterp, Verhoeven, Koper, & ten Hoor, 1991; Montoye, Kemper, Saris, & Washburn, 1996; Tryon, 1985, 1991; Tryon & Williams, 1996; U.S. Department of Health and Human Services, 1996). Unfortunately, they do not share a common unit of measure. *Continuous performance tests* are instrumented measures of sustained attention (e.g., Conners, 1992). Several instrumented tests of impulsivity exist. Barratt's (1981, 1985) time-estimation task measures the accuracy with which participants can correctly guess measured amounts of elapsed time. Complex reaction time has been used as a measure of impulsivity (Exposito & Andres-Pueyo, 1997). The stop signal test measures the delay at which a stop signal fails to counteract a start signal and has also been used to measure impulsivity (Logan & Cowan, 1984; Logan, Cowan, & Davis, 1984; Logan, Schachar, & Tannock, 1997).

Unlike all of the other methods for data collection just reviewed, the measurement properties of instruments can be evaluated under highly controlled laboratory conditions independent of human behavior. Timers can be compared to calibrated standards. Activity monitors can be placed on pendulums or put into spinners. Studies that attempt to evaluate the measurement properties of instruments using people confound subject variation with instrument variation. For example, the reliability of activity monitors cannot be properly evaluated using people because people cannot repeatedly perform exactly the same movements with anywhere near the same degree of precision that laboratory devices can. Subject variability can be several times larger than instrument variability and consequently severely attenuates reliability estimates. Tryon (1991, pp. 9–11) shows that special methods are needed to evaluate instrument reliability.

*Instrument validity* pertains to the operational specifications of the instrument, which are again best determined under laboratory conditions. For example, step counters are intended to be worn at the waist and to count steps taken by people. The best way to evaluate the consistency of a single device to repeated stimulation is to produce up and down movements with known properties using a laboratory device. People's gait is far less regular than such a mechanical device and will confound gait variability with instrument variability.

The remaining question is whether the device, a step counter in this case, adequately measures the behavior(s) one is interested in. Can a step counter correctly identify the steps taken by all people all of the time or do they sometimes take steps that are too small to be detected? An activity monitor placed at the waist cannot be expected to measure wrist activity. No single instrument placed at anywhere on the body can measure all aspects of human activity.

Operational definitions are not generally considered when instruments are used beyond specifying the make and model numbers. We do not generally think about the measurement units employed by the devices we use. Nor do we think about instruments as a possible source of new theory. This following section raises these and other related issues.

### Instrument Driven Theory

We normally think of measurement in service of theory. Science is typically presented with theory generating hypotheses and research being conducted to evaluate them. Measurement specifics are frequently relegated to minor details and are typically printed in smaller print in accordance with their lesser stature. However, sometimes instrumentation advances impact theory in unplanned, but important ways that either open new areas of inquiry or decisively settle long-standing theoretical disputes. Sometimes instruments enable theoretical changes that might not have otherwise occurred. These are instances of what is here called *measurement driven theory*. A few examples from established sciences are used to illustrate these points because clinicians have less experience with instruments than do other scientists.

*Physics/Astronomy.* Harwit (1981) documented the role played by instruments in the generation of new ideas in astronomy. These novel ideas were almost always unanticipated by existing theory. For example, children playing in the shop of a Dutch spectacle maker named Lippershey (Boorstin, 1983, p. 314) discovered the telescope. He observed that the children were able to enlarge a distant weather vane by properly spacing selected lenses. Telescopes were first sold in Paris in 1609, and by the end of that year, Galileo had constructed his own 30 power telescope. This device increased the number of visible stars by a factor of 10, resulting in the conclusion that the universe was much larger than had been thought. The moon was seen to have a rough and uneven surface rather than the smooth polished surface as believed by the then current theory. The centuries-old debate concerning the substance of the Milky Way was definitively settled to be a mass of stars (p. 320). Saturn was observed to have an oval rather than the theoretically expected circular shape. Venus was observed to have phases like our own moon, thereby fostering the Copernican model of our solar system.

All planets were thought to be inert until 1955, when Bernard Burke and Kenneth Franklin unexpectedly detected radio waves from Jupiter (Harwit, 1981, p. 38). A similar unexpected radio wave measurement in 1967 by Anthony Hewish and Jocelyn Bell established an entirely new type of astronomical body for theoretical analysis.

Farmelo's (1995) account of Röntgen's discovery of X rays clearly illustrates instrument driven theory. Röntgen accidentally discovered X rays while studying streams of electrons called cathode rays. The first theories of X rays did not emerge until several months after Röntgen's discovery and therefore could not have guided his inquiry. This scientific advance was considered so important that Röntgen won the Nobel Prize in physics in 1901.

**Biology.** Biologists had no conception of bacteria and other very small life forms prior to the invention of the microscope. Antoni van Leeuwenhoek was among the first investigators to systematically use a microscope. He began his studies by simply examining a variety of specimens. No pre-existing theory guided his inquiry. Nevertheless, Leeuwenhoek made seminal discoveries in microbiology, embryology, histology, botany, and crystallography using his new instrument. Some of his observations disproved accepted theory of his day. For example, his detection of spermatozoa helped disprove the accepted theory that semen provided fertilizing vapors. Visualization of spermatoza revealed a specific causal biological entity. Robert Hooke's (1635–1703) cellular theory was developed only after he examined a thin slice of cork under the microscope.

**Medicine.** Modern medicine differs from its precursor in that it understands disease in terms of measurements and analyses conducted in natural science laboratories. Certain medical disorders were unknown prior to certain instrumentation because they are defined entirely in terms of measurements made by instruments (cf. Davidsohn & Henry, 1974). For example, *anemia* is defined as having less than 13.5 grams of hemoglobin per decaliter (gm/dl) in adult males and 12.0 gm/dl for adult females (Davidsohn & Henry, 1974, p. 181). This condition has no meaning apart from a measure of weight and a measure of liquid volume. Hypo- and hypertension are distinguished from normal blood pressure as measured by a sphygmomanometer. Cutoff values for diagnosing these disorders are given in terms of the measurement units employed by this device (mm Hg). No pre-existing theory of excessive arterial pressure was tested by constructing a sphygmomanometer. Rather, it appears that clinical application of the sphygmomanometer caused physicians to become aware of the health consequences of hyper- and hypotension.

### Reasons Why Instruments Can Produce Conceptual Change

Several reasons exist as to why new instruments can stimulate conceptual change. One reason is that instruments extend our senses in new and sometimes unanticipated ways. Instruments quantify, sometimes at precisely timed intervals, and thereby reveal temporal patterns at time indices vastly different from ordinary experience and consequently may yield unexpected information. The total unfamiliarity of what is revealed by the new instrument explains why theory is unable to anticipate and guide these developments. For example, high-speed photography can be played back slowly to reveal details of events

that would ordinarily happen too quickly to be perceived. Time-lapse photography is used to "speed up" events so that we can perceive changes that
would ordinarily happen so slowly as not to create the impression of systematic change. Use of lasers to pulse chemical reactions into partial completion
is another example. Obtaining brain scans from conscious subjects provides
new information about which areas of the brain mediate certain psychological
functions.

A second reason why instruments can lead us in new theoretical directions
stems from the organizing function of theory. By structuring our thought and
perception, theory also blinds us to alternative possibilities. Instruments and
research generally, can present us with unanticipated data patterns that force
us to think in new ways. In other words, instruments are not bound by the
limits of current theory. They sometimes penetrate unconsidered alternatives,
present us with unexpected, anomalous results, and thereby focus our attention
where no theory previously directed us.

Third, instruments are selective in what they measure because of how they
are constructed. Instruments consistently collect data in accordance with design
parameters that include their units of measure. For example, accelerometers
measure movement and not inattentiveness so they cannot confuse one concept
for the other as human observers can. Instruments observe more objectively
and consistently than people do. For example, measured activity is not always
concordant with rated activity (cf. Tryon & Pinto, 1994). People are much more
easily distracted than are instruments. In sum, investigators should consider
using instruments to obtain their data and not reflexively use the other forms
of data collection already reviewed.

## TYPES OF PSYCHOLOGICAL SCALES

*Nominal scales* use numbers as names. Athletic uniforms are a case in point.
Number 7 designates a specific player. Nothing is quantified; no measurement
has occurred. We are not concerned with such scales.

*Ordinal scales* entail rank-order information. The fastest runner is designated as 1, the next fastest runner is designated as 2, etcetera, through the
slowest runner, designated $N$. Numbers reflect ordinal position. We know that
runner 1 is faster than runner 2 and that runner 2 is faster than runner 3 but
we cannot say more. Perhaps runner 1 came in way ahead of runner 2, who
was just a step ahead of runner 3. Alternatively, the top reader in a class, the
number 1 reader, may not be able to read a newspaper. This can happen when
all persons in a class do not read very well. No necessary connection exists
between being number 1 and being good. Similarly, one can come in last and
be very good. For example, the last-place person in the national spelling-bee
finals is probably an excellent speller. The last-place sprinter in the Olympic

100-meter dash is probably faster than 99% of the world's population. In short, ordinal data are meaningful only in context.

*Interval scales* presume a unit of measure that is equal across the measurement scale. This is the case with a thermometer. A difference of one degree entails the same amount of heat whether it is from 10 to 11 degrees, or 20 to 21 degrees. Most psychological tests presume equal interval scaling. IQ units are frequently understood to be equally meaningful across the scale. The IQ unit between 130 and 131 is presumed to be equivalent to the IQ unit between 50 and 51. Similarly, the depression increase on the Beck Depression Inventory from 25 to 26 is presumed to entail the same increase in depression as a change from a score of 10 to 11. The equality of measurement units assumed by interval scales is questionable when applied to most psychological tests. There is no good way to settle this issue because measurement units have not been defined in psychology as they have been defined in other sciences. This issue is of sufficient importance that the units of measure section is devoted to it.

*Ratio scales* are interval scales with an absolute zero. It is not twice as hot on a summer day when it is 100°F than in the autumn when it is 50°F even though 100 is twice 50. This is because both the Fahrenheit and Centigrade temperature scales have arbitrary rather than absolute zero points. O°C is just the point at which water freezes; not the point of no heat. That would be absolute zero, which is $-459.69°F = -273.16°C$. The Kelvin scale takes this point as zero and uses the centigrade unit. Hence, water freezes at 273.16°K. Ratio scales support ratio inferences. 300°K is twice as hot as 150°K and half as hot at 600°K. A person with an IQ of 150 is not twice as smart as a person with an IQ of 75 because IQ tests do not have an absolute zero point. Most psychological tests lack an absolute zero point and therefore cannot support ratio statements.

## UNITS OF MEASURE

The unit of measure is fundamental to the measurement process in at least two ways. First, and foremost is that measurement units define the fundamental quanta or packets of what is being measured. They specify a standard amount of the phenomenon being assessed, and in so doing make a theoretical statement about what is being measured. For example, Tryon and Williams (1996) defined activity in units of acceleration. This physics perspective differs markedly from a biological understanding of activity as calories of metabolic heat energy expended, as well as various psychological perspectives based on perceived movement. Acceleration and calories have well-defined measurement units. Their different definitions reflect different conceptions about what is being measured. Acceleration pertains to movement, whereas calories pertain to heat.

## Measurement Units in Psychology

Psychophysics endeavors to translate physical units into psychological units. Although scaling techniques were derived for estimating the magnitude of psychological response, standard measurement units were not derived. Psychometricians have developed many psychological tests but have not defined any standard measurement units. The $z$ score is perhaps the closest that psychologists have come to a standard unit of measure. Other scores such as $T$ scores are derived from $z$ scores where the $Mz$ score is always zero and the standard deviation ($SD$) is always 1.0 (Hinkle, Wiersma, & Jurs, 1994). College SAT and GRE scores are obtained by multiplying $z$ scores by 100 and adding 500. Intelligence quotients are derived by multiplying $z$ scores by 16 and adding 100 (Anastasi, 1988). MMPI results are reported in terms of $T$ scores. One advantage is that patients' scores on depression can be directly compared to their scores on schizophrenia despite vast theoretical differences in what is being tapped. Disparate concepts are measured on the same scale using the same measurement unit. A $T$ score of 70 on the Depression scale and a $T$ score of 70 on the Schizophrenia scale implies that the person is as depressed as he/she is schizophrenic. Such a conclusion can easily be questioned.

Effect sizes are standardized differences between means. Clinicians have chosen to express effect sizes in terms of $z$ scores. They divide the difference between the $M$s of the experimental and control groups by the $SD$ of the control group or by the pooled $SD$. This expresses the difference in terms of the number of $SD$ units by which the two groups differ. The $z$ score is a theoretical, two-edged sword. Its positive benefits include the ability to quantitatively compare the relative standing of subjects across qualitatively disparate measurements. All measurements for all subjects are placed on the same $-3$ to $+3$ scale centered on zero, with zero being the average. The primary negative consequence is the loss of the original measurement unit. The numerator of the $z$ score equals the difference between a person's score and the $M$ score and is therefore expressed in original measurement units. The denominator of the $z$ score equals the $SD$ expressed in the same units of measure. Hence, the original units of measure cancel, resulting in a unitless measurement. All theory construction effort devoted to the development of measurement units is discarded. Any unit of measure that may have been developed is replaced by the $SD$. One reason why this result is problematic is because the size of the measurement unit is not constant but is dependent on who was measured; it differs with every new group of subjects. The $SD$ changes as people are added or dropped from a given group and it changes from one testing to the other. Imagine the quandary that could be created in physics by making the length of a meter stick depend on who or what is measured. It is difficult to estimate the confusion clinicians have created by linking unit size to subjects studied; yet clinicians appear content to routinely allow measurement units to continuously change in unknown and unpredictable ways without question.

Johnston and Pennypacker (1980, p. 128) stressed the theoretical importance of units for psychology. They articulated a behavioral approach to seeking natural units and recommend the following six measurement aspects: (1) latency measured in time units, (2) duration measured in time units, (3) countability measured in cycles, (4) frequency measured in cycles per unit time, (5) celeration measured in cycles per unit time per unit time, and (6) interresponse time measured in time per cycle. Time is mentioned in five of the six suggested units. The concept of *behavioral cycle* is the new unit. A behavioral cycle is defined as persisting until a point is reached where the cycle can start over (cf. Johnston & Pennypacker, 1980, p. 126). Rather than define a unit of measure in reference to two points on a continuum, as with the thermometer, this approach is based on the concept of *periodicity*. Like the sine or cosine trigonometric functions, different values obtain throughout the first rotation around the unit circle but repeat once the start point is encountered a second time. Although any position can be chosen as the starting point in the trigonometric example, some behavioral reference points may be better than others as a point of origin. The time to return to a start point would then quantify the duration of one cycle. The inverse of this time would equal the frequency of this event.

The aforementioned approach assumes that psychology requires new fundamental units of measure. Tryon (1991, pp. 1–22) recommends applying the meter-kilogram-second (mks) system of measurement used in physics to measure behavior. He calls this extension of behavioral assessment *behavioral physics*. Because behavior entails movement in space over time, it can be described in physical terms. For example, pedometers are usually calibrated in terms of miles or kilometers walked. Accelerometers are calibrated in terms of $g$ where $g = 9.80616$ m/s/s at sea level at $45°$ latitude; the rate with which objects freely fall to the ground there. Although some devices attach to the wrist or ankle, the waist is an especially important site of attachment because it corresponds to the body's center of gravity, which allows one to ascribe the person's body mass in kilograms to this point. Integrating vertical acceleration over time yields velocity; which integrated over time gives distance moved; which multiplied by weight yields work energy in joules. Dividing work energy either by total seconds of wearing-time yields power in watts. Tryon (1991, pp. 138–141) describes how calories of energy expended by activity can be calculated from measures of vertical acceleration about the waist.

This approach to measuring behavior has at least two benefits. First, it solves the unit problem by adopting well-defined and accepted measurement units. It seems efficient to pursue this course simultaneously with exploring new psychological units rather than to hold psychological research in abeyance until progress has been made on the unit issue. Second, it may be that substantial progress can be made by reconsidering psychology from the perspective of mks units. Psychology is assumed to be a natural science by some investigators.

In general, physical instruments that quantify behavioral and psychological states make use of the mks measurement system. Reaction time is the classic example. Response rates, latencies, and forces placed on operant manipulanda are measured in terms of the mks system. Computer administered personality tests and neuropsychological exams and rehabilitation programs employ mks units. All physiological measures such as EEG, skin conductance, temperature, blood pressure, etcetera, are defined in mks units. Biofeedback modalities are also definable in mks units. Some activity monitors report distance walked whereas others integrate forces of acceleration detected at the site of attachment. Brain imaging of resting or psychologically active subjects also reports in these units.

Our challenge lies in deriving units for measurements for constructs currently tapped by psychological tests. Units of measure could be introduced into the assessment of intelligence in the following way. Beginning from an information processing theory of intelligence, one might define the characters per sec that can be processed on a digit-symbol (or similar) task as a measure of intelligence. For example, a computer-administered, digit-symbol task could be formulated so that the first key press activates a count-down timer, which would terminate the task when time expires. The number of correct and incorrect responses plus total digit symbols processed would be the dependent variables. The unit of measure for these data would be digits/sec. Time, the denominator, is the primary or constant metric whereas the number of digits processed within each unit would vary and thus would constitute the secondary or variable unit. One would explain variation in total numbers of responses as a function of experimental conditions or subject selection.

Alternately, the time taken to process each correct and/or incorrect digit symbol could be tallied. The constant unit of measure now is the response. The number of ms necessary to complete each response varies. One would explain variation in time as a function of experimental conditions or subject selection.

## Reliability, Validity, and Accuracy

The purpose of this section is to demonstrate that our concepts of *reliability* and *validity* are distorted by the absence of measurement units such that it is possible to develop a measurement device that is completely reliable and valid but inaccurate (cf. Tryon, 1991, pp. 5–6). This problem is eliminated once a measurement unit is introduced.

The absence of standard units of measure allows the following validity paradox to result (cf. Tryon, 1991, pp. 5–6). Imagine that five different investigators construct their own thermometer. Assume that each investigator independently establishs the reliability of their device by demonstrating that repeated measures of the same object yield approximately the same results. Imagine that each investigator performs validity studies where they compare readings taken from water heated by a constant flame for varying periods of time, obtaining progressively greater readings and consequently perfect rank-order validity coefficients. Each investigator would therefore be confident that he or she had a highly reliable and valid instrument. Finally, imagine all five investigators meet at a convention where they gathered to reveal their highly reliable and valid thermometers to each other. When presented with a beaker of room temperature water they insert their thermometers and to everyone's shock, read five very different temperatures! How can this be if each device is highly reliable and valid. Sharing their validity data, investigators find that each one of their devices is very highly intercorrelated with each of the other four devices so this is not the issue. What then is the problem? Are we to conclude that temperature is a multivariate construct and that each investigator is measuring one facet of multidimensional space?

Failure to explicitly define a unit of measure does not mean that no unit of measure is operative. None of the investigators defined a unit of measure but that did not prevent their using different implied measurement units. By choosing glass tubes of different diameters and lengths and inserting different amounts of mercury, or other substances, into different size reservoirs at the bottom of each thermometer, the absolute heights of each column of substance in each thermometer was different even when they were placed in a single medium having a single temperature. Some investigators may have used bimetalic strips connected to pointers with their own read-out scale, thereby further augmenting discrepancies among devices.

Establishing a unit of measure through calibration completely resolves the problem. Place all five devices in ice and mark each dial. Then place all five devices in boiling water and mark each dial. Finally, divide the intervening distance into 100 equal parts thereby creating five centigrade thermometers. When replaced into the previous room temperature beaker of water, all five devices will now indicate the same, or very similar, temperature.

If investigators working with highly reliable and valid instruments can encounter such empirical conundrums as single beakers of water with five simultaneously different temperatures, then even greater confusion can be expected when working with phenomena that are more complex.

### Assessing Instrument Reliability

Psychometric reliability and validity are based on correlational methods. These methods fail when applied to instruments. This failure raises fundamental questions. Consider what happens when coefficient alpha is calculated on the results when 12 activity monitors (subjects) are presented with the same stimulus 10 times (items). If these devices have been manufactured to a high standard and/or if they have been calibrated to function alike, then all 10 readings for each device will be highly similar. This range restriction attenuates the correlations among devices for each of the 12 activity monitors. The corresponding reliability coefficient becomes essentially zero when all of the devices are performing as desired! Coefficient alpha becomes zero, and can even become negative under these conditions. Look at the formula already given. Coefficient alpha becomes zero when the variance of the test equals the sum of the variances of the items. The term within parentheses becomes $1 - 1 = 0$ under these conditions. Coefficient alpha becomes negative as the sum of the item variances exceeds the test variance.

Tryon (1991) suggested an alternative index of reliability for use with instruments. It is based on the coefficient of variation (CV) which equals the standard deviation of a set of repeated measurements divided by the $M$ of the measurement set times 100 to express the result as a percentage. Repeated measurements must form a scatter plot whose diameter is an acceptably small fraction of the $M$ value to be considered reliable. Since CV is an error proportion as is $1 - r^2$, the two can be equated (i.e., $CV = 1 - r^2$). Solving for $r$ yields the following equation:

$$r = \sqrt{1 - CV}$$

## RELIABILITY OF MEASUREMENT: GENERALIZABILITY THEORY

A limitation of classical test theory is that it deals only with random measurement error (Suen, 1990). How is systematic error handled, that is, error that systematically raises or lowers test scores? As noted earlier, systematic error is unlikely to prove problematic when all test scores are affected equally. However, systematic error can become a problem when it affects the scores of only some individuals. Consider the following example. Judges are trained to rate infant affect as positive, negative, or neutral during mother–infant interaction. Suppose that despite standardized training procedures, certain judges are more prone to rate affect as positive or negative, as opposed to neutral (e.g., misinterpreting a grimace as a smile). If not all judges rate all infants, the scores of only some infants will be affected, systematically biasing their results. Classical test theory is not equipped to handle this problem. It assumes that all measurement error is random, and that systematic error has been controlled for by standardizing test conditions. Nevertheless, as the example illustrates, systematic error can still creep in. Unlike classical test theory, generalizability theory is concerned with identifying and quantifying specific sources of measurement error, for example, due to the tendencies of certain judges or types of test conditions. These sources are referred to as *facets* (Suen, 1990).

Facets can be either random or fixed (Suen, 1990). Facets are random when their levels are considered a random sample of all possible levels of the facet. Imagine that three judges rate essays written by students. If the judges can be considered a random sample of all potential judges who might have been employed to rate essays, the judges' facet is a random one. Similarly, if the essays can be considered a random sample of all possible essays that might have been written by the students, the essays facet can be considered a random one. The advantage of random facets is that it allows us to make generalizations about the broader domain from which the specific levels (e.g., the actual judges or essays used in the study) were randomly sampled. For example, we can determine the amount of systematic measurement error associated with judges or essays in general. A generalizability study requires at least one random facet.

In contrast, facets are fixed when all future administrations use exactly the same levels of the facet. For example, if all future studies used exactly the same three judges to rate the students' essays, the judges facet would be considered fixed. The advantage of using fixed facets is that it reduces measurement error. It is equivalent to standardizing test conditions. On the other hand, fixed facets make it more difficult to make generalizations about the object of measurement. If we were to use the same three judges to rate the essays of all future students, we could only make generalizations about students' essays as rated by these three judges, not about essays that might be rated by any randomly selected judge. Thus, the choice to use random versus fixed facets involves a trade-off between generalizability and measurement error.

In classical test theory, there is only one reliability coefficient per test, reflecting the degree to which the test's scores are free from measurement error. In generalizability theory, there can be as many reliability coefficients as there are sources of measurement error (facets; Suen, 1990). A corollary of this is that in classical test theory, there is only one true score—the reliability coefficient is the squared correlation of the observed score with the true score. In generalizability theory, the true score is dependent on the testing situation (Suen, 1990). Different testing situations may introduce different sources of measurement error, and therefore imply different true scores for the same individual.

It should be evident that generalizability theory has much in common with considerations of experimental design. In generalizability theory, the goal is to devise a measurement design that enables one to identify and estimate the magnitude of different sources of error variance. This is known as a *G study* (Suen, 1990). The results of the G study inform decisions about the ultimate design of the experiment, known as the *D study* (Decision study; Suen, 1990). For example, a G study might be used to determine the amount of measurement error associated with any randomly selected judge, and a D study might be used to decide how many judges to employ to achieve a satisfactory level of reliability.

From a statistical point of view, generalizability theory is based on an analysis of variance (ANOVA) framework (Suen, 1990). In ANOVA, the variance of a group of scores can be decomposed into several population variance estimates, known as "mean squares." In the simplest example, a one-way ANOVA, two or more groups are compared on some variable of interest. For example, schizophrenics, bipolar disorder, and unipolar depressed patients might be rated by one judge on a 10-point scale of cognitive disturbance. These scores can be decomposed into two sources of variance: between group variance, reflecting the deviation of each group's $M$ from the $M$ of all patients (the grand $M$), and within group variance, reflecting the deviation of each individual's score from the $M$ of his own group. In ANOVA, we are interested in the ratio of between group variance (the $M$ square between groups) to within group variance (the $M$ square within groups) as a way of testing hypotheses about differences in group means. For example, do schizophrenics, bipolar depressed, and unipolar depressed patients differ in their level of cognitive disturbance?

In generalizability theory, we use the $M$ squares to estimate the magnitude of different sources of test score variance in the population (Suen, 1990). Typically, we wish to estimate the amount of variance associated with different sources of systematic measurement error (e.g., systematic differences between the judges in ratings of cognitive disturbance), random measurement error, and trait variation; that is, variation in the trait we are interested in measuring (e.g., cognitive disturbance; Suen, 1990). Imagine a slight variation on the study just described. Two judges rate the cognitive disturbance of a single group of psychiatric patients using a 10-point scale. Here there are two different sources of variance in the cognitive disturbance scores: subjects (i.e., patients) and judges. In other words, both subjects and judges can contribute to systematic variation in the test scores. Under most circumstances, the variance between subjects would be considered trait variation—it is what we are interested in studying, and is therefore referred to as the *object of measurement*. If this were the case, the variance between judges would be considered a potential source of systematic measurement error (i.e., a facet). In this example, there is a single source of systematic error, judges, so this study would be referred to as a single-facet design with two levels (Suen, 1990). There are two levels to the facet because there are two judges. We could introduce additional facets into the design, for example, by asking the judges to rate the patients at two points in time, or to make two different ratings of cognitive disturbance, one based on peculiar word usage, the other on flight of ideas.

Although in most studies we are interested in trait variation as the object of measurement, we might also be interested in studying judges' perceptions of cognitive disturbance. In this case, judges would become the object of measurement, whereas subjects would become the source of systematic error (the facet). It all depends on whether we wish to make generalizations about the cognitive disturbance of subjects or the perceptions of judges—hence the term, *generalizability theory* (Suen, 1990). If we are interested in the cognitive disturbance of subjects as the object of measurement, we would like trait variation to be as large as possible—that is, as much variation in subjects' cognitive disturbance as possible—and interjudge variation to be small. If, on the other hand, we are interested in studying the perceptions of judges as the object of measurement, we would like trait variation to be small and interjudge variation to be large.

In this example, there is a third source of variation: random measurement error. Random error is the interaction of subjects and judges (Suen, 1990). Although some judges may give higher average ratings than other judges, they may not do so uniformly. A variety of idiosyncratic factors may affect the rating that a particular judge gives to a particular subject (random error). Thus, there are three sources of variance in this single facet design and three corresponding $M$ squares to estimate them: trait variation ($M$ square between subjects), systematic measurement error ($M$ square between judges), and random error (the residual $M$ square, which reflects the interaction of subjects and judges).

If the object of measurement is subjects, the following formula can be used to estimate the reliability coefficient (Suen, 1990):

$$r_{11} = \frac{MS_{subjects} - MS_{residual}}{MS_{subjects}}$$

Conceptually, this formula estimates the proportion of variance in the test scores of subjects that can be considered "true score" variance. In fact, in the case of a simple, one-facet design, this formula would produce a reliability estimate that is identical to Cronbach's alpha (just think of the judges as "items" in the formula for alpha; Suen, 1990). However, generalizability theory is far more flexible than classical reliability theory. For example, various variance components could be adapted to estimate the reliability of ratings under the following conditions: There is only one judge, who rates all subjects; each judge rates only a single subject; different numbers of judges rate each of the subjects, etcetera. And, of course, the design could be modified to study the effect of adding facets, changing the number of levels within each facet, and so forth.

## VALIDITY OF MEASUREMENTS

### Construct Validity

There are three main types of test validity: construct validity, content validity, and criterion-related validity (Nunnally, 1978; Suen, 1990). In psychometric theory, construct validity is usually considered the most important (Nunnally, 1978; Suen, 1990). *Construct validity* refers to the question of whether a test measures what it purports to measure (Nunnally, 1978; Suen, 1990). In psychology, we are usually interested in measuring abstract theoretical entities that are known as "constructs." For example, clinicians have developed tests to measure such abstract entities as locus of control, extraversion, field independence, and so on. To the extent that a construct is well defined, it is possible to generate hypotheses about the construct—its causes, effects, and correlates. *Construct validation* is the process of testing these hypotheses through the use of empirical data. If the hypotheses are confirmed, the construct validity of the scale is supported. In essence, then, construct validation involves the accumulation of evidence about a network of hypothesized relationships stemming from a construct, which is measured by a test (Nunnally, 1978; Suen, 1990).

As an example, suppose we developed a new measure of trait anxiety. Based on our knowledge of this construct, we generate the following operational hypotheses. Individuals with higher scores on our trait anxiety test will show greater physiological reactivity, as demonstrated by laboratory measures of heart rate and skin conductance; more avoidant behavior, when observed in a naturalistic setting; and greater emotional instability, as measured by a self-report questionnaire. We can test predictions by correlating scores on the trait anxiety test with each of these dependent variables. The resulting Pearson correlation coefficients (or alternatively, regression coefficients) are referred to as *validity coefficients* (Lord & Novick, 1968; Nunnally, 1978). If the validity coefficients are found to be statistically significant, the hypotheses are confirmed, and the construct validity of the trait anxiety test is supported.

### Convergent and Discriminant Validity

A more sophisticated means of investigating the construct validity of a test is by examining its convergent and discriminant validity (the latter is sometimes known as *divergent validity*; Campbell & Fiske, 1959; Suen, 1990). *Convergent validity* means that alternative measures of the same construct should be highly intercorrelated (Campbell & Fiske, 1959; Suen, 1990). *Discriminant validity* means that measures of different constructs should be, at most, moderately intercorrelated (Campbell & Fiske, 1959; Suen, 1990). In other words, convergent validity coefficients should be larger than discriminant validity coefficients—a test ought to be more highly associated with other measures of the same construct than with measures of different constructs. In the example presented, the test of trait anxiety ought to be more highly correlated with other measures of anxiety than with measures of depression. If, on the other hand, two scales that ostensibly measure different things are highly intercorrelated (i.e., poor discriminant validity), it means that they are actually measuring the same construct, or very highly overlapping constructs. In that case, the test in question would be in need of revision.

The terms, convergent and discriminant validity, were introduced by Campbell and Fiske (1959). Campbell and Fiske (1959) also proposed a framework for assessing the convergent and discriminant validity of a test, known as the multitrait, multimethod matrix (MTMM). To perform an MTMM, one needs to measure at least two constructs using at least two methods. For example, we might measure the constructs of anxiety and depression using two methods: self-report inventory, and clinical interview. In the MTMM matrix, convergent validity is assessed by the correlation between the same traits using different methods (known as monotrait–heteromethod correlations). In this example, there are two traits being measured and therefore two convergent validity coefficients: the correlation between the self-report inventory and interview measures of anxiety, and the correlation between the self-report and interview measures of depression. These correlation coefficients should be at least moderately high. Discriminant validity is assessed by the correlation between different traits using different methods (heterotrait–heteromethod correlations), and by the correlation between different traits using the same methods (heterotrait–monomethod correlations). The discriminant correlations should be lower than any of the corresponding convergent correlations. For example, to demonstrate the convergent and discriminant validity of the two anxiety measures, one would need to show the following. The correlation between the two methods for assessing anxiety, self-report inventory, and clinical interview (i.e., the convergent correlation), should be higher than the correlations between anxiety and depression, as measured with the same method or with different methods (i.e., the discriminant correlations).

Another way to think about convergent and discriminant validity is that we want most of the variance in our tests to be accounted for by the substantive constructs that underlie them (i.e., trait variance) and little variance to be accounted for by the methods that we use to assess them (i.e., method variance). If the scores on our tests are mostly attributable to trait variance and not to method variance, the convergent and discriminant validity of tests will be supported by the MTMM matrix. Recently, more technically advanced procedures have been developed for analyzing the data in the MTMM matrix, involving the use of confirmatory factor analysis (Cole, 1987; Schmitt & Stults, 1986). *Confirmatory factor analysis* enables one to formally partition the variance in the matrix into factors that are associated with traits, and factors that are associated with methods. In the just mentioned example, there would be two trait factors, one for anxiety and one for depression, and two method factors, one for self-report inventory and one for clinical interview. The size of the factor loadings reflects the relative contribution of the various trait and method factors to each test in the matrix. If the trait factors produce higher loadings than the method factors, the convergent and discriminant validity of the tests is supported (Cole, 1987; Schmitt & Stults, 1986).

Construct validation can be a lengthy, time consuming process. A single study rarely settles the question of a test's construct validity (Nunnally, 1978; Suen, 1990). The reason for this is that the theoretical entities we study in psychology are often complex and difficult to measure. Consequently, some authors have viewed construct validity as a gradual or even a never-ending process (Nunnally, 1978; Suen, 1990).

Some authors have argued that construct validity subsumes all other forms of validity, such as content and criterion-related validity (Nunnally, 1978). This is because all psychological tests measure some underlying theoretical entity. On the other hand, theory can play a greater or lesser role in some instances. For example, if we create a test to measure achievement in an eighth grade history class, theory is of little practical importance. Instead, we are concerned with insuring an adequate sampling of the course's content. Hence, content validity will be of primary importance. Similarly, if we develop a test to screen job applicants for a sales position, we are usually interested in predicting performance, not in building theories. Hence, predictive validity, a form of criterion-related validity, will be of primary importance, not a test's construct validity.

## Content Validity

Content validity refers to the question of whether the items on a test adequately reflect the domain of content for which they were written (Nunnally, 1978; Suen, 1990). In other words, do the items on a test constitute an adequate sample of the domain of interest? There are two aspects to sampling adequacy: relevance and representativeness (Suen, 1990). A test is relevant when all of its items are within the domain of interest. A test is representative when its items reflect the essential characteristics of the domain it represents in the proper proportion and balance.

Content validity is difficult to demonstrate empirically. For this reason, it is sometimes considered the weakest form of validity (Nunnally, 1978; Suen, 1990). Nevertheless, it is extremely important, because tests that lack content validity often lack construct validity as well. Content validation usually involves the following steps: (a) detailed and thorough delineation of the domain of content, and (b) judgments of experts about the relevance and representativeness of the items for the domain (Nunnally, 1978; Suen, 1990). The latter can be quantified using statistics that index the degree of interrater agreement, such as Cohen's kappa (Cohen, 1960) and the intraclass correlation coefficient (Shrout & Fleiss, 1979). In practice, content validity is often assumed by the test's developer, who is a presumably an expert in his area of interest and has thoroughly investigated the domain prior to test development. Nevertheless, formal content validity procedures can sometimes be very helpful, particularly when a test is being developed to assess a novel content area. As a general rule, content validity should be assured prior to actual test construction by specifying the domain of content and formulating an adequate plan for test construction (Nunnally, 1978; Suen, 1990). Specifying the domain of content is usually achieved by reviewing the relevant literature as well as the content of other, similar tests. In the educational field, a "table of specifications" or "test blueprint" is sometimes constructed that specifies the cognitive skills to be measured (Nunnally, 1978; Suen, 1990). Focus groups can sometimes be useful when the domain of content is a novel one. For example, if one were developing a screening test to identify women who were potential victims of domestic violence, women with histories of domestic violence might be interviewed to generate item content.

Content validity is sometimes confused with face validity. *Face validity* refers to whether a test contains items that appear appropriate to the casual observer (Nunnally, 1978; Suen, 1990). In other words, does the test appear to be valid in a superficial sense? Face validity can be important when trying to enlist respondent cooperation. Tests that appear inappropriate or irrelevant can be off-putting to respondents. So, although content validity concerns the judgments of experts about the relevance and representativeness of test content, face validity concerns the judgments of lay people (i.e., nonexperts).

### Criterion-Related Validity

*Criterion-related validity* addresses the question of whether scores on a test are related to some defined criterion measure of interest (Nunnally, 1978; Suen, 1990). Criterion-related validity often arises in the context of making decisions about people, where predicting some type of performance is at issue (Nunnally, 1978; Suen, 1990). For example, tests like the Scholastic Aptitude Test (SAT) are used to make decisions about college admission, and personnel selection tests are used to make decisions about hiring employees. In both examples, tests are used to select individuals on the basis of their expected future performance. In these examples, the criterion variable—the variable that we are trying to predict—is college grade point average and job performance, respectively. In criterion-related validity, we are less concerned about the theoretical relationship between the test and the criterion than in the case of construct validity. In fact, in the traditional view, the criterion variable is chosen under the assumption that its relationship to the selection test is self-evident. For example, it is self-evident that college grade point average is a valid measure of undergraduate performance, and should be related to a well-designed achievement test like the SAT.

There are two types of criterion-related validity, *concurrent* and *predictive validity* (Nunnally, 1978; Suen, 1990). There is little substantive difference between them. In concurrent validity, the criterion is measured at the same time that the test is given. In predictive validity, the criterion is measured at some future time. In both cases, criterion-related validity is indicated by the size of the correlation coefficient (or regression coefficient) between the test and the criterion variable, that is, the validity coefficient. In general, validity coefficients for predictive validity will be smaller than for concurrent validity, because the passage of time will affect performance on the criterion variable (Nunnally, 1978; Suen, 1990). However, the temporal relationship between test administration and criterion measurement makes little theoretical difference.

The key issue with respect to criterion-related validity concerns the adequacy of the criterion measure (Nunnally, 1978; Suen, 1990). There are several points to consider. First, unreliable criterion measures can spuriously lower validity coefficients, because measurement errors can attenuate the correlation between variables. A formula known as the "correction for attenuation" can be used to estimate the correlation that would have been attained, if measures of perfect reliability had been employed (Nunnally, 1978; Suen, 1990). However, this formula is no substitute for using reliable criterion measures in the first place. Second, validity coefficients can also be lowered due to a restricted range of values in the criterion measure (Nunnally, 1978; Suen, 1990). This often occurs when tests are used to select individuals and the performance of those persons selected is assessed later. For example, if a threshold score is used to make college admission decisions, only a restricted range of individuals—those who score above the threshold and gain admission—will be measured on the criterion variable, namely college grade point average. Thus, the correlation between test scores and college performance may be artificially lowered. Finally, criterion-related validity is more difficult to accomplish that it appears, because it is often difficult to find reliable and valid measures of performance (Nunnally, 1978; Suen, 1990). For example, supervisors' ratings of job performance can be undermined by personal factors, such as supervisors' racial or gender biases.

## Phantom Measurement

Psychological tests entail "phantom measurement" because they reliably measure more than their validity coefficients suggest. For example, it is not uncommon for a good test to have a reliability coefficient of .9, which means that pretest scores predict approximately $.9^2 = .81 = 81\%$ of the variance in posttest scores. These tests typically have validity coefficients of approximately .3. This means that gold-standard criteria or validity indices explains approximately $.3^2 = .09 = 9\%$ of test scores. Hence, reliable variance is nine times greater ($81\% \div 9\% = 9$) than what the test has been shown to measure. It follows that the test is consistently, and by implication, validly measuring other psychological facets than are recognized. Conceptualizing validational criteria in multidimensional terms would likely increase validity coefficients. Multiple $R$-squared is either equal to or greater than simple $r$-squared, thereby increasing the proportion of variance accounted for and decreasing the degree of phantom measurement.

## MEASURING OUTCOMES

Any of the methods of collecting data described can be used to measure outcome. The type of measuring device used to measure outcome will therefore not be discussed further here.

Outcome can be evaluated with a posttest only research design (Cook & Campbell, 1979, pp. 96–103) but they do not permit strong causal inferences because the absence of initial assessment allows for the possibility that the experimental and control groups began at different points. ANOVA can be used to evaluate pre- and posttest scores for both groups. Pre-test scores can be used as a covariate if initial differences in pre-test scores exists.

Difference scores (post–prescores) frequently seems to be an intuitively obvious method of measuring change. However, they present many persistent problems and should generally be avoided (Bereiter, 1963). Thorndike (1924) reported a spurious negative correlation between an initial score and a gain score (post–prescore). This occurs because both measurements share the same error scores, because the same test is used twice, but the error scores for the gain scores are negative when the error scores for the initial test are positive, and vice versa. Lord (1963) noted that people who score very low initially typically can show larger gain scores than people who score initially very high. This can be thought of as a *ceiling effect*. Starting high leaves little room for increases. People who initially start high can show larger decreases than those who start low. This can be thought of as a *floor effect*. Starting low leaves little room for decreases. Regression toward the $M$ is another factor that occurs in all situations where the correlation between the posttest and pretest scores is not perfect. The next formula illustrates how this phenomena works. Let the pretest be called $X$ and the posttest be called $Y$. Let both variables be transformed into $Z$ scores where:

$$Z_x = \frac{X - \overline{X}}{S_x}$$

and

$$Z_y = \frac{Y - \overline{Y}}{S_y}$$

then

$$Z_y = rZ_x$$

When $r = .5$, a pretest $X$ score that is $Z_x = +3.0$ $SD$ above the mean predicts a posttest $Y$ score that is $Z_y = .5(3.0) = 1.5$ $SD$ above the mean. Notice that the posttest score is only half as far above the mean as is the pretest score, showing a negative change. The opposite occurs for pretest scores below the $M$. When $Z_x = -3.0$, $Z_y = .5(-3.0) = -1.5$, which is also closer to the $M$. Hence the term, *regression toward the mean*. Combining measurement errors of pre- and posttest scores with ceiling and floor effects with regression toward the mean causes difference scores to be unreliable indicators of change.

Lord (1963) provided the following general formula for calculating the reliability of difference scores where $r_{gg}$ is the reliability of gain scores, $r_{xx'}$ is the reliability of the pretest score, $r_{yy'}$ is the reliability of the posttest scores, $S_x$ and $S_y$ are the standard deviations of the pre- and posttest scores, and $r_{xy}$ is their correlation.

$$r_{gg'} = \frac{S_y^2 r_{yy'} - 2S_y S_x r_{xy} + S_x^2 r_{xx'}}{S_y^2 - 2S_y S_x r_{xy} + S_x^2}$$

If we let $S_x = S_y = 1$, as is the case when the data are converted to $Z$ scores using the formulas just cited, and set $r_{xx'} = r_{yy'} = r_{xy}$ .8, then $r_{gg} = [1(.8) - 2(1)(1)(.8) + 1(.8)] \div [1 - 2(1)(1)(.8) + 1] = 0$. Said otherwise, when the correlation between the pre- and posttests equals the reliability of the two tests, then the reliability of the change scores becomes zero. However, If we continue to let $S_x = S_y = 1$, and continue to set $r_{xx'} = r_{yy'} = .8$ and but reset $r_{xy} = 0$, then $r_{gg} = [1(.8) - 2(1)(1)(0) + 1(.8)]/[1 - 2(1)(1)(0) + 1] = .8$. We see that the reliability of the gain scores now equals the acceptably high reliability of the pre- and posttest scores. However, the change scores are now meaningless because the zero correlation between pre- and posttest scores indicates that they are measuring different things and this provides an "apples to oranges" comparison.

Wainer and Messick (1983) and Collins and Horn (1991) provided extensive discussions of other problems associated with measuring change. They also provide a variety of opinions regarding how change should be measured that cannot be readily summarized here.

## SUMMARY

Measurement is fundamental to science. Measurement quality limits the scientific value of every study. This chapter informed the reader about fundamental measurement issues. All measurements entail some degree of error. Classical test theory understands that observed measurements are composed of a true score plus error. Reliability is the ratio of true score variance to observed score variance. Coefficient alpha is a popular measure of test reliability. Alternatives to alpha were also discussed. The standard error of measurement is correspondingly defined as the average amount that observed scores would be expected to deviate from true scores because of random error. Parallel tests are defined as having the same true score and equal observed score variances.

Composite measures, aggregates, have higher reliability and validity coefficients because measurement errors associated with individual measurements partially cancel one another. It was proposed that variables can be rank ordered on the basis of how many repeated measurements are necessary to achieve a chosen level of reliability. This was called the $K$ scale because $K$ represents the number of times a base test is lengthened when using the Spearman-Brown formula. Aggregation also increases validity coefficients.

Development of univariate and multivariate operational definitions was discussed. Methods of collecting data covered included interviews, questionnaires, behavioral observation, psychological tests, and physical instruments. Activity measurement was used to illustrate physical measurement. The usual methods of calculating reliability cannot be used with instruments because such instruments are much more alike than people are. More importantly, reliability and validity of instruments can be established under controlled laboratory conditions. Psychometric properties of psychological tests, interviews, observation, etcetera, can only be established by giving them to people. Operational characteristics of instruments can be evaluated apart from people. Instruments sometimes provide unexpected data that set the occasion for theoretical developments and changes. This process was referred to as instrument driven theory. Examples from physics, astronomy, biology, and medicine were provided. Reasons why instruments can change our conceptual understanding were discussed. Instruments extend our senses; they objective meaning and they are not bound by theoretical expectations.

Nominal, ordinal, interval, and ratio scales were discussed. Interval and ratio scales presume a fixed, and preferably standard, measurement unit. Psychophysics attempted to develop psychological units of measure. Other attempts to establish measurement units in psychology were reviewed. Investigators who use $z$ scores discard measurement units so that disparate measures can be combined. An example was presented where highly reliable and valid measures were inaccurate in that they disagreed across investigators. This problem disappeared with the introduction of a fixed measurement unit.

Measurement reliability was expanded though a discussion of Generalizability Theory. Multiple reliability coefficients can be calculated depending on measurement objectives. Concepts of convergent and discriminant validity were discussed. The multitrait–multimethod approach to understanding and evaluating construct validity, and content and criterion-related validity were discussed. The issue of phantom measurement was introduced; it derives from the fact that reliability coefficients almost always exceed validity coefficients; this means that tests consistently measure other factors than what they were intended to measure.

Measuring outcomes was discussed; in particular, the measurement of change was considered, and the unreliability of change scores was discussed in detail.

## REFERENCES

Ambrosini, P., & Dixon, J. F. (1996). *Schedule for Affective Disorders & Schizophrenia for School-Age Children (K-SADS-IVR).* Philadelphia: Allegheny University of the Health Sciences.

Anastasi, A. (1988). *Psychological testing* (6th ed.). New York: Macmillan.

Angold, A., Cox, A., Rutter, M., & Siminoff, E. (1996). *Child and Adolescent Psychiatric Assessment (CAPA): Version 4.2—child version.* Durham, NC: Duke Medical Center.

Barratt, E. S. (1981). Time perception and cortical evoked potentials among male juvenile delinquents, adolescent psychiatric patients, and normal controls. In K. Roberts, R. Hays, & L. Soloway (Eds.), *Violence and the violent individual* (pp. 87–95). New York: Spectrum Publishers.

Barratt, E. S. (1985). Impulsiveness defined within a system model of personality. In C. D. Spielberger & J. N. Butcher (Eds.), *Advances in personality assessment* (Vol. 5, pp. 113–132). Hillsdale, NJ: Lawrence Erlbaum Associates.

Beck, A. T., & Speer, R. A. (1987). *Beck Depression Inventory.* San Antonio, TX: The Psychological Corporation.

Bereiter, C. (1963). Some persisting dilemmas in the measurement of change. In C. W. Harris (Ed.), *Problems in measuring change* (pp. 3–20). Madison, WI: The University of Wisconsin Press.

Boorstin, D. J. (1983). *The discoverers.* New York: Random House.

Bouten, C. V., Westerterp, K. R., Verduin, M., & Janssen, J. D. (1994). Assessment of energy expenditure for physical activity using a triaxial accelerometer. *Medicine and Science in Sports and Exercise, 26,* 1516–1523.

Campbell, D. T., & Fiske, D. W. (1959). Convergent and discriminant validity by a multitrait–multimethod matrix. *Psychological Bulletin, 56,* 81–105.

Cohen, J. (1960). A coefficient of agreement for nominal scales. *Educational and Psychological Measurement, 20,* 37–46.

Cole, D. A. (1987). Utility of a confirmatory factor analysis in test validation research. *Journal of Consulting and Clinical Psychology, 55,* 584–594.

Collins, L. M., & Horn, J. L. (1991). *Best methods for the analysis of change: Recent advances, unanswered questions, future directions.* Washington, DC: American Psychological Association.

Conners, C. K. (1992). *Continuous performance test computer program.* North Tonawanda, New York: Multi-Health Systems, Inc.

Cook, T. D., & Campbell, D. T. (1979). *Quasi-experimentation: Design & analysis issues for field settings.* Chicago: Rand McNally.

Davidsohn, I., & Henry, J. B. (1974). *Todd-Sanford clinical diagnosis by laboratory methods* (15th ed.). Philadelphia: W. B. Saunders.

Endicott, J., & Spitzer, R. L. (1978). A diagnostic interview: The Schedule for Affective Disorders and Schizophrenia. *Archives of General Psychiatry, 35,* 837–844.

Epstein, S. (1979). The stability of behavior: I. On predicting most of the people much of the time. *Journal of Personality and Social Psychology, 37,* 1097–1126.

Epstein, S. (1980). The stability of behavior: II. Implications for psychological research. *American Psychologist, 1980, 35,* 790–806.

Epstein, S. (1983). Aggregation and beyond: Some basic issues on the prediction of behavior. *Journal of Personality, 51,* 360–392.

Exposito, J., & Andres-Pueyo, A. (1997). The effects of impulsivity on the perceptual and decision stages in a choice reaction time task. *Personality and Individual Differences, 22,* 693–697.

Farmelo, G. (1995). The discovery of X-rays. *Scientific American, 273*, 86–91.

First, M. B., Spitzer, R. L., Gibbon, M., & Williams, J. B. W. (1995). *Structured Clinical Interview for Axis I DSM-IV Disorders—Patient Edition* (SCID-I/P, ver. 2.0). New York: New York State Psychiatric Institute, Biometrics Research Department.

Freedson, P. S. (1991). Electronic motion sensors and heart rate as measures of physical activity in children. *Journal of School Health, 61*, 220–223.

Gulliksen, H. (1950). *Theory of mental tests.* New York: Wiley.

Hambleton, R. K., Swaminathan, H., & Rogers, H. J. (1991). *Fundamentals of item response theory.* Newbury Park: Sage Publications.

Harwit, M. (1981). *Cosmic discovery: The search, scope, and heritage of astronomy.* New York: Basic Books.

Hinkle, D. E., Wiersma, W., and Jurs, S. G. (1994). *Applied statistics for the behavioral sciences* (3rd ed.). Boston: Houghton Mifflin Co.

Hodges, K. (1997). *Child Adolescent Schedule (CAS).* Ypsilanti, MI: Eastern Michigan University.

Holden, R. R., Fekken, G. C., & Cotton, D. H. G. (1991). Assessing psychopathology using structured test-item response latencies. *Psychological Assessment, 3*, 111–118.

Holden, R. R., Woermke, C., & Fekken, G. C. (1993). Enhancing the construct validity of differential response latencies for personality test items. *Canadian Journal of Behavioral Science, 25*, 1–12.

Johnston, M. M., & Pennypacker, H. S. (1980). *Strategies and tactics of human behavioral research.* Hillsdale, NJ: Lawrence Erlbaum Associates.

Laporte, R. E., Montoye, H. J., & Caspersen, C. J. (1985). Assessment of physical activity in epidemiologic research: Problems and prospects. *Public Health Reports, 100*, 131–146.

Logan, G. D., & Cowan, W. B. (1984). On the ability to inhibit thought and action: A theory of an act of control. *Psychological Review, 91*, 295–327

Logan, G. D., Cowan, W. B., & Davis, K. A. (1984). On the ability to inhibit simple and choice reaction time responses: A model and a method. *Journal of Experimental Psychology: Human Perception and Performance, 10*, 276–291.

Logan, G. D., Schachar, R. J., & Tannock, R. (1997). Impulsivity and inhibitory control. *Psychological Science, 8*, 60–65.

Loranger, A. W., Sartorius, N., Andreoli, A., Berger, P., Buchleim, P., Channabasavanna, S. M., Coid, B., Dahl, A., Diekstra, R. F. W., Feguson, B., Jacobsberg, L. B., Mombour, W., Pull, C., Ono, Y., & Regier, D. (1994). The International Personality Disorder Examination: The World Health Organization/Alcohol, Drug Abuse, and Mental Health Administration international pilot study of personality disorders. *Archivers of General Psychiatry, 51*, 215–224.

Lord, F. M. (1963). Elementary models for measuring change. In C. W. Harris (Ed.), *Problems in measuring change* (pp. 21–38). Madison, WI: The University of Wisconsin Press.

Lord, F. M. & Novick, M. R. (1968). *Statistical theories of mental test scores.* Reading, MA: Addison-Wesley.

Markus, H., Crane, M., Bernstein, S., & Siladi, M. (1982). Self-schemas and gender. *Journal of Personlality and Social Psychology, 35*, 63–78.

Markus, H. & Wurf, E. (1987). The dynamic self-concept: a social psychological perspective. *Annual Review of Psychology, 38*, 299–337.

Meijer, G. A. L., Westerterp, K. R., Verhoeven, F. M. H., Koper, H. B. M., & ten Hoor, F. (1991). Methods to assess physical activity with special reference to motion sensors and accelerometers. *IEEE Transactions on Biomedical Engineering, 38*, 221–229.

Melanson, E. L., Jr., & Freedson, P. S. (1996). Physical activity assessment: A review of methods. *Critical Reviews in Food Science and Nutrition, 36*, 385–396.

Montoye, H. J., Kemper, H. C. G., Saris, W. H. M., & Washburn, R. A. (1996). *Measuring physical activity and energy expenditure* (pp. 72–96). Champaign, IL: Human Kinetics.

Mueller, J. H., Thompson, W. B., & Dugan, K. (1986). Trait distinctiveness and accessibility in the self-schema. *Personality and Social Psychology Bulletin, 12*, 81–89.

Nunnally, J. M. (1978). *Psychometric theory* (2nd ed.). New York: McGraw-Hill.

Pfohl, B., Blum, N., & Zimmerman, M. (1995). *Structured Interview for DSM-IV Personality SIDP-IV.* Iowa City, IA: University of Iowa.

Popham, S. M., & Holden, R. R. (1990). Assessing MMPI constructs through the measurement of response latencies. *Journal of Personality Assessment, 54,* 469–478.

Reich, W. (Ed.) (1996). *Diagnostic Interview for Children and Adolescents–Revised (DICA-R) 8.0.* St. Louis: Washington University.

Robins, L. N., Helzer, J. E., Croughan, J., & Ratcliff, K. S. (1981). National Institute of Mental Health Diagnostic Interview Schedule: Its history, characteristics, and validity. *Archives of General Psychiatry, 38,* 381–389.

Sattler, J. M., & Mash, E. J. (1998). Introduction to clinical assessment interviewing. In J. M. Sattler *Clinical and forensic interviewing of children and families: Guidelines for the mental health, education, pediatric, and child maltreatment fields* (pp. 3–44). San Diego, CA: Jerome M. Sattler.

Schmitt, N., & Stults, D. M. (1986). Methodology review: Analysis of multitrait–multimethod matrices. *Applied Psychological Measurement, 10,* 1–22.

Segal, D. L. (1997). Structured interviewing and DSM classification. In S. M. Turner & M. Hersen (Eds.), *Adult psychopathology and diagnosis* (3rd ed., pp. 24–57). New York: Wiley.

Shrout, P. E., & Fleiss, J. L. (1979). Intraclass correlations: Uses in assessing rater reliability. *Psychological Bulletin, 86,* 420–428.

Suen, H. K. (1990). *Principles of test theories.* Hillsdale, NJ: Lawrence Erlbaum Associates.

Thorndike, E. L. (1924). The influence of chance imperfections of measures upon the relation of initial score to gain or loss. *Journal of Experimental Psychology, 7,* 225–232.

Tryon, W. W. (1985). The measurement of human activity. In W. W. Tryon (Ed.). *Behavioral assessment in behavioral medicine* (pp. 200–256). New York: Springer.

Tryon, W. W. (1991). *Activity measurement in psychology and medicine.* New York: Plenum.

Tryon, W. W. (2002). Activity level and DSM-IV. In S. Turner & M. Hersen (Eds.), *Adult psychopathology and diagnosis* (4th ed., pp. ??). New York: Wiley.

Tryon, W. W., & Pinto, L. P. (1994). Comparing activity measurements and ratings. *Behavior Modification, 18,* 251–261.

Tryon, W. W., & Williams, R. (1996). Fully proportional actigraphy: A new instrument. *Behavior Research Methods Instruments & Computers, 28,* 392–403.

U.S. Department of Health and Human Services. (1996). *Physical activity and health: A report of the surgeon general.* Atlanta, GA: U.S. Department of Health and Human Services, Centers for Disease Control and Prevention, National Center for Chronic Disease Prevention and Health Promotion, (Superintendent of Documents, S/N 017-023-00196-5, P.O. Box 371954, Pittsburgh, PA 15250-7954).

Wainer, H., & Messick, S. (1983). *Principles of modern psychological measurement: A festschrift for Frederic M. Lord.* Hillsdale, NJ: Lawrence Erlbaum Associates.

# 3

# Sampling Issues

Karl A. Minke
Stephen N. Haynes
*University of Hawaii at Manoa*

What is the average age of single mothers in the United States? How often during the day does a hyperactive child leave his or her desk? What problems are faced by persons who have been sexually assaulted? All of these are questions about universes of people, time periods, or behaviors. The obvious way of answering them would be to observe the *population*, or entire universe of elements being examined. But such an approach is clearly impractical and, in many instances, impossible. To answer these questions using the entire population, we would have to interview all single mothers, observe the hyperactive child continuously throughout the day, and assess all persons who have been sexually assaulted. Instead, we must be satisfied with observing a subset of the populations in which we have an interest. Based on our observations of the subset, or *sample*, we want to make inferences about the characteristics of the entire population from which that sample was taken.

Understanding issues associated with taking samples to make inferences about populations is important in counseling and clinical practice in several ways. In clinical settings we often must estimate the general behavior of a client from only small samples of his or her behavior, in a small sample of situations, and in only a limited sample of possible time periods. In research settings, often we must estimate the effects of a treatment using only a small sample of clients and from a small sample of behaviors that might be affected by the treatment. Critical reading of the research literature providing the empirical basis for the procedures we employ requires that we understand the strengths and limitations of the sampling procedures with respect to the generalizations made by the researchers.

When people think of samples, they usually think of subsets of populations of individuals. But we often are interested in generalizing our observations to universes other than the universe of people. For example, what about the universe of settings? Are the depressive symptoms observed in a client in a mental health center indicative of that client's depressive symptoms at home, or while at work, or around family members? What about the universe of time? Are observations made at particular times of day valid across the entire 24-hour period, or at least are they valid across people's waking hours? Are the particular behaviors noted at the time of observation representative of the population of behaviors exhibited by a given individual? Are a person's depressive symptoms the same in the morning as in the evening? In these examples, we have chosen a few persons, behaviors, settings, or times in order to draw inferences about people, behaviors, or times in general. Sampling considerations are important because they affect the generalizability of our conclusions—the inferences we can draw and the confidence we can place in these inferences.

Suen and Ary (1989) have suggested that the three basic questions that must be considered when developing a basic sampling plan are "who to observe," "what to observe," and "when to observe" (to which we add "where to observe"). It must be recognized that answers to each of these questions involve sampling considerations from larger populations (populations of subjects, behaviors, settings, and time), and permissible generalizations regarding these four aspects will depend on the way in which each sample is constructed. Although most of the discussion to follow focuses on sampling from populations of persons, it should be recognized that the principles and issues can be generalized as well to sampling situations of behaviors, environmental settings, and time.[1]

Sampling issues arise in most types of empirical research. The goal of most survey and descriptive research is to estimate *parameters*. Parameters are characteristics of populations (e.g., what percentage of college students make use of campus mental health services) as opposed to characteristics of samples (e.g., what percentage of college students enrolled at Universities X, Y, and Z in 1998 visited the campus counseling center?). We often are interested in making inferences about group differences. Our ability to conclude that a population has changed as a function of some intervention or manipulation (e.g., does gradual exposure reduce the subjective fear and avoidance behaviors of persons with agoraphobia?) or to conclude that two specific populations differ meaningfully along some dimension (is the incidence of posttraumatic

---

[1] In clinical assessment, we are also concerned with generalization across "states" of the client. For example, are observed interactions of a marital couple obtained when the couple is happy representative of their interactions when they are distressed?

stress disorder among sexually assaulted persons the same for males as for females?) is dependent on the sampling procedures we have employed.

Paradoxically, again because of practical considerations, there are times when we can describe a population more accurately by using sampling procedures, at least partially, than by attempting to observe every member of that population. The Bureau of the Census, for example, recognizes that a significant number of individuals are missed every 10 years when it attempts to identify every individual in the country. Using mailed questionnaires, door-to-door surveys, and follow-up calls, the Bureau estimates that approximately 4 million people were not counted in the 1990 census (Hogan, 1990). The undercount is particularly serious, in that many of those missed by the census were the poor, children, and ethnic minorities, and the census is used to redraw Congressional districts, distribute federal aid, and monitor the implementation of civil rights statutes. Statisticians have argued that the accuracy of the census could be improved by taking a sample of those not responding, then aggressively attempting to contact them. The information obtained would then be used to estimate the 10% of the population undercounted. Although the sampling plan was considered for the 2000 census, the Supreme Court ruled that the plan was unconstitutional, at least as proposed, because the census is also used to allocate the number of members of the House of Representatives available to each state, and statistical sampling is explicitly prohibited for this purpose.

We need to recognize, however, that whenever samples are used to obtain information about populations, our conclusions will only be approximations to the true characteristics of the population. The accuracy with which we can make inferences about populations by looking at samples is dependent on a number of factors: the methods we use to obtain the sample, the variability in our measures, and the size of the sample. These are the topics of focus in the remainder of this chapter. Specifically, we will look at the power we gain in generalizing results to populations when we can select our samples randomly and how we can improve our ability to generalize when we add some refinement and complexity to our random sampling strategy. We will consider a variety of sampling methods which have been employed when random sampling is not possible. Many times we are interested in comparing multiple samples. We will discuss how to minimize bias and reduce the variability of our measures in these comparisons by matching our samples. And finally, we will consider the issues involved in choosing an appropriate sample size.

## THE BASIC SAMPLING PLAN: SIMPLE RANDOM SAMPLING

The first step in developing a sampling plan is to define the population of interest, the population from which we wish to take our samples. This would seem to be an easy, almost self-evident task, but, in fact, can be incredibly difficult. In order to take a sample from a population, we need to identify a *sampling frame*, a list of all members of the population. The *elements* of our sample, then, will be the members of the population that are chosen from the sampling frame. The sampling frame provides an operational definition of our population.

When we wish to sample from a population of times for a client (i.e., time sampling), the sampling frame consists of all times of interest. Sometimes, the sample frame may be all times of the day. An example would be when we wish to measure a client's depressed mood throughout a 24-hour period. At other times, the sampling frame may be specific times of the day. An example would be when we wish to sample interactions between a parent and his or her child with oppositional behaviors that occur after school. Regardless of the specific times of interest, the sampling frame affects our decisions about which times to sample in order to derive estimates of the client in the times of interest—the target times.[2]

The sampling frame is seldom an accurate specification of the population about which we wish to make inferences. Any sampling frame is likely to place restrictions on the population, and any inferences made from a sample based on that frame are necessarily limited to that frame. For this reason, a distinction needs to be made between target and study populations. The *target population* is the one about which we want to make inferences. The *study population* is the one from which we actually take our sample and is operationally defined by the sampling frame we utilize.

For example, let's assume we want to obtain a sample of citizens of a given local municipality. What might be an appropriate sampling frame? One possibility might be the tax rolls for the city. However, only a portion of the citizenry would pay property taxes—those actually owning property. Another possibility would be voter registration lists. Again, only a portion of the members of a community vote (according to the Washington Post, only 63% of the population was registered to vote in the last presidential election, and only 47% actually voted). A popular sampling frame in situations such as this is the phone book. Of course, not everyone has a phone. In addition, one phone number typically serves multiple individuals, and some method must be devised to handle this situation. All but the last sampling frame, by definition, would exclude children and adolescents.

---

[2]Time and setting sampling often overlap. Sampling at particular times (e.g., of parent–child interactions after school, of thoughts prior to going to sleep) often involves sampling in particular settings. Further, time sampling during a particular setting often involves division of the total time sample into smaller time periods to aid data collection and analysis. For example, we might measure how a parent responds to a child's oppositional behavior by observing and recording several child and parent behaviors, every 15 seconds, for 30 minutes, during suppertime. The data acquired can be in the form of the behavior rates, the time-course of behavior (such as systematic changes in rate over time), latencies, or conditional probabilities (e.g., the probability that a parent will provide attention to a child, given the occurrence of an oppositional behavior).

Which sampling frame we choose in this situation should be influenced by the question we are asking, the inferences we wish to draw. What if we are interested in determining community support for the building of a new community mental health center? The tax rolls or the voter registration list may be appropriate sampling frames, since the funding is likely to come from municipal taxes and might well need to be approved by voters at the next municipal election. If we are interested in determining how many people in the community experience stress in their daily lives, the phone book may be more appropriate. The point is, any sampling frame will result in biases in the way a target population is defined, and any inferences made from a sample based on that frame are necessarily limited to study population defined by that frame.

So, study populations have a number of limitations when we realize that our real interest almost always lies with target populations. Study populations are dependent on practical considerations, which impose biases on the degree to which they are representative of the target populations of interest. One major limitation placed upon our ability to approximate the target population with our sampling frame is that imposed by ethical requirements. In particular, the necessity for informed consent necessarily limits our study population to those individuals willing to participate, at least when engaging in non-archival research. This becomes particularly problematic when trying to draw inferences about socially sensitive behaviors—sexual abuse and assault, domestic violence, criminal activity, and illegal substance use. The necessity of informed consent can also limit our ability to use time and setting sampling. For example, if we wish to videotape the social behaviors of a child who is hyperactive in a classroom, we must obtain permission from the parents of other children who may appear in the videotape.

The operation of these limitations can be seen in the following example. Let us assume we are interested in identifying a sample of individuals who have experienced sexual assault to determine the effects of such assault. No general sampling frame covering the spectrum of such victims is available. One possible sampling frame might be developed through police records. But the use of police records would exclude persons who were assaulted but did not report the assault to the police. Another possible sampling frame could be individuals utilizing sexual assault treatment centers. Such a frame would consist primarily of individuals who were most severely affected by the assault, however. Another possibility would be to conduct a door-to-door interview to identify potential participants in our study, but that method would exclude persons who were uncomfortable acknowledging that they had been sexually assaulted.

Given that the study population is almost always different on some dimensions from the target population, how do we improve our ability to generalize from samples of the study population back to the target population? There is no simple answer to this question. Obviously, the closer the study population approximates the target population (i.e., the more dimensions on which they are matched), the safer we will be in drawing conclusions about our target population. But as we have seen, it is not always possible to find a sampling frame that is very representative of the population in which we are interested.

One way out of this dilemma is through replication, but of a systematic sort. If multiple studies are conducted using different sample frames to approximate the target population (i.e., if different study populations are employed) and similar results are obtained, we understand the degree to which results can be generalized. For instance, if we wished to draw inferences about the characteristics of persons seeking services from a student counseling center, inferences might vary, depending on whether the sample included counseling centers from large universities, community colleges, private colleges, higher education institutions located in large urban centers versus those located in college towns, and so on. Conducting multiple studies utilizing sampling frames reflecting these differences would provide information about the degree to which our conclusions apply to the target population of interest, that is, students seeking counseling center services in general. To the degree that results are the same with these different study populations, our confidence is increased that our conclusions apply to our target population. To the extent that results differ, we can place limits on our generalizations regarding the target population.

In time-sampling, our ability to generalize accurately from time-samples of behavior to the population of interest (e.g., how does a parent respond to a child's oppositional behavior) is also affected by the number of time-samples taken. Parents may respond differently to children in different situations. Acknowledging this potential for setting biases, the more time-samples of behavior that we take and the longer the total time in which the behavior is measured, the more confident we can be that the derived measures are accurate estimates of the target behaviors. For example, we will be more confident of our inferences if we observe parent–child interactions for 60 minutes across 10 days versus 1 day, or if we observe for only 5 minutes each day. We discuss the issue of sample size in time-sampling further in the section on "Sample Size."

Differences between the target and study populations raise an important principle in interpreting and reporting results from studies that involve sampling. Results from studies that involve sampling are applicable to the target population only to the degree to which the parameters of the sample and target population are similar. Thus, if we are studying a sample of sexual assault victims from a sexual assault treatment center, our inferences are limited to those seeking treatment, unless it can be demonstrated that the data are generalizable to all sexual assault victims.

Once the sampling frame has been decided on, the next step is to identify the particular elements that will constitute our sample. *Elements* are the members of the study population that are chosen from the sampling frame to actually be included in our study. For instance, if we are conducting a face-to-face survey of persons visiting campus counseling centers, the elements of our sample would be the particular individuals selected to be interviewed.

It is essential that the sample be representative of the sampling frame if we are going to be able to generalize from our sample back to the study population. A sample is *representative* to the extent that the distribution of its characteristics parallel those of the larger study population. The basic threat to representativeness is bias. A *biased* sample is one in which the distribution of characteristics differ systematically from that of the study population. In our example regarding persons seeking services from a university counseling center, inferences would be biased if based primarily on male participants, assuming that males and females seek such services in approximately equal proportions. In our example of sampling the depressed mood of a patient throughout the day, our data would be biased if based only on samples taken while the client was at work, or only in the afternoons, or only when the client had time to fill out the self-monitoring forms. The data we would derive could accurately measure depressed mood at those times, but would provide an inaccurate measure of the client's typical depressed mood throughout the day.

The primary method of controlling for potential bias is to utilize some form of *probability sampling*, sampling in such a way that the investigator can specify, for each member of the population, the probability that it will be included as an element in the sample. The basic technique of probability sampling is *simple random sampling*, sampling in such a way that every individual in the population has an equal probability of being included as an element. Members of a population will differ on a wide variety of variables, some of which are likely to affect the measurements we are taking. By taking random samples we are assuring that the range of possible values these potential biasing variables can take have a probability of being included in our sample. Thus, our sample is more likely to be representative of the population. For example, children attending a given elementary school will vary on a wide variety of dimensions: age, grade level, gender, prior experiences, personality variables, and so forth. Let us say we wanted a sample of these children for a study to determine the effects of a school-wide incentive program on homework compliance. We could increase the probability that different values on these factors would be included in our sample, thus reducing bias, by selecting children randomly from the list of students attending the study school. The beauty of this approach to the control of bias is that it is not necessary that we be able to identify the potential biasing factors. In other words, it controls for both known and unknown sources of bias.[3]

Simple random time sampling is often used in self-monitoring of clinically important behaviors (see Special Section in *Psychological Assessment* on

---

[3]The logic of statistical inference requires random sampling for just these reasons. When we seek statistical justification for conclusions we reach about populations in our research, we must be sure that we have selected our samples randomly from the populations in which we are interested.

self-monitoring, Cone, 1999, 411–497). For example, a timetable wristwatch or hand-held computer can be programmed to give random cues throughout the day. Upon this intermittent cue (e.g, a short tone) the client can record his or her mood, recent social exchanges, smoking urges, or food intake.

It must be recognized, however, that simple random sampling controls for bias only in the long run. The characteristics of the elements of any single sample may differ dramatically from the study population. For instance, a sample of individuals visiting a university counseling center will include males and females, students and faculty of different class standings and academic ranks, and individuals who differ on a host of other variables. By chance, if simple random sampling is employed, the sample could wind up consisting primarily of freshman students or male assistant professors. Similarly, a few random time-samples could wind up sampling primarily from times of higher-than-average depressed mood states or from periods of particularly negative social exchanges.

There are several ways of reducing the risk of non-representativeness when using simple random sampling techniques. One is to reserve the use of simple random sampling to situations where the study population is relatively homogeneous with respect to variables likely to influence the measurements we are taking. In time sampling, we can restrict our sampling frame to specific settings. Another is to increase sample size, as noted earlier with respect to time sampling procedures. The larger the sample, the more likely it is to be representative of the population from which it is taken. Yet another technique is to replicate the study using a new sample from the same population. To the extent that the results are comparable, we can be more confident that our samples are representative of the population of interest.

The last two methods are particularly useful when we cannot identify potential biasing variables ahead of time. Larger samples are more likely to be representative of the study population and to include examples of all relevant dimensions, even those occurring only occasionally in the study population. In a similar fashion, each time we take a new sample, we increase the probability that we have included relevant factors in our study, even if we do not know what those particular factors might be. To the extent that our study population differs on those factors, there is always some possibility that they can introduce bias if not included in our sample.

## ADDING COMPLEXITY TO RANDOM SAMPLING

As we have seen, sample plans based on simple random sampling can provide results that are unrepresentative of the target population, particularly when small samples are used. Although simple random sampling is sometimes used in time-sampling, because of the conditional nature of most clinical phenomena (i.e., they are usually more likely to occur in some settings than in others) we are most often interested in measuring events during particular times or settings. For example, we could have a watch timer set to go off at random times throughout the day, signaling a client to record his or her mood. However, we may be most interested in measuring the mood of a client after a distressing exchange with a supervisor or spouse. Thus, time-sampling is seldom implemented in such a way that every time period across the day has an equal probability of being included. Furthermore, simple random sampling procedures require an easily identified sampling frame for their implementation. However, some populations do not have readily identified sampling frames associated with them. To deal with these types of problems, two alternative probability sampling techniques have been developed: stratified random sampling and cluster sampling. Both methods are examples of probability sampling, in that the probability that a given element of the population will be included in the sample can be specified, but the probability is not the same for each element.

## Stratified Random Sampling

Perhaps the most common way of increasing representativeness when using probability sampling is to take a *stratified random sample*. In this situation the sampling frame is divided into subcategories, or strata, based on specific, important characteristics, then random samples are taken from each stratum. The sub-categories, to the extent that they represent variables correlated with the measures of interest, will be more homogeneous, thereby reducing the likelihood of bias. For example, consider our example regarding users of a university counseling center. Students and faculty differ on a wide variety of measures. When using simple random sampling, the proportion of students and faculty in the sample may not represent the proportion as it exists in the study population, thus biasing the results. One way of dealing with this problem would be to divide the sampling frame into students and faculty, then randomly sample from each category, the sample sizes reflecting the proportion of each type of individual seeking services as it exists in the study population.

Let us assume we are interested in assessing the effectiveness of a new treatment for seriously mentally ill, hospitalized patients. Our sampling frame might consist of a list of patients released from the hospital over the past 2 years, and we might be calculating recidivism rates for these patients. But we might well expect these rates to differ depending on their diagnoses. Therefore, we could divide the sampling frame into diagnostic subcategories, then randomly sample from each subcategory separately.

Stratified random sampling concepts can also be applied to time- and setting-sampling. For example, if we want to measure a client's blood pressure during the day, and we know that his or her blood pressure varies across home-alone, home-with-spouse, and work settings, we could insure that readings in each situation are included in our sample by taking random samples in each setting separately.

This technique has a special advantage. We would not expect each category to be equally represented in our hospital population nor would we expect our blood-pressure-monitoring client to spend an equal amount of time in each setting. By letting sub-sample sizes reflect the proportion of each category as it exists in the hospital or throughout the day, we are assuring a representative sample across these dimensions.

Stratified random sampling becomes particularly important when some sub-categories represent a small proportion of the overall population (e.g., Schizophrenia, Catatonic Type; highly stressful social situations). These categories may not be represented in our sample at all when using simple random sampling, particularly with smaller sample sizes. Developing a stratified random sample guarantees that all sub-categories will be represented.

Another reason for constructing stratified random samples is that the purpose of the study may be to explore explicitly differences due to the stratifying variable. For example, we might be interested in determining whether there are differences in recidivism rates across the diagnostic categories of patients found in a mental hospital. In our blood pressure monitoring example, we might be interested in determining whether there are differences in blood pressure across home and work settings. Under these circumstances, to assure that each category is represented equally in our analyses, we might want to take a equal number of patients or blood-pressure readings from each category rather than let sub-sample sizes parallel the relative sizes of the categories in their respective populations.

In addition, it is possible to construct our sampling plan in such a way that we have multiple strata. In our mental hospital example, we might want to include sex as well as DSM diagnosis as a stratifying variable. Or we might want to include social context (alone vs. with others) as well as setting (home vs. work) when trying to identify the factors that affect a client's blood pressure. In the case of the mental hospital study, we would break each diagnostic sub-category in our sampling frame into two sub-categories, one for males and one for females. For example, if we were interested in five DSM categories, our sampling frame would be broken into 10 sub-groups before taking our random samples, each sub-group representing a particular diagnostic category/gender. As before, the specific sample sizes can be either proportional or disproportional to the representation of the sub-groups in the population, depending on the question being asked in the research and the population to which we wish to generalize our conclusions.

## Cluster Sampling

Sometimes it is difficult, if not impossible, to find a sampling frame that is representative of the population about which we wish to make inferences. One solution to this problem, which retains the advantages of random sampling, is to utilize *cluster sampling*. In cluster sampling, the sampling frame consists not of individual elements, but of definable groups, or clusters, of elements. Let's say we are doing a study to determine drug use among early adolescents in a state. No list of early adolescents exists. However, we could obtain a list of all middle schools in the state, and, within each school we could identify seventh-grade homerooms. In cluster sampling, we would first take a random sample of schools; schools represent clusters of students, and it is the list of schools that is our initial sampling frame. Then, we could either survey every student in the seventh-grade homerooms located in the schools selected, or we could take another random sample, this time of the students within the homerooms. The list of students in the various homerooms would constitute a second sampling frame.

It should be noted that we are not restricted to simple random sampling at each stage. For example, we could stratify the middle schools into urban and rural, and we could stratify the students in the homerooms into sex, socioeconomic background, and so on. Whether or not we do so would depend on issues of representativeness, potential bias, and/or whether we were interested in differences related to the stratifying variables.

As implied previously, cluster sampling can occur in stages, a technique referred to as *multistage sampling*. For example, it is hard to imagine any sampling frame for residents of the United States that would not be too unwieldy to be of any practical use. When doing national surveys, the Gallup Poll uses multistage sampling, beginning by randomly sampling zip codes. Then, from each of these zip codes, a random sample of streets is obtained. Finally, a random sample of addresses is taken from each street (McBurney, 1994). Notice that the study population defined in this way is not necessarily a good representation of our target population. For instance, a sample such as this would exclude the homeless, persons "in transit," and so on.

## NON-RANDOM SAMPLES

Although random sampling is the primary method of obtaining representative samples from populations in which we are interested, there are times when such methods are difficult or impossible to employ. In addition, sometimes the purpose of collecting the sample is not best served by randomly selecting the units from the population. A variety of non-random sampling techniques have been developed and are used in certain types of research of clinical interest.

### Systematic Sampling

As mentioned earlier, random sampling techniques allow for valid inferences about the study populations from which the samples are taken with a specified probability of making an error and provide representativeness when many samples are taken. However, any single sample may, by chance, be quite unrepresentative of the population from which it was taken. A common technique for improving representativeness in a single sample is *systematic sampling*. In systematic sampling, one either starts at the beginning of the sampling frame or at a random location in the list, then takes every *n*th entry as an element in the sample.

As an example where systematic sampling may be appropriate, let us assume we want a sample of patients admitted to a large hospital in a given year. Our sampling frame would be the admissions roster, where patients are listed in terms of date of admission. In this case we probably would begin at the top of the roster and then select, perhaps, every fifth patient. This would be easier and less time-consuming than taking a formal random sample, particularly if many patients were admitted. In addition, different types of patients tend to be admitted at different times of the year. Certain types of injury (e.g., injury due to skiing accidents) are more common in the winter than in the summer, for example. Systematic sampling would guarantee representativeness across the 12-month period.

Systematic sampling methods can also be used in time-sampling. An example is the situation where the aggressive or delusional speech of a psychiatric inpatient, as observed by a staff member, is measured at the top of every hour. This method of time sampling is referred to as "momentary time sampling" (Hawkins, Mathews, & Hamdan, 1999; Odom & Ogawa, 1992).

Although systematic sampling is often used to improve representativeness, it can also introduce serious bias. Problems can arise when there are periodic or cyclic orderings in the sampling frame. For instance, different types of patients tend to be admitted at different times during the day. Certain types of surgery are scheduled for early morning, for example. Since admissions rosters are arranged chronologically, both across and within days, it is possible that different types of patients could be over- or under-represented in our sample. Judd, Smith, and Kidder (1991) pointed out an extreme example. What if a sampling frame consisted of married couples, where the husband is always listed before the wife? Depending on whether *n* is odd or even, the sample would consist entirely of males or females. Analogously, momentary time samples of a mental hospital patient may not tap into important periodic situations that affect aggressive or speech behaviors, such as scheduled interactions with the ward staff.

## Convenience Sampling

A very common sampling strategy is to take *convenience samples* (sometimes called *accidental samples*), samples based on the availability or accessibility of research participants or ease of obtaining data from a client. Most surveys we encounter in the popular media are of this sort. TV news shows ask us to vote on a variety of issues by dialing 1-900 numbers, web sites give us buttons to push to express our opinions about controversial topics, and so on. Convenience samples are taken by scholarly researchers as well. For instance, convenience samples are often used in clinical research, where the researcher has access to a particular school or clinic or access to a particular data set collected by others.

A classic example of convenience sampling used in formal research is the Hite Report (1987) on romantic relationships in women. Shere Hite mailed 100,000 questionnaires to women belonging to various women's organizations (voting and political groups, church groups, professional groups, etc.) located in 43 of the 50 states. Her return rate was quite low (a common problem with mail surveys); only 4.5% responded. Nevertheless, this left her with 4,500 respondents. The research has been severely criticized because of the sampling plan she employed (Shaughnessy & Zechmeister, 1990). The problem has to do with representativeness. Hite was attempting to draw conclusions about women in general within the United States. But most women do not belong to formal women's groups, individuals who are dissatisfied with their lives were probably more likely to respond, and so on.

Clinical assessment involving self-report instruments in the natural environment is often done using convenience time-sampling. For example, we often ask a client to indicate his or her level of depression, anxiety, physiological arousal, or marital satisfaction, at night, just before going to bed. This sampling method is chosen because it is easier for clients to provide the information (they are more likely to comply with the assessment task). However, as suggested earlier, such a sample regime may not provide measures that represent the targeted variables throughout the day.

Most popular media surveys are examples of a form of convenience sampling frequently called haphazard sampling. *Haphazard samples* are those in which essentially everyone who responds is included. When you are invited to vote on a controversial issue by phoning an 800 number or to express your opinion about the topic of the day on a news website, you are part of a haphazard sample. Haphazard samples are typically limited by size or by time. In other words, either the first $x$ number of respondents are included, or everyone who responds within a given time period is part of the sample.

Because everyone who responds is included, even if they respond multiple times, haphazard samples can lead to bizarre results. In 1997 *Time* magazine took a poll to determine who the public thought should be selected for Man of the Century for their January 2000 issue. Editors were surprised to see that they were deluged with nominations for Ataturk, the founder of modern Turkey, receiving over 200,000 nominations for him in just one day. He received more votes than Winston Churchill, Henry Ford, and Einstein. He was even the leading candidate in the category of Entertainers and Artists. It was later determined that a campaign was launched by Turkish journalists to flood the magazine with repeated nominations for the Turkish patriot.

A version of haphazard sampling, designed to increase representativeness, is called quota sampling. In *quota sampling* categories are established for participant dimensions deemed important for the question being asked. Everyone who responds is selected until a category is filled, or its sample size quota has been met. For example, if we want to assure that sex is equally represented in our sample, and our total sample size is to be 500, we would accept the first 250 females and the first 250 males who responded, ignoring all later respondents.

Some have argued that most psychological research employs convenience sampling (e.g., Whitley, 1996). For example, the use of subject pools in psychology departments, the basis of much research in psychology, can be viewed as a form of convenience cluster sampling. The cluster (the introductory psychology class) is selected because it is convenient, then random samples are taken from those students in the class who are willing to volunteer for research studies.

What we are really talking about here is the distinction made earlier between study populations and target populations. Study populations are almost always selected based on practical considerations—for convenience. However, if we use random sampling techniques when taking samples from those study populations, we are justified in generalizing back to the study populations, as defined by our sampling frame. The ability to generalize back to our *target* population, however, is ultimately dependent on replication with different study populations. It is still the case, however, that unless the study populations selected for replication differ from one another along a variety of dimensions, we still may end up with a body of knowledge concerning the behavior of a limited set of individuals, such as college freshmen, rather than people in general.

We can make similar inferential errors in time sampling when repeated samples are biased in a consistent manner. For example, if we are interested in using behavioral observation measures to identify the factors that maintain a child's self-injurious behaviors (e.g., by observing how a teacher responds to instances of self-injurious behavior), but do repeated observations in only highly demanding school situations, our inferences are limited to the maintaining factors that operate in that setting. Our data may be consistent across time samples, indicating satisfactory reliability of measures. However, the study samples and setting may be more narrow than the target samples and settings, thereby limiting the generalizability of our inferences.

With the rapid explosion of the worldwide web, the Internet is being used increasingly as a source for research participants. Research using the Internet almost always uses convenience sampling techniques. We must be particularly careful when taking convenience samples from Internet users. For instance, unless special care is taken, people can respond multiple times, thus strongly biasing our results. Even when respondents are limited to one-time participation, such as by the use of "cookies" to reject multiple responses from the same site, other problems remain with Internet surveys. Most Internet surveys involve quota sampling. Under these circumstances, one source of bias comes from different rates of log-on among individuals visiting a particular site. A major concern regarding Internet research centers around representativeness— to what extent are Internet users representative of meaningful populations to the behavioral researcher (Babbie, 2001).

### Snowball Sampling

There are times when we are interested in populations that are not easily identified or located. For example, what if we were interested in studying the homeless culture or in interviewing persons engaged in illegal activities? A sampling method that might be appropriate in this situation is *snowball sampling*. Initial elements of the sample are identified through convenience sampling or through acquaintances of the researcher that meet the criteria of the ultimate sample. Each of these respondents is asked to identify others who might be willing to participate in the project. Thus, the sample "snowballs" until the desired sample size is obtained.

For instance, let us assume we are interested in doing survey research on sexual orientation issues, and we need to obtain samples of individuals from the lesbian/gay/bisexual/transgender community. Sampling frames for this population would be extremely difficult to identify. It might be possible to obtain a convenience sample by asking for research volunteers through advertisements in community newspapers directed at the lesbian/gay/bisexual/transgender population, but is likely that only a small, biased subset of that community read such publications and a smaller number yet would be willing to participate in our project for fear of having their sexual orientation disclosed. Further, such publications are available only in larger urban communities. Under these circumstances we might identify a subset of openly gay individuals, invite them to complete our survey, but then ask them to provide copies of our survey to friends and acquaintances who are also part of the LGBT community.

### Purposive Sampling

A final non-random sampling technique that is employed under special circumstances is *purposive sampling*. In purposive sampling we rely on our subjective judgment to identify specific individuals from the population in which we are interested. Qualitative research methods often rely on this sampling technique. Individuals judged as prototypes of the population are selected for use with such techniques as focus groups and case studies. Whitley (1996) distinguished between identifying the typical case and the critical case when employing this technique. Selecting presumed typical cases would be particularly appropriate when establishing focus groups. For example, if one wished to set up a focus group of individuals using a student counseling center, participants might be chosen based on the degree to which the investigator believed they were typical or representative of those using the center. So, the investigator would probably select individuals of different genders, with different class standing, and with different problems.

Critical cases may be particularly appropriate for case studies. Someone studying children who bring guns to school would probably interview selected students suspended for such an act based on the interesting features of the individual case rather than on any concern for identifying the typical case. Regardless of the use to which such samples are to be put, however, it must be remembered that their selection is ultimately subjective, and our ability to generalize back to larger populations is severely limited.

Examples of purposive sampling with respect to time and setting are *critical time sampling* and *critical event sampling*. Often, we are interested in obtaining measures of a client during particular times of the day, or in particular settings. For example, troublesome parent–child interactions may occur mostly at bedtime or at suppertime. In such a case, it is not important that the information obtained from our samples be generalizable to other times or settings. We sample parent–child interactions primarily during these critical times and settings because the data we will acquire are the most useful for planning treatment strategies and the most sensitive to treatment effects.

## USING MATCHED SAMPLES

The discussion to this point has focused primarily on single samples, such as might be identified for survey research or other research methods designed primarily for descriptive purposes. Many times, however, we are interested in research methods that require the use of multiple samples. Treatment outcome studies are a classic example (Kazdin, 1998). In the simplest case, two groups are sampled from the same population, then the independent variable (treatment) is imposed on one of them (the Experimental Group), to determine if it produces differences over the performance of the second group (the Control Group). Our ability to infer that any differences observed between the two groups after treatment is due to our treatment is partially dependent on the two groups originally being samples of the same population.

In this instance our inferences about the populations from which our samples are drawn can be improved by matching elements of our samples on basic characteristics correlated with our dependent measure. Consider a study designed to evaluate a treatment procedure for depression. A good strategy might be to match treated and untreated depressed participants on initial level of depression, because treatment outcome is usually correlated with initial severity. By matching participants on such characteristics we are controlling for potential bias due to the matched factors and, in addition, we are increasing the precision of the statistical test we use to evaluate our results.

Statistical tests, in general, consist of constructing a ratio where the denominator estimates the amount of variation in our scores due to unknown or uncontrolled variables. The smaller the denominator, the larger will be the ratio, and the greater will be the probability that we will conclude a significant difference exists between groups or across time. Therefore, the smaller the denominator, the more sensitive or powerful the experiment will be said to be. By matching subjects, we are reducing variance due to the matching variable from our experiment. In other words, we are reducing the size of the denominator (the error term), thereby making the experiment more sensitive.

The amount of variance reduction can be seen in the following formula, which represents mathematically our estimate of the unaccounted-for variance when we have matched samples:

$$\left( \frac{s_1^2}{n_1} + \frac{s_2^2}{n_2} \right) - 2r_{1.2} \sqrt{\frac{s_1^2}{n_1} * \frac{s_2^2}{n_2}}$$

The $s^2$ terms represent estimates of the variance of the scores in the populations from which each sample is taken, the $n$ terms are the sample sizes associated with each of these estimates, and r stands for the correlation between our two samples that results from the matching process. This formula is complicated, and the details are not important to this discussion. What *is* important, however, is that the left side of the expression represents our estimate of uncontrolled variance when samples are independent, and the right side represents the reduction in our estimate of uncontrolled variance realized by matching our samples. Note that the reduction is dependent on the correlation between our two samples. The higher the correlation between the two samples on the measure being taken, the greater the reduction in error variance.

An extreme, but common, form of matching is to use the same individuals for both experimental and control groups, for example, by taking pre- and post-measures. The first author once ran a series of studies that utilized semantic differential ratings as the dependent measure. Semantic differential scales are a form of Likert scale, where individuals are asked to rate items on 7-point bipolar scales, such as "pleasant–unpleasant" or "weak–strong." Individual differences with respect to ratings on these scales are not the same as for many other types of rating scales. For example, on many scales some individuals rate everything positive while others tend to rate everything more negative.

Under these circumstances, when taking two ratings from each individual (e.g., having participants rate more than one item or taking test–retest ratings on the same item), the correlation across individuals will be positive. With semantic differential ratings, however, some raters tend to rate most things toward the middle of the scale while others rate things at the extremes. In this case, the correlation across individuals will be negative. The first author was puzzled to find that he consistently had smaller error terms when he ran independent groups than when he had the same individuals give ratings under the different conditions, until he examined more carefully the mathematical underpinnings of his statistical analysis. Close examination of the equation for determining unaccounted-for variance with matched samples indicates that the reduction only occurs if the correlation between the two samples is positive. A negative correlation will actually inflate the error term.

Survey research is often concerned with changes in descriptive characteristics of a population across time. Political polls across the course of a campaign are good examples of this. The pollsters are interested in differences in attitudes toward issues and candidates as the campaign progresses. Again, in most cases, this requires multiple samples taken from the same population at different points in time. Since we want to conclude that changes observed in our measures are due to passage of time, it is important to assume that the different samples are representative of the same basic population. The most common survey design to track changes in a population across time is the *successive cross-sectional design*. In a simple cross-sectional design, a sample of a population is taken at one point in time. The purpose of this design is description— either to describe the characteristics of a population at the time the sample is taken or to describe differences between two or more sub-populations. A good example of this design is the Kinsey Report (Kinsey, Pomeroy, & Martin, 1948; Kinsey, Pomeroy, Martin, & Gebhard, 1953), designed to describe the sexual behavior of American men and women.

Over 40 years later another survey was taken, the Sex in America survey (Laumann, Gagnon, Michael, & Michaels, 1994). Results of this survey have been examined to determine if there had been significant changes in sexual behaviors and mores across the preceding 50 years. Thus, this could be regarded as a successive cross-sectional design. For such a design to be valid, however, it is important that the sampling plan be the same for both surveys. The authors of the Sex in America survey argued that Kinsey's sampling techniques overrepresented the urban population, particularly on the east coast, and underrepresented rural and western populations. When they changed their sample, however, in an attempt to be more representative, they weakened the ability to assess directly changes in behavior across the time period. Changes observed could be due to changes in composition of the sample. One way to deal with this problem is to draw a sub-sample from the second large sample that matches the characteristics of the original sample.

The parallel to repeated measures designs in survey and other descriptive research is the longitudinal design, in which the same individuals are observed repeatedly at different points in time. A common design used in clinical outcome research consists of obtaining pre-treatment measures, measures at the end of treatment, and measures at follow-up. In the ideal case, the successive samples are perfectly matched, since they involve the same individuals. However, a major problem must be guarded against. Care must be taken to remove from the analysis any individual for whom measures at any of the observation times are missing. Individuals tend to drop out of treatment programs, and even those who complete treatment are not always available for follow-up. Unless data from these individuals are removed completely from the data set, systematic bias is likely to be introduced across sampling times. Participants who drop from the study may come from a different sub-sample than those who remain (e.g., they may differ in severity of disorder, current life stressors, or marital status). Thus, the original sample and the final sample are from different populations.

There are many times when random assignment of subjects to experimental and control groups is not feasible. In other words, sampling experimental and control participants for participation in a study is not being done from equivalent populations. This is the so-called *non-equivalent control group design* and is probably the most popular of the quasi-experimental designs (Johnston & Pennypacker, 1993). For example, in the past few years there has been an increased interest in the effects of special educational programs such as participation in learning communities during the freshman year for enhancing the academic experience of college students. Because it is not possible to randomly assign students to classes, a common design is to take a random sample of students who elect to enroll in a learning community their freshman year and a random sample of students entering the same year who do not select the learning community experience.

Clearly there is a strong selection factor operating. Any differences in academic performance observed between the two groups could be due to other factors that might distinguish individuals who select experimental programs from those who do not. An appealing strategy might seem to be to match individuals in the two samples on factors suspected to serve as alternative explanations of any differences observed. Thus, one might wish to match students in the two groups on SAT scores, ethnic background, or gender, for example. There are a number of problems with this strategy, however. To the extent that the two groups differ heavily on the matching dimension, the resulting sample may be severely restricted in size because of the inability to find appropriate matches. Matching on one variable might produce a mismatch on another. For example, if there are strong differences in SAT scores among students who attended different high schools, matching on high school could produce a mismatch on SAT scores. Finally, of course, even after matching has occurred, it is still possible that differences between the two groups are due to variables not identified at the time the design was set up (Cook, 1993).

A better strategy might be to leave the groups unmatched, but to use the non-equivalent control group to test for alternative hypotheses to account for any differences that might be observed (Kerlinger, 1986). For example, to determine if differences between freshmen in an enhanced learning environment and those in traditional classrooms might be due to differences in initial academic ability rather than differences in academic programs, we could see if the two groups differed on SAT scores. If there are significant differences, SAT scores could account for the differences observed between the two groups on academic performance. If there are not, we can rule out differences in academic ability as an alternative explanation for the results obtained. This strategy has been employed successfully in a program much like the one described to evaluate the impact of learning communities at the University of Hawaii.

One situation in which matching might seem particularly appropriate is when employing a pretest–posttest non-equivalent control group design. A classic example of this research strategy can be found in the Rogers and Dymond (1954) study designed to evaluate the effectiveness of client-centered therapy. The experimental group consisted of a sample of individuals who asked for appointments at a university counseling center; the control sample consisted of paid volunteers who were not seeking psychotherapy but who were told they were participating in research investigating personality. Both groups were rated on a variety of scales designed to measure mental health before experimental subjects entered therapy and again after therapy was completed.

The major finding of the study was that the experimental sample improved significantly in average performance on most scales between pretest and posttest, and the control group did not. The study has been severely criticized, however, because of the selection factor involved. Students seeking help would be expected to have poor mental health scores, while students enrolled in undergraduate courses probably would have average scores. In other words, for the control students to improve an equal amount would require that they score super-mentally-healthy on the posttest.

One way out of that dilemma might seem to be to match students in the experimental and control groups on their pretest mental health scores. Judd et al. (1991), however, have pointed out the fallacy of this strategy. Because matching would require selecting of control students from the lower end of the self-concept score distribution for that group, regression will almost assuredly occur, and control group means would improve independent of any intervention. In addition, students seeking treatment are different in many other ways from those seeking treatment, even if severity levels of the presenting behaviors are controlled for.

## SAMPLE SIZE

Whether investigating the significance of differences among sample means, as in multi-group studies, or attempting to estimate population parameters, as is usually the case in much current clinical outcome research and survey and descriptive studies, the degree of confidence that we can place in our conclusions is affected by the size of the samples we employ. Because the larger the sample, the more closely we are approximating the population from which the sample is drawn (unless the sample is biased), it should come as no surprise that, in general, the larger the sample, the greater the precision with which we can estimate the true parameters.

In traditional group comparison methods, we formulate two hypotheses. The first is the null hypothesis, which states that our samples are drawn from equivalent populations. Equivalent populations are those for which the distributions of our measure on a population level have the same shape, dispersion, and central tendency. Most populations in which we are interested are normally distributed on the measures of interest. Dispersion refers to the degree to which the scores differ from one another, and central tendency refers to where the majority of the scores fall in the distribution. Specifically, we usually assume the same shape and dispersion (as measured by the variance or standard deviation) and hypothesize commonality of central tendency (usually measured by the mean). Under our assumptions, if the hypothesis of no difference in means is correct, the samples represent equivalent populations. The alternative hypothesis states that the populations from which our samples are drawn are not equivalent in terms of central tendency, either because of pre-existing differences or because of some manipulation we made with respect to one or more of the groups.

We either reject the null hypothesis of no differences among the population means, or we suspend judgment. Notice that there are two types of decision errors we can make in this situation. Either we can reject the null hypothesis when it is really true in nature (a Type I error), or we can fail to reject the null when it is really false (a Type II error). Traditionally, there has been much more concern with the first type of error than the second. The probability of making a Type I error is specified by $\alpha$, our level of significance chosen for our statistical test.

In the past 10 years or so, there has been an increased focus on the problem of making a Type II error, that is, failing to detect a difference that really exists. The probability of making a Type II error is called $\beta$, and $1 - \beta$ is called the *power* of the test. Beta (and thus power) is dependent on several factors: the size of the effect as it actually exists in the real world (usually measured in standard deviation units or by a correlation coefficient), the $\alpha$ we select for our experiment (our chosen level of significance), and the size of the samples we employ. It has become increasingly common for journals and grant application review boards to require a power analysis for research being considered for publication or for funding. In other words, reviewers want to assure that sample size was (or will be) large enough to detect a difference if it really exists.

Computation of minimum sample size needed for given values of $\alpha$, $\beta$, and effect size is relatively straightforward for simple statistics, and tables are available for determining this number directly (Cohen, 1988). Cohen also has detailed discussions regarding selecting $n$ sizes in more complex designs, where estimating effect size can be more complicated. Use of an effect size statistic rather than a simple estimate of mean difference expected is important in these analyses. Any difference, regardless of how trivial, will be found significant if the sample size is large enough. Effect size statistics speak to the magnitude of the effect. In technical terms, effect size indicates the proportion of variance in our measure that is accounted for by the variable being studied.

In recent years it has been argued that traditional null-hypothesis-testing models are inappropriate for the development of psychology as a science (e.g., Cohen, 1994; Schmidt, 1996). Instead, it has been suggested that researchers should focus on estimating population parameters (called point estimation) rather than engaging in formal statistical hypothesis testing. This approach recommends that in place of null hypothesis testing, investigators report estimates of parameters along with appropriate confidence intervals. To the extent that these intervals do not overlap, one can conclude a true difference. Although the specific criticisms of null hypothesis testing are open to debate (e.g., Frick, 1996), the alternatives suggested have been recognized as an appropriate methodological approach for psychological journals, and we should be seeing more and more such techniques appearing in the literature in the future.

Paralleling this position, in clinical outcome research there has been a shift from determining whether a treatment has a statistically significant effect (can the null hypothesis be rejected?) to determining how strong that effect is. Researchers calculate the size of effect due to treatment, then develop confidence intervals around these effect sizes. This approach can be applied across experiments through meta-analysis, and, it has been argued, leads to a more accurate body of knowledge within the field. As mentioned earlier, our ability to estimate a population parameter, such as magnitude of effect of a clinical intervention on a specific clinical outcome measure, is also dependent on sample size. The larger the sample, the better the estimate, assuming our sample is unbiased.

Most survey research is designed to obtain estimates of population parameters as well. What percentage of recent divorcees have depression problems? How satisfied are clients of a mental health clinic with the treatment received? The concept of margin of error is not foreign to anyone following the polling that takes place during an election year. Percentage of individuals who intend to vote for a given candidate according to results of a survey of potential voters is reported, along with a percentage, such as 5%. This establishes a confidence interval for the estimate and means that the true percentage will fall anywhere within the interval with a given probability. When the percentage leaning toward each of two candidates is reported, the race is considered a "dead heat" if the intervals overlap. For example, if the poll indicates that 43% favor Candidate A and 47% favor Candidate B, with a 3% margin of error, the candidates are tied. The true percentage of individuals favoring Candidate A is anywhere from 40%–46% and favoring Candidate B is anywhere from 44%–50%. Computation of confidence intervals is dependent on the standard deviation of scores and sample size. Again, this can be a complicated task, depending on the scale of measurement employed, the actual survey design used, and whether or not a correction for sampling without replacement is utilized. Pedhazur and Schmelkin (1991) has a good discussion of how to estimate population standard deviations under a variety of these conditions.

It must be remembered, however, that point estimation procedures are accurate only to the extent that we obtain unbiased samples. Confidence intervals and margins of error can be misleading to persons reading the results of studies using these methods. If a study reports a large sample size and a small distribution of scores, the confidence interval will be small, but if the sample is biased, a great deal of inferential error can still occur.

As we noted earlier, confidence in our inferences about the target population in time sampling is also affected sample size. In this case sample size refers to the number and duration of time samples. Consider the precision with which we can estimate a client's daily mood by sampling 1, 5, 20, or 50 times a day, or by sampling 2, 10, or 60 minutes.[4] The more samples of an event that we obtain, or the longer the samples, the more likely it is that our obtain measures are accurate estimates of the population parameters (e.g., the "true" mood of the client during a day).

The precision of estimates from time sampling is complicated by the dynamic nature of the measured events—measured events can change systematically or unsystematically over time. Consequently, the number and duration of time samples necessary to draw accurate estimates is affected by the dynamic characteristics of the measured phenomena.

Figure 3.1 illustrates three time series—plots of time-sampled data—that differ in their variability and slope. Just as confidence in estimates from samples

---

[4]In time sampling, many methodological considerations, in addition to sample size, will affect precision of our estimates. Precision may be affected by the reactive effects of assessment (mood may be affected by the process of measuring it), the practicality of obtaining multiple measures, the validity and precision of the measurement instrument, and effects such as response biases associated with multiple measures.

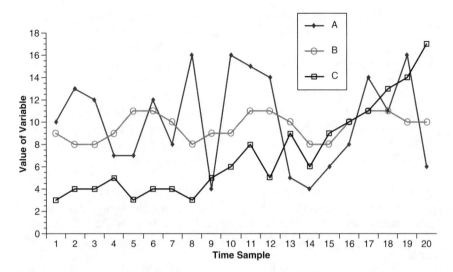

FIG. 3.1.    Three time series that differ in variability and slope. "Value" may refer to rate, intensity, duration, or other dimension of the measured event.

of persons depends on the number of persons sampled and the dispersion of measures across persons, confidence in estimates from samples of time depends on the number of time-samples and the dispersion of measures across time. As we can see from Fig. 3.1, we can be more confident of our estimates of variable B than of variable A. Because of its higher variability over time, it would be necessary to obtain more measures of variable A than of variable B.

Variable C illustrates systematic changes in the measured variable over time. To capture the dynamic quality of variable C, we may need to sample the variable across more time periods, to estimate important dimensions—the slope and cylicity of the variable. These dynamic aspects are particularly important in clinical assessment because they can indicate the operation of important causal variables in a client's life—for example, something is happening to affect a client's mood, or the way a parent responds to a child. Methods of analyzing time-series data are discussed in Collins and Horn (1991), Gaynor, Baird, and Nelson-Gray, (1999), and Wei (1990).

## SUMMARY

In clinical research, we seldom have the opportunity to observe the entire population about which we wish to draw conclusions, whether the population is of a group of people or time periods in which behavior of a given individual can occur. Therefore, we need to take samples from the population and then make inferences about the nature of the population given that sample. These inferences will only be approximations of the populations of interest, however, the accuracy of which will depend on the sampling methods employed, the variability in our measures, and the size of the sample.

We begin the sampling process by identifying our sampling frame, the list of all the elements that comprise the population from which our sample will be taken. The sampling frame operationally defines our study population, which is seldom exactly the same as our target population, the population about which we wish to make inferences. Therefore, we must be cautious in the conclusions we draw about the target population of interest.

Our ability to draw inferences about even our study population is dependent on the degree to which our sample is unbiased. The primary method of controlling for potential bias is the use of some form of probability sampling. Simple random sampling controls for bias in the long run, but may result in a biased sample in any specific instance. For this reason, sampling plans often involve taking stratified random samples, assuring that important characteristics are represented in the sample studied. Cluster sampling, another variant of probability sampling, is usually employed when it is difficult to identify a sampling frame that is directly representative of the population of interest.

A variety of non-random sampling techniques are employed in clinical settings as well, either because of difficulties in obtaining random samples or because of special research needs. Non-random techniques discussed in this chapter included systematic sampling, convenience sampling, snowball sampling, and purposive sampling. All of these techniques must be employed with some caution, since all of them, by their very nature, introduce bias into the sample.

Many times a research question requires multiple samples to be taken, for example when we want to look for differences among two or more groups or when we want to study changes in a population across time. We often can improve our inferences by utilizing research designs that match elements of our samples on important characteristics. Care must be taken, however, when using matching procedures with quasi-experimental designs such as the non-equivalent control group design.

The larger the sample size, the more closely the sample approximates the population of interest and the more accurately we can estimate the population's parameters. An important parameter in clinical research is effect size. In clinical outcome research, there recently has been a shift away from determining whether a treatment has a statistically significant effect to determining how strong that effect is. Researchers calculate the size of effect due to treatment based on their sample data, then develop confidence intervals around these effect sizes. It also is becoming increasingly common to conduct power analyses before running a study to determine the minimum sample size needed to detect an effect of expected magnitude.

## REFERENCES

Babbie, E. (2001). *The practice of social research* (9th ed.). Belmont, CA: Wadsworth.

Cohen, J. (1988). *Statistical power analysis for the behavioral sciences* (2nd ed.). Hillsdale, NJ: Lawrence Erlbaum Associates.

Cohen, J. (1994). The earth is round ($p < .05$). *American Psychologist, 49*, 997–1003.

Collins, L. M., & Horn, J. L. (Eds.). (1991). Best methods for the analysis of change. Recent advances, unanswered questions, future directions. Washington, DC: American Psychological Association.

Cone, J. S. (1999). Self-Monitoring (Special Section). *Psychological Assessment, 11*, 411–497.

Cook, T. D. (1993). A quasi-sampling theory of the generalization of causal relationships. In L. Sechrest & A. G. Scott (Eds.), Understanding causes and generalizing about them. *New Directions in Program Evaluation.* San Francisco: Jossey-Bass.

Frick, R. W. (1996). The appropriate use of null hypothesis testing. *Psychological Methods, 1*, 379–390.

Gaynor, S. T., Baird, S. C., & Nelson-Gray, R. O. (1999). Application of time-series (single-subject) designs in clinical psychology. In P. C. Kendall, J. N. Butcher, & G. N. Holmbeck (Eds.), *Handbook of research methods in clinical psychology* (2nd ed., pp. 297–329). New York: John Wiley & Sons, Inc.

Hawkins, R. P., Mathews, J. R., & Hamdan, L. (1999). Measuring behavioral health outcomes—A practical guide. New York: Kluwer Academic/Plenum Publishers.

Hite, S. (1987). *Women and love: A cultural revolution in progress.* New York: Knopf.

Hogan, H. (1990, May). *Post-enumeration survey: An overview.* Paper presented at the Population Association of America meeting, Toronto, Canada.

Johnston, J. M., & Pennypacker, H. S. (1993). Strategies and tactics of behavioral research (2nd ed.). Hillsdale, NJ: Lawrence Erlbaum Associates.

Judd, C. M., Smith, E. R., & Kidder, L. H. (1991). *Research methods in social relations* (6th ed.). Fort Worth, TX: Harcourt Brace Jovanovich, Inc.

Kazdin, A. E. (1998). *Research design in clinical psychology* (3rd ed.). Boston: Allyn & Bacon.

Kerlinger, F. N. (1986). Foundations of behavioral research (3rd ed.). Orlando, FL: Holt, Rinehart, & Winston.

Kinsey, A. C., Pomeroy, W. B., & Martin, C. E. (1948). *Sexual behavior in the human male.* Philadelphia: Saunders.

Kinsey, A. C., Pomeroy, W. B., Martin, C. E., & Gebhard, P. H. (1953). *Sexual behavior in the human female.* Philadelphia: Saunders.

Laumann, E. O., Gagnon, J. H., Michael, R. T., & Michaels, S. (1994). *The social organization of sexuality: Sexual practices in the United States.* Chicago: The University of Chicago Press.

McBurney, D. H. (1994). *Research methods* (3rd ed.). Pacific Grove, CA: Brooks/Cole.

Odom, S. L., & Ogawa, I. (1992). Direct observation of young children's social interaction with peers: A review of methodology. *Behavioral Assessment, 14*, 407–441.

Pedhazur, E. J., & Schmelkin, L. P. (1991). *Measurement, design, and analysis: An integrated approach.* Hillsdale, NJ: Lawrence Erlbaum Associates.

Rogers, C. R., & Dymond, R. F. (1954). *Psychotherapy and personality change.* Chicago: University of Chicago Press.

Shaughnessy, J. J., & Zechmeister, E. B. (1990). *Research methods in psychology* (2nd ed.). New York: McGraw-Hill.

Schmidt, F. L. (1996). Statistical significance testing and cumulative knowledge in psychology: Implications for training of researchers. *Psychological Methods, 1*, 115–129.

Suen, H. K., & Ary, D. (1989). *Analyzing quantitative behavioral data.* Hillsdale, NJ: Lawrence Erlbaum Associates.

Wei, W. W. S. (1990). Time series analysis—Univariate and multivariate methods. Redwood City, CA: Addison-Wesley Publishing Company, Inc.

Whitley, B. E. (1996). *Principles of research in behavioral science.* Mountain View, CA: Mayfield Publishing Company.

# 4

# Validity: Making Inferences from Research Outcomes

Joseph R. Scotti
Tracy L. Morris
Stanley H. Cohen
*West Virginia University*

The poetic parody, *Hiawatha Designs an Experiment* (Kendall, 1959/1973), cleverly illustrates the critical relation between reliability and validity. Hiawatha, the mighty hunter, demonstrates that he is able to repeatedly shoot his arrows in tight groups such that the "average point of impact [is] very near the spot he aimed at" (p. 331). Unfortunately for Hiawatha, despite his great consistency, he always misses the target. Thus, although reliable, his shots are not valid. In research, this translates into use of reliable measures and experimental procedures that can be replicated by other researchers, but finding the resulting data do not hit the mark in terms of our confidence that we have manipulated or measured the variables of interest. Our goal in research is to control as many variables as is feasible so that we may reveal the relations among a smaller set of variables. As the reader will see, this is not such a simple process.

In this chapter, we review four aspects of validity that are central to our confidence in our research designs and the resulting ability to interpret and generalize the outcomes. These are internal validity, external validity, statistical conclusion validity, and construct validity. We present these types separately, but the attentive reader will note similar issues across them, leading to our later discussion on the relations among these forms of validity. A key source for the multiple factors that need to be considered in these forms of validity is the classic work of Campbell and Stanley (1963), with recent elaborations by Shadish, Cook, and Campbell (2001).

## INTERNAL VALIDITY

*Internal validity* refers to the extent to which we may feel confident about inferences that we draw from an investigation regarding causal relations among variables, especially that the independent variable is responsible for the observed effect or outcome (Campbell & Stanley, 1963; Christensen, 1997). With respect to drawing conclusions about the effectiveness of interventions, internal validity is of paramount importance. The issue at hand is how confident one can be that observed changes following an intervention or experimental manipulation were indeed "caused" by the intervention and were not, instead, due to the influence of *extraneous* variables; that is, "any variable other than the independent variable that influences the dependent variable" (Christensen, 1997, p. 229). In order to demonstrate a causal relation, it is necessary to rule out alternative explanations for the observed findings. The range of alternative explanations includes demand characteristics, expectancies, and a host of other threats to internal validity, as originally outlined by Campbell and Stanley (1963; see also Shadish et al., 2001).

### Demand Characteristics

It has been demonstrated time and again that the *demands* of the research situation can affect participant responding. Commonly referred to as the *demand characteristics* of an experiment, these represent cues that are inadvertently provided by the experimental situation or treatment setting that may influence how the participants react. Research participants are volunteers who likely are favorably inclined toward the research process by virtue of having volunteered in the first place, and these participants will typically want things to "go well" for the investigator. Assessments administered at baseline may sensitize, or alert, participants to the objectives of the investigation, even when researchers attempt to keep participants naive (i.e., uninformed) as to those purposes. For instance, on entering a treatment study, the participant might be asked to complete self-report measures of depression and general distress—the content of which are not easily disguised as to their purpose (e.g., "How often in the last week have you felt sad?"). Clearly, any treatment investigation would have the objective of decreasing symptoms of depression and distress. Participants can easily discern this and may even react to their own self-observation about their levels of depression and distress. The outcome then, may be a reduction in these symptoms simply due to reactivity or the implicit "demand" that treatment will lead to improvement—regardless of the intervention (Shadish et al., 2001).

Additionally, participation of human subjects in a research study requires that they actively provide their *full and informed consent* (American Psychological Association [APA], 1992; Kerlinger & Lee, 2000). Regulated by federal guidelines, informed consent provides a general overview of a study (be it experimental, treatment, observational, or survey): its goals and purposes; procedures that will be involved; and the expected risks, benefits, and costs to the participant, if any. Such information can alert participants to the content of the study, and their common sense and general knowledge may lead them to believe they should respond in certain ways (even when this belief may be inaccurate and even contrary to the experimenter's hypotheses). This is not to say that participants should not be informed about the research in which they are going to participate; they must be in order to control abuses and minimize—or at least alert participants to—any risks (see Kerlinger & Lee, 2000, for a discussion of deception, fraud, and abuse in scientific research). Thus, it becomes incumbent on the experimenter to consider what information goes into the consent form—without misrepresenting the study—and what effects this may have on the behavior of the participants. For instance, consider the potential differential impact of simply the study's title on the consent form. Titling one's study, *Severe Sexual Abuse and its Role in Causing Mental Illness*, would raise much different concerns for a participant than the sufficiently descriptive title, *The Relation of Life Events to Current Concerns*, especially for those participants who have a history of sexual abuse.

Closely related to the issue of demand characteristics is that of *subject roles*. In his discussion of the literature on this threat to validity, Kazdin (1998) noted several roles that research participants might adopt, including: (a) *the good subject*, who wants to give information consistent with the perceived goals of the investigator; (b) *the negativistic subject*, who seeks to provide information that is contrary to the perceived hypotheses; (c) *the faithful subject*, who attempts to follow instructions to the letter and not let their preconceived notions affect the research; and (d) *the apprehensive subject*, who is concerned about their performance and how he or she may be judged. Kazdin (1998) noted the concern over participants assuming these various roles and how this may impact on research outcomes (causing effects that are not due to the independent variable), but evidence for such effects is difficult to gather and remains equivocal.

### Experimenter Expectancies

Clearly, investigators also have expectations as to the outcome of their study, and these expectations may influence outcome. This is not to say that investigators purposefully bias their findings, for that would be a serious breach of ethics with severe consequences for professional standing. Rather, experimenters may engage in behavior that unwittingly biases, skews, or otherwise alters the outcome in their favor (that is, in support of their hypotheses). This "self-fulfilling prophecy" has come to be commonly known as the *Rosenthal Effect*, after Robert Rosenthal, a social psychologist who wrote about this problem in the 1960s (see Kazdin, 1998; Shadish et al., 2001). If investigators are aware to which group participants are assigned, they inadvertently may treat participants in the two groups differently, such as being more enthusiastic and responsive to participants in the group receiving the treatment the investigators expect to be more effective, and being unenthusiastic and even unintentionally pessimistic with those in the "less favored" comparison treatment groups. For example, Scotti, Evans, Meyer, and Walker (1991), in a meta-analysis of the developmental disabilities intervention literature, found that the same intervention classes were consistently found to be *less* effective when they were used as the secondary comparison treatment in a study than when they were the primary intervention of interest to the author of a study. Although other interpretations for this finding are possible, it points to the need to ensure that research assistants who have direct contact (i.e., observing, rating, testing, or treating) with participants avoid being aware of a participant's group assignment or of experimental hypotheses, and that *procedural reliability* (i.e., the consistency of implementing procedures as designed) is routinely evaluated.

As a further example, let us look at an investigation of the influence of parenting practices on child depression. The study involves two groups of children and their parents: (a) children with high levels of depression (Depressed), and (b) children without any symptoms of depression (Nondepressed). Observers watch videotapes of structured interactions between each child and his or her parent, and then provide ratings of child and parent affect and various aspects of parenting behavior (e.g., criticism vs. praise, guidance on a task vs. taking over the task). If observers are aware of which participants are in the Depressed group and which are in the Nondepressed group, this may influence ratings of child and parent behavior. For example, if the observer is having difficulty assigning a score on a Likert rating of negative affect (e.g., such as on a 5-point scale from *not at all sad* to *very sad*), and the observer is aware that the child being rated is in the Depressed group, then the observer may be more likely to assign a rating consistent with depression (i.e., *very sad*). Likewise, observers who are aware of group membership may perceive parents of children in the Depressed group as displaying higher rates of criticism.

To control for such experimenter bias, persons assigning ratings, performing observations, completing assessments, or implementing treatments of participants should not be informed about group assignment (typically referred to as *blind* or *masked* assignment). When the research design is set up so that neither the front-line investigator (the person having direct contact with participants) nor the participants themselves know to which group they have been assigned, this is called a *double-blind* study.

## Threats to Internal Validity

In their classic text, Campbell and Stanley (1963) identified eight categories of extraneous factors that may influence internal validity (see Shadish et al., 2001, for further elaboration on variants of these eight categories, and others).

*History.* Participants may be exposed to certain life events between the several points of measurement (e.g., Time 1 and Time 2; or Times 1, 2, 3, and 4) in the study that may impact the results. Studies involving repeated measurements over long periods of time (such as at 1, 6, and 12 months following a traumatic motor vehicle accident) are more susceptible to history effects than those studies in which data are collected over shorter time periods (such as a 1-week retest interval). For example, let us say that a social science researcher is attempting to assess the impact of a campus-wide multimedia campaign (e.g., posters on campus, announcements in class, displays in the campus newspaper) to decrease drinking and driving among college students. She chooses the campus of ABC University to conduct her study. During the course of the study, a well-known popular music celebrity is killed while driving under the influence of alcohol. If, at the end of the campaign (i.e., the intervention), the investigator observes lower rates of drinking and driving among the college students on the campus of ABC University, it may be quite difficult for her to discern whether the lower rates were a direct result of the campus media campaign or a result of the national media attention concerning the consequences of drinking and driving that occurred in the wake of the celebrity's death.

One means for ruling out such group history effects is to include a *control group* that does not receive the intervention (we use the term, *control group*, in this chapter in the general sense, and are not distinguishing between "true" control groups created via random assignment and comparison groups formed by other means—procedures that are discussed elsewhere in this text). In this case, a different campus of comparable size and demographics—XYZ University— would be monitored for rates of drinking and driving but would not receive the campus-wide media campaign. If the rates of drinking and driving decrease dramatically at both campuses, then the possibility exists that the recent burst of media attention may have played a part. However, if reductions in drinking and driving are only observed in the treatment group—that is, at ABC University—then the investigator may feel more confident that the change in behavior was a consequence of her campus-wide media campaign.

Unfortunately, history effects may not manifest themselves equally across all participants. This is sometimes referred to as a *local history effect*, being more prevalent in one group than in another (i.e., an interaction). For example, imagine you are administering a program designed to improve the social interaction of preschool children. You have taken care to randomly assign the children to treatment (e.g., pairing socially skilled and nonskilled children) and control (e.g., providing access to extra toys) groups. However, unknown to you during the course of the study, the mothers of three children in your control group began arranging play dates for their children and made active attempts on their own to improve the social interaction of their children. At the conclusion of the study, these three children have made drastic improvements in social interaction, thereby diminishing posttreatment differences between your treatment and control groups. Such an example illustrates the importance of obtaining information on processes relevant to the outcome of your investigation. In this case, it would have been useful for you to obtain information on social contacts occurring outside of the context of the study (i.e., the preschool classroom), and to consider whether, at the initial assessment, participants should be given more explicit instructions about maintaining their typical routines throughout the course of the study.

With respect to the latter issue of typical routines, internal validity of investigations of new medication treatments for reducing blood pressure have been compromised when it was found that participants in such studies often independently made drastic changes in their exercise habits following study initiation. As increased exercise can lower blood pressure, investigators could not be certain if it was the change in exercise or the addition of the medication (or even the combination) that was leading to reduced blood pressure in the treatment group because increased exercise by the control group participants reduced any differences between them and the participants in the treatment group. Thus, it became important for investigators to instruct participants to maintain their typical course of behavior while enrolled in the study.

Finally, consider the impact on a study of anxiety, depression, stress, or posttraumatic stress of the events of September 11, 2001. The collapse of the World Trade Center itself, along with the crashes in Pennsylvania and into the Pentagon, was a nearly unbelievable calamity of historic proportions. Any psychological study already in progress at that time will need to be analyzed for potential effects and differences in both treatment and control groups that could be attributed to all participants being impacted by the disaster in some way. Complicating the analysis are the multiple ways that people might be affected, from watching the dramatic events unfold on television, to having friends or relatives who lived or worked in New York City, to the injury or death of loved ones. Furthermore, in our research group, we postponed the start of a study on the reliability of the self-report of traumatic stress symptoms because of the apparent increase in overall stress and psychological symptoms even some months after September 11, as the continuing events of the war on terrorism unfolded.

***Maturation.*** Maturation effects are those that occur over the normal passage of time rather than as a result of experimenter imposed changes. These may be thought of as normal growth, such as children growing taller and heavier with age; typical developmental progression, such as children learning to crawl, stand, walk, and run in that order; or typical social and general knowledge gains, such as changes in social behavior and language use over time with exposure to role models and learning opportunities.

For example, as children age, their word knowledge improves; that is, they speak and understand a greater number of words. This is not simply the effect of passing time, but of what events normally occur over time, such as continuing verbal interaction with adults, learning to read, and attendance at school. (The passage of time is, in itself, never a factor in change; it is what events or processes occur during the passage of time.) If one were implementing a 6-month course of intervention designed to improve the verbal ability of 5-year-old children (such as an early head start program to help children perform better academically as they enter kindergarten), it would be necessary to demonstrate that any gains made were not merely a function of expected developmental changes as a result of typical learning opportunities. Instead, one would want to show that improvements were *in addition to* those that could be expected due to maturation: that is, greater gains in verbal ability over the same time period. In such a study, it is necessary, as it is with history effects, to include a comparison control group that would help rule out maturation as a possible cause for the observed changes at the conclusion of a study. Thus, the control group in this study would not receive the intervention designed to improve verbal ability, but still would be expected to show improvement in verbal ability at a level that typically occurs during normal development or maturation. The intervention group would be expected to show improved verbal ability above that demonstrated by the control group; that is, the effects of maturation plus the intervention program.

**Testing.** Completion of pretest assessments may affect participant's performance on later testing. Let us return to the example just used regarding word knowledge among 5-year-old children. If at the time of the pretest, we asked the children to give the meaning of ten words, and then asked the meaning of those same ten words at posttest, it is quite possible that exposure to these words at pretest will have affected performance at posttest. Following the pretest administration, children may recall words with which they were not familiar and may ask their parents the meaning of those words when they return home. Thus, readministration of those same ten words may not be an adequate assessment of the children's general level of word knowledge.

Repeated testing also provides one more opportunity for demand characteristics to play themselves out. Participants in a study on social anxiety may feel badly that they are not really improving at all (such as those in the control group), or may think they are not improving as fast as they should. In either case, they may wish to "help out" the researcher by reporting fewer symptoms on the follow-up assessment than they think they remember reporting on the initial assessment. This sort of behavior is made easier by being familiar with the instruments being used by virtue of having previously completed them one or more times over the course of the study. Also, repeated testing may lead to fatigue or frustration effects, whereby participants do not carefully complete measures because they are simply tired of doing them over and over. Thus, it is important to attend to the length, difficulty, and administration frequency when selecting outcome measures.

***Instrumentation.*** Changes in measurement devices, instructions, or methods of administration may affect the outcome of a study. Let us say you are interested in minimizing testing effects in the word knowledge study just described. You decide to use different sets of words for the pre- and posttest assessments of the effects of your intervention on children's word knowledge. It is crucial that this alternate set of items be equivalent to the original set in terms of difficulty (i.e., alternate or parallel form reliability). Otherwise, any observed differences in performance may be a result of differences in instrumentation rather than due to actual treatment effects. Thus, you would want to create a large pool of words that represent different levels of word knowledge, with similar difficulty within each level. The pre- and posttests would then use a different representative sample of words from that larger pool.

Likewise, for observational studies, changes in the adherence of the observers (both within and between observers) to the original behavioral code may affect the outcome of the study. For instance, over the course of the study, Observer A may begin to interpret the definition for "talking out loud in the classroom" more leniently than Observer B (e.g., Observer B records any time the child speaks in the classroom, while Observer A only records what he feels is "loud" and fails to record what he thinks is whispering or quietly talking to oneself). Thus, over time, the two observers no longer agree with one another. In such cases, it is necessary to periodically assess for *observer drift* (via regular calculation of interrater reliability/agreement coefficients) to ensure that observers are adhering to the original definitions in the behavioral observation code provided by the principal investigator. Observers may even be *recalibrated* by having them periodically observe a standard training videotape and comparing their data to a *criterion* or "gold standard;" that is, the values for each code that were obtained by several well-trained observers (such as the principal investigator).

***Statistical Regression.*** On repeated testing, there is a statistical tendency for the scores of any given sample to regress (i.e., move closer) toward the mean for the population on any given measure. This occurs because samples selected for research studies are rarely truly random or representative of the general population. Often participants are selected based on extreme scores on a measure of clinical concern, such as anxiety, self-esteem, or frequency of compulsive behaviors. For groups that are selected on the basis of extremely high scores (such as the children in the Depressed group in the parenting practices study, described earlier), it would not be unusual for scores on subsequent testing to be lower than the initial testing—for the group as a whole. Thus, reductions in scores may be the result of statistical regression rather than indicative of change resulting from the intervention. It is important to note that this is a *group* statistical phenomenon and that it reflects the fallibility—or less than perfect reliability—of observed scores on our measures. The score for any given individual may move slightly up or down on subsequent testing; it is the sample *group mean* that is likely to demonstrate the phenomenon of regression. The more extreme the sample selected, the greater the possibility for regression. Thus, it would be important to include a control group that begins with similarly extreme test scores—and that will also show regression of those scores in the direction of the population mean. Success of the intervention or experimental manipulation would then be demonstrated by the treatment group showing changes that exceed those seen in the control group (i.e., regression plus treatment effects vs. regression alone).

**Selection.** Participants in group comparison studies should be functionally equivalent to each other on all relevant variables at the outset of the study. It is important for investigators to determine which variables may impact on outcome and to match the groups accordingly. Too often, investigators rely on random assignment to groups in the hope that all potentially relevant variables will be evenly distributed across the groups. Random chance suggests that many variables will be so distributed, but key variables of interest should not be left to such chance. For instance, age, gender, socioeconomic status, educational level, and ethnicity can play important roles in the response to many psychological and social science manipulations. The more we know about such differential effects, the more important it is that groups are matched on these variables—or that they even become variables to manipulate in their own right (such as assessing the effects of treatment on a group of older vs. younger adults, or White vs. African-American children). Typically, this strategy also decreases within group variability and thus increases the power of our statistical analyses (discussed later).

Formal subject *matching* involves ensuring, for example, that not only is the mean age of the participants in each group the same, but that there are equal numbers of participants within each of several age levels within each group (e.g., such as each group having 20 participants in each of the 20 to 30, 31 to 40, 41 to 50, and 51 to 60 age brackets). Age in itself is a complex variable that actually reflects number of years of life experience, different levels of exposure to key events (e.g., number of traumatic life events), health status, educational level (and the knowledge base at the time of that educational attainment), occupation, and a host of other variables—many of which also reflect the generation within which a person was born and matured and the opportunities available at that time (such as the increased likelihood over successive generations of attending college). Variables likely to be related to the outcome measures in the study should be controlled by matching or manipulation (i.e., creating relevant groups). It is other nuisance and potentially confounding variables that may largely be unknown at the time of the study that we should rely on to be distributed across groups according to chance through random assignment.

*Mortality.*   Mortality can, unfortunately for the participant, literally mean the death of one's research subject. More typically, mortality refers to those instances in which participants withdraw (i.e., drop out) from a study before it is completed. The longer and more involved a study is, the higher the rate of participant mortality or attrition. If participant mortality is not equivalent across groups, or is high across the entire study, the validity of observed differences between groups becomes questionable. For example, imagine you are conducting a study of the comparative efficacy of two treatments to reduce anxiety. You randomly assigned your participant volunteers to one of two groups. The first group, CBT, receives a fairly standard Cognitive-Behavioral Treatment package in which *in vivo* exposure is delivered and participants are expected to complete complex homework assignments on a weekly basis. The second group, Support, involves participation in a weekly anxiety support group with no assigned homework. Over the course of the study, 37% of the CBT participants and 8% of the Support participants drop out. Posttreatment results indicate more improvement on measures of clinical concern (e.g., state/trait anxiety, avoidance of feared situations) for the CBT group than for the Support group.

Given the different mortality rates in the two groups in this study, one might question the validity of the results as it is possible that only the most motivated participants, or those with the lowest levels of anxiety, continued with the CBT treatment for the duration of the study—potentially biasing the outcome. Post-hoc comparison of the participants who dropped out of the study, in terms of pretreatment levels of anxiety, motivation, etcetera, becomes necessary. You will also want to compare those participants who remained in the study—in both groups—on the same pretreatment measures. If no relevant differences can be ascertained, then you may have more confidence in your results, although this does not rule out other *unmeasured* differences. Examination of the reasons that participants give for dropping out may greatly assist in development of more consumer friendly treatments (such information may be obtained in debriefing or exit interviews or through mailed questionnaires—if one can still locate those participants and they are willing to provide the information). No matter how "good" a treatment may be from a research perspective, it will be of no practical value if very few clients are willing to complete the program.

*Selection Interactions.*   Selection methods may interact with the other threats to internal validity already listed, thus further biasing the results. For example, selection may interact with history in a selection-history threat. Returning once again to our study of word knowledge among 5-year-old children, let us suppose that children were assigned to treatment and control groups based on the classroom to which they had already been assigned by the school. In one classroom, the teacher played videotapes of *Sesame Street* (with segments designed to enhance word knowledge) each day, whereas this activity did not occur in the other classroom. Results may be positively biased toward the intervention program if the treatment group were also the group that was exposed to the *Sesame Street* videotapes. Alternatively, any actual treatment effects artificially may be obscured if the control group children were the ones exposed to the videotapes.

Selection-instrumentation threats may come into play, for example, in an observational study if two observers are assigned to different groups and the rater for one group demonstrates more observer drift than the rater for the other group. When observations are conducted live in real time (vs. from video tapes), it is imperative that all raters be up to par (in terms of agreement with the observation code) and consistent with one another, for there is no going back to recode the data (thus the preference for many researchers to videotape observations for later coding).

A number of the aforementioned threats to internal validity point out the need for assessment of *procedural reliability* or *treatment validity*, with the key issue being that the study (be it an intervention, survey, or laboratory experiment) be conducted exactly as designed. When investigators increasingly depart from implementing the research protocol as designed—even unwittingly—increasing uncertainty as to the source of effects—if any even remain—creeps into the interpretation of outcomes. When control group participants receive aspects of the intervention (even by their own independent initiation) and treatment group participants do not fully receive the intervention (through incomplete participation or investigator departures from protocol), the result is *diffusion of treatment* (Kazdin, 1998). A very unfortunate instance of this occurring was witnessed by the first author when he was an undergraduate research assistant serving as an observer in a study on classroom token economies. Partial analyses midway through the study showed improvements in student behavior in several treatment classrooms, but no improvement in one of the treatment rooms. As it was eventually revealed, the teacher in that latter room was violating the intervention protocol by only implementing the intervention when the research assistants arrived to gather observational data on student behavior, rather than maintaining the intervention throughout the school day, as planned. Obviously, this haphazard implementation undermined confidence in the resulting data and the conclusions that could be drawn from it.

## EXTERNAL VALIDITY

While internal validity refers to the ability of the researcher to be confident that outcomes observed in the experiment were due to the variables that he or she manipulated, *external validity* refers to the ability of the researcher to say anything about the results beyond the particular people, settings, times, measurements, variables, and characteristics of that single study. This is *generalizability*, and it is the preeminent goal of most research: what we can say about the world in general, rather than just about our specific research study. However, as Campbell and Stanley (1963) pointed out, "logically, we cannot generalize beyond . . . [the] . . . limits" (p. 17) or circumstances of our particular study, that is, the particular confluence of events and variables that are present in a single study. We can, however, create conditions increasingly favorable to generalizing beyond our study by attempting to make the characteristics of our participants and procedures as representative of the population and conditions of final interest as is possible. Thus, laboratory studies of depression among college students are less representative and generalizable to clinical depression in older adults who reside in nursing homes than are survey studies of community dwelling, older adults, or laboratory studies of older adults who actually reside in nursing homes. Consider this as an issue of sampling from a population (be that of people; or settings, ranging from the contrived conditions in the laboratory to the practical aspects of the mental health clinic; or experimental procedures) and hoping that the sample is fully representative of that population so that conclusions about the sample can be extended back to that population. The closer the study is to the population of interest, the more confidence we have in our ability to generalize. A key component here is experimental replication, which we discuss at another point in this chapter.

Although there is some argument on this point (see Kazdin, 1998), internal validity has been considered to be the "basic minimum, without which any experiment is uninterpretable: Did in fact the experimental treatments make a difference in this specific experimental instance?" (Campbell & Stanley, 1963, p. 5). Without a positive answer to this question, external validity may be irrelevant. But once answered, the results of a particular study are only of academic interest if they are not generalizable. As with internal validity, however, there are multiple threats to our ability to make the necessary generalizations, to which we now turn.

As a case in considering the threats to external validity, imagine that you completed your thesis research in 1990. The study was conducted with a large sample of undergraduate students at a small, midwestern community college. Through use of a paper-and-pencil survey, you determined that there was a strong negative correlation between participant knowledge of the ways in which HIV can be transmitted between sexual partners and of the effects of HIV infection, and the number and frequency of risk behaviors (i.e., anal intercourse, intercourse without the use of condoms, multiple sexual partners) in which participants reported having engaged. From this relation between knowledge and risk behavior (the more knowledge, the lower the level of risky sexual behaviors) you determine that education about HIV would be a powerful solution to the spreading HIV/AIDS crisis (you are, of course, assuming that the causality is not in the other direction: lower levels of risk-taking behavior leads to increased knowledge). Ten years later, your thesis mentor continues to urge you to publish this study, but you wonder if the study can still make a meaningful contribution to the AIDS literature and to worldwide AIDS intervention. You wonder about how generalizable the findings are: that is, the external validity of the study. The next several sections look at some issues to consider as you decide whether to publish this research.

**Sample Characteristics.** You have completed this study on the relation between HIV/AIDS knowledge and risk behavior on a specific sample: undergraduate students at a small, midwestern community college, in the year 1990. Consider that this sample is not only students at a community college, but is also primarily White, 17 to 20 years of age, without children, from rural or suburban areas, of middle-class backgrounds, and perhaps more conservative than people in other parts of the United States. These data are also from 1990, a time when certain aspects of HIV transmission were less generally known, and what was known was treated with more skepticism than today—over 10 years later. Now, consider the population to which you would like to generalize your results. You are not interested in only informing young, White, middle-class, midwestern community college students about HIV/AIDS, but more generally helping a diverse range of other people, including those of other ethnicities, cultures, ages, socioeconomic conditions, and geographic locations (not only in the United States, but around the world). Would you be willing to bet that knowledge and risk behavior holds the same relation now (over 10 years later) with either a highly similar sample, or a sample of college students from a large west-coast university (more ethnically diverse and perhaps more liberal, but of generally similar cultural and economic backgrounds), or a group such as might be found in sub-Saharan Africa (nearly exclusively Black, but representing numerous tribal and cultural differences, especially with regard to sexual behavior and male–female roles; substandard economic conditions; lack of access to birth control in general and condoms in particular; and high rates of illiteracy)? You likely would not be willing to bet on this relation holding over such differences in sample characteristics, nor over the time period involved. You would be reluctant to suggest huge investments of time, effort, and funds in an HIV/AIDS awareness campaign if you could not be sure that the relation would hold.

This, in essence, is the issue of external validity as it applies to sample characteristics: Can we generalize the results of one study sample to the population from which it was drawn or to other populations? This is a critical point because we should not be allowing our research samples to define the population of ultimate interest; rather, the population of interest should define who (or what) we sample to study. The more similar the sample and population, the more confidence we have; the more diverse the sample and the population, the less confidence we should have in our ability to generalize. In basic animal

research, the issue is one of how well the behavioral, motivational, physiological, neurological, or pharmacological findings with rats, pigeons, monkeys, and
other infrahuman subjects can be generalized to humans. The more divergent
from humans (such as great apes vs. goldfish), the more difficult the assumption of generality. Much of clinical and counseling research is, of course, done
with humans. But even here there can be great diversity between the persons
under study and the population of ultimate interest. College students, as in the
aforementioned example, are often the participants in clinical and counseling
research due to their relative ease of access to researchers, many of whom
are located at major research universities. Sometimes it is the college student
population to which one wants to generalize the results of a study, such as in
the case of understanding the best methods for studying or presenting lecture
material, or in addressing the stresses and psychopathology that are evident
on college campuses. (Even here, however, it is important to note that not
all colleges, nor college students, are the same; they may differ along several
demographic dimensions.) Most often, however, we seek to generalize from
college student participants to the general population. The question then is
whether that generalization is warranted; is there a threat to external validity
due to the characteristics of the study sample?

Another issue is that most research to date has focused on such convenience
samples of college students, but even in general population studies, in which
the vast majority of the sample, or even the population, is White, problems of
generality are evident. When minority participants are included, they are often
underrepresented with respect to their proportion in the population at large,
and are rarely the sole focus of a particular study. Thus, we know very little
from typical research studies—and, correspondingly, there is little external
validity—about minority populations. When such research is conducted, we
find similarities as well as differences (see Rabalais, Ruggiero, & Scotti, 2002,
for a discussion of the potential differential effects of trauma on children by
minority status). It is critical to consider both ethnic differences as well as cultural differences. Within the United States, people of different ethnicity may
have more in common culturally than persons of the same ethnicity who were
raised in different countries and thus vastly dissimilar cultures. The issue of
gender is similarly understudied. Many factors are involved here, and psychological research is only just beginning to incorporate them into the design of
studies.

Compounding the issues here are that potential participants in the population under study may *self-select* themselves for participation—or non-
participation—in research. In a recent study on the effects of motor vehicle
accidents (MVAs) on children ages 7 to 13 years, we reviewed the emergency
room (ER) records of children brought to the hospital following an MVA. The
ER records indicated that in some 20% of admissions, another child or adult
had died in the accident. However, less than 5% of our final study sample

represented MVAs involving a death. Parents or guardians of the children who were in crashes involving a fatality had self-selected out of the study, potentially for fear that the study would be too stressful for the child (or even themselves, as the parents/guardians were asked to participate, as well), or because of the increased distress being exhibited by the child (or the family in general). Thus, some caution needs to be taken in the final interpretation of the results and in generalizing the findings to the wide range of accident severity, from mild fender-benders to fatal crashes.

This latter example points out an interesting aspect of external validity: It typically involves interactive effects among variables, whereas internal validity may be considered to be experimental main effects (Campbell & Stanley, 1963). Thus, the question of importance becomes how specific the effects of the independent variable are to the limited set of conditions under study— conditions that may not adequately represent the full range of interest. In the MVA study just discussed, the effects that we found might well be limited to the levels of accident severity and certain pre-existing child and family characteristics of the study participants. Due to participant self-selection, we were not able to fully evaluate the potential differential effects of increasingly severe accidents and pre-existing pathology on the independent variables.

***Stimulus Characteristics and Settings.*** Returning to the study of HIV/ AIDS knowledge and risk behavior, it is not only important to consider who the participants in the study were, but the characteristics of the study itself; that is, how the study was conducted. Assume that this paper-and-pencil survey was given in a typical college classroom with multiple participants present at the same time. This seems innocuous enough, and the students may generally expect that their responses to the survey not only will be confidential but anonymous as they are not providing any identifying information on the survey forms.

Consider, however, how features of the room, the researcher, the manner of conducting the survey, and the wording of the questions on the survey itself may affect the responses of the participants. Imagine if the space in which the survey was done was a room at the college health center or counseling center, and the walls in the room and adjacent hallways were decorated with posters related to physical and mental health in general, and HIV/AIDS awareness and prevention in particular. Seeing such posters just prior to the survey could affect the participants in a number of ways. Some posters might even contain information (e.g., "Prevent HIV with condoms") that would be reflected in their responses on the knowledge test, suggesting that they had some information about HIV/AIDS prevention that they might not otherwise have known prior to seeing the posters. Or perhaps as a result of seeing the posters or being in a health center, the participants are less likely to admit—even anonymously— that they engage in high-risk sexual behaviors.

Similar types of subtle influences might result from the demeanor or statements made by the researcher while distributing the surveys (e.g., "I am conducting this survey because preventing HIV/AIDS by reducing risky sexual behaviors is a matter of life and death."). Even wording of the items on the survey might influence the likelihood of participants admitting to certain sexual practices. For example, think about the differences in asking: "Have you ever had oral sex?" versus "Would you ever have oral sex?" versus "Oral sex means placing your mouth on another person's genitals. Would you ever do that?" These questions ask similar things, but differ in time frame and intentionality (reporting what you have done versus your intent to do something in the future), and the level of explicitness (in the pursuit of clarity). Furthermore, participants may be more or less likely to report about certain sexual behaviors (from underreporting to exaggerated reporting) depending on whether participation was on an individual or group basis, the person with whom they came to the study, the strength of the evidence that responses are anonymous, whether the researcher was the same or opposite gender, and whether the researcher remained in the room. Many of these factors may make little to no difference in responding, but in combination could bias the results.

Suddenly, a simple survey takes on many of the characteristics that could be further studied in a formal experimental design that varied any one or more of these factors in combination and simply sought to analyze how responses varied by condition (see Dillman, 2000). For instance, the researcher might want to study the influence on survey responses of the presence versus the absence of posters related to the content of the study, or the effects of individual versus group participation, or even cross these two factors in a two (Posters: Present vs. Absent) by two (Participation: Individual vs. Group) design. The primary goal in such a study would not be understanding the relation between knowledge and risk behavior, but of understanding how the conditions under which a survey is completed affects whether participants will indicate whether they engage in certain HIV-risk behaviors, and thus how that changes the apparent relation between knowledge and risk taking (an example of how the factors considered in external validity can be interactive with the independent variable). Assuming that there is no effect of these conditions, the researcher could then summarize across all conditions and more confidently speak to the relation between knowledge and behavior.

***Reactivity to Research Participation.*** This factor has been referred to as the reactive effects of experimental arrangements (Campbell & Stanley, 1963; Kazdin, 1998), and the reactivity of assessment (Kazdin, 1998), but might simply be thought of as the participants knowing that they are in a research study and how that knowledge affects their behavior within the confines of the study. The question then arises as to how well the researcher can generalize from the behavior of a participant who knows he or she is being studied, observed, or evaluated to the behavior of people in general (let alone those particular participants) outside of the research setting. That is, generalizing from "public" to "private" behavior, or from the laboratory to the field (Campbell & Stanley, 1963), or vice versa (Shadish et al., 2001).

This ability to generalize may, in part, depend on what it is that is being studied or the conditions under which it is studied—again, an interactive effect. Consider the example of adults who are seeking treatment for depression at a community mental health center (CMHC) and expect to receive benefit from that treatment. These adults are already different from a group that might be receiving treatment relatively unaware of what that means, such as young children whose parents are attending a parenting skills group. Asking the adults at the CMHC to participate in a treatment research study first raises the issue of self-selection, then brings up the factors already discussed under demand characteristics. Then one needs to consider how often assessment occurs and how intrusive the demands of the intervention are, both of which may repeatedly remind the participants that they are in a treatment study, making any related effects just that much more salient. Compare this, then, to a retrospective chart review in which after 5 years of conducting a very similar treatment protocol, a clinician at the CMHC wishes to review and summarize his patients' records for evidence of changes in levels of depression from pre to post-treatment. In this situation, patients are not aware that their clinical data are now being summarized in a program evaluation study, and thus would clearly not be reactive to the research. (The reader should know that such retrospective research still requires review and approval by an Institutional Review Board for the Protection of Human Subjects, and is *not* a method for avoiding proper prior scrutiny and consent: Clinical treatment, even outside of the research situation, requires the full informed consent of the patient [APA, 1992].)

Given this potential reactivity, Evans (1986) outlined several different types or classes of information that are important when we consider that many research studies—perhaps the great majority—within clinical and counseling psychology involve to greater or lesser degrees the self-report of the participants concerning some aspect of their behavior. Evans has classified these self-reports into four types: (a) private but potentially verifiable events (e.g., "I had eggs for breakfast," "I used a condom when I had sex last night"); (b) private nonverifiable events (e.g., "I dreamed about my father last night," "I thought about using a condom before I had sex last night"); (c) private but potentially accessible internal events (e.g., "My hands got sweaty when I saw a movie that had a car accident in it," "My heart beat faster when I was having sex"); and (d) attitudes, opinions, and beliefs (e.g., "I am a religious person," "I believe that condoms should be used during sex to prevent HIV infection"). Each of these is an example of the type of self-report questions that might be asked of participants in a research study and to which they might differentially react. Each also has problems as to its verifiability and thus its susceptibility to "distortion" (intentional or otherwise) during a research study—thus affecting external validity.

In the first instance, a private event, such as eating eggs or wearing condoms, is *potentially verifiable* if someone took the trouble to directly observe the behavior. Of course, we might be more inclined to request—and the participant more inclined to allow—direct observation of the behavior of eating than of having sex. But if we have permission to observe, there is still the issue of participants knowing they are being observed within the context of a research study, raising the possibility that they have altered their typical behavior as a result (whether or not they are aware of having done so—another issue altogether). The trick would be to observe without the participant's knowledge, which, of course, is not possible as participants must provide informed consent for such observation. What is critical here, however, is that the participant is reporting on behavior that potentially could have been observed if we had arranged it. This differs dramatically from the second type, *private but nonverifiable* events or behavior. This second category refers to the self-report of covert behavior, especially of cognitions. Here, direct observation clearly is of no use because cognitions cannot be observed; they can only be reported on in more or less indirect ways (e.g., introspection vs. information processing speeds). One can, of course, report their cognitions to the researcher—and that is what is being done in self-report items such as "I think about the traumatic event several times each day," or "I feel ashamed." But the question will remain as to whether the report of one's cognitions is itself the event of interest or a potentially distorted report of the event of interest.

If the private event is an internal one that is potentially accessible—such as heart rate or muscle tension—we are essentially back to the first type of self-report, with the exception that now we not only need to arrange observation, but also special instrumentation. For instance, we might be measuring heart rate and muscle tension in the laboratory and attempt to verify the participant's statement, "My heart is beating faster and my muscles are tense." Two important problems arise here, however. The first is that participants may not be very good at recognizing physiological changes within their own bodies and thus accurately reporting about those changes. The second problem is how the question is worded. A participant may report that their heart is beating faster and the appropriate transducer may indicate a 15 beat per min increase in heart rate. However, what if the researcher asks the participant, "Tell me when you are feeling more anxious," on the assumption that anxiety is equivalent to increased physiological arousal (an issue related to construct validity)? Two new problems then arise. First, is *arousal*—in the form of increased heart rate—necessarily equal to *anxiety*? Might it not also be the result of "excitement" or physical activity? Second is the problem of response synchrony/desynchrony (Evans, 1986; Lang, 1968). It simply is the case that overt motor behavior, covert behavior (such as cognitions and emotions), and physiological responses do not necessarily fully covary with each other. One can have an accelerated heart rate, be thinking they are fearful and anxious, and still perform a supposedly feared task, such as touching a snake or public speaking. Our participant may notice that his heart rate is increasing—and the transducer indicates such—but he does not feel or report being anxious. (This is also a problem of what Cone, 1978, referred to as a *method-content confound.*)

In the final case, surveys of attitudes, beliefs, and opinions are often conducted on the basic premise that these self-reports express preferences, intentions, and tendencies to act in certain ways. Again, it is important to ask how overt behavior corresponds to those self-reports. How can we verify a person's claim to be religious? Do we follow them and observe whether they attend church, synagogue, or mosque regularly? Do we look for random acts of kindness? How do we define "religious" in order to verify the self-report of religious beliefs? The belief that people should wear condoms during sex may be easier to verify by observing whether people who state such beliefs actually wear condoms. But there are still a multitude of reasons why a particular person may or may not wear a condom during any particular act of sex (e.g., simple human fallibility, having sex with one's mate, and attempting a pregnancy, etc.).

The point of the foregoing is that we cannot take for granted that people are good reporters of their own behavior, engage in behavior that is consistent with their self-reports, nor are unaffected by the fact that they are being asked to report on themselves within the context of a research study (or even within the context of clinical treatment). People, whether as research participants or clients, are likely to differentially react to the situation of being evaluated, raising the issue of how generalizable their responses are to the situations of ultimate interest. One may think that the closer one is to measuring directly observable motor behavior the better; and that as one moves away to the various types of self-report, problems of accuracy increase. However, whether motor behavior or self-report, reactivity is an issue.

*Multiple Treatment Interference.* Often in clinical research, an investigator wishes to compare the differential effectiveness of two competing interventions, rather than just the simple comparison of treatment versus no treatment. Such comparisons can involve a no-treatment control group and participants who receive either Treatment A or Treatment B, enabling comparisons among the two treatments relative to each other and to no treatment at all. Alternately, one might administer both treatments to the participants, such as in comparing the independent and combined effects of anxiolytic medication and exposure therapy in the treatment of a simple height phobia. Here, Group A might receive mediation for several weeks and then a course of virtual reality exposure therapy (VRET; see Rothbaum, Hodges, & Smith, 1999), whereas Group B might first receive VRET and then medication. Finally, Group C might receive a combined treatment: medication with VRET. In all cases, improvement is evaluated by repeatedly assessing, before and after each treatment phase, the participants' willingness to approach and remain in a high place (which in itself raises the issue of testing effects, an aspect of internal validity).

In this example, several potential problems might arise due to the interactive, and even interfering, effects of the interventions. Consider that in Group A, medication might be effective in reducing anxiety and allowing the participants to approach and remain in high places (such as a glass elevator in a tall hotel lobby). When medication is removed and VRET is implemented, additional improvement may not be forthcoming for a critical reason that potentially is unrelated to the effects of the medication: In the course of assessing the effects of medication, the participants have essentially had a successful exposure to the feared stimulus and have remained in a high place without experiencing anxiety—the critical active component of VRET. Alternately, consider that Group B, after treatment with VRET, is no longer anxious in high places; thus, the original presenting problem is no longer present. Thus, ceasing VRET and starting medication will have no additional benefit. Finally, the placement of Group C on anxiety-reducing medication may well remove a critical boundary condition for exposure therapy: the increase and then habituation/extinction of anxiety in the presence of the feared stimulus. That is, if medication inhibits the anxiety response, the conditions for effectively implementing VRET are not present.

The end result of these various ways in which the multiple treatments might interfere with each other is that it both becomes difficult to tease out the effects of each intervention, and whether it is the interventions themselves or the various ways they were ordered and combined that resulted in the final outcomes measured some months later in the follow-up phase of the study.

***Other Factors.*** The aforementioned VRET and medication study illustrates a host of other, related, threats to external validity. These factors include novelty effects, test sensitization, and the timing of measurement. Conducting therapy using a virtual reality computer program is both a unique and novel idea, and a potential problem. Consider first the differential response that people who are naive versus experienced computer users or video game players may have to this technology. Second, the client or research participant may react more favorably or with a more positive treatment outcome simply because of the novel nature of the treatment and use of high technology. As such strategies become more common, the novelty effect may be reduced. Indeed, it may also be that as the technique and technology become more familiar (and thus more routine) to the therapist or investigator, they will be less consistent and enthusiastic in its application, also reducing the effects.

Issues concerning test sensitization and timing of measurement are both evident in the VRET/medication study due to repeated assessment of progress via behavioral observation of approaching and remaining in a high place. In this case, the assessment is confounded with the VRET treatment, as both involve approaching and remaining in a high place. Furthermore, the measure is quite transparent in terms of being obvious as to the desired final outcome. The question, relevant to external validity, is whether less frequent assessment or a different method of assessment would be associated with different findings. Finally, we might ask whether the effects of the treatments are evident at the points in time at which the investigator completes the assessment. Can we expect the effect of either treatment to be evident by the conclusion of their respective intervention phases? It may not be until some months later at the end of the follow-up phase—at which point medication has been discontinued but the skills learned in VRET continue to be utilized—that the differential effectiveness of VRET over medication becomes evident. But, even then we cannot be sure that the times we have selected for administering the assessments are representative of all those times at which we might have evaluated the outcomes (i.e., why a 6-month follow-up, vs. 3 months or 12 months?).

## STATISTICAL CONCLUSION VALIDITY

Finally, you have completed your experiment or treatment. You have carefully considered the possible threats to the internal and external validity of the research design. The design was such that you are confident of the conceptual basis for the effects you anticipate. However, what is the extent to which the effects can be demonstrated by the statistical analyses carried out by the researcher, if they even exist and can be detected at all? This is the issue of *statistical conclusion validity* and it largely depends on decision making, statistical tests, and the amount of variability in the study.

### Hypothesis Testing, Effect Size and Power

In conducting a study, it is the generally hoped for outcome that the *null hypothesis* ($H_O$) will be rejected or shown to be false (i.e., *null* meaning "zero" or "nothing"). The null hypothesis is the prediction of no differences—in the population—between the various groups within a study, be those treatment versus no treatment conditions (e.g., behavior therapy vs. a wait-list control), or multiple levels of a treatment (e.g., length of treatment, such as 0, 4, 8, or 12 sessions of behavior therapy; or dose, as in 0, 100, 200, 400 mg per day of a prescribed antidepressant medication). We want our study to accurately reflect the conditions in the world outside of our specific experimental arrangements; that is, to have external validity and generalizability. Thus, we want to correctly identify a difference between the groups or levels in our study when such a difference really exists in the world (i.e., the population of interest, rather than just our sample from that population). Conversely, when such a difference does not really exist in the world, we do not want to find a difference within our study. We can never fully know the *true state of the world* (that is, the characteristics of the population); we can only attempt to generalize from our study to the world and hope to make valid (i.e., true and accurate) conclusions. As such, there are four conditions that reflect the correct and incorrect decisions that we can make about the real world as a result of the outcome of our study, as shown in Table 4.1, where the validity of our statistical conclusions falls into Cells A and D.

In the typical psychological research study, we make decisions about the presence or absence of an effect due to our manipulation or treatment by comparing the *mean level* of responding between groups, such as Stress Inoculation Therapy (SIT) versus a Support Group in the treatment of generalized anxiety disorder (GAD), either across time (e.g., SIT vs. Support at pretest, posttest, and follow-up), within subjects (e.g., the course of generalized anxiety symptoms within a no-treatment group over successive 3-month intervals), or among a variety of combinations of these and other designs. We may use one (e.g., state anxiety) or multiple (e.g., state anxiety, role functioning, worry diary) outcome measures (i.e., the dependent variables) in evaluating effects, generally seeking to find where groups or levels are, or are not, different. In a study of the effects of SIT versus a Support Group, we would test the statistical null hypothesis of no difference in level of anxiety between the groups at the pretest, and lower levels of anxiety in the SIT group as compared both to the SIT group itself at the pretest and the Support Group at the posttest and/or follow-up. We evaluate these differences with tests such as ANOVA and the familiar $t$ test. An $F$ ratio or $t$ is derived, and the obtained value is compared to a table with the appropriate *degrees of freedom* (reflecting number of groups and sample size) and *alpha* ($\alpha$) level. The most commonly used minimum alpha is $\alpha = .05$, meaning that we accept that the results (i.e., a difference between the groups such as were found in the study) could only have happened by chance in 5 out of 100 instances of conducting this same study when it is the case that the null hypothesis is indeed true (i.e., that no differences exist in the population—the "real world"). Thus, we conclude an effect due to our manipulation or treatment; that is, we are rejecting a chance occurrence in our particular sample as the explanation of our results. If we conclude that there is a difference when there really is not a difference, we have made a *Type I Error* (see Table 4.1, Cell C). We can reduce the likelihood of a Type I Error by using a smaller alpha level, such as $\alpha = .01$ or $.001$ (meaning the results would have occurred by chance in 1 of 100, or 1 of 1,000, instances). However, as we decrease alpha, we increase the chance of a *Type II Error* (*beta*, $\beta$, Cell B in Table 4.1), accepting the null hypothesis when there really is a difference.

TABLE 4.1

Comparison of Statistical Decisions Based on the Results of the Study to the True
State of the World Regarding Differences Between Groups (or Levels) in a
Research Study

| | | The True State of the World | |
| --- | --- | --- | --- |
| | | *No Difference*<br>($H_O$ is True) | *Difference*<br>($H_O$ is False) |
| | *No Difference*<br>(Accept $H_O$) | **A**<br>Correct Decision (True Negative)<br>We decide "No Difference" when there really is no difference<br>(Accept $H_O$ when it is True; $1 - \alpha$) | **B**<br>Incorrect Decision (False Negative)<br>We decide "No Difference" when there really is a difference<br>(*Type II Error:* Accept $H_O$ when it is False; $\beta$) |
| *The Decision Based on the Study* | | | |
| | *Difference*<br>(Reject $H_O$) | **C**<br>Incorrect Decision (False Positive)<br>We decide there is a difference when there really is no difference<br>(*Type I Error:* Reject $H_O$ when it is True; $\alpha$) | **D**<br>Correct Decision (True Positive)<br>We decide there is a difference when there really is a difference<br>(Reject $H_O$ when it is False; $1 - \beta$, *power*) |

Our ability to avoid making a Type II Error is referred to as *power* ($1 - \beta$, Cell D in Table 4.1).

The possibility arises, as can be seen in Cell C and Cell D of Table 4.1, that we have made either a correct or incorrect decision in terms of whether, in the "real" world, our manipulation would continue to make a difference in levels of anxiety. We have made a decision based on the *effect size* within our study and have attempted to generalize that decision to the world (i.e., to the population of other instances of using SIT to reduce levels of anxiety in persons with GAD). Simply put, effect size is the difference between the means on some measure (in this case, mean scores on a measure of state anxiety) of the groups under consideration, divided by their standard deviation (the reader will likely recognize this as related to the *t* ratio in which the pooled variance is used as the denominator; like the *t* ratio, sample size plays a role in effect size). This results in a *change score* in terms of standard deviation units. What is a meaningful effect size? Cohen (1988) suggested that, for the behavioral sciences, effect sizes approximating 0.2, 0.5, and 0.8 represent small, medium, and large effects, respectively, although these are somewhat arbitrary cut points.

TABLE 4.2
Mean State Anxiety and Effect Size Comparisons ($SD = 15$) for Two Groups at
Pretest, Posttest and Follow-up

| | Measurement Point | | | Effect Size within Group | |
|---|---|---|---|---|---|
| | | | | Pretest to Posttest | Pretest to Follow-up |
| | Pretest | Posttest | Follow-up | | |
| Stress Inoculation Group | 20 | 16 | 10 | 0.27 | 0.67 |
| Support Group | 21 | 20 | 22 | 0.07 | 0.07 |
| Effect size between groups | 0.07 | 0.27 | 0.80 | | |

Let us say the mean scores in this study at three points in time are those depicted in Table 4.2. It can be seen that the difference between group means at the pretest (i.e., after random assignment to groups and before conducting the intervention) is small: 0.07 standard deviation units. The Support Group does not change much over the course of the study, as measured by comparing pretest to posttest, and pretest to follow-up. The SIT Group shows large changes over the course of the study when considering the effect sizes both within the group across the measurement periods (Effect Size = 0.67 for the pretest to follow-up comparison), and between the groups at each point in time (Effect Size = 0.80 at the follow-up). Given these effect sizes, we would be confident in saying that SIT had the effect of lowering state anxiety scores over the course of the study, as compared to the Support Group treatment (in which state anxiety did not change). We would then also make the assumption that this effect is likely to carry over to the "real world." That is, SIT would decrease anxiety in other people with GAD who received the same intervention.

Consider, however, the impact of variability on these effect size scores. We have assumed in this example that the standard deviation is 15. If the standard deviation were 30, all effect sizes would be cut in half. Given the same difference between mean scores, larger standard deviations—that is, more variability in the sample—will result in correspondingly lower effect sizes and thus greater difficulty rejecting the null hypothesis (i.e., power) and asserting that there was an effect due to treatment. As more variability enters the study, the mean differences between conditions, groups, levels, or measurement points will have to be larger and larger to find a meaningful effect. It should be evident, then, that variability is a key factor in effect size, and thus a threat to statistical conclusion validity—our ability to find a difference when it really exists. What, though, are those sources of variability? They are many.

**Sample Size.** Simply put, as the size of a sample increases, the variance tends to decrease because outliers (i.e., extreme scores) have less and less impact on the calculation of measures of central tendency (i.e., mean, median, mode) and variability (i.e., standard deviation and variance). With very large samples, the sample variance (and other statistics) approaches that of the population from which the sample was drawn. Sample statistics—be they percentages, means, variances—are estimates of the population parameters. By the principle of randomization, it is likely that small samples will deviate more from the population parameters than will larger and larger samples (see Kerlinger & Lee, 2000, for an example of this principle).

Thus, when we draw a sample of persons—such as those with GAD, in this case—we run the risk that a small sample (e.g., 10-20 persons per group) has both high variance and is not representative of the population back to which we wish to generalize our findings. If small samples are likely to have larger variability in scores (and thus larger variances and standard deviations), then the resulting effect sizes will be smaller, as we have already shown with the example in Table 4.2.

The answer, then, to this threat to statistical conclusion validity is to use as large a sample as is feasible. All else being equal, larger sample sizes increase power. What is feasible will depend on research funding, time, estimates of effect sizes and power from similar prior studies, and adequate sampling procedures. Sampling in a truly random fashion from the general population would be the optimal process, but one rarely achieved and—in most psychological studies—even more rarely attempted. Substitutes for the true random sample are other sorts of probability samples, including stratified samples, cluster sampling, and systematic sampling—all beyond the scope of this chapter (see Kerlinger & Lee, 2000). More often, nonprobability samples are employed, being samples of convenience or even accident (Kerlinger & Lee, 2000), such as college students or consecutive admissions to a particular outpatient clinic. These harken back to threats to external validity, and, in such cases, the characteristics of the samples need to be clearly described and caution used in interpretation and generalization.

***Subject Heterogeneity.***  The persons who participate in a research study can differ widely on a number of dimensions that are seemingly unrelated to the variables of interest. This is the issue of heterogeneity of subjects (Kazdin, 1998) or "units" (Shadish et al., 2001). As we discussed, increased variability is related to decreased effect size, all else being equal. When participants differ by age, gender, socioeconomic status, culture and ethnicity, and even co-morbid medical or psychological disorders, the degree of variance increases in the sample. This is a double-bind of sorts. How do we utilize a homogeneous sample to reduce variability and enhance our chances of finding an effect (internal validity), yet ensure that our sample and the study results are generalizable back to the population of interest (external validity)? Given the increasing importance of including research participants other than White, middle-class males in research, solutions to the problem of heterogenous samples need to be utilized.

One method is to evaluate as many features as is both theoretically and practically reasonable. Obtaining basic demographics (e.g., age, gender, ethnicity, education, income, etc.) is the standard. But other features to consider include history of psychological disorders, prior treatment, medications, family psychiatric history, and readiness for change (Prochaska, DiClemente, & Norcross, 1992), among a host of other variables that might impact on the severity, complexity, and intractability of a disorder as exhibited by persons within a treatment study, not to mention their level of willingness to participate and expectations for improvement (both of which might reflect the consistency with which the participants will implement components of the intervention, thus affecting its efficacy). Once, measured, such variables can be used as covariates or as grouping factors or levels in their own right, such as older versus younger participants; African American compared to White participants; or levels of "readiness" to change pathological, maladaptive, or inappropriate behavior. Although subject heterogeneity increases variability and decreases effect size, using these demographics as covariates or grouping factors can reduce that variability and thus increase effect size and statistical conclusion validity.

*Variability in Procedures.*   What in other contexts has been referred to as treatment fidelity or procedural reliability can be a critical feature in the conduct of a research study. The basic question here is whether each of the researchers involved in a study followed the exact same protocol each time the procedures were implemented. Was the skin sufficiently cleaned and abraded prior to attaching skin conductance electrodes? Were the instructions clear and presented to each participant in the same manner? Were all stimulus cards available and presented in the requisite order? Was VRET implemented in the same manner by all therapists in the study? The more the agreed on standard research protocol is deviated from, the greater the amount of variability in the study and thus the lower the power.

Clearly, in the real world, variability will not be easily controlled, such as when an intervention package becomes widely used—with greater or lesser consistency—by large numbers of therapists. The research setting is our opportunity to minimize that variability and implement procedures "as designed," giving the best chance to demonstrate the effect of an intervention or experimental manipulation.

*Unreliable Measures.*   Just as intervention procedures that are not faithfully implemented can introduce unwanted variability into the research study, so can the very measures that are being utilized to evaluate the effects of those procedures. Assessment measures need to follow rather rigorous procedures for establishing their psychometric properties and demonstrating that they consistently measure what they are believed to be measuring (see Nunnally &

Bernstein, 1994). Unlike poor Hiawatha, the measures need to be both consistent (reliable) and accurate (valid) in hitting the target.

Test–retest reliability is what the reader will most commonly associate with the idea of consistency: Does the test give essentially the same score for the same person on multiple occasions? It is important to remember that reliability falls off over time; the longer the period between test and retest, the lower the correlation between two scores. Additionally, the optimal test–retest period may vary according to the construct being measured. Intelligence will be more stable than quality of life, which will be more stable than state (i.e., current) anxiety, allowing test–retest intervals of months, weeks, or minutes, respectively. Additionally, measures should have internal consistency, that is, they should all point to the same construct. Thus, we look for moderate to high correlations among items on a scale; the lower the interitem or item-scale correlations, the less likely the items are measuring the same thing and the greater the error variance. As reliability of instruments falls off, statistical conclusion validity becomes increasingly threatened—a warning to remember for the investigator who develops and uses his own measure without also taking time to establish its psychometric properties.

*Return to Type I Error.*   Much of the foregoing has noted threats to statistical conclusion validity due to variability from several critical sources. Another method for controlling—or increasing—that threat relates to Type I Error ($\alpha$). As noted, if we want to reduce the chance of concluding that there is a difference between groups in the population (the "true state of the world") when there really is no difference, we can reduce alpha from .05 to .01 or .001 (realizing that Type II Error now increases). However, the flip side is also true: If we increase alpha from .05 to .10, we are *increasing* the chance of finding a difference when there really is no difference. Unfortunately, this latter situation can occur unintentionally when the investigator makes multiple comparisons among groups and measures within a study, increasing what is known as *experiment-wise error*. Simply put, as the number of statistical comparisons increases, the chance likelihood of finding a significant difference, when it does not really exist, also increases. This is a bit like rolling dice: With more and more rolls, the desired number (within the limits of the die) will eventually come up. Several different procedures exist for controlling for experiment-wise error, including the use of preplanned orthogonal comparisons, more conservative significance tests (e.g., Scheffé), or adjusting the alpha level for individual comparisons so that their combined total does not exceed $\alpha = .05$ for the entire study (e.g., Bonferroni correction). These types of adjustments reduce the threat to statistical conclusion validity and enhance our faith in the results of our study.

Unfortunately, the researcher can make a number of other errors that negatively impact on decision error and thus, statistical conclusion validity. First, although many statistical procedures are considered to be quite robust to violations of their basic assumptions (such as homogeneity of variance between groups, and normal vs. highly skewed distributions), as those violations accumulate, validity decreases. As journal reviewers and dissertation committee members, we also have seen a second error occurring all too often: uninformed or excessively conservative use of statistical tests. For instance, in an attempt to be rigorous, a researcher may have required that an overall ANOVA be statistically significant before conducting preplanned, orthogonal comparisons (acceptably conservative, but not necessary), or may have followed the significant ANOVA with the conservative use of a Bonferroni correction for the already conservative post hoc Scheffé tests on preplanned comparisons (an excessively conservative strategy), or have used a two group analysis when the data actually represent a repeated measures design (unnecessarily conservative, if not improper). Although the reader may not be wholly familiar with these procedures, they each result in perhaps being overly cautious in the evidence required to reject the null hypothesis. This is, of course, the researcher's prerogative, but the result is to reduce the likelihood of finding a significant difference when it in fact exists (Type II Error, Cell B in Table 4.1). Thus, statistical consultation may be a useful step in ensuring that basic assumptions are met and proper analyses are conducted so as to maximize statistical conclusion validity.

## CONSTRUCT VALIDITY

At this point in a study in which internal and external validity have been considered, and there is confidence in the statistical conclusions one has drawn from the results, the question arises as to whether the intervention and its outcome are really a result of the construct that the investigator thought was being manipulated and measured in the first place. This is the question of *construct validity*, "the extent to which the abstract construct can be inferred from the operational definition of that construct" (Christensen, 1997, p. 207). The operational definition applies equally to the measures and procedures utilized in the study. At the level of measurement, say we are attempting to evaluate the level of posttraumatic stress disorder (PTSD) symptoms present in a clinical sample prior to and following treatment. We need to establish the traditional forms of validity for any psychometric measure, including face, content, concurrent, convergent, and divergent validity in order to be fully confident that our measures of PTSD are indeed assessing that diagnostic category and not anxiety in general or co-morbid problems such as depression, substance abuse, or social withdrawal (see Nunnally & Bernstein, 1994).

Of most relevance to experimental research is to similarly ensure the construct validity of the manipulations. For example, in a study of differential fear to trauma-relevant stimuli in accident-related PTSD, we might want to first ensure that the stimuli are salient enough to elicit fear, that they are indeed relevant to the traumatic event under consideration (e.g., motor vehicle accidents), and that some other aspect of the stimuli does not better account for the fear than does "trauma-relevance." Finally, one has to carefully define what is meant by the term, or construct, of *fear*, as it can be operationally defined in several ways (see Evans, 1986; Lang, 1968). First, one might consider fear to be *avoidance behavior*, that is, moving away from a particular stimulus. Second, fear might be defined by *physiological arousal*, as measured by increases in skin conductance (i.e., sweat on the palms). One might also define fear as an *emotion* that includes both physiological arousal and avoidance behavior, but also a critical evaluative component in which the person thinks, "I am afraid." These and other ways of operationally defining this apparently simple construct have important implications both for the design of the study and generalization across studies.

Following each of the above points in turn, some of the following procedures and considerations might be implemented. First, the investigator will need to consider how to decide whether someone does or does not exhibit PTSD. This diagnostic decision may vary according to whether a self-report measure is used, as compared to a formal structured interview, and what cut-off scores are used on the measures to indicate presence/absence or even severity of PTSD. Second, the investigator would need to decide on the type of stimuli that will be used in this study: words relevant to accidents (e.g., "crash"), pictures of accidents, audiotaped vignettes describing accidents, or videotapes of accidents. One may also consider the level of graphic detail to be included. These considerations get at the salience of the stimuli, but one may also want to consider which type of stimuli are most like those that a person with accident-related PTSD will encounter and which may thus produce the same fear response they experience in daily life. Third, it will likely be useful to conduct a small pilot study in which persons with and without accident-related PTSD rate how relevant to accidents in general the stimuli are. Then it might be considered as to whether some other aspects of the stimuli could cause arousal, besides accident relatedness, such as the novelty of the stimuli or simply their graphic nature. That done, the method by which one defines fear determines how the stimuli will be presented and fear will be measured. If fear is defined as avoidance, then stimuli have to be presented in such a way that participants can terminate the stimuli. If fear is physiological arousal, then the skin conductance response needs to be measured during discrete stimulus presentations. Finally, if fear is an emotion, it will also be important to have the participant rate their level of fear.

The essential problem in construct validity, then, is being sure to match the experimental materials and procedures to how one is defining the construct. If I define fear as an emotion, but only measure changes in skin conductance, then I have not fully evaluated the construct and the results will not be generalizable to that construct as defined. A clear problem is that there is no single way to operationally define a construct, as just seen, although all constructs need to have empirical support. Thus, we also encounter the problem of attempting to generalize across published studies that have defined the construct in slightly different ways (e.g., fear as avoidance behavior vs. physiological arousal). We may well find that those slightly different definitions lead to different methodologies and potentially to conflicting results or interpretations.

In considering these issues, Kazdin (1998) suggested that the investigator keep in mind the following questions when considering the issue of construct validity: (a) What is the intervention or experimental manipulation? and (b) How or why did the intervention/manipulation lead to the observed results or outcome? As Shadish and colleagues (2001) noted, there are a "host" of threats to construct validity when considering these issues. A number of those threats are actually ones that we have already discussed under internal and external validity, including reactivity to the experimental situation, reactivity of observation and the problems of self-report, experimenter expectancies, novelty, subject roles, unreliable measures, procedural reliability, and treatment diffusion. When these threats impinge on the internal and external validity of a study, they are also raising the question of whether the intervention was implemented as specified, and thus whether it—or some other confounded factor—was responsible for the outcome. Even the most well-developed operational definitions are in jeopardy if the study is not implemented in a manner consistent with those definitions or sufficient other factors arise to influence the results.

Several other threats are more specific to construct validity *per se*, these having been illustrated in the aforementioned example. For instance, *inadequate explication of constructs* refers to clear operational definitions for materials and procedures that can be adhered to in the study. In the aforementioned study, this includes the manner for deciding on a diagnosis of PTSD, the stimuli and their presentation format, and the operational definition of fear. *Construct confounding* occurs when more than one construct is being measured in a study and one or more of them are not adequately defined, potentially resulting in overlap among constructs such that outcomes cannot be properly attributed. In this study of PTSD, the investigator might also add a comparison group of persons with panic and agoraphobia, so that comparisons can be made between persons with PTSD and another psychiatric disorder in an attempt to show that the results are not simply related to "having psychological difficulties." This is a critical manipulation and at least two problems can arise. First, the diagnostic measures used to determine group membership may not have adequate discriminant validity; thus, some persons with PTSD may end up in the panic with agoraphobia group, and vice versa. Second, the diagnostic criteria for these two disorders have a number of arousal and avoidance criteria in common. It is possible that it is these two symptom clusters that are responsible for the differential fear response to the experimental stimuli, rather than the particular history of trauma experienced by the PTSD group; however, if the results show no differences between the groups, the investigator will not be able to determine this relation due to the confound (or overlap). If a psychiatric comparison group is desired, it should thus be one with minimal overlap of symptoms with PTSD.

This example also illustrates the issues of *mono-operation and mono-method bias* (Shadish et al., 2001) or *single operations and narrow stimulus sampling* (Kazdin, 1998). Here the issues have to do with how construct validity is established. In validating the existence of a construct (which in psychology is rarely something we can directly observe or put our finger on), it is necessary to *triangulate* on it, or come at it from various directions or means. In demonstrating the psychometric properties of a measure of depression, for instance, it is not enough that it have face and content validity (i.e., look like it measures depression and have a sampling of items that ask about symptoms of depression). The measure must also agree (correlate) with other purported measures of depression (convergent validity), show lower correlations with measures that do not purport to assess for depression (divergent validity), and to able to discriminate depressed from nondepressed individuals. Once this process has been completed, we can be more confident in the claims of the construct validity of the measure. In a research study, the same principles apply; we should have more than one means of establishing that we are manipulating or measuring the constructs of interest.

Thus, in establishing group membership in this study of PTSD, it is not sufficient only to use a self-report measure of PTSD. We may also want to use a structured clinical interview for PTSD. Even better, we may want to use a structured interview that not only establishes PTSD as a credible diagnosis, but one that also rules out other potentially confounding diagnoses. We will then have established group membership through multiple methods. Similarly, even if we define fear in this study as physiological arousal, we may want to measure heart rate changes in addition to skin conductance, providing multiple measures of the construct of fear as being physiological arousal (as operationally defined in this case). Finally, we will not want to present stimuli that are only related to accidents, but perhaps also neutral stimuli and other stressful stimuli that are not accident related. Additionally, we may want to present these categories of stimuli through several means—such as printed words and audiotaped vignettes. Such a range of procedures was followed in work by Scotti and colleagues (see Scotti, Morris, Ruggiero, & Wolfgang, 2002; Scotti, Ruggiero, & Rabalais, 2002), and it enhanced the overall confidence in procedures, methods, and outcomes, creating a comprehensive *multimethod multitrait matrix* (see Nunnally & Bernstein, 1994).

## SUMMARY

It should be clear to the reader that the four forms of validity covered here not only overlap in the issues that threaten them, but display a moderate to high degree of interrelation such that attempts to reduce threats to one form of validity may increase threats to one or more other forms of validity. For example, we have already noted that failure to implement the study as designed and to control for a host of threats to internal validity may well obviate the need to even consider the other forms of validity. Alternately, as experimental controls become more and more rigorous, the situation also becomes more and more artificial, which reduces our ability to generalize to real world situations (external validity). Increasing sample size enhances external and statistical conclusion validity, but can then lead to an unwieldy study that begins to falter in its adherence to the research protocol (internal validity), possibly then also threatening construct validity and adding back variability that impinges on statistical conclusion validity. Finally, although homogenous samples can enhance internal validity and reduce variability (thus increasing effect size), they usually do not have much external validity. However, as diversity is added to the samples, making them more generalizable to the population, variability is added, again decreasing effect size, unless blocking or covariation procedures are introduced—but this then becomes a definitional issue under construct validity.

The reader may thus want to consider the multiple threats to validity in two ways. First, this list of threats (and many others; see Shadish et al., 2001) might best be considered as a somewhat fluid taxonomy that can be displayed in a grid, crossing threats to validity with the types of validity. Within the grid, threats can be rated as being primary and secondary factors under each type of validity, being shifted around to some degree as various threats increase or are controlled. Second, the reader should realize that in a fluid model where control of one threat can increase other threats, it simply is not possible to conduct "the perfect research study." Such an animal does not exist: All research is flawed! Thus, the researcher considers and weighs various threats and validity issues and seeks to do the best study under the conditions. What then becomes critical in social science research—as in the "hard" sciences—is the process of *systematic replication*. No one study can fully answer the question of interest to the researcher. A series of studies (by that researcher or by colleagues in the field who likely have competing hypotheses) builds the evidence that is ultimately needed. Each study replicates portions of the ones before it, extends certain features (e.g., stimuli, methods, samples), and controls different aspects of threats to validity. It is the weight of the combined evidence—not the results of a single study—that finally moves the field from research hypotheses to theories and laws. Each researcher along the way, attending to various aspects of threats to validity, accumulates evidence, pro and con, to that final end.

# REFERENCES

American Psychological Association. (1992). Ethical principles of psychologists and code of conduct. *American Psychologist, 47*, 1597–1611.

Campbell, D. T., & Stanley, J. C. (1963). *Experimental and quasi-experimental designs for research.* Chicago: Rand McNally.

Christensen, L. B. (1997). *Experimental methodology* (7th ed.). Boston: Allyn & Bacon.

Cohen, J. (1988). *Statistical power analysis in the behavioral sciences* (2nd ed.). Hillsdale, NJ: Lawrence Erlbaum Associates.

Cone, J. D. (1978). The Behavioral Assessment Grid (BAG): A conceptual framework and a taxonomy. *Behavior Therapy, 9*, 882–888.

Dillman, D. A. (2000). *Mail and Internet surveys: The tailored design method* (2nd ed.). New York: Wiley.

Evans, I. M. (1986). Response structure and the triple-response mode concept. In R. O. Nelson & S. C Hayes (Eds.), *Conceptual foundations of behavioral assessment* (pp. 131–155). New York: Guilford.

Kazdin, A. E. (1998). *Research design in clinical psychology* (3rd ed.). Boston: Allyn & Bacon.

Kendall, M. G. (1973). Hiawatha designs an experiment. *Journal of Applied Behavior Analysis, 6*, 331–332. (Reprinted from *The American Statistician, 13*, 1959)

Kerlinger, F. N., & Lee, H. B. (2000). *Foundations of behavioral research* (4th ed.). New York: Harcourt Brace.

Lang, P. J. (1968). Fear reduction and fear behavior: Problems in treating a construct. In J. M. Schlien (Ed.), *Research in psychotherapy* (Vol. 3, pp. 90–102). Washington, DC: American Psychological Association.

Nunnally, J. C., & Bernstein, I. H. (1994). *Psychometric theory* (3rd ed.). New York: McGraw-Hill.

Prochaska, J. O., DiClemente, C. C., & Norcross, J. C. (1992). In search of how people change. *American Psychologist, 47*, 1102–1114.

Rabalais, A., Ruggiero, K., & Scotti, J. R. (2002). Multicultural issues in the response of children to disasters. In A. M. La Greca, W. K. Silverman, E. M. Vernberg, & M. C. Roberts (Eds.), *Helping children cope with disasters and terrorism* (pp. 73–99). Washington, DC: American Psychological Association.

Rothbaum, B. O., Hodges, L., & Smith, S. (1999). Virtual reality exposure therapy abbreviated treatment manual: Fear of flying application. *Cognitive and Behavioral Practice, 6*, 234–244.

Scotti, J. R., Evans, I. M., Meyer, L. H., & Walker, P. (1991). A meta-analysis of intervention research with problem behavior: Treatment validity and standards of practice. *American Journal on Mental Retardation, 96*, 233–256.

Scotti, J. R., Morris, T. L., Ruggiero, K. J., & Wolfgang, J. (2002). Posttraumatic stress disorder. In M. Hersen (Ed.), *Clinical behavior therapy: Adults and children* (pp. 361–382). New York: Wiley.

Scotti, J. R., Ruggiero, K. J., & Rabalais, A. E. (2002). The traumatic impact of motor vehicle accidents on children. In A. M. La Greca, W. K. Silverman, E. M. Vernberg, & M. C. Roberts (Eds.), *Helping children cope with disasters and terrorism* (pp. 259–291). Washington, DC: American Psychological Association.

Shadish, W. R., Cook, T. D., & Campbell, D. T. (2001). *Experimental and quasi-experimental designs for generalized causal inference.* New York: Houghton Mifflin.

**II**

**Research Strategies**

# 5

# Group Designs

Jill T. Ehrenreich
*University of Central Florida*

Alan M. Gross
*University of Mississippi*

Historically, group designs were not the favored methodology of psychologists and psychiatrists. In actuality, many of the early developments in experimental psychology are based on designs reflecting *ideographic* perspectives—those focused on the study of individuals and exemplified by case studies and single-case experimental designs. For instance, Pavlov, Wundt, and Piaget all derived basic propositions regarding human capacities and behavior through various forms of single case investigation (Kratochwill & Mace, 1984). However, since the 1950s, the field of experimental psychology has steadily moved toward a preference for a *nomothetic* view in research design—a perspective concerned with uncovering more general statements and laws about behavior. At the heart of the nomothetic perspective is the desire to examine persons in groups, so that the researcher may comprehend how people *on average* will react to a particular set of experimental conditions (Hampton, 1998).

The movement toward a preference for group designs may be seen as both an indictment of single-case methodology and a compliment to the flexibility of group designs in evaluating a variety of psychological phenomena. For example, most researchers attempting to investigate a set of individuals are apt to notice the wide variability that human beings demonstrate, in everything from clothing choice to sexual preference to even the most basic perceptions of the same event. Single case methods have been criticized for failing to account fully for the potentially unlimited amount of variation present among individuals, and, therefore, for failing to accurately assess whether the variables under investigation in a particular study are the only variables that have a central role in observed outcomes (Kratochwill & Mace, 1984). In other words, some single case methods lack *internal validity*, or the experimental controls necessary to determine whether experimental conditions, and not some extraneous influence or difference specific to the individual being investigated, account for changes observed (Kazdin, 1998). The potential for an extraneous or individually mediated influence significantly impacting the results of some single case investigations may also make the variables of interest in such studies difficult to define and their results hard to replicate. Conversely, group designs, by virtue of investigating behavior in the aggregate assume that, all else being equal, most extraneous sources of variation should average out across sufficiently sized groups.

In addition, case study methods of investigating individuals rarely involve an active or systematic manipulation of variables, instead utilizing a more fundamental description of some ongoing human activity. By contrast, many, though not all, group method designs allow the researcher to deliberately exert experimental control over the investigation of human behavior, by systematically manipulating an *independent variable* in order to observe some potential change in a *dependent variable*. Similarly, the rise of group methodology can also be traced, historically, to an increased need and desire for statistical evaluation of behavior in psychological research. In general, changes in single cases are not evaluated using inferential statistics, but rather through observation of differences in behavior over time. Following Sir R.A. Fisher's (1925) introduction of the analysis of variance and its associated research methodology, investigators such as Underwood (1949) have underscored the value of evaluating psychological theories through tightly controlled and statistically evaluated group experiments. This perspective on research design, sometimes known as the *hypothetico-deductive* or *confirmatory approach*, also espouses the value of establishing internal validity via random assignment of participants to groups, in an attempt to assure equality among the group participants, and the use of statistical methods to detect whether an observed difference in group behavior is greater than that which would be expected to occur by chance alone (Howard, Orlinsky, & Lueger, 1995). While the hypothetico-deductive approach has widely noted flaws in both its logic and execution, its continuing acceptance in the psychology literature stands as a primary motivation to select a group research design in order to evaluate some event of interest.

Furthermore, while some group designs are the result of applying a hypothethico-deductive approach or conducting a *true experiment*—in which the independent variable is manipulated in different ways across groups, random assignment is used to assign participants to groups, and experimental control is exerted through endeavoring to keep variables outside of the independent variable constant—there are certainly other types of group designs that can test scenarios in which the conditions of a true experiment cannot be met. For example, group designs may be utilized to test *quasi-experimental conditions*, where random assignment to groups is not possible. Other forms of group design, such as *longitudinal, cross-sectional*, and *sequential* designs, allow the researcher to employ groups in order to describe changes in development. Therefore, group designs give the investigator both the design flexibility and the statistical tools to evaluate psychological processes in a variety of systematic ways.

## BETWEEN-SUBJECTS DESIGNS

One clear realization of the hypothetico-deductive school of thought is the *between-subjects* experimental design. In essence, when an investigation is designed to evaluate a variable between subjects, the researcher is examining how different groups of individuals perform under the conditions of some experimental manipulation, to determine whether the unique sets of procedures for each group has any differential effect on the dependent variable (Hampton, 1998). The most common example of this design is that in which one group, in an *experimental condition*, is exposed to a particular treatment (or independent variable) hypothesized to impact the dependent variable in some specific way, while another group, in a *control condition*, is not exposed to any active treatment. After this differential exposure to the independent variable, the groups are then compared with each other in regard to any change in the dependent measures. This basic formula for a between-groups design may vary widely in terms of both the number of variables investigated and the nature and number of the control or comparison groups employed. However, no matter the size or scope of the between-groups design, the basic notion of presenting groups with different conditions in order to observe changes in another variable or set of variables remains the same.

### Group Equivalence

In general, a vital aspect of between-groups design is assuring that the groups under investigation are essentially "equivalent" prior to introducing any experimental manipulation, so that the only major differences between an experiment's groups are those introduced by the investigators. However, as previously indicated, human beings present investigators with an infinite number of differences with which to contend. Any number of these individual differences could be related to an experiment's independent variable(s) or could even be responsible for group differences on measures associated with dependent measures. Therefore, the experimenter must endeavor to ensure that groups are as similar as possible along these potentially *confounding* or interfering factors *before* an experimental intervention is introduced, in order to conclude that differences found among groups *after* an intervention is applied are actually due to the experimental intervention alone (Kazdin, 1998). For example, an investigator who does nothing to promote group equivalence before giving a proposed conduct disorder treatment to one group of adolescents and no treatment to a control group of adolescents has no systematic way of assuring that the groups did not already greatly differ on a myriad of factors, such as intelligence or openness to change, that might eventually effect therapy outcome.

Therefore, researchers attempting to conduct an ideal between-subjects experiment will endeavor to keep everything, outside of the experimental conditions, that could impact results constant across groups. Group design researchers have traditionally employed *random assignment* in order to assure some measure of group equivalence in between-subjects design research. *Matching* is a second strategy for assuring some measure of group equivalence regarding a specific variable, and is typically used when that factor is believed to impact the dependent variable or interact with independent variables in a way that requires it be expressly balanced across groups. Although some consider matching strategies more of an alternative strategy in traditional between-subjects research, especially because of some dissimilarities regarding the statistical analysis of matched groups versus traditional between-subjects groups, it will be discussed in this section, due to its overall popularity as a group equivalence strategy.

**Random Assignment.** Random assignment of participants to groups is a process of assuring that all members of an experiment's sample are equally likely to be in any one of the groups used in the study. The effort to randomly assign participants to groups may be accomplished in a number of ways. However, one common method involves using a random number generator that produces a set of random numbers, corresponding to the number of groups available, to assign to participants. An investigation that utilizes three groups, then, would need a list of randomly generated 1s, 2s, and 3s (e.g., a random list of these numbers might appear as 1,2,2,3,1,2,3,2,1,3). Then, the investigator could simply assign participants to a group number in accordance with this random number list. Using the list just presented, this procedure would involve assigning the first participant into the first group, then the next participant to the second group, with the third participant also in the second group, and so on. Obviously, such a procedure would not ensure that the experimenter would have an equal number of persons in each group, although there are methods of random assignment that will place an equal number of persons into each group (see Kazdin, 1998).

In general, random assignment is a simple procedure that may be the best method of bolstering the internal validity of an experiment and addressing the unexpected nuances of human behavior that might cause unintended group differences (Kazdin, 1998). However, random assignment is not only difficult to utilize in many applied settings, such as schools or mental health clinics, where the assignment of participants to groups may be out of the investigator's control, but neither can it completely guarantee the researcher that groups will not unintentionally differ in some important way. Notably, the smaller a sample that the experimenter utilizes, the more likely it is that groups will differ on some possibly confounding variable, despite attempts to randomly assign participants to groups. In fact, Hsu (1989) concluded that a study with a total sample of 20 to 40 participants is unlikely to exhibit group equivalence across a range of variables, such as age or gender, that may have an unwanted impact on the investigation's results. Therefore, use of groups with larger sample sizes will help to alleviate concerns about gaining the anticipated benefits of random assignment procedures.

*Matching.* There are many situations in which the investigator does not wish to leave the equivalence of a certain variable in doubt. In these cases, it may be advisable to use *matching* to group participants together based on their presentation of certain characteristics, then distribute them in such a way that an equal number of persons with differing levels of that characteristic are represented in each of the groups utilized. An example of a situation in which matching would be appropriate would be the investigation of a family systems treatment versus a behavioral treatment for adults with substance abuse disorders. The experimenters in this instance may be concerned that participants' cognitive abilities will impact the outcome of treatment and, therefore, wish to keep the range of cognitive ability equivalent across treatment groups. Kazdin (1998) identified two strategies for assuring equivalence on this type of variable. First, the experimenter might give the participants a pretreatment measure of cognitive ability, match individuals with identical scores, and then randomly assign matched participants to the groups. However, this procedure may prove difficult, because very few participants with identical cognitive ability scores may be available, and the potential result could be that multiple participants are needlessly discarded from the study. Alternatively, Kazdin (1998) suggests another methodology for matching participants that would involve ranking all individuals on the pretreatment measure and then, based on the number of groups in the study, randomly assigning *blocks* of participants to the groups. For example, in the substance abuse treatment study just described, we would first rank all the participants from highest to lowest cognitive ability score. Next, since this study involves two treatment groups, we would pair the participants (creating blocks of participants), starting with the two highest scores represented, and randomly assign each member of that first block to one of the two groups available. This procedure would assure that (a) cognitive ability would be almost equivalently represented among treatment groups and (b) that all the participants available would be utilized. In addition, random assignment of matched participants to groups can be used when the variable hypothesized to impact with the experimental manipulation is categorical in nature (i.e., gender, ethnicity, etc.).

Matching may be helpful when the investigators feel confident that a variable not directly under investigation will interfere with or interact with treatment effects; however, matching procedures, particularly when accomplished via a pretreatment measure, may prove inadequate for controlling the nuisance variable. Most commonly, problematic scenarios arise due to the tendency of individuals to *regress to the mean* or average score on any measure given to participants. That is, over time, it is likely that an individual's score on a given questionnaire or other measure of a variable, such as depression or anxiety, will become more average upon retesting. Therefore, matching participants to groups based on such pretreatment scores may ultimately prove inaccurate, particularly if multiple participants are matched based on extremely high or low scores on pretreatment assessment measures.

## Some Examples of Between-Subjects Design

The ultimate success or failure of a particular experiment most often lies in the strength of the design itself. In the interest of learning to select an appropriate between-subjects design and evaluate the quality of such designs, we now consider three common forms of between-subjects design: pretest-posttest control group designs, posttest-only control group designs, and factorial designs, along with the strengths and weaknesses of these various approaches to between-subjects methodology. Additionally, we consider variants of these approaches that incorporate quasi-experimental conditions and some general considerations that must be examined before choosing this alternative design approach.

*Pretest-Posttest Control Group Design.* The pretest-posttest control group design is the methodology that most often comes to mind when discussing between-group design methods and is also a very popular design choice for clinical psychology research. This design generally consists of two groups, formed using random assignment, with one group receiving some treatment or experimental condition, while the other does not. Groups are tested both prior to experimental treatment (pretest) and following treatment (posttest), with changes inferred from differences between pretest and posttest scores on the measures given. This design is particularly popular in treatment research, because the pretest-posttest format allows the experimenter to assess changes in the severity and frequency of relevant symptoms in both the presence of either an active treatment or no treatment at all (Kazdin, 1998).

The pretest-posttest control group design has multiple advantages. Given that the interval of time between pre- and posttest remains the same for both groups, researchers using this design are generally assured that their groups are similar with regard to exposure to common changes or specific events in the environment surrounding the experiment (also referred to in clinical research as *history* and *maturation*, respectively), and testing factors related to the pre- and posttests themselves, thereby bolstering the internal validity of the investigation (Kazdin, 1998). With a sufficiently large sample and use of random assignment, the likelihood that results are due to nuisance or extraneous variables is also minimized.

The use of a pretest alone is a major methodological strength of this design approach. In fact, Kazdin (1998) outlined the several advantages associated with pretest usage. First, using a pretest allows the researcher to match participants between groups on some variables of interest. A second factor, somewhat related to the first, is the ability to match participants along various levels of some variable, so that a range of that factor is represented equivalently in both groups. Third, the use of a pretest allows the investigator to utilize the pretest for more advanced statistical purposes, such as using pretest scores in an analysis of covariance. Finally, Kazdin (1998) has suggested that the use of a pretest may allow the investigator to examine individual behavior more specifically. For example, in an experiment where loss of participants, or *attrition*, was particularly high, the researcher may wish to further examine pretest scores to uncover whether attrition was related to a particular pattern of symptom severity or some other factor of interest (e.g., Were persons with particularly high or low scores more apt to withdraw from the investigation?).

Although the usage of a pretest does make this a particularly strong design approach, the pretest-posttest control group design is not without its flaws. In fact, the primary objection to this approach has much to do with the difficulties inherent in administering additional tests to participants. The administration of pretests alone are unlikely to impact the outcome of this type of investigation, since all participants receive the same pre- and posttests, at approximately the same time. However, what might vary between groups in this approach is the effect of the pretest on members of each group, a process known as *pretest sensitization*. For instance, if a pretest requires participants to answer a multitude of questions about their mood, this measure might somehow uniquely prepare participants in the experimental condition for an upcoming depression treatment. Therefore, even with positive results for this treatment, relative to control participants, it would be difficult to say whether participants in this condition improved due to the impact of the treatment alone; it may have been the combination of pretest and treatment that worked wonders for their mood. Kazdin (1998) suggested that the only way to avoid pretest sensitization with this design is to space out the pretest and experimental manipulation phases of the investigation, so that the impact of the pretest is lessened by time. However, this approach may be undesirable for other reasons. Specifically, the accuracy of a pretest may be minimized or statistical regression factors may come into play, when the interval between testing and manipulation is increased (Kazdin, 1998).

**Posttest-Only Control Group Design.** This design is essentially the same as the previously discussed approach with the major difference being the absence of a pretest administration. Again, random assignment of participants to groups is used, with an experimental treatment given to one group, while the other group typically serves as a control group, receiving no active treatment. After the experimental intervention is complete, a posttest is administered to measure the impact of the treatment.

Without the benefit of a pretest, the researcher obviously has little way to tell if participants differed on these measures between groups, prior to the intervention. However, there are many occasions in which a pretest is simply not practical. Foremost among the instances in which a pretest would be less desirable is when concerns about pretest sensitization are significant. For example, if a pretest would clearly impact performance on a laboratory measure, or has been shown to impact an intervention to be applied immediately following the pretest, then it might be advisable to omit this initial measure. Moreover, Kazdin (1998) pointed out that a very large sample, randomly assigned to groups, might allow the investigators to feel that their participants are likely to be equivalent along most variables, even without confirming this on pretest measures. In other instances, a pretest may simply be too time-consuming to justify its usage. For example, some standardized clinical interviews may take up to several hours to effectively administer, a factor which might make them difficult pretests to give to a large group of participants.

However, the absence of a pretest does tend to make this design a less popular choice among clinical researchers (Kazdin, 1998). Specifically, when the investigator wishes to evaluate the utility of a treatment approach for a particular disorder, it is frequently too important to specify where participants stand with regard to relevant factors associated with the diagnosis or treatment, to omit the pretest administration. Moreover, even with a larger sample size, most researchers tend to prefer that group equivalence on such variables is an assurance, rather than just a likelihood, before conducting a time- and/or labor-intensive investigation.

**Factorial Designs.** The designs just discussed are methods for assessing the impact of a single independent variable or multiple levels of a single independent variable through the usage of an experimental group and a control group. These designs tend to address more simple and specific questions about a treatment or behavior. While such designs are often more powerful due to their very simplicity, in many instances the researcher wishes to ask questions about two or more independent variables in the same experiment. For example, a researcher conducting an experiment investigating the impact of a speaker's characteristics on audience ratings of speaker competence might wish to simultaneously examine ratings for speakers of different ethnicity and gender. In such an experimental scenario, the investigator may utilize a *factorial design* to simultaneously test two or more variables (in this case, gender and ethnicity), each with two or more levels (male vs. female speaker and Caucasian vs. African American speaker; Kazdin, 1998). This specific experimental scenario is referred to as a 2 × 2 factorial design, since two different levels of two independent variables are being examined in relation to ratings of speaker competence. However, factorial designs may have as many levels and independent variables as the investigator wishes to examine. In fact, such flexibility is a major strength of this design approach. Specifically, in treatment studies, where the desire to test multiple variables (i.e., client factors, therapist factors, setting factors, etc.) in a minimum amount of time may be quite great or the literal and statistical *interaction* between such variables is of primary concern, a factorial design may be a good methodological choice (Kazdin, 1998).

Although testing multiple independent variables in the same experiment may seem an economical and practical choice by the researcher, there are some disadvantages to such an approach. For example, as the number of independent variables increases, the more participants an experiment will require to achieve adequate *power*, or the ability to actually detect an experimental effect when one truly exists. As we discuss later in the chapter, researchers can choose to incorporate some within-subjects components into their factorial designs to help alleviate the need for a much larger sample size. However, beyond the physical demands of monitoring numerous levels of multiple independent variables simultaneously, untangling the statistical influence of the three or more interactions between such variables can prove difficult, if not simply impossible. More importantly, it is vital to know that experimental treatments are useful at their most fundamental level, before attempting to add other variables or dismantling an intervention to study its nuances. Because the basic logic of this type of experimentation is rooted in the attempt to actually try to falsify our own hypotheses, the more levels and variables that one adds to the experimental mix, the more difficult it will be to determine whether or not hypotheses are accurate. Therefore, initial experiments about a phenomena should be focused on establishing a robust effect demonstrating that a treatment or manipulation is a powerful force under the experimental conditions specified. Once this initial proposition is met, then between-subjects factorial designs may be efficacious to test the conditions under which the treatment or manipulation is effective (Hampton, 1998).

### Quasi-Experimental Conditions and Between-Subjects Design.

*Quasi-experimental variables* are experimental factors that cannot be directly manipulated, such as gender, age, or social class. When the investigator wishes to examine such factors as independent variables, it is always necessary to treat these variables as between-subjects factors, since it is virtually impossible for participants to effectively alter such characteristics just so that they may be evaluated under the different conditions of a researcher's experiment (Hampton, 1998).

Just as commonly, the researcher in psychology simply runs into situations at hospitals, schools, and clinics that do not allow them to randomly assign participants to groups. Campbell and Stanley (1963) referred to investigations such as these, in which the experimenter is simply unable to exert the experimental control necessary to conduct a true experiment, as utilizing *quasi-experimental design*. Most often, such designs are identical to the pretest-posttest control group design or posttest-only control group design, with the only exception being the absence of randomization during group formation (Kazdin, 1998). While such approaches still allow the investigator to test their independent variable's impact on the dependent variable, without random assignment the internal validity of such studies may be impacted due to uncontrolled differences between groups. Kazdin (1998) asserted that quasi-experimental designs themselves are not inherently flawed. It is merely the inability to "rule out" possibly confounding factors as rival interpretations that continues to haunt such an approach. In fact, the more an investigator can do to eliminate such alternative explanations, methodologically, the stronger quasi-experimental designs become. One way of increasing the internal validity of quasi-experimental designs is to utilize what Campbell and Stanley (1963) call a *patched-up control group*. Patched-up control groups are added to quasi-experimental designs to examine some prominent threat to internal validity, such as the history or maturation factors indicated previously. These control groups may vary greatly in their effectiveness and are obviously still limited by the lack of random assignment problematic throughout this type of design. Nevertheless, when a specific internal validity factor comes into question in quasi-experimental designs, such control groups may provide one manner of investigating potential confounds.

## WITHIN-SUBJECTS DESIGNS

Up to this point, this chapter has discussed *between-subjects design* approaches, in which various participants are assigned to different groups, such as an experimental treatment group and a control group, and their scores on relevant measures are then compared to see if the independent variable, or experimental intervention, had some anticipated effect. Between-subjects methods have the potential to be statistically powerful and allow the researcher the design flexibility to make several relevant comparisons regarding group performance. However, the practical difficulties often inherent in attempting to create the group equivalence necessary to make the most adamant statements about a between-subjects effect, such as time, setting, or sample size limitations, may make these design approaches a less desirable choice for some researchers. Moreover, certain types of research questions require that an individual subject perform under all of the experimental conditions available in a given investigation. Experiments that are performed in this manner are often referred to as *within-subjects designs*. That is, the same participants perform in all of the conditions of a given experiment, then subject scores are compared in the aggregate within the various conditions presented, to determine the extent of a given effect (Hellier, 1998). These designs are also commonly called *repeated measures designs*, since the same participants are measured repeatedly, at least once in every condition.

### Some Examples of Within-Subjects Design

*Testing Multiple Levels of a Single Independent Variable.* Often, the researcher in a particular investigation wishes to examine many levels of a single independent variable within a single experiment. Examples of this type of investigation are commonly found in the psychophysiology literature, when an investigator is attempting to uncover what level or threshold of a particular stimulus is necessary to produce a given physiological effect. Such experiments might prove unwieldy in a between-subjects format. For instance, if a researcher wished to find out what level of illumination resulted in a human's subjective report of brightness, he or she might need to test multiple levels of illumination to allow participants to make fine discriminations in brightness. If this researcher determined that 15 levels of illumination were needed to accurately determine the threshold of "brightness," then a between-subjects design would demand at least this number of subject groups to make an accurate statistical conclusion. If a powerful test could only be constructed by including 30 participants in each group, the resulting between-subjects experiment would require (30 participants × 15 groups) a minimum of 450 participants. In many settings, this sample size would be extremely difficult to procure. Therefore, psychophysiology researchers may choose a within-subjects approach, whereby each participant would be exposed to every level of the independent variable which, in this case, constitutes exposure to 15 levels of illumination (Hellier, 1998). If the researcher chose to use a within-subjects design in this scenario, all participants would be repeatedly measured as they report the perceived brightness of each level of illumination, and the judgments offered by each participant may be compared within the same subject.

*Pretest-Posttest Within-Subjects Design.* A special case of within-subjects design is demonstrated by the *pretest-posttest within-subjects design* (Hellier, 1998). In this approach, a pretest measuring the dependent variable is given to all participants, followed by the presentation of an experimental condition to those same participants reflecting only one independent variable (or one level of the variable). A posttest is then given, again measuring the dependent variable. This design is necessarily different from the between-subjects version of a pretest-posttest design, in that there is only one group of participants utilized. Although this design choice may seem a practical one with which to evaluate the effectiveness of smaller-scale programs, such as an aggression intervention embedded within a larger milieu preschool program, the lack of a comparison or control group makes this design necessarily lacking in internal validity. That is, it is very likely that results could be caused by other uncontrolled changes in the environment or within the group, and these possibilities are wholly unmeasured in this design.

*Factorial Within-Subjects Design.*    Similar to the between-subjects variant of factorial designs, the *factorial within-subjects design* differs from previously discussed design approaches due to its simultaneous examination of two or more independent variables. For example, this design approach could be utilized to examine whether reaction time in a computerized task presenting negatively valanced stimuli is mediated by the type of stimuli presented, such as words (lexical cues) vs. human faces (facial cues), or the speed of stimuli presentation (ranging from 500 msec to 1200 msec). In this instance, the same group of participants is exposed to several levels of two different independent variables (form of stimulus presented [lexical vs. facial cue] and speed of stimulus presentation [several levels between 500 msec and 1200 msec]) within the context of repeatedly measuring the same dependent variable (reaction time).

Conceptually, the factorial within-subjects design differs from the between-subjects form of factorial design mainly in that the within-subjects format allows all participants to be repeatedly measured along all levels of each independent variable, whereas the between-subjects form still compares performance between groups of participants receiving different experimental conditions. Also similar to the between-subjects factorial design, the number of independent variables included in this within-subjects approach is really only limited by the feasibility of the study itself and, thus, this form of factorial design may prove an economical choice for many psychological investigations.

## Strengths of Within-Subjects Designs

Within-subjects designs are quite popular in psychology (Hellier, 1998). Part of this popularity is the likely result of their appropriateness for research questions, such as those in psychophysiology, where it might be necessary for a whole group of participants to be exposed to all experimental conditions. However, Hellier (1998) outlined four specific advantages that within-subjects designs hold for the researcher. The first of these strengths is the possibility for increased statistical *power* using a within-subjects design. As power refers to the potential for detecting an effect where one actually exists, any degree to which variability might be reduced that could potentially obscure this effect should increase the power of the experiment. Within-subjects designs obviously make use of the same participants across all conditions. Therefore, the variability which might be present between two groups of participants is eliminated and power is maximized. Second, within-subjects designs are more economical than between-subjects designs, in many instances, due to the *smaller number of participants* required to produce an effect in a within-subjects approach. This advantage is exemplified by the illumination study discussed previously, which required only 30 participants to test the 15 conditions, within-subjects, but needed 450 participants to test those same conditions, between-subjects. A third benefit, somewhat related to the last, associated with the within-subjects approach is the savings in *time and money* that a within-subjects design can offer next to very large scale investigations, such as the 450 between-subjects illumination study cited previously. Hellier (1998) also suggests that when lengthy instructions or training might be necessary for participants to take part in a study, the time-saving benefits of a within-subjects design may be even more attractive. A fourth benefit discussed by Hellier (1998) is the ability of participants in within-subjects designs to *serve as their own control*. As previously discussed, in a between-subjects investigation it is always best to use matching or random assignment to bolster equivalence across groups, thereby minimizing the possibility that nuisance variables will confound the effect. However, in a within-subjects approach, there no purpose in matching along specific factors, since the same individuals participate in all conditions. A participant's scores in one condition are simply being compared with his or her own scores in another condition. Thus, in the within-subjects paradigm, participants act as their own controls.

### Weaknesses of Within-Subjects Designs

On a practical level, within-subjects designs hold much promise for the clinical researcher. However, a trio of concerns regarding the potential influence of experimental context on an investigation, often known as *order effects* or *context effects*, raise some serious issues about this design's utility (Greenwald, 1976). These effects all arise from the fact that, during a within-subjects investigation, participants must complete all of the experimental conditions in some particular order (Hellier, 1998). Therefore, the possibility exists that the experimental arrangements in one condition might impact or sensitize participants to the tasks in the next condition. If this occurs, then we are no longer just considering the effect of a treatment condition alone, but rather the interaction of that treatment with the order in which it was presented. There are generally three order or context effects that may be addressed in the planning of a within-subjects design: *practice effects*, *sensitization effects*, and *carry-over effects* (Greenwald, 1976).

To better understand these effects, let us imagine a study in which there are four semi-distinct facets of the experiment that all individuals will participate in: (a) Drink Beverage A during a 10-minute period of time, (b) Play computerized chess game for 20 minutes, (c) Drink Beverage B during a second 10-minute period of time, and (d) Play the 20-minute chess game a second time. The point of this study may be to measure performance change from the first chess game to the second. However, participants are also exposed to three unique facets of the experiment prior to the final chess game, all of which may actually hurt the validity of any effects found across the performance-based measures. For example, if a participant performs better on the second chess game than the first, the improvement may have been due to nothing more than a *positive practice effect*, or the benefit gained from having practiced the chess game before. A *negative practice effect* might also be take place in this scenario, with performance on the second chess game suffering in some way from fatigue or disinterest gained sometime during the previous experimental conditions. Unfortunately, a researcher might interpret either a positive or a negative practice effect as simply the result of the experimental manipulation, when the reverse or some combination of practice and the expected effect may be occurring.

In order to illustrate *carryover effects*, let's now presume that Beverage A contains a drug hypothesized to optimize chess-playing ability, and Beverage B is a placebo, with no drug content. If performance is worse during the second chess game, the researcher might conclude that the miracle chess drug works to improve your chess playing skills. However, it is possible that the "chess playing drug" also has some large withdrawal effect that substantially worsens natural chess playing abilities during the interval of time when the second game was played. In other words, the effects of the drug from the first condition "carried over" into the second chess game administration and obscured the measurement in that condition (Mitchell & Jolley, 1996).

In addition to positive and negative practice effects and carryover effects, a *sensitization effect* may occur if, after receiving several conditions or treatments, the participants become aware of the nature of the independent and dependent variables under investigation. As a result, participants might guess what the experimental hypothesis could be and attempt to behave more or less in accordance with this hypothesis. In our example, if participants guess that the first drink is somehow increasing their chess playing skill, they might also realize that the second drug is a placebo, or at the very least, not having a similar effect on their abilities. At that point, they may attempt to perform even better in the second chess game than they would have under normal or control conditions, to see if they are truly able to perform up to the high level seen in the first chess game. Conversely, participants, now "aware" that the drug improved their chess-playing ability, may feel demoralized and perform even worse than would be expected under control conditions. Therefore, a sensitization effect, or a heightened awareness of the experimental variables, may pose a serious threat to the internal validity of a within-subjects design.

## Addressing the Limitations of Within-Subjects Designs

There are certainly steps one can take to address the order effect limitations of within-subjects designs. To minimize a positive practice effect, the experimenter may offer an extensive practice period to all participants, in an effort to maximize the benefits of practice prior to administering the experimental tasks. Fatigue and other negative practice effects may combated by making experimental materials brief or more entertaining for participants. Carryover effects, such as those due to the withdrawal symptoms produced by the chess-playing drug, may be minimized by lengthening the interval between experimental tasks, so that the drug is no longer in effect during subsequent tasks (Mitchell & Jolley, 1996). However, a researcher should be cautious and not necessarily lengthen the interval too much, so as to maintain strict control over the experimental conditions and not enter additional, unwanted variance into the experiment.

Mitchell and Jolley (1996) discuss three specific ways in which sensitization effects may be reduced. First, levels of the independent variable presented may be kept as similar as possible to one another, so as not to make participants overtly aware of the changes. For example, in the illumination experiment, the investigator could keep the levels of brightness very close to one another during the perception task, to keep the purpose of presenting varying levels of illumination more ambiguous. Second, the levels of the independent variable may be altered in a gradual or surreptitious way, such as asking the participant to exit the room while the illumination level is changed. Third, the use of a good placebo treatment is essential, if a placebo condition is utilized. In other words, the placebo condition should not unduly arouse the suspicions of participants regarding its differential impact on the dependent variable.

Although each of these strategies is somewhat effective in combating the effects of order, the only true way to rid a within-subjects designs of these effects is to alter the sequence of the treatments presented. In our chess-playing example, you could accomplish this by randomly determining which beverage will be served first for each subject. Unfortunately, the difficulty with randomizing the order of treatment presentation is that you are unlikely to gain an even number of participants completing treatments in each order specified, with this likelihood decreasing even further as the sample size decreases. The most effective way of addressing the issues associated with randomizing treatment presentation order is to introduce a between-subjects factor into the within-subjects design, through a process called *counterbalancing*. Since a within-subjects design utilizing counterbalancing necessarily falls under the category of a mixed design, it will be now be discussed in the next section of this chapter.

## MIXED DESIGNS

As just implied, *mixed designs* are typically those that combine aspects of both between- and within-subjects designs. Although mixed designs might take one of many forms, the two types discussed in this section include *counterbalanced designs* and *mixed factorial designs*.

### Counterbalanced Designs

Clearly, some measures must be taken to eradicate order effect limitations inherent in many within-subjects design. As just discussed, randomization alone may be an ineffective strategy for addressing order problems, because it may leave the researcher with unbalanced groups of participants. That is, the result of randomization may be the production of two or more groups, containing a possibly uneven amount of participants, that have received different treatment orders. Moreover, by creating groups of participants, each receiving a different order of treatment, you are introducing a between-subjects factor associated with treatment order into a repeated measures experimental context. A more effective way of accomplishing this goal with a more equal distribution of treatment order across groups is to counterbalance, so that order effects are balanced between conditions with a roughly equivalent number of participants receiving the treatment conditions in each order specified.

*Complete Counterbalancing.* With *complete counterbalancing*, the researcher creates enough groups to present all possible combinations of experimental conditions an equal number of times (Hellier, 1998). Therefore, if you have two groups of stimuli to present in a given task, such as a group of pictures demonstrating happy faces and another group displaying angry faces, then you would randomly assign exactly half of the participants to see the angry faces first, then the happy faces, while the other half receives the happy faces first. The difficulties with complete counterbalancing begin to mount as the number of presentation orders increases (Hellier, 1998). For example, in order to present seven experimental conditions in every possible combination in which they could occur, you would have to utilize at least 5,040 participants (i.e., $7! = 7 \times 6 \times 5 \times 4 \times 3 \times 2 \times 1$), to have even one participant completing the conditions in each potential order.

In therapy research, this type of completely counterbalanced design is frequently referred to as a *crossover design* (Kazdin, 1998). In the crossover design, participants are randomly assigned and evenly distributed to as many groups as there are treatments to compare. Assuming that you are only comparing two treatments, each group would receive the two therapeutic conditions in a completely counterbalanced manner, with assessments or observations occurring not only pretest and posttest, but also before switching or crossing over to the second treatment.

With the between-subjects factor of order present in a completely counterbalanced design, the investigator can now statistically evaluate interactions between the order of treatment presentation and the treatments themselves. That is, the researcher may assess statistically the question of whether order is really impacting treatment, perhaps due to factors such as practice or sensitization. However, since few investigators have the rest of their natural lives available to collect data for single experiments with multiple conditions to counterbalance, some incomplete counterbalancing measures have been developed to address order concerns in a more parsimonious fashion.

***Incomplete Counterbalancing.*** In an investigation testing four treatment conditions (i.e., treatments W,X,Y,Z), complete counterbalancing seems impractical. Kazdin (1998) reiterates that simply randomizing treatment order is inadequate, particularly for investigations with smaller sample sizes, since it is very possible that treatment order will fall into some systematic and possibly confounding pattern. For example, in an experiment testing treatments W, X, Y, and Z with only 10 participants it is very possible that one treatment will randomly fall into the same ordinal position on multiple occasions (i.e., Treatment X presented in the fourth position for eight of 10 participants).

Alternatively, the researcher could use a *Latin Square design* to assure that a subset of treatment order possibilities are each presented to a roughly equivalent number of participants. For example, the researcher could specify four particular orders in which treatments W, X, Y, and Z could appear, then randomly assign participants to four groups, with each receiving one of the four treatment orders selected (Kazdin, 1998). This treatment arrangement is only effective if each treatment is presented in a given position only once. Therefore, the number of groups, number of treatments, and orders of treatment presentation are equal. Kazdin (1998) used a "Latin Square" to illustrate this relationship between treatments, order, and groups (see Table 5.1).

A Latin Square, such as the one indicated in the table, will allow the researcher to make comparisons to see whether an effect is due to order (columns), group (rows), or to the effects of the treatments or interventions themselves (Kazdin, 1998). However, this design clearly exempts a great many treatment *sequences* from testing. This may become an important factor if the researcher believes that certain effects will only occur with particular treatment sequences. For example, Treatment X never directly follows Treatment Y in

TABLE 5.1
Treatment Presentation in a Latin Square Design

| | *Treatment Order* | | | |
|---|---|---|---|---|
| *Sequence* | *1* | *2* | *3* | *4* |
| I | W | X | Y | Z |
| II | X | W | Z | Y |
| III | Y | Z | X | W |
| IV | Z | Y | W | X |

*Note.* From Kazdin, 1998.

the design specified in the table. Therefore, this design could not eliminate the possibility that such a sequence would influence the effects found. In such a case, the investigator may wish to follow-up this type of investigation with additional research examining these alternative hypotheses.

## Mixed Factorial Design

We have already alluded to the possibility that one can combine between-subjects and within-subjects independent variables into the same factorial design, referred to as a *mixed factorial design* (Mitchell & Jolley, 1996). To imagine this design, let's suppose that the researcher is hoping to study the effects of blindness and practice effects on a maze learning (dependent variable) in mice. The investigator in this case may believe that blindness typically occurs "between-subjects," that is, it effects some members of the population, but not others, while practice may be considered a "within-subjects" variable that could be acquired by any participant (Mitchell & Jolley, 1996). To study the between-subjects variable in this mixed design, the researcher would want to randomly assign half of the mice to be blinded, perhaps through the administration of a drug with this effect, while the other half remain sighted. Next, the within-subjects variable, practice, would be administered by having the mice in both conditions run the maze a fixed number of times. Finally, all participants would then be assessed on the dependent measure. The statistical analyses available for such a design allow the investigator to test for both main effects and interactions. In this case, that means the researcher may test to see how blindness alone, practice alone, and the interaction of blindness and practice effect maze learning (Mitchell & Jolley, 1996).

Mixed designs such as the one exemplified above can be of great benefit in terms of reducing the sample size necessary for a powerful study of a given set of variables, while simultaneously allowing for the appropriate design steps to be taken for two discrepant types of variables within a single experiment. For example, the combined benefits of randomly assigning participants to conditions and having individuals participate in all levels of the within-subjects variable, all in the same study, cannot be underestimated.

## CROSS-SECTIONAL, LONGITUDINAL AND SEQUENTIAL DESIGNS

Frequently, a researcher in psychology wishes to describe the manner in which a particular condition or behavior develops. Although there are multiple variants of each design, investigators concerned with development most often employ some form of *cross-sectional design*, in which the functioning of persons in different age groups is compared simultaneously, or a *longitudinal design*, where the performance of a single group of individuals is repeatedly assessed over time (Sigelman, 1999). One prominent criticism of both cross-sectional and longitudinal approaches surrounds the frequent differences in results that these two methods have produced regarding the same phenomena. For example, Yerkes (1921) administered the *Army Alpha Test*, a test of cognitive ability, using a cross-sectional design, to persons representing a variety of age groups, up to a maximum age of approximately 60. His results indicated that cognitive ability appeared to be highest around the age of 20, then steadily decreased to lower points around age 50 or 60. This result was generally believed accurate until Owens (1953) produced a longitudinal study suggesting that middle-aged persons actually scored higher than younger persons on most measures of cognitive ability. Assuming that this result has little to do with the instruments selected to test cognitive ability, how could both findings possibly be correct? To get to the bottom of such discrepancies, we now consider the strengths and weaknesses of each design approach. Moreover, a third design type, *sequential design*, that combines elements of both cross-sectional and longitudinal approaches, will be considered as an effort to improve some of the weaknesses of the two former design strategies.

### Cross-Sectional Design

Cross-sectional designs attempt to simultaneously compare individuals of different age groups regarding some variable of interest. For example, a researcher could examine recall of a simple reading passage cross-sectionally by giving that passage, at roughly the same point in time, to three groups of children, ages 5, 7, and 9. The average recall score for each group of children could then be compared to see whether age differences exist in recall scores *between* these three groups. A common misunderstanding regarding such results is to infer that the data resulting from cross-sectional research tells us how people develop as a function of age (Sigelman, 1999). However, in truth, this data carries with it a *cohort effect* which makes such descriptive information about development difficult to glean from this design. Cohort effects are differences between groups of individuals that due to one group, or *cohort*, being born around the same time and experiencing a unique historical context (Sigelman, 1999). For example, persons who are now 75 years old belong to a cohort that experienced a vastly different historical context to their development than persons who are now 25 years old. The difficulty with cross-sectional research is that when you measure some variable by giving it to both 25-year-olds and 75-year-olds simultaneously, it is impossible to tell whether the differences found reflect a true developmental change associated with growing older (an *age effect*) or are simply a cohort effect of being born into different eras of time (Sigelman, 1999). These hopelessly entangled age and cohort effects help to explain some of the discrepancies regarding Yerkes' (1921) cognitive ability findings, since a 60-year-old in the 1920s was likely to have experienced a vastly different education than a person who was only 20 at that time. Without overly digressing into the history of education, generational changes regarding the value placed on education across social classes and safeguards available to keep children in school were likely to produce a very different educational background for a 20-year-old versus a 60-year-old in 1920. Therefore a cohort effect, associated with differing educational history, may have partially confounded Yerkes' findings. Moreover, even without cohort effects, cross-sectional designs merely test age differences in functioning at one point in time. Therefore, such designs tell us nothing about exactly how a person changes over the developmental period (Sigelman, 1999).

So, if cross-sectional designs are so flawed, why do developmental researchers continue to make use of them? The answer is likely to be found in their simplicity and ease of administration. Relative to other approaches to developmental group design, cross-sectional designs allow the researcher to collect some basic information about age differences in functioning within a single test administration and without significant concerns regarding the loss of subjects or aging of instruments over time (Sigelman, 1999).

## Longitudinal Design

To test the development of the previously introduced reading recall variable longitudinally, the investigator in this experiment would start with a single group of five-year-olds and *repeatedly measure* that same group of children on the recall task at ages seven and nine. By doing so, the researcher would get an idea of how reading recall changes or develops for this particular group of children. Clearly, such a longitudinal approach would have some genuine practical benefits, particularly in regard to investigations hoping to demonstrate whether certain traits or tendencies in childhood develop into associated behaviors later in life (Sigelman, 1999). More importantly, longitudinal designs can tell the researcher a great deal about similarities and differences in the development of particular variable.

However, longitudinal studies also have some serious flaws in their design and execution. On the design end, longitudinal data suffers from interpretive difficulties, related not to cohort effects, but rather to *time of measurement effects* (Sigelman, 1999). Time of measurement effects are the result of changes in attitudes, trends, or the influence of historical events on society as a whole, rather than a specific cohort. Any time data are collected longitudinally, the development of the individuals measured is necessarily influenced by the historical trends and events around them. Therefore, in longitudinal designs, age effects and time of measurement effects cannot be reliably detangled (Sigelman, 1999). On the practical end, a longitudinal investigation may take years and a large amount of money to produce effectively. Attrition may also be a problem with such studies, as participants may be lost through a variety of mechanisms over time, including drop-out or even death. Moreover, the testing one uses to assess a certain variable may prove inadequate or obsolete as time passes following its initial usage in a longitudinal study. Even if instruments do not *decay* in this manner, repeated testing with the same measures may prove extremely problematic if practice or sensitization effects come into play in the interpretation of resultant data.

This information surely casts doubt on the validity of the Owens (1953) study of cognitive ability, as well. Perhaps some historical changes occurring during the administration of the Owens investigation produced higher scores among individuals when they completed the cognitive ability measure in middle age. Or, it may be possible that some practice with a cognitive ability instrument gave persons an advantage after the years of repeated testing they experienced with such measures. Moreover, it is also possible that persons in this particular sample who were less bright simply dropped out of the study over time, for one reason or another, leaving a smarter and smaller sample remaining to test during middle adulthood. Whichever the case, it is clear that a different methodology is required to test these types of developmental questions without the many flaws inherent in the cross-sectional and longitudinal approaches.

## Sequential Design

Sequential designs allow the researcher to combine both cross-sectional and longitudinal approaches into a single design. In doing so, the effects of age, cohort, and time of measurement can finally be separated or independently investigated (Sigelman, 1999). For instance, if the researcher in the reading recall study now wished to examine this behavior sequentially, he or she would begin by first measuring the five-, seven-, and nine-year-olds cross-sectionally, then simply re-test these same three cohorts longitudinally, as they get older (e.g., at two- or three-year intervals). The resultant data would tell the researcher which effects were due to actual developmental trends or age effects, whether those developmental trends differ by cohort, and if the data indicate any shift reflecting some time of measurement influence. Such time of measurement effects would suggest that an environmental or historical event affected all under investigation, regardless of cohort (Sigelman, 1999).

Use of a sequential design can also help in settling the debate between the cognitive ability and age trend results seen in Yerkes (1921) cross-sectional study and Owens (1953) longitudinal analysis. Schaie (1996) conducted a series of sequential analyses, by testing cognitive ability with groups of 22- to 70-year-olds, cross-sectionally, then repeating this testing every seven years. Begun with one sample in 1956, this same sequential strategy has been repeated with samples acquired in 1963, 1970, 1977, and 1984 (Schaie, 1996). Schaie's data suggest that, in fact, cognitive ability measures are quite susceptible to cohort effects, when collected cross-sectionally. That is, it appears that the most recently born persons, across samples, tend to perform better on most cognitive ability measures than those born in earlier generations. Overall, age trends in this data indicate that most persons tend to gain, though quite modestly, in cognitive ability, through their 50s, with a notable drop-off in ability only becoming steep sometime in the 80s (Schaie, 1996).

Thus, sequential studies are an excellent methodology for resolving debates about discrepant findings in cross-sectional and longitudinal data regarding the development of some aspect of functioning. However, because behaviors in a sequential design must be investigated over a lengthy period of time, these investigations may suffer from the instrument, attrition, and cost-related disadvantages encountered with a purely longitudinal approach. They can also be quite complex and difficult for other investigators to replicate or accurately repeat in the future.

## DISTINGUISHING BETWEEN GROUP AND INDIVIDUAL RESULTS

The very purpose of studying behavior in groups is to reveal something about average tendencies or performance within a given population. The reasoning behind this group approach was detailed earlier in this chapter. Although the statistical tools associated with many group designs only allow inferences to be made based on changes in group means on relevant measures, it is all too tempting to conclude that a statistically significant result in a group design tells the reader exactly how all *individuals* in that sample tended to behave (Jacobson & Truax, 1991). In fact, a group result tells us very little about how each individual in the sample behaved, since scores are averaged within groups. Moreover, exceptional individual scores, often called statistical *outliers*, are routinely purged from group data sets due to the strong individual influence that an extreme score might exert upon averaged scores, like obscuring a treatment effect altogether. Overall, then, the individual score or behavior seems to be of minimal value in assessing a group effect.

The great problem with such logic is that, in psychology, and particularly in psychotherapy research, we are very concerned about how the individual client responds to a particular experimental treatment. Conger (1984) and others have gone as far as to say that, if the purpose of psychotherapy is to produce some meaningful result for the individual, then such a goal may not be attainable within a treatment program derived from a group study in which the treatment was shown to enhance the average performance of some clinical sample versus a control condition. That is, group results relay little about *clinical significance*, or the practical value of an effect, for individual consumers of a treatment (Kazdin, 1998). In other words, a statistically significant result tells the reader virtually nothing about the practical benefit of that treatment for individuals because such findings do not generally reveal anything about the *magnitude* of change (i.e., how big the change was) or the *generalizability* of that change to other settings or circumstances. Moreover, it is very important to recognize that a statistically significant effect regarding average performance could genuinely mean that all group members improved with a given treatment in a particular setting, but it also may indicate that some individuals changed substantially, while others did not improve or even deteriorated slightly under treatment (Conger, 1984).

There are steps that an investigator might take to better uncover the individual sources of change within groups. For example, the distribution of scores or effects may be investigated after the experimental conditions and preliminary analyses are complete, to determine the exact pattern of improvement in a given group. If differential changes are found, then the researcher would simply need to qualify the benefits of treatment in terms of those who did not improve, or follow up such results with further experimentation about the sources of clinical improvement. Conger (1984) indicates that the better plan might be to specify "clinically relevant performance variables" *a priori*, or before experimentation, and explore eventual treatment effects in terms of how individuals in both groups responded along these measures. However, the lesson to be learned here is largely for the consumer of group treatment literature. Even with the best usage of random assignment or the tightest experimental controls in place, to presume that a group effect either applies to all members of the sample measured or always generalizes to the greater population belies both the typical goals and scope of group research.

## ILLUSTRATION AND ANALYSIS OF A CLASSIC
## GROUP OUTCOME STUDY

Sloane, Staples, Cristol, Yorkston, and Whipple (1975) produced a clinical outcome study regarding the relative benefits of psychoanalytic therapy versus behavior therapy, utilizing a design with both between-subjects and longitudinal elements, that is widely considered to be the most comprehensive and well-executed investigation of its kind (Heimberg & Becker, 1984). Approximately 90 outpatients seeking or referred for mental health services, between the ages of 18 and 45, and judged to be suitable candidates for therapy, were matched by gender and problem severity and then randomly assigned to either a behavior therapy, psychoanalytically oriented therapy, or a wait-list/minimal contact control group. These participants were assessed on a variety of personality and diagnostic measures, during pretreatment, four months into treatment, and again, at a 1-year follow-up assessment. Informants for these assessments included not only the participant, but also the therapist and a close relative of the participant (Sloane et al., 1975).

The majority of the participants (approximately two thirds) were assigned neurotic disorder diagnoses, and the remaining third were diagnosed with personality disorders, based on interactions between the participant and a research assistant conducting an initial, structured interview with the client and close relative. Inclusion criteria, also judged during the initial assessment, included: (a) status as a psychiatric patient without symptoms of extremely severe disturbance, (b) a desire to receive psychiatric services, (c) appropriateness for psychotherapy, as determined by the initial assessor, and (d) age between 18 and 45 years (Sloane et al., 1975). Following initial assessment, clients were matched along the variables previously indicated and randomly assigned to one of the three treatment groups. The wait-list control group agreed to abstain from the receipt of any therapeutic services for approximately four months, at which time they were entered into treatment. This control group might also be aptly called a minimal contact group (versus a no-treatment control group), because these participants also received some follow-up, compliance assessment-oriented phone calls from the research assistant during the four-month wait-list period. Notably, although not designed to be a treatment of any kind, some participants in the wait-list control group indicated that such phone calls had some personal therapeutic value (Sloane et al., 1975). Both the experimental psychoanalytic and the behavioral treatments were defined prior to treatment and all participating therapists agreed to generally adhere to these approaches as outlined. Additionally, therapists considered expert in these respective clinical approaches (i.e., Wolpe, Lazarus, and Serber for behavior therapy; Urban, Vispo, and Freed for psychoanalytically oriented therapy) were utilized as primary clinicians for each participant, in an attempt to further insure appropriate exposure to the treatment selected (Heimberg & Becker, 1984). Tape recordings of session contact were made and reviewed to assure compliance with the general treatment protocol, though therapists were given much latitude with regard to the specifics of session content.

The results of this investigation suggest that, according to a variety of posttreatment measures, those participants in either psychoanalytic therapy or behavior therapy tended to improve, relative to control group participants (Sloane et al., 1975; Heimberg & Becker, 1984). On average, those in the behavior therapy group evidenced slightly greater improvement on ratings of adjustment and social functioning, relative to the other treatment group and the control group. At a one-year follow-up assessment, both behavior therapy and psychoanalytic therapy participants continued to report sustained improvement, beyond that indicated by control participants, with no significant differences found between the two primary treatment groups. Overall, the Sloane et al. (1975) investigation concludes that both behavior therapy and psychoanalytic therapy are efficacious treatment approaches for neurotic and personality-disordered clients, with behavior therapy perhaps evidencing a slight advantage over psychoanalytically oriented approaches in some arenas.

***Analysis of Sloane et al. (1975).*** Fine critical analyses of this seminal treatment study (e.g., Bergin & Lambert, 1978, Heimberg & Becker, 1984, Kazdin & Wilson, 1978) already exist in the psychology literature and their points of praise and contention are certainly worthy of review. In general, these analyses of Sloane et al. (1975) address some design issues. However, many of the excellent points made regarding this investigation concern additional issues more aligned with clinical outcome research than a pure analysis of the design. For example, Kazdin and Wilson (1978) endorse Sloane et al. (1975) as an outstanding investigation, maintaining that the study reflects the following strengths: (a) the usage of trained, expert therapists, (b) attempts at random assignment (although matching makes this procedure less robust in producing overall group equivalence), (c) a large sample size with an enthusiastic membership, (d) the inclusion of what was initially designated a no-treatment control group, (e) an appropriate follow-up assessment period, and (f) few participants lost to attrition. Additional praise from Bergin and Lambert (1978) indicates that: (a) matching of participants adds *a priori* assurance of group equivalence on some relevant treatment factors, (b) the usage of a clinical population promotes the generalizability of results to the treatment settings in which it is most likely to be used, (c) some attempts to check the integrity of treatment were used, accomplished via a review of treatment tapes, and (d) a wide variety of informants and measures utilized in the assessment of treatment outcome provide a wealth of potential information regarding treatment outcome.

Heimberg and Becker (1984) support most of these contentions, but also raise some important concerns regarding this investigation. For example, they question whether the measures utilized for assessment purposes, though large in number, actually yield any operational specificity regarding the details of ongoing behavior problems among participants. Second, the research assistant in this investigation, who conducted all of the initial interviews and was responsible for the general assignment of participants to conditions, was not *blind* to treatment selection (Heimberg & Becker, 1984). That is, the research assistant, who was a psychoanalytically trained therapist and aware of participants' histories, may have knowingly or unknowingly placed participants believed to be most appropriate for psychoanalytic treatment into that group, potentially giving a slight edge to the therapists utilizing such treatment. In addition, the "appropriateness for psychotherapy" condition for inclusion in the investigation is criticized by Heimberg and Becker (1984) as another potential source of bias against the behavior therapy group. Importantly, a fourth and very salient difficulty identified by Heimberg and Becker (1984) is the placement of wait-list control group participants into treatment, following the four-month assessment. As a result, the control group essentially disappears from this investigation and, while relevant data might have been achieved from this control group at the four-month follow-up, the eight months of therapy that the control group received prior to the one-year follow-up greatly reduces the validity of those comparisons with experimental treatment groups. Conversely, the investigators may have included a different type of control or comparison group, such as one receiving supportive or theoretically inert treatment for one year. However, such a strategy also holds multiple ethical and practical limitations.

The investigators in this analysis might have also selected an alternative design strategy, such as a crossover design (Kazdin, 1998), that would have allowed more comparisons regarding treatment to be made within-subjects. Moreover, the researchers might have more deliberately entered the control group participants into the experimental therapy conditions, by randomly assigning participants to one of the two experimental treatment groups, following the four-month delay. Such a control group strategy still maintains many of the follow-up assessment limitations seen in Sloane et al. (1975), but would be an ethical way of establishing that treatments were effective during another temporal period.

Overall, this investigation is an excellent model of group outcome research. However, the difficulties of gleaning individual findings from such results remain prominent. For example, how does a clinician use this information in a practical therapy context? More specific investigation, establishing and operationally defining the clinical correlates of therapeutic change for each of these groups would allow clinicians to more reliably determine which approach to select for what clients, based on the delimiting factors present in their particular context. As far as these latter goals are concerned, group designs may leave much to be desired in establishing the practical relevance of a given treatment approach.

## REFERENCES

Bergin, A. E., & Lambert, M. J. (1978). The evaluation of therapeutic outcomes. In S. L. Garfield & A. E. Bergin (Eds.), *Handbook of psychotherapy and behavior change: An empirical analysis* (2nd ed.). New York: Wiley.

Campbell, D. T., & Stanley, J. C. (1963). Experimental and quasi-experimental designs for research and teaching. In N. L. Gage (Ed.), *Handbook of research on teaching.* Chicago: Rand McNally.

Conger, A. J. (1984). Statistical considerations. In M. Hersen, L. Michelson, & A. S. Bellack (Eds.), *Issues in psychotherapy research* (pp. 285–312). New York: Plenum Press.

Fisher, R. A. (1925). *Statistical methods for research workers.* Edinburgh, Scotland: Oliver & Boyd.

Greenwald, A. G. (1976). Within-subjects designs: To use or not to use? *Psychological Bulletin, 83,* 314–320.

Hampton, J. (1998). Between-subjects versus within-subjects designs. In J. Nunn (Ed.), *Laboratory psychology: A beginner's guide* (pp. 15–38). East Sussex, England: Psychology Press.

Heimberg, R. G., & Becker, R. F. (1984). Comparative outcome research. In M. Hersen, L. Michelson, & A. S. Bellack (Eds.), *Issues in psychotherapy research* (pp. 251–283). New York: Plenum Press.

Hellier, E. J. (1998). Within-subjects designs. In J. Nunn (Ed.), *Laboratory psychology: A beginner's guide* (pp. 39–57). East Sussex, England: Psychology Press.

Howard, K. I., Orlinsky, D. E., & Lueger, R. J. (1995). The design of clinically relevant outcome research: Some considerations and an example. In M. Aveline & D. A. Shapiro (Eds.), *Research foundations for psychotherapy practice* (pp. 3–47). West Sussex, England: John Wiley & Sons.

Hsu, L. M. (1989). Random sampling, randomization, and equivalence of contrasted groups in psychotherapy outcome research. *Journal of Consulting and Clinical Psychology, 57,* 131–137.

Jacobson, N. S., & Truax, P. (1991). Clinical significance: A statistical approach to defining meaningful change in psychotherapy research. *Journal of Consulting and Clinical Psychology, 59,* 12–19.

Kazdin, A. E. (1998). *Research design in clinical psychology* (3rd ed.). Needham Heights, MA: Allyn and Bacon.

Kazdin, A. E., & Wilson, G. T. (1978). *Evaluation of behavior therapy: Issues, evidence, and research strategies.* Cambridge, MA: Ballinger.

Kratochwill, T. R., & Mace, F. C. (1984). Time-series research in psychotherapy. In M. Hersen, L. Michelson, & A. S. Bellack (Eds.), *Issues in psychotherapy research* (pp. 171–225). New York: Plenum Press.

Mitchell, M., & Jolley, J. (1996). *Research design explained* (3rd ed.). Orlando, FL: Harcourt Brace College Publishers.

Owens, W. A., Jr. (1953). Age and mental abilities: A longitudinal study. *Genetic Psychology Monographs, 48,* 3–54.

Schaie, K. W. (1996). *Intellectual development in adulthood. The Seattle longitudinal study.* New York: Cambridge University Press.

Sigelman, C. K. (1999). *Life-span human development* (3rd ed.). Pacific Grove, CA: Brooks-Cole.

Sloane, R. B., Staples, F. R., Cristol, A. H., Yorkston, N. J., & Whipple, K. (1975). *Psychotherapy versus behavior change.* Cambridge, MA: Harvard University Press.

Underwood, B. J. (1949). *Experimental psychology.* New York: Appleton-Century-Crofts.

Yerkes, R. M. (1921). Psychological examining in the U.S. Army. *Memoirs: National Academy of Science, 15,* 1–890.

# 6

# Correlational Methods

### Gerald Goldstein
*VA Pittsburgh Healthcare System and University of Pittsburgh*

*Correlational methods* deal with relationships among phenomena as they exist in natural situations. A correlation can be defined in numerous ways: as the strength of association between phenomena, as the degree to which one phenomenon can be predicted from another phenomenon or as the degree to which phenomena covary. In a sense, it is a scientific version of the kinds of natural observation in which one relates one thing to another. Underlying these observations, we generally can find some theoretical inference concerning those relationships. For example, the clinician may observe that clients with alcoholism often have fathers with histories of alcoholism. A formal study of this observation would involve obtaining information about alcoholism status in clients and their fathers. We can then tabulate these data in what is called a contingency table of the type shown in Table 6.1. It can be seen there that the alcoholic clients had alcoholic fathers far more frequently than the nonalcoholic patients. We can therefore say that there is a high correlation between alcoholism in parent and child. However, in research applications, it is necessary to know how high. The value typically used to express how high the correlation is, or the strength of association, is called the *correlation coefficient*. A correlation coefficient is an index of the strength of association between two variables. It is a number that can range between $-1$ and $+1$. A value of zero reflects complete absence of correlation; a $-1$ indicates a perfect negative correlation whereas $+1$ represents a perfect positive correlation. A positive correlation occurs when both values go up (e.g., height and weight in children) and a negative correlation occurs when one value goes up as the other

**161**

TABLE 6.1
Alcoholic Father

|                    |     | Yes | No |
|--------------------|-----|-----|-----|
|                    | Yes | 12  | 3  |
| Alcoholic Client   |     |     |    |
|                    | No  | 2   | 14 |

goes down (e.g., days of drought and the size of a wheat crop). Correlations are rarely perfect and most correlation coefficients are values such as .67 or −.35. The problem then becomes one of evaluating strength of association from these values. Statistical significance is one way. The other way of evaluating strength is by considering amount of explained variance. The *statistical significance* of a correlation coefficient involves the determination at a particular confidence level as to whether or not the coefficient is different from zero. Typically, statistical analysis in the behavioral sciences utilizes the .05 (occurrence by chance 5 times out of 100) or .01 (1 time out of 100). Thus, working at the .05 level, a given correlation coefficient would be significant if it could occur by chance less than 5 out of 100 times. Nonsignificant correlations are sometimes referred to as *zero-order correlations*. The statistical significance of a single correlation coefficient is often considered to be a relatively trivial matter in most research, but particularly, when the purpose of the research is that of generating predictions from an unknown variable to a known variable, statistically significant correlation coefficients can have exceedingly low predictive value. Generally, a more important consideration is the percentage of explained variance. That percentage is the squared correlation coefficient. Thus, a correlation coefficient of .40 yields 16% explained variance. That is, 16% of the variance in the unknown variable can be accounted for by variance in the known variable. The remaining variance in the unknown variable has to be accounted for by unknown factors. Sometimes statistically significant correlations explain very little variance.

Generally, correlation coefficients are based on the mathematics of what is called *regression analysis*. Regression provides estimates of unknown $y$ values from known $x$ values through the generation of equations. Thus, application of a regression equation can provide a predicted score for the unknown variable based on the known variable score. The correlation coefficient is a measure of the gain in precision of predicting $y$ from knowledge of $x$. Thus, a coefficient of zero means absolutely no gain, whereas +1 or −1 means complete predictability. It is often useful for the investigator to examine regression equations diagrammatically so that the pairing of $x$ and $y$ variables can be seen in individual cases. This step may be accomplished by plotting a scatter diagram or scattergram. On a scattergram, the $x$ scores are plotted along the $X$ axis and the $y$ scores along the $Y$ axis. Individual score pairs are plotted as points at their meeting places. Thus, the point for a score of $x = 5$ and $y = 6$ would be plotted at 5 units along the $X$ axis and 6 units up the $Y$ axis. The scattergram is helpful in providing a picture of what the bivariate distribution looks like. That is, one can tell at a glance whether it is linear in which case the $x$ variable increases or decreases directly with the $y$ variable, or curvilinear, in which case there is a bend in the distribution such that the $y$ variable goes up to a point and then begins to go down. Some distributions are random, with no discernible relationship between the two variables.

There are many variants of regression analysis and many types of correlation coefficients. The major reason for choosing among the various types has to do with the mathematical assumptions on which the statistic is based. Most notably, there is an assumption of linearity of the bivariate distribution for most correlation coefficients. However, many strong associations may not be linear. They may be U shaped or have some other configuration. Appropriate statistics have been devised for situations in which the assumption of linearity cannot be made. We go no further into the mathematics of regression and correlation here, because these matters are covered in extensive detail in numerous statistics texts (e.g. Rosner, 1990).

Simple correlational research designs are those in which there is a single $x$ variable and a single $y$ variable. The strength of association between these variables is measured with the appropriate correlation coefficient, and evaluated by the presence or absence of statistical significance or by amount of explained variance. Strength of association is not entirely synonymous with predictability.

## MULTIPLE AND PARTIAL CORRELATION

It is frequently necessary to deal with more than one correlation at a time. That is, the investigator may be interested in interrelationships among more than one bivariate at a time; for example, the relationship among age, height, weight, and blood pressure. If we paired each of these variables, there would be 16 possible pairs. However, six of them repeat themselves (e.g. height vs. weight and weigh vs. height), and four cases would represent the correlation of the variable with itself. Therefore, there would be only six meaningful correlations. In general, the number of intercorrelations is equal to (number of tests) $2 - 1$ divided by 2. The correlations are generally represented in a table called a *correlation matrix*. Table 6.2 provides an example of a correlation matrix. Note the triangular shape of the matrix reflecting the fact that redundant correlations are generally not entered, nor are the "1s" that reflect the correlation between the variable and itself. When working with multiple variables, it is often useful to construct a correlation matrix in order to look for patterns of relationships among variables; that is, clusters of variables that are highly correlated among

TABLE 6.2
Intercorrelations Among Age, Height, Weight, and Blood Pressure

|        | Age | Height | Weight | Blood Pressure |
|--------|-----|--------|--------|----------------|
| Age    | 1   | .85    | .78    | .63            |
| Height |     | 1      | .91    | .57            |
| Weight |     |        | 1      | .45            |
| BP     |     |        |        | 1              |

themselves, but not with other variables. In the case of large matrices, factor analysis, to be described, is often helpful.

The situation often arises in which it is thought that a combination of many factors may be contributing to a single outcome or criterion. The procedure for performing this kind of evaluation is called *multiple regression and correlation*. Instead of an *x* variable and a *y* variable, there are at least two *x* variables and one *y* variable. It is possible to compute regression equations and correlation coefficients for these situations, but the mathematics is far more complex than is the case for bivariate correlation. Using the example just mentioned, suppose we wanted to know the correlation between the combined effects of age, height, and weight on blood pressure. Age, height, and weight are then characterized as predictor or independent variables and blood pressure is called the criterion, or dependent variable. A multiple regression equation is written with the independent variables on the left hand side and the dependent variable on the right hand side. The correlation coefficient is called multiple $R$, or simply $R$. $R$ is not simply an additive function of the simple correlation coefficients but rather, reflects the interaction of the weights they contribute to the multiple regression equations. These weights, sometimes called *beta weights* or *partial regression coefficients*, are used in calculating $R$. It is also possible to compute individual predicted $Y$ scores from the regression equation. Some investigators use the so-called residual scores, or differences between actual and predicted scores, in their analyses. The major reason for their use is that when estimating scores from a regression equation, the accuracy of the estimate may depend on the location of the score on the distribution. Typically, extreme scores are estimated with relatively less accuracy. Before leaving this topic, it should be emphasized that although these multivariate procedures are quite powerful, they often require large numbers of subjects. As a general rule of thumb, a ratio of 10 subjects to one variable is desirable.

As indicated, two variables are sometimes correlated with one another within the context of both being correlated with a third variable. For example, two abilities may be correlated with one another because they are both correlated with general intelligence. The method used to evaluate this third variable effect is called *partial correlation*. Thus, one can compute the correlation between reading and mathematics ability, accounting for the variance associated with general intelligence. This third variable is called a *covariate* or a *control variable*. The coefficient derived from this process is called the *partial correlation coefficient*. It is an index of the strength of association between two variables following removal of the variance produced by a third variable. Partial correlation may be extended by utilizing several covariates. In the present example, one might want to use general intelligence and years of education as covariates. Partial correlation is particularly useful in behavioral research when one wants to account for variance contributed by some demographic variable. Thus age, education, and socioeconomic status are often used as covariates. The application of partial correlation is commonly seen in prospective or retrospective field studies when there is a need to adjust or correct the data for some demographic variable. For example, one may wish to attribute some characteristic to a particular diagnostic group, but subsequently find that the characteristic is sensitive to age, educational, or gender differences. It then becomes appropriate to use these variables as covariates in partial correlation analyses. As a rather dramatic example of the effects of such an analysis, Goldstein, Zubin, and Pogue-Geile (1991) studied the degree of association between length of hospitalization and cognitive decline in schizophrenic inpatients. They initially computed simple correlation coefficients and found many robust correlations between performance on cognitive tests and years of hospitalization. However, when they repeated these analyses using chronological age as a covariate, these robust relationships essentially disappeared and they had to conclude that there was no significant association between years of hospitalization and cognitive decline. However, as people remain hospitalized, they also get older, and it seems that advancing age was the key factor in producing the decline rather than institutionalization. In this case, the application of partial correlation helped to detract from the correctness of a hypothesis that had some support in the literature.

## STRUCTURAL EQUATION MODELING, PATH ANALYSIS, AND FACTOR ANALYSIS

In recent years, very sophisticated approaches have been taken to the problem of causality based on the structural equation modeling mathematics originally presented in Jöreskog (1979). The method of *path analysis* deals directly with the matter of causality. It is a mathematical method designed to assess the direct causal contribution of one variable to another. The output of a path analysis is a network diagram that contains an array of boxes representing the variables used in the study connected by two headed arrows on which the correlations between the variables are presented. A good example is found in a study by Burns and Eidelson (1998), in which the question of whether depression and anxiety share a common cause was investigated. Through a sophisticated correlational study in which path analysis was used, they concluded that depression and anxiety were phenomenologically distinct, but may share a common cause described as *negative affect*.

The most elegant and complex form of correlational analysis is a procedure called *factor analysis*. This correlational method is probably found in its most elegant form in psychometric research concerning relationships among abilities. Historically, this research began with the study of the structure of intelligence. At one time, there was a great debate over whether intelligence was a global ability or a series of separate functions. The scientific activity associated with this debate largely involved factor analytic methods, with the database consisting of subscales of intelligence and related mental ability tests. The names of Spearman, Burt, and Thurstone are most prominently associated with this movement.

Factor analysis is both an art and a science, and requires advanced training to master. It is rather commonly used now because of the general availability of statistical packages designed for use on high-speed computers, but interpretation of the output of these packages is often problematic for the individual who lacks appropriate training. As indicated, a correlation matrix can be inspected to see which correlation coefficients cluster together; that is, are correlated with each other but not with other clusters of correlations. For example, if we had a correlation matrix containing intelligence test subscales, one might note that the verbal tests are correlated with each other, but not with the performance tests, for which the reverse is true. Factor analysis is a formal method of doing this clustering. The mathematical procedures employed to do a factor analysis may be divided into two components: one to derive the factor matrix and the other that rotates the matrix to an interpretable structure. This distinction is important because there are numerous paradigms for doing the initial factoring as well as numerous methods of rotation. With some restrictions, it is possible to interchange initial factoring methods and rotation methods. Thus, factoring Method A may be used in combination with rotation Methods A, B or C. The investigator needs to choose one of each, and ideally, to provide some rationale for that choice.

The "bottom line" of a factor analysis for most behavioral science investigators is called the matrix of rotated factor loadings. A factor is what the mathematics of the method used determines to be a cluster of correlations, as already discussed. A *loading* is the correlation between an individual variable and the factor. The matrix of rotated factor loadings tells us how many meaningful factors were extracted, and what the loading pattern is. Ideally, the goal of rotation should be that of obtaining simple structure, or a matrix, in which the individual variables load on unique factors. A factor analysis solution, in which the same test loads substantially on several factors, is often not helpful, particularly when one is seeking the underlying dimensions of the series of measures under investigation. A good general introduction to factor analysis can be found in Rummel (1970).

Our ideas about the nature of factor analysis have changed in recent years. Methods have been developed for what is called *confirmatory factor analysis*, that allow for testing of specific hypotheses through factor analysis. Investigators now often make the distinction between exploratory and confirmatory factor analysis in describing their work. In contemporary behavioral investigation, factor analysis is mainly viewed as an exploratory procedure, to be followed by more specific experimental investigations. It is commonly used as a data reduction method when the investigator has an excessively large number of variables and has to make sense out of how they relate to each other. A large correlation matrix can be bewildering, and factoring can provide a much more coherent picture of the structure of the data. It is also possible to reduce the number of variables used in subsequent studies through factor analysis. The two most commonly used ways of doing this are to only use the variables with the highest loadings on each factor, or to use factor scores. *Factor scores* are the scores of each subject on each factor.

It is now widely accepted that exploratory factor analysis should be followed by further experimental study, but that one can learn more from the factor analytic procedure itself by using confirmatory factor analysis. This method is also based on structural equation modeling and is used to test specific hypotheses. It is used when something is already known about the data, usually based on exploratory analysis, and more information is desired about the relationship among the variables. Confirmatory factor analysis is used to discover the underlying or latent variables that explain the relationships among the observed variables. It is conducted by proposing a number of models for this latent structure and applying them to actual data. Statistics are available to assess the goodness-of-fit of the different models as applied to the data set. The best model is the one that has the best goodness-of-fit. As an example, Allen, Goldstein, and Mariano (1999) did a confirmatory analysis of the Halstead Category Test, a neuropsychological test of abstraction ability. After contrasting different models, they found that a three-factor model provided the best fit.

Our emphasis thus far has been on correlation of tests and other methods, but one can also correlate people. We do this naively when we say things like John is like Harry because they are both tall and have red hair. When we do this more formally, it is called *classification*: John and Harry have schizophrenia because they have delusions, hallucinations, bizarre language, and meet other criteria. Classification is based on similarities and differences, but may be accomplished in a variety of ways; for example, intuitively, using objective rules, or empirically. The two most widely used empirical methods are called $Q$ type factor analysis and cluster analysis. In either case, they can be thought of as factor analyses of people rather than tests. As in the case of factor analysis of tests, these methods are complex, and require special training to use. In the biological and behavioral sciences, cluster analysis has been widely used to develop subtypes of a disorder. Within any general disorder, there may be enough variability to infer that there are distinct, identifiable subgroups that have the disorder, but have it in varying forms. Cluster analysis, in particular, appears to be growing in popularity, apparently because of its growing availability in statistical computer packages.

Cluster analysis, like factor analysis, contains a number of paradigms, or mathematical methods of clustering. Although all the clustering methods are based in some way on similarity, the way in which the clusters are formed vary. There are also many methods for determining similarity, such as using the correlation coefficients or distance measures. The most popular method is called *Squared Euclidean Distance*. Cluster analyses generally proceed by going through the cases and grouping them by similarity, thereby creating a hierarchical treelike structure called a dendogram. Usually, a number of clusters or groupings of cases can be discerned on the dendogram, but there are also statistical methods available to aid in determining the number of clusters identified. This process is used to determine the internal validity of various proposed numbers of clusters. Internal validity is high when the clusters are clearly spatially separate. After that is accomplished, external validity is evaluated. It has to do with the relationship between pertinent variables not included in the cluster analysis, and is usually evaluated with analysis of variance, using cluster membership as the independent variable. For example, clusters may differ significantly in age or general intelligence. Ideally, they will differ with regard to some variable that is relevant to further understanding of the heterogeneity that exists in the sample. In clinical research, we generally want to obtain external validity with some relevant clinical criterion such as age of onset of illness or family history. Recently, cluster analysis has been extensively used in the areas of identifying subtypes of learning disability (Fletcher & Satz, 1985), and understanding the cognitive heterogeneity found in schizophrenia (Seaton, Goldstein, & Allen, 2001).

## CORRELATION AND CAUSATION

Probably the most controversial issue involved in correlational data analysis has to do with the matter of causality. There is a commonly stated dogma that correlation is not causation. Because the correlation coefficient relating $A$ to $B$ is high, that does not mean that $A$ causes $B$. The reasons for absence of causality may be simple co-occurrence of phenomena with no actual cause-and-effect relationship, or the presence of a third variable that is correlated with the two variables under study, but that is the real causal variable. For example, loss of teeth may be correlated with slowing of gait, but it might seem apparent that one does not cause the other. It seems more likely that the high correlation coefficient occurs because both variables are correlated with age. It may be recalled that this issue became particularly controversial during the time of early research on cigarette smoking and cancer. Despite the high correlations found, it was nevertheless argued by some that smoking was not the cause of cancer. The argument was based on the considerations just raised. Either smoking and cancer frequently co-occurred in the same people, without evidence of a direct cause and effect relationship, or alternatively, that both the inclination to smoke and cancer were actually caused by a third, unknown variable. Thus, many scientists view correlational research as merely descriptive in nature, and definitive, causative findings must await specification of clearly defined independent and dependent variables followed by experimental interventions.

It is noted that independent and dependent variables are often not specified in correlational research. They may be either implied but not specified, or the investigator may simply be seeking relationships among phenomena without any need for specification. In this regard, a distinction may be made between what may be termed transitive and intransitive correlation. In transitive correlation, the relationship between two variables is reciprocal. One cannot say that one is the independent and the other the dependent variable, nor can it be reasonably stated that one variable is the cause and the other the effect. The correlation between abilities would be an example of a *transitive relationship*. Because mathematical and reading abilities are highly correlated cannot be interpreted to mean that one ability caused the performance level of the other. They both, in fact, may have been caused by other considerations such as quality of education or general intelligence. But if one considers the correlation between size the of a wheat crop and amount of rainfall, no reasonable person would argue that wheat growing causes it to rain. Thus, the relation between correlation and causation would appear to resolve to logical analysis specifying independent and dependent variables, or the lack of pertinence of that distinction to the matter under study. For example, in exploratory factor analysis, there is typically no interest at all in independent and dependent variables, because the purpose of the analysis is purely that of seeking relationships among variables. In summary, although one should not naively assume that correlation implies causation, neither should one naively assume that it does not imply causation. The mathematics of correlation are neutral to the matter of causality, and the issue can only be dealt with through logical analysis of the variables under consideration, particularly with regard to their transitive or nontransitive relationship. However, the methods coming from structural equation modeling may allow us to deal with the issue of causality directly from the data analysis.

## CORRELATION IN BEHAVIORAL RESEARCH

The two most extensive areas of correlational research in the behavioral sciences are in psychometrics and epidemiology. *Psychometrics* is the branch of behavioral science that has to do with the development and application of objective assessment and evaluation procedures. *Psychiatric epidemiology* technically deals with the incidence and prevalence of mental disorders, but is actually a broader field that does community and cross-cultural longitudinal and cross-sectional studies of mental illness. Both of these fields make extensive use of correlational methods, but in different ways.

### Psychometrics

There are three major applications of correlational statistics in psychometrics. They are determination of reliability, validity, and interrelationships among tests or test items. *Validity* is the appropriateness of a test for the purpose for which it is used. Tests may be used for classification, prediction of future performance or, in clinical contexts, as an aid to diagnosis and prognosis. The extent to which they perform these functions well is referred to as their validity. Validity is generally established by correlating scores from the test under scrutiny with what is referred to as a criterion. A *criterion* is a quantified measure of the outcome that the test is purported to predict. Within the context of psychiatric research, the criterion used is frequently expert clinical judgment. Depending on the level of sophistication of the psychometric research being accomplished, varying criteria may be established for the reliability of those judgments. For example, a stringent criterion might be complete agreement on the judgment among three board-certified psychiatrists. Many psychological tests such as the Minnesota Multiphasic Personality Inventory-2 (MMPI-2; Butcher, Graham, Dahlstrom, Tellegen & Kaemmer, 1989) have been validated against clinical judgments of this type. In this case, what we obtain is called concurrent validity, or the ability of the test to predict to a contemporary criterion. Another type of criterion-related validity is called *predictive validity*. Tests are often used to predict future performance, such as level of functioning on a job or treatment outcome. In this case, there must be a waiting period between administration of the test and acquisition of the outcome information that is used as a criterion. In both concurrent and predictive validity establishment, a validity coefficient, which is in fact a correlation coefficient, is typically computed in order to determine the degree of association between the test scores and the criterion ratings. Low coefficients suggest that the test is not suitable for the purpose for which it is being used. There is no hard and fast rule for determining acceptability of a validity coefficient, but we are generally impressed when they get into the .8 to .9 range, and unimpressed when they are less than about .6.

Reliability has to do with the stability or consistency of an instrument. The concept of *reliability* cannot be intuited as readily as that of validity, probably because the stability of instruments we use clinically on a routine basis is assumed. However, imagine a thermometer that gave readings that were different over the course of a day even though evidence was available that the patient's temperature had not changed at all. What we would have is an unreliable thermometer, and we would probably discard it. In the case of psychometric procedures, the problem is that it is not scientifically justifiable to presume that a new psychological test is a stable measuring instrument that provides consistent data. Part of test development always includes a determination of degree of stability. That procedure is referred to as *establishing the reliability of the test*.

In psychometrics, there is a distinction between two types of reliability, both of which are assessed with the correlation coefficient. The first type is *internal consistency* and the other is *repeatability*. A test typically consists of numerous items that are thought to measure some trait or other dimension. If it does so reliably, then various alternate or parallel forms of the test should agree with each other. Within the framework of our present discussion, we mean that the scores should be highly correlated with each other. Thus, one method of determining reliability involves administering both alternate forms to the same group of individuals and computing the correlation coefficient between the two sets of scores. If alternate forms are not available, the single test itself can be split in half and the odd numbered items can be correlated with the even numbered items. Determining reliability in this manner provides information concerning the internal consistency of the test. A statistic called Cronbach's alpha (Cronbach, 1951) is now commonly used to index internal consistency rather than a regular correlation coefficient.

The matter of repeatability comes closer to the thermometer example. If the subject does not change, then we would want a measure to provide about the same scores over numerous testing occasions. This kind of evaluation is done with what is called the test–retest reliability method. It simply involves giving the same subjects the same test on at least two occasions, and computing correlations between the scores obtained the first time with those obtained the second time. This method, although commonly used, is somewhat hazardous. First of all, retesting often produces a "practice effect," such that the subject may improve on the second testing as a result of experience with the first testing. This problem is somewhat attenuated by the fact that the mathematics of correlation are based mainly on the relative rankings of scores, and as long as the rankings remain stable across testing occasions, the correlation should not be greatly affected. Thus, it is possible that the average score for the group may be substantially higher on the second testing occasion than it was on the first, but the correlation coefficient may nevertheless be quite high. In clinical situations the test–retest method is often not applicable because of the high probability of there being rapid fluctuations in the conditions of patients. The test–retest method really depends on sampling in a stable population.

The common wisdom is that there cannot be validity without reliability, because an unstable procedure cannot predict accurately to any criterion. It is nevertheless quite possible to have satisfactory reliability without validity. If one used the bull's-eye of a target as an analogy for the criterion, one could consistently hit some precise area time after time, but that area may be quite distant from the bull's-eye. As in the case of validity, there is no commonly accepted single value for determining whether a reliability coefficient is satisfactory or not. However, there is a helpful statistic in psychometrics called the *probable error of measurement*. Without going into detail, it is generally assumed that there is some error in testing so that a single test score is viewed as a point in a range of scores. That range is a function of the test's reliability. Thus, changes in test scores may reflect actual change in the subject or chance fluctuations within the probable error of measurement. Reliability is considered to be unsatisfactory to the extent that the probability of error of measurement of the score of a single subject ranges over an entire distribution of scores.

### Reliability of Judgment

Here we consider the situation in which decisions are reached not by administering quantitative tests but through the process of clinical judgment. From the point of view of quantification, clinical judgments are different from tests in that they constitute nominal rather than metric scales. That is, a phenomenon is said to be present or absent, and the clinician is, in essence, the test. The role of correlation in this context is frequently that of assessing the reliability of these judgments. Reliability of clinical judgment may be evaluated by having a clinician make nominal judgments concerning the same case over several occasions, by having a clinician make judgments and then contrasting them with nominal judgments made by a procedure different from clinical judgment, or by contrasting the clinical judgments made by more than one clinician concerning the same case, assuming that these judgments are made independently. In psychiatry, the third alternative is the most commonly used one. We therefore take examples from those kinds of comparisons, and try to show that the evaluation procedure used is quite comparable to procedures used in determining the reliability of quantitative tests.

Most of us are familiar with the problem of the reliability of psychiatric diagnosis, and with the major effort made by the science and profession of psychiatry to improve that reliability, leading ultimately to the development of the objective diagnostic criteria codified in the Diagnostic and Statistical Manual of Mental Disorders (DSM-IV; American Psychiatric Association [APA], 1994). Because there are few objective criteria for most of the mental disorders, in the sense of definitive laboratory or related biological indicators, the emphasis was placed on the application of structured clinical interviews, and the extent of agreement among clinicians on conclusions reached on the basis of these interviews. It is noted that the interviews were typically not used as psychological tests yielding quantitative scores, but rather as procedures used

TABLE 6.3
A Kappa Table

|  |  | Schizophrenic | Nonschizophrenic |
|---|---|---|---|
| Judge 1 |  |  |  |
|  | Schizophrenic | 12 | 4 |
| Judge 2 |  |  |  |
|  | Nonschizophrenic | 2 | 12 |

to aid clinical judgment. Thus, the representative research study was one in which two or more clinicians independently interviewed the same patients and made judgments concerning their diagnoses. As Cohen (1960) pointed out, it then becomes possible to view the clinicians as analogous to alternate forms, and the judgments as analogous to test scores. The statistical problem then becomes quite similar to what is involved in determining the reliability of psychological tests. The major difference is in the nature of the data, which is on a metric scale in the case of psychological tests and on a nominal scale in the case of clinical judgment.

Let us begin with the simplest possible case to develop an example: Two clinicians make independent judgments concerning the presence or absence of a single diagnosis. How well do they agree with one another (i.e., what is their interjudge reliability?) Let us say that they both independently interviewed 30 patients, and had to judge whether or not these patients had schizophrenia. Their data can be cast in a 2 × 2 contingency table (Table 6.3). Note that the agreements are on one diagonal and the disagreements are on the other. There is 80% agreement (24/30). Does that figure constitute satisfactory reliability? In order to answer that question, the first matter to consider is that some of the agreement could have occurred by chance. In this case, the judges would agree with each other by chance half the time. Is 80% significantly better than 50%?

As simple as the question may seem, no statistic was generally available to answer the question until the statistician Jacob Cohen (1960) published a paper describing a statistic called *kappa*. Those familiar with contingency tables might suggest that chi-square would be the appropriate statistic for determining significance, and that the chi-square related correlation coefficients, the phi or contingency $C$ coefficients, would be the appropriate reliability coefficients. However, Cohen pointed out that chi-square tests for association, not agreement. Indeed, it would be possible to obtain a highly significant chi-square if there were complete disagreement between the judges. A statistic was needed that dealt with only the values along the agreement diagonal, testing the null hypothesis that the obtained proportions of agreement could have occurred by chance. Kappa is computed with the following equation. That is, it is equal to the number of agreements obtained subtracted from the number of agreements that

$$k = \frac{fo - fc}{1 - fc}$$

would be obtained by chance divided by 1 minus the number of agreements that would be obtained by chance. Kappa may range from 0 to 1, with 1 representing perfect agreement. The hypothesis that an obtained kappa is significantly different from zero may be obtained by converting kappa to a $z$ score and referring to a normal distribution table. Testing for the significance of a difference between two kappas can be accomplished in a similar manner. Kappa can be generalized beyond the $2 \times 2$ table situation. Various elaborations of kappa, including a weighted kappa in which seriousness of disagreement can be quantified, is presented in Fleiss (1981).

As in the case of the correlation coefficient, the finding that kappa is significantly different from zero is often trivial, because such significance can occur in the presence of substantial disagreement. Citing a study of Landis and Koch (1977), Fleiss presents a rating scale for kappas in which values above .75 reflect excellent agreement; values below .40 represent poor agreement and values in between represent fair to good agreement exceeding chance expectation.

## Epidemiology

As Bromet, Davies, and Schulz (1988) illustrated, psychiatric epidemiology is not restricted to rate estimation. In addition to that area of investigation, which they term *descriptive epidemiology*, there is also an analytic and experimental epidemiology. *Analytic epidemiology*, with which we are mainly concerned here, includes case control, longitudinal, and prospective studies. It is largely concerned with causes of rate differences in different groups, and so looks at risk factors, the natural history of various disorders, the role of environmental factors, and prediction of outcome. Implicitly or explicitly, much of this research is correlational in nature. A typical clinical research design in psychology or psychiatry may have a group comparison component, generally based on diagnosis, but once the groups are established, the remainder of the procedure is correlational in nature. Chapter 5 and chapter 6 of Fleiss (1981) provide information concerning specific statistical methods that are useful in naturalistic, prospective, and retrospective studies.

Let us use a risk study as a simple example. What is the risk of developing schizophrenia if one has a schizophrenic parent? As in examples already used above, we can cast the data in a $2 \times 2$ contingency table as follows (Table 6.4). It will be noted that 12 of the 26 schizophrenics had schizophrenic parents,

TABLE 6.4
Schizophrenic Parent

|                 |     | Yes | No |
| --------------- | --- | --- | -- |
|                 | Yes | 12  | 14 |
| Schizophrenic   |     |     |    |
|                 | No  | 8   | 16 |

8 of the 24 nonschizophrenics had schizophrenic parents, and the remaining 16 did not have schizophrenic parents. It would be appropriate to use the phi coefficient in this case as the measure of association. However, Fleiss (1981) described a statistic that is a measure of association but is more meaningful in risk research. It is called the *odds ratio*, and provides an estimate of the probability that B will occur when A is present and when A is absent. In this case, we would have the odds of there being a schizophrenic offspring when there was a schizophrenic parent. Information in this form may be more useful to the investigator than it would be in the form of a correlation coefficient.

Zigler and Glick (1986) utilized correlational evidence quite extensively in their work on the relationship between premorbid competence and psychiatric hospitalization. In one analysis, they tested the hypothesis that more competent individuals, as measured by a scale they developed, would be hospitalized at a later age than would less competent individuals. They correlated age at first hospitalization with score on the competence test and obtained correlation coefficients that were somewhat consistent with the hypothesis. They also factor analyzed their premorbid competence scale, finding that it was multifactorial rather than based on a single dimension. Three factors were identified: one representing education and occupation, the second received high loadings only from age and marital status, and the third reflected employment history.

A matter of particular interest in clinical research is prognosis, or prediction of outcome. In prospective studies designed to evaluate accuracy of prediction, a mixed design is often devised in which both group comparison and correlational methods are used. The groups may be divided along numerous dimensions, but perhaps diagnostic or treatment variables are used most often. In the case of treatment research, the question may involve either comparisons of different treatments or simply an active treatment against a placebo control. The specific treatment effect may be directly evaluated with group comparison statistics, but components of the study that may be characterized as more "epidemiological" in nature would involve correlational statistics. For example, in many treatment studies, although the active treatment group may have improved relative to the control group, not all of the patients in that group get better, or some patients do not improve as much as others. If pertinent demographic, diagnostic, and other clinical data are collected, then it is possible to correlate these data with outcome. Such questions as to whether age is associated with treatment response, or whether women improve more than men, or whether a particular laboratory finding is associated with outcome may be answered in this manner. These analyses aid in refining the findings and in specification of those individuals for whom the treatment is most promising.

Sometimes the investigator is simply interested in prediction from baseline data to outcome. Such questions as "What patient characteristics are most predictive of outcome following treatment for depression?" are typical of those asked in this type of research. The most direct way of answering this question is by the method already described of obtaining the predictive validity of tests. Here, the tests are replaced by the baseline measures, and the criteria are measures of outcome, which are obtained sometime after the baseline period. In many instances, univariate predictors are not adequate, but it is possible to use multiple predictors by applying multiple regression and correlation methods if enough subjects are available. Sometimes outcome is also complex, and cannot be sufficiently captured by one variable. For example, relief from symptoms, return to work, and improved family relations may all be outcomes of some treatment. While separate regression equations could be computed for each criterion, a more elegant way of analyzing the data would be to employ an advanced statistical procedure called *canonical correlation*. Canonical correlation permits more than one variable on both the left- and right-hand sides of the multiple regression equation, thereby allowing for associating multiple predictors with multiple criteria.

Outcome is sometimes conceptualized as change on the same measure. Such a conceptualization is extremely common in treatment research. Treatment with a nutritional supplement may change blood count; treatment with a neuroleptic may change the Brief Psychiatric Rating Scale score, etcetra. It may appear that change can be directly evaluated by taking the difference between a measure taken on the first occasion and measures taken on subsequent occasions. Although that is sometimes true, it is unfortunately not always true; the basic reason is that not all phenomena lie on equal interval scales. Probably the best way to illustrate this point is with an athletic example. An accomplished runner may set a new world record on the basis of a fraction of a sec, while an amateur runner may improve running time by several sec over many occasions without the same significance. Running times are therefore not on an equal interval scale. At the extreme limit of human performance, changes of fractions of a second appear to require substantially more ability and effort than do changes at less extreme points in the range of performance. Some time ago Lacey (1956), making the same observation in the case of psychophysiological measurements, characterized this phenomenon in a general way as the "law of initial values." How then do we evaluate change if the significance of a particular magnitude of change varies with the point on the scale at which it lies? A commonly used procedure is sometimes called *correction for baseline* and involves the use of correlation. More specifically, it involves the regression equation relating initial values to values obtained on subsequent occasions. Taking a two-occasion example, we can solve a regression equation and compute a correlation coefficient by relating the scores of a sample on the first occasion to their scores on the second occasion. The regression equation allows us to predict second occasion $y$ scores from performance on the first occasion $x$ scores, as we have discussed previously. We then compare this predicted score with the score actually obtained, and take the difference between them. This difference is known as a *residual change score*. Large residual change scores mean that the subject has changed substantially beyond what would be predicted for an individual with his or her initial level. Small residual change scores mean the opposite, and any change obtained is not much different from what would be predicted from initial performance. Thus, we have factored initial performance out reasonably well, and obtain a purer measure of meaningful change through the use of correlation and regression.

## A CLASSICAL SERIES OF CORRELATIONAL STUDIES

Perhaps one of the more exciting areas of correlational research has involved the factor analytic studies of the structure of higher brain function. The beginnings of this research began with Ward Halstead (1947), who published the first factor analysis of a series of what are now referred to as neuropsychological tests. These tests were shown to be sensitive to brain dysfunction, and the question became one of what abilities they measure. Halstead's factor analysis contained four factors that he termed *central integrative field, abstraction, power,* and *directional*. It is generally agreed that in more familiar terminology, these factors are *memory, abstract reasoning, attention,* and a number of *perceptual and motor skills*, probably including language. As a whole, they constituted what Halstead called *biological intelligence*, basically meaning abilities that assured adaptation to the environment. This seminal work was the first effort made to provide an empirically, quantitatively based organization of higher brain function.

Halstead's factor analysis was accomplished before the era of high-speed computers and was based on a rather small sample. However, over many years, up to quite recently, efforts have been made to repeat that factor analysis with reasonably good replication. Using modern technology, more sophisticated mathematics, and large samples, investigators typically arrived at four factor solutions that could be described as *memory, abstraction, attention,* and *perceptual and motor skill factors*. The factor structure has held up in samples of neuropsychiatric patients, and patients with alcoholism (Goldstein & Shelly, 1971, 1972). A confirmatory factor analysis was done with a modified battery (Newby, Hallenbeck, & Embretson, 1983). Although this study was aimed at comparing different models, the authors concluded that a conceptual scheme of receptive and expressive, memory, and cognitive processes can be developed into a relatively well-fitting model. Their terminology seems relatively equivalent to the original memory, abstraction, and directional factors. These studies are of importance because they illustrate how factor analytic investigation has the potential of providing a structural organization of abilities that held up over many years, in several settings, and with different populations.

## SUMMARY AND FUTURE DIRECTIONS

In this chapter, we introduced some basic concepts of regression and correlation, and have provided some illustrations of how these methods are typically applied in behavioral research. We took illustrations from psychometrics and from descriptive, epidemiological studies in the behavioral sciences, but regression and correlation were used in essentially all applications of statistical methods. It should be emphasized that although the term, *correlational research*, has some connotations of being merely descriptive, exploratory, and preliminary, probably more often than not, correlational methods are used in combination with group comparison, experimental studies. Sometimes a stated preference for "experimental" rather than "correlational" studies may be based on some degree of mathematical naiveté. For example, one may compare two groups on some measure and determine whether or not their means differ significantly from each other using a student's $t$ test or some similar group difference statistic. If they are not significantly different from each other, that probably means that the scores obtained by one group are reasonably highly correlated with the scores of the second group. A correlation coefficient can be computed from precisely the same data that were evaluated by the $t$ test. The point is that the use of correlational statistics should not produce the assumption that the research being done is preliminary, exploratory, or purely descriptive.

As specialized fields in statistics develop, they tend to become increasingly mathematically complex. That appears to be the case in correlation and regression, but we should nevertheless point out that this area has not been completed and research producing new methods is still being actively conducted. Furthermore, there are outstanding needs for new developments that are only in their early stages. For example, there is a great need for methods that can deal with multivariate analysis of nonlinear relationships.

In conclusion, correlation and regression are important statistical tools that are applicable in a variety of research settings. It is probably inappropriate to think of their use as restricted to a particular type of research that is generally characterized as descriptive, naturalistic, hypothesis-seeking, or preliminary. The mathematics of correlation and regression are neutral to the kind of research in which the investigator is interested. Furthermore, new developments in this mathematics are changing our previously held views of correlation.

## REFERENCES

Allen, D. N., Goldstein, G., & Mariano, E. (1999). Is the Halstead Category Test a multidimensional instrument? *Journal of Clinical and Experimental Neuropsychology, 21*, 1–8.

American Psychiatric Association. (1994). *Diagnostic and statistical manual of mental disorders (DSM-IV)*. Washington DC: Author.

Bromet, E. J., Davies, M., & Schulz, S. C. (1988). Basic principles of epidemiologic research in schizophrenia. In H. A. Nasrallah (Ed.), *Handbook of schizophrenia, Volume 3*. (pp. 151–168). Amsterdam: Elsevier.

Burns, D. D., & Eidelson, R. J. (1998). Why are depression and anxiety correlated? A test of the tripartite model. *Journal of Consulting and Clinical Psychology, 66*, 461–473.

Butcher, J. N., Graham, J. R., Dahlstrom, W. G., Tellegen, A. M., & Kaemmer, B. (1989). *MMPI-2 manual for administration and scoring*. Minneapolis: University of Minnesota Press.

Cohen, J. (1960). A coefficient of agreement for nominal scales. *Educational and Psychological Measurement, 20*, 37–46.

Cronbach, L. J. (1951). Coefficient alpha and the internal structure of tests. *Psychometrika, 16*, 297–334.

Fleiss, J. L. (1981). *Statistical methods for rates and proportions, Second Edition*. New York: Wiley.

Fletcher, J. M., & Satz, P. (1985). Cluster analysis and the search for learning disability subtypes. In B. P. Rourke (Ed.), *Neuropsychology of learning disabilities* (pp. 40–64) New York: Guilford Press.

Goldstein, G., & Shelly, C. H. (1971). Field dependency and cognitive, perceptual and motor skills in alcoholics: A factor-analytic study. *Quarterly Journal of Studies on Alcohol, 32*, 29–40.

Goldstein, G., & Shelly, C. H. (1972). Statistical and normative studies of the Halstead Neuropsychological Test Battery relevant to a neuropsychiatric hospital setting. *Perceptual and Motor Skills, 34*, 603–620.

Goldstein G., Zubin J., & Pogue-Geile, M. F. (1991). Hospitalization and the cognitive deficits of schizophrenia: The influences of age and education. *Journal of Nervous and Mental Disease, 179*, 202–206.

Halstead, W. C. (1947). *Brain and intelligence*. Chicago: University of Chicago Press.

Joreskog, K. G. (1979). *Advances in factor analysis and structural equation models*. Cambridge MA: Abt Books.

Lacey, J. I. (1956). The evaluation of autonomic responses: Toward a general solution. *Annals of the New York Academy of Science, 67*, 123–164.

Landis, J. R., & Koch, G. G. (1977). The measurement of observer agreement for categorical data. *Biometrics, 33*, 671–679.

Newby, R. F., Hallenbeck, C. E., & Embretson, S. (1983). Confirmatory factor analysis of four general neuropsychological models with a modified Halstead-Reitan battery. *Journal of Clinical Neuropsychology, 5*, 115–134.

Rosner, B. (1990). *Fundamentals of biostatistics*. Boston: PWS-Kent.

Rummel, R. J. (1970). *Applied factor analysis*. Evanston IL: Northwestern University Press.

Seaton, B. E., Goldstein, G., & Allen, D. N. (2001). Sources of heterogeneity in schizophrenia: The role or neuropsychological functioning. *Neuropsychology Review, 11*, 45–67.

Zigler, E., & Glick, M. (1986). *A developmental approach to adult psychopathology*. New York: Wiley.

# 7

# Single Subject Designs

Kurt A. Freeman
*Pacific University, Portland, Oregon*

As is evidenced by the adoption of the scientist-practitioner or local clinical-scientist models by graduate programs in clinical and counseling psychology, it is clear that the role of research is vitally important in graduate training. Thus, whether planning a career as a researcher or a practitioner, graduate students are expected to gain an understanding of, and an appreciation for, research methodology. Further, as both beginning graduate students and seasoned researchers are aware, the goal of scientific inquiry is to help understand the phenomena of interest in more precise, complete terms. Related to the topic of the present volume, this general goal translates into scientific inquiry that elucidates the conditions resulting in human distress, as well as the methods by which that distress can be alleviated. In other words, research methodologies should assist in understanding the cause–effect relationships between various life events and situations and the clinical phenomena with which clients present. Such an understanding can be developed either via group or single subject design methodologies, depending on the particular questions of interest and constraints present. This chapter focuses on the latter methodologies.

The primary goal of this chapter, therefore, is to provide the reader with a discussion of single subject experimental designs. Specifically, an introduction to the various single-subject designs (SSDs) currently described and utilized is provided in terms of the processes involved in their utilization, as well as the benefits and weaknesses of each. This chapter also includes discussion of SSDs in both the context of psychological research that forwards our understanding of human behavior and the treatment of problems that arise, as well as in guiding clinical practice.

## USES AND MISUSES OF SINGLE SUBJECT DESIGNS

Both historically and currently, SSDs are often considered synonymous with behaviorism, behavior therapy, and behavior analysis. In fact, Yates (1970) put forth that behavior therapy is defined in relation to the single-subject methodology. Further, within both the basic and applied branches of behavior analysis (a particular subdiscipline of behavioral psychology based on Skinner's philosophy of radical behaviorism), researchers almost exclusively rely on the use of single-subject methodologies in their practices, as a quick perusal of any issue of journals devoted to these issues demonstrates (e.g., *Journal of the Experimental Analysis of Behavior, Journal of Applied Behavior Analysis*).

However, although typically linked to behavioral subdisciplines of psychology, there is nothing inherent in single-subject methodologies that preclude their use by researchers and clinicians who operate from other perspectives. In fact, examples of the use of single-subject methodologies can be found in numerous fields, including social work (Kazi, Mantysaari, & Rostila, 1997; Nugent, 1992), education (Scruggs, Mastropieri, Cook, & Escobar, 1986), and cognitive rehabilitation following brain insult (Benedict & Wechsler, 1992; Evans, Emslie, & Wilson, 1998), for example. Such widespread and diverse use of these methodologies attests to their utility. Further, there have been numerous calls for increased use of SSDs in various aspects of psychology, including sports psychology (Hrycaiko & Martin, 1996), rehabilitation psychology (Aeschleman, 1991), and counseling (Lundervold & Belwood, 2000), and across various disciplines, including occupational therapy (Campbell, 1988), pharmacology (Cook, 1996), and even zoo research (Saudargas & Drummer, 1996), just to name a few. Clearly, then, an understanding of SSDs is important for graduate trainings starting their careers within clinical or counseling psychology, regardless of theoretical orientation.

Despite the apparent recognized utility of such designs across diverse fields within and outside of psychology, there remain multiple misconceptions and myths about their strengths and weaknesses (Aeschelman, 1991). These misconceptions likely produce two outcomes: (a) continued assumptions that these research methodologies are useful only if one is operating from a strictly behavioral paradigm, and (b) assumptions that SSDs are not as scientifically rigorous as group research methodologies. First, Aeschelman (1991) suggested that many people consider single-subject methodologies to be synonymous with case studies. However, such an assumption about the similarity between the two suggests naiveté in one's understanding of the methodologies. Case studies in psychology typically are considered to be in-depth analyses of a particular person, facilitating clinical case formulation based on hypotheses about the causal variables in a client's presentation but not necessarily scientifically analyzing cause–effect relationships. In contrast, SSDs involve direct manipulation of important (potentially) causal variables to determine their effect on the particular phenomena of interest. Thus, the latter methodology involves a scientifically rigorous approach to analyzing human behavior. Although there exists similarity between the two approaches (i.e., both involve in-depth analysis that includes observation over time), the difference in methodological rigor between them makes it impossible to consider them as synonymous. Further, case studies typically rely on the analysis of qualitative data, whereas single subject research designs rely on quantitative data (Hilliard, 1993).

Considering SSDs to be synonymous with case studies results in the view that the former lacks internal validity (Aeschelman, 1991). Although case studies are accurately rejected on scientific grounds because of concerns regarding poor internal validity, with perhaps the exception of one design (the simple A–B design soon discussed), SSDs do in fact control for threats to internal validity in a variety of ways. Specifically, through use of repeated measurement of behavior across time, repeated demonstrations of the impact of independent variables, and intra- and interparticipant comparison, single-subject methodologies control for threats to internal validity such as maturation and history effects, for example. Extraneous variables that threaten internal validity are assumed to be constant across baseline and treatment conditions, and thus any notable differences across the conditions can be attributed to the independent variable. Together, these factors provide adequate protection against threats of internal validity in a manner that is just as effective as group-design methodologies.

A second common misconception of SSDs described by Aeschleman (1991) is that these designs lack external validity. In other words, some individuals hold the assumption that, because single subject research analyses involve a relatively small number of participants (often only one or a few people) the results are not applicable to a larger population. However, this assumption rests on the premise that a prerequisite of generality is the use of random sampling to select participants. Although a means of addressing generality, random sampling is by no means the only method. Further, most group design research fails to use true/comprehensive random sampling and thus suggesting this, as an argument against the use of SSDs, would also provide the argument against most group design research.

SSDs do, however, address external validity through two types of replication: direct and systematic (Sidman, 1960). *Direct replication* is accomplished by demonstrating the impact of the independent variable across participants with similar characteristics. As the number of replications of the impact increases across participants, the extent of generality is identified (McReynolds &

Thompson, 1986). *Systematic replication*, or replication that involves varying some aspect of the original experimental conditions, is also used to address external validity. Thus, using single subject methodologies to demonstrate replication of treatment effects across clinical disorders, settings, clinicians, and so forth allows for the assessment of the extent to which the findings are externally valid.

Third, SSDs are often erroneously considered to be appropriate only for research in the area of behavior modification (Aeschelman, 1991). As has been previously mentioned, however, there is nothing inherent in the designs that such need be the case. In other words, these methodologies are not constrained by psychological theory. Rather, the primary constraint is that there must be a dependent variable that can be measured repeatedly. If an investigator can satisfy this requirement, then the use of a SSD is theoretically possible, regardless of the particular paradigm of psychology from which the psychologist operates.

Finally, Aeschelman (1991) pointed out that SSDs are misperceived as not being scholarly. He suggested that this is due primarily to the fact that investigators utilizing SSDs typically rely on visual inspection as the mode of analysis, rather than statistical analysis. Without debating the relative merits of this argument, during the past 20 years, there has been increasing use of statistical analysis in the interpretation of data gathered via single subject research (Foster, Jarema, & Poling, 1999).

## CHARACTERISTICS OF SINGLE-SUBJECT RESEARCH DESIGNS

When evaluated from a group design perspective, SSDs may be considered limited in scope and application, or even meaningless. For example, as already mentioned above, it has been argued that single subject designs are limited in terms of internal and external validity (Aeschleman, 1991). However, such concerns are grounded in the group design perspective, and taking such an approach may be misleading (Hilliard, 1993). In order to appreciate the complexity and utility of the various SSDs, it is important that one understand their fundamental premises and characteristics.

### Single Subject Research as Intrasubject Research

Hilliard (1993) distinguished between two types of research—intersubject (variation across subjects) and intrasubject (variation within subjects). Single subject research can best be viewed as primarily (although not exclusively) the latter. In other words, use of single subject methodologies within a research paradigm involves an avoidance of aggregation of obtained data across cases and instead is based primarily on demonstrating experimental control through replication of the impact of an independent variable on a case-by-case basis.

As such, the participant serves as his or her own control and performance is compared across different conditions.

Given the focus on intrasubject variability as the primary issue of importance, SSDs are particularly relevant for psychotherapy research (Hilliard, 1993). Typically, psychotherapy involves repeated interactions between the therapist and client as a means of producing change. Further, there is typically a period of assessment in which the therapist learns about the client's presenting problems (analogous to the baseline period in research scenarios) and treatment, during which the therapist creates certain conditions in an effort to produce change in the client's presenting problem. Like the SSD, psychotherapy as a process allows for comparison across conditions. In this way, the focus on intrasubject variability, which is at the center of SSDs, is directly applicable to process-oriented psychotherapy research. As Hilliard (1993) stated, "the term *process* implies the temporal unfolding of variables within therapeutic dyads" (p. 374). Thus, for investigators interested in understanding the influence of particular variables as causal mechanisms of change within psychotherapy, SSDs may be important as methodologies.

### Repeated Observation of Phenomena of Interest

SSDs share in common repeated observation of the phenomena of interest across time under standard conditions (Holcome, Wolery, & Gast, 1994). Specifically, measurement of the dependent variable occurs multiple times, across at least two separate conditions, which are usually referred to as *baseline* and *intervention*. Such a method of data collection is based on the assumption that to determine whether the dependent variable differs from one condition to the next requires an observation of the multiple data points within each condition.

Within the framework of behavior analytic research, the dependent measure utilized typically is some form of observable behavioral phenomena. One may observe the aggressive behavior of a young child, the smoking behavior of an adult, or the duration of crying by a depressed client—all of which are examples of overt behavior observable to another individual. However, as discussed, there is nothing inherent within the SSDs that require the independent variable be of such form. End products (e.g., weight loss), scores on questionnaires (e.g., obtained scores on the Beck Depression Inventory), or subjective ratings (e.g., measurements of anxiety using the Subjective Units of Distress Scale) could be repeatedly obtained within single-subject research, thus allowing for inferences regarding the impact of the independent variable. In fact, multiple examples abound regarding the use of various types of dependent measures within a single-subject research paradigm (e.g., Glicksohn, Gvirtsman, & Offer, 1997; Nugent, 1992).

## Replication of the Experimental Effect

In order to fully demonstrate adequate internal validity, SSDs (again with the exception of the simple A–B design) set as the standard repeated demonstration of the impact of the independent variable as the measure of experimental control. Support for the interpretation of the independent variable as the cause of the change in the dependent variable increases each time that it is demonstrated that the latter changes as a function of a change in the former. Because of this, then, each participant in single-subject research is repeatedly exposed to baseline and treatment conditions. This is in stark contrast to the most common group design used in psychological research—the between groups design. In the between groups design, the experimenter compares the aggregate level of the dependent variable(s) across at least two groups: the comparison group, which is not exposed to the independent variable, and the treatment group, which is. In such a design, the experimenter rarely introduces, withdraws, and reintroduces the independent variable while obtaining measurement of the dependent variable across conditions. Instead, there is reliance on statistical analysis to determine whether the obtained difference would occur by chance versus as a result of the treatment.

## Changing One Variable at a Time

Another essential tenet of SSDs is that only one variable should be altered at a time when moving from one phase of the experiment to the next (Barlow & Hersen, 1984; Hersen, 1982). For example, if a researcher were determining effective interventions for treating nocturnal enuresis, the investigator would want to introduce only one intervention (e.g., the urine alarm) at the start of the treatment phase. If more than one variable is changed, then it becomes impossible to determine which variable is the operative one in terms of producing any change in the dependent variable. Continuing this example, using two strategies such as decreasing evening fluid intake and introducing a particular behavioral intervention (e.g., the urine alarm) at the same time would result in a situation in which it would be impossible to determine which produced any noted improvements that occur. Thus, unless the investigator is actually evaluating an intervention with multiple components (see upcoming discussion), standard practice is to hold all variables constant except for one independent variable as the investigation moves from the baseline to the treatment phase.

Although the general guideline is to only change one variable at a time as one moves from baseline to treatment, as with any rule, there are exceptions. Specifically, if a researcher is interested in the combined effect of several independent variables, then it is acceptable to vary more than one variable. For example, Freeman and Piazza (1998) were interested in the effects of a combined intervention for treating food refusal, and therefore introduced several strategies as a "package" intervention. In this way, the authors were able to determine the impact of the combined treatment on the targeted behavior. It should be noted, however, that if investigators are using such an approach, all independent variables should be introduced simultaneously, rather than progressively. In this way, the package intervention essentially becomes one independent variable. Although by using a package treatment, it is impossible to determine which component of the intervention is producing the change, or whether it is the components in concert, such an approach does allow the investigator to determine if the combined intervention directly impacts the dependent variable. Thus, if simply assessing the impact of a package intervention is the goal of the research, such an approach is appropriate.

### Commentary

As should be evident thus far, SSDs are scholarly methodologies that allow investigators to determine adequately whether an independent variable produced a change in the specified dependent variable(s). Through replication of the treatment effect and intrasubject comparison, the designs allow for adequate control to threats of internal validity. Further, through intersubject comparison and direct and systematic replication, generality of the findings is established.

With the basic underlying principles of the SSDs explained, the reader should have a more complete appreciation for the utility of such designs. Next, issues regarding baseline measurement are discussed.

## CHOOSING A BASELINE

With few exceptions, the researcher utilizing a SSD initiates the process by completing a period of observations of the dependent variable as it occurs in the absence of the independent variable. Conventionally, this first phase of the analysis is referred to as the *baseline* and is labeled with an *A*. It is the data pattern of the dependent variable, which emerges during this phase of the research, that serves as the point of comparison for patterns of data during other (often treatment) conditions. Ideally, the researcher is interested in establishing a consistent, stable pattern of data during the baseline condition. When this is accomplished, it facilitates the process of comparing baseline against later conditions. Often in "basic" research, investigators are concerned with establishing a baseline period in which the dependent variable is observed under tightly controlled conditions that produce patterns of data with little variability (e.g., Perone, 1991; Sidman, 1960). For example, basic researchers may specify the minimal degree of variability across baseline points as a means of establishing a criteria for a stable baseline (e.g., less than 5% fluctuation for three consecutive sessions). Baseline conditions and observations would thus continue until the experimenter is able to create the appropriate conditions so as to produce such a pattern of behavior. Various definitions of stability have been proposed for use within basic laboratory research (for a review, see Perone, 1991).

In contrast to basic research paradigms, applied researchers typically conduct a baseline phase in which the dependent variable is observed in naturally occurring conditions (Barlow & Hersen, 1984; Hersen, 1982). Rather than creating the conditions to produce baseline responding, the applied researcher often is simply documenting the occurrence of the dependent variable in the typical environment. Thus, it can be quite difficult to obtain the level of control over environmental conditions necessary to produce patterns of data with minimal fluctuation. Further, applied researchers, because they are often working with human participants who may be experiencing significant distress, may not have the luxury of continuing baseline observations until a narrowly defined pattern of data emerges. As such, the definition of "stability" or "pattern" is typically viewed differently when in the applied context. This is not to suggest that applied researchers should not be vigilant in minimizing or eliminating variability in data patterns due to measurement errors or other extraneous variables that are controllable (and for which control over is warranted). Rather, the point is that the acceptable amount of control, and thus the level of variability, differs considerably across basic and applied research environments. The remaining discussion focuses on issues primarily relevant to applied research situations.

When conducting baseline observations, applied researchers are interested in gathering a sample of the dependent variable sufficient to serve as a standard against which to compare patterns of data produced during other conditions. To date, however, there remains no definitive criterion for the "right" length of baseline. The most important consideration when attempting to determine whether one's baseline observation period is adequate is that of consistency in data patterns. Once a pattern of consistency in the desired direction has developed (i.e., if the baseline pattern is increasing if you expect your independent variable to produce decreases, or visa versa), it may be prudent to introduce the independent variable. Convention is to consider a minimum of three data points as sufficient for determining whether consistency or pattern exists (Barlow & Hersen, 1984). However, the interested readers could easily and quickly find published examples of single-subject research in which there were fewer baseline observations. Further, one could just as easily find examples of baseline periods containing significantly more than three observations. Thus, although most single-subject researchers strive for a minimum of three baseline data points, the ultimate criteria of being able to adequately assess the impact of the independent variable prevails.

Although various combinations and permutations could occur, several basic patterns of baseline have been described (Barlow & Hersen, 1984; Hersen, 1982). Each pattern of baseline has particular implications for the interpretation

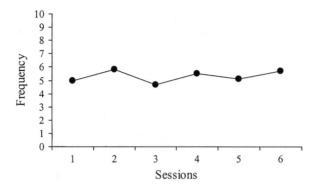

FIG. 7.1. The stable baseline. Hypothetical data demonstrating slight, but negligible variation in data patterns.

of the impact of the independent variable. The stable baseline is depicted in Fig. 7.1, utilizing a 6-point baseline observation period with hypothetical data. As is evident, there is slight but minimal variation across data points. There is no significant increasing or decreasing trends across observations, essentially resulting in a straight line. Application of the independent variable following this baseline period would result in unambiguous interpretation of its effect. That is, one would easily be able to determine if there had been no change (i.e., data patterns are essentially the same during treatment), improvements (i.e., data patterns either increased or decreased, depending upon the goal of the intervention), or worsening (i.e., again, data pattern either increased or decreased, depending on the goal of intervention).

The second general pattern of baseline is the increasing or decreasing baseline, with the change representing worsening of the problem. Take, for example, a situation in which a researcher was measuring the rate of aggressive acts displayed by a youth at recess (see Fig. 7.2, top graph). An increasing baseline pattern would document more frequent occurrence of the aggressive acts as baseline continued, suggesting that the behavior is worsening over time. Alternately, Fig. 7.2 (bottom graph) demonstrates a decreasing trend. In this hypothetical situation, the figure depicts a decrease in the $M$ number of hours spent outside the home across weeks by a client presenting with agoraphobia. In both situations (i.e., increasing and decreasing trends), the pattern depicts a worsening of the problem. Both are acceptable baseline patterns for treatment comparison because one is able to make meaningful interpretations of the impact of the independent variable. Specifically, if the independent variable produces a reversed pattern of data (i.e., decreasing in the number of aggressive acts or increase in hours spent outside the home), then the original pattern serves as an adequate comparison. An increasing or decreasing baseline trend become problematic, however, when the independent variable

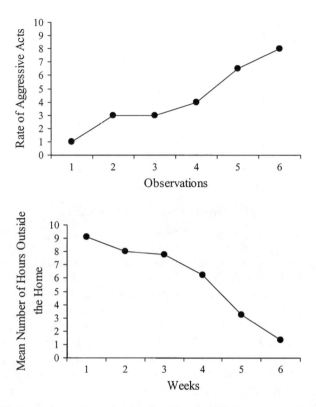

FIG. 7.2.   The increasing or decreasing baseline. Hypothetical data on aggressive acts demonstrating an increasing baseline (top graph). Hypothetical data on the *M* number of hours spent out
of the home by a client with agoraphobia demonstrating a decreasing baseline (bottom graph).

does not produce a reversal in the direction of the behavior pattern. According
to Hersen (1982) "if treatment were detrimental to the patient, it would be
difficult to determine whether the data in the intervention phase simply represent a continuation of the trend begun in baseline or whether they indicate
further deterioration due to the treatment" (p. 176). However, if there were a
marked shift in the slope of the data (significantly steeper in either direction),
one would be able to determine that the independent variable was having an
adverse impact on the dependent measure.

   In contrast to increasing or decreasing trends that represent a worsening in
the dependent measure, the same data patterns that indicate improvements are
troublesome as baseline patterns. Returning to the aforementioned examples,
one would not want a baseline that indicates a decreasing trend in aggressive
acts or an increasing trend in the *M* number of hours outside the home. These
data patterns are problematic as points of comparison because one could not
determine whether continued improvements following the introduction of the

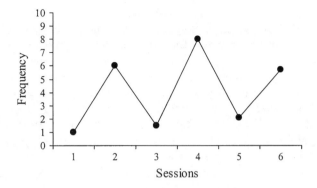

FIG. 7.3.   The variable baseline.

treatment are the result of naturally occurring factors (i.e., those that were resulting in the initial improvement) or of the systematically controlled treatment.
It has been suggested that marked changes in slope would indicate significant
impact of the independent variable (Hersen, 1982); however, given that data
obtained in single-subject research are typically analyzed via visual inspection,
it may be difficult to detect intervention effect in such a manner.

The fourth pattern of baseline is the variable baseline (see Fig. 7.3). Given
the difficulties in establishing tight experimental control over environmental variables, this is a frequent baseline pattern seen in applied research. As
demonstrated in Fig. 7.3 with hypothetical data, no consistent trend is noted,
although there is a consistent pattern of alternating between high and low data
points. Although one could aggregate the data in a manner that minimizes the
variability (e.g., by averaging the data collected over a 2-day period), this simply masks the variability and does not alter the basic pattern. Sidman (1960)
recommended that, when a researcher is faced with such a pattern in baseline
data, the researcher should seek out and eliminate the extraneous factors that
produce such variability. However, as has already been mentioned, this may
be difficult or excessively time consuming for the applied researcher.

The utility of the variable baseline as a point of comparison depends on the
impact of the independent variable. If the treatment conditions produce a decrease in the variability of the data pattern and a change in the desired direction,
then it is appropriate to conclude that the treatment had the desired impact.
However, if variability is reduced but the problem remains at unacceptable
levels, then interpretation of the independent variable as useful would not be
warranted. In this latter situation, although the dependent measure is impacted
by the independent variable, the impact is not in the desired direction. Thus,
one would not want to retain the treatment.

Another pattern of baseline is the variable–stable baseline. Here, the pattern
is initially variable, but then becomes stable. Such a pattern may be achieved

by extending the baseline observation period for sufficient length so as to have the dependent measure come under the control of the baseline conditions. Such an approach might be warranted, for instance, if baseline conditions are novel to the participant. Because the independent variable is introduced following a period of stability, interpretation of its impact is the same as with the stable baseline—unambiguous. However, although perhaps the ideal scenario when initially obtaining variable data, practical and/or ethical constraints may limit the applied researcher's ability to extend baseline to a sufficient length to establish stability (e.g., as in the case of a brief inpatient hospitalization, or when the dependent measure is severe, self-injurious behavior).

The stable–variable baseline presents particular challenges as point of comparison. This pattern is essentially the opposite of the variable–stable baseline. Although unstable patterns of baseline data are not in and of themselves problematic, the stable–variable pattern suggests the influence of extraneous variables introduced after the initiation of baseline measurement. Thus, some factor that has a marked impact on the dependent variable is occurring in an uncontrolled way. This may make it difficult to evaluate the impact of treatment, as the extraneous variable may interfere with the independent variable.

### Commentary

As should be evident, there are numerous patterns in data that can emerge during baseline observations (Barlow & Hersen, 1984; Hersen, 1982). In contrast to basic research paradigms, there are no standards or specifications for the appropriate baseline length and variability. Rather, the overarching function of the baseline—as the point of comparison across phases—serves as the guide to determining when adequate baseline data have been collected. With the exception of the stable and worsening baseline patterns, other possible patterns present some potential problems when one uses them for comparison purposes.

In the next two sections, the discussion of SSDs is extended beyond baseline observation to encompass methods of introducing the independent variable that allows for appropriate comparisons.

## "CLASSIC" SINGLE SUBJECT WITHDRAWAL DESIGNS

### The Simple A–B Design

As previously mentioned, the hallmarks of SSDs include repeated observation of the behavior interested across time and systematic changes in independent variables. The least complex SSD utilized to accomplish these goals is the A–B design. With this design, the experimenter collects measures of the dependent variable during the baseline and then again during the treatment condition. Thus, the effect of the independent variable is demonstrated once.

The simple A–B design has been criticized due to its lack of experimental rigor. Specifically, inclusion of only one phase of each of the components (i.e., baseline and treatment) decreases the ability of the investigator to adequately assess experimental control or internal validity. Theoretically, it is possible that a change in an extraneous variable affecting the individual occurred concurrently with introduction of the treatment conditions. If and when this occurs, then it is impossible for the investigator to make causal inferences about the impact of the independent variable separate from the impact of the extraneous example. Take, for example, a situation in which a clinician is working with an adolescent experiencing difficulties sustaining attention during academic tasks. Suppose, after gathering baseline data on off-task behavior during school, the clinician initiates instruction on compensatory strategies to address the attention problems. Coinciding with this psychological intervention, parents of the youth also seek services with their pediatrician, who prescribes a psychopharmacological intervention (e.g., Ritalin©). If off-task behavior decreases, the clinician will be unable to determine whether this change is due to the compensatory strategies, the Ritalin©, or a combination of both.

As illustrated in the just cited example, one can see that the simple A–B design does not provide adequate protection against various threats to internal validity. As such, the design is often considered a correlational design (Hersen, 1982). In other words, due to lack of experimental rigor, one cannot make inferences about the causal role of the independent variable. However, the A–B design can be useful given certain circumstances, and does offer advantages over the uncontrolled case study methodology. Specifically, for problems that have been resistant to change for significant periods of time, noticeable changes that occur during the B phase of the study offers some support for the intervention as the causal mechanism. Further, the A–B design is well suited for certain situations in which practical or ethical limitations decrease one's ability to remove the intervention as a means of demonstrating experimental control. For example, when treating severe, life-threatening, self-injurious behavior, the investigator may not have the luxury of returning to baseline conditions following successful decrease in the behavior during the treatment phase.

## The A–B–A Design

The A–B–A design corrects the primary limitation of the A–B design by including a phase that involves a return to the original baseline conditions. Removal of the intervention to return to baseline serves as a means of confirming experimental control over the dependent measure by allowing for repeated demonstration of experimental effect. That is, if observations reveal that the dependent measure returns to a pattern that is similar to the original baseline, then the experimenter can make stronger assumptions about the causal role of the independent variable. Given the assumption that extraneous variables remain relatively constant across all phases of the experiment, this return to baseline patterns is said to be due to the withdrawal of the independent variable. In contrast to the A–B design, with which one must be concerned about the possibility of a change in extraneous variables coinciding with the introduction of the treatment phase, such a concern does not exist when using the A–B–A design. Although this may happen once, the possibility of another change in extraneous variables occurring at precisely the same time that the intervention is both introduced and withdrawn is so remote that it typically does not constitute a realistic threat to internal validity.

Although the A–B–A design corrects for problems of the simple A–B design, it is not without its limitations. Specifically, it may be problematic to complete an investigation while the participant is exposed to baseline conditions, particularly if one is addressing clinical issues. Let us return to the already mentioned example of the youth with attention problems. Assume that an A–B–A design was used, in which the B phase consisted of effective use of compensatory strategies. Completing the investigation while the participant was exposed to baseline conditions would be problematic if those conditions produced a return in data patterns similar to the original baseline. In this example, the youth would be left to deal with his problems without the aid of intervention. Although perhaps not required to demonstrate experimental control, ethically it would seem prudent to reintroduce the intervention so as to address the presenting complaint.

### A–B–A–B Design

By introducing an additional treatment phase, the investigator creates the A–B–A–B design. This design has also been referred to as the *equivalent time-samples design* (Campbell & Stanley, 1966), the *withdrawal design*, and the *reversal design* (Kazdin, 2001). This design controls for the limitation of the A–B–A design by reintroducing the treatment conditions. Additionally, the design is more methodologically rigorous due to the fact that two opportunities occur to compare the behavior patterns during baseline and treatment conditions (that is, B to A and A to B).

To illustrate the A–B–A–B design, consider an example from the literature. Friman et al. (1999) recently investigated the impact of an intervention for bedtime behavior problems exhibited by two children, age 3 and age 10 years. Both children exhibited bedtime problems in the form of calling out from their bedrooms and physically exiting the rooms after their parents had put them to bed for the night. The behavior problems occurred at a frequency and duration that interferred with family functioning (e.g., the parents were unable to have quality time together, the children were obtaining too little sleep). In all phases of the study, the participants' parents collected data on frequency of crying and leaving the room once the children were placed in bed. Baseline data were collected across 15 days, during which time parents were instructed to respond to the bedtime problems as they would typically. Treatment began on the 16th day and involved parents providing each child with a "bedtime pass," good for one free trip outside of the room past bedtime. The pass was a laminated $3'' \times 5''$ note card. At the beginning of treatment, the parents explained to the children that they could use their pass for one trip out of the bedroom each night, but that the trip had to be to accomplish a specific task (e.g., get a drink of water, get another hug). Once the pass was used, it was relinquished to the parents, and no further trips were allowed. The pass was returned to the child the subsequent night. During intervention, the parents were instructed to ignore all crying and to simply physically guide the child back into his room if he were to leave without the use of the pass. Results of the experimental analysis are presented in Fig. 7.4.

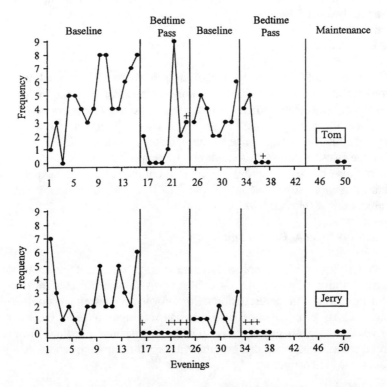

FIG. 7.4. Nightly frequency of crying and leaving the room for the 3-year-old child (top) and the 10-year-old child (bottom). From "The Bedtime Pass: An Approach to Bedtime Crying and Leaving the Room" by Friman et al., 1999, *Archives of Pediatric and Adolescent Medicine, 153,* 1027–1029, Fig. 1. Copyright ©1999 by *Archives of Pediatric and Adolescent Medicine.* Reprinted by permission.

Inspection of the data obtained during baseline indicates that somewhat variable, but increasing trends, were noted in the dependent measure for both participants. Following introduction of the intervention, a marked decrease in the targeted behavior occurred, to zero for the 10-year-old participant. Thus, it was demonstrated quite clearly with both participants that the behavior changed in the desired direction during the initial intervention phase. This is tempered slightly, however, with the 3-year-old participant. For him, as intervention continued, the behavior problems began to increase again after the initial decrease. Reintroduction of the baseline conditions (i.e., withdrawal of the bedtime pass) resulted in the increased occurrence of the bedtime behavior problems, which decreased to zero for both participants on the readministration of the intervention. Obtaining zero rates of behavior with the 3-year-old participant during the second intervention phase adds strength to the determination of experimental control given the initial variability in the first intervention phase. Furthermore, the noted improvements continued to be present when follow-up data were collected 3 weeks later.

## The B–A–B Design

Although typically single-subject research starts with an initial baseline period, there may instances in which this is not feasible. For instance, perhaps the investigator is only able to gather data after some form of intervention is put into place. Or, perhaps a participant's behavior problems are so severe that attempts at intervention are needed immediately. In either case, it is possible to use the B–A–B design. Although not as complete as the A–B–A–B design (i.e., because it does not allow for repeated comparisons of the experimental effect), it is more advantageous than the A–B–A design because it ends on a treatment phase (Hersen, 1982).

## Variations of the A–B–A Designs

The underlying strategy employed to demonstrate functional control using the various withdrawal designs (e.g., A–B–A, B–A–B), the repeated introduction and withdrawal of the intervention, allows for various extensions of the basic designs. Thus, perhaps endless permutations or formations of the basic components of the designs can be created to address particular questions of interest. Several examples of such designs are considered next, although the list is not meant to be exhaustive.

*A–B–A–B–A–B design.* The basic components of the A–B–A design can be extended resulting in multiple withdrawals and administrations of the independent variable (e.g., the A–B–A–B–A–B design). Using such a design adds further support for the demonstration of functional control of the independent variable over the dependent variable. By demonstrating multiple times that the data patterns change in the expected direction when the treatment is added and withdrawn, the researcher can be more confident that the effect is due to the particular treatment variables. Although this might not be necessary when the treatment effect is large (i.e., when there are significant differences in the data pattern between baseline and treatment conditions), repeatedly demonstrating the desired effect may be necessary when the effect is small (i.e., when the difference between the two conditions is small). Observing minimal or moderate changes multiple times may provide more convincing evidence that the independent variable is producing the impact, above and beyond natural variability.

**A–B–A–C–A–C design.**    The basic A–B–A design also can be extended by introducing a condition in which the effects of a second independent variable are assessed (e.g., as with the A–B–A–C–A–C design). In such a design, the investigator compares the impact of treatment conditions B and C on the dependent variable. However, with such a design, one is not able to compare the relative effects of the different independent variables because they are confounded by the extraneous variable of time (Hersen, 1982). Further, order effects may confound the findings. That is, perhaps the conditions present in C only have an impact after the participant is exposed to the conditions present in B. With such a design, one is unable to determine whether this is the case, and thus there is a threat to the internal validity of the study. If completing intersubject comparisons, one can control for this by using a counterbalancing technique (i.e., Participants 1 and 3 are exposed to the conditions in the following order: A–B–A–C–A–C, whereas Participants 2 and 4 are exposed to them in the following order: A–C–A–B–A–B). By using counterbalancing, the research is able to determine whether the independent variables produce similar effects regardless of order of presentation. Thus, if all participants respond to condition C in similar ways regardless of when they were exposed to this condition, than one has greater confidence in the effect of C alone.

**Interaction Designs.**    As stated earlier, single-subject research typically involves a change in only one variable at a time across conditions. This rule can be applied in a way that allows the investigator to evaluate the combined effects of multiple independent variables by using a withdrawal design. Specifically, by introducing a condition in which two independent variables are present, it becomes possible to assess the impact of the combined intervention relative to a single intervention. In some situations, a particular treatment may produce minimal impact, or may produce an impact that is less than that desired. By extending the basic components of the A–B–A design, one can assess the impact of adding additional treatment components on the dependent variable.

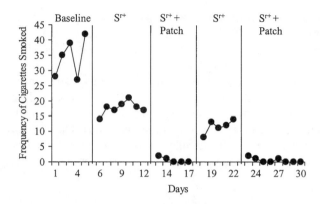

FIG. 7.5.   Number of cigarettes smoked per day. Hypothetical data of the assessment of interventions for smoking.

Assume, for example, that a researcher is interested in treating smoking. Fig. 7.5 shows hypothetical data in this scenario. After establishing a baseline of the number of cigarettes smoked per day, the impact of a reinforcement-based treatment is evaluated. As is shown, although the number of cigarettes smoked decreases somewhat, the desired goal of zero cigarettes smoked is not achieved. Thus, the investigator adds an additional component to the intervention–the use of a nicotine patch. This results in a condition labeled BC because it involves both components (i.e., reinforcement + nicotine patch). As shown in Fig. 7.5, the combined intervention results in decreases in the dependent variable to zero. When the investigator withdrawals the nicotine patch, the data patterns return to being similar to the original treatment phase. Finally, the combined intervention is reintroduced, resulting the elimination of the smoking. As illustrated, it is possible to demonstrate the impact of the combined intervention with such a design. Put another way, one is able to investigate the relative impact of condition C over condition B. The number of combinations is theoretically endless, potentially resulting in conditions such as BCD, BCDE, and so forth.

## STAGE-PROCESS DESIGNS

Although the withdrawal designs have proven remarkably useful in scientific inquiry, partly because of the flexibility in applying in multiple ways the basic concepts of repeated observations and replication of experimental effect, there are situations in which their use is not appropriate. Withdrawal designs may be considered inappropriate due to a variety of reasons (e.g., ethical, practical). As mentioned earlier, withdrawal of a treatment may be unethical if the behavior problem is severe or life threatening. Also, it may not be possible to withdraw or remove certain therapeutic strategies. For example, once instructions have been given to a participant, it is impossible to remove them. Although the research could stop giving them in a particular condition, the fact that they were given earlier could result in a change that is not removable. As another example, if the intervention results in behavior that is supported beyond the treatment conditions, then withdrawal of the intervention may have no impact on the behavior. For instance, if a clinician teaches someone to be appropriately assertive, the reactions of others likely will maintain those behaviors regardless of whether the clinician removes the intervention. In this scenario, the lack of a return to baseline data patterns might suggest a lack of functional control of the independent variable. However, such is likely not the case; rather, other controlling variables continue to maintain the behavior patterns in the absence of the intervention. Because of these limitations, various other SSDs are used. These include the alternating treatment designs, multiple baseline designs, and changing criterion designs.

## The Multielements Design

The *multielements design* (also referred to as the *simultaneous treatment designs* or the *alternating treatments design*) differs from other SSDs in that multiple conditions (i.e., baseline and treatment conditions, two or more treatment conditions) are conducted in rapid succession, with the order of presentation typically determined through random selection, and compared against each other (Miltenberger, 2001). For example, perhaps baseline conditions are in effect one day, treatment conditions the next, and so forth. Thus, unlike the withdrawal designs, the effects of the different experimental conditions are evaluated across the same time frame. This helps eliminate the possibility of extraneous variables influencing the dependent variable during only one of the experimental conditions. In other words, any extraneous variable is going to impact the dependent variable during all conditions because they are occurring essentially in conjunction. Thus, the extraneous variable could not be the cause of any differences noted across conditions.

With the multielements design, often there are three phases: baseline, comparison (rapid alternation between two or more conditions), and the use of the effective intervention (Holcombe, Wolery, & Gast, 1994). In some situations, however, the baseline might not be necessary. This may be particularly true if one of the comparison conditions is a baseline condition. One treatment condition is judged to be superior if it produces data patterns in the expected direction at a level that is greater than other conditions. Another component of the multielements design is that an equal number of sessions of each condition should be conducted. To ensure discriminated responding across conditions, researchers often pair separate but salient stimuli with each condition. This design may be particularly useful if the investigator is comparing interventions that have an immediate effect, and when the dependent measure is particularly sensitive to changes in stimulus conditions (i.e., reversible; Holcombe et al., 1994).

As an example of use of the multielements design, consider a recent paper by Anderson, Freeman, and Scotti (1999). In this investigation, the authors used a multielement design to assess the impact of different assessment conditions on the problem behavior of three children with developmental disabilities (a methodology referred to as a *functional analysis*). As part of a larger assessment, participants were exposed to multiple analog conditions designed to simulate conditions occurring in the children's environment to determine consequent variables maintaining targeted behaviors. In the attention condition, the therapist delivered brief verbal attention contingent on the occurrence of targeted problem behavior. In the tangible condition, participants were allowed 20 sec access to preferred stimuli contingent on misbehavior. The demand condition involved ongoing instructions, which were terminated for 20 sec contingent on targeted misbehavior. Finally, the control condition involved positive verbal attention every 20 sec, access to preferred stimuli, and no demands. The control condition served as the comparison condition. Sessions were 15 sec in length and conditions were presented in a multielement format in random order, except that identical conditions were not conducted consecutively. Rates of problematic behavior for one participant (Ann) are presented in Fig. 7.6.

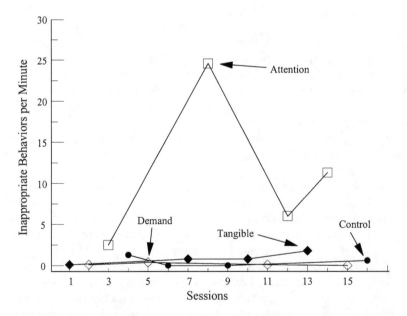

FIG. 7.6. Rate per min of inappropriate behaviors across assessment conditions. Adapted from "Evaluation of the Generalizability (reliability and validity) of Analog Functional Assessment Methodology" by Anderson, Freeman, & Scott, 1999, *Behavior Therapy, 30,* 21–30, Fig. 1. Copyright ©1999 by *Behavior Therapy.* Reprinted by permission.

As is shown, Ann was exposed to each condition four times. Data show that rates of inappropriate behavior were higher in the attention condition as compared to in the others. Thus, the researchers were able to hypothesize that contingent attention likely was a factor that maintained the occurrence of the participant's inappropriate behaviors. Environmental factors used in the other conditions (e.g., contingent escape from demands, contingent access to tangibles) appeared to have lesser of an effect on Ann's problematic behavior as evidenced by lower rates during those assessment conditions.

In the just cited example, the multielements design was used to compare different assessment conditions to determine which contained the factors that were most affecting the target behavior problems. In addition, this design can be used to compare a treatment condition to baseline (e.g., Freeman & Piazza, 1998), or to compare multiple treatments (e.g., Kahng, Iwata, DeLeon, & Wallace, 2000). Such an approach allows the investigator to assess which intervention may prove to be the most effective in changing the targeted dependent variable. The benefit of such a design over other designs is the ability to make such treatment comparisons in a relatively short amount of time.

## Multiple Baseline Designs

There are three types of multiple baseline designs: (a) multiple baseline across behaviors, (b) multiple baseline across persons, and (c) multiple baseline across settings (Hersen, 1982; Miltenberger, 2001). With the multiple baseline design across behaviors, the investigator evaluates the impact of an intervention across different behaviors emitted by the same person. As such, this is a within-subjects design. The intervention is applied sequentially to the different (presumably) independent behaviors. The second design, multiple baseline across persons, involves the evaluation of the impact of a particular intervention across at least two individuals matched according to relevant variables, who are presumed to be exposed to identical (or at least markedly similar) environments. For example, the investigator may compare an intervention across two students who attend math class with a particular teacher, one who attends in the morning and one who attends in the afternoon. Finally, with the multiple baseline-across-settings design, a particular intervention is applied sequentially to a single participant or group of participants across independent environments (e.g., home and school).

Technically, there must be at least two separate dimensions (i.e., behaviors, settings, or persons) present to utilize a multiple baseline design, although convention suggests a minimum of three or more. Multiple baseline designs are characterized by the presence of only two conditions: baseline and treatment. However, unlike the simple A–B design, treatment is introduced in such a way that one is able to evaluate experimental control of the independent variable. As stated by Hersen (1982) "the multiple baseline design across behaviors is a series of A–B designs, with every succeeding A phase applied to one targeted behavior until treatment has finally been applied to each" (p. 190). Although stated in reference to the multiple baseline-across-behaviors design, the same is true for the other multiple baseline designs. With these designs, the baseline condition is extended for increasing lengths of time as the intervention is introduced with the other dependent variables. Thus, these designs are particularly useful for studying irreversible effects, because replication is achieved without withdrawal and reintroduction of the independent variable (Perone, 1991).

An assumption underlying the multiple baseline designs is that the various dependent measures (i.e., behaviors, settings, persons) are functionally independent. If this is the case, a change in one dependent variable as a result of the change in the independent variable should not produce changes in the other dependent variables. Treatment effects therefore are inferred when the dependent measure changes only when the intervention is applied to it. Variables still exposed to the baseline conditions should show little to no change when the treatment is introduced with the other dependent variables. In this way, the multiple baseline designs are weaker than other designs (Barlow & Hersen, 1984; Hersen, 1982). Specifically, experimental control is inferred based on the comparison of nontreated dependent variables as compared to the treated variables and thus is not demonstrated directly.

If the dependent variables are not functionally independent (i.e., introduction of the treatment with one variable produces changes in the other variables), then the ability to establish experimental control is compromised. Determining a priori whether dependent variables are independent can be difficulty, however. Thus, an investigator may select targeted variables that are not best suited for the use of the multiple baseline designs. Take, for example, a situation in which the dependent measures are three problematic behaviors (i.e., talking out of turn, throwing spit wads, getting out of seat without permission) of a student in a classroom. As an intervention, the investigator teaches the student's teacher to respond in a particular way to the behaviors (e.g., verbal reprimand), and evaluates the impact of the intervention using a multiple baseline design. It is possible that the student will learn to change each of the behaviors simply by exposure to the treatment for one behavior. Therefore, if the teacher first provides verbal reprimands when the student talks out of turn, the other behaviors may change as well. As this example illustrates, as an artifact of the lack of independence, introducing the intervention with one variable may produce changes in the other variables, resulting in the inability to demonstrate experimental control. This is problematic because the intervention may be the controlling variable in this situation, but the investigator is unable to demonstrate that such is the case in a convincing manner.

Kazdin and Kopel (1975) provided three recommendations for addressing problems of dependence across dependent variables. First, they recommend selecting dependent measures that are as topographically distinct as possible as a means of increasing the likelihood that they are independent. However, such an approach still relies on successful "guessing," as topographically distinct behaviors may still be functionally related. Second, they suggest that investigators utilize four or more baselines as compared to two or three. Their argument is that, by increasing the number of baselines, the investigator is decreasing the likelihood of selecting measures that are not independent. However, as pointed out by Hersen (Hersen, 1982; Barlow & Hersen, 1984), the probability of interdependence may be enhanced with a larger number of dependent variables. Finally, Kazdin and Kopel (1975) recommended that, when faced with the occurrence of dependence across variables, the investigator withdraw and then reintroduce the independent variable. By doing so, it may be possible to demonstrate adequate experimental control. Although the investigator originally may have selected the multiple baseline design to avoid using a withdrawal design, this may be necessary to adequately demonstrate control.

***Nonconcurrent Multiple Baseline Design.*** The presumption of the multiple baseline designs is that the measurement of the different dependent variables occurs simultaneously. In this way, the designs control for threats to internal validity as such as history effects. However, there may be situations in which it is particularly difficult to obtain simultaneous observations on multiple individuals who meet the specified criteria, thus limiting one's ability to utilize the multiple baseline-across-persons design. This may be particularly true in applied or clinical research (Hayes, 1985). In such situations, it may be possible to utilize the nonconcurrent multiple baseline design, originally described by Watson and Workman (1981).

With the nonconcurrent multiple baseline-across-persons design, the investigator predetermines the length of each of baselines (e.g., 3, 6, 9 days). Then, when a participant with the requisite features is available, he or she is exposed to a baseline period that is randomly assigned. From this point, the methodology is conducted in the same manner as the simple A–B design—baseline observations are conducted (for the predetermined length of time), followed by the application of treatment. In this manner, the researcher continues to obtain baseline and treatment data from multiple participants, allowing for adequate between-persons comparisons. If a participant fails to display an acceptable baseline pattern, that individual would be dropped from the formal investigation, although their eventual reaction to treatment may still be useful as a replication (Watson & Workman, 1981).

Some (e.g., Harris & Jenson, 1985a, 1985b) argued that the nonconcurrent multiple baseline design across persons is equivalent to a series of A–B designs with replication. This nomenclature has been recommended due to the fact that multiple baseline designs rely on simultaneous data collection as a means of demonstrating adequate control over threats to internal validity. As described earlier, by showing that the change in the dependent variable changes only when the treatment is introduced, the investigator has confidence in the causal relationship. This is strengthened when data with several individuals are collected simultaneously because the design controls for history effects. Harris and Jenson (1985a, 1985b) argued that the nonconcurrent multiple baseline design does not control for such effects because the data are not collected across individuals simultaneously; thus, the individual is not exposed to the same environment.

By varying the length of baseline, however, the nonconcurrent multiple baseline design does control for threats to internal validity (Hayes, 1985; Mansell, 1982). Specifically, each time that the investigator demonstrates that the dependent measure changes when the treatment is introduced, regardless of the length of baseline, the likelihood that an extraneous variable produced the change for each participant is greatly reduced. Further, by using increasing lengths of baseline, the researcher controls for the possibility that the exposure to baseline conditions naturally produces changes in the dependent measure. Thus, although generally considered one of the weaker SSDs, the nonconcurrent, multiple baseline-across-persons design can serve as a useful methodology if other factors limit the ability to utilize a more stringent design.

## Changing Criterion Design

The changing criterion design shares features with both the simple A–B design and the alternating treatments design (Hersen, 1982; Miltenberger, 2001). Specifically, this design is characterized by the presence of only one baseline and one treatment phase. However, what differentiates this design from the A–B design is that the treatment condition is defined by the sequential introduction of different performance goals. In other words, the treatment phase is applied until the targeted dependent variable achieves a specified level of performance. At that time, the goal (i.e., criterion) of performance is altered and the intervention continues until the behavior again achieves the desired level. Changes in the criterion occur until the dependent measure is occurring at the desired terminal level. As such, the changing criterion design is particularly well suited for situations in which the investigator is interested in evaluating shaping programs that are expected to result in increases or decreases in the dependent measure (e.g., decreased cigarette smoking, increased level of exercise; Hersen, 1982). Evaluation of the intervention as the causal agent occurs through two comparisons: between the occurrence of the dependent measure during baseline and treatment, and between the occurrence of the dependent measure across the different levels of the intervention. If the dependent variable changes in the desired direction only when the criterion changes, then the investigator can have confidence in the controlling nature of the independent variable.

## SUMMARY

In the current chapter, an overview of the basic characteristics of various single-subject research designs has been provided. SSDs are distinguished by several features, including repeated observation of the dependent variable, replication of treatment effects, intrasubject and intersubject comparisons, and systematic manipulation of independent variables. Further, direct and systematic replications are used to establish the generality of the findings. Together, these features allow the investigator to guard against, or to detect when present, threats to internal and external validity. Although misconceptions continue to abound regarding their limitations (Aeschelman, 1991), SSDs are scholarly and do allow for the demonstration of experimental control of the independent variable over the dependent variable. Thus, their use in psychological and psychotherapy research can allow investigators to answer questions of interest in a manner that meets the requirements of the scientific method.

A particular strength of SSDs is their flexibility, allowing an investigator to change the purpose of the study when warranted as the investigation progresses (Barlow & Hersen, 1984; Holcombe et al., 1994). Assume, for example, that baseline data are variable. Rather than simply moving to the treatment phase in which the impact of a particular intervention is assessed, the investigator may wish to determine the source of the variability. In this way, the investigation then becomes an extended assessment that involves the identification of extraneous variables affecting the dependent variable. Once this is done, then the researcher may wish to introduce a treatment (which, consequently, may be more effective now that sources of variability have been identified and can be accounted for).

Or perhaps the researcher was initially interested in the impact of a particular intervention on the dependent variable. For instance, perhaps a researcher is investigating the impact of "time out" as an intervention for a noncompliant child using an A–B–A–B withdrawal design. Baseline data are collected on the rate of compliance per day. Then, use of time out as a consequence for noncompliance is introduced, which produces no change in the occurrence of the noncompliance. If this were a group design, the investigator would need to continue to utilize the exact procedures across all participants so as to assure experimental integrity, or consider the research as unacceptable and stop the experiment altogether. With the SSDs, however, the investigator can extend the original lack of findings by evaluating another treatment (e.g., praise for compliance). Specifically, if there is no difference in the occurrence of the dependent variable between the initial baseline and treatment phases (A and B phases), it would be appropriate to introduce the second intervention (C phase) without returning to the original baseline conditions. If this produced an effect, then, withdrawal of the intervention would involve a return to the B phase. In other words, because data patterns do not differ between A and B, it is possible to use B as the comparison against patterns during the C phase. Thus, SSDs may be more economical than group designs in that they are malleable and changeable based on the data obtained.

In this way, single subject designs are useful not only in the context of psychological research, but also in the context of demonstrating the effectiveness of clinical interventions (Hilliard, 1993). Psychotherapy as a process involves first hypothesis building (i.e., developing reasonable explanations for the client's current conditions) and then hypothesis testing (i.e., assessing the effectiveness of an intervention expected to be effective based on the original hypothesis). Initial interventions may not be effective, and thus clinicians may experiment with others until improvements are noted. Flexibility of SSDs can allow clinicians to collect data and manipulate variables in a way that allows for adequate demonstration of therapeutic outcome as a result of specific interventions. Therefore, their use within psychotherapy results in the clinician truly operating as a scientist–practitioner.

In conclusion, I presume the reader now has a more complete understanding of the underlying assumptions and basic characteristics of SSDs. Although often misunderstood, their utility is exemplified by the fact that there are frequently calls for more single-subject research in various fields of psychology and beyond (e.g., Cook, 1996; Hrycaiko & Martin, 1996; Lundervold & Belwood, 2000). Not only are they useful for explicit research purposes, but they can also be used to assist practitioners in determining the impact of their efforts. Because of this, understanding the SSDs is important for both researchers and clinicians alike.

## REFERENCES

Aeschleman, S. R. (1991). Single-subject research designs: Some misconceptions. *Rehabilitation Psychology, 36*, 43–49.

Anderson, C. M., Freeman, K. A., & Scotti, J. R. (1999). Evaluation of the generalizability (reliability and validity) of analog functional assessment methodology. *Behavior Therapy, 30*, 21–30.

Barlow, D., & Hersen, M. (1984). *Single case experimental designs: Strategies for studying behavior change* (2nd ed.). Elmsford, NY: Pergamon.

Benedict, R. H., & Wechsler, F. S. (1992). Evaluation of memory retraining in patients with traumatic brain injury: Two single-case experimental designs. *Journal of Head Trauma Rehabilitation, 7*(4), 83–92.

Campbell, D. T., & Stanley, J. C. (1966). *Experimental and quasi-experimental designs for research and teaching.* Chicago: Rand-McNally.

Campbell, P. H. (1988). Using single-subject research design to evaluate the effectiveness of treatment. *The American Journal of Occupational Therapy, 42*, 732–738.

Cook, D. J. (1996). Randomized trials in single subjects: The N of 1 study. *Psychopharmacology Bulletin, 32*, 363–367.

Evans, J. J., Emslie, H., & Wilson, B. A. (1998). External cuing systems in rehabilitation of executive impairments in action. *Journal of International Neuropsychology, 4*, 399–408.

Foster, T. M., Jarema, K., & Poling, A. (1999). Inferential statistics: Criticized by Sidman (1960), but popular in the *Journal of the Experimental Analysis of Behavior*. *Behaviour Change, 16*, 203–204.

Freeman, K. A., & Piazza, C. C. (1998). Combining stimulus fading, reinforcement, and extinction to treat food refusal. *Journal of Applied Behavior Analysis, 31*, 691–694.

Friman, P. C., Hoff, K. E., Schnoes, C., Freeman, K. A., Woods, D. W., & Blum, N. (1999). The bedtime pass: An approach to bedtime crying and leaving the room. *Archives of Pediatric and Adolescent Medicine, 153*, 1027–1029.

Glicksohn, J., Gvirtsman, D., & Offer, S. (1997). The compensatory nature of mood: A single-subject time-series approach. *Imagination, Cognition, & Personality, 15*, 385–396.

Harris, F. N., & Jenson, W. R. (1985a). AB designs with replication: A reply to Hayes. *Behavioral Assessment, 7*, 133–135.

Harris, F. N., & Jenson, W. R. (1985b). Comparisons of multiple-baseline across persons designs and AB designs with replication: Issues and confusions. *Behavioral Assessment, 7*, 121–127.

Hayes, S. C. (1985). Natural multiple baselines across persons: A reply to Harris and Jenson. *Behavioral Assessment, 7*, 129–132.

Hersen, M. (1982). Single-case experimental designs. In A. S. Bellack, M. Hersen, & A. E. Kazdin (Eds.), *International Handbook of Behavior Modification and Therapy* (pp. 167–203). New York: Plenum Press.

Hilliard, R. B. (1993). Single-case methodology in psychotherapy process and outcome research. *Journal of Consulting and Clinical Psychology, 61*, 373–380.

Holcome, A., Wolery, M., & Gast, D. L. (1994). Comparative single-subject research: Descriptions of designs and discussions of problems. *Topics in Early Childhood Special Education, 14*, 119–145.

Hrycaiko, D., & Martin, G. L. (1996). Applied research studies with single-subject designs: Why so few? *Journal of Applied Sports Psychology, 8*, 183–199.

Kahng, S., Iwata, B. A., DeLeon, I. G., & Wallace, M. D. (2000). A comparison of procedures for programming noncontingent reinforcement schedules. *Journal of Applied Behavior Analysis, 33*, 223–231.

Kazdin, A. E. (2001). *Behavior modification in applied settings* (6th ed.). Belmont, CA: Wadsworth/Thomson Learning.

Kazdin, A. E., & Kopel, S. A. (1975). On resolving ambiguities of the multiple-baseline design: Problems and recommendations. *Behavior Therapy, 6*, 601–608.

Kazi, M. A. F., Mantysaari, M., & Rostila, I. (1997). Promoting the use of single-case designs: Social work experiences from England and Finland. *Research on Social Practice, 7*, 311–328.

Lundervold, D. A., & Belwood, M. F. (2000). The best kept secret in counseling: Single-case (N = 1) experimental designs. *Journal of Counseling and Development, 78*, 92–102.

Mansell, J. (1982). Repeated direct replication of AB designs. *Journal of Behavior Therapy and Experimental Psychiatry, 13*, 261.

McReynolds, L. V., & Thompson, C. K. (1986). Flexibility of single-subject experimental designs. Part I: Review of the basics of single-subject designs. *Journal of Speech and Hearing Disorders, 51*, 194–203.

Miltenberger, R. G. (2001). *Behavior modification: Principles and procedures*. Belmont, CA: Wadsworth/Thomson Learning.

Nugent, W. R. (1992). The affective impact of a clinical social worker's interviewing style: A series of single-case experiments. *Research on Social Work Practice, 2*, 6–27.

Perone, M. (1991). Experimental design in the analysis of free-operant behavior. In I. H. Iversen & K. A. Lattal (Eds.), *Experimental analysis of behavior, Part I* (pp. 135–171). Amsterdam, Netherlands: Elsevier Science Publishers.

Saudargas, R. A., & Drummer, L. C. (1996). Single subject (small N) research designs and zoo research. *Zoo Biology, 15*, 173–181.

Scruggs, T. E., Mastropieri, M. A., Cook, S. B., & Escobar, C. (1986). Early intervention for children with conduct disorders: A quantitative synthesis of single-subject research. *Behavioral Disorders, 11*, 260–271.

Sidman, M. (1960). *Tactics of scientific research*. Boston, MA: Authors Cooperative, Inc.

Watson, P. J., & Workman, E. A. (1981). The non-concurrent multiple-baseline across-individuals design: An extension of the traditional multiple-baseline design. *Journal of Behavior Therapy and Experimental Psychiatry, 12*, 257–259.

Yates, A. J. (1970). *Behavior Therapy*. New York: Wiley.

# Program Evaluation

Mark M. Greene
*Retired head of Mark M. Greene & Associates,
a planning and evaluation consultancy*

*Program Evaluation* fits well in a volume dealing with research in clinical and counseling psychology. First, the concept of program evaluation is not initially well understood. Second, the term, program evaluation, elicits so many different responses that it would make a fine addition to existing clinical projective techniques. Third, when understood and properly defined, program evaluation can enhance many aspects of a clinical program. Fourth, more and more practitioners are being asked to conduct evaluations or, more likely, have evaluations conducted on the programs for which they are responsible. Thus, a knowledge of the evaluation process is invaluable to the practicing clinician.

## SOME DEFINITIONS

Because the term, program evaluation, does mean so many different things to different people, we need to pare down the possibilities and begin with a consideration of what program evaluation is not:

- A single data collection method or instrument;
- A data collection effort scheduled at the end of a program cycle;
- A series of judgments made about the worth of a program.

Program evaluation, as defined within the present context, is: The systematic development of data to serve the information needs of a program. In a word, program evaluation is a planned effort to collect data to support a range of decisions within and about a program. Those decisions are usually made by someone other than the "program evaluator."

How is the term, program, defined? A program is an institutional or societal response to a problem or a challenge that consists of one or more relatively uniform interventions designed to address a problem or challenge. Typically, a program serves a known population and focuses on a limited array of problems within that population. Unlike projects (which tend to have limited resources and a limited time frame), programs can be long-lived. Example: The psychological assessment unit at a local hospital can be considered a program because:

- It was developed in response to a particular problem (i.e., what is the psychological status of the clients at entry, during their stay and upon exit?);
- It employs a relatively uniform set of procedures (the "acceptable" assessment procedures within the unit have largely been defined);
- Those procedures are limited to assessment (rather than treatment);
- It deals with a known population (clients entering, residing in and leaving the hospital);
- It is relatively enduring. The assessment unit has been around for a long time and will continue to exist for the foreseeable future.

How then does program evaluation fit into the foregoing definition of a program? The fit is very easy to see if one considers the life cycle of the typical program:

- It begins when a need is identified and a solution is proposed;
- It progresses through a development or testing phase;
- It gets implemented;
- It is transformed (to accommodate another need) or is terminated.

The type of information needed to guide or support program decisions throughout the life-cycle varies from stage to stage. The data considered so essential when the *need* is being identified will *not* serve to guide program decisions during the *development stage* when materials and procedures are being tested and revised. Later in the present chapter, a model that anticipates the different decisions (and hence the informational needs) of a program across its entire life cycle is presented.

## NEEDS ANALYSIS

Question: What do the following bits of dialogue have in common?

"Is anything wrong?"
"How are you feeling today?"
"What brings you here today?"

The questions might well have be asked by a parent, a physician and a clinician, respectively. All three questions are aimed at determining whether or not a problem exists. As such, they represent the initial step in the three-step process known as *needs analysis*.

The first step in the needs analysis process is that of problem detection. From the perspective of the individuals asking the foregoing questions, a decision must be made:
"Does the person in front of me have a problem or face an opportunity?" If *Yes* (a problem detected), then I will ask further questions; if *No* (a problem not detected), then I will discontinue the questioning.

From the standpoint of evaluation, these questions yield data that will support a decision to continue or to discontinue the questioning. Note that in this example, the decision was a small one; yet, it still required data—albeit highly informal data. This, then, is the essence of program evaluation: the provision of timely data in service of a decision that must be made.

The second step of the needs analysis process entails diagnosis and consists of two parts. In the first part, more formal data are collected to support the decision regarding the nature of the problem or opportunity. From the perspective of the questioner, the issue becomes: What is the specific problem (or opportunity) being considered? The data collected during this step (often from a variety of sources) yields a formal statement of the problem as follows: The *value element* is very often the force which drives the problem. Not many individuals care about the butterflies in Table 8.1, but change the butterflies to whales in Alaskan waters or salmon in the northwest and the perceived importance of the problem may change significantly.

Indeed, one of the outcomes of the diagnostic step (in a community setting) is a report on the proportion of community members who consider the problem to be important or unimportant. Thus, the evaluator must be prepared to assist with the decision regarding the priorities among various problems.

The second part of the diagnostic step involves a more detailed analysis of the problem. That is, given the formal statement of the problem, the task then becomes one of identifying or developing a "theory of the problem." In the case of the children with dental caries, one theory might be that watching television before bedtime gave rise to the problem—not a very plausible theory. Another

TABLE 8.1
A Formal Statement of The Problem/Opportunity

---

A formal statement of the Problem/Opportunity should contain the following elements:
  Who—An indication of the population affected by the problem.
  What—An indication of the problem or opportunity at hand.
  Intensity—An indication of the severity or the cost of the problem.
  Condition or limits—An indication of the boundaries of the problem.
  Value—An indication of the underlying precept or "core belief" that makes the problem a problem.
    This is the element which makes a problem more important or less important. It is rarely explicit.

*Example 1*
  *Who*—Monarch butterflies
  *What*—Are declining in number
  *Intensity*—By 12% each year.
  *Conditions or limits*—Monarch butterflies in the west over the past 10 years
  *Value*—There should be no decline in natural populations.

*Example 2*
  *Who*—The children
  *What*—Have dental caries
  *Intensity*—At least 12% of the children are affected
  *Conditions or limits*—Children within the present community between the ages of 3 and 6 years
    of age.
  *Value*—No child should have dental caries.

---

theory might be failure to include whole-grain cereals in the diet caused the problem—again, a plausible but not a probable theory.

What is required here is an explication of the causal factors and a statement of how the causal factors combine to produce the formally stated problem. In the absence of a theory of the problem, any solution to the problem is as good as any other solution. It is the theory of the problem that dictates the solution. For example, if the problem is aggressive behavior on the part of children in a family, the solution (or intervention) that is posed might well be (a) medication—if the theory of the problem centers about internal chemical imbalances; (b) counseling—if the theory of the problem centers about a lack of communication or understanding; or (c) behavior modification—if the theory of the problem centers about a history of behavioral reinforcement. From the perspective of the evaluator, the key task becomes one of assisting the decision makers to make their theories of the problem explicit. In this instance, the problem theories of the decision makers constitute the "data" to be collected.

The third step of the needs analysis process is prescription of a solution. As noted, solutions must be based on the underlying theory of the problem. The formal solution statement is but a restatement of the problem theory to include causal factors and mechanism by which the new or realigned factors combine to produce a different outcome.

Example :

Factor $A$ + Factor $B$ $\longrightarrow$ Problem (Factor $D$)

(Icy Roads) + ("Summer" Driving Habits) $\longrightarrow$ Accidents

Factor $A$ + Factor $B$ − Factor $C$ $\longrightarrow$ Reduction of Problem (Factor $D$)

(Icy Roads) + ("Summer" Driving Habits)
  − (Winter Warning Signs) $\longrightarrow$ Reduced Accidents

In the foregoing example, the solution was not to eliminate icy roads; rather, it focused on changing the driving habits through the posting of warning signs. It is also true that the icy road factor could have been altered (by sanding).

Perhaps the most important point for the budding clinician to note here is that each proposed solution (or prescription) is really a hypothesis to be tested. Like any good experiment, the hypothesis is stated as: Given conditions (Factors $A$ and $B$ which are the control variables), the introduction of Factor $C$ (The independent variable) will produce a change in Factor $D$ (the dependent variable). Factor $C$ is the proposed solution and its statement represents the endpoint of the needs analysis.

## GOAL CLARIFICATION

There are many aspects of a program that require clarification. The presenting problem itself needs to be clarified, along with the underlying value that makes the problem a problem, the priority attached to any particular problem, the "theory of the problem," and the restatement of the problem theory (in terms of a testable hypothesis). In addition, the overall goal of the proposed program needs to be clearly established (written in concrete is not phrasing it too lightly).

In all of this clarification work, there are three rubrics to keep in mind:

1. The evaluator can assist with the format of the goal statement, but must never be the originator of a program's goal statement. The final goal statement must be a product of the decision makers.
2. A goal is not an objective. Goals represent the direction a program intends to take; objectives represent milestones. Goals do not contain precise statements of how they are to be measured; objectives do. The reason here is that changes in (measurement) technology may occur between the onset of a program and its demise some decades later. In such an

TABLE 8.2
Goals, Non-goals and Objectives

Nonexample
*The goal* of the program is to reduce travel time on the road through the sale of improved buggy
   whips to drivers.

Example
*The goal* of the Title I Program is to improve students' reading performance.

The objective of the Title I Program is to improve (pretest to posttest) performance of at least 75% of
   the students on the 1992 version of the XYZ standardized test of reading by 15% or more within
   1 year.

---

    instance, the program would lose credibility in later years if it were tied
specifically to an obsolete means of measurement.

3. Goals do not include a "how to" statement. That is, goals do not specify
   the means by which they are to be attained. As already noted, programs
   tend to be long term and technology or methodology can change. Once
   more, tying a program to a specific methodology may cause the program
   to lose credibility over the long run (see Table 8.2).

    The evaluator who assists program planners in formulating their goals will
provide a valuable service by applying these three rubrics.

## FORMATIVE AND SUMMATIVE EVALUATION

Until the late 1960s and early 1970s, evaluation was largely considered to be
an "end of program" phenomenon. During that era, however, Michael Scriven
became a strong advocate for differentiating the functions of evaluation (cited
in Shadish, Cook, & Leviton, 1991). In his classic description, Scriven likened
*formative evaluation* to the information available to a coach or team player
from the scoreboard during the game, which could be used to form or shape
decisions made while the game was still in progress. *Summative evaluation*
was described as the final result posted to the scoreboard at the end of the
game: it summarized the outcome of the game.

    This was (and remains) an important distinction—rather like an explorer
discovering that the Mississippi River has tributaries. In the same vein, it is
also true that the tributaries have tributaries. That is, it is now useful to think of
several varieties of information that would fall within the *formative* category
and several varieties that would fall within the *summative* category (and some
that would fall into both). In the paragraphs to follow, a model of evaluation
employed by me over the past 20 years is detailed. The model encompasses both
formative and summative aspects of program evaluation while incorporating
them into the life cycle of a program.

## THE THREE-PHASE MODEL OF EVALUATION

One need not spend many years in the evaluation business to realize that programs and projects have definite life cycles. In general, formal programs progress through the following sequence. Phase I is termed *generation* and consists of the planning, acquisition, or development of a program from needs assessment to the point of service delivery. Phase II is *implementation*: the delivery of the program services and the tracing of apparent effects on the client population. Phase III is *causation*: the development of evidence that the program (and only the program) produced the apparent effects on the client population.

Within each of the foregoing phases, there are important program activities—each of which has its own informational need. The three phases and their associated program activities have been outlined in Table 8.3.

Table 8.3 provides an initial view of the Three-Phase Model. In brief terms, the activities in Phase I trace the program's solution from drawing board through development, testing, and refinement. In Phase II, the activities extend from the delivery of the program (in a clinic or a classroom) to the clients' applications of the program content in their life situation and ends with an examination of the apparent impacts on other individuals or agencies with whom the client is associated.

Phase III essentially replicates the activities of Phase II but from a more rigorous point of view. Essentially, the activities in Phase III focus on proof

TABLE 8.3
Three Phases of Programs and The Activities Associated with Each Phase

| *Program Phase* | *Program Activities* | | |
|---|---|---|---|
| *Phase I*<br>Generation | A. Needs<br>Assessment | B. Acquisition or<br>development of<br>program | C. Testing and<br>refinement of<br>program services,<br>material |
| *Phase II*<br>Implementation | A. Provision of<br>service to client<br>population.<br>Immediate,<br>apparent effects<br>on clients<br>measured | B. Client application<br>of knowledge,<br>skill, concepts or<br>resources in<br>life-situation | C. Apparent impacts<br>on other<br>individuals or<br>agencies measured |
| *Phase III*<br>Causation | A. Experimental<br>proof of impacts<br>of program<br>service on client<br>population | B. Experimental<br>proof of changes<br>in client<br>performance in<br>life situation | C. Experimental<br>proof of impacts<br>on other<br>individuals or on<br>agencies. |

that the program (and only the program) caused the apparent effects noted:

+In the clinic or the classroom (Phase IIA),

+In the client's life situation (Phase IIB),

+Among other individuals or agencies with whom the client is involved (Phase IIC).

As evidenced by the entries in Table 8.4, the work of a program changes throughout its life cycle. For example, the major task of the program in Phase II (implementation) is to provide services to participants from the client population. Moreover, the tasks in Phase II also include monitoring the delivery of services, gauging the apparent impacts of those services, and client follow-up outside of the clinic or classroom. It must be acknowledged that not all programs adhere to such a sequence. In some instances, there is an emphasis on delivery of services. In other instances, there is some interest in learning about the immediate, apparent impacts of a program on the participants (Phase IIA). Sometimes the only apparent impact of interest is client attitude toward the service. In other instances, a more complete regimen is followed in which client attitudes, perceptions, knowledge, and/or skills are assessed within Phase IIA, with additional follow-up in Phases IIB and IIC. At this point, it should be abundantly clear that each activity has its own informational requirement. And that is where evaluation comes in.

Recall that at the beginning of this chapter, evaluation was defined as development of data to serve the informational needs of a program. Given that program activities change over time, how is it possible to anticipate the informational needs across the entire program cycle? The answer to this question is simplicity itself: Each activity within the program cycle gives rise to a predictable issue and that issue provides the basis for evaluation planning.

### Evaluation Issues

*Evaluation issues* are broadly stated areas of inquiry. They represent the areas in which program decisions will be made. Evaluation issues are the engine of inquiry; they focus the data collection effort in the areas of greatest concern. To illustrate: The XYZ Program focuses on fine motor skill training for a special client population. New instructional materials are being developed: That is, the program is in Phase IC. One evaluation issue facing the staff is: To what extent are the new instructional materials effective when used with the client population? Another evaluation issue is that of material revision: To what extent do the materials need to be revised before being implemented with the entire client population?

TABLE 8.4
Amplification of Detail Within the Three Phase Model

| Program Phase | Program Activities | | |
|---|---|---|---|
| *Phase I*<br>Generation | A. Needs assessment<br><br>Needs are identified. A Problem statement is formalized. A "theory of the problem" is detailed and a general solution is proposed. | B. Acquisition or Development of Program<br><br>Specifications for the program's solution are developed, reviewed, and refined.<br><br>An initial version of the program's solution is developed or acquired from other sources. The acquired solution may be adapted or adopted intact. | C. Testing and Refinement of Program Services, Material<br><br>The program's solution is tested with a sample from the client population.<br><br>Refinements to the program's specifications and/or the solution may be made.<br><br>The program's solution is produced preparatory to implementation. This includes staff preparation. |
| *Phase II*<br>Implementation | A. Provision of service to client population.<br><br>The services are delivered to the client population (e.g., in clinic or classroom setting).<br><br>The delivery of services are monitored to assure that the program's solution is being implemented as designed.<br><br>Immediate, apparent impacts are studied. | B. Client application of knowledge, skill, concepts, or resources in life situation.<br><br>Client application of program content outside the classroom or clinic setting is monitored.<br><br>Apparent changes in client performance in life situation are monitored. | C. Impacts on other individuals or agencies<br><br>Apparent impacts on others in the client's life situation are monitored (e.g., family, co-workers).<br><br>Apparent impacts on agencies in the client's life situation are monitored (e.g., reduction in disciplinary actions taken by an employer, reduction in visits to emergency rooms). |

(Continued)

TABLE 8.4
(Continued)

| Program Phase | Program Activities | | |
|---|---|---|---|
| Phase III<br>Causation | A. Experimental proof of impacts of program service on client population.<br><br>Same as IIA above, but with experimental proof of effects. | B. Experimental proof of changes in client performance in life situation.<br><br>Same as IIB, but with experimental proof of effects. | C. Experimental proof of impacts on other individuals or on agencies.<br><br>Same as IIC, but with experimental proof of effects. |

Note that both of the foregoing evaluation issues share two characteristics. First, both are stated in a neutral manner. Thus, the inquiry, which represents the heart of the evaluation effort, is launched in an unbiased manner. Note that the first issue did *not* ask: How successful are the new instructional materials with the client population? An inquiry based on such a question begins with the assumption that the materials will be successful and hence might well fail to take into account the possibility that the materials are not successful. In a word, the evaluation issue must launch an inquiry that is open to both positive and negative outcomes.

The second characteristic of the two foregoing evaluation issues is that they contain no statement of measurement methodology. Selecting the method(s) for conducting the inquiry comes after the evaluation issue has been identified. There are at least two reasons for this: (a) Preselecting the data collection methodology usually results in a misdirected data collection effort, thus the most vital evaluation issues within a program may be overlooked or inadequately addressed; (b) Such preselection severely limits the scope of any inquiry and analysis. Selecting the method of inquiry prior to identifying the area of inquiry calls to mind the renowned comic sequence: Ready! Fire! Aim!

## THE ISSUE DRIVES THE METHODOLOGY; THE METHODOLOGY MUST NOT DRIVE THE ISSUE

I was once hired to evaluate a bilingual education program. The program had been in operation for some time. The program staff had developed its own "test" to measure student learning. The content of the test was "all over the map." It was not at all consistent with nor representative of the course content. In this case, the staff had preselected the measurement methodology and that methodology did not comport at all with the evaluation issue: To what extent did the participating students acquire the program's knowledge and skills? As a result, there was no valid way to answer the impact issue.

Earlier it was noted that by taking into account the life cycle of a program, it is possible to anticipate some of the issues that arise during each phase. Table 8.5 contains just such a set of predictions.

Table 8.5 expands on the previous table by presenting examples of the issues associated with each program activity. These are unique to the individual activity and can be anticipated. A word of caution is in order; the issues suggested within Table 8.5 have been provided as illustrations, they do not comprise the entire set of issues that might be identified for any single program activity. Nor does Table 8.5 provide any hint about the methods that might be employed to study any of the issues. That aspect of evaluation planning is deferred until the relevant issues have been identified.

## Methodology

Presuming that the issues important to the program have been identified, how is methodology determined? For better or for worse, methodological considerations (in the real world) are always a compromise between three competing factors. *Factor 1* is the "penetration" of any given method or measuring device. Consider for example the penetration of a test of intelligence. Can a standard I.Q. test accurately reveal the full breadth and width of an individual's intelligence or are there some aspects of individual intelligence (such as "social intelligence") that are not covered? Or, consider personality inventories. If one administers the Minnesota Multiphasic Personality Inventory (MMPI-2; Butcher, Dahlstrom, Graham, Tellegen, & Kaemmer, 1989) to a client, do the results accurately reveal the entire psychological make up of the client? Or are there aspects of the client's personality that are not encompassed by the instruments?

Think now of a project that is developing new instructional materials— perhaps a manual for administering a new psychological test. A test of the manual is conducted using a sample of experienced counselors. This is called a pilot test. With modern techniques, it is possible to record the eye movements of the pilot test subjects as they study the manual. Such a record would reveal which sections of the manual required additional attention by the subjects. An alternative technique would be to have the subjects make note of those sections that required more study. The essential difference between the two techniques is the level of detail required by the pilot study: Are data to be collected on every eye movement of every subject on every line within the manual? Or would a set of marginal notes suffice? The difference is one of penetration.

On a broader scale, consider surveys. For the most part, surveys are based on samples of the larger population. Does a carefully drawn random sample

TABLE 8.5
The Three Phase Model with Evaluation Issues Common to Each Activity

| Program Phase | Program Activities | | |
|---|---|---|---|
| *Phase I*<br>Generation | A. Needs Assessment<br><br>Issue: What is the extent or intensity of the problem?<br><br>Issue: What is the cost of the problem? | B. Acquisition or Development of Program<br><br>Issue: What are the specifications of the program solution?<br><br>Issue: To what extent are the specifications present in the adopted program? | C. Testing and Refinement of Program Services, Material<br><br>Issue: To what extent does the program require revision?<br><br>Issue: For which categories of clients does the program work? For which categories does it not work?<br><br>Issue: To what extent is the program staff able to implement the program? |
| *Phase II*<br>Implementation | A. Provision of service to client population. Immediate, apparent effects on clients measured.<br><br>Issue: To what extent was the program implemented as planned?<br><br>Issue: To what extent did the program yield the expected results on the clients? | B. Client application of knowledge, skill, concepts or resources in life-situation<br><br>Issue: To what extent did the clients apply the program's knowledge, skills or attitudes at home?<br><br>Issue: To what extent was there an apparent change in the client's behavior in the family? | C. Apparent impacts on other individuals or agencies measured.<br><br>Issue: To what extent was there an impact on the client's family or co-workers?<br><br>Issue: To what extent was there an impact on the agencies with which the client is involved? |
| *Phase III*<br>Causation | A. Experimental proof of impacts of program service on client population<br><br>Issue: To what extent was the program implemented as planned? | B. Experimental proof of changes in client performance in life situation.<br><br>Issue: To what extent did the clients apply the program's knowledge, skills, or attitudes at home? | C. Experimental proof of impacts on other individuals or on agencies.<br><br>Issue: To what extent did the program—by itself—have an impact on the client's family or co-workers? |

(Continued)

TABLE 8.5
(Continued)

| Program Phase | Program Activities | | |
|---|---|---|---|
| | Issue: To what extent did the program—by itself—yield the expected results on the clients? | Issue: To what extent did the program—by itself—produce a change in the client's behavior within the family? | Issue: To what extent did the program—by itself—have an impact on the agencies with which the client is involved? |

provide an accurate view of the population? (Although sampling techniques provide reliable results if repeated over the long run, most surveys are single "snapshots in time" and are not repeated over the long run.) The key point here is that although some data collection methods (which include both design and instruments) are highly accurate, all are subject to penetrability limits.

*Factor 2* is the reliability and the validity of the measurement approach. In the case of standardized instruments (such as intelligence tests and personality inventories), the publishers provide indices of accuracy (validity coefficients) and repeatability (reliability coefficients). These indices represent results of instrument trials in the hands of well-trained professionals. Do such indices hold up when the instruments are administered by nonprofessionals under "ambient" conditions? It should be evident that the quality of the data derived from any measurement approach is influenced greatly by three characteristics: (a) the quality of the data collection instrument, (b) the quality of the data collection effort, and (c) the quality of the subsequent data recording and analysis procedures. And, in turn, these elements are greatly influenced by the third factor.

*Factor 3* is the matter of resources for data collection. If the resource budget is ample, then "high end" data collection methods (which presumably have greater penetrability, higher reliability, and greater validity), can be used. Moreover, professionally trained staff can be used to collect, reduce, analyze, and interpret the data. If, however, resources are scarce, data collection methods employed may have less depth (e.g., one page of questions on the survey form and a much smaller sample) and may be collected by "volunteers." For example: Is there a difference between a physical exam (complete with CAT scan) undertaken at the Mayo Clinic and the exam given at an outpatient clinic in a small, rural town?

The challenge confronting the evaluator is to balance each of these three factors and to produce solid information which can support the decision making process. Quite independently of the foregoing challenge, there is a positive side to the question of methodology. In particular, measurement methodology is

TABLE 8.6
A Tool for Classifying Evaluation Methods

Evaluation methods:
—include data collection instruments.
—include data collection procedures (i.e., who, how many, when, timing, and frequency).
—may be classified as *formal* or *informal*
   Formal = Involves a data collection instrument; is planned, scheduled, and results are documented.
   Informal = No instrument per se, spur of the moment, no plan for documenting results.
—may be classified as *active* or *passive*
   Active = The source of the information must do something extra to generate the data (e.g., take a test, answer a questionnaire).
   Passive = The source of information does nothing extra to generate the data (e.g., client interacts with family while counselor observes, client attends school, and attendance record is generated).

Examples of Data Collection Procedures

|  | *Informal* | *Formal* |
|---|---|---|
| Passive | *Clinician's observation | *Tabulation of behaviors |
|  | *Incidental observation | *Guided observation |
|  | *Environmental scanning | *Attendance |
|  | *Informal conversations | *Review of client history |
|  | * | * |
| Active | *Debrief clients after session | *Test, Personality Inventory |
|  | *Ask questions of counseling group | *Attitudinal Questionnaire |
|  | *Ask for show of hands | *Respond to phone survey |
|  | *Ask for volunteers | *Client demonstrates new skill through role play |
|  | * | * |

*From your own experience, list at least one example for each of the four quadrants.

abundant and is often limited only by one's imagination. In one study reportedly conducted within a museum, the evaluation issue was: Which are the most popular exhibits? The methodology was not a headcount of viewers, nor a study of "average time spent in front of each exhibit." The methodology of choice was based on building maintenance records; that is, the records of floor tile replacements. It was reasoned that the most popular exhibits were those where the foot traffic was heaviest, resulting in more frequent replacement of floor tiles. (Webb, Campbell, Schwartz, & Sechrest, 1966).

Table 8.6 contains a tool for thinking more broadly about data collection methods. And Table 8.6 contains some examples of the use of the tool.

***An Evaluation Planning Template.*** This section began with a discussion of formative versus summative evaluation. Next the Three-Phase Model, which encompasses both formative and summative elements, was discussed. The key points within the Three-Phase Model are: (a) programs have a life cycle, (b) each stage of the life cycle is defined by activities, (c) each activity has some predictable evaluation issues, and (d) it is important to identify the evaluation issues before selecting a data collection method. There are many data collection methods from which to make a selection. In the concluding part of this section, these concepts are combined in a sample evaluation plan.

A sample program is used to illustrate the Three-Phase Model. The Gentle Mental Counseling Center (a fictional name) operates the Outreach Program. The program is in its third year of a 5-year program grant. The purpose of the grant is to provide counseling, training and in-home assistance for troubled families. The specific assistance to be provided within the program focuses on three areas: parenting skills, anger management skills, and communication skills within the family. The assistance is based on a weekly counseling and a weekly instructional session conducted by the clinicians at the center. The work of each clinician is followed by a weekly home visit by a clinical assistant from the center.

The Outreach Program has been through the needs assessment and program development stages. It is now in Phase 2 (Implementation) and the following evaluation issues are receiving the most attention:

Issue 1. To what extent are the clinicians delivering the program as planned?

Issue 2. To what extent are the participants acquiring the parenting, anger management and communication skills within the weekly instructional sessions?

Issue 3. To what extent are the participants employing the skills at home?

Issue 4. To what extent are there changes in the way the participating families interact at home?

The plan for collecting data for each of the four issues is presented in Table 8.7.

## EVALUATING IMPLEMENTATION ADHERENCE

Earlier it was stated that a program is an institutional or societal response to a problem or opportunity. It was further stated that a program is defined as one or more relatively uniform interventions designed to address a problem or opportunity. The key phrase within that definition is "relatively uniform." This means that the program operates pretty much the same way across sites and (to some extent) across time. By way of contrast, the "program" that provides a different, ever-evolving set of services to clients at each of several locations is not a program at all—it is a collection of projects. Under such

TABLE 8.7
Sample Section of Evaluation Plan for The Gentle Mental Outreach Program

| Program Phase | Evaluation Issue | SubArea of Issue | Data Collection Method | Data Collection Detail |
|---|---|---|---|---|
| IIA | 1. In class delivery of program as planned | 1a. Parenting Skills | Topic checklist | Completed after each session by instructor. |
| | | | Guided observation checklist | Completed once every three sessions by center supervisor. |
| | | 1b. Anger management skills | Topic checklist | Completed after each session by instructor |
| | | | Videotape of session | Video review checklist completed after each session by supervisor. |
| | | 1c. Communication skills | Topic checklist | Completed after each session by instructor. |
| | | | Process observer with monitoring checklist | Process observer monitors every other session. |
| II A | 2. Parents acquire skills in class | Parenting, anger management and communication skills | Participant role plays | Each participant role plays each skill. Instructor records skill attainment or nonattainment on individual client skills record. |
| II B | 3. Parents employ skills at home | Parenting, anger management and communication skills | Clinical assistant records family interactions in homebased on guided observation form. | Prior to service, clinical assistant employs guided observation form on at least four occasions in the home (baseline established). Observations continue during instructional phase. |

(Continued)

TABLE 8.7
(Continued)

| Program Phase | Evaluation Issue | Subarea of Issue | Data Collection Method | Data Collection Detail |
|---|---|---|---|---|
| II B | 4. Changes in family interactions in the home. | Family interactions | Clinical assistants complete the XYZ family interaction form based on observations in the home. | The XYZ family interaction form is completed prior to service and at the conclusion of service. At least two clinical assistants must make the observations to complete the form for each family. |

circumstances, there can never be an answer to the question: Did this program impact the problem or challenge for which it was designed? It is rather like a medical practitioner who tries to cure a patient by employing a random series of medications. If the patient is finally cured, what particular regimen affected the cure? No one knows, so the results may never be duplicated. Even worse is the situation where a program's tightly controlled solution actually works and is subsequently adopted at other sites. The sites that change the solution or intervention (sometimes without realizing it) find that the solution does not work; It does not work because it was not implemented as designed. A major challenge to the evaluator, therefore, is to assist the program staff in defining the program's solution and to help them monitor the fidelity of that solution.

The reader should now return to Table 8.5 and examine cells IB and IC. The entries therein refer to *specifications* for the program's solution. Specifications represent the formula for the program's solution. Taken together, they comprise a written description of the program intervention. There are a number of advantages to having such a written description:

- Those who authorize the intervention are able to communicate clearly with those who design it;
- Those who implement the intervention know exactly what is expected;
- Those who adopt the intervention know the original "recipe" for the program;
- Those who supervise (or otherwise monitor) the program have a solid understanding of the original intent or design;

* Those who evaluate the intervention can learn the extent to which the planned program was actually implemented. Such knowledge is critical if the effectiveness of the program is to be assessed.

Therefore, quality control of a program begins with a written description.

Table 8.8 consists of 21 dimensions (there are many more) that can be used to describe program interventions. Not all dimensions (or specifications) are relevant to all programs. Yet the consideration of each of the dimensions casts a very bright light on the question, "What are the essential elements of the program?"

In applying the entries in Table 8.8 to any particular program, two questions should be asked of each dimension: (1) Is this dimension applicable to the program under consideration?, and (2) If so, what is the program's position[1] on this dimension?

By way of example, if dimension 21 (cost limits) were under consideration, the answers might be: (1) yes, and (2) program services are limited to an expenditure of no more than $800 per client.

Assume that a program staff identifies the relevant dimensions and identifies the program position on those dimensions; what have they accomplished and what do they do with the results? First, in establishing a position on a given dimension, the staff will have created a specification. And taken in sum, collection of specifications will constitute the official program description. Such a description represents the standards for the program. Second, specifications can easily be converted into a program monitoring guide. The monitoring guide can be used to assure the quality and fidelity of the program. It can also be used by other (adopting) agencies as they attempt to replicate the program elsewhere.

Table 8.9 contains a sample of the monitoring guide for the Gentle Mental Counseling Center's Outreach Program.

## EVALUATING IMPACT

Programs in the social service area can have many impacts. They can impact the participants, they can impact participant families, they can impact other institutions and agencies, and they can impact the staff who operate them. Within the present section, five kinds of program impacts are explored.

---

[1] Keep in mind that the dimensions represent variables. Accordingly, it is not necessary select a single value for the variable; a *range* of values along the dimension is a legitimate option. For example, if the dimension of duration (how long the services last for a client) is selected, it is not necessary to select a single value (such as 6 months). Rather, selecting a range (such as 3 to 9 months) is allowable. The important thing is to establish the limits of the variable.

TABLE 8.8
Program Specifications

| *Dimension* | *Description* |
| --- | --- |
| 1. Client objectives | 1. The outcome objectives. The expected results. What clients will be able to do when they have completed the program. The level of proficiency of each successful client. |
| 2. Client population | 2. The group or groups to be served by the program. Those for whom the program was designed, developed, and delivered. |
| 3. Client characteristics | 3. The known characteristics of the clients. Are they highly motivated? Are they self-aware? Are they well educated? Are they adults? Are they children? |
| 4. Client prerequisites | 4. The screening criteria. The answer to the questions: Who gets into the program? Who does not get into the program? |
| 5. Client roles/tasks | 5. What are the tasks and responsibilities of the client? What should the client be doing while enrolled in the program? Is the role active? Is the role passive? |
| 6. Content domain | 6. What are the major concept areas in which services are to be provided? What is the scope of program offerings? What are the limits of the program's offerings? |
| 7. Client grouping | 7. The configuration of services to individuals or groups. If services are provided in group format, what are the criteria for establishing groups? |
| 8. Program point of view | 8. The theoretical or practical stance the program takes toward clients and services. Example: Does the counseling program operate from a cognitive or a Rogerian point of view? Do program practices include dream therapy? Behavior modification? What varieties of therapy are in? What varieties of therapy are out? |
| 9. Service model | 9. The usual and customary sequence of transactions (steps) that the clients will experience as they progress through the program. At what points in the sequences are decisions to be made? On what data are the decisions to be based? What are the criteria for each decision? Who is authorized to make those decisions? (use a flow chart here.) |
| 10. Duration | 10. The period over which the average client is to be served. |
| 11. Intensity | 11. How often and for what length of time the average client is to be served. Example: Two sessions per week with each session 50 min in length. |
| 12. Media mix | 12. The major means by which the services are to be delivered. One to one meetings with the counselor? Biblio therapy? At-home readings coupled with weekly small group discussions? Take-home workbook and monthly meetings with the counselor? |
| 13. Verisimilitude | 13. For use with training and skill development programs. The extent to which the instructional activities resemble the life situation and circumstances of the client. Example: Realistic role play versus group discussion of skills. |

(Continued)

TABLE 8.8
(Continued)

| Dimension | Description |
|---|---|
| 14. Instructional materials | 14. The basic instructional materials (e.g, the client text or the service provider's guide) used in the program. The hand-out materials distributed to clients. |
| 15. Service provider qualifications | 15. The essential qualifications required for each category of the program's service providers. License required? Educational or language requirements? Special experience required? |
| 16. Service provider role/tasks | 16. The functions, tasks, responsibilities, and authority level of each category of service provider. How the roles relate to one another. |
| 17. Assessment procedures | 17. Data collection forms and assessment instruments to be used. The scope, frequency, and content of client assessments within the program. |
| 18. Record system | 18. Provision for maintaining data about the clients and the program per se. |
| 19. Linkage to client's home, school, job or other agencies | 19. Liaison arrangements with other individuals and agencies who deal with the client. |
| 20. Plan for follow-up | 20. Arrangements for follow up with the client after leaving the program. |
| 21. Cost limits | 21. The cost boundaries of the service. Is there a minimum? Is there a maximum? Is there an expected average cost? |

## Immediate Impacts on Participants

The reader is referred to Table 8.5. Within Table 8.5, Phase IIA, represents the first occasion in which impacts are mentioned. Within Phase IIA, clients are provided with the program's service. That service may be instruction, it may be counseling, it may be some other intervention. In most programs, it is anticipated that at the point of service delivery, the client or participant will somehow be changed. And to the extent that such change occurs, the program is said to have had impact.

What kinds of change or impacts are anticipated at the point of service delivery? Kirkpatrick (1959a, 1959b, 1960a, 1960b) presented a hierarchy of outcomes consisting of four levels; reaction, learning, behavior, and results. Kirkpatrick suggested that changes at the point of service delivery could be expected in participant attitudes or reactions (Level 1) and in participant knowledge or skills (Level 2). Within the context of the Three-Phase Model, such changes are referred to as apparent impacts. Remember, Phase II does not encompass experimental findings. Accordingly, the prudent evaluator holds the findings at this point rather lightly. Although apparent impacts may be very encouraging and may be consistent with the program's predictions, they ordinarily do not constitute "hard evidence" of program effectiveness.

TABLE 8.9
Sample Monitoring Guide for The Gentle Mental Outreach Program

| Program Element | Specification | If Present, Expect to Observe | Rating |
|---|---|---|---|
| 4. Client prerequisite | 4a. Participating families with two adults and at least one child. | 4a. Each participating family composed of two adults and one or more children.<br><br>See program enrollment form | 4a. Percentage meeting criteria:_____ |
| | 4b. Each family must have been referred by either the court or the State's Family Services Division. | 4b. Copy of court order or State Family Services Division referral form in each client file. | 4b. Percentage meeting criteria:_____ |
| 6. Content domain | 6. Clinicians conduct at least three small group instruction sessions for each cohort of clients encompassing the program's 12 key parenting skills. | 6a. Clinicians conducting at least three small group instruction sessions for each cohort of clients.<br><br>See signatures on completed topic checklists.<br>6b. The sessions encompass the program's 12 key parenting skills.<br><br>See completed topic checklists and supervisor's guided observation list | 6. Number of completed client cohorts:_____<br><br>6a. Percentage of cohorts in which clinicians presented at least three sessions on the topic:_____<br>6b. Percentage of completed cohorts in which all 12 skills were presented:_____ |
| 10. Duration | 10. Each family to be served between six and nine months. | 10. Entry and exit dates of client on program enrollment forms indicating service between six and nine months. | 10a. Closed cases: Percentage meeting criteria:_____<br><br>10b. Current cases: Percentage not exceeding nine month limit:_____ |

With the foregoing warning in mind, what "impacts" can be expected from program participants at the point of service delivery? Apparent changes in attitude and skill or knowledge attainment can be detected, provided that care has been taken to assess the participants on a pre and post basis with an appropriate instrument. An even stronger claim for immediate program impacts can be made if a "chain of evidence" can be established. The chain would run something like this: (a) The participant did not possess certain knowledge/skills or attitudes prior to entering the program: (b) The program provided special services (instruction, training, counseling, etc.) to the participant. The delivery of these services was documented: (c) The participant exhibited certain knowledge/skills or attitudes on completing the program. This chain of evidence makes for a stronger claim of program impacts, but does not yet constitute hard proof of such impacts.

### Intermediate Impacts of the Program

Let us move ahead to Phase IIB of the Three-Phase Model. This phase deals with the participants' application of the acquired knowledge, skills or attitudes away from the site of service delivery—perhaps in their home, school or on the job. To make the further claim of program effectiveness, it is necessary to ascertain that the participant actually applied those things learned from the program. To push the point further, a program claim of effectiveness should also establish the extent to which applying those things learned made a difference in the participant's life situation.

Thus, the chain of evidence would look like this:

A. The participant did not possess certain knowledge/skills or attitudes prior to entering the program.
B. The program provided special services (instruction, training, counseling, etc.) to the participant. The delivery of these services was documented.
C. The participant exhibited certain knowledge/skills or attitudes on completing the program.
D. The participants employed the program's knowledge/skills or attitudes in their life settings. The application was documented.
E. The application of the knowledge/skills or attitudes was accompanied by a change in performance, interaction, or effectiveness in the life setting. The changes were documented on a pretest and posttest basis.

Again, the foregoing chain (Link A to Link E) makes for a fairly strong claim, but by itself does not constitute hard proof of program impact. Still, most of the educational and training programs with which the writer is familiar barely achieve Links A–C in the chain.

## Secondary Impacts of The Program

In Phase II C of the Three-Phase Model, the secondary impacts of the program become a matter of concern. Within Phase II C, the impacts on other individuals, other institutions and other agencies can be assessed. The notion here is that a participant who now possesses the concepts or skills or attitudes provided by the program not only has applied those things, but the application has impacted others. For example, parenting skills acquired in a program have been applied at home and as a result, the participant is a better parent, the family is more cohesive, and the authorities (e.g., family services workers or the courts) remove the family from the active caseload roster. This would be a tremendous apparent impact, but to make the claim for it, the chain of evidence would have to contain the following links:

A. The participant did not possess certain knowledge/skills or attitudes prior to entering the program.
B. The program provided special services (instruction, training, counseling, etc.) to the participant. The delivery of these services was documented.
C. The participant exhibited certain knowledge/skills or attitudes on completing the program.
D. The participants employed the program's knowledge/skills or attitudes in their life settings. The application was documented.
E. Application of the knowledge/skills or attitudes was accompanied by a change in performance, interaction, or effectiveness in the life setting. The changes were documented on a pretest and posttest basis.
F. A change in status (e.g., status on a family dynamics rating scale) reduced to "normal" range; family no longer considered as part of court caseload, absenteeism from job reduced; children no longer considered as "at risk" in school, observed, and status is documented. This requires assessment of status on pretest and posttest basis.

It is important to observe here that it is difficult to claim the impacts in Link F in the absence of any of the preceding links. That is, one cannot say: "We delivered the parenting skills program and as a result the children are no longer considered to be at risk students in school." The entire chain is necessary but not sufficient to make such a claim.

## Experimental Proof of Impacts

As noted in Table 8.4, the three cells in Phase III have content which parallels the that of the three cells in Phase II. The difference is that Phase III requires a much more rigorous approach to claims and to proof than does Phase II. For example, in Phase IIIA, the evaluation issue is not merely about changes in the attitudes or performances of the participants at the point of service delivery, but whether it was the program and only the program that brought about those changes. Regardless of the quality of the data collection instruments and techniques in Phase II, there are always plausible, competing explanations for the results. This is why the claims in Phase II (regardless of the strength of the chain of evidence) can never be accepted as final proof of program impact. The purpose, then, of Level III, is to eliminate any competing explanation for the results that were obtained; and this is accomplished by experimental designs.

Experimental designs are simply arrangements for collecting data that eliminate competing explanations for the results which are obtained. Non-Example: (a) Participants complete the pretest, (b) Program services provided to the participants, (c) Participants complete the posttest, (d) Result: Participants demonstrate pretest-posttest gain, (e) Claim: The program caused the gain.

Aside from the foregoing claim, how else might the result have occurred? (a) The participants were more familiar with the test on the second occasion and therefore performed better on the posttest; (b) The participants were simultaneously enrolled in another program which covered the same content; (c) The participants were distracted by a holiday at the time of the pretest. The participants were able to concentrate better on the posttest.

A stronger case for program effectiveness is illustrated in the following example: (a) Participants randomly assigned to two groups; (b) All participants complete the pretest at the same time; (c) Program services provided to only one of the groups; (d) All participant complete the posttest at the same time; (e) Result: Participants receiving program services make larger pretest-posttest gains than participants in the other group; (f) Claim: The program was the cause of the larger gain.

In the foregoing example, use of a contemporaneous control group eliminated three competing explanations. Thus, within Phase III, the use of an experimental design (plus monitoring of program processes) is required for "hard evidence" of program impact. The challenge facing the program evaluator is two-fold:

1. The case has to be made that program claims of impact are weak in the absence of experimental designs.
2. Feasible substitutes for pure experimental designs have to be found or developed. Five such designs are discussed in the next section.

### Reduction of The Initial Problem

It will be recalled that programs were defined as responses to societal problems or challenges. And in an earlier part of this chapter, the reader was admonished to exercise care in documenting the extent of the initial problem (see Table 8.1).

This is called *establishing a baseline*. Careful attention to that particular detail pays big dividends in the long run. Here is why. *If it can be shown that the severity or intensity or frequency of the problem has been reduced, the program can make a stronger case for claiming impact.* That is the headline. The details, however are subject to the same limitations for claiming impact that were noted in all three elements of Phase II. There are thus two general approaches that may be taken to laying claim for a reduction of the initial problem:

1. Establish the chain of evidence that shows step by step that the program was implemented as planned, that the participants acquired the knowledge, skills, or attitudes at the point of delivery, that the participants employed what they had learned, and that their life situation was changed. Although this does not constitute final proof of program effectiveness, it is a strong argument.

2. Do all of the aforementioned, but within the context of an experimental design that reduces or eliminates competing explanations for results that show improvement over the initial baseline. In the end, this "hard evidence" approach to assessing program impacts hinges on three factors: (a) The desire for and commitment to finding a causal link between the program intervention and the program outcomes; (b) Availability of resources (time and money) to plan and execute an appropriate experimental design; (c) Feasibility of employing an appropriate design within the context of the program.

Unfortunately, within the experience of the writer, factors A and B are rarely encountered in programs outside of education and academia. Thus, what is known about most programs is that they have some apparent effects on the participants. What is not known—with any degree of assurance—is that the programs are solely responsible for creating those effects.

## QUASI-EXPERIMENTAL DESIGNS

Experimental designs are simply arrangements for conducting observations in a given situation. Usually this means collecting the observations, which are called data, in such a manner that the effect of a variable can be discerned. The desired state of affairs is one in which the observer can state with assurance: "It was this variable and this variable alone that accounts for any change." Traditionally this has meant that the study met the requirements for establishing causality as described in Chapter 1, meaning a traditional experimental design with random assignment, control groups, and considerable control by the experimenter. That some degree of assurance can be obtained without full experiment was recognized by Campbell and Stanley (1963). The most recent incarnation of that work is Shadish, Cook, and

Campbell (2002), in which many experimental and quasi-experimental designs are described.

The good news is that here are many ways to arrange for observations that will permit the observer to make such a statement. The bad news is that most observational arrangements or designs that would permit such a statement are not feasible outside of a laboratory setting. For example, consider the classic randomized pretest–posttest design:

1. A pool of participants is identified.
2. Participants from the pool are randomly assigned to one of two groups.
3. Both groups are pretested contemporaneously.
4. One group receives the treatment (or program services); the other does not.
5. Both groups are posttested contemporaneously.
6. The pretest–posttest performances of the two groups are compared and any significant differences are attributed to the treatment.

Under this arrangement, the following assumptions can be made:

- Participants were selected for the pool based on characteristics pertinent to the study (e.g., all were college sophomores enrolled in their first course in psychology).
- Assignment to the two groups was made on a random basis. This permits the observer to assume that the two groups are initially equal in talent, skill level, motivation, etcetera. (This can be checked by comparing the pretest scores of the two groups.)
- Because group assignment was random, it is assumed that the two groups were equivalent in their familiarity with the test instrument.
- Because both the pretests and the posttests were administered in a contemporaneous manner, neither group has an advantage due to seasonal or other potentially distracting events.
- Because of random assignment, it is assumed that the two groups were (initially) equivalent in their familiarity with the treatment.
- Only one group received the treatment and this was the only way in which the two groups differed.

Given these assumptions, it is fair to conclude that any differences between the pretest–posttest gains of the two groups can be attributed to the treatment that one group received.

Note that in this classic design, the observer exercises a great deal of control. The harsh reality is, however, that the ability to exercise such control is largely limited to private and academic research enterprises. Most programs operate in the public arena where such control is not available. Consider the public outcry that would arise if public school students were randomly assigned either to the new experimental reading group or to the control group. Random assignment is not an option in most public settings. As an armchair exercise, the reader is invited to revisit the classic experimental design just mentioned with one change: eliminate the random assignment and substitute intact classrooms of students. What happens to the conclusion that can be drawn?

Most programs, as we know them, are conducted in the public arena. Further, the controls that are available in a laboratory setting are often not available to public programs. This means that even with the most favorable outcomes, it is difficult to make the claim that the program was solely responsible for such outcomes.

Given these circumstances, is there anything that can be done? The answer is *yes*—if a compromise is accepted. The compromise consists in finding an arrangement that moves the evaluation in the direction of a true experimental design, but does not entail such a design. The observational or data collection arrangements that perform this task are called quasi-experimental designs. These designs provide a higher level of proof of program effectiveness than that provided by the apparent results alone. At the same time, such designs yield results that are suggestive but not entirely conclusive. In the paragraphs that follow, five such designs are described. Again, note that each is capable of strengthening the claim that a program caused a certain effect, but they do not constitute final proof of the matter. These all represent actual evaluation projects conducted by the author.

1. *Normative comparisons.* Where the program deals with an area (such as reading) for which standardized tests are available, normative comparisons are possible. Here is how the design works: In developing the standardized test, the publisher typically tries out the test with a national sample of students. The selected sample is usually chosen to be closely representative of students enrolled in each grade throughout the nation. Tests are administered on two occasions (specific dates in the fall and spring of the year). The results are used to create test norms. Norms essentially represent the distribution of student performances within each grade level in the fall and in the spring. Local programs can then administer the tests on a fall–spring basis (using the anniversary dates of the publisher's norming study). Local program scores can then be compared with the published test norms. This means that the standardized test norms serve as a surrogate control group for the program. This is by no means a perfect solution, but it can strengthen the claim that the program is having an impact upon its participants.

2. *Normative comparison—local version.* I was once involved in a migrant education program. The program sought to provide preschool and kindergarten educational services to youngsters between 4 and 6 years of age. The program

had at least two unique features: (1) the children's families were migrant workers who moved on an annual cycle between Mexico and the Pacific Northwest. They did not remain in one location for any extended period of time; (2) The program staff made the instructional program portable. That is, wherever a few of the families settled (temporarily), the educational program would operate. This was made possible by recruiting and training some of the mothers of the participating families to deliver the program's instructional content. There were at least two major challenges in evaluating the program: First, there were no standardized tests (with convenient norms) that were appropriate for this particular group of students. Second, there was no control group for this unique set of students. The solution to this dilemma was to create a set of program norms. That is, every participating child was given the program's test on entry. The test closely mirrored the program's instructional content. Because the children ranged in age between 4 and 6 years, it was possible to establish a set of norms for children from this unique population. The norms were organized by age group. The entry scores represented children who had never been exposed to the program's instruction, so the scores could be used as benchmarks. For example, students who entered the program at age 4 years and 6 months would be tested and their test results would be accumulated within the 4 year, 6 month category. If some of these same students completed the program a year later, they would be posttested and their results compared with the scores of students who entered at age 5 years, 6 months. In this way, each entering student helped to provided an estimate of "untreated" student performance from the same population and at a specified age level. Does this design represent a compromise? *Yes.* Did it strengthen the claim that the program was having a positive effect on the participants? *Yes again.*

3. *Pretest–posttest design with comparison group.* In some circumstances, there are no standardized tests with norms that can be used to assess program impact. Nor is random assignment to treatment and control groups possible. Sometimes the only available alternative is comparison of the program participant's performance with similar individuals elsewhere. This may mean using an intact group whose circumstance parallel those of the program participants. Consider the situation in which training in interpersonal communication skills are to be provided to all members of a clinic. Suppose further that it is possible to measure the effect of the training. Because the clinic wants to make the program available to all employees, there is no possibility of obtaining a control group within the clinic. How are the impacts of the program measured?

Begin by locating a clinic that approximates the size and specialty areas of the first clinic. Secure their participation in the study (perhaps by promising to provide the training to them at a later date at a reduced fee). Next, collect data on the demographic characteristics of employees at both clinics, then pretest the employees of both clinics at the same time. Provide the training to the first clinic. Posttest the employees of the two clinics at the same time.

While the staff members of the second clinic are not an ideal control group, they represent (particularly if the demographic characteristics of the two groups match) a comparison group. The closer the two groups are in terms of matching characteristics and initial test performance, the stronger the claim for program effectiveness.

4. *The delayed entry design.* Sometimes, as in the just cited example, the program is designed to serve the entire pool of participants. How does one obtain a comparison group under these circumstances? The delayed entry design may help here. It is useful when the entire cadre of participants is to be provided with the treatment. Because it usually not possible to provide services to everyone at once, the participants are divided into two groups. (Because no one will be denied the treatment, it may be possible to make random assignments to the two groups.) Begin with the first group of participants taking the pretest. Next provide them with the treatment. At the conclusion of the treatment, posttest them. The second group is pretested twice, provided with the treatment, and then posttested. The dual pretesting of the second group is timed to coincide with the pretests and posttests of the first group. In effect, all participants receive the treatment, but a true experimental design has been incorporated into the procedure.

5. *Multiple baseline.* In some situations, the program participants are unique. In a special education program, for example, each of the participants exhibited a unique constellation of symptoms. Moreover, the educational "prescription" for each child was also unique. The problem was how to demonstrate program impact. The program was fortunate in that the designers had compiled a vast catalogue of motor, language, social, and academic skills. Moreover, each of the skills was written as a behavioral objective. Thus, when a skill was included in a student's prescription, the instructor knew what the skill was, how well the student was to perform the skill, how the skill was to be tested, and the conditions under which the skill was to be tested.

Although it is true that the program might have claimed credit for each prescribed skill attained, the staff chose a somewhat more rigorous design. In this instance, they chose a multiple baseline design. The design worked like this:

1. An individual prescription was developed for each student.
2. The individual prescriptions contained a unique collection of objectives.
3. When it was appropriate to begin work on an objective, the instructor tested the student's performance on the objective.
4. If the student met the criteria for the objective, the student was tested again.

A rule was applied to the results: If a student passes the pretest for the objective on two successive tries, the objective is marked as "mastered,"—but the program claimed no credit for the mastery. If the student failed to pass the two pretests, then instruction was provided. After instruction, the student was tested again. In this case as well, the student had to pass the test twice before the objective was marked as "mastered." Under these circumstances, however, the program could claim credit for the student's learning.

The multiple baseline design also found application in an English as a second language (ESL) program where the mixture of native languages was very broad. In this instance as well, the program was designed for a unique population, was skill based, and was individually paced.

In conclusion, in the real world of everyday programs, it is not always possible to exercise the level of control over data collection protocols that one might find in a laboratory. However, the use of quasi-experimental designs can lend strength to the causal claims of programs.

## BENEFIT COST ANALYSIS

On occasion, the topics of program effectiveness and money intersect in a discussion. Within the present section, two avenues leading from that intersection are presented.

### Cost Effectiveness Analysis

The purpose of *cost effectiveness analysis* is to determine the cost of producing a given result. The analysis is typically undertaken after the program intervention. However, if the program's effects can be estimated a priori, then an analysis that yields tentative results might be undertaken in advance.

A cost effectiveness analysis is easy to conceive but difficult to implement. At the simplest level, a program effect (or outcome) is determined and weighed against the resources required to produce that effect. For example, the director of the Gentle Mental Outreach Center has decided that each of the 10 recently hired employees should complete the center's new employee orientation course. The course costs $5 per session and is attended by all 10 of the new employees. The only "evaluation" for the course was "smile sheets" (postcourse surveys of student reactions). Nine of the 10 participants indicated that they were happy (smiling) when they left the session.

$$\text{Cost Effectiveness} = \frac{\text{Cost of The Session}}{\text{Known Effects of The Course}}$$

$$\text{Cost Effectiveness} = \frac{\$5.00}{9 \text{ Smiles}} = \frac{\$.55}{\text{Smile}}$$

Thus, it cost the Center about 55¢ to produce each smile.

The example illustrates two difficulties with the cost effectiveness model. First, the model is a model. It does not know or care how it is applied. Provide a nonsensical effect, calculate the cost to produce that effect, and you wind up with a ridiculous answer. The better course of action would be to measure the meaningful effects of the program and to use them in the analysis.

The second difficulty here is that the cost of the course was not $5. The $5 figure represented the cost of reproducing materials for the course. A more complete compilation of the course costs might have included the following elements:

- *Administrative costs*
  Wage/salary/benefits while preparing for and attending the course.
  Opportunity Costs: Income not earned by center during course.
- *Staff trainer costs*
  Wage/salary/benefits while preparing for and attending the course.
- *Participant costs*
  Wage/salary/benefits while attending the course.
  Substitute worker costs—To cover positions of those attending.
- Instructional materials costs (development and reproduction)
- Facility costs (prorated use of training room)
- Equipment costs (prorated use of overhead projector)
- Refreshments
- Miscellaneous expenses.

The foregoing list is not intended to deter anyone from undertaking a cost effectiveness analysis. Rather, its purpose is to serve as a reminder that getting a handle on the costs of a training course or indeed a clinical intervention requires a bit of sleuthing. Once a set of costs have been developed, the prudent evaluator will check them with the organization's accounting office. It is very discouraging to conduct a cost effectiveness analysis only to have a detractor state, "Yes, but your cost figures do not include A, B or C."

## The Benefits Analysis

The purpose of a *benefits analysis* is to determine the value of an intervention. In contrast to cost effectiveness analysis, benefits analysis requires that a dollar value be attached to the effects or impacts of a program. When such effects or impacts are cast in terms of dollars, they are known as benefits.

The Benefits Analysis consists of five basic steps: (1) Place a value on the problem, (2) Place a value on the result, (3) Find the difference between (1) and (2), (4) Find the cost of the solution or intervention, and (5) Make the calculations.

The foregoing steps are illustrated in the following example:

*Situation.* The Smith Clinic operates an employee assistance program (EAP). Through the program, they offer counseling services to employees of an nearby accounting firm. The contract between the clinic and the firm provides for limited counseling services. That is, for any of the firm's employees who seeks or is referred for counseling, the clinic will provide up to five sessions per calendar year. The accounting firm wants to know if the EAP contract represents a worthwhile expenditure of funds.

*Step 1.* Place a value on the problem. The initial problem facing the accounting firm was the high rate of absenteeism. By their calculations, employee absenteeism, over and above sick leave, represented about 15% of the firm's annual personnel costs. Moreover, the 15% figure was consistent over the preceding 3 years. Thus, if the personnel budget was $1 million per year, the annual cost of the problem was $150,000 (.15 × $1,000,000).

*Step 2.* Place a value on the result. The EAP program has operated for about $2\frac{1}{2}$ years. Moreover, the personnel cost figures for those 2 years are available. In the first year of operation, the absentee rate (and hence personnel costs) were reduced by 5% overall. This translates to a cost of the problem at the end of year 1 of about $100,000 (15% − 5% = 10%; 10% of $1,000,000 = $100,000).

Even better results were obtained at the end of the second year of program operation with a further reduction of the absentee rate to 7% overall. This means that the absentee problem was costing the firm about $70,000 at the end of year 2 (15% − 5% − 3% = 7%; 7% of $1,000,000 = $70,000).

*Step 3.* Find the difference between (1) and (2). For year 1, the difference between the initial cost of the problem and the cost of the problem at the end of the first year was $150,000 − $100,000 = $50,000. This figure represents the year 1 benefit of program. For year 2, the difference between the initial cost of the problem and the cost of the problem at the end of the second year was: $150,000 − $70,000 = $80,000. This figure represents the year 2 benefit of program.

*Step 4.* Find the cost of the solution or intervention.. The annual cost of the EAP contract was $60,000.

*Step 5.* Make the calculations.

$$\text{Benefit to cost ratio for year } 1 = \frac{\text{Year 1 benefit}}{\text{Annual cost of program}}$$

$$= \frac{\$50,000}{\$60,000} = .83$$

A benefit to cost ratio of less than 1.0 means that the costs of the program were greater than the benefits derived. The EAP did not "pay for itself" in terms of absentee costs saved in the first year.

$$\text{Benefit to cost ratio for year 2} = \frac{\text{Year 2 benefit}}{\text{Annual cost of program}}$$

$$= \frac{\$80,000}{\$60,000} = 1.33$$

A benefit to cost ratio of more than 1.0 means that the benefits of the program were greater than the costs incurred. The EAP more than "paid for itself" in terms of reduced absentee costs in the second year.

Another calculation that can be made is called the return on investment (ROI). The ROI represents an extension of the benefits to cost ratio. It follows the formula:

$$\text{ROI} = \frac{\text{Benefit} - \text{Cost}}{\text{Cost}}$$

Applying the ROI formula to the EAP program, we find:

$$\text{ROI} = \frac{\text{Year 1 benefit} - \text{Annual cost of program}}{\text{Annual cost of program}}$$

$$= \frac{\$50,000 - \$60,000}{\$60,000} = \frac{-\$10,000}{\$60,000} = -.17$$

This means that as an investment, the EAP program during the first year demonstrated a "loss" of about 17%.

How did the program fare in Year 2?

$$\text{ROI} = \frac{\text{Year 2 benefit} - \text{Annual cost of program}}{\text{Annual cost of program}}$$

$$\text{ROI} = \frac{\$80,000 - \$60,000}{\$60,000} = \frac{\$20,000}{\$60,000} = +.33$$

This means that as an investment, the EAP program during the second year demonstrated a "gain" of about 33%. In other words, the accounting firm not only got it's original investment back, but it also made a gain of 33% in the process.

A final word of caution is in order. Program claims for effectiveness are not strengthened merely because indices of program effectiveness have dollar signs in front of them. That is, every bit of care that was required to make other claims about program impacts (recall the "chains of evidence") must still be observed when dealing with cost effectiveness or cost benefit issues. In addition, programs that extend beyond a year or two must include the time value of money in these calculations. That is, they must correct for the pre-vailing inflation or deflation rate, usually expressed as changes in the cost of living. These corrections go beyond the scope of this chapter, but it is im-portant to remember that the results of cost effectiveness analyses, benefit analyses, and especially, return on investment analyses, are heavily influenced by the economic times in which the analyses were conducted. Wait a few years and a program that could not be justified economically may well be worthwhile; the economic merit of a program is separate from its scientific merit.

## REFERENCES

Aliger, G. M., & Janak, E. A. (1989). Kirkpatrick's levels of training criteria: Thirty years later. *Personnel Psychology, 42*, 331–342.

Butcher, J. N., Dahlstrom, W. G., Graham, J. R., Tellegen, A. M., & Kaemmer, B. (1989). *MMPI-2: Manual for administration and scoring.* Minneapolis: University of Minnesota Press.

Campbell, D. T., & Stanley, J. C. (1963). *Experimental and quasi-experimental designs for research.* Chicago: Rand McNally.

Kirkpatrick, D. M. (1959a). Techniques for evaluating training programs. *Journal of American Society for Teaching & Development, 13*(11), 3–9.

Kirkpatrick, D. M. (1959b). Techniques for evaluating training programs: Part 2-learning. *Journal of ASTD, 13*(12), 21–26.

Kirkpatrick, D. M. (1960a). Techniques for evaluating training programs: Part 3-behavior. *Journal of ASTD, 14*(1), 13–18.

Kirkpatrick, D. M. (1960b). Techniques for evaluating training programs: Part 4-results. *Journal of ASTD, 14*(2), 28–32.

Shadish, W. R., Cook, T. D., & Leviton, L. C. (1991). *Foundations of program evaluation: Theories of practice.* Newbury Park, CA: Sage.

Shadish, W. R., Cook, T. D., & Campbell, D. T. (2002). Experimental and quasi-experimental designs for generalized causal inference. Canton, MA: Houghton Mifflin.

Webb, E. J., Campbell, D. T., Schwartz, R. D., & Sechrist, L. J. (1966). *Unobtrusive measures.* Skokie, IL: Rand McNally.

# Meta-Analysis

Joseph A. Durlak
Inna Meerson
Cynthia J. Ewell Foster
*Loyola University Chicago*

The most commonly used research methodology in psychology is not a randomized true experiment, a quasiexperimental design, or a correlational study; it is a literature review. Think about this for a moment. Every student doing a masters thesis or doctoral dissertation completes a literature review; so does every researcher who prepares a research report or a grant proposal. The format, depth, and type of review that is conducted in each case varies but all reviews have the same general goals: to critically examine a body of research, reach some conclusions, and suggest guidelines for future work. Literature reviews parallel steps taken in most individual studies: a research question is posed, a population is selected, data are collected, analyzed, and interpreted, and conclusions are reached. The general intent is to complete this entire task in a scientifically rigorous manner in order to increase the validity of the data and conclusions. Rigor is achieved by following the basic standards of the scientific method as closely as possible and these standards focus generally on such things as objectivity, precision, clarity, and reproducibility. Good science has these features and exceptional science has all of these characteristics plus creativity and insight.

The purpose of this chapter is to discuss the major steps involved in conducting a scientifically rigorous meta-analysis, which is one format for a literature review. Table 9.1 lists the five major steps of a meta-analysis and also contains critical questions to consider regarding each step. In general, the more satisfactorily each part of the review is handled, the more scientifically rigorous the review becomes. Two important points should be stressed before continuing,

TABLE 9.1

Major Steps and Issues in Conducting Scientifically Rigorous Meta-Analyses

---

Step 1. Formulating the research question.
      Was the purpose of the review clearly described?
      Were a priori hypotheses offered?
      Were research questions reasonable, important, and testable?

Step 2. Obtaining a representative study sample.
      Were inclusionary criteria explicit?
      Were multiple search strategies used to locate studies?
      Were unpublished reports obtained?

Step 3. Deriving maximal information from individual reports.
      Was the experimental rigor of primary studies considered?
      Was the extent of missing or limited information acknowledged?
      Were coding procedures reliable?

Step 4. Conducting appropriate analyses.
      Was one effect per study used per research question?*
      Were effects weighted for analyses*
      Were statistical outliers identified?*
      Were studies grouped appropriately for analyses?
      Were plausible rival explanations for the results evaluated?
      Was the practical significance of outcomes assessed?

Step 5. Reaching conclusions and guiding future researchers.
      Were necessary qualifications in the conclusions offered?
      Where relevant, did the author distinguish between "no evidence of effect" vs.
        "evidence of no effect"?
      Were critical directions for future research presented?

---

*Note:* The features marked with an * apply specifically to meta-analyses while the others apply to all types of reviews.

however. First, the elements in Table 9.1 apply to all types of literature reviews (narrative and meta-analytic) except for the specific considerations relevant to the statistical analyses of effect sizes. Therefore, Table 9.1 can be a useful guide for both the consumers and producers of different types of reviews. Second, each section of a review is important and affects the final product. Reviews are as strong as their weakest section and the failure to attend adequately to each aspect of the process can jeopardize a review's validity. Well-done statistical analyses cannot compensate for an inadequate literature search or poorly constructed research questions.

## HISTORY AND DEFINITION OF META-ANALYSIS

Statistical procedures that are now recognized as meta-analysis were present in a few scientific papers as early as 1904, but some landmark meta-analyses that appeared in education, psychotherapy research, and industrial organizational psychology in the 1970s are generally credited with introducing this approach to the social sciences (Cooper & Hedges, 1994). Meta-analyses is now very popular and by the late 1980s, over 200 meta-analyses were appearing every year in the social sciences. Fortunately, substantial procedural and statistical refinements have been made in meta-analytic methods as their popularity increased so that the literature on meta-analysis is now highly sophisticated.

*Meta-analysis* is a literature reviewing procedure that quantifies and translates the results of individual studies into a common index of effect. Meta-analysts typically present the pooled or *M* index of effect for all studies and then attempt to identify the factors that influence variability in outcomes (frequently called *moderators*). There is always variability in outcomes in any research area. If there was not, there would be no need for the review in the first place because we would already know that most research produces the same results.

This chapter focuses on meta-analyses using standardized *M* differences as the index of effect. This type of meta-analysis, sometimes called treatment meta-analysis, is the most common approach to assess the impact of treatments, programs, or interventions. Although other types of designs can be accommodated (see upcoming text), we discuss between-group designs in which an intervention is compared to some type of control group (no-treatment, waiting list, or attention placebo).

## Basic features of Standardized *M* Effects

The standardized *M* difference, also called *d*, *g*, or the term we use here, effect size (ES), is calculated by subtracting the *M* of the control condition from the *M* of the intervention condition at posttest and dividing by the pooled *SD* of the two groups at posttest. Some reviewers have used only the *SD* of the control condition to calculate effects, although Hedges and Olkin (1985) demonstrated that the pooled *SD* provides the best estimate of the true population effect and thus should be used. Higher values of an ES are preferred because they indicate the intervention group changed more than the controls. Lacking *M*s and *SD*s, ESs can be calculated from more limited information, if, for instance, the sample sizes, *p* levels, or *t* or *F* values are provided. Lipsey and Wilson (2001), Wolf (1986) and Holmes (1984) offered useful formulae for these alternative calculations.

The prime advantage of an ES is its ability to translate the magnitude of effect into a standardized common metric across studies. That is, the ES is based on *SD* units, the unique data obtained in each study is converted into these units, and the resultant ES reflects just how strong or powerful an intervention has been. The latter is a very different issue than whether the results of an individual study achieved significant findings according to traditional probability levels. There is no direct relationship between the magnitude of effect and its initial statistical significance; significant results at the .05 level can reflect small effects, whereas nonsignificant findings can produce relatively high effects.

For instance, suppose a *t* test in a study was conducted on 50 participants in a treatment group and an equal number of controls but failed to reach the .05 level of significance. The original researcher might conclude that the treatment was not effective. However, given a modest *M* difference and pooled *SD* produced by the two groups, a statistically nonsignificant ES might range anywhere from, say, −.39 (if treated participants did more poorly than controls) to +.39. This is a large range of possible effects but a meta-analysis can provide a precise *M* across a set of studies. Put another way, a meta-analysis can easily produce results that are not discernable when looking at the statistical significance of each study's findings.

Theoretically, an individual ES can be any value, but most typically fall between −.50 and +1.50. Lipsey and Wilson (1993) presented a useful context for judging the average effects obtained in treatment meta-analyses. They analyzed the results of 156 meta-analyses of between-group designs evaluating behavioral, psychological, and educational treatments that collectively involved approximately 9,400 studies and over 1 million participants. The overall *M* ES from these meta-analyses was .47, with a *SD* of .28. In other words, $\frac{2}{3}$ of the *M* effects obtained in the social sciences fall somewhere between .19 and .75; only about 16% of effects are higher than .75 and an equal proportion are lower than .19. Furthermore, and most important, only .006% of *M* effects were negative in sign (i.e., less than zero). The latter finding is reassuring because it indicates that, overall, virtually none of the interventions examined in the 156 analyses was making the treated group worse than controls. This can certainly happen in a single study, but rarely when the results are averaged across studies.

## Effects from Other Designs

It is also possible to calculate standardized *M* differences in one group pretest–posttest designs and one group posttest only designs. As one might expect from the absence of any control group, ESs coming from such designs are typically higher than those produced by between-group designs, although they are rarely as high as those from within-subject designs (see upcoming text). In some cases, reviewers might wish to compare two treatments against one another; these between-treatment ESs may be up to 50% lower than those produced by control group designs (Kazdin & Bass, 1989). This is not surprising because one would expect less of a difference if both groups had received some intervention.

A meta-analysis of data from single-subject designs can also be done (e.g., from reversal or multiple baseline designs). The methods of calculating effects in such cases depend on what assumptions can be made about the data such as the homogeneity of the variances across baseline and intervention phases. Busk and Serlin (1992) discussed these issues. Effects from single-subject designs are often considerably higher than those from group designs. One survey of

150 published effects found that half of them were above 9.20; 25% were greater than 17.0, and only 25% were less than 4.90 (Matyas & Greenwood, 1990). Effects coming from the different types of designs just described should not be combined in the same analysis because of the way these ESs are calculated and the designs on which they are based. Analyses containing a mixture of effects from treatment-control group designs, single-group designs, single-subject designs and between-treatment designs are hopelessly confounded and the results are impossible to interpret. DuPaul & Eckert (1997) and Kavale, Mathur, Forness, Rutherford and Quinn (1997) offered good examples of how to keep ESs from different designs separate in a review.

### Other Indices of Effect

The second most commonly used index of effect is the product moment correlation ($r$)and its variants, which range in value from $-1.0$ through zero to $+1.0$. Rosenthal (1991) offered a good explanation of this approach.

Effects can also be expressed as odds-ratios, which portray the magnitude of effect against the standard or typical odds of 1.0 or no effect. Odds ratios can be any positive nonzero value, although $M$ odds ratios reported in reviews rarely exceed 10 or so. An odds ratio of 2.12 for a successful treatment would mean the typical person in the treatment group is 2.12 times more likely to fall into a positive dichotomous outcome category, for example, is 2.12 times less likely to experience a stroke following a heart attack if treated with a certain procedure.

It is important to keep in mind that depending on the available information, $r$s, ESs, and odds ratios can be computed from the same studies. These metrics are simply different ways to express effect sizes and their use depends on the research area under study. When both important study characteristics and outcomes are continuous variables, $r$ is frequently used; when most study characteristics are categorical in nature (e.g., type of treatments or presenting problems) and most outcomes are continuous variables, ES is used. Finally, when important outcomes are dichotomous such as life or death, or complete remission of symptoms or not, then odd ratios (and sometimes risk ratios or relative risk ratios) can be useful. Reviews in medicine frequently employ the latter indices (Cooper & Hedges, 1994).

## MAJOR STEPS IN A META-ANALYSIS
## STEP 1: FORMULATING THE RESEARCH QUESTION(S)

It is very important to begin the review with specific a priori hypotheses because such hypotheses are useful for identifying the parameters of the research field, coding studies for critical information, focusing the statistical analyses, and reaching specific conclusions. In contrast, vague or fuzzy research questions tend to lead to vague or fuzzy answers. In fact, if you do not have specific research questions you want to answer, why do the review in the first place?

In other words, the choice in beginning a review is between a reasoned hypothetical deductive approach guided by specific hypotheses or a post-hoc fishing expedition. The former is clearly preferred because if you throw your line into the water enough times while fishing, eventually you will catch something (i.e., something will come out significant). Without hypotheses to guide the analyses, however, it is hard to tell if you have caught a prized fish, a tiny fish that should be tossed back, or just some seaweed or an old tire. As Jackson (1980) stressed, "Rigorous hypothesis testing is as desirable in reviews as it is in primary research" (p. 455).

There are several ways to generate good hypotheses and most come from an initial inspection of the relevant literature. In other words, the best literature reviews are generated by a good working knowledge of the research area. What important theories and practices predominate in the area? What conceptual, procedural, or clinical factors might be responsible for the inconsistent findings that have emerged to date? Do any particular investigations suggest the possibility of some important variables that could be examined in the literature as a whole? What controversies exist in the field? What are the methodological challenges facing investigators? These types of questions often lead to good hypotheses that can be tested in the review.

Authors should present and explain their specific research questions in the introduction to the review. These questions can then be immediately judged in terms of their reasonableness, importance, and testability, and how their potential answers will advance the field in terms of theory, practice, or policy.

## STEP 2: CONDUCTING A GOOD LITERATURE SEARCH

The second major aspect of a meta-analysis involves conducting a systematic literature search to locate relevant studies. The intent should *not* be to do a comprehensive or exhaustive search for every study. It is impossible to locate every single relevant report, particularly all unpublished works. Rather, the goal should be to obtain a representative sample of studies. Unfortunately, because reviewers are not always careful in searching for studies, it should not be surprising that reviews ostensibly examining the same research area can end up analyzing largely nonoverlapping literatures and thus reach different conclusions.

For instance, two early meta-analyses of the child therapy outcome literature, one with 64 outcome studies (Casey & Berman, 1985), and the other containing 105 studies (Weisz, Weiss, Alicke, & Klotz, 1987), only had 24 studies in common. In another case, six different reviews of student evaluations of teacher effectiveness examined 98 different studies but no single study appeared in all six reviews (see Abrami, Cohen & d'Apollonia, 1988).

How does one obtain a representative sample of studies for review? The questions to keep in mind regarding a good literature search are listed in Table 9.1. The reviewer starts first with explicit inclusionary criteria to specify precisely what types of studies are relevant. The presence of clearly formulated research questions guides the development of inclusionary criteria that are reasonable, relevant, and defensible. Frequently, inclusionary criteria concentrate on such matters as the types of interventions, populations, problems, and outcomes to be examined. For instance, will all types of therapies be included, or only those targeting a specific population or problem. What is the timeframe for the review?

Once the inclusionary criteria are established, multiple search strategies are essential to capture representative reports. The three most productive strategies are: (1) manual searches of key journals (i.e., reading the abstracts and procedure sections of all articles published in several major journals over a specific time period); (2) examination of the references lists of all obtained studies and previous literature reviews; and (3) computer generated searches of multiple databases (e.g., MEDLINE, Psych INFO), The first two approaches typically yield the most studies and reviewers should never depend exclusively on computer-generated searches because of their unreliability. Computer searches typically generate many false positives (irrelevant studies) and miss too many true positives (relevant investigations).

This fact is unknown to many researchers and deserves some discussion. There are several reasons why computer searches are not the most reliable search strategy. First, they are incomplete and do not include all possible sources of information. It may seem impressive that two frequently used data bases, MEDLINE, and Psych LIT, cover over 3,600 and 1,300 journals, respectively, and add new sources periodically, until one realizes there are over 6,000 computer databases and over 20,000 possible sources for medical and social science research (Cooper & Hedges, 1994). Second, some databases inadequately sample books and book chapters, which can be a good source for studies. Third, databases do not contain the most recent studies because of the time lag involved in their updating. Fourth, each data base has its own terminology, which almost never corresponds exactly to the reviewer's interests and needs. Fifth, and finally, the way reports are included in the database depends on the individual judgment of the indexer so the process is never completely uniform and free from error or bias. There is no guarantee, for instance, that a study testing the theory of reasoned action, using a behavioral group intervention, targeting African-American junior high schoolers, and assessing behavioral changes in safe sexual practices will be retrieved using search terms that match each of these study dimensions.

In fact, computer searches can be the poorest search strategy. Some meta-analyses using multiple search strategies suggest that only a small percentage of included studies were obtained by computer searches (6 to 20%), whereas the majority of relevant research was located through manual journal searches and inspection of reference lists of previous reviews and individual reports (Durlak, 2000). Computer data searches can complement but should never replace other methods of searching for studies.

## Unpublished studies

Finally, caution must be attached to any meta-analysis examining only published studies because of the existence of publication bias; that is, the tendency for published studies to report better outcomes than unpublished studies. Analyzing only published data would therefore overestimate the true effect. Although publication bias has frequently appeared in the social sciences, medicine, and education (Dickersin, 1997), it does not always occur. Therefore, it is always an important empirical question that bears examination in each review whether publication bias is present in the research area of interest. This question cannot be answered without including unpublished work.

There are many different types of unpublished studies: technical reports, conference presentations, doctoral dissertations, and so-called file drawer studies, which are completed studies that researchers have done, but for one reason or another have never got around to publishing. Some reviewers contact those who have published in the field to obtain completed but as-yet unpublished work. Sometimes this strategy can capture additional studies but much depends on the cooperation of the original researchers.

Unpublished doctoral dissertations probably represent the best source for unpublished work in many areas for several reasons. Other types of unpublished work are both difficult to obtain and their prevalence is difficult to estimate. How many file-drawer studies actually exist in any area? In contrast, *Dissertation Abstracts* contains a listing of all dissertations completed each year at American and Canadian institutions, so the reviewer can gauge how many unpublished dissertations are relevant and should be sampled. Furthermore, most dissertations can be obtained free of charge through interlibrary loan agreements, and dissertations often contain more extensive and specific procedural details and data than published papers. This could be due to the committee's insistence on complete details and/or the doctoral candidate's desire to be as thorough as possible.

In summary, in the second stage of the review process, rigorous reviews have clear inclusionary criteria, use multiple strategies to find relevant research, and include unpublished work in the study sample.

## STEP 3: MAKING MAXIMUM USE OF STUDY INFORMATION

After relevant studies are collected, reviewers must make several decisions when drawing information from studies, some of these decision are easy to make but others are very difficult. Meta-analysts code studies on different variables and then later use the coded information to search for possible moderators. Therefore, it is essential that the coding process include the most important variables, be explicit, and can be replicated by others. Authors often make the instructions and definitions for coding systems available to interested readers.

The typical steps in coding include: (1) developing a clear coding protocol (which includes coding forms and operational definitions of coded variables); (2) training raters to mastery in the coding process (which often requires modification of the initial coding scheme to clarify ambiguous elements); (3) keeping a logbook of coding problems and resolution of coding disagreements; and (4) reporting data to support the reliability or reproducibility of the coding process. Lipsey and Wilson (2001) offered useful examples in this regard.

Different procedures for estimating reliability are possible and Hartmann (1982) discussed the utility, calculation, and defensibility of different procedures. It is highly recommended to use reliability estimates that are corrected for chance agreements (e.g., kappa coefficients) for all categorical codes (e.g., if two different types of presenting problems are coded, coders would agree half the time by chance). Furthermore, coding schemes should always contain a category for missing or uncertain information because such situations invariably arise (see later discussion in text). If coding occurs over a long time period (i.e., several months or more), it is a good idea to assess reliability more than once, and not tell raters beforehand which studies will be selected for reliability checks. Otherwise, coders might relax or change their standards over time, but take more care when they know their data are going to be checked for reliability.

But exactly which variables should be coded in each study? The primary goal of coding is to code all variables that potentially could moderate study outcomes. Usually, this means different methodological aspects of studies, and various theoretical, procedural, and clinical features. Once again, a priori hypotheses are useful in directing attention to the most important information that should be collected.

## STEP 4: CONDUCTING APPROPRIATE ANALYSES

Although there can be exceptions depending on the intent of the review and the research area evaluated, specific questions to keep in mind regarding the analyses of ESs are noted in Table 9.1.

TABLE 9.2
Selected Effect Size Outcomes for Group Therapy Studies

| Study | Behavioral | Parent Ratings | Teacher Ratings | Sociometrics | Achievement | Child-Report | Mean Effect | Per Study |
|---|---|---|---|---|---|---|---|---|
| Observations | | | | | | | | |
| 1 | 1.34 | .50 | .56 | — | .12 | .75 | .65 | |
| 2 | — | .50 | .80 | — | .05 | .60 | .49 | |
| 3 | .75 | .23 | .20 | .10 | — | .20 | .30 | |
| 4 | .80 | .45 | — | .50 | — | — | .58 | |
| 5 | — | .20 | .15 | — | .00 | .70 | .26 | |
| 6 | 3.45 | — | — | — | — | — | 3.45 | |
| | | | | | M Effect Across Studies | | .96 | |
| M Effect by outcome measure | | | | | | | | |
| | 1.59 | .38 | .43 | .30 | .06 | .56 | | |

Note: If the outlier effect size from Study 6 is removed, the M effect across studies drops to .46.

## One Effect Per Research Question

One important decision is how to draw ESs from studies for analysis. A cardinal rule in meta-analysis is to average multiple effects within each study so that each investigation produces only one effect per analysis. Multiple analyses always occur in a meta-analysis, but each time the studies should be contributing the same number of data points. For example, Table 9.2 presents the effect sizes achieved by six hypothetical child and adolescent group therapy studies on different outcome measures. If the meta-analyst were interested in the effect of group treatment in general, the M effects in column 8 would be used. The effects in column 8 are the average effects derived from all outcomes within each study. If these effects were not averaged at the study level, then among the six investigations, study 1 and study 3 would contribute five data points each for their five measures, whereas study 6 could only contribute one. By using study as the unit analysis, that is, by averaging across all outcomes in the same study, each study contributes one effect in the analysis.

In another analysis, the effects from each study can be averaged for each of the different type of outcomes (columns 2 through 7 in Table 9.2). In contrast to the first research question above (i.e., how effective is treatment overall?), these data provide crucial information on a different research question (i.e., how do effects vary depending on the type of outcome measure?). For this analysis behavioral observational data from four studies (1, 3, 4, and 6) would be averaged (M ES = 1.59), parent ratings from 5 studies would be averaged (M ES = .38), and so on. Keeping the basic principle of one effect per study in mind, other combinations of effects could be done if, for example, the meta-analyst wanted to compare outcomes between behavioral and cognitive behavioral treatments, and so on.

Special circumstances arise in some studies that permit modification of the aforementioned considerations. For instance, some studies evaluate two distinctly different forms of intervention (e.g., a behavioral and a client-centered treatment). It is then acceptable to calculate individual effects for each of these treatments in the same study because the treatment constructs differ and the same subjects are not being treated in the two conditions. ESs can be calculated by comparing each treatment against the controls. In this case, each major type of intervention contributes one effect per analysis.

## Weighting of Effects

Weighting procedures should be used when combining effects across studies and many meta-analysts follow Hedges and Olkin's (1985) suggestion that these weights should consist of the inverse of the variance of each effect. Basically, this weighting procedure is heavily dependent on the study sample size and gives more weight to studies involving more participants because effects based on larger samples are more reliable.

Weighting often makes a difference in clinical areas where many small samples predominate. For example, unweighted ESs in three different meta-analyses have been between 23 to 33% *larger* than unweighted effects (Durlak, 2000). The reader might wish to reduce any reported unweighted $M$ effects by 25% or so to gain a more conservative (and likely truer) estimate of the magnitude of effect.

## Statistical Analysis of Mean ESs

Reviewers now routinely calculate and report confidence intervals (CIs) around mean ESs. CIs portray the range of effects one might expect at a certain $p$ level (e.g., .05). $M$s with CIs are easy to interpret: $M$s differ significantly from zero if their CIs do not include zero, and two means differ significantly from one another (again at a predetermined probability level) if their CIs do not overlap. An example is provided later in this section.

## Identifying Outliers

An *outlier* is an atypical ES. Outliers are often defined as being $\geq 2$ $SD$s from their respective mean. Outliers are the bane of meta-analysts because they strongly influence the variability of effects in a group of studies and thus make it extremely difficult if not impossible to obtain homogeneity (see upcoming text). For example, the ES from study 6 in Table 9.2 (3.45) is much higher than all other effects. Removing these high effects would drop the overall $M$ study level ES from .96 (with a $SD$ of 1.23) to a more reasonable mean of .46 and $SD$ of .33.

***Dealing With Outliers.***   Different strategies can be used to deal with outliers. First, they can be removed from the statistical analyses, which is perfectly legitimate and is sometimes done by individual researchers in their studies. There is no hard and fast rule but if many data points are outliers (e.g., $\geq 15\%$) great care should be exercised in reaching any conclusions about the total data set. Second, outlier values can be Windsorized, that is, recomputed as less extreme scores. This can be done by letting them equal less extreme effects in the same tail of distribution (e.g., they could be set equal to other high but less extreme effects). Third, the analyses could be done with and without the outliers, which is a type of sensitivity analysis. In this case, the reviewer is saying: "Well, we have some unusual results (i.e., some outliers); here are the findings when they are included and when they are excluded." Fourth, if there are many outliers, the entire distribution of effects could be normalized through a logarithmic transformation or another procedure.

Outliers should never be totally ignored, however. The number and types of outliers should be described and the reviewer should strive to seek a possible explanation for their occurrence. On one hand, outliers could simply be error or noise in the data, or be the result of a unique population, procedure, or outcome assessment. On the other hand, patterns occurring among outliers might signal important phenomena. Perhaps certain treatments are highly effective, or some problems or client populations can be treated much more effectively. This would be important to discuss. (Outliers are usually positive in sign.)

## Grouping Studies for Analyses

Because studies vary in their outcomes, reviewers are invariably faced with a critical decision: How can I investigate variability in study effects in a scientifically sound manner? There is probably no other aspect of meta-analysis that has generated more criticism and disagreement than how to group studies appropriately for analysis. Meta-analysts make very different types of decisions in these cases, which can have far-reaching implications for their results and conclusions. Critics contend that some reviewers have combined studies that should not be combined because they are measuring distinctly different constructs and will thus produce inaccurate or misleading results. This is the so-called "apples and oranges" criticism of meta-analysis. For example, one should not combine studies of massage therapy with psychotropic medication to assess the value of treatment for depression. You should not combine treatments for adults and children to see if treatment works, and so on. These examples are obvious, but in many situations scientists can reasonably differ about what to combine with what. It is not always easy to decide how different interventions (or populations, or outcome measures, etc.) have to be before the corresponding studies should be analyzed separately. Is there a systematic approach that can guide the reviewer in this respect and confirm or disconfirm the reviewers' choice about how to group studies? Fortunately, there is. In brief, this approach involves model testing.

The meta-analyst can apply 1 of 3 possible models to the data: fixed effects, random effects, and mixed effects. The choice of which model to apply is based on what is believed to contribute to variability in effects in addition to sampling error. Sampling error always applies because the individual studies in the review have not involved all possible participants, but have only sampled a portion of the relevant population. Basically, if the reviewer believes that another source of variability comes from systematic differences that could explained by coded study features, then a fixed effect model is used. If variability is likely due to random effects, which cannot be identified, then a random effects model is used, and if variability is presumed to result from both systematic and random differences among the studies, a mixed-effects model is more appropriate.

The following discussion explains fixed-effects model testing, keeping in mind that the basic goal in all models is to ascertain the factors that contribute to variability in effects. Fixed-effects model testing is appropriate if one wishes to reach conclusions specifically about the types of studies that are being reviewed, rather than all types of possible studies, and one's assumption is that reviewed studies are estimating one "fixed" population effect. Lipsey and Wilson (2001) offered further explanation about the different assumptions and statistical features of model testing.

## *Q* Statistic and Homogeneity Testing

The core of the fixed effects approach revolves around the $Q$ statistic, or homogeneity test, a statistic distributed as a chi square variable whose degrees of freedom are based on the number of studies in the analysis minus one. Basically, the $Q$ statistic examines if the variability of ESs produced by a group of studies is greater than one would expect beyond the contribution of sampling error. The $Q$ statistic is often described as a homogeneity test because it can be interpreted as determining if a group of independent studies produces a homogeneous (i.e., common) estimate of the population effect. Alternatively, the results of the test could suggest that study outcomes are being influenced by more than chance or sampling error (i.e., there are one or more possible moderators among the studies). This would mean there is not a single homogeneous group of studies yielding one common effect but a heterogeneous group that contains two or more subgroups of studies whose effects likely differ. In other words, there are apples and oranges (and perhaps some other fruit) in the larger group. In an important switch to most statistical tests, a nonsignificant $Q$ result is preferred because it indicates homogeneity among study effects, whereas a significant result indicates heterogeneity.

A fixed-effects model testing approach to meta-analysis can be expressed as an internal dialogue of a reviewer that goes as follows:

> I have examined this research literature beforehand, and I have a model in mind, that is, one or more hypotheses to explain why different findings have been reported. Using meta-analysis I cannot only quantify the overall effect, but quantify and compare the effects of my hypothesized variables. I expect that when I look at *all* the studies, the effects will be heterogeneous based on the $Q$ statistic, but when I subdivide the total sample into smaller subgroups based on my hypothesized variables (i.e., moderators), each subgroup will then yield homogeneous effects and their mean effects will differ from each other. This would suggest I have identified some important moderators of outcome, that is, my hypothesis was correct.

Once again, notice the importance of hypotheses in the aforementioned situation. Literally hundreds of analyses can be done in a meta-analysis by repeatedly combining and recombining studies and comparing their results so that reviews guided by specific hypotheses avoid a post hoc search for homogeneity and significant differences among study groupings. In summary, model testing using the $Q$ statistic provides a systematic, statistical way to verify whether or not the reviewer's grouping of studies is justified.

The $Q$ statistic is analogous to ANOVA in the sense that a total $Q$ value for all studies combined equals the sum of $Q$ between and $Q$ within for the same studies when they are subdivided. The desired result is a significant total $Q$ that can be subdivided into separate, nonsignificant $Q$ withins for each study grouping, and a significant $Q$ between. A significant $Q$ between would indicate the subgroups yield significantly different effects. In other words, you only achieve homogeneity when studies are divided appropriately for analysis.

Table 9.3 illustrates this feature of the $Q$ statistic and is based on a review of group therapy studies for children and adolescents (Meerson & Durlak, 2000). The $Q$ statistic for all 236 reviewed studies ($Q$ total = 331.30) indicates significant heterogeneity among study outcomes. We hypothesized that the theoretical orientation behind the group treatment would moderate outcomes and to test this hypothesis, the type of treatment used in each study was used to divide the studies into three categories: behavioral, cognitive behavioral, and nonbehavioral. Using the .05 probability level, we then recomputed the $Q$ statistic for each subgroup of studies ($Q$ withins). As noted in the top half of Table 9.3, the $Q$ within was nonsignificant (reflecting homogeneity of effects) for cognitive behavioral and nonbehavioral forms of treatment. There was also a significant $Q$ between ($df$ for $Q$ between is the number of groups minus one) indicating there were significant differences in mean ESs among the three treatments. Notice that the value for $Q$ total equals the values of $Q$ between plus the three $Q$ withins ($331.3 = 55.55 + 137.43 + 74.64 + 63.68$).

The means and CIs for each treatment are presented in the lower half of Table 9.3. Each treatment produced a $M$ effect that was significantly different

TABLE 9.3
Illustration of the $Q$ Statistic and Homogeneity Testing

| Statistic | Number of Studies | Value | Significant at .05 |
|---|---|---|---|
| $Q$ total | 236 | 331.30 | Yes |
| $Q$ withins for treatments | | | |
| Behavioral | 76 | 137.43 | Yes |
| Cognitive behavioral | 80 | 74.64 | No |
| Nonbehavioral | 80 | 63.68 | No |
| $Q$ between treatments | | 55.55 | Yes |

$M$ Effects and Confidence Intervals for Different Treatments

| Treatment | Mean | Confidence Intervals |
|---|---|---|
| Behavioral | .56 | .49 to .64 |
| Cognitive behavioral | .38 | .31 to .44 |
| Nonbehavioral | .23 | .17 to .29 |

than zero (no CI included zero), but the main focus of the hypothesis centered on differential treatment effects. Because none of the CIs for any two treatments overlapped, inspection of the data indicated that behavioral treatment produced significantly higher $M$ ESs than cognitive behavioral and nonbehavioral treatment, and cognitive behavioral treatment produced significantly higher ESs than nonbehavioral treatment.

Although it is not discussed here, weighted multiple regression analyses can also be used to search for variables that explain variability in effects (see Lipsey & Wilson, 2001). Regression analyses are particularly helpful in estimating the relative importance of several moderators simultaneously, and when many of the possible moderators are continuous in nature rather than categorical (e.g., number of treatment sessions).

There is one important qualification to be made. It is usually difficult to obtain homogeneity for every subgroup of studies because there is still much we do not know about the effects of interventions, important information might be missing from the primary studies, and so on. After all, not every hypothesis generated in individual experiments is confirmed either. Notice that the $M$ effect for behavioral treatment in Table 9.3 is heterogeneous (the $Q$ statistic is significant.) Therefore, meta-analysts are sometimes left with having to interpret some findings from heterogeneous studies. Although homogeneity is preferred, contrary to popular opinion, it is possible to interpret findings from heterogeneous study groups. The types of interpretations that can be made under such circumstances often depend on one's ability to rule out the most plausible rival explanations for the obtained results, a topic we turn to next.

## Ruling Out Rival Explanations

Just like in an individual experiment, it is wise not to jump to conclusions in a meta-analysis about the veracity of one's hypotheses until other possible explanations for the findings have been ruled out. There could be several reasons why the results in Table 9.3 might suggest the superiority of some treatments over others, quite apart from the inherent potency of the compared treatments.

The most likely influences on the variability of ESs generally fall into 4 areas: sampling error, study artifacts, methodological features of the studies, and confounds among study characteristics. These four factors can be treated as plausible rival explanations for the variability of outcomes. We have already described how sampling error can be attended to via $Q$ testing, and the other three factors should also be considered before reaching any final conclusions.

**Study Artifacts.**    There are many different types of study artifacts ranging from unreliable outcome measures to imperfect implementation of a treatment (see Hunter & Schmidt, 1990, for more details). It may not be possible to assess the effect of all possible artifacts but their possible relevance should be noted by the meta-analyst. For example, the unreliability of outcome measures is one type of artifact. Basically, an individual ES is calculated as if the outcome measure on which it is based is perfectly reliable (i.e., $r = 1.0$) which, of course, is an idealistic assumption. However, it is possible to correct ESs for unreliability using the formula: corrected ES = original ES divided by the square root of the measure's reliability. This formula indicates that the lower the reliability of the measure, the more an ES could be adjusted upward. For instance, suppose an effect of .50 was originally obtained from an outcome measure whose reliability was .64. The corrected ES would become 25% higher, or .625 (i.e., .50 divided by .80), which indicates the substantial influence of unreliability on ES estimates.

**Methodological Features.**    It is reasonable to assume that the way primary studies have been designed might be related to effect sizes, but reviewers must make decisions about which methodological features to consider, and how to examine their contribution. Some authors use a univariate, whereas others employ a multivariate approach. That is, the impact of design features are assessed one at a time in some cases, whereas in other reviews, several method variables are used simultaneously to judge the overall quality of studies, which are then placed into categories of low, medium, and high quality studies to compare their outcomes. Unfortunately, there are no universal standards with respect to methodology (different areas usually require somewhat different procedures and safeguards) so authors do not always choose the same experimental criteria to evaluate studies. Some commonly used method variables include general design considerations (quasiexperimental vs. randomized designs), reactivity of measurement procedures, and use of psychometrically adequate assessments.

Sometimes the results of methodological variables are surprising. In some reviews, studies using randomized designs have produced higher effects than quasiexperimental designs; sometimes the latter have produced significantly higher effects, and sometimes there has been no difference (Durlak, 2000). The results for the impact of methodological features should not be misinterpreted. If quasiexperimental designs yield the same magnitude of effect as randomized true experiments, this does not sanction or encourage greater use of the former. Most scientists prefer randomized trials whenever possible; it just means that quasiexperiments are not biasing study outcomes either upward or downward compared to randomized designs.

***Confounds in Study Features.***   Study features are rarely distributed randomly or independently across studies. Thus, it can be a challenge to deal with studies that vary simultaneously in both study features and outcomes. For instance, the finding in Table 9.3 that behavioral, cognitive–behavioral, and nonbehavioral group treatments produced significantly different ESs could be due to other variables confounded with one or more of these treatments. Perhaps, one of the treatments was disproportionately applied to those with milder (or more severe) problems, or one was more often conducted by the most experienced group leaders. To make things more complicated, method and clinical characteristics can also be confounded. Maybe behavioral treatments were more often evaluated in methodologically sounder studies, which were freer from bias or error, and hence more sensitive to treatment effects. A reviewer is not responsible for examining every possible combination or permutation of variables, but should examine the most plausible rival explanations for the results.

One way to rule out alternatives is to divide studies according to different variables and then examine the outcomes. The logic of such analyses requires the potential confound to significantly influence outcomes and be disproportionately distributed among treatments. For example, because randomized and nonrandomized designs produced similar outcomes in our group therapy meta-analysis, this variable cannot serve as an explanation why one treatment was more effective than another.

In summary, a meta-analyst should be thinking as follows: "Although model testing has confirmed my initial hypotheses, I have a checklist of other possible explanations for these same outcomes. If I can rule out each other possibility, I will have stronger empirical support for my findings."

## Practical Significance

There is no straightforward relationship between an ES and its practical significance. A high ES does not always mean intervention has produced clinically significant changes in functioning. A good meta-analysis will attempt to provide some information on the practical importance of obtained effects. Usually, the practical significance of ES depends on the way outcomes have been measured and presenting findings for different types of outcomes can be helpful.

For example, a $M$ effect of .20, which seems low, can be important if it is based on such outcomes as suicide attempts, commission of serious crimes, psychiatric hospitalizations, and so on. To illustrate how this is so, it is helpful to calculate the binomial effect (Rosenthal & Rubin, 1982). This can be done by the reader in any case when $M$ effects are presented.

The binomial effect expresses the success rates for intervention and control groups expressed in proportions and is calculated from a Pearson $r$. (Within the ranges often obtained in meta-analyses, ESs can be converted to an $r$ by simply dividing by 2.) Success rates for the intervention and control groups are then found through the following formula: 50% plus and minus $r/2$, respectively. For example, suppose we wanted to calculate the binomial effect for a serious suicide attempt, which yielded a $M$ ES of .20 in a hypothetical meta-analysis. Using the above formula, the $M$ ES of .20 converts to an $r$ of .10 and the success rates would be 55% for the treated group and 45% for the controls (50% $\pm$ .10/2). In this case, "success" refers to no serious suicide attempt. Although a 55% success rate might seem low, it is actually 22% higher among treated than untreated clients (i.e., 55% is 22% higher than 45%). Because suicide attempts are such an important clinical outcome, the impact of treatment has considerable practical significance in this case. Rosenthal (1991) described instances when ESs as low as .02 have literally translated into life or death decisions regarding medical treatment.

Another way to assess practical significance is by calculating effects using normative data, which can be done for studies containing normed outcome measures. For example, in a review of cognitive behavioral treatments, we found 23 studies using at least one normed outcome measure (Durlak, Fuhrman & Lampman, 1991). A normative effect size (NES) was calculated as the $M$ of the treatment group minus the $M$ of the normed group divided by the latter's $SD$. At pretreatment, the $M$ NES was 1.55, but at post treatment, it was only .50. In this case, lower NESs are preferred because they indicate less of a difference between treated groups and normals. Our results indicated that treated groups were functioning much nearer to the levels of normal controls following intervention than before, although the post $M$ effect of .50 still indicated room for improvement among the treated samples. Overall, however, these findings suggested intervention was producing practical benefits for participants. Trull,

Nietzel and Main (1988) offered another example of how normative data can be used to assess the practical significance of effects in a meta-analysis.

## STEP 5: REACHING CONCLUSIONS & GUIDING FUTURE RESEARCH

Reviewers often strive to reach conclusions on major themes and important issues relevant to their central research questions, for example: How effective in this treatment? Which theory has received the most support? What implications do the findings have for future research, practice, or policy? Three factors are often relevant to qualifying one's conclusions: (a) the inclusionary criteria used to select the study sample, (b) missing information in the primary studies, and, (c) the statistical power of the analyses.

For instance, if the literature search did not include certain types of treatments, populations, or problems, the results cannot be generalized to these excluded areas. Although this seems elemental, authors are not always careful in tempering their conclusions. Wampold et al. (1997) concluded that different types of treatments did not yield significantly different results, but because they included only three child and family therapy studies, their results clearly do not apply to these types of treatments. If a table of the major study characteristics of reviewed studies has been provided, readers can judge for themselves the generality of conclusions across different populations, treatments, and problems.

It is also usually necessary to limit conclusions and generalizations because of missing information in the study sample. The typical situation is that only some reviewed studies contain all the needed information; some studies might have most of the required data, but many studies will be missing something of relevance and interest. This loss of information can be critical. For example, in one review, we could not investigate our hypothesis about the influence of program implementation on outcomes because very few studies contained any information at all on implementation (Durlak & Wells, 1997).

In some notable cases, meta-analysts have reached surprising conclusions based on nonsignificant results. That is, they have concluded that there are no significant differences as a function of different treatments, therapists, or presenting problems. The data may support such conclusions (although one must be cautious in promoting a null hypothesis), but it is important to consider the contribution of statistical power to such analyses.

Statistical power in a meta-analysis is based on the same factors that affect power in an individual study: (1) the effect size one is expecting, (2) the probability level of the analysis, and (3) sample size. In a meta-analysis, sample size involves both the number of studies in the analysis and the number of participants within these studies. Hedges and Pigott (2001) have provided useful guidelines for calculating the level of statistical power in a meta-analysis when comparing mean effects and assessing homogeneity. Unfortunately, reviewers may ignore matters of statistical power when offering their conclusions.

In other words, when it comes to negative results, reviewers should distinguish between "no evidence of effect" and "evidence of no effect" (Oxman, 1994). Evidence of no effect requires that a sufficient number of studies exist (i.e., there is sufficient statistical power) to put a research question to a fair test. For instance, there are enough studies of Treatment A to say this treatment is ineffective. By contrast, "no evidence of effect" refers to situations in which there are insufficient data for a fair test. If there are only a few evaluations of Treatment A, there are not enough data to reach any conclusion, one way or another about treatment impact.

*Guiding Future Research.* The contribution of well-done reviews goes beyond reaching conclusions about past research and extends to offering useful guidance for future studies. The assessments possible in a meta-analysis permit reviewers to highlight gaps and limitations in prior studies that should be corrected by future investigators. For example, which treatments, populations, or problems deserve more attention? Which theories need more analysis? Which competing interpretations of outcomes need clarification? Authors can also offer suggestions on how to improve research in general through more rigorous and sensitive ways to design and evaluate individual experiments. Finally, authors can pose specific research questions for others to answer. Reviews often generate more questions than they answer because the inspection and analysis of data from multiple studies during the review process has given the author insights into the field that were not immediately apparent. In summary, the best reviews consider the past, the present, and the future. Prior studies are used to ascertain the current status of research with an eye toward improving the next generation of studies.

## AN EXAMPLE OF A META-ANALYSIS

To illustrate some of the points just discussed, an example of a recently completed meta-analysis is presented (Meerson & Durlak, 2000). Space does not permit a full description of this review, so a few major points are emphasized. Parenthetical comments are used to highlight important principles.

### Formulating the Research Questions

The goal of the meta-analysis was to examine the impact of group therapy for children and adolescents with adjustment problems. Our major prediction was that the type of group treatment would moderate outcomes, specifically that both behavioral and cognitive behavioral treatments would produce significantly higher mean ESs than nonbehavioral treatment. We also predicted there would be publication bias, that is, that unpublished reports would yield significantly lower ESs than published studies. Finally, we predicted that studies using experienced group therapists would yield significantly higher ESs than studies using inexperienced therapists. (The basis for each of these hypotheses would be explained in the introduction to the meta-analysis.)

## Obtaining Representative Studies

Our primary inclusionary criteria were the following: (a) a between-group design in which the effects of group therapy were compared to some type of control condition (waiting list, no treatment, or attention placebo); (b) the study was reported in English and appeared by the end of 1999; and (c) participants were identified as having some type of adjustment problem. Prevention programs were not included, nor were family therapy studies or interventions that focused only on academic problems. (It is often helpful to mention a few exclusionary criteria.)

We used three strategies to locate published reports (manual journal searches, examination of reference lists, and computer searches). The first two strategies identified 70% of our eventual, published study sample. (In other words, depending on computer searches exclusively would have reduced our data set by over half.) To obtain unpublished studies, we did both computer and hand searches of three randomly selected years of *Dissertation Abstracts* (1 year in the 1970s, 1 year in the 1980s, and 1 year in the 1990s). Our final study sample consisted of 236 evaluations of group therapy treatments including 54 unpublished dissertations (23% of the total sample). Our study sample was over 4 times larger than any previous review of group therapy and the only one to sample unpublished literature. (In other words, we seemed to have secured the most extensive and representative sample of group studies yet evaluated in the literature.)

## Coding of Studies

We coded each study on 50 different variables that included methodological aspects of study design, and various characteristics of the populations, presenting problems and treatments. (We inform readers that a copy of our coding scheme was available on request.) A randomly selected 20% of the studies was independently coded by another rater and coefficient kappa corrected for chance did not dip below 70% for any variable (i.e., it appears that acceptable reliability was obtained.)

## Analysis of Outcomes

We used a fixed effect model in our analyses because we believed that systematic differences existing among studies would be the main contributor to significant variability in effects. The overall unweighted $M$ effect from all studies was .61, but the $M$ weighted ES was .41. Weighted ESs were used in all subsequent analyses. (Using unweighted ESs would have overestimated the overall effect of group treatment by 49%). Although the confidence intervals around the weighted overall $M$ did not include zero, indicating that group therapy in general produced a significantly positive impact, the $Q$ total was significant. (This indicated heterogeneity of ESs in our total sample and suggested the need to search for possible moderators.) We then divided the studies according to the variables in our hypotheses.

The data relevant to our first major hypothesis that type of treatment would moderate outcomes have already been presented in Table 9.3. Our hypothesis was largely supported; homogeneity was obtained for cognitive behavioral and nonbehavioral treatments, and the confidence intervals indicated significant $M$ differences between each major type of treatment. (We did not predict, however, that behavioral treatment would generate the highest $M$ ES.)

Our other two hypotheses were also supported. Dissertations yielded significantly lower ESs than published studies and studies using experienced therapists produced significantly better results than those using inexperienced therapists. The relevant data are presented in Table 9.4. (If you have followed the discussion about CIs, you should be able to confirm the aforementioned statements by examining Table 9.4.)

Apparently, there is significant publication bias in the reporting of group therapy outcomes. (If we had omitted dissertations, it would have been impossible to discover this fact, and our reporting of data from only published studies would have overestimated the overall effect of group intervention.) There is a major limitation, however, in our finding regarding group experience. (Can you tell what it is by comparing the data in Tables 9.3 and 9.4?)

TABLE 9.4
Results for Other Hypothesized Variables in the Group Therapy Meta-Analysis

| Variable | Number | M | Confidence Intervals | Significant Q |
|---|---|---|---|---|
| Source of Publication | | | | |
| Published study | 182 | .42 | .37 to .46 | Yes |
| Unpublished dissertation | 54 | .20 | .11 to .30 | No |
| Leaders' Group Experience | | | | |
| Experienced | 51 | .50 | .43 to .59 | No |
| Inexperienced | 20 | .30 | .24 to .42 | Yes |

The limitation is that only 71 of the 236 studies (only 30%) provided any information on therapists' previous group therapy experience. (In other words, critical information relevant to one of our hypotheses was missing from most studies.)

**Ruling Out Rival Hypotheses.** To rule out some alternative explanations for our results, we assessed whether the three types of treatment were confounded with some other major variables. For instance, the three treatment groups contained a comparable number of unpublished dissertations and experienced group therapists so these variables could not explain why the three treatments differed in outcome. Also, we did not find different outcomes when we recombined studies according to several methodological variables such as general type of design (randomized or not), type of outcome measures used, nature of the presenting problems, and so on. (It is always possible that method variables may impact outcomes as much as or more than any theoretical or clinical variables and this should be examined.)

## Reaching Conclusions

Our major conclusions are that group therapy in general is an effective intervention for children and adolescents with adjustment problems and that the type of treatment is an important determinant of outcomes. Publication bias does occur in this literature; effects from published studies are twice the magnitude of those from unpublished dissertations. It is possible the latter occurs because dissertations use more inexperienced therapists (perhaps the person doing the dissertation). Although there was some support for our prediction that experienced therapists would obtain better results than inexperienced therapists, 70% of the reviewed studies did not report the experience level of the group leaders. Future investigators should study the effect of the leaders' previous group experience on outcome and design studies that could help elucidate the factors that make some forms of group treatment more effective than others. There are some other limitations among current group therapy studies that should be addressed in future research; only 25% conducted any follow-up and most follow-up periods were very brief (i.e., less than 2 months), and only 24% treated members of any minority group. (Although this brief presentation hardly does justice to the discussion section in a meta-analysis, consistent with earlier comments, it is important to discuss the major findings, their limitations, and how future research can advance the field, by, for instance, assessing variables that have so far been overlooked or understudied.)

By clarifying the current state of knowledge on the effects of group treatment, practitioners may judge how far to trust the techniques they use, and researchers are alerted to questions that require additional research. In this way, meta-analysis furthers both science and practice.

**Further Reading**

The interested reader who wishes to learn more about meta-analysis can consult several sources that explain the different facets of meta-analysis in greater depth and contain plenty of practical details and useful examples (Cooper & Hedges, 1994; Durlak, in press; Hunter & Schmidt, 1990; Lipsey & Wilson, 2001).

## REFERENCES

Abrami, P. C., Cohen, P. A., & d'Apollonia, S. (1988). Implementation problems in meta-analysis. *Review of Educational Research, 58*, 151–179.

Busk, P. L., & Serlin, R. C. (1992). Meta-analysis for single-case research. In T. R. Kratochwill & J. R. Levin (Eds.), *Single-case research design and analysis* (pp. 187–212). Hillsdale, NJ: Lawrence Erlbaum Associates.

Casey, R. J., & Berman, J. S. (1985). The outcome of psychotherapy with children. *Psychological Bulletin, 98*, 388–400.

Cooper, H., & Hedges, L. V. (Eds.). (1994). *Handbook of research synthesis.* New York: Russell Sage Foundation.

Dickersin, K. (1997). How important is publication bias?: A synthesis of available data. *AIDS Education and Prevention, 9*, 15–21.

DuPaul, G. J., & Eckert, T. L. (1997). The effects of school-based interventions for attention deficit hyperactivity disorder: A meta-analysis. *School Psychology Review, 26*, 5–27.

Durlak, J. A. (2000). How to evaluate a meta-analysis. In D. Drotar (Ed.), *Handbook of research in pediatric and clinical child psychology* (pp. 395–407). New York: Kluwer Academic/Plenum.

Durlak, J. A. (in press). Basic principles of meta analysis. In M. Roberts & S. S. Ilardi (Eds.), *Methods of research in clinical psychology: A Handbook.* Malden, MA: Blackwell.

Durlak, J. A. , Fuhrman, T., & Lampman, C. (1991). Effectiveness of cognitive-behavior therapy for maladapting children: A meta-analysis. *Psychological Bulletin, 110*, 204–214.

Durlak, J. A., & Wells, A. M. (1997). Primary prevention mental health programs for children and adolescents: A meta-analytic review. *American Journal of Community Psychology, 25*, 115–152.

Hartmann, D. P. (Ed.). (1982). *Using observers to study behavior: New directions for methodology of social and behavioral sciences.* San Francisco: Jossey-Bass.

Hedges, L. V., & Olkin, I. (1985). *Statistical methods for meta-analysis.* New York: Academic Press.

Hedges, L. V., & Piggot, T. D. (2001). The power of statistical tests in meta-analysis. *Psychological Methods, 6*, 203–217.

Holmes, C. T. (1984). Effect size estimation in meta-analysis. *Journal of Experimental Education, 52*, 106–109.

Hunter, J. E., & Schmidt, F. L. (1990). *Methods of meta-analysis: Correcting error and bias in research findings.* Newbury Park, CA: Sage.

Jackson, G. B. (1980). Methods for integrative reviews. *Review of Educational Research, 50*, 438–460.

Kavale, K. A., Mathur, S. R., Forness, S. R., Rutherford, R. B., Jr., & Quinn, M. M. (1997). Effectiveness of social skills training for students with behavior disorders: A meta-analysis. *Advances in Learning and Behavioral Disabilities, 11*, 1–26.

Kazdin, A. E., & Bass, D. (1989). Power to detect differences between alternative treatments in comparative psychotherapy outcome research. *Journal of Consulting and Clinical Psychology, 57*, 138–147.

Lipsey, M. W., & Wilson, D. B. (1993). The efficacy of psychological, educational, and behavioral treatment: Confirmation from meta-analysis. *American Psychologist, 48*, 1181–1209.

Lipsey, M. W., & Wilson, D. B. (2001). *Practical meta-analysis.* Thousand Oaks, CA: Sage.

Matyas, T., & Greenwood, K. M. (1990). Visual analysis of single-case time series: Effects of variability, serial dependence, and magnitude of intervention effects. *Journal of Applied Behavior Analysis, 23*, 341–351.

Meerson, I., & Durlak, J. A. (2000, June). Effectiveness of group psychotherapy with children and adolescents: A meta-analytic review. Paper presented at the 31st Annual Meeting of the Society for Psychotherapy Research, Bloomingdale, IL.

Oxman, A. D. (1994). Checklists for review articles. *British Medical Journal, 309*, 648–651.

Rosenthal, R. (1991). *Meta-analytic procedures for social research* (Rev. ed.). Newbury Park, CA: Sage.

Rosenthal, R., & Rubin, D. B. (1982). A simple, general purpose display of magnitude of experimental effect. *Journal of Educational Psychology, 74*, 166–169.

Trull, T. J., Nietzel, M., T., & Main, A. (1988). The use of meta-analysis to assess the clinical significance of behavior therapy for agoraphobia. *Behavior Therapy, 19*, 527–538.

Wampold, B. E., Mondin, G. W., Moody, M., Stich, F., Benson, K., & Ahn, H. (1997). A meta-analysis of outcome studies comparing bona fide psychotherapies: Empirically, "All must have prizes." *Psychological Bulletin, 14*, 203–215.

Weisz, J. R., Weiss, B., Alicke, M. D., & Klotz, M. L. (1987). Effectiveness of psychotherapy with children and adolescents: A meta-analysis for clinicians. *Journal of Consulting and Clinical Psychology, 55*, 542–549.

Wolf, F. M. (1986). *Meta-analysis: Quantitative methods for research synthesis.* Beverly Hills, CA: Sage.

# III

# Research Practice

# 10

# Ethical Guidelines in Research

Catherine Miller
*Pacific University, Forest Grove, Oregon*

As a student, when you are first learning how to conduct research, it is unlikely that ethical issues are your foremost considerations. With so much to learn about the steps of conducting research, research design, and statistical analyses, research ethics may sound like an important, but not a pressing, subject. In this chapter, I hope to disabuse you of the idea that ethical principles may be thought of, if at all, as a final step in research design. It is not true that ethical issues are mutually exclusive from research issues; on the contrary, it is reasonable to argue that "ethics and scientific inquiry are very closely interrelated" (Rosenthal, 1994, p. 127). Researchers should recognize that methodology and ethics must work together, as reflected in this statement by Sieber (1992):

> The ethics of social research is not about etiquette; nor is it about considering the poor hapless subject at the expense of science or society. Rather, we study ethics to learn how to make social research "work" for all concerned. The ethical researcher creates a mutually respectful, win–win relationship with the research population. (p. 3)

Before delving further into research ethics, consider the following examples of three controversial research projects. Think about your response to these studies as if you were a subject. Would you want to participate in these studies? Does your answer change depending on the potential value of the study in increasing our knowledge base? Is it possible to design these studies to avoid the ethical dilemmas the researchers faced?

In 1963, Milgram conducted a study on obedience in order to assess human response to the commands of authority figures (as cited in Adair, Dushenko, & Lindsay, 1985). In this study, subjects were designated as "teachers" and given the task of teaching other subjects (designated "learners") pairs of words. Teachers and learners were placed in separate rooms, where they could hear but not see each other. When a learner gave an incorrect answer, the teacher was instructed by the researcher to administer increasing levels of electric shock to the learner, even when the learner could be heard begging the teacher to stop hurting him or her. Unbeknown to the teachers, the learners were actually confederates of the researcher; the learners were not shocked but instead only acted as if they were harmed. Milgram found that the majority of subjects would administer what they believed to be very painful shocks to others when instructed to do so by an authority figure.

In 1972, Zimbardo conducted a study on the effect of role-playing (as cited in Myers, 1992). He divided college student subjects into "prison guard" and "prisoner" roles. A mock prison setting was constructed in the basement of a college building and both sets of subjects were told to enact their roles on a regular basis. The study had to be suspended after only 6 days when the researcher discovered that the students had enacted their roles too well. Some of the guards were becoming aggressive toward the prisoners, and some of the prisoners were showing signs of depression.

As a final example, Campbell, Sanderson, and Laverty (1964; as cited in Adair et al., 1985) conducted a study in which subjects were administered a drug that produced a temporary interruption of breathing without being fore-warned of this effect. The purpose of the study was to assess human responses to traumatic situations. The experience was not reported to be painful but was considered horrific and traumatizing by subjects.

These three studies were controversial and presented some troubling ethical dilemmas. For example, is it ever acceptable to deceive subjects in order to study a worthwhile topic? How can researchers balance the rights of individuals with the contribution of research toward the advancement of knowledge (Sieber, 1992)? These studies did report important findings that contributed to our knowledge of human behavior (Myers, 1992). The issue for current researchers is to consider how such information may be obtained in the most ethically acceptable manner.

The prior studies illustrate two of the main points of this chapter. First, ethical dilemmas will inevitably arise when doing research (American Psychological Association [APA], 1982). It is not possible to design a study in which no ethical issues will be encountered. Second, the quality of the design directly affects the ethicality of the study (Rosenthal, 1994). The lower the quality of the research, the less ethically justified we are in using human subjects as participants. Most investigators would agree that even "perfectly safe research in which no participant will be put at risk may also be ethically questionable because of the shortcomings of the design" (Rosenthal, 1994, p. 127). It should be clear that invalid or inadequate research has no benefit and is therefore not appropriate to be conducted with human subjects (Azar, 2000).

Because the attempt to reconcile research and ethical issues is difficult, some researchers may forgo conducting a particularly worthwhile study due to the complex ethical issues involved. Rather than wrestle with thorny ethical issues, it is possible that researchers may abandon a worthwhile study on important social issues if that study involves ethically questionable practices, such as the use of deception. However, not conducting important studies may be just as ethically problematic as employing questionable ethical practices. Researchers are encouraged to consider "the ethical implications of the *failure* to conduct ethically ambiguous studies that might reduce violence, prejudice, mental illness, and so forth" (Rosnow, 1990, p. 179, italics added). Although wrestling with ethical dilemmas is difficult at times, researchers must continue to do so rather than foregoing worthwhile and useful research.

Despite a desire for clear and unequivocal guidance from ethics codes, researchers should recognize that there are no real right and wrong answers contained in ethical principles. Instead, investigators must consider both the advantages and disadvantages of conducting a potential study (APA, 1982). It is common that researchers face situations in which one ethical principle conflicts with another (see APA, 1982, p. 18, for examples). As a researcher, you must remember that "there is more than one vantage point from which the ethical evaluation of a study can be made" (Rosnow, 1990, p. 179). In other words, look to the ethical principles to provide guidance but do not expect unambiguous answers to every ethical dilemma (Sieber, 1998).

## HISTORY OF RESEARCH ETHICS

In order to understand current ethical principles related to research, it is important to briefly examine the history and evolution of legislation governing research activities and the formation of ethical codes. It was not until 1947 that the importance of ethical principles in research was acknowledged formally. At that time, the public first became aware that physicians and scientists had conducted biomedical experiments on prisoners in Nazi concentration camps during World War II (Schmidt & Meara, 1996). The two main objections to these studies were that the experiments had no scientific merit and that the scientists employed prisoners involuntarily as subjects (Sieber, 1992; Tuthill, 1997). Examples of experiments conducted in the concentration camps included assessing human responses to poisons, high altitude, extreme temperatures, and infections (Tuthill, 1997).

Twenty-three of these scientists were investigated at the Nuremberg Trials of Nazi war criminals (Keith-Spiegel, 1983; Sieber, 1992). Some of the Nazi scientists correctly argued at the trials that no international law or code of ethics existed that prohibited their behavior (Portland State University [PSU], 1999[1]). Dr. Leo Alexander, a physician from the United States working with the prosecution during the Nuremberg Trials, submitted a report in 1947 that outlined the standards of legitimate and ethical research (PSU, 1999). As a result of these trials and Dr. Alexander's report, the Nuremberg Code was developed, which outlined how research with human subjects must be conducted (Keith-Spiegel, 1983; Sieber, 1992).

The Nuremberg Code emphasized that "certain basic principles must be observed in order to satisfy moral, ethical, and legal concepts" (as cited in PSU, 1999, p. 37). Out of the 10 principles outlined in the Nuremberg Code, first and foremost, the Code emphasized that scientists must have the informed consent of any human subject in research (Sieber, 1992; Tuthill, 1997). Virtually no room for exceptions was noted, as the Code stated that "the voluntary consent of the human subject is absolutely essential" (as cited in Keith-Spiegel, 1983, p. 182). Other principles emphasized in the Nuremberg Code included the following: "a favorable risk/benefit ratio, the avoidance of harm and suffering, protection of subjects from injury, the necessity that investigators be qualified scientists, and freedom for subjects to withdraw at any time" (Schmidt & Meara, 1996, p. 114).

The effect of the Nuremberg Code on current research standards cannot be overemphasized. That initial code influenced both federal regulations as well as current ethical principles promulgated by the American Psychological Association (APA; 1992a) and the American Counseling Association (ACA; 1995). I discuss the effect of the Nuremberg Code on federal regulations first and then address the impact of the Code on ethical guidelines.

## Federal Regulations

On the federal level, the United States Congress passed the National Research Act (Public Law 93-348) in 1974 (Schmidt & Meara, 1996; Sieber, 1992). This act had two important provisions regarding research. First, the act created the National Commission for the Protection of Human Subjects in Biomedical and Behavioral Research (Schmidt & Meara, 1996; Sieber, 1992). Second, the act mandated the formation of institutional review boards (IRBs) in each university or other organization that conducts biomedical or behavioral research involving human subjects and receives federal funding for research (Sieber, 1992).

The National Commission for the Protection of Human Subjects in Biomedical and Behavioral Research (hereafter referred to as the National Commission)

---

[1]Portland State University has an excellent summary of the history and requirements of IRBs contained in their IRB application packet. To obtain a copy of this packet, please visit PSU's website at *http://www.gsr.pdx.edu/rsp* and then click to "human subjects."

held hearings from 1974 to 1977 regarding ethical problems in human research (Schmidt & Meara, 1996). As one part of the hearings, commissioners examined problematic research studies, such as the Tuskegee Syphilis Study (as cited in Sieber, 1992). This study was begun in 1932 and continued until 1972 in an effort to assess the degenerative course of syphilis. Primarily rural, African-American males from impoverished backgrounds were recruited as subjects in this longitudinal study. In an effort to prevent any disruption of data, the subjects were not given any treatment for syphilis, even one became available (penicillin was widely known to cure syphilis by 1943; Sieber, 1992). In addition to examining specific studies, the National Commission's hearings focused on problematic but commonly used research practices. For example, the hearings found that deceptive practices were frequently employed in research studies, due to "the assumption . . . that subjects neither suspected deception nor could be harmed by it" (Sieber, 1992, p. 7).

On the basis of these hearings, the National Commission developed specific recommendations for research with human subjects (Sieber, 1992). In 1978, the National Commission published a report entitled "The Belmont Report: Ethical Principles and Guidelines for the Protection of Human Subjects of Research" (reprinted in a report from the Office for Protection from Research Risks, 1993). The report came to be known simply as the Belmont Report, after the Belmont Conference Center of the Smithsonian Institution in Washington, DC, where the National Commission met (Schmidt & Meara, 1996).

The Belmont Report identified three basic ethical principles that are still important today when conducting research with human subjects: respect for persons, justice, and beneficence (Schmidt & Meara, 1996; Sieber, 1992). The principle of respect for persons mandates that researchers must protect the autonomy and individuality of all persons (Sieber, 1992). Included in this concept is the idea that that those people who are not autonomous (e.g., children, developmentally delayed adults) should be treated fairly, with respect and courtesy (Sieber, 1992). The principle of justice involves the idea of "fair distribution of costs and benefits among persons and groups (i.e., those who bear the risks of research should be those who benefit from it"; Sieber, 1992, p. 18). Finally, the principle of beneficence emphasizes the importance of "maximizing good outcomes for science, humanity, and the individual research participants while avoiding or minimizing unnecessary risk, harm or wrong" (Sieber, 1992, p. 18). The idea of beneficence is contained in cost-benefit analyses of research projects (Rosenthal, 1994). This concept states that each study must be examined through "cost-utility analyses designed to determine if the known or suspected damage entailed in a study can be justified by the utility (or benefit) that accrues from its completion" (Pomerantz, 1994, p. 135).

In 1981, the United States Department of Health and Human Services (DHHS) issued regulations regarding human subjects that incorporated principles contained in the Belmont Report. This 1981 report is entitled, "Protection of Human Subjects," and is contained in Title 45, Part 46, of the Code of Federal Regulations (as cited in Schmidt & Meara, 1996). Although changes have been made to this code, the principles of beneficence, justice, and respect for persons are still emphasized in the revisions (Schmidt & Meara, 1996).

In addition to forming the National Commission, the Research Act of 1974 mandated the establishment of Institutional Review Boards (IRBs) at all universities and agencies that accept federal funding (Sieber, 1992). The purpose of these boards is to review research proposals in order to prevent ethically questionable research from being conducted with human subjects (Sieber, 1992). Due to the Research Act, no research with human subjects may be conducted without written IRB approval (Schmidt & Meara, 1996). The specific steps involved in obtaining IRB approval are discussed in a later section of this chapter.

## Ethical Codes

The Nuremberg Code had a strong influence on the development of formal ethical guidelines by APA and ACA. APA's first publication of a general ethics code for psychologists in 1953 encouraged psychologists to (a) engage in ethical research practices by stating that investigators are responsible to protect subjects' welfare; (b) fully inform subjects of risks involved in the research; (c) allow subjects to decline to participate; (d) use deception only when necessary; and (e) maintain confidentiality of research subjects (APA, 1953; as cited in Schmidt & Meara, 1996). In 1966, APA started an ad hoc committee to further examine research ethics (APA, 1982). This committee developed a set of principles to guide research; in 1973, APA distributed a booklet containing these principles entitled, "Ethical Principles in the Conduct of Research With Human Participants" (APA, 1973; as cited in APA, 1982). In 1978, APA established a Committee for the Protection of Human Subjects in Psychological Research; this committee took the place of the ad hoc committee and "was charged to make annual reviews and recommendations about the official APA position on the use of human participants in research" (APA, 1982, p. 12). Subsequent revisions of both APA's booklet and general ethical guidelines have been published, with increased emphasis and clarification of statements regarding ethical principles (Blanck, Bellack, Rosnow, Rotheram-Borus, & Schooler, 1998; Schmidt & Meara, 1996).

APA's general ethics code was last revised in 1992; in this revision, research guidelines are contained in standard 6 (APA, 1992a). Overall, the current ethical guidelines emphasize the importance of protecting the welfare of all research participants. Specifically, the guidelines state that researchers must plan studies in such a way as to protect "the rights and welfare of human participants, other persons affected by the research, and the welfare of animal subjects" (APA, 1992a, standard 6.06). Other guidelines emphasize that use of deception in studies should be minimized, that IRB approval must be obtained prior to conduction research, and that subject confidentiality should be maintained (APA, 1992a).

ACA has developed a similar set of ethical guidelines for counseling students and master's level counselors who are engaged in research projects (ACA, 1995). These research ethical guidelines are contained in Section G of the ACA Ethical Codes and emphasize that investigators must protect the rights of research participants and must take reasonable precautions to avoid causing harm to research subjects (ACA, 1995). The guidelines also admonish researchers to be sensitive to diversity issues, to obtain consent from every subject to participate in research, to avoid deceptive practices, and to keep subject information confidential (ACA, 1995).

## ETHICAL ISSUES ENCOUNTERED BY RESEARCHERS

It should be clear from the previous discussion that ethical issues are important in designing sound research. The question then centers on how researchers can ensure that they adhere to ethical codes and legal requirements when designing a study. In other words, how can investigators make sure that their research is done ethically? In this section, I first review basic ethical issues that every researcher should know. Next, I review several applied issues involved in research. Areas to be addressed include the following: (a) IRB approval process, (b) informed consent, (c) children's participation in research, (d) confidentiality and privacy of subjects, (e) deception in research, (f) use of animal subjects, and (g) use of the Internet to conduct research.

### Basic Ethical Issues in Research

There are some obvious ethical mistakes that investigators might make, particularly when first conducting research. First and foremost, it is imperative that researchers never fabricate data or falsify results. The data should be reported honestly, even if the results do not support the initial hypothesis. This may sound like a simple guideline to follow, but even advanced researchers have disregarded it in the past. For example, after his death, it was discovered that Sir Cyril Burt had published fictitious data in his identical twin studies (as cited in Koocher & Keith-Spiegel, 1998). This discovery not only discredited Burt's work but also hurt the entire field of psychology (Koocher & Keith-Spiegel, 1998). It is understandable that certain contingencies, such as grant funding or job requirements, may make it tempting to falsify data, even slightly, in order to get a study published. However, researchers should note that this is one of the few unequivocal ethical guidelines: Do not, no matter how tempted, alter or falsify research results (APA, 1992a).

Related to the fabrication of data are the concepts of *data dropping* and the *exploitation of data*, practices that are ethically questionable (Rosenthal, 1994). Data dropping involves procedures such as outlier rejection (dropping outlying data without informing readers) and subject selection (subset of data not used in analysis and not reported in article; Rosenthal, 1994). Exploitation of data or data torturing involves "snoop[ing] around in the data" (Rosenthal, 1994, p. 130) in an effort to find any possible statistically significant results.

In reporting hypotheses or results, there are several ethically questionable practices that should be avoided. First, researchers should not engage in "hyper-claiming," a procedure wherein investigators "tell . . . our prospective participants, our granting agencies, our colleagues, our administrators, and ourselves that our research is likely to achieve goals it is, in fact, unlikely to achieve" (Rosenthal, 1994, p. 128). In addition, researchers should avoid the temptation to engage in "causism," which refers to "the tendency to imply a causal relationship where none has been established" (Rosenthal, 1994, p. 128). The bottom line, according to Rosenthal (1994), is that it is unethical to inflate the importance of your own data in reports of your study.

Another simple but often overlooked guideline in the reporting of research involves the citing of prior studies or ideas. Always give credit to the originator of work or ideas (APA, 1994). When a work is quoted verbatim, remember to place quotation marks around the statement(s). If you are not quoting the exact words of another, you may paraphrase prior work (APA, 1994). Paraphrasing may be defined as summarizing a passage or changing word order; researchers should be aware that these passages must still be cited (APA, 1994). The very serious ethical violation of plagiarism may be leveled at researchers who report ideas or prior work without appropriate citations (APA, 1992a).

APA guidelines spell out other ethical requirements of researchers (APA, 1992a, 1994). For example, only take authorship credit for work you actually did and do not withhold data from other researchers who wish to verify your conclusions. Avoid duplication publication of the same study. In other words, do not present as original data in one article data that have been presented elsewhere. If a study has been published in one journal, do not attempt to publish the same study or a large part of that study in another journal. In the same vein, avoid publishing one study in the mass media and then submit the same study to a psychological journal. Although not clearly prohibited by APA, avoid submitting one study to more than one conference unless the conference audience is widely divergent. The above recommendations serve to conserve resources, such as journal space and reviewer effort (APA, 1994). In addition, these recommendations avoid "distort[ing] the knowledge base by making it appear there is more information available than really exists" (APA, 1994, pp. 295–296).

## IRB Approval Process

As previously mentioned, institutional review boards (IRBs) were formed by the National Research Act of 1974. Currently, most IRB committees are monitored by the Office for Protection from Research Risks (OPRR), a federal office within the National Institutes of Health (Schmidt & Meara, 1996). One exception involves drug-related research, which is administered nationally by the Food and Drug Administration (FDA; Sieber, 1992). Institutions not in compliance with federal law regarding IRBs may lose any federal funding of their programs, including financial aid to students (Sieber, 1992).

IRB committees generally consist of five or more members from varying backgrounds (Sieber, 1992). The job of the IRB is to "review, evaluate, and approve or disapprove investigations that include human research subjects" (Tuthill, 1997, p. 232). Although each IRB committee is responsible for developing specific policies regarding review protocol and meeting schedules (Sieber, 1992), some commonalties across committees may be found. In general, in order to have a study approved by an IRB, the following conditions must be met: "the risks are minimal; the risk-benefit balance is reasonable; the selection of subjects is equitable; informed consent will be sought and documented; subjects' safety and privacy are adequately protected; and the rights and welfare of particularly vulnerable subjects are respected" (Tuthill, 1997, p. 233). All of the requirements for IRB approval are consistent with current ethical guidelines and prior federal reports (e.g., the Belmont Report).

The majority of studies involving human subjects, even pilot projects, must be reviewed by IRBs (Sieber, 1992). However, it is possible that a review is not required in every situation. Such a case might occur if the data would not be published or otherwise disseminated, or if archival data are obtained from another researcher and no identifiers are employed (PSU, 1999).

If data will be disseminated, two types of reviews are possible: expedited or full committee reviews (PSU, 1999). The type of review needed depends heavily on the amount of potential risk to which human subjects are exposed in the proposed study (Sieber, 1992). Researchers are encouraged to consider any possible areas of risk, as "few things concern an IRB more than an investigator who blithely states that no risk is involved in proposed research" (Sieber, 1992, p. 79). In order to increase the likelihood of IRB approval, researchers should review each proposed study on the following categories: inconvenience, physical risks, psychological risks, social risks, economic risks, and legal risks (Sieber, 1992). Inconvenience refers to the possibility of subject boredom or frustration when participating in a study. Physical risk refers to the likelihood that a subject may incur some physical injury by research participation. Psychological risk refers to the possibility that some subjects may experience depression, anxiety, or some other uncomfortable emotional reaction to study participation. Social and economic risks refer to the likelihood that subject information may be exposed to the public and negative consequences may ensue, such as social rejection or loss of employment. Finally, legal risk refers to the possibility that a subject may incur some legal liability for study participation (Sieber, 1992). An example of the latter risk is the potential for having to report to proper authorities any child abuse statements made by a subject during the research project.

An expedited review may be requested for research involving no more than minimal risk (PSU, 1999). In 1974, the National Commission defined the term, *minimal risk*, to mean that "the probability and magnitude of harm . . . anticipated in the research are not greater . . . than those ordinarily encountered in daily life" (Tuthill, 1997, p. 244). As the name implies, an expedited review takes less time, as it typically does not require a meeting of the full board. Instead, the study proposal is reviewed by a subset of committee members. Examples of research that might qualify for expedited review include surveys, program evaluation, and research on cultural beliefs and social behavior (PSU, 1999). A review of the full board is required for research that involves some potential risk to human subjects. Such reviews typically take 4 to 6 weeks, due to the wait time involved in scheduling a full board meeting (PSU, 1999).

There are two main steps in obtaining IRB approval that must be considered well in advance of data collection, as researchers may not collect data from human subjects without IRB approval in writing (Schmidt & Meara, 1996). Because each committee develops its own procedural rules, the first step in obtaining IRB approval is to obtain a packet from your institution's IRB office. The packet will contain information about meeting dates and institutional requirements. Review the meeting times carefully, because the IRB at your institution may only meet a few times per year and boards will not typically receive proposals later than their announced deadlines. Once meeting times and deadlines have been ascertained, the second step is to prepare a proposal containing all of the information required by the IRB. In general, committees require that a study proposal include the following items: a description of the study's purpose and methods, a copy of the informed consent form, and a copy of any questionnaires or survey materials (PSU, 1999). Specific instructions on preparing this proposal should be contained in your institution's IRB packet.

Once a study has been approved, any changes made to the procedure, informed consent form, or questionnaires must be approved by the IRB (PSU, 1999). Generally, the committee requires researchers to send any changes along with a letter to the board that describes the reasons for the changes. The board will then meet to determine whether the changes are approved. In addition, if the study is a longitudinal one, the IRB will review the study on an annual basis, which requires researchers to submit updates to the IRB board on a regular basis. Finally, each IRB requires researchers to maintain all study records and data for a minimum amount of time (generally 3 years after the completion of the study; PSU, 1999). As previously stated, it is imperative that researchers obtain a copy of the institution's IRB procedures and requirements to ensure that specific guidelines are followed.

### Informed Consent

One of the main pieces of information required in order to obtain IRB approval is documentation that each human subject has been given information about the study, has been given an opportunity to ask questions about the study, and has expressly consented to participate in the study. This concept is known as *informed consent* (Schmidt & Meara, 1996). Although this has long been a familiar term in psychological treatment literature, this concept as it applies to research projects received much attention only after Milgram's 1963 study (Adair et al., 1985).

Informed consent to participate in a research project is documented by having each subject read information about the study, ask questions about the study, and sign a consent form. It is imperative that each subject sign a consent form, as "federal law requires that informed consent to experimentation be documented in writing" (Tuthill, 1997, p. 231). The intent behind informed consent forms is the protection of each person's welfare and the desire that subjects should leave a research study with the feeling that it has been a positive experience that he/she would repeat (Sieber, 1992).

In order to participate in a research study, subjects must consent to do so voluntarily, knowingly, and intelligently (Koocher & Keith-Spiegel, 1998). Voluntariness implies that "consent is obtained without exercising coercion or causing duress, pressure, or undue excitement or influence" (Koocher & Keith-Spiegel, 1998, p. 417). To ensure the voluntary nature of consent, APA ethical guidelines clearly prohibit the use of excessive rewards or inducements for participation in research, as that might serve as a coercive force (APA, 1992a). In addition, APA guidelines state that students must not be coerced into participating as subjects by the promise of extra credit but instead must be given alternatives to earn extra credit (APA, 1992a).

The concept of *knowledge* implies that potential subjects should be given all of the relevant information about a study needed to make a decision on whether or not to participate and be given the opportunity to ask questions about the study. It is important to understand that "failure to disclose material facts when obtaining a patient's consent [for research] is fraud" (Tuthill, 1997, p. 228). Per APA guidelines, this body of information must be conveyed in simple language that is easily understood by participants (APA, 1992a). This generally means the consent form should require no more than a 7th grade reading level (PSU, 1999).

The idea that subjects should consent intelligently implies that potential participants have "the capacity to comprehend and evaluate the information that is offered to them" (Koocher & Keith-Spiegel, 1998, p. 419). This concept suggests that only competent adults can legally sign an informed consent form. This issue is addressed further in this chapter in the discussion on employing minor research participants.

Specific information must be contained in the informed consent document. In general, according to APA ethical guidelines, the form must clarify the nature of the particular study and the responsibilities of each party (APA, 1992a). The guidelines further state that researchers must disclose to participants any foreseeable risks as well as limits on confidentiality before the subject agrees to participate in the study (APA, 1992a).

More specific guidelines were issued in 1971 by the Department of Health, Education and Welfare (DHEW; as cited in Keith-Spiegel, 1983). This report instructed researchers to include the following six elements in informed consent forms:

(1) a fair and understandable explanation of the nature of the activity, its purpose, and the procedures to be followed, including an identification of those that are experimental; (2) an understandable description of the attendant discomforts and risks that may reasonably be expected to occur; (3) an understandable description of any benefits that may reasonably be expected to ensue; (4) an understandable disclosure of any appropriate alternative procedures that may be advantageous for the participant; (5) an offer to answer any inquiries concerning the procedures to be used; and (6) an understanding that the person is free to withdraw his or her consent and discontinue participation in the project or activity at any time without prejudice (as cited in Keith-Spiegel, 1983, p. 186).

In addition, other specific elements have been recommended to satisfy the informed consent requirement, including the following:

(1) an invitation (as opposed to a request or demand) to become a participant along with a clear definition of the role the person is being asked to play as a participant; (2) informing the prospective participant as to why he or she has been selected, including any consequences of being found eligible; [and] (3) an offer to the potential participant of consultation with a third party during the decision-making process (Keith-Spiegel, 1983, p. 186).

In summary, current experts in this field recommend that all of the following items be included in an informed consent form to ensure IRB approval:

(1) the purpose(s) of the research and the procedures to be used; (2) the nature of subject participation, including the length of time involved, frequency of sessions, and location of the study; (3) any potential risks and discomforts to the subject, how these risks will be managed, and the treatment available for any research-related injury; (4) possible benefits the subject or others may receive from the research; (5) alternative treatments if the research has a treatment component; (6) the extent of the subject's

anonymity in records that are being kept; (7) a description of any compensation offered; (8) the subject's rights, including the right to terminate participation at any time without losing benefits to which the subject otherwise would be entitled; (9) a statement indicating that participation is voluntary; (10) a statement that the subject has the right to ask any questions about the study and procedures; (11) the name of the researcher and his/her affiliation, as well as a way for the subject to contact the researcher; (12) methods for contacting the institution's IRB committee; and (13) a statement that each subject will receive a signed copy of this form for his or her own records. (PSU, 1999; Tuthill, 1997)

Researchers may not place any language in a consent form that implies any loss of subjects' legal rights. According to the United States Department of Health and Human Services (1983)

no informed consent, whether oral or written, may include any exculpatory language through which the subject is made to waive or appear to waive any of the subject's legal rights, or releases or appears to release the investigator, the sponsor, the institution, or its agents from liability from negligence. (as cited in Adair et al., 1985)

Clearly, a large amount of information must be communicated to potential subjects prior to their agreeing to participate in a research study. Baker and Taub (1983; as cited in Mann, 1994) found that the average length of consent forms doubled from 1975 to 1982, in order to include more information about subject rights and confidentiality. Given the large amount of information contained in consent forms, it is important to consider whether subjects fully comprehend the material prior to signing their consent. It is clear from the preceding discussion that valid consent cannot be obtained unless subjects understand the consent form (Mann, 1994). There is some concern that longer and more detailed consent forms, although technically correct in covering all of the required consent elements, may not be comprehended by subjects. Instead, longer forms may be employed by investigators to protect themselves against charges of ethical violations and may "mistakenly lead some investigators to shift responsibility for ethically questionable practices from themselves to the subjects" (Adair et al., 1985, p. 61).

Although little research has been done on the ability of subjects to understand consent form information, one study that did examine this issue found that subjects are better able to correctly answer questions regarding research when the consent form is shorter (Mann, 1994). Eighty-three undergraduate students in introductory psychology classes were given one of three forms that required a twelfth-grade reading level: long consent form, short consent form, and information sheet. In the consent form conditions, subjects read standard consent forms and signed their agreement to participate in the study. In the information sheet condition, subjects read standard consent form information but were not asked to sign the form. Each subject then completed a questionnaire designed to test subjects' knowledge of the information on the forms, including information on the particular study as well as information on research in general (e.g., What happens if you change your mind about wanting to be in this study?). Mann found that subjects answered more questions correctly when given the shorter consent form. In any of the three conditions, however, subjects answered only 60% of questions correctly. Mann concluded that subjects comprehend longer consent forms less well than shorter forms and that subjects agree to participate in studies for which they do not understand specific information (Mann, 1994). This act of signing a form for which the conditions are not understood belies the whole idea of informed consent. This study should suggest to investigators that long, complex consent forms must not be used in the mistaken belief that more information absolves the researchers' responsibilities; instead, clearer and more concisely written consent forms are needed to protect subject welfare.

### Children's Participation in Research

Many interesting questions arise when employing children as subjects in a research project (Keith-Spiegel, 1983; Oesterheld, Fogas, & Ruttan, 1998). For example, do children have the legal right to consent to participate in research? Do children really understand what is involved when they agree to participate in research? At what age do children feel they have the right to say no to an adult's request? How do children feel after participating in research? Although not all of these questions have been clearly answered, I attempt to outline the variety of ethical issues that researchers may face when employing child subjects and provide some recommendations.

Today, children are universally seen as an especially vulnerable population, one that must be protected in research settings (Keith-Spiegel, 1983; Oesterheld et al.,1998). However, the concept of children needing protection in research settings is relatively new (Keith-Spiegel, 1983). Children were not specifically mentioned in the Nuremberg code; in fact, the subject was not expressly addressed until 1977, when the National Commission issued recommendations in a report entitled, "Research Involving Children" (as cited in Keith-Spiegel, 1983). Recommendations included having parents sign informed consent forms for children under the age of 21 as well as having children give age-appropriate assent (agreement to be a research subject; Keith-Spiegel, 1983; Oesterheld et al., 1998).

Currently, parents or other legal guardians must provide consent for child participation in research, as children "have not been accorded the legal capacity to enter into such contracts with investigators" (Keith-Spiegel, 1983, p. 185). Although the legal requirement for parental consent is clear, investigators still struggle with the possible implications of this requirement. In any such situation, what a parent desires and what a child needs may be in conflict. Assuming that parents always hold the best interests of their child as their primary concern belies "the fact that statistics on child abuse, neglect and other negative influences perpetrated by parents are appallingly impressive" (Keith-Spiegel, 1983, p. 187).

Regarding the concept of assent, guidelines from DHEW state that children, age 7 or older, should sign a written assent form agreeing to participate in research (as cited in Keith-Spiegel, 1983). Use of the term, *assent*, implies that children may not completely understand the nature and purpose of the particular study or their involvement in it (Keith-Spiegel, 1983). However, researchers are encouraged to provide information to the child about the particular study and ascertain the child's wishes about participating. If a child does not want to participate in a study, despite parental consent, researchers are encouraged to forego employing that child as a research subject (Koocher & Keith Spiegel, 1998).

When employing child subjects, one controversial area involves the distinction between therapeutic and nontherapeutic research (Keith-Spiegel, 1983). *Therapeutic research* has been defined as research that will directly benefit the individual child, whereas *nontherapeutic research* can be considered research that will not gain the child anything (Keith-Spiegel, 1983). Some authors argue that children should participate only in therapeutic research (Oesterheld et al., 1998), whereas others argue that children may participate in nontherapeutic research only if full informed consent from the child is obtained (Keith-Spiegel, 1983). Most authors are in agreement that the "profound dilemmas posed by competency and other consent issues when research participants are minors are far from resolved" (Keith-Spiegel, 1983, p. 206).

From the previous discussion, it is clear that more ethical dilemmas are introduced than are decided by using children as research subjects. However, "to suggest that research utilizing minor participants should be foreclosed until such time as the dilemmas are fully resolved would neither be in the best interests of science nor of minors themselves" (Keith-Spiegel, 1983, p. 206). Clearly, when employing child subjects, researchers must be vigilant as to the inevitable ethical dilemmas and must always strive to protect the welfare of this vulnerable population.

## Confidentiality and Privacy of Research Participants

Typically, the identity of research subjects and the responses generated by subjects are kept confidential (Koocher & Keith-Spiegel, 1998). As previously specified, in order to obtain IRB approval, researchers must delineate the limits of confidentiality to their subjects. In addition, IRB requirements state that investigators must inform subjects of any possibility that data or names of participants could be obtained by others (Koocher & Keith-Spiegel, 1998). In order to satisfy informed consent requirements, it is imperative that "the investigator ... be comprehensive and truthful in providing potential research participants with information about the possible uses of the data that might be material to their decision to participate in the study" (Kelman, 1977, p. 172).

In order to protect confidentiality, researchers are encouraged to identify subjects by numbers or not record identifying information at all (Koocher & Keith-Spiegel, 1998). Remember that if confidentiality has been promised to subjects, "investigators must scrupulously adhere to the guarantees of confidentiality that they have made to research participants" (Kelman, 1977, p. 173).

Although most authors would agree with the importance of keeping data and identifying information as confidential, there is little agreement as to how researchers should handle a disclosure by a research participant about issues such as child abuse or intended harm to self or others. In those instances, "obligations of research investigators are even more ambiguous" (Koocher & Keith-Spiegel, 1998, p. 429) than the obligations of a clinician hearing such reports. It appears that such reports cannot be considered privileged information and must be reported to authorities (PSU, 1999). Most state law requires that psychologists report statements indicating imminent harm to others or child abuse (Koocher & Keith-Spiegel, 1998). It would behoove each researcher to examine the laws in a particular state to assess state legal requirements before beginning any study that might involve such disclosures. If such statements are to be reported, subjects must be informed about the possible reporting requirements in the informed consent form (PSU, 1999).

### Use of Deception in Research

The concept of *informed consent* requires that subjects be given full disclosure of information about the study before deciding whether or not to participate in the study. However, many studies employ deception, which by definition compromises the idea of informed consent (Koocher & Keith-Spiegel, 1998). It is not possible to fulfill the ethical requirement of fully informed consent when deception is utilized, as "deceived subjects [clearly] are not informed" (Adair et al., 1985, p. 70).

Proponents of deceptive research practices argue that deception allows for useful information to be obtained that could not be obtained in any other way (Koocher & Keith-Spiegel, 1998). Critics argue that deception essentially condones lying and increases the likelihood that subjects will become more suspicious and jaded about the candor of researchers (Koocher & Keith-Spiegel, 1998). Critics have also argued that deception violates the individual's right to choose to participate, abuses the basic interpersonal relationship between experimenter and subject, contributes to deception as a societal value and practice, and ultimately leads to loss of trust in the profession and science of psychology (Adair et al., 1985). Finally, authors have criticized deceptive practices as being a questionable base for development of the discipline and as being contrary to our professional roles as teachers or scientists (Adair et al., 1985). One of the reasons that the debate is ongoing regarding the use of deception is that there has been very little research on the effects of deceptive practices on subjects. The research that has been done generally has not supported the idea that deception harms or distresses research participants (see Koocher & Keith-Spiegel, 1998, for examples of research on this issue). Sullivan & Deiker (1973; as cited in Adair et al., 1985) stated that "research has shown . . . that subjects do not evaluate . . . deception nearly as negatively as we might expect" (p. 61).

Deception has been used frequently in research studies (Adair et al., 1985), although its use may be declining in recent years (Koocher & Keith-Spiegel, 1998). Deceptive practices employed by researchers "range markedly from outright lies or concealment of risks to mild or ambiguous misrepresentations or omissions" (Koocher & Keith-Spiegel, 1998, p. 420). Examples of deceptive practices include the following: (a) offering inaccurate information about the nature of the study, (b) concealing information from participants, (c) employing confederates, (d) making false guarantees regarding confidentiality or some other important issue, (e) misrepresenting the identity of the investigator, (f) providing false feedback on subject performance, (g) encouraging subjects to deceive themselves about the study's purpose, (h) using placebos, (i) misrepresenting the scope of the study, (j) employing concealed observations or recordings, and (k) not informing participants that they are in a study (Koocher & Keith-Spiegel, 1998). Such practices are often used in conjunction with each other in one study (Koocher & Keith-Spiegel, 1998).

Although APA ethical codes allow for the use of some deceptive practices, deception of subjects about significant aspects of the projects, such as possible physical risks of participation in the study, is never justified (APA, 1992a). In addition, the guidelines clearly state that the use of deception must be justified by the prospective scientific value of the study (APA, 1992a). Finally, APA guidelines encourage researchers to consider alternatives to deception before employing such practices (APA, 1992a). Alternatives may include the use of role-play or naturalistic observation (Koocher & Keith-Spiegel, 1998). One promising alternative to deception is the use of some form of forewarning in the informed consent form (Koocher & Keith-Spiegel, 1998). In other words, by signing the consent form, the subject has agreed to be deceived within the research project.

If deceptive practices are employed in a study, APA ethical principles state that the researcher must debrief the participants no later than at the end of data collection (APA, 1992a). This "coming clean" procedure is typically called *debriefing* but has also been referred to as *postinvestigation clarification, dehoaxing, desensitization,* or *disabusing* (Koocher & Keith-Spiegel, 1998). The overall goal of debriefing "is to correct any misconceptions or supply any information purposely withheld" (Koocher & Keith-Spiegel, 1998, p. 421). In addition, debriefing may be utilized to "reduce negative aftereffects [and] prevent arousal of negative feelings toward investigators" (Gurman, 1994, p. 139).

There has been very little research conducted on the concept of debriefing. For example, only one study has been conducted that documents the need for some type of debriefing with subjects. Gurman (1994) conducted a survey with undergraduates and found that 10% of the subjects reported feelings of anxiety and resentment after completing only initial screening questionnaires. Based on this study, Gurman (1994) advocated for use of debriefing techniques with all subjects, including those who are screened out by initial questionnaires. No research exists as to the effectiveness of debriefing (Koocher & Keith-Spiegel, 1998), and very little information is available about different methods of debriefing. Although the concept is mentioned in many research projects, only one author has provided detailed instructions on how to debrief a subject (Mills, 1976; as cited in Adair et al., 1985). This author advocated for face-to-face debriefing sessions lasting up to 20 min with each subject. He also advocated for telling each subject why deception was necessary, the purpose of the particular study, and which deceptions were used. Because little research has been done in this area, it is not possible to state that Mills's method is the most effective form of debriefing.

## Use of Animal Subjects

Currently, millions of animals are used in research projects annually (Koocher & Keith-Spiegel, 1998). Consideration for animal welfare in research projects can be traced to the 1960s. At that time, APA published a position paper on the use of animals in research studies (as cited in Koocher & Keith-Spiegel, 1998). In 1981, a revision of the ethical principles of psychologists included a section on animal welfare in research (APA, 1981; as cited in Koocher & Keith-Spiegel, 1998). Recently, APA published a booklet in 1992 entitled "Guidelines for Ethical Conduct in the Care and Use of Animals" (APA, 1992b). These guidelines emphasize that psychologists should ensure that their work with animals is justified on the basis of its prospective scientific, educational, or applied value (APA, 1992b). In addition, the guidelines state that psychologists must ensure the welfare of all animals employed in a research project, must treat animals humanely, and must ensure assistants are well trained in animal care. Finally, the ethical guidelines emphasize that painful or distressing procedures may be employed only after the researcher has considered alternatives to such procedures (APA, 1992b).

Despite the advances in our knowledge of neurological aspects of behavior by using animals in research projects, such work is not without its detractors (Koocher & Keith-Spiegel, 1998). The primary criticism against animal use in research studies is that most such research is "trivial and inhumane" (Koocher & Keith-Spiegel, 1998, p. 430). As a critic of animal research, one author pointed out that "we cannot justify the worthwhileness of the study of animals because of the similarities between them and humans while, at the same time, morally justifying it on the basis of differences" (Ulrich, 1991). Due to at least in part to increasing sensitivity to animal welfare, it appears that use of animal subjects in psychological research has been decreasing recently (Koocher & Keith-Spiegel, 1998).

## Use of the Internet in Conducting Research

The Internet is being increasingly used to collect data on human subjects (PSU, 1999), due to the potential to obtain information from a wide range of subjects with little cost of time or money (Frankel & Siang, 1999). Research conducted online typically falls into one of two categories: (1) studies that investigate usage patterns of the World Wide Web (e.g., by monitoring Web-based inter-actions in chat rooms); and (2) online surveys or experiments (Azar, 2000).

Although this tool may prove to be a boon to researchers, ethical issues involved in using the Internet to conduct studies are just now beginning to be discussed. What is clear is that "the same ethical principles that bind researchers in the real world apply in cyberspace" (Azar, 2000, p. 50). In other words, the principles of informed consent, confidentiality, and debriefing when employing deception must still be considered (Michalak & Szabo, 1998).

Ethical issues are difficult to manage when conducting research on the Internet (Azar, 2000). Although researchers agree that following ethical guidelines is important, at least one researcher has questioned "how readily guidelines developed for traditional research will transfer to that performed in cyberspace" (Jones, 1994; as cited in Michalak & Szabo, 1998, p. 71). For example, how do researchers ensure that a prospective subject has read and understood the informed consent form? With data suggesting that subjects do not understand all of the consent form when presented it in person (Mann, 1994), how can researchers ensure that consent given online is really an informed one? Further, how can researchers determine that the person signing the form is legally capable of providing consent (i.e., not a child)? Currently, "there is no standardized method for collecting and validating informed consent online" (Azar, 2000, p. 51).

Other examples of thorny ethical dilemmas online include how to manage issues of deception and confidentiality. Regarding confidentiality, some level of anonymity is inevitably lost when e-mail is employed to obtain survey data (J. Thomas, personal communication, November 9, 2000). Some authors have argued for allowing subjects to remain *semianonymous*, with identification occurring only in the e-mail address but no names or postal addresses employed (Michalak & Szabo, 1998). When deception is utilized, a researcher has the ethical obligation to debrief subjects by providing them with relevant information concerning the true nature of the study (Koocher & Keith-Spiegel, 1998).

It is difficult if not impossible to ensure that adequate debriefing is done when subjects "can click away from your site and disappear for good in an instant" (Azar, 2000, p. 50).

Although there are no definitive answers to ethical dilemmas posed by online research, preliminary discussions of the issues involved have been started. In November 1999, the American Association for the Advancement of Science (AAAS) issued a report entitled "Ethical and Legal Aspects of Human Subjects Research on the Internet" (Frankel & Siang, 1999). This report was sponsored by the agency that oversees IRBs, OPRR, and was intended to delineate the many ethical issues presented by online research. The report concludes with further research questions that must be answered before these ethical dilemmas may be solved.

In addition to OPRR's report, other authors have attempted to provide suggestions for employing the Internet in research (Childress & Asamen, 1998; Smith & Leigh, 1997). For example, to ensure informed consent, a researcher might advertise his or her study on the Web and ask prospective subjects to send their name and address to researcher over e-mail. Once the e-mail was received, the researcher would then mail two copies of the informed consent form for the subject to sign. The subject would be instructed to sign both forms, to keep one copy for his or her own records, and to return one copy to the investigator's address. Once the researcher receives the signed copy, the subject is sent a password that allows him or her to participate in the study. Another option might be to use a portal, wherein the subject must click on a button saying, "I agree," after reading the informed consent form. Once the button is clicked, the subject could gain access to the research page. However, neither alternative guarantees that the subject you get is the subject you want (i.e., one who fits your study criteria, one who can legally give informed consent; PSU, 1999; Smith & Leigh, 1997).

Overall, despite the current excitement and the promise of quick responding, researchers must keep in mind that some studies are just not appropriate for the Internet (PSU, 1999). Much more discussion and resolution of the unique ethical challenges facing researchers who conduct online studies is needed before widespread use of this technology can be categorically encouraged.

## SUMMARY

In this chapter, I reviewed basic research ethics and considered some evolving issues, such as the employment of children as research participants and the increasing use of the Internet to conduct research studies. Although not all of the issues discussed have clearly defined answers, I hope that a review of potential ethical dilemmas will prompt researchers to consider ethical issues early in research design.

The bottom line is that sound research methodology cannot exist without following ethical principles of research (Sieber, 1992). Ethical issues should be considered when first discussing study ideas and should be repeatedly attended to throughout design planning. It is likely in our litigious society that more researchers will be held accountable for their ethically questionable actions with research subjects. At least one author has introduced the term, *malresearch*, that is consistent with the idea of malpractice in the clinical realm (Keith-Spiegel, 1983). Use of this legalistic term is an attempt to emphasize to investigators the importance of considering ethical issues in research, as they may be found negligent when engaging in unethical research practices (Keith-Spiegel, 1983).

As a researcher, it is imperative that you are conversant with ethical regulations regarding research, with your institution's IRB requirements, and with federal law governing research with both human and animal subjects. In your research lab, it is highly recommended that the following documents be clearly visible and read by all research assistants: "Ethical Principles of Psychologists" (APA, 1992a); "Ethical Principles in the Conduct of Research With Human Participants" (APA, 1982); "Guidelines for Ethical Conduct in the Care and Use of Animals" (APA, 1992b); and the "Publication Manual of the American Psychological Association" (APA, 1994).

Researchers should not consider ethical considerations to be the enemy. Investigators should recognize that "ethical and research procedures are not on an inevitable collision course [but] the conflict between them will not disappear with inattention" (Adair et al., 1985, p. 70). In other words, investigators should turn their focus on studying the effects of ethical guidelines on research. Further research is needed in many areas, including the limits of children's competency to assent to research, the effect of deception on subjects, and the comprehension level of informed consent forms. In order to facilitate research into these areas, Adair and colleagues (1985) suggested that authors should include information on ethical issues in journal articles. For example, including information on informed consent forms, debriefing procedures, and specific deception techniques in any journal article written on a study might provide other researchers with needed data on the effects of ethical guidelines on research. Until the aforementioned are studied empirically, researchers are advised to contemplate ethical issues concurrently with methodology issues. The best researchers should recognize that "sound ethics and sound methodology go hand in hand" (Sieber, 1992, p. 4).

## REFERENCES

Adair, J. G., Dushenko, T. W., & Lindsey, R. C. L. (1985). Ethical regulations and their impact on research practice. *American Psychologist, 40*, 59–72.

American Counseling Association. (1995). *Code of ethics and standards of practice.* www.counseling .org/resources/codeofethics.htm

American Psychological Association. (1982). *Ethical principles in the conduct of research with human participants.* Washington, DC: Author.

American Psychological Association. (1992a). Ethical principles of psychologists and code of conduct. *American Psychologist, 47,* 1597–1611.

American Psychological Association. (1992b). *Guidelines for ethical conduct in the care and use of animals.* Washington, DC: Author.

American Psychological Association. (1994). *Publication manual of the American Psychological Association* (4th ed.). Washington, DC: Author.

Azar, B. (2000). Online experiments: Ethically fair or foul? *Monitor on Psychology, 31*(4), 50–52.

Blanck, P. D., Bellack, A. S., Rosnow, R. L., Rotheram-Borus, M. J., & Schooler, N. R. (1998). Scientific rewards and conflicts of ethical choices in human subjects research. In A. E. Kazdin (Ed.), *Methodological issues and strategies in clinical research* (2nd ed., pp. 655–669). Washington, DC: American Psychological Association.

Childress, C. A., & Asamen, J. K. (1998). The emerging relationship of psychology and the Internet: Proposed guidelines for conducting research. *Ethics and Behavior, 8*(1), 19–35.

Frankel, M. S., & Siang, S. (1999, November). *Ethical and legal aspects of human subjects research on the Internet.* www.aaas.org/spp/dspp/sfrl/projects/intres/main.htm.

Gurman, E. B. (1994). Debriefing for all concerned: Ethical treatment of human subjects. *Psychological Science, 5,* 139.

Keith-Spiegel, P. (1983). Children and consent to participate in research. In G. B. Melton, G. P. Koocher, & M. J. Saks (Eds.), *Children's competence to consent* (pp. 179–211). New York: Plenum Press.

Kelman, H. C. (1977). Privacy and research with human beings. *Journal of Social Issues, 33*(3), 169.

Koocher, G. P., & Keith-Spiegel, P. (1998). *Ethics in psychology: Professional standards and cases* (2nd ed.). New York: Oxford University Press.

Mann, T. (1994). Informed consent for psychological research: Do subjects comprehend consent forms and understand their legal rights? *Psychological Science, 5,* 140–143.

Michalak, E. E., & Szabo, A. (1998). Guidelines for Internet research: An update. *European Psychologist, 3*(1), 70–75.

Myers, D. G. (1992). *Psychology.* New York: Worth Publishers.

Oesterheld, J. R., Fogas, B., Ruttan, S. (1998). Ethical standards for research on children. *Journal of the American Academy of Child and Adolescent Psychiatry, 37*(7), 684–685.

Office for Protection From Research Risks, United States Department of Health and Human Services. (1993). *Protecting human research subjects: Institutional review board guidebook* (2nd ed.). Washington, DC: Author.

Pomerantz, J. R. (1994). On criteria for ethics in science. *Psychological Science, 5,* 135–136.

Portland State University. (1999, September). *Application guidelines for research involving human subjects.* Portland, OR: Author.

Rosenthal, R. (1994). Science and ethics in conducting, analyzing, and reporting psychological research. *Psychological Science, 5,* 127–134.

Rosnow, R. L. (1990). Teaching research ethics through role-play and discussion. *Teaching of Psychology, 17,* 179–181.

Schmidt, L. D., & Meara, N. M. (1996). Applying for approval to conduct research with human participants. In F. T. L. Leong & J. T. Austin (Eds.), *The psychology research handbook: A guide for graduate students and research assistants* (pp. 113–126). Thousand Oaks, CA: Sage Publications.

Sieber, J. E. (1992). *Planning ethically responsible research: A guide for students and internal review boards.* Newbury Park, CA: Sage Publications.

Sieber, J. E. (1998). Will the new code help researchers to be more ethical? In A. E. Kazdin (Ed.), *Methodological issues and strategies in clinical research* (2nd ed., pp. 639–654). Washington, DC: American Psychological Association.

Smith, M. A., & Leigh, B. (1997). Virtual subjects: Using the Internet as an alternative source of subjects and research. *Behavior Research Methods, Instruments, and Computers, 29*(4), 496–505.

Tuthill, K. A. (1997). Human experimentation: Protecting patient autonomy through informed consent. *The Journal of Legal Medicine, 18,* 221–250.

Ulrich, R. E. (1991). Animal rights, animal wrongs, and the question of balance. *Psychological Science, 2,* 197–201.

# Reviewing the Literature and Evaluating Existing Data

Matt J. Gray
*National Center for PTSD*
*Boston Veterans Affairs Medical Center, Boston, Massachusettes*

Ron Acierno
*National Crime Victims Center*
*Medical University of South Carolina, Charleston, South Carolina*

Never before has so much information been so easily available to so many people. Such a wealth of data brings with it new requirements of those who endeavor to be scholars, specifically, the ability to sift through studies of varying quality and extract the most pertinent information. In the absence of a systematic approach to searching the literature, this task can be difficult at best. The aim of this chapter is to help readers systematize an approach to reviewing the literature. To this end, we enumerate important factors in deciding what to review. We briefly describe traditional research databases and their usage, as well as nontraditional options for obtaining information. Of course, not all information is good information. As such, critical evaluation is an essential part of the literature review process. Accordingly, guidelines for evaluating published work are described. Finally, when an investigator has critically reviewed the literature and has selected that subset of information most central to his or her research purposes, the essence of this body of work must be efficiently and parsimoniously conveyed to others. Consequently, this chapter concludes with suggestions for expressing the results of a critical literature review.

## DECIDING WHAT TO REVIEW

Like most skills, conducting successful literature searches becomes easier with practice. Neophyte researchers experience frustration resulting from the double task of having to familiarize themselves with the key elements of a new topic, as well as having to learn methods required to learn about that area. Students attempting to gain mastery of a particular topic or domain are often faced with the difficulty of not knowing enough about that topic to conduct a focused, manageable search. Because they are unfamiliar with nomenclature in a field, novice researchers often have difficulty narrowing their search and zeroing in on essential information, not to mention information of high quality. Although there is no substitute for expertise and familiarity with one's area, accessing the appropriate information does not need to be a hopelessly complex endeavor. Moreover, it is not necessary to master this skill through trial and error. Judicious planning and a systematic approach can benefit all researchers, regardless of their experience, in conducting thorough but efficient literature reviews.

Familiarity with a topic or domain will, in no small measure, affect the focus of a reviewer's search. Student researchers who are just beginning to study some particular phenomenon (e.g., PTSD) will necessarily need to take a more "macro" or wide focus approach to searching the literature. Reading sources such as texts and book chapters that provide broad, global summaries of the phenomenon will be a necessary precondition to the formulation of sufficiently specific research questions and hypotheses. Attempting to circumvent this groundwork will yield untenable hypotheses and ill-formulated research questions. Although broad reviews are typically not detailed enough to permit development of specific research questions, they usually inform the reader of areas in need of further resolution. This can be a jumping-off point for new researchers. More specifically, reference sections of these chapters and overviews are excellent places to start looking for actual empirical articles.

Familiarity with a topic or domain will, in no small measure, drive a reviewer's search. Investigators such as student researchers who are just beginning to study some particular phenomenon (e.g., PTSD) will necessarily need to take a more macro approach to reviewing the literature. Reading sources such as texts and book chapters that provide broad, global summaries of the phenomenon will be a necessary precondition to the formulation of sufficiently specific research questions. Once an individual has a working knowledge of the domain he or she wishes to study, and at least a rudimentary idea of variables that may be important in elucidating or expanding previous efforts in that domain, the next step is to turn attention to the literature in order to determine what work in that area has already been done. The breadth of one's review will depend on the author's purposes. If the writer is attempting to provide a relatively comprehensive review of an area for the purposes of a thesis, dissertation, or review article, the search will invariably be broad. By contrast, focused research articles do not require exhaustive literature reviews, provided that key constructs are presented and that no core concepts or contradictory findings are omitted. Indeed, it is not necessary for a researcher to summarize all prior studies bearing on the present investigation, provided that central arguments and considerations have been adequately addressed.

Similarly, the intended audience is an important consideration when deciding what to review and discuss. Although this is seldom a consideration when initially designing a study, it is often relevant when deciding on a journal to which one's work will be submitted. Typically, there are many different journals or outlets that may be appropriate for communicating results of a particular study. However, each outlet will have a different focus and will therefore require a literature review that is specific to that particular journal. (These foci are typically outlined in the "instructions to contributors" page, which is usually found at the very beginning or very end of each issue of the journal.) For instance, consider an investigator who has recently found that the types of attributions (i.e., causal explanations) that people offer for traumatic events influence the likelihood that they will develop PTSD. Traditionally, attributions have been studied predominantly by social psychologists. The researcher may opt to submit his or her findings to a journal such as the *Journal of Applied Social Psychology*. Alternatively, he or she may decide to submit the findings to a more clinically oriented journal, such as the *Journal of Traumatic Stress*. This decision will have important implications for informing one's literature search and review. Quite obviously, if the investigator submits to the *Journal of Traumatic Stress*, the basic features of PTSD need not be discussed in any great detail. Reviewers and subscribers of this publication are well-versed in this area. The author would do well instead to focus the review on attributional theory and its potential applicability to PTSD. Similarly, if the individual submitted findings to the *Journal of Applied Social Psychology*, more space would be devoted to describing PTSD at the expense of attributional theory, as the readership would be sufficiently familiar with the latter but not the former.

Finally, the breadth of one's literature search also depends on the topic of interest. Although a review on virtually any topic could benefit from searching all relevant databases, some areas, by their very nature, demand such a thorough approach to ensure adequate coverage. Most notably, topics that span multiple disciplines such as psychology, psychiatry, and pharmacology would require the researcher to review multiple databases. By way of example, we did a very brief search of two popular databases (PsychINFO and Medline) that can be accessed through most university libraries. We were interested in finding studies that discussed usage of the drug, sertraline, in treating PTSD. By entering the search terms, *sertraline* and *PTSD*, PsychINFO produced 15 articles and Medline produced 13 articles. Although it might be tempting to conclude that PsychINFO produced all of the articles that Medline did as well as two others that Medline did not produce, this is not the case. Only five articles overlapped in both databases. Thus, 10 of the articles found by searching PsychINFO would have been neglected if we only relied on Medline. Similarly, eight of the articles on Medline would have been ignored had we only used PsychINFO.

When one considers the fact that there are numerous other databases (e.g., Grateful Med) that might address topics such as PTSD and sertraline, it is readily apparent that relying exclusively on a single database may result in a very spotty review of the literature. This potential problem becomes even more pronounced when one considers that this was a very specific, narrow search. Most literature reviews necessarily need to be broader. For instance, had we conducted a specific investigation evaluating the efficacy of sertraline in treating PTSD, we certainly would not review only those articles focusing on sertraline as a treatment of PTSD. To orient the reader, it would be necessary to briefly touch on other pharmacological interventions that have been used to treat PTSD, as well as a discussion of why sertraline might prove to be a better choice than other antidepressants. It may even be necessary to discuss the efficacy of pharmacological interventions relative to other forms of treatment, such as psychotherapy. It is easy to see how the just mentioned "spottiness" that results from exclusive reliance on a single database can quickly become compounded when one conducts anything but the narrowest of searches.

To summarize, the breadth and depth of a review are typically dictated by considerations such as the intended audience, focus of the journal, the author's familiarity with the domain, and the extent to which the topic is addressed by multiple disciplines. As a general rule of thumb, a broader search will be required when the author is not (a) intimately familiar with the domain; (b) when the journal to which the manuscript is being submitted does not focus exclusively on that topic; (c) when the review is for the purposes of a review article, thesis, or dissertation; and/or (d) when the topic is addressed by multiple disciplines.

## FINDING INFORMATION: SEARCHING DATABASES, THE INTERNET, AND OLD-FASHIONED DETECTIVE WORK

Libraries will differ with respect to accessible databases, but most will include Medline (clinical medicine abstracts), PsycINFO or PsycLIT (psychology and psychiatry abstracts), and ERIC (education abstracts) among other disciplines. A greater variety of health-related databases is generally available through medical university libraries. These may include Grateful Med, CINAHL (nursing and allied health abstracts), CANCERLIT, Current Contents (basic sciences, clinical medicine, behavioral sciences, agriculture, and environmental sciences), and HEALTHSTAR (health planning and administration abstracts), among others. It may be necessary to visit a medical school library (in person or online), if your college library's offerings are limited.

Although different databases have varied search rules and procedures, they tend to operate along similar lines. Once you are fluent with one, it is generally an easy transition to perform related searches on other databases. For purposes of this chapter, we describe strategies and procedures for conducting literature searches with PsycINFO, including techniques to broaden and narrow searches. Although the techniques are specific to that database, you will likely find the procedures identical or highly similar when using other electronic databases.

PsycINFO is produced by the American Psychological Association. It includes abstracts and citations for journal articles pertaining to psychology, psychiatry, and behavioral science from over 1,300 journals in 29 different languages. It also provides citations and abstracts for books and edited book chapters. This database is updated monthly. Databases like PsycINFO allow users to search for abstracts by keyword, topic, author, journal, date, and title. The default search is by keyword. At the "search" prompt, the user enters a word or phrase most descriptive of the type of information he or she wishes to access. As a general rule of thumb, it is best to start with very broad and general descriptors to increase the likelihood of capturing articles of interest. The user can then narrow the focus by combining descriptors or specifying subsets of articles within the broader domain that are of particular interest. Starting with a very focused, narrow search will likely produce many good references, but it will also prematurely exclude important references. Remember, prior to "hitting the computer databases," a review article or chapter should be consulted to (a) familiarize the novice researcher about the topic of interest; (b) provide direction about what is relevant and what has already been done; and (c) provide keywords that may be helpful when subsequently searching the databases.

How does one go about narrowing or broadening a search? When multiple searches have been conducted using singular keywords or phrases, the intersection of these searches (i.e., using the word, "and," between keywords) can narrow a search and the combination (i.e., using the word, "or," between keywords) can broaden a search. Each database will have a set of reserved words (known as *Boolean operators*), such as "and," "or," and "near" which, when used in conjunction with keywords at the search prompt, are interpreted to be search commands rather than keywords. This point is best illustrated by way of example. Returning to our example of searching for previous work examining the relationship between attributions and PTSD, we might begin by entering the search term, *PTSD*. This produces 5,168 citations that include the term, PTSD, somewhere in the abstract, title, or keyword list. Realizing that some abstracts may not contain the acronym, PTSD, but may instead contain the full disorder name, we conduct another search using the phrase, "posttraumatic stress disorder." The database displays the number of articles containing the word, "posttraumatic," as the second search, the number of articles containing, "stress," as the third search, and the number of articles containing the word, "disorder," as the fourth search. It then displays the number of abstracts or citations that include all three words as search #5, as this set of words is what we actually requested (i.e., not the separate words in isolation).

Clearly there is likely to be extensive overlap between these searches. By combining the first search and the second by entering #1 or #5 (or retyping the search terms separated by the word "or"), our search is broadened and 6,290 records are produced. The net result is that all articles containing "PTSD" or "posttraumatic stress disorder" are captured, but redundancies in the initial searches are eliminated. This is clearly an unwieldy number of abstracts to peruse, but we must reemphasize the importance of starting with very broad categories and then narrowing the searches as necessary.

This is accomplished when we begin to specify the subset of the PTSD literature in which we are most interested. Once again, however, it is best to maximize the likelihood of accessing relevant articles by maintaining a broad focus before focusing the search by combining topics. Specifically, we want to first capture, as efficiently as possible, the entire domain of articles relevant to attributions. As such, we repeat the aforementioned steps by conducting separate searches for "causes," "attributions," "explanations," and so forth. Then we combine each of these searches (simultaneously eliminating redundancies) by employing the combination word, "or" (e.g., #6 or #7 or #8). This produces 28,361 articles. Now we have 6,290 PTSD articles and 28,361 attribution articles. Although these numbers are a bit staggering, bear in mind that the intersection of these domains (i.e., the subset of PTSD articles we are interested in) is likely to be quite small. By using the search combination word, "and," we only capture those articles that pertain to PTSD and attributions. When we actually performed this combination, the net result was a much more manageable 127 citations. Had we used the "or" combination term, we would have captured all articles that included either PTSD or attributions (and related terms). This would have combined the totals of the two searches. It should be obvious by now that the combination word, "and" results in smaller numbers of references. By contrast, the combination word, "or," aggregates searches and serves to broaden the focus. The word, "or," is useful when the topic for which you search has multiple names (e.g., treatment, or intervention, or therapy). Once you have accessed a manageable number of references, you can review them and mark those of particular interest (i.e., references for articles that you will ultimately want to obtain) either by pressing the enter key, or using the "mark record" option. The marked records can then be printed, saved to a floppy disk, or emailed to your account.

If the researcher is not sure what other descriptors might be relevant, databases such as PsycINFO typically include electronic thesauruses of related search terms. If there is a particular subset of articles that the investigator is decidedly uninterested in, he or she can use the word, "not," to exclude certain topics. For instance, if we were interested in accessing the intersection of PTSD and attributions in the literature, but did not want to wade through numerous unpublished dissertations, we could take the final search term just mentioned and add, "not dissertation," to the search. Because PsycINFO includes abstracts of unpublished dissertations, this search would further narrow the final search by excluding any reference that included the word dissertation in the citation (i.e., all citations denoted as dissertations). One can also specify the language (e.g., "PTSD and English in la"), if foreign language journals are not desired. (La is the search term that specifies the language of the publication.) Depending on the default settings, the searches you conduct may only produce citations and not abstracts of the articles. Quite obviously, there is usually not enough information in the title to determine whether obtaining the full article would be worthwhile. This is easily remedied by selecting "abstracts" under "retrieved record options."

Finally, it can be cumbersome to conduct separate searches for all variations of a word. For example, a researcher interested in attributions may inadvertently overlook important articles if he or she only enters the word, "attributions," at the search prompt. This is because the abstract may not contain that specific variation or the word. Some authors may discuss "attributional style," some may note, for instance, that trauma victims often "attribute" the traumatic event to supernatural factors, and so forth. Fortunately, it is not necessary to perform numerous iterations of a search for each possible variation of the search term. PsycINFO and similar databases allow the researcher to find all words that begin with the same root word, by truncating the search term. In this specific example, the researcher can simply enter "attrib*" or "attribut*," and the database will be searched for all citations containing any word beginning with these initial letters—including attribute, attribution, attributional, etcetera. (The specific symbol used for truncation will differ among databases.) This feature can save the investigator considerable time when conducting extensive literature searches involving numerous possible descriptors. Although this overview of strategies for searching electronic databases is by no means comprehensive, it should allow the novice literature reviewer to conduct relatively efficient searches. With practice, large databases can be searched quickly but comprehensively.

## Internet Searches

Confining literature searches to traditional databases accessible through one's local library may be too limiting, as many databases are only available via the Internet. In the area of PTSD, an invaluable database of trauma-relevant research articles and theoretical reviews is only available online. Specifically, the Published International Literature on Traumatic Stress (PILOTS) is a freely accessible database maintained by the National Center for Posttraumatic Stress Disorder. It includes over 18,000 articles available via the Internet from the Dartmouth library. It does not simply contain the subset of PTSD articles that would be accessible on PsycINFO or PsycLIT. Although there is a fair amount of overlap, there are articles typically unique to each database. In a brief comparison of PILOTS and PsycLIT, several identical trauma-relevant searches were conducted with each database (Kubany, 1995). Neither database was consistently superior with respect to the number of articles yielded. On some topics, PILOTS yielded more citations and on other topics, PsycLIT yielded a greater number of citations. Exclusive reliance on a single database may unnecessarily confine one's search. Those seeking comprehensive information are advised to search the Internet for nontraditional sources of information such as online databases.

As readers are no doubt well aware, the Internet is the gateway to a wealth of information (varying widely in quality, of course). Although there may not be the same assurances of quality that are typically afforded by traditional peer-reviewed journals, it would be a mistake to conclude that quality information is unattainable via the Internet. In fact, a compelling case could be made for the notion that exclusive reliance on traditional print journals may exclude, or at the very least delay, important information and data bearing on a particular research area. Increasingly, investigators are utilizing electronic media to disseminate research findings. The considerable delays from submission to publication in traditional scientific journals have led to the advent of electronic, peer-reviewed journals. This medium allows manuscripts to be submitted electronically, disseminated to reviewers electronically, and "published" electronically. The elimination of mailing delays and the time that it takes a journal to go to press substantially accelerates the research dissemination process.

The American Psychological Association established its first solely electronic journal, *Prevention and Treatment*, in 1998. Submissions to the journal as well as readership have increased exponentially since that time. It has recently been asserted that it is now the most widely accessed APA journal, as articles "get anywhere from 10,000 to 50,000 hits each" (Carpenter, 2000, p. 72). Because electronic journals are accessed via the Internet, it is possible to determine how many times a given article has been accessed, which arguably provides direct information about the impact of a given investigation. This feature is unique to electronic journals.

Within the field of PTSD, the electronic journal, *Traumatology*, is exemplary of this novel approach to research dissemination. Established in 1995, it was developed for the more expedient communication of findings from the scientific study of trauma, posttraumatic sequelae, and methods for the alleviation of trauma-related suffering. It augments information available from traditional outlets by focusing more on research and treatment approaches that are in progress or under development. Perhaps the most appealing feature of this electronic journal is its remarkably rapid "turnaround time." Specifically, from submission of a manuscript to publication, the "entire process should not take more than 30 days" according to information provided on the website through which the journal is accessed, www.fsu.edu/~trauma.

While e-journals are in their infancy, the concept is certainly promising. There is no reason to suspect that such nontraditional outlets will necessarily be lacking in quality or rigor. Of course, it is still incumbent on researchers to scrutinize methods and results to determine whether the authors' conclusions are warranted. The mere appearance of an article in a peer-reviewed journal (traditional or electronic) is not an absolute guarantee of quality. Regardless of the medium, the individual reviewing the literature must rely on his or her own research and critical thinking skills when evaluating published research.

The Internet also provides access to invaluable information that may not be represented in peer-reviewed journals or texts. Although great caution should be exercised when reviewing this information, it would be imprudent to dismiss this source of potentially very useful information. It is becoming increasingly common for experts in the field to develop Websites devoted to the scholarly treatment of their area of expertise. University of Oregon professor, David Baldwin, for instance, has produced Trauma Information Pages, which provide an abundance of information for researchers and laypersons alike. In addition to very broad overviews of trauma and its consequences, the Trauma Information Pages, www.trauma-pages.com, provide numerous links to electronic mailing lists that allow professionals to discuss issues pertinent to trauma, trauma-focused databases (including PILOTS), trauma organizations, treatment manuals, full-text research articles, and trauma readings. This Website also includes an online bookstore, which enables the researcher to purchase books and other resources. The National Center for PTSD also has a very comprehensive, user-friendly Website, www.ncptsd.org, that, like the Trauma Information Pages, provides an impressive array of resources for trauma professionals and laypersons alike. Both sites come close to offering "one-stop shopping" for those seeking trauma information. Most subfields of psychology will no doubt be similarly represented on the Internet. To overlook such comprehensive compendiums of information is to unnecessarily encumber one's quest for pertinent information. Although it would be unwise to rely on such resources exclusively, they can be invaluable in directing researchers toward resources that would be neglected using more traditional search strategies.

## Evaluating Published Work

As mentioned previously, the greatest challenge in reviewing literature is not finding information about a given topic. The greatest challenge is to focus the search and narrow the enormous body of related sources to only those that are of high quality and central to your purposes. The strategies just outlined should facilitate this process. Even when you have this subset of most pertinent information, your work as a reviewer is only partially complete. Keeping in mind that not all information is good information, your next task is to critically evaluate the information gleaned from your literature search. You must decide whether conclusions reached by authors are warranted, based on the quality of the studies represented. Are there alternative explanations? Do the research methods used allow for such conclusions? What information is lacking? We now focus on guidelines to use when evaluating published work. As a literature reviewer, you are in a position to scrutinize the area as a whole—methods, findings, strengths, shortcomings, and necessary directions for future research. Every investigation has limitations and shortcomings. Although there is no perfect study, there are basic characteristics that must be present in order for a study to be maximally informative. These necessary features are now discussed.

### Sample Characteristics

The composition of the study sample has important implications for conclusions that may be drawn. First and foremost, it is important to ascertain how the participants for a given study were selected. Were they randomly selected from the population at large? Were they recruited on the basis of convenience (e.g., undergraduate students at the investigator's university)? Did the participants respond to advertisements? If so, did the advertisements appear in widespread publications, or only publications likely to be encountered by a small subset of the population of interest? The method of sample selection that allows the greatest degree of generalizability while simultaneously minimizing the likelihood of bias is random selection. Because this is often a cumbersome and expensive approach to sample selection, it tends to be the exception rather than the rule. It is important to note that although the likelihood of bias is minimized with this method, it is not entirely eliminated. This is especially true to the extent that the sample is small. If the United States population is characterized by an even gender split and I randomly sampled 100 of them, I would likely get approximately 50 males and 50 females (or very close to that ratio). Occasionally, a strictly random sample of 100 Americans may result in a sample of say, 35 males and 65 females. This sample is biased in that it is not representative of the population at large. Such an outcome is not very likely, but it is possible. Thus, random selection minimizes but does not fully eliminate the possibility of obtaining an unrepresentative (i.e., biased) sample of the population of interest. However, the greater the sample size, the more likely a random sample will be representative.

It is important to point out that, despite advantages afforded by random selection, volunteer samples can be equally informative. If an experimenter is investigating the effectiveness of a novel smoking cessation program, he or she may elect to solicit volunteers via an advertising campaign. If the program proves to be effective, the experimenter can justifiably contend that individuals who volunteer for this treatment are precisely those that would seek treatment for this type of problem. Many other populations may not benefit from this intervention. For instance, cardiac patients who go through this program at their physicians' insistence may prove to have little success. It would be necessary to replicate this hypothetical investigation with a sample of (perhaps reluctant) cardiac patients, in order to assert that the program is effective for this population. The investigator may only be interested in designing a treatment program for those motivated enough to volunteer for treatment. If he or she utilizes this method of participant selection and confines his or her conclusions to this population, volunteerism is not a confound or problematic method of sample selection. The method of sample selection that is appropriate depends fully on the investigator's purposes. Results of the investigation may generalize to other populations, but this cannot be asserted with any degree of certainty without replication.

Obviously, the makeup of a sample has important implications for the conclusions that can be drawn from an investigation. It is not essential that the sample mirrors the population at large. What is essential is the explicit recognition that the results of an investigation may not generalize to samples or populations that are dissimilar to the one actually studied. Thus, the process of sample selection must be outlined by the investigator. If a researcher finds that social support following a motor vehicle accident reduces the likelihood that an individual will develop PTSD, it is important to recognize that this relationship may not hold true for survivors of natural disasters. In conducting a critical review of the literature, one should always attend to whether the author is appropriately confining his or her conclusions to the population actually studied (e.g., motor vehicle accident victims), or whether the author is inappropriately generalizing his or her findings to broader or dissimilar populations. Although the findings may, in fact, be applicable to populations other than the one studied, this is an empirical question that requires explicit investigation. One should not simply assume that findings will generalize to similar populations. Conflicting results in the literature may be owing to differences in sample composition.

## Control Conditions and Assignment of Participants to Conditions

Control conditions need not be present for a study to have value, depending on the purpose of the investigation. If the researcher is merely attempting to describe a phenomenon or is simply attempting to show an association between or among variables (correlational research), control conditions may not be necessary. If however, the investigator is attempting to evaluate causality between or among variables, control conditions are necessary but not sufficient for doing so.

When reviewing published work, pay special attention to the language used by the author. Implicit in the discussion section is the interpretation of the findings that the author believes to be most justifiable. It is not uncommon to review articles in which the author makes stronger conclusions than are warranted by the methods. In particular, pay attention to words such as "caused," "resulted in," "led to," "produced," and so forth. Such phrases typically impart the notion that the manipulated variable influenced participant scores on dependent measures. The extent to which extraneous factors are accounted for via control groups will determine whether such statements are justifiable.

Certainly, it is impossible to control for all possible extraneous factors or rival explanations for a finding within the context of a single experiment. This is precisely the reason that a single experiment cannot establish causality, no matter how well controlled it may be. It is essential, however, that especially strong rival hypotheses be addressed in the experimental design. Appropriate control conditions are necessary to rule out competing explanations for a phenomenon.

Most importantly, participants in the experiment should be randomly assigned to experimental conditions to minimize the potential for systematic bias, unless there is a compelling practical or ethical constraint that prohibits random assignment. When random assignment is not possible, the investigator should make an effort to demonstrate that the treatment and control conditions were similar on important variables prior to the experimental manipulation. Otherwise, differences following the experimental manipulation are arguably uninterpretable. That is, they may be due to experimental manipulation (i.e., the treatment) or to differences in those variables employed to assign subjects to conditions. Even if hypothesized differences between experimental and control conditions are found following experimental manipulation, without random assignment of participants or demonstration of premanipulation similarity, the resulting differences could well have been preexisting. That is, the manipulation may have been wholly ineffective—the groups may have differed systematically on the dependent variables prior to the experiment.

The importance of adequate control groups is perhaps best demonstrated by turning to examples from the literature. Although badly confounded experiments rarely get published, it is not uncommon for important confounds to be overlooked by authors and journal reviewers alike. Within the area of PTSD for instance, there is a burgeoning literature on hypothesized memory deficits for traumatic events in those with PTSD. In a critical commentary on this literature, Shobe and Kilhstrom (1997) noted that much of this work is badly confounded and that such conclusions are often premature at best and quite possibly untenable. In order to claim that individuals with PTSD have significant memory deficits for experienced traumatic events, it is not sufficient to document that individuals with PTSD have difficulty recalling details of the traumatic event. It must be shown that individuals without PTSD that have experienced similar events do not have similar difficulties. Accordingly, a trauma-exposed group of individuals without PTSD would be a necessary control group, but this control is often lacking in studies of this type.

Suppose that an investigation compared individuals with PTSD to trauma-exposed individuals without PTSD and found that the former had more difficulties producing detailed accounts of their traumatic events. Would it then be appropriate to conclude that individuals with PTSD have greater memory deficits for traumatic events? Technically, yes—but this conclusion may be misleading. Implicit in this assertion is that this deficit is specific to traumatic events (i.e., that painful trauma memories are repressed by those with PTSD). Although this implicit notion may be true, there are other equally viable possibilities. This deficit may not be trauma specific. Given that a number of cognitive deficits—including more generalized, non-trauma-specific memory deficits—have been documented in PTSD populations (e.g., Yehuda et al., 1995), it may be that the experiment is simply highlighting a more global cognitive skill deficit among PTSD participants. In order to contend that traumatic memories are "repressed," it would be advisable to not only include a no-PTSD group as a control, but also to compare both groups' memories for other types of events, such as pleasant events. In this manner, it would be possible to ascertain whether differences between the groups are trauma specific, or whether they are more global in nature. Of course, it would be important to ensure that the traumatic and nontraumatic events occurred at approximately the same point in time. It does little good to document greater memory deficits for traumatic events that occurred years ago relative to nontraumatic events that occurred relatively recently. Clearly, this would not allow determination of whether differences between groups were owing to the type of event (traumatic versus nontraumatic) or whether they were owing to the passage of time (recent events vs. events from long ago). Although this may seem to be a rather obvious confound, Shobe and Kihlstrom (1997) documented widely cited, influential investigations that possess this very same error. A thoughtful, critical review of the literature was responsible for illuminating common methodological flaws in this area of the literature.

Continuing with the aforementioned example, even if a study found that a PTSD group exhibited significant memory deficits relative to a trauma-exposed group without PTSD, and even if this difference were only found for traumatic memories but not other types of memories studied, it would still be premature to conclude that repression of traumatic memories is a problem associated with PTSD. Although such a finding has never been published, a problem with this hypothetical scenario is that such a finding might not be specific to PTSD. This phenomenon could be true of other psychopathologies as well. PTSD is not the only disorder that can ensue following trauma. Major Depressive Disorder, for instance, is also a common consequence of trauma. Accordingly, it may be necessary to include a trauma-exposed Depression group (without PTSD), in order to determine whether this (hypothetical) phenomenon is unique to PTSD, or whether it is true of psychopathology in general.

Certainly, there are many potential explanations for even seemingly straight-forward associations. Only those that are especially likely confounds need be explicitly addressed via the experimental design. Because of practical consid-erations and other constraints, it is typically not feasible for any single study to control for more than a couple of likely confounds—even if there are many that ultimately should be controlled. However, as a critical reviewer, you are in a position to determine whether some obvious confound is consistently ne-glected across studies. You will only be able to do so, however, if you attend closely to experimental design and use of appropriate controls when digesting the results and conclusions of a line of inquiry. That is, the experiment should "control" for all possible sources of variance except those under study. This is best accomplished by randomly assigning patients to groups. If this is not possible, this can be accomplished by assessing whether subjects differ in each group in the study. Finally, even if all of these factors exist, conclusions should be limited to those allowed by the experimental design and manipulation, and not unjustifiably extrapolated.

## Power, Effect Size, and Nonsignificant Findings

When reviewing the results of an empirical investigation, do not be convinced that a result is large or meaningful just because the author deems it to be "highly statistically significant." It is entirely possible for a relationship between or among variables to be highly significant in the statistical sense, but to have little or no practical meaning whatsoever. The level of statistical significance arguably tells one as much about the sample size as it does about the magnitude of the effect.

By way of a very simple example, let us assume that we conducted a corre-lational investigation in which we were interested in the relationship between symptoms of PTSD and symptoms of depression. If we administer an inven-tory of PTSD symptoms and an inventory of depressive symptoms to a group of participants, our results and conclusions certainly depend on the magnitude of the association between these variables, but they also depend greatly on the size of our sample. Assume that the true magnitude of this association is a correlation of .30. Had we administered these questionnaires to a sam-ple of 30 individuals, a .30 Pearson's $r$ correlation would not be significant by conventional standards. The $p$-value associated with this effect using only 30 individuals is .10. Because the conventional standard for statistical signifi-cance is an alpha level of .05 or less, we would conclude that the association between these two variables is not statistically significant. Had we conducted the exact same study and found the exact same magnitude of association be-tween PTSD and depression (i.e., $r = .30$), but studied a sample of 40 indi-viduals instead of 30, the $p$ value would be .05, even though the strength of the relationship remains unchanged. Using conventional standards we would now conclude that there is in fact a statistically significant relationship between these variables. It is not uncommon for researchers to implicitly (and erroneously) convey to the reader that the alpha level connotes the magnitude of the association between variables. Continuing with our hypothetical study, had we employed a sample of 70 individuals, the .30 correlation is now significant at the .01 alpha level. If we had slightly over 100 participants, our .30 correlation would be significant at the .001 alpha level. Note that the actual magnitude of the association between PTSD and depression has not changed in any of these scenarios. The strength of the relationship has remained constant across these studies—that is, $r = .30$. Whether we used 30 participants or over 100 participants, the proportion of variance in one variable (e.g., depression) accounted for by the other variable (PTSD) is 9%. It is the correlation coefficient that truly tells us how strong the relationship between these two variables is. But the $p$ value changes dramatically depending on the sample size.

The lesson to be learned from all of this is that you should not be persuaded that a finding is practically or theoretically meaningful simply because the author uses phrases such as "highly significant" in reference to the $p$ value. He or she may be telling you more about sample size than the actual magnitude of the relationship between variables. If the researcher is fortunate enough to have access to very large samples, even very small associations can be "highly statistically significant." It has been pointed out elsewhere that a Pearson $r$ of .10 is statistically significant using conventional standards, if the sample consists of 1,300 participants (Cohen, 1990). This is arguably a very minuscule association. Only 1% of the variance in one measure is accounted for by the other measure when the association is this minute. Yet if we attended only to the $p$ value as authors would often have us do, we might be left with the impression that the two variables were meaningfully associated when they were not. We would have been duped by "significant" associations that resulted as a byproduct of a very large sample size.

In short, fairly large, meaningful, and important relationships can be deemed "not significant" if the researcher carelessly conducts an investigation with a very small sample. Similarly, fairly meaningless and minuscule relationships can be deemed "significant" if the investigator had the good fortune to have access to a very large sample. When reviewers of the literature bearing on a particular phenomenon remark that the "findings are mixed," they are typically noting that some studies have yielded significant results whereas some have not. It is often implied in such reviews that the phenomenon in question may not actually exist. It could well be the case that the findings are fairly uniform, but that some investigators used large enough samples for the association to meet the statistical criterion for significance and some did not. Focusing only on $p$ values does not allow the reviewer to determine which of these two possibilities is more tenable.

Always remain keenly aware that the use of the word, "significant," tells you almost nothing about the strength of a relationship between or among variables of interest, when this distinction is based solely on a $p$ value. The reader must ascertain the meaningfulness of the association by focusing on the *effect size*—the strength of association between or among variables. If the investigator did not include this information, it can be easily calculated for any statistic of interest. Although it is beyond the scope of this chapter to explain such computations, a very comprehensible text has been written by Jacob Cohen (1988) and is highly recommended.

As a final word on the matter, strength of association measures (i.e., effect sizes), while still being more informative than $p$ values, cannot by themselves inform us about the importance of a finding. As a general rule, the larger the effect size, the more important the finding. This is not invariably true, however. There are occasions when very small effects can be extremely important and there are times when very large effects can be quite meaningless. With respect to the former, in a widely cited example of a very important, yet very small association, the Steering Committee of the Physicians' Health Study Research Group (1988) documented that regular aspirin usage significantly reduces the risk of having a heart attack. The effect size was inordinately small ($r = .03$)—much smaller than conventional standards for a small effect. However, because this study had a sample size in excess of 22,000 individuals, this small association was statistically significant by even the most stringent criterion ($p < .001$). This is not simply an example of a meaningless and minuscule effect that happens to be significant only because of an enormous sample size, however. It is certainly true that this tiny effect size is only statistically significant because of the enormous sample size. However, because this study documented a potentially life saving intervention, the importance of this small effect is profound. The experimental group and the placebo control group each consisted of approximately 11,000 individuals. Only 1% of all participants had a heart attack over the course of the study. Specifically, 104 individuals who regularly took aspirin had heart attacks compared to 189 in the placebo group. Although these numbers are paltry relative to the number of participants in the entire study (hence the inordinately small effect size), the ability to reduce the risk of having a heart attack by nearly $\frac{1}{2}$ is surely quite important. Clearly, in matters of life and death, even very small effects can be quite meaningful.

On the flip side of the coin, very large effect sizes may sometimes be of little practical importance. Suppose we were interested in reducing self-injurious behaviors in a group of individuals that frequently engage in these types of behaviors. In determining whether our intervention is effective, we might randomly assign half of the individuals to the treatment condition and half to the wait list control condition. We would want to determine the baseline rate of self-injurious behaviors in the groups prior to implementing treatment. Let us say that each group each group averaged 15 self-injurious behaviors per day, with a *SD* of 4. After our intervention, we find that the wait list control group remains unchanged, but the participants in the experimental condition now average 13 instances of self-injurious behavior per day. Our intervention resulted in a $\frac{1}{2}$ *SD* reduction in self-injurious behavior. Reducing a problem behavior by a half a standard deviation is generally regarded as a relatively large effect. In this instance, however, it is questionable whether the intervention would be considered meaningful. Arguably, 13 self-injurious behaviors per day is not appreciably better than 15 such behaviors per day.

In short, focusing only on statistical significance in reviewing the literature can often mislead the reviewer. Attention to effect size will generally be much more fruitful. However, even effect size may not convey the full meaning of an association. One must also consider the practical implications of an association no matter how small or large it might be statistically. A thorough review of the literature involves a great deal more than simply counting those studies that do and do not yield statistically significant associations.

Much of what we have been discussing (though not explicitly stating) thus far is the importance of statistical power. *Power* is defined as the probability of detecting an association that actually exists between or among variables. It should be obvious from the examples just cited that the sample size greatly affects the likelihood of rejecting the null hypothesis (i.e., finding a statistically significant association among variables). A large sample size will lead to increased statistical sensitivity (i.e., power). Using the Cohen (1988) text, it is generally quite easy to compute power for a wide array of statistics.

For the purposes of reviewing the literature, it is not necessary to routinely analyze power. It may be more helpful when reviewing mixed or nonsignificant findings. Was the association nonsignificant because the effect is truly minuscule, or was there insufficient power to detect the association? The answer to this question will clearly have profound implications for the findings of your review. Even if you do not formally compute the power of the investigations you review, it will certainly be informative to compare the sample sizes. These will give you a rough idea of which studies may have suffered from low power. It may be that the investigators did not employ a large enough sample to detect the association. Unfortunately, reviewers too often collude with careless experimenters in assuming that nonsignificant findings result because the variables under investigation are not meaningfully associated. It is often the case that the variables are meaningfully associated, but the study suffers from low power (usually resulting from small sample size).

Given the enormous impact that statistical power can have on the outcome of an investigation, readers may assume that this issue is seldom neglected by authors of published studies. Unfortunately, such an assumption is wholly incorrect. In one of his earliest treatises on the matter, Cohen (1962) reviewed the average power of studies in the 1960 volume of the *Journal of Abnormal and Social Psychology* and found that the *M* power to detect medium effect sizes was .48. Stated differently, the published studies in that volume had only a 48% likelihood of detecting moderate associations that actually existed in the population. At that time, issues of power and effect size were not routinely stressed in statistics courses. Although power analysis has been increasingly emphasized to the point that it is now standardly taught in statistics and research design courses, this has not translated into a demonstrable increase of power in recent studies. In a much more recent discussion of the matter, Cohen (1992) observed that the matter of power is still largely ignored, and that the power of more recent studies is not appreciably greater than it was at the time of his seminal review. For a brief, but relatively thorough tutorial of power analysis, the reader is referred to Cohen (1992).

## APPROPRIATENESS OF DESIGN, MEASURES, AND ANALYSES

An investigation may have adequate power, adequate control groups, and appropriate participant selection and assignment procedures, but may still fail to adequately address the stated goals of the study. As a reviewer, you may encounter a very well-designed study that is better equipped to address a question other than the one posed by the experimenter.

By way of example, in reviewing epidemiology studies bearing on the prevalence of PTSD, Breslau and colleagues (1998) rightly noted that many investigations employed methods that likely produced spuriously high prevalence rates of PTSD. Specifically, they noted that the modal approach to establishing the conditional probability of developing PTSD given exposure to a traumatic event, was to ask individuals to report their worst or most upsetting experiences. Researchers then assessed PTSD symptoms resulting from that experience to calculate conditional probabilities of developing the disorder given exposure to that trauma. It is clear that this method may artificially inflate the various conditional probabilities of developing PTSD associated with different traumas. This is because individuals are much more likely to develop symptoms of PTSD related to their worst traumatic experience in comparison to other potential PTSD-eliciting events that they may also have encountered. Accordingly, in designing their investigation, Breslau and colleagues (1998) estimated conditional probabilities of developing PTSD in response to various traumas, by obtaining an exhaustive trauma history from participants, and then randomly selecting one trauma offered by each individual and ascertaining symptoms pertaining to that traumatic experience. This method, coupled with the impressive sample size (2,181) likely provides the most accurate conditional probabilities of developing PTSD in response to specific types of trauma. These researchers found that the conditional probability of developing PTSD in response to any traumatic experience (i.e., the overall prevalence of PTSD given some traumatic experience) was 9.2%, although some traumatic events (e.g., rape) were much more likely to result in PTSD and some (e.g., motor vehicle accidents) were much less likely to culminate in PTSD.

Published studies are easier to evaluate to the extent that they utilize multiple, appropriate measures of the constructs under investigation. Our measures tap into the constructs that we seek to measure, but they do not equal those constructs. The Beck Depression Inventory (Beck, 1996), for instance, is the most widely used paper-and-pencil measure of depression. It contains questions that address the major features of the disorder and it converges well with structured interviews and other sound measures of depressive symptomatology. An individual's score on this measure approximates his or her level of depression, but cannot fully explicate his or her experience. Accordingly, multiple measures of the same construct are often useful in providing the most fine-grained analysis of an individual's functioning. If two measures (each tapping into a different construct) are not significantly associated, it may be the case that the constructs are not meaningfully related to one another. Alternatively, specific measures may not correlate with each other, but conceivably, other measures of the same constructs might be associated.

Measures should also reflect current conceptualizations of the construct of interest. Researchers should not continue to use an instrument simply because it has been used frequently in the past. As the science advances, our measures should reflect these developments. The Impact of Events Scale (IES; Horowitz, Wilner, & Alvarez, 1979), a measure of trauma-related pathology was designed before PTSD was even recognized as a formal diagnostic entity. Because it was designed prior to the advent of the PTSD diagnosis, it only taps into two of the three PTSD symptoms clusters that define the disorder—intrusions (re-experiencing), and avoidance. It does not assess hyperarousal symptoms. It was nonetheless a very useful measure as it demonstrated good convergence with PTSD diagnoses. Relatively recently, the IES has been revised to more closely match diagnostic criteria, including hyperarousal symptoms (IES-R; Marmar, Weiss, Metzler, Ronfeldt, & Foreman, 1996). There are a number of other psychometrically sound paper-and-pencil measures of PTSD symptoms that have also been around for some time (e.g., the Modified PTSD Symptom Scale; Falestti, Resnick, Resick, & Kilpatrick, 1993). It is not uncommon however, to read studies that still utilize the original IES, even when the data were collected well after the development of arguably superior measures of PTSD.

If you encounter conflicting findings in the literature, pay attention to the measures used. Also pay attention to the reported psychometric properties of the measures. If none is reported, be suspicious. Do some investigations include more recent, thorough, or valid measures of the construct? All else being equal, these results may be more accurate. Again, do not simply conclude that findings are mixed. Scrutiny of methods and measures may commend some investigations over others.

Finally, evaluate whether the analyses performed were appropriate to the design and stated purposes of the investigation. A brilliantly conceived, diligently designed investigation is all for naught if the data are not appropriately analyzed. As one of innumerable possible examples, consider the practice of artificially dichotomizing continuous measures. That is, researchers will often administer a continuous measure such as the Beck Depression Inventory, but instead of analyzing it as a continuous measure, they will use a cut-point to artificially establish groups. For instance, those with a score below 15 might comprise a low-depression group, whereas those with a score of 16 or greater would comprise a high-depression group. The investigator might then use these groups in conducting an analysis of variance examining the impact of group status on some other continuous measure (e.g., a measure of intelligence). This practice is inexplicably common, despite the fact that there is typically no good reason for doing such a thing. More troubling is the fact that investigators unwittingly jeopardize their own investigations when they engage in this practice. Associating two continuous measures is invariably more powerful than artificially dichotomizing a continuous measure in the service of performing a group-based statistical analysis. Some researchers wrongly assume that an ANOVA affords stronger inferences of causality than does a correlational analysis. Causal inferences depend on the experimental design, not the statistics used in analyzing the resulting data. Not only does an ANOVA using artificially categorized data not allow any greater inferences of causality, it often obscures meaningful relationships that do exist. Dichotomizing continuous measures results in a significant reduction of power, equivalent to eliminating upwards of $\frac{2}{3}$ of one's sample (Cohen, 1983).

In summation, when evaluating the literature, do not passively accept conclusions proffered by the authors. Although these conclusions may be correct, it is sometimes easier for an objective observer to generate alternative explanations. An exclusive focus on $p$ values will result in a very suspect review of the literature. By attending to critical features of the sample, design, measures used, statistical analyses, as well as issues such as statistical power and effect size, you will be in a position to reconcile discrepancies in the literature and specify directions for future research.

## EXPRESSING THE RESULTS OF THE LITERATURE REVIEW

Once you have thoroughly but efficiently searched the literature for pertinent information and you have contemplated the methodological merits and shortcomings of studies yielded from your literature search, you must convey this information to others. Whether you are writing an introduction for a brief research report or a more comprehensive review article, the written literature review should not be an exhaustive study-by-study summary of relevant research. Instead, it should parsimoniously convey the core issues, selectively providing examples where appropriate.

It is advisable to jot down notes about each article that you read in order to facilitate your written review later. You will want to note the title, authors, and year of publication in your notes, as well as key features that distinguish each study from others you have read, such as experimental design, sample size, and measures used. Include important extraneous factors that were or were not controlled, as well as strengths and weaknesses of the design and analyses. Although this may seem to be a burdensome additional step, it will save you a great deal of time in the long run. You will not have to spend as much time wading through a stack of articles later in order to find the example that you wish to use. Moreover, you will be in a better position to organize your written review. When you read over very brief summaries that you have produced, important themes will emerge that will serve to focus your review. Consistent methodological weaknesses across studies will become readily apparent. This will allow you to make a more compelling case for the importance of your investigation if you are writing a manuscript for the purposes of disseminating results of your empirical investigation. If you are simply writing a review of the literature, you will be in a better position to specify necessary directions for future research.

Before writing a single word, you should always construct an outline. Even if your literature review is very short (e.g., for the purposes of a brief report) and you know which points you wish to discuss and which are the most pertinent examples from the literature, this point can not be emphasized strongly enough. It is easy for your written work to take on a life of its own without this imposed structure. As such, your review may be brief but rambling instead of brief and cohesive. Even if you do not have a tendency to ramble, you may neglect important themes or examples in the absence of an outline.

In constructing your outline from the summaries of articles you have made, you do not need to address all of the shortcomings in an area of inquiry. Instead, you should select no more than three or four areas that are most lacking or are most relevant to your investigation. Once you have identified these themes, do not describe every relevant example from the literature in a study-by-study fashion. Describe the general issue and cite only the most prominent examples.

For most purposes, it is much better to be selective and efficient rather than exhaustive. Being succinct and being comprehensive need not be mutually exclusive. As a literature reviewer, you should be comprehensive when accessing and reading relevant work. But you can certainly convey the central themes in a succinct fashion by citing only the most pertinent examples. You can and should refer interested readers who may desire more detailed information to other sources. Your task is to orient the reader to key issues. You need not take it upon yourself to thoroughly and exhaustively educate the reader on these issues.

The best written literature reviews adopt a "funnel" approach. That is, they are sufficiently broad in the beginning in order to quickly orient the reader to the subject matter. As the review progresses, it should quickly narrow to the specific focus of your research. As mentioned earlier in this chapter, the audience is a key consideration in determining exactly how broad the beginning of the review should be. To reiterate, a journal that focuses exclusively or primarily on a particular phenomenon (e.g., *the Journal of Traumatic Stress*) will not require an extensive overview of PTSD. Literature reviews for more general journals will require at least a cursory discussion of the general phenomenon or disorder you are addressing. Once the reader is sufficiently oriented to the larger domain, you must quickly and efficiently focus the review to your specific purposes. Page space in journals is precious. While there may be many tempting tangents, you must be painstakingly selective in your commentary.

## SUMMARY

In sum, the literature review should not be viewed as a chore or a necessary evil in the process of research. Unfocused, unsystematic, or sketchy reviews will surely be cumbersome for the author and reader alike. In contrast, attention to detail and a critical eye will ensure that you have no shortage of research ideas. Importantly, this attention to detail will also enable you to make a compelling case for the contributions of your work when communicating your ideas to others.

## REFERENCES

Beck, A. T. (1996). *The Beck Depression Inventory—Second Edition*. San Antonio, TX: The Psychological Corporation.

Breslau, N., Kessler, R. C., Chilcoat, H. D., Schultz, L. R., Davis, G. C., & Andreski, P. (1998). Trauma and posttraumatic stress disorder in the community. *Archives of General Psychiatry, 55*, 626–632.

Carpenter, S. (2000). APA's electronic journal gains momentum. *Monitor on Psychology, 31*, 72.

Cohen, J. (1962). The statistical power of abnormal-social psychological research: A review. *Journal of Abnormal and Social Psychology, 65*, 145–153.

Cohen, J. (1983). The cost of dichotomization. *Applied Psychological Measurement, 7*, 249–253.

Cohen, J. (1988). *Statistical Power Analysis for the Behavioral Sciences—Second Edition*. Hillside, NJ: Lawrence Erlbaum Associates.

Cohen, J. (1990). Things I have learned (so far). *American Psychologist, 45*, 1304–1312.

Cohen, J. (1992). A power primer. *Psychological Bulletin, 112*, 155–159.

Falsetti, S. A., Resnick, H. S., Resick, P. A., & Kilpatrick, D. G. (1993). The Modified PTSD Symptom Scale: A brief self-report measure of post-traumatic stress disorder. *The Behavior Therapist, 16*, 161–162.

Horowitz, M. J., Wilner, N., & Alvarez, W. (1979). Impact of Event Scale: A measure of subjective stress. *Psychosomatic Medicine, 41*, 209–218.

Kubany, E. S. (1995). Searching the traumatic stress literature using PILOTS and PsycLIT. *Journal of Traumatic Stress, 8*, 491–494.

Marmar, C. R., Weiss, D. S., Metzler, T., Ronfeldt, H., & Foreman, C. (1996). Stress responses of emergency services personnel to the Loma Pricta earthquake Interstate 880 freeway collapse and control traumatic incidents. *Journal of Traumatic Stress, 9*, 63–85.

Shobe, K. K., & Kihlstrom, J. F. (1997). Is traumatic memory special? *Current Directions in Psychological Science, 6*, 70–74.

Steering Committee of the Physicians' Health Study Research Group (1988). Preliminary report: Findings from the aspirin component of the ongoing physicians' health study. *New England Journal of Medicine, 318*, 262–264.

Yehuda, R., Keefe, R. S. E., Harvey, P. D., Levengood, R. A., Gerber, D. K., Geni, J., & Siever, L. J. (1995). Learning and memory in combat veterans with posttraumatic stress disorder. *American Journal of Psychiatry, 152*, 137–139.

# 12

# Planning Data Collection and Performing Analyses

Jay C. Thomas and Lisa Selthon
*Pacific University*
*Portland, Oregon*

This chapter provides the beginning researcher with a set of guidelines for how to actually set up and conduct a research study. It is based on the authors' experience in conducting numerous research studies and program evaluations and in the senior author's experience in working with many students on masters theses and doctoral dissertations. The content of the chapter reflects what we have found to be the most troublesome phases of conducting a study, particularly from the perspective of a student faced with their first research project. We will use an example from an actual small-scale study conducted in an anxiety disorders clinic.

The data you collect in any study needs to be analyzed before it can be understood. The first step is to develop hypotheses about what these data will show. Presumably this was done before the data was collected, although in archival studies, the researcher may be taking advantage of existing data and would state hypotheses after the data are assembled, but prior to analysis. Having your hypotheses stated before you begin the analysis endows the results and the conclusion from the study with credibility.

The second step in developing such understanding is to create a plan for the analysis. Parts of this plan can be completed before you collect any data and it should be complete in its first draft form before any analysis begins. As the analysis proceeds, the plan may be modified to fit unexpected conditions in the data or to allow for follow up on unexpected findings. There are advantages to having a plan and modifying it as needed; these include (a) examining all relationships you expected to observe, and (b) the analysis proceeds in a reasonable order so that conclusions are not prematurely accepted. Once the plan is set and the analyses begin, there is the problem of how to evaluate the evidence as it bears on the hypotheses. Quite often this is left to rejecting or not rejecting the null hypothesis, using common significance-testing methods. However, there are other, more powerful and useful methods that should be considered. Finally, there is the problem of conducting exploratory or secondary analyses. These were not preplanned, but arise from patterns of results noticed by the researcher during the initial data-analysis process.

## STEP 1. STRUCTURING CREATIVITY: WRITING HYPOTHESES

We begin by writing the hypotheses for the study. It is important to state hypotheses before beginning the analysis to increase the credibility of conclusions. A *hypothesis* is a tentative statement describing a relationship between two or more variables of interest. Hypotheses that are research oriented are usually stated in a way that implies that two or more variables will be related. They also identify the nature of the relationship. In an experimental or quasiexperimental study, causal relationships will typically be specified. For a simple example, a study comparing the effects of home and clinic based treatments for obsessive–compulsive disorder (OCD) may have as its research hypothesis Clients receiving home based treatment will show greater improvement in symptoms as measured by the Yale–Brown Obsessive Compulsive Scale (Y-BOCS; Goodman et al., 1989a, 1989b) than clients receiving clinic-based treatment. Notice that this hypothesis specifies who will change, what is related to or causes the change (form of treatment), what will change (symptoms as measured by the Y-BOCS), and the direction of change (improvement).

The world we live in is diverse and ever-changing. Being able to generate hypotheses that are creative can allow researchers to explore new areas and therefore discover or establish new relationships between variables. If science is to enhance our understanding, then it is necessary for researchers to move beyond observed facts. Stating hypotheses allows the researcher to specify patterns of data that are expected and ultimately to compare the data against these expectations.

Developing hypotheses first requires an understanding of theories that attempt to account for what is already known. Isaac Newton once wrote "If I have seen further it is by standing on the shoulders of giants" (Newton, cited in Oxford Dictionary of Quotations, 1979). The literature review (chap. 11) is intended to allow the researcher to identify and become familiar with the work preceding the current study. Having mastered the existing literature, the researcher is ready to begin generating hypotheses about the topic of their own study. Your ability to make a significant contribution to the knowledge base of your field depends on your ability to integrate previous work and go beyond it (McGuire, 1997).

Current research literature tends to focus on testing hypotheses rather than on creating hypotheses. McGuire (1997) reported that the neglect of teaching/and/or participating individuals how to creatively develop hypotheses results from a lack of strategies. He encourages psychologists to generate creative hypotheses that will allow research to move beyond merely testing hypotheses, and provides 49 creative heuristics that can aid in generating them.

McGuire (1997) organized his 49 heuristics into five categories, which recommend that researchers be sensitive to provocative natural occurrences, look at direct and mediated inference, reinterpret past research, and collect new or analyze old data. As an example of the first category, Bahrick, Parker, Fivush, and Levitt (1998) examined how Hurricane Andrew's devastation of parts of Florida and its resultant stress affected young children's memories of a natural disaster. By comparing the extent of damage in each child's neighborhood with the child's memory of the hurricane a few months later, the authors were able to show that the specificity of the memory depended on the extent of the natural stressor in an inverted-U function. This study has important implications in many areas of psychology, not the least of which is its relevance to the repressed memory debate of the 1990s. Bosma, Stansfeld, and Marmot (1998) provided an example of the second category of heuristic. They examined data from a prospective cohort study of the British Civil Service (Whitehall II; Marmot et al., 1991). The data included measures of the degree to which each participant had control over their work as well as gender and personality data. Ten years after the initial data collection, the researchers gathered data on the incidence of heart disease. Job control had a direct effect on the risk of developing heart disease (low job control leads to higher risk) and this was not impacted by personality. Recently, Kluger and Tikochinsky (2001) re-examined the conclusions of many studies throughout the field of psychology. They found that several well-accepted conclusions about the lack of an effect could not be sustained by the available data. In other words, psychologists have often been too quick to accept the null hypothesis of no effect. This exemplifies the type of heuristic of reanalyzing old data or results.

## STEP 2. DESIGNING THE STUDY

The previous chapters of this book presented a number of methods for designing a research study. The researcher needs to choose a basic design and modify it based on the nature of the hypotheses, resources available for the research, and circumstances under which the results will be used. Clinical trials of a new medication, for example, will involve many researchers from a variety of disciplines, several sites, months or years to accomplish, and an extensive subject pool. Such research will typically have a very complex design, accompanied by very complex analysis procedures. A master's thesis, having a single investigator, a small budget, and a time frame measured in a few months will typically utilize a much simpler design and analyses. In choosing a design, remember that a purpose of science is to make the world understandable. It is easy to design a study that is so complex it is difficult to comprehend the results (we have done this). As the eminent methodologist, Jacob Cohen (1990), advised, researchers should keep their designs and analyses as simple as possible.

The design of a study should include an evaluation of the ethical issues in conducting the research, obtaining or developing all of the measures to be used in the study, developing informed consent forms, and requesting and obtaining approval from the appropriate institutional review board (IRB; see chap. 10). Data collection may not begin until the IRB has either approved the study or found it exempt from the need for review.

## STEP 3. CREATING A WORK PLAN AND DEVELOPING A CODE BOOK FOR DATA ANALYSIS

If you are about to embark on your first research project, you should understand that it will involve stress. Theses and dissertations, in particular, are always stressful. One way to combat the stress is to keep this fact in mind; it helps to know that you are not alone in this regard. A second way to combat this stress is to reduce the distress (those factors that make stress wearing and unpleasant), and increase eustress (those factors that can make research productive and even exhilarating). The single most distressing thing in a research project is the chaos and uncertainty, which comes from not having a good work plan and code book at the start. You can substantially reduce your own stress and that of your advisor or co-workers if you spend a little time developing a work plan and a code book. It is not uncommon for professional research and evaluation organizations to set aside 10% to 20%, or more, of a project's budget for project management. The time spent developing the work plan and code book, as well as keeping track of progress, research group meetings, and sessions with your advisor, can all be thought of as project management and can be charged to this budgeted time.

Depending on the project, the work plan can be a formal document or a simple paper and pencil list of things to do. The latter may suffice in a small project with just a few variables, whereas the work plan for a large analysis may take several weeks or more to develop. The work plan should include starting and ending dates, a description of the work scope (what is to be done), and who is responsible for each phase of work. An easy way to do the scheduling is to use a Gantt chart, where the project tasks to be completed are listed on the vertical axis and the time tasks are to be completed are measured along the horizontal axis (Frame, 1987). This graphic representation can be used for project control as well as time management. Gantt charts are useful because they are simple and relatively easy to develop. Figure 12.1 is a Gantt chart that lists the tasks involved in doing a representative research project. Both the planned and the actual task completion goals are represented, which allows for examining schedule variance in a project's tasks. As you can see in this example, the actual dates that tasks began and ended are slightly off the planned dates. However, the overall timeframe was similar to the projected estimate.

Our practice is to develop a three-ring binder with a tabbed section devoted to each section of the work plan. Modern technology might allow just using electronic records, although we have never found that efficient. A hard copy has the advantage of being accessible anytime and it is easy to add notes or changes as needed. We recommend the following sections:

1. Description of the study: title, date, who worked on it, how the data were obtained, purpose, and other information you want to know in the future.

2. The work plan itself: schedule (including Gantt chart), procedures, and responsibilities of each person involved. These are updated periodically as needed.

3. A copy of the instruments used (surveys, tests, inventories, etc.). Usually you want to identify the variable name used in the data file associated with each item and scale. If you are using other forms of data, such as physiological recording, describe each variable and how it is obtained. If special procedures need to be followed, they should be included in this section.

4. An up-to-date list of computer files created during the study and analysis. This list should include the file name, type of file (i.e. what format, such as ASCII, Excel, Access, SPSS, etc.), what the file was used for, important variables in the file, any modifications made to the file, and any files that link to this one. In a large project, it may be wise to devote a page to each file.

5. The code book. The code book is a document that specifies how the data are to be coded prior to analysis. It also describes changes made to the data, such as the computation of a new variable from one or more existing ones, for example, the summation of a scale score. The code book will be described soon.

6. Basic statistics and frequency tables for each variable (obtained after all data are collected).

7. The next several sections would be devoted to each phase of the analysis. For a thesis or dissertation you, would probably have a tab for each hypothesis. You would create a summary of results for each phase/ hypothesis.

324

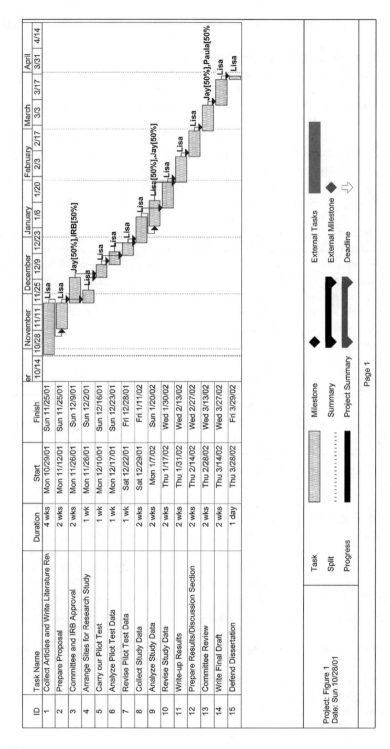

FIG. 12.1.

8. Additional findings not otherwise classified.

9. A copy of the raw data. Identifying information should be removed.

10. A list of data coding decisions by subject. This section includes documentation of any decisions made by the researcher(s) about data values for a specific participant. For example, a subject makes a mark midway between two anchors on a Likert-style response form, say between two and three. You need to record how this problem was dealt with; the response could be coded as a 2, 3, 2.5, or as missing data. The code book will include the decision rules; this section describes the application of these rules to particular cases.

**The Code Book**

The code book describes how data are to be coded for input into the database, usually in a computer. Even the simplest data collection instrument will have decisions to be made when entering the data. For example, demographic information such as gender of the respondent is generally coded as 0 and 1 (or 1 and 2). The code book tells which gender is a 0 and which is a 1. It will also tell how to code a nonresponse. Other forms of demographic information often require more complex coding schemes; for example, race/ethnic origin or marital status may have several categories.

There are even decisions to make about how to code improperly completed forms. The importance of having these rules established as early as possible in the process was shown in the recent presidential election between George W. Bush and Albert Gore. One of the issues raised before the courts involved the lack of standards for deciding what was a vote and what was not a vote during the Florida recount process controversy. You run into many similar decisions in research. Sometimes, for example, a respondent will check off a point midway between two of the numbers on a Likert scale. Do you allow responses of 2.5? How about 2.75? Often a respondent will leave one item on a multiitem scale blank. You can leave it as missing, but if the items are totaled in a scale, that person's score may be misleadingly low and certain types of analysis may give misleading results if there is much missing data. Researchers have developed many methods for dealing with missing data, some of which get quite sophisticated. Two common methods are to replace the missing data with the midpoint of the scale, or alternatively, to replace the missing data with the average response from the other items. Either of these may result in a distortion of the respondent's actual attitude (opinion, etc.). Any time you have to use any interpretation of a response, write it in colored pencil or pen on the original data collection instrument. Write it so that your notes do not cover up anything the respondent wrote. Also, note the problem and decision in the last section of the data binder. This makes it easy to determine where changes were made and to undo them if that proves necessary.

Sometimes data are obtained from some mechanical or electronic source, such as a scanner (like the ones used to grade multiple-choice tests), Internet or Intranet, or received from someone else who has already entered the data. These often come in the form of ASCII or ".txt" files. Depending on how it was set up, it may not be a simple matter to input the data into an analysis program without stating the format of the data. That is, some variables may be represented by a single digit, others by more than one. Fractions will generally be in the form of decimals. Often, the data file will not include the decimals. You have to tell your computer where they go and this information must be in the code book.

Open-ended questions and qualitative data will require careful planning of response codes. You can sometimes predict what many responses will be and can plan codes for those. Other codes may be developed after you have examined a number of responses. Your coding scheme should be flexible enough to handle these improvised codes. The code book should be updated as soon as one of these codes is invented.

Greene (1994) provided several rules for developing codes. First of all,

1. The codes must be objective. You do not want to use subjective interpretation during the coding process, which could eventually bias your results.

2. The codes must encompass all of the cases. This excludes cases that fall out of the data pool due to not being answered during data collection.

3. The codes must be meaningful. It would be difficult to interpret the results if there is no meaning to the data you are analyzing.

4. The codes need to enhance rather than complicate the analysis of the data.

5. Coding must also economize the data. You want to make sure that all the necessary data information is included without extraneous variables that can complicate the analysis.

6. Coding must also yield reliable, therefore repeatable, results. In doing so, the coding process must not add bias to the data or distort the data in any way.

7. The codes must be neutral and they must be documented. Both of these guidelines will help eliminate any confusion during the analysis and interpretation processes.

8. The coding process is aimed at being helpful. Therefore the codes must be developed with ease of application in mind. An overly complex coding system will not only be frustrating, but may lead to inaccurate results during the interpretation process.

9. Codes must consist of mutually exclusive categories and they may have to accommodate multiple responses. A common example of failing to account for multiple responses has occurred frequently in the collection of data on racial or ethnic heritage. Many people are multicultural in origin and forcing a single choice is not appropriate. Thus, current methods for collecting this data allow for multiple responses.

## STEP 4. DATA COLLECTION

There are several steps to consider when preparing to collect data. First, one needs to plan for the data collection in the work plan. Second, data collection procedures and instruments need to be tried out on a pilot sample. Once this planning and trial has taken place, the third step, actual data collection, can proceed. In Step 4, during the data collection process and immediately following it, it is necessary to code the data (see the code book section). When all data are collected, then Step 5, data editing, can take place. This is where the data are checked and assessed for accuracy. Unusual values, such as an age of 102, need to be checked against the original documents. If there is more than one data editor, then it is necessary to make sure that they all are editing the same way and using the same data reduction rules. Again, the code book should be precise enough that all editors know what decisions to make. The final data are then entered into the data analysis program being used.

## STEP 5. DATA VERIFICATION

Data sometimes are entered incorrectly. The data input person is responsible for checking work to verify that it is error free. But, mistakes sometimes happen. So, you should plan to sample the original data sheets and compare them to what has entered the data file. The sample would normally include the first two or three subjects' data, data from one or two subjects near the middle of the file, and the last two subjects. This will tell you if any major errors have occurred. You also want to randomly sample from the remaining subjects to determine the prevalence of errors. If you begin finding errors, the only solution may be to double check all of the data (if you paid for the data entry and it turns out to be low quality, you want to be sure and record the mistakes and corrections).

## STEP 6. BASIC STATISTICS

This step includes calculating basic statistics (averages, measures of variability), frequencies, histograms, and performing assumption checks. The first step in actual analysis is to look at the basic statistics that describe the variables. This would include the sample size, $M$, $SD$, median, lower and upper quartiles, quartile range, and minimum and maximum quartile range. Not only are these data to be used in writing the results, but they also will help identify any strange or unexpected characteristics in the data. This latter inspection is assisted by frequency tables and histograms. You should be checking the data to see if it will sustain the assumptions of any tests that you plan to run.

## STEP 7. CHECK RELIABILITY

If you have the necessary data and sufficient subjects to make it worthwhile, the next step is to check the reliability of your measures. This may include internal consistency, stability (test–retest), interrater, or even generalizability indices. The only exception to doing the reliability checks at this point is if you are planning to do item analyses, a factor analysis, or some other scale development procedure. If so, those analyses would precede the reliability checks. Generally, you should provide confidence intervals for the reliabilities. Formulas for these intervals for coefficient alpha are given in Feldt, Woodruff, and Salih (1987).

## STEPS 8 AND BEYOND. TESTING HYPOTHESES

Steps 8 and beyond involves actually testing the hypotheses. Finally, you get to the planning of the analyses you wanted to do in the first place. For each one, describe the method to be used, variables to be included, assumptions (check them if you have not already done so), alpha levels you will accept, and power analysis methods to be used. Remember, if you are performing $M$ comparisons to specify preplanned comparisons if at all possible. This way you have documentation that you really did preplan the comparisons.

If you are doing a theory testing type study (e.g. confirmatory factor analysis or structural equation modeling) the work plan should include the expected coefficients or relationships needed to test the theory.

As you proceed with data analysis, new ideas emerge. It is easy to get sidetracked following them up and forgetting to finish what you intended to do.[1] Conditions and people vary, but the best advice is to keep track of the new ideas by adding sections or subsections to the work plan. This way you can finish the planned work and still remember the great inspirations or important questions that struck you midway through an analysis. Such analyses are known as *secondary* or *exploratory analyses*. Such analyses are often discouraged as being *data snooping*, an unethical and improper process consisting of going through the data and performing all possible tests and comparisons. However, secondary analyses are appropriate so long as they are recognized for what they are and not considered as credible evidence until replicated in a later study.

As part of planning the testing of hypotheses, we encourage you to think about the nature of the tests being performed. The null hypothesis significance testing (NHST) procedure taught in most introductory statistics courses has

---

[1]There are numerous stories in science about great discoveries being made while following up an anomalous finding. We do not want to miss out on our own great discoveries, so be ready to follow the leads. Just remember to finish what you originally started as well, just in case the great discovery does not pan out.

come under significant attack. There are several reasons for this, but what they all have in common is that the NHST rarely tells us what we want to know. Over the years, several alternatives have been suggested. In evaluating whether to rely on NHST or one of the alternatives, it is important to remember that data are analyzed for different reasons, and these reasons bring different requirements to the analysis process. The distinction between studies done for the sole purpose of the advancement of science and those done to allow decisions to be made in a local situation has bedeviled the significance-testing procedure since the 1940s (Gigerenzer, 1993). The alternatives to significance testing are also apt to appeal to different researcher's perspectives. The recent distinction between "efficacy" versus "effectiveness" studies (Seligman, 1995; see also chapter 13, this volume) implies that each will require somewhat different analysis treatments. The costs and benefits of different decisions and their associated errors must be considered.

The assumed role of the single study must be taken into account in deter-mining the rules to be used for inference. Studies whose primary purpose is to advance science should rarely be seen as contributing results that can be relied upon to stand alone (Schmidt, 1992). Local decision-making studies may have a substantial research tradition to draw on and the methods employed to evaluate the data should take this into account. This distinction alone implies that differ-ent methods may be needed in different situations. In our view, the automatic application of NHST has resulted in the retardation of psychology both as a sci-ence and in its application. Because it is important that students recognize the limits of the NHST procedure, in this section we present a few of the many alter-natives to NHST. The methods we have chosen to present are those that are the most readily understandable to students and do not represent an exhaustive list.

1. *Plot data rather than presenting them as tables plus F and p values* (Loftus, 1996) The easiest suggestion is to eliminate much of the mathemati-cal analysis and present graphs of the data rather than summary statistics and significance tests. This has been the custom for many years in single-subject research designs (chap. 7) and has worked well in those situations. This proce-dure gets away from the binary choice of the NHST and forces the researcher and reader to evaluate the data on its form, which is often more interesting than the summary statistics. The disadvantage is the lines on the graph as drawn by graphics programs generally misrepresent the data. The line that truly rep-resents the data is rather thick and fuzzy due to sampling and measurement errors (cf. Schmidt & Hunter, 1996); it is not the thin line you usually see in journal articles. Graphs are often drawn showing the confidence limits or at least sampling error around the points on the line and these are more use-ful for comparison's sake. Unfortunately, this results in the same problem as evaluating confidence intervals (see upcoming text).

2. *Provide confidence intervals* (CIs; Cohen, 1994; Loftus, 1996; Wilkinson and the Task Force on Statistical Inference, 1999). In the two-group case, or when presenting correlations, the CI provides all of the information of the

significance test plus additional information. Unlike the NHST, the CI places limits on what the credible values of the population parameters may be. So, although the NHST provides no information on the nature of the alternative hypothesis (Goodman & Royall, 1988), the CI at least describes the range in which it may fall.

This method helps move the researcher and reader away from a strict binary choice toward considering a range of possibilities. It also provides some information on the ability of the data to allow effects to be seen. A very wide CI suggests that the study had little power. Correcting the CI to reflect errors of measurement enhances this effect. However, as a disadvantage, the use of CI's continues the use of an arbitrary cutoff. If "God loves the .06 nearly as much as the .05" (Rosnow & Rosenthal, 1989), then God would love the 96% CI nearly as much as the 95% CI. A second disadvantage is that CIs may not lead to understanding, particularly when there are more than two groups to be compared.

3. *Report actual p levels, not alpha levels.* For those who are not sure yet what to do, an alternative is to simply report the obtained $p$ value from the study. This was the procedure recommended by Ronald Fisher in his later years (cited in Gigerenzer, 1993). In this case the $p$ value is set after the study is completed, rather than setting $\alpha$ prior to analyzing the data. This method removes the problem of choosing significance levels after the fact by legitimizing that practice. Using the actual obtained $p$ reduces some of the emphasis on the accept/reject dichotomy. A $p = .056$ seems more acceptable alongside a $p = .049$, than a $p > .05$ against a $p < .05$. Using this method eliminates $\alpha$ as a choice point. There are four advantages to this technique. First, the reader is able to make up his or her own mind. Although the researcher may find $p = .06$ a cause for rejecting the null hypothesis (Ho), the reader may not. If, as Pearson and Neymann (cited in Gigerenzer, 1993) believed, the $\alpha$ level should be set based on a cost-benefit analysis of Type I and Type II errors, this allows for easier assimilation by readers with a different cost-benefit function than the original researcher. Second, some forms of meta-analysis require the use of $p$ values for combining the data from studies. The obtained $p$ would make it possible for a meta-analyst using one of these methods to incorporate the data into their study. Third, a reader who wishes to use the data to compute a liklihood ratio can easily do so. The fourth advantage is it encourages an emphasis on the probability of results given the theory (null hypothesis) rather than the probability of the theory given the results.

There are four major disadvantages to this method. First, the results may be misleading. For parametric statistical methods, it is well known that the violation of most assumptions will change the $p$ value somewhat; usually it is actually larger than the reported value. However, given a strict $\alpha$ level, this is not much of a problem because the degree of change is seldom enough to exert much influence on the decision. But, when $p$ values are to be reported as obtained, it is not clear that there is an interval of error around this value and that this interval is most likely asymmetric. The second disadvantage is that reports and tables are apt to appear cluttered and more important information obscured. This is more of a challenge to the art of writing well than to statistics. The third disadvantage is that it does not force a change away from NHST, it simply results in an anarchy of floating, or fuzzy, or nonexistent decision rules. The fourth disadvantage is the method provides no information about the probability of the theory (alternate hypothesis), given the data. This is sometimes of more interest than the opposite conditional probability.

4. *Equivalency testing* (Rogers, Howard, & Vessey, 1993). This method was developed in the pharmaceutical industry for comparing a new alternative drug to a standard drug. If the new drug is cheaper, easier to administer, or has fewer side effects, it is not necessary that it result in clinical effects superior to the standard drug. It is enough that it achieved comparable results. The strategy of the method consists of determining an interval around zero difference within which the researcher will accept a finding that the two treatments are equivalent. This is done statistically by relying on sample sizes and desired confidence levels (e.g., 95% confidence) much as in setting confidence levels. The method is a little more complicated statistically because you have to specify the noncentrality parameter corresponding to each upper and lower limit.

Clearly, if you want to "prove the null hypothesis," but want to emphasize statistical over clinical significance, this is the method to use. There is one big disadvantage to this method. A detailed procedure corresponding to the $Z$ test procedure has been worked out and presented. Extension to other distributions (e.g., $t$) is not available yet to the nonmathematically precocious. Also, in its current manifestation, equivalency testing is limited to two groups.

5. *Likelihood ratios* (Goodman & Royall, 1988). Use of likelihood ratios (LR) is a Bayesian technique in which the probability that a result comes from a population in which the null hypothesis is true (e.g., the difference between groups is zero) is compared to the probability that a result comes from a population in which the parameter is some other value *identified in advance*. The alternative parameter (the *prior*) may be based on previous research, such as from a meta-analysis, or may reflect the amount of change necessary for a practical effect to appear. Goodman & Royall (1988) gave the example of a study testing a blood pressure drug in which it was previously determined that a 10-point reduction in pressure would be clinically significant. In the example, the observed change is compared to populations with both zero difference and a 10-point difference. Goodman and Royall (1988) provided guidelines for determining whether the evidence favors one or the other hypotheses. The strength of the method lies in LRs concentrating attention on the strength of the evidence for and against the proposition of interest rather than the evidence against a null hypothesis nobody cares about. This advantage is so strong that LRs should always be considered when a reasonable prior can be established.

The Achilles' heel of LRs is the prior value against which the hypothesis of no effect is compared. If the prior comes from a sensible source, such as the effect needed for practical results or from good quality, trustworthy, and relevant prior research, there is no problem. When a strong justification cannot be given for the prior, the LR may be nonsense.

6. *Effect size estimates.* There are a variety of effect size measures that could be used in place of NHST. Four basic types are (1) those based on shared variance or variance explained (e.g., eta$^2$, omega$^2$, $r^2$); (2) those that measure the distance between $M$s in terms of $SD$s (e.g., Cohen's $d$, Hedges' $g$); (3) those intended to show the practical impact of an effect (e.g., the binary effect size estimate (Rosenthal & Rubin, 1982); and (4) those intended to increase understanding, especially among statistically naive readers (e.g., the "common language" effect size (Dunlap, 1994; McGraw & Wong, 1992). Descriptions of all of these effect sizes is beyond the scope of this chapter, although none is particularly difficult to calculate. Effect sizes are not dependent on the power of a study (Judd, McClelland, & Culhane, 1995), eliminating one problem with significance tests. They also tell about the strength of the effect, which is usually of primary interest. The second category of effect size estimates allows for a determination of the effects of a cutoff, say in a predictor variable, or a criterion variable. Variance based effect sizes can be incorporated into meta-analyses (if corrected for restriction of range and unreliability) without further manipulation. Unfortunately, effect sizes do not provide all of the information one would like and the issue of sampling error is still present. There is no way to relate size and importance, as even very small effects can have important ramifications (Prentice & Miller, 1992; Rosenthal, 1990). Effect sizes cannot be compared from one study to another unless the variances of the samples studied are equal (Judd et al., 1995). Thus restriction of range and base rates of occurrence are limitations on the generalizability of these statistics.

7. *Emphasize practical or clinically significant change instead of statistically significant change.* To say that an effect is statistically significant is to say that results as extreme as those which were observed would occur only rarely if the null hypothesis were true. Under the best of circumstances, this does not tell us whether the observed effect is large enough to make any practical difference. For this reason, clinicians have not found NHST very useful in guiding their work and have recently developed alternative methods. We present these in the next section.

Not all of the aforementioned methods are mutually exclusive so a researcher may choose to report more than one. It is currently recommended to report $p$ values or CIs along with effect sizes (Wilkinson, 1999) and certainly graphs such as those Loftus (1996) championed can be reported along with any of the methods just presented. The choice depends on the nature of the data and the type of generalizations to be made. Because the authors of a study should expect that it will eventually be included in a meta-analysis, effect sizes and exact *p* values or CIs should generally be reported in every study. For studies conducted to facilitate local decision making, the LR, RC, and clinically significant change procedures should be given predominant consideration. Because they are not commonly covered in statistics textbooks, the following section presents clinical significance and reliable change concepts in some detail.

## MEASURING CLINICAL SIGNIFICANCE AND THE RELIABILITY OF CHANGE

Neil Jacobson and colleagues (see, e.g., Jacobson & Truax, 1991) argued that instead of relying on statistical significance alone for evaluating the efficacy or effectiveness of treatments, researchers should look at the extent of practical change in clients. Although rooted in standard statistical methodology, their techniques differ in putting an emphasis on the degree of change made by individuals, not the average change found in groups. This, of course, is the information the practitioner really cares about and is potentially much more useful than a finding that a significant change was noted.

The Jacobson group identified two separate issues regarding change. The first issue is concerned with whether an individual can be said with some confidence to have actually changed. The simplest way to think of this is to think of a sort of significance test, such as a $Z$ test. The $Z$ test is simply

$$Z = \frac{\overline{X}_1 - \overline{X}_2}{\sigma_{\overline{X}diff}}$$

In that case, the typical standard is to look for a large enough difference so that it is unlikely to occur by chance more than 5% of the time. In the normal distribution, this occurs at 1.96 *SD*s from the point of no difference. So, the first step is to look for a change of 1.96 *SD*s. However, life is not so simple because this fails to take into account the fact that the outcome measure is usually not measured perfectly, but contains some error and, so, has less than perfect reliability. Second, because the treatment may affect the variability of outcomes, it is possible that the *SD*s of the pretreatment and posttreatment conditions differ. In statistical analysis this may pose problems and, at the least, means that the researcher must use a pooled *SD*.[2] When dealing with individual change we can simplify this problem by just using the pretreatment *SD*. This *SD* is then corrected for the unreliability of the outcome measure,

---

[2]The pooled *SD* is just the weighted average of the *SD*s. Strictly speaking, it uses the degrees of freedom associated with each *SD* rather than the *n* in the calculations.

then multiplied by two. Consequently, the reliable change is defined as:

$$RC = \frac{x_2 - x_1}{s_{diff}}$$

$x_2$ is the posttest, $x_1$ is the pretest, and $s_{diff}$ is defined as:

$$s_{diff} = \sqrt{2(s_E)^2}$$

$s_E$ is just the standard error of measurement, i.e., $s_E$

$$= s_1 \sqrt{(1 - r_{xx})}.$$

$S_1$ is the *SD* of the outcome measure at pretreatment. Finally, $r_{xx}$ is just the test–retest reliability of the outcome measure. The researcher simply calculates the RC for each subject. Any subject's RC that exceeds 1.96 is said to have shown a reliable change.

The second issue regarding change identified by Jacobson, and Truax (1991) was whether the amount of change, reliable as it may be, meant anything in a practical sense. For this purpose, they proposed a set of three statistically derived indices that address a very straightforward question: Does the individual appear on the outcome measure more like someone who is in need of therapy or more like someone who is part of the general, nonclinical population?

The three indices, named $a$, $b$, and $c$, all attempt to answer the same question. They differ from one another only in the amount of information used. Index $a$ uses the least information. It would be used when only the most minimal information is available. Index $b$ relies on more information than $a$ does, but it again is a stopgap measure for use when insufficient information is available. Index $c$ is the full-information figure and should be used whenever possible. Because they all attempt to do the same thing, we will only cover $c$ here.

Index $c$ attempts to allow the classification of treated patients into two groups, those who now seem more like people who have not been treated and those who seem more like people who have been treated. Imagine a graph showing the distributions of outcome scores for people who need treatment and those who do not. Further imagine that the distributions look like normal curves. It is easier that way, and besides, Jacobson, and Truax (1991) based their development of indices on that assumption. If the two curves are so far apart that they basically do not cross one another, it is simple to take an individual's score and see to which group they belong. If the curves overlap to the point that they are almost identical, it is impossible to tell which group someone is a member of. Usually, we would expect that, at most, the distributions would have some but only a little overlap, if only because there are probably some people in the nonclinical group who could use treatment, but have not obtained it. So, the trick is to find the point where the curves cross. A person who falls on the dysfunctional side of that point is considered to be more like those who need treatment and a person who falls on the other side is thought to be more

TABLE 12.1
Calculations for the Reliable Change Index

| Outcome Measure | $s_1$ | $r_{xx}$ | SEM | sdiff |
|---|---|---|---|---|
| Obsessions | 1.95 | .88 | .675 | .955 |
| Compulsions | 4.56 | .89 | 1.512 | 2.139 |
| Total score | 6.95 | .91 | 2.085 | 2.949 |

like those who do not need treatment. We calculate $c$ using the following fairly simple formula:

$$c = \frac{s_0\overline{x}_1 + s_1\overline{x}_0}{s_0 + s_1}$$

where $s_0$ and $s_1$ are the SDs of the dysfunctional and functional groups and $x_1$ and $x_2$ are the Ms of those groups.

The researcher calculates the value for $c$, then compares each individual's outcome score to it. If the functional group has the higher score, then if the individual's score is above $c$, that person is deemed to be like other functional people. If not, the individual is thought to be dysfunctional.

## A Real Life Example

Warren and Thomas (2001) examined the effectiveness of a cognitive–behavioral treatment for obsessive–compulsive disorder (OCD) in a private practice setting. The outcome measure consisted of three scores from the Yale–Brown Obsessive Compulsive Scale (Y-BOCS); Obsessions, Compulsions, and Total Scores (note that the total score is not independent of either obsessions or compulsions and so the results will be influenced by both). The sample consisted of 19 of 26 OCD patients who completed treatment at a private anxiety disorders clinic.

Table 12.1 shows the calculation of the $s_{diff}$ for the RC.[3] Calculating the RC from each client's measured change divided by the $s_{diff}$ showed that 84% showed a reliable change in reducing obsessions, 53% reliably reduced compulsions, and 84% reduced their total score. No subjects showed an increase.

Table 12.2 shows the basic calculations for the $c$ index. The dysfunctional comparison group is the patients themselves prior to treatment. The functional comparison group is a nonclinical norm group from the Y-BOC's manual.

---

[3] An RC should be calculated using the retest reliability of a measure. In this case we relied on internal consistency measures because test-retest data was not available. The RC estimates are probably an underestimate.

TABLE 12.2
Calculations for the $c$ Index

| Y-BOCS Scale | $s_0$ | $s_1$ | $m_0$ | $m_1$ | $s_0+s_1$ | $s_0 \times m_1$ | $s_1 \times m_0$ | $c$ |
|---|---|---|---|---|---|---|---|---|
| Obsessions | 3.21 | 1.95 | 2.130 | 11.500 | 5.16 | 36.915 | 4.1535 | 7.95 |
| Compulsions | 2.85 | 4.56 | 1.550 | 11.500 | 7.41 | 32.775 | 7.068 | 5.38 |
| Total score | 5.46 | 5.64 | 3.680 | 23.000 | 11.1 | 125.58 | 20.7552 | 13.18 |

TABLE 12.3
Effects of Treatment: Obsessions

| | Posttreatment, Dysfunctional | Posttreatment, Functional | Row % |
|---|---|---|---|
| Pretreatment, dysfunctional | 4 | 15 | 100% (i.e. all dysfunctional at start) |
| Pretreatment functional | 0 | 0 | 0 |
| Column % | 25% (dysfunctional at start and end) | 75% (functional at end) | |

Note: Entries represent number of clients.

TABLE 12.4
Effects of Treatment: Compulsions

| | Posttreatment, Dysfunctional | Posttreatment, Functional | Row % |
|---|---|---|---|
| Pretreatment, dysfunctional | 9 | 8 | 89% (dysfunctional at start) |
| Pretreatment functional | 0 | 2 | 11% (functional at start) |
| Column % | 47% (dysfunctional at start and end) | 53% (functional at end) | |

Note: Entries represent number of clients.

Table 12.3, 12.4, and 12.5 show the result of applying the $c$ index from obsessions to the subjects.

The interpretation of these results is that over $\frac{1}{2}$ ($\frac{3}{4}$ in the case of obsessions) of the OCD patients are indistinguishable from normal controls at the end of therapy. The rest will still be to some extent more like the dysfunctional group. The RC analysis indicated that, for the most part, even these people are improved over their pretreatment status.

TABLE 12.5
Effects of Treatment: Total Score

| | Posttreatment, Dysfunctional | Posttreatment, Functional | Row % |
|---|---|---|---|
| Pretreatment, dysfunctional | 9 | 9 | 95% (dysfunctional at start) |
| Pretreatment functional | 0 | 1 | 5% (functional at start) |
| Column % | 47% (dysfunctional at start and end) | 53% (functional at end) | |

*Note:* Entries represent number of clients.

## Issues in the Determination of Clinical Significance

The $c$ index, or any similar index can prove to be a valuable source of information. It can also be misleading because it only considers the statistical relationship between groups, not the behavioral change. Thus, it depends entirely on the content validity of the outcome measures, that they incorporate all of the behavioral information required to assess change. Of course, few measures have perfect content validity and this is rarely assessed in any event. A second issue arises with the interpretation of *clinically significant* as consisting of a change so that the patient no longer looks like a patient and instead looks like a member of the general population. In some cases, a successfully treated client is able to return to a semblance of a normal life, even though some issues remain. So, the clinical significance index needs to be considered in the light of other information. For example, in the Warren and Thomas (2001) study, the therapist indicated whether each client was considered a treatment success or failure. There are many problems with using such ratings by psychotherapists, but such ratings do provide a guide for the potential errors made by both the therapist and the index. There was a tendency for the $c$ index to be more conservative than the therapist, considering a patient still dysfunctional even if the therapist considered the therapy a success. Given the validity problems with the therapists' measure, such results suggest a fertile area of future investigation.

## REFERENCES

Bahrick, L. E., Parker, J. F., Fivush, R., & Levitt, M. (1998). The effects of stress on young children's memory for a natural disaster. *Journal of Experimental Psychology: Applied, 4*, 308–331.

Bosma, H., Stansfeld, S. A., & Marmot, M. G. (1998). Job control, personal characteristics, and heart disease. *Journal of Occupational Health Psychology, 3*, 402–409.

Chambless, D. L., Caputo, G. C., Bright, P., & Gallagher, R. (1984). Assessment of fear in agoraphobics: The Body Sensations Questionnaire and the Agoraphobic Cognitions Questionnaire. *Journal of Consulting and Clinical Psychology, 52*, 1090–1097.

Cohen, J. (1990). Things I have learned (so far). *American Psychologist, 45*, 1304–1312.

Cohen, J. (1994). The Earth is round ($p < .05$). *American Psychologist, 49*, 997–1003.

Dunlap, W. P. (1994). Generalizing the common language effect size indicator to bivariate normal distributions. *Psychological Bulletin, 116*, 509–513.

Feldt, L. S., Woodruff, D. J., & Salih, F. A. (1987). Statistical inference for coefficient alpha. *Applied Psychological Measurement, 11*, 93–103.

Frame, J. D. (1987). Managing projects in organizations. San Francisco, CA: Jossey-Bass.

Gigerenzer, G. (1993). The superego, the ego, and the id in statistical reasoning. In G. Keren & C. Lewis, (Eds.) *A handbook for data analysis in the behavioral sciences: Methodological issues* (pp. 311–339). Hillsdale, NJ: Lawrence Erlbaum Associates.

Goodman, S. N., & Royall, R. (1988). Evidence and scientific research. *American Journal of Public Health, 78*, 1568–1574.

Goodman, W. K., Price, L. H., Rasmussen, S. A., Mazure, C., Fleischmann, R. L., Hill, C. L., Heninger, G. R., & Charney, D. S. (1989a). The Yale–Brown obsessive compulsive scale: Part I. Development, use and reliability. *Archives of General Psychiatry, 46*, 1006–1011.

Goodman, W. K., Price, L. H., Rasmussen, S. A., Mazure, C., Fleischmann, R. L., Hill, C. L., Heninger, G. R., & Charney, D. S. (1989b). The Yale–Brown obsessive compulsive scale: Part II. Validity. *Archives of General Psychiatry, 46*, 1012–1016.

Greene, M. (1994, August). *Data coding.* Paper presented at Columbia Northwest Chapter, National Society for Performance and Instruction, Portland, OR.

Jacobson, N. S., & Truax, P. (1991). Clinical significance: A statistical approach to defining meaningful change in psychotherapy research. *Journal of Consulting and Clinical Psychology, 59*, 12–19.

Judd, C. M., McClelland, G. H., & Culhane, S. E. (1995). DATA ANALYSIS: Continuing issues in the everyday analysis of psychological data. *Annual Review of Psychology, 46*, 433–465.

Kluger, A. N., & Tikochinsky, J. (2001). The error of accepting the "theoretical" null hypothesis: The rise, fall, and resurrection of commonsense theories in psychology. *Psychological Bulletin, 127*, 408–423.

Loftus, G. R. (1996). Psychology will be a much better science when we change the way we analyze data. *Current Directions in Psychological Science, 5*, 161–170.

Marmot, M. G., Davey Smith, G., Stansfeld, S., Patel, C., North, F., Head, J., White, I., Brunner, E. J., & Feeney, A. (1991). Health inequalities among British civil servants: The Whitehall II study. *Lancet, 337*, 1387–1393.

McGraw, K. O., & Wong, S. P. (1992). A common language effect size statistic. *Psychological Bulletin, 111*, 361–365.

McGuire, W. C. (1997). Creative hypothesis generating in psychology: Some useful heuristics. *Annual Review of Psychology, 48*, 1–30.

*Oxford Dictionary of Quotations, 3rd Edition.* (1979). New York: Oxford University Press.

Prentice, D. A., & Miller, D. T. (1992). When small effects are impressive. *Psychological Bulletin, 112*, 160–164.

Rogers, J. L, Howard, K. I., & Vessey, J. T. (1993). Using significance tests to evaluate equivalence between two experimental groups. *Psychological Bulletin, 113*, 553–565.

Rosenthal, R. (1990). How are we doing in soft psychology? *American Psychologist, 45*, 775–776.

Rosenthal, R., & Rubin, D. B. (1982). A simple, general purpose display of magnitude of experimental effect. *Journal of Educational Psychology, 74*, 166–169.

Rosnow, R. L., & Rosenthal, R. (1989). Statistical procedures and the justification of knowledge in psychological science. *American Psychologist, 44*, 1276–1284.

Schmidt, F. L. (1992). What do data really mean? Research findings, meta-analysis, and cumulative knowledge in psychology. *American Psychologist, 47*, 1173–1181.

Schmidt, F. L., & Hunter, J. E. (1996). Measurement effects in psychological research: Lessons from 26 research scenarios. *Psychological Methods, 1*, 199–223.

Seligman, M. E. P. (1995). The effectiveness of psychotherapy: The *Consumer Reports* study. *American Psychologist, 50*, 965–974.

Warren, R., & Thomas, J. C. (2001). Cognitive-Behavior therapy of OCD in private practice. *Journal of Anxiety Disorders, 15*, 277–285.

Wilkinson, L., & the Task Force on Statistical Inference. (1999). Statistical methods in psychology journals: Guidelines and explanations. *American Psychologist, 54*, 594–604.

# IV

# Special Problems

# 13

# Effectiveness Versus Efficacy Studies

Paula Truax
Jay C. Thomas
*Pacific University, Forest Grove, Oregon*

Both the research and practice of clinical psychology have undergone dramatic changes throughout the last century. During the first half of the century, both psychotherapy and the concomitant effectiveness research were largely unstructured. Typically, diagnostic categories were unreliable; treatment strategies were poorly defined; measurements were not standardized, and subjects were not randomly assigned to treatment conditions. Although these early efforts to investigate the effectiveness of psychotherapy began a valued tradition of holding psychotherapists accountable for their outcomes, the lack of methodological rigor led to some discouraging conclusions about psychotherapy effectiveness. Hans Eysenck, a pioneer in psychotherapy outcome research, conducted two large-scale qualitative literature reviews in 1952 and 1960 in which he concluded that, with the exception of behavior therapy, psychotherapy adds little or nothing to the simple passage of time or treatment by a general medical practitioner (Eysenck, 1952). Not surprisingly, Eysenck's findings elicited a wave of concern in the psychological community about the validity of the research that led to these bleak conclusions. Of paramount concern was the fact that the vast majority of the reviewed studies had uncontrolled designs, weak methodology, ill-defined subject groups, insufficiently described treatments, unidimensional outcome measures, and no follow-up data. Critics of Eysenck's findings argued that the studies had such low internal validity that it would be impossible to conclude anything regarding the effectiveness of psychotherapy. This uprising catalyzed a movement toward efficacy studies focused on enhancing internal validity.

TABLE 13.1
Criteria for Empirically Validated Treatments: Well-Established Treatments

---

I. At least two good group design studies, conducted by different investigators, demonstrating
   efficacy in one or more of the following ways:
   A. Superior to pill or psychological placebo or to another treatment.
   B. Equivalent to an already established treatment in studies with adequate statistical power.
Or
II. A large series of single-case design studies demonstrating efficacy. These studies must have
   A. Used good experimental designs.
   B. Compared the intervention to another treatment as in I.A.
Further criteria for both I and II:
III. Studies must be conducted with treatment manuals.
IV. Characteristics of the client samples must be clearly specified.

---

*Source:* Division 12 Task Force, 1995, p. 21. (as cited in Nathan & Gorman, 1998).

During the 1970s and 1980s, randomized controlled clinical trials (RCTs) became state of the art. These studies were characterized by random assignment to conditions, blind pretest and posttest assessment, carefully defined subject groups, manualized treatments, multimodal standardized outcome assessments, and extensive follow-up data. By the early 1990s, a number of qualitative and quantitative reviews had established that psychotherapy was not only better than nothing (L. Luborsky, Singer, & L. Luborsky, 1975; Smith & Glass, 1977), but that some therapies were better than others (cf. Nathan & Gorman, 1998). As it became more apparent that not all therapy was equal for all problems, treatment guidelines began to develop. Prominent among these was the American Psychological Association's (APA) Division of Clinical Psychology Task Force development of criteria for classifying treatments as empirically validated treatments (EVTs; see Table 13.1; Division 12 Task Force, 1995). These guidelines emphasized the importance of an EVT having empirical support from well-controlled research designs that used treatment manuals and homogeneous samples. Within these guidelines was the implicit reminder that clinicians have an ethical responsibility to maximize the chances their clients will improve by using empirically supported treatments.

Although this movement toward uniform standards for establishing efficacy brought about important changes in the practice of psychotherapy, many believe that RCTs are poor analogues for real-world clinical practice. Clinicians are often faced with clients having complex problems, session limits, limited training opportunities, and a need for flexible interventions (Chorpita, Barlow, Albano, & Daleiden, 1998; Seligman, 1995). Although therapy's efficacy had been demonstrated repeatedly in the laboratory, questions were raised about therapy's effectiveness as it is conducted in the real world. These concerns prompted increased concern toward assessing the effectiveness of therapy as it is really practiced using heterogeneous samples, with realistic training requirements in actual clinical settings addressing questions that are of interest to clinicians. Proponents of effectiveness research as a follow up to well-controlled efficacy studies proposed revised practice guidelines that emphasized the importance of establishing the community feasibility, acceptability, effectiveness, and cost-effectiveness before they are classified as empirically supported (Chambless & Hollon, 1998). This movement has also been supported by the primary funding source for mental health research: the National Institute of Mental Health (NIMH). Until recently, the NIMH's Psychotherapy Treatment Research Program has funded primarily well-controlled clinical trials; however, its most recent focus has been a shift to funding and supporting effectiveness research (Street, Niederehe, & Lebowitz, 2000).

The methods just described have come to be known as *efficacy* and *effectiveness* research. Each places different emphasis on the importance of experimental control versus generalizability.

The goal of efficacy research is to establish cause and effect relationships between independent (e.g., intervention) and dependent variables (e.g., symptoms). To conclude that one variable (e.g., behavioral intervention for sleep) has actually caused a change in another variable (e.g., number of hours sleeping each night) requires special attention to experimental control or *internal validity*. The research must be conducted in such a way that the investigator can be reasonably certain that something else (e.g., antidepressant medication) did not bring about any observed changes in the targeted variable (e.g., sleep). Hence, both random error and systematic error must be minimized. This requires close control over subject groups, treatments, and assessments. The result, unfortunately, is that the findings may not generalize to the general client or clinician.

The goal of *effectiveness* research is to assess how well interventions work in the real world. With effectiveness research, there is a premium on the generalizability or the *external validity* of findings. The effectiveness researcher is invested in evaluating the impact of interventions in the community, thereby producing findings that will apply to real clients and therapists in real clinical settings. The trade off of reduced experimental control is increased variance and a reduced ability to test cause and effect relationships. The next section describes each in more detail. Later we show how a possible reapproachment can be accomplished.

## EFFICACY RESEARCH

### What is It?

John Stuart Mill (as cited in Cook, Campbell, & Peracchio, 1990), a mid-1800's philosopher, wrote that the more closely a hypothesis test meets the following three conditions, the more confidently cause and effect conclusions can be drawn: (1) covariation of independent and dependent variables; (2) time precedence of cause, and; (3) the presence of no other plausible alternative explanation. For example, if researchers wanted to know if a behavioral intervention for insomnia in depressed clients improved sleep, they would need to establish that increases in intervention intensity were associated with improvement in sleep (covariation). They would also want to demonstrate that improvement in sleep followed the treatment (time precedence of cause) and that no other treatment, life circumstance, mood change, bed change, room temperature change, pajama change, etcetera could account for the change in the number of hours slept. To this end, efficacy research requires that the treatment be potent and that random error and confounding variables be minimized.

To design an efficacy study, the researcher must first create a potent intervention, unpolluted by unintended factors. First, only therapists who believe in the research treatment should participate. Lack of allegiance to the research protocol may result in a less potent or competent intervention (Luborsky et al., 1999). Second, all therapists must be carefully trained to do exactly the same thing with each of their clients. This requires a detailed treatment manual, comprehensive training, and supervision. Finally, it must be determined that therapists are adhering to the manual and not inadvertantly inserting interventions from another protocol. This is typically done by having trained objective observers watch and code videotapes of sessions and evaluate adherence to the treatment protocol.

Next a homogeneous, well-defined subject group must be assembled. All members should be of similar age, gender, socioeconomic status, and ethnic identification. Similarly, all members should meet criteria only for the condition for which they are being treated. They also should not be participating in any other treatment at any point during their participation in the research project. This way, outcome results cannot be blurred by other problems or other treatments.

Subjects would then be randomly assigned to either the treatment or no treatment control group. The control group provides the necessary contrast to rule out rival plausible alternative explanations (Campbell & Stanley, 1963). The random assignment aims to equate the two groups so that and posttest differences can be attributed only to the research intervention. The presence of the control group allows the researcher to assess how the simple passage of time affects targeted symptoms. Without a control comparison, a researcher may erroneously conclude that a treatment had been effective when in fact subjects would have made the same progress due to maturation, history, regression toward the $M$ or simply participating in the pretest and posttest assessments.

Assessment should be accurate and unbiased. First, this requires using instruments that have demonstrated *reliability* and *validity*. That is, repeated administrations of the instrument will produce similar outcomes provided the measured variable is stable (reliability) and the instrument measures what it was designed to measure (validity). Second, any human raters involved should be blind to the conditions that subjects are assigned to because that knowledge could affect both intake and exit interviews.

In summary, necessity of establishing a cause and effect relationship in efficacy research requires that treatments, subjects, and instruments be as pure as possible so that covariation and time precedence of cause can be established while ruling out other plausible alternatives. A violation in even one area can draw any of these requirements into question.

### Defining an Example: The BICID Model

It may be easiest to understand these concepts in the context of an example. A recent research interest for both of the present authors has been to develop and test a behavioral intervention for depression with significant insomnia. Although empirically supported behavioral interventions exist for depression and for insomnia, they have not been formally combined or researched. For depression, one of the most effective and lasting interventions is behavioral activation (cf. Jacobson et al., 1996). For insomnia, the most effective and durable intervention in multiple studies is stimulus control (e.g., bed is associated only with sleep) combined with sleep hygiene (e.g., positive sleep habits; Morin, Culbert, & Schwartz, 1994). Although insomnia is often considered a symptom of depression that resolves with appropriate treatment of mood, thought, and activity, clinical observations combined with a literature review suggest that insomnia may contribute uniquely with the development, maintenance, and recurrence of depression. For example, insomnia is: (a) one of the most common symptoms of depression (Ohayon, Shapiro, & Kennedy, 2000); (b) often a precursor to recurrent episodes of depression (Perlis, Giles, Buysse, Tu, & Kupfer, 1997); (c) frequently remains a problem even when the depression is resolved (Breslau, Roth, Rosenthal, & Andreski, 1996); and (d) often interferes with behavioral treatment for depression because the client is too fatigued to engage in behavioral interventions. Traditionally, antidepressant medication has been the treatment of choice for depression with significant insomnia probably because even the most effective psychotherapies (e.g., cognitive behavioral therapy) have been less effective than medication at resolving insomnia (cf. Keller et al, 2000). This finding is not really surprising in light of the fact that current empirically supported psychotherapies for depression do not directly address insomnia. In an effort to improve treatment for depression with insomnia, we have developed a combination intervention entitled Behavioral Intervention for Combined Insomnia and Depression (BICID). Table 13.2 illustrates the interventions under independent variables and variables of interest under dependent variables. In the process of deciding on a research methodology to address these questions, we have had to carefully consider a variety of factors, including the importance of establishing causality,

TABLE 13.2
Hypothetical Behavioral Intervention for Combined Insomnia and
Depression (BICID)

---

*Independent Variables*
1. Stimulus control (i.e. subjects are not allowed to stay in bed longer than 15 minutes not sleeping in an effort to disassociate the bed with tossing and turning and reassociate the bed with sleep).
2. Sleep hygiene (i.e. subjects are encouraged to change sleep habits through avoiding alcohol and caffeine, establishing a regular bed and waking time, avoiding naps, avoiding sugar or heavy foods before bedtime, exercising moderately during the day and avoiding exercise 2–3 hours before bed, etc.)
3. Round the clock activity planning (i.e. subjects learn how to increase pleasurable and mastery activities while decreasing depressive activities through carefully planning their day-time and bed-time schedules)

*Dependent Variables*
1. Sleep efficiency (i.e. Number of hours asleep/number of hours in bed)
2. Depressed mood

---

the importance of generalizability, resources, and feasibility. These issues are addressed throughout this chapter in the context of both efficacy and effectiveness research.

## Efficacy Research and the BICID Model

If the primary goal of the study were to establish a causal relationship between BICID and the observed outcomes, we would want to rule out all possible alternative causes of change. This would require an efficacy study. First, we would need to define our research question. We would have to decide whether we wanted to know if BICID is better than nothing (no-treatment control group) or whether BICID is better than another treatment. Because research has already demonstrated that behavioral activation for depression and behavioral interventions for insomnia are individually better than a no-treatment control group, there would be little point in having a no-treatment control group for this study. Instead, we would probably want to choose an existing efficacious treatment, such as behavioral activation only, as our control group. The research question would then be: "Is the combination of behavioral interventions for insomnia and depression better than behavioral activation for depression alone?" Second, we would, develop detailed treatment manuals specifying the exact interventions, what portion of therapy should be spent on each one, and methods for deciding how to handle a variety of subject reactions and issues. Without this, our therapists may operate very differently from one another. Third, we would decide what variables we wanted to assess and select well-established reliable and valid measures. Problematic instruments could unnecessarily increase error variance and result in obscuring any findings. For this study, we might choose the Beck Depression Inventory-II (BDI-II; Beck,

Steer, & Brown, 1996) and the Structured Clinical Interview (SCID-1) for the DSM-IV (First, Spitzer, Gibbon, & Williams, 1997a) to assess depression and the Pittsburgh Sleep Quality Index (PSQI; Buysse, Reynolds, Monk, Berman, & Kupfer, 1989) to assess sleep variables. Fourth, we would define inclusion and exclusion criteria so that our sample would be pure. We would, for example, want to make sure that all subjects crossed a certain threshold for depression and insomnia symptoms and that other problems were ruled out (e.g. taking medication for a medical illness that reduces sleep, depression due to bereavement, anxiety disorders, alcohol, or drug use). We would also want to ensure that our subjects did not participate in other treatments while they were completing our treatment. Otherwise, any number of factors could affect depressed mood and insomnia other than our interventions. Fifth, these selected subjects would then be randomly assigned to the BICID group or the behavioral activation group. If nonrandom processes, such as subject choice or pre-exiting groups, were used (e.g., individuals at one clinic are used as the treatment group and individuals at another clinic are used as a control group), we could not be certain that our groups were not inherently different in ways that could have affected our outcome (e.g., income or severity). Sixth, our pretest and posttest interviewers would be blind to subjects' treatment conditions, thoroughly trained, and scrupulously monitored to ensure reliability and validity of the interviews. This way, we could assess the extent to which our interviewers were arriving at similar and unbiased conclusions. Finally, to confirm therapists' adherence to the treatment manual and their competence in the methodology, videotapes of treatment sessions would be coded. If, after carefully controlling all these variables, we observed that subjects in the BICID condition improved more than those in the behavioral activation condition, we could conclude that our interventions had been responsible (or caused) what we observed.

This example illustrates a glimmer of the complexity involved in an efficacy study. Yet, through the hard, conscientious work of many researchers, efficacy research has advanced the field of counseling and psychology far beyond the early attempts to demonstrate that psychotherapy had something to offer.

### What Has Efficacy Research Done for Us?

Efficacy research using RCTs has significantly increased the credibility of clinical psychology. Prior to this research, there was a great deal of skepticism about the efficacy of psychological interventions. Following several decades of efficacy research, clinicians and consumers can both confidently conclude that some psychotherapeutic interventions are effective for some problems. Although a comprehensive review of empirically supported interventions is beyond the scope of this chapter, a few notable examples follow (see Nathan & Gorman, 1998, for a comprehensive review). Cognitive behavioral therapy (CBT) for depression, for example, has been repeatedly demonstrated to produce recovery rates between 53% and 83% (W. E. Craighead, L. W. Craighead, & Ilardi, 1998). Likewise, CBT including exposure to feared stimuli has been shown to be more effective than other interventions for anxiety disorders in numerous clinical trials (Barlow, Esler, & Vitali, 1998). In Panic Disorder, for example, approximately 81% to 87% are panic-free after CBT, including exposure to feared physiological symptoms (Barlow et al., 1998). Conduct disordered children appear to benefit more from behavioral interventions than nonbehavioral interventions for both internalizing and externalizing concerns (Weisz, Weiss, Han, Granger, & Morton, 1995).

Along with the simple knowledge of what treatments work the best for which problems has come a number of additional improvements that have changed the practice of clinical psychology. Some of these include refinement of diagnostic categories and assessment as well as the production and dissemination of manualized treatments.

### Problems With Efficacy Research

Although clinical psychology owes a great debt to the efficacy research revolution, many have become increasingly concerned about the generalizability of efficacy research to the real clinical setting (cf. Stricker, 2000). These concerns have typically focused on differences between research and community therapists, clients, settings, and questions of interest. As a result, clinicians have tended to not read or apply research findings in their clinical practices.

*Therapists.* A growing body literature suggests that the majority of community therapists rarely conduct treatment exactly according to any particular treatment manual (Kendall & Chu, 2000). According to Addis and colleagues (Addis, Wade, & Hatgis, 1999), the six most commonly reported reasons for therapists not conducting therapy according to manuals are: (1) a lack of focus on the therapeutic relationship, (2) inadequate attention to client needs, (3) feeling incompetent to conduct manualized treatments, (4) believing that they are already doing effective therapy and do not need to learn new methods, (5) fears about the affects of manuals on dictating practice and reducing clinical innovation, and (6) concerns about feasibility. Instead, therapists report that when they begin with a treatment manual, they use it flexibly to address their assessments of clients' concerns. They may, for example, change the length of treatment, add or subtract different empirically supported interventions, add nonempirically supported interventions, or combine interventions from more than one treatment manual (Clarke, 1995). They may also collaborate with a number of treatment providers (e.g. physicians, psychiatrists, psychologists, occupational therapists, etc.). Community therapists usually do not have the same access to training and supervision that research therapists have. Researchers in efficacy studies often spend 8 to 20 hr training their therapists with one treatment manual for one type of clients. They also have regular clinical supervision ranging from 2 to 8 hr per month. Community therapists often do not have time or financial resources to gain extensive training in all of the treatment manuals they would need to sufficiently address the needs of their varied caseloads. Regular supervision focused on mastering one particular type of therapy is also rare in community settings.

*Clients.* Inherent in many clinicians' concerns is that fact that research subjects are often not representative of the clinical population (Goldfried & Wolfe, 1996). The typical treatment outcome efficacy study excludes as many as 50% to 60% of those who express interest in the study due either to lack of interest in study procedures on the potential subject's part (Hofmann et al., 1998), or to the client not meeting the narrow diagnostic criteria (Haberfellner, 2000; Humphreys & Weisner, 2000; Mitchell, Maki, Adson, Ruskin, & Crow, 1997; Schneider, Olin, Lyness, & Chui, 1997). These findings suggest that efficacy studies may generalize to only a minority of actual clients. Community clients are likely to be more severe, have more comorbid diagnoses, have more personality disorders, tend to be lower income, and are more often from minority populations (cf. Matt & Navarro, 1997). Not surprisingly, the variables that separate research and community populations are also the variables most often associated with negative psychotherapeutic outcomes (Brent, Kolko, Birmaher, Baugher, & Bridge, 1999; Hirschfeld, et al., 1998; Mynors-Wallis, & Gath, 1997; Shea et al., 1990). These findings suggest that clinicians' concerns about the generalizability of efficacy research to the real clinical setting may be well founded.

*Settings.* The research setting itself may also set treatments delivered in efficacy studies apart from real practice. Recruitment, random assignment, fee schedules, expectations regarding research, contact with a variety of members of a research team, and facilities may all affect outcomes in treatment outcome studies. First, subject recruitment does not mirror the way that average clients seek services. Subject recruitment usually involves subjects responding by phone to newspaper advertisements for subjects. In contrast, regular clinic clients call a clinic to make an appointment when their distress has escalated to a point that they feel they need help. It may be speculated that the distress threshold that leads to the call is higher for the regular clinic client than the research subject. The research subject called because they were "interested," whereas the clinic client called because they were "distressed." Second, the way subjects are assigned to therapy in a research study differs from assignment to a therapist in the community. By definition, research subjects in RCTs are randomly assigned to treatment. This means that participating subjects agree at the outset that they are willing to let someone else decide the identity of their therapist and the type of treatment they will receive. Community clients often shop carefully for a therapist and choose a therapist based on comfort and agreement with the therapist's philosophy. If the study involves a control group, all subjects must agree that they are willing to take the chance that they will not receive any treatment at all for a period of time. Again, it could be argued that only subjects who are less distressed would be willing to take a chance that their therapy would be delayed. Third, treatment in research studies is usually very low cost or free of charge to participants. Clinic clients either pay for service or have insurance that covers some or all of the cost for a limited number of sessions. The number of sessions in most research protocols (e.g., 12 to 20 sessions) often exceeds contemporary sessions limits (e.g., 8 to 10 sessions). The result is that research subjects can usually be guaranteed that they will have the financial resources to complete the treatment protocol. Clinic clients may run out of sessions or money before treatment is complete. Fourth, subjects may be influenced by the implicit expectations of the researchers skewing either actual or reported outcomes. An interesting study by Norenzayan and Schwarz (1999) gave two groups of research participants identical paper and pencil instruments regarding explanations for a mass murder. The only difference between the two groups was the letterhead; one group had Institute of Social Research and the other had Institute for Personality Research. Both groups gave significantly different responses to questions skewed in the direction of the department in which they thought the study was being held. Thus, subjects in research studies may be motivated to tell researchers what they want to hear. If they know they are in a study for a depression and insomnia treatment project, they may want to show the researcher that they can get less depressed. Community clients often do not have similar specific expectations that may affect their responses to outcome questionnaires. Fifth, research participants often have contact with more than one member of a research team. They often participate in a phone screening with one person, an interview with a second person, therapy with a third person, and follow-up interviews with additional people. This dilution of allegiance may affect a subject's investment and potential for attrition differentially from the clinic client who has contact with only one therapist. Finally, the setting itself is often different between research and community settings. Often, research subjects come to a university for some or all of their assessment and treatment. Simply being in a university setting may affect the way the subjects feel about the quality and scientific validity of their treatment. In sum, research settings are significantly different from community settings in important ways that may differentially affect outcome.

***Questions of Interest.*** Not only are the therapists, clients, and settings different, the questions addressed by researchers may not be questions of interest to the stakeholders in clinical practice (Clarke, 1995). Newman & Tejeda (1996) pointed to four groups of stakeholders: consumers, practitioners, service managers, and policymakers. Each of these stakeholders has unique interests in the practice of psychotherapy. Consumers are concerned with the cost and the effect on functioning. Practitioners and service managers want to know which interventions will be most effective with which clients, given the resources available, and policymakers want to know which interventions are feasible and effective for different population groups. Treatment outcome research typically does not deal with the questions of special interest to these groups, particularly issues regarding (a) how to increase cost-effectiveness; (b) how to deal with session limits; (c) how to best intervene with comorbid client diagnoses; (d) how to best coordinate and combine care modalities (e.g., psychologists, occupational therapists, etc.); and (e) how to best coordinate client wishes into treatment planning. Newman and Tejeda (1996) noted that efficacy research has generally done a poor job of addressing these questions. Instead, efficacy research tends to focus more on theoretical questions (e.g., cognitive vs. behavioral; family vs. individual intervention) that may have more academic than practical appeal.

***Clinicians Do Not Read Efficacy Research.*** Given the lack of correspondence between research and clinical practice, it is perhaps no surprise that clinicians often do not read efficacy research (Nathan, 2000). It seems that clinicians may feel that efficacy research has little to offer them and that researchers do not have the interests of the practicing clinician at the forefront of their decision making (Addis et al., 1999). One researcher even proposed that "there appears to be an inverse relationship between the frequency with which a treatment form is actually used by practitioners and the frequency with which that treatment has been studied" (Parloff, 1979, p. 304).

***Clinicians Are Affected by Efficacy Research.*** Despite the facts that efficacy research may be a poor analogue for real practice and that clinicians do not read efficacy research, the results of efficacy research may have a profound impact on the practices of community clinicians (Goldfried & Wolfe, 1996). This is particularly true within the world of managed care, where cost effectiveness is paramount. Frances (1994) predicted that "Within this decade, most real-world psychotherapy will be based on treatment manuals that are adaptations of those that have been prepared for research studies" (p. 279). In some managed care organizations, therapists who use empirically supported interventions are more likely to get contracts or be invited to join panels than those who do not. Likewise, compared to therapists who do not focus on empirically supported treatments, therapists who use empirically supported approaches may be more likely to get extensions on requests for sessions that exceed the session limits. Additionally, managed-care's definition of session limits has also been defined, in part, by efficacy research that suggests that 50% of clients will make most of their progress in the first eight sessions (Howard, Kopta, Krause, & Orlinsky, 1986). Unfortunately, half of the clients seeking services will not fall into this category, yet community clinicians must find a way to provide effective care to all of their clients.

***Efficacy Research is Impractical.*** Because of the experimental rigor, efficacy research can also be impractical. Efficacy research is both time consuming and expensive. Typically, researchers will devote 50% to 100% of their time toward designing, implementing, and seeking funding for a single efficacy study. The budget for large-scale RCTs with adequate power may easily exceed 1 million dollars. When one considers the sum spent across studies combined with the fact that some of this research may not address questions of relevance to either improving care or reducing this yearly figure, the amounts are daunting. The advent of managed care in the last 10 years has further catalyzed the need to bridge the gap between efficacy and clinical practice. As clinicians are forced to do more with less, the need to have clinically relevant research has also increased. Properly done efficacy research requires skills and resources that only clinicians who specialize in research can bring; this creates a situation in which practicing clinicians find it difficult to make meaningful contributions to the research literature. This combination of factors has led to a new and growing movement toward effectiveness research.

## EFFECTIVENESS RESEARCH

### What is Effectiveness Research?

Effectiveness research is differentiated from efficacy research by its focus on external rather than internal validity. Where efficacy research puts a premium on experimental control, effectiveness research emphasizes generalizability. The primary question vexing effectiveness researchers is: How well does this treatment work in the real world? Effectiveness research may use broader subject inclusion criteria to allow for a more heterogeneous sample. Real clinic therapists may be used with training and supervision that are more typical or feasible for practicing clinicians. Assessment procedures may also be briefer and more similar, in terms of time and effort, to actual clinical assessment. Therapists may be given more choices about how to apply treatment manuals so that the study treatment can more closely mimic how therapy is actually done. Treatments and assessments may be conducted in real clinical settings rather than laboratories, addressing questions that take all stakeholders into account while aiming to improve the effectiveness and efficiency of client care.

## Balancing Internal and External Validity

Although pure generalizability is a seductive goal, the price of increasing generalizability is usually a reduction in experimental control and loss of internal validity. Such reduction leaves the researcher open for concerns that the targeted treatment may not have actually brought about the observed outcome. Instead, any positive, neutral, or negative findings can easily be attributed to uncontrolled variables. Although establishing a cause and effect relationship may be less important in studies that are verifying the effectiveness of treatment already deemed efficacious in previous research, attention to internal validity remains of concern.

One of the earliest high profile effectiveness studies generated significant controversy about the balance between internal and external validity. Martin Seligman (1995) reviewed a retrospective *Consumer Reports* (CR) survey of their readers' opinions about psychotherapy. CR received 20,000 surveys back from 180,000 originally mailed; 7,000 answered mental health questions, and 2,900 had actually seen a mental health professional. Survey respondents answered a number of questions about their experiences including what kind of therapy they had, how long it lasted, specific and global improvement, as well as satisfaction. The findings in this survey study suggested that clients benefited from therapy, but that long-term therapy was more effective than short-term therapy. Medication did not appear to enhance psychotherapeutic outcomes and no psychotherapeutic orientation outperformed any other. Although this study may characterize the epitome of generalizability (i.e., real therapists, real clients, real clinics, flexible treatments, real assessments), numerous critics asserted that the internal validity of the study was insufficient to conclude anything. Jacobson and Christensen (1996) stated that the CR study is:

> similar in many ways to H. J. Eysenck's (1952) controversial report on the effectiveness of psychotherapy, a study that has been rejected by the field despite the fact that it avoided some of the methodological shortcomings of the CR study. It would be a mistake to put forth a design rejected the in the 1950s as an exemplar of good effectiveness research, especially when better alternatives exist. (p. 1031)

Some of the problems that Jacobson and Christensen (1996) emphasized were the unreliability of retrospective data, the unrepresentative sample that returned the survey, the absence of a control group, and the use of unreliable instruments.

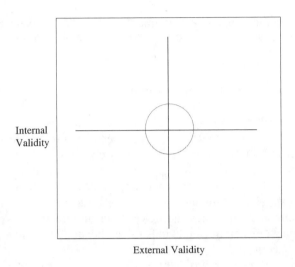

FIG. 13.1. Theoretical depiction of the relationship between internal and external validity in effectiveness and efficacy research.

The argument surrounding the balance between internal and external validity is much like the issue of reliability and validity for outcome instruments. An instrument must be reliable (i.e., yield the same result on repeated applications for a stable variable) before the issue of validity (i.e., the instrument is measuring what it was designed to measure) can be established. Similarly, adequate internal validity is a necessary but not sufficient condition for establishing external validity. That is, you must be able to conclude with reasonable certainty that your independent variable was responsible for the observed change in the dependent variables before there is anything worthwhile to generalize to the population at large. Good effectiveness research simultaneously maximizes both external and internal validity (Hoagwood, Hibbs, Brent, & Jensen, 1995). Stricker (2000) pointed out, however, the relationship between internal and external validity is orthogonal. As one increases, the other decreases (see Fig. 13.1). Ideally, each would reach the highest level possible without appreciably diminishing the other. Methods for balancing control and generalizability for effectiveness research are addressed now for sampling, assessment, treatment, design, data analyses, and research questions as they apply to effectiveness research.

### Sampling

Generalizability can be maximized through recruiting a representative sample from the targeted population. This requires knowledge of the pertinent variables in this targeted population, and sufficiently broad inclusion criteria to avoid unnecessarily excluding representative members. It also requires recruitment procedures that successfully capture this group. If, for the BICID study (see Table 13.2), our goal was to generalize the findings to adult community mental health outpatients, the inclusion criteria should accurately reflect the community clients with whom clinicians would use this intervention. Because community outpatient clients vary substantially in the severity, comorbidity, and concomitant treatments, clients should not be excluded on this basis. Instead, inclusion criteria may mirror the same issues that would influence a community clinician's choice to use BICID with their clients. Because clinicians typically treat the primary presenting concern first (Oxman, 1997), inclusion criteria for the effectiveness study may be simply depressed mood and insomnia as primary presenting concerns. Individuals would only be excluded if they had a competing condition that would make them unlikely to benefit from the intervention. Hence the effectiveness sample would have ample variability in severity and comorbidity. Recruitment should then take place in the community outpatient setting and may involve direct referrals from clinicians or study advertisements in the agencies themselves.

Although this method may produce a representative sample, the substantial variability may obscure any meaningful findings. Hence, internal validity may be enhanced through careful assessment of all variables likely to have a substantial impact on outcome (e.g., severity, comorbidity, chronicity, ethnicity, socioeconomic status). This way, the relative contribution of these variables can be addressed in regression or factorial models in the data analysis phase. Clarke (1995) described a sampling method for effectiveness research that he called the "donut model" (Clarke, 1995). Although a broad group of subjects is recruited, those subjects who represent pure cases (the donut hole) are used to address the efficacy questions while the more heterogeneous clients (the outer donut) are used to assess the effectiveness of the interventions. He also suggests comparing the outcome for these two groups in factorial analysis models. Sampling models such as these allow researchers to preserve internal validity while simultaneously addressing questions of generalizability. The outer ring also serves as a form of cross-validation for the results of the donut hole sample.

## Assessment

Outcome research relies on accurate assessment of outcomes and moderators. In efficacy research, such assessment has typically involved long interviews and questionnaire batteries at the beginning and end of treatment, as well as progress assessment throughout treatment. Although these assessments are often central to investigating important research questions, some research suggests that assessment alone changes the course of therapy (Ahava, Iannone, Grebstein, & Schirling, 1998; Sharpe & Gilbert, 1998). Community clinicians and agencies rarely perform such comprehensive assessments because they are often not feasible or relevant for clinical decision making. Thus, an efficacy study that couples a manualized treatment with a large battery of instruments may be essentially testing a different therapy than the one used in practice. Effectiveness researchers have the delicate task of balancing adequate measurement with feasibility, so the research methods can be mirrored in practice.

To satisfy research goals, effectiveness research should be based on established normed, reliable, and valid instruments. The instruments should be established and in common use, so the samples and findings of the effectiveness study can be compared to efficacy studies and other research. Instruments should be reliable and valid to prevent random noise in a study that is already fraught with a myriad of uncontrolled variables.

To address the needs of clinicians and clients, the need for comprehensive assessment should be balanced with the need for brevity and utility. This balance can be achieved by leanly targeting the assessed variables, and then choosing instruments and assessment schedules that adequately address these variables briefly. The first step in pairing down the assessment time is prudently choosing the variables to be assessed. While any number of variables may be interesting, the question in effectiveness research is, "What variables are necessary to address the research questions?" (e.g., severity, comorbidity, concomitant treatment, chronicity, ethnicity, socioeconomic status). The effectiveness researcher should conscientiously "trim the fat" and not fall prey to the temptation to throw in just one more questionnaire to "see what happens." Instead, efficient measures that adequately assess the variables should be used. Multiscale instruments may be used, for example, in the place of separate questionnaires for several related variables. The Brief Symptom Inventory (BSI; Derogatis, 1993a) is an example of one such instrument. It marries comprehensiveness (10 subscales of psychiatric symptomology, and a summary score of overall distress), frequent use (Derogatis, 1993b), and good reliability and validity (Derogatis, 1993a), with brevity (53 items). Likewise, briefer or more clinician-friendly versions of measurements may be substituted for their longer versions. Many well-known instruments have briefer versions with good psychometric properties. The SCID-CV (First et al., 1997b) may be used in place of the much longer, more cumbersome research version of the SCID. Similarly, instruments like the BDI-II (Beck et al., 1996) and the 36-item measure of physical and psychological health [SF-36]; Ware, Snow, Kosinski, & Gandek, 1993) have well-researched brief versions: Beck Depression Inventory-Short Form (BDI-SF; A. T. Beck & R. W. Beck, 1972) and SF-12 (Ware, Kosinski, & Keller, 1995), respectively. The administration schedule can also be calibrated to maximize generalizability and internal validity. For example, longer assessment batteries may precede and follow treatment, whereas short forms of established instruments may be used to assess therapeutic progress at each session.

Assessment should be clinically useful. Assessment should target variables of interest to clients and therapists and the data from the instruments should be available to them. This may be accomplished by having automatic computer scoring readily available or by using instruments that are easily hand scored by the client or therapist. The therapist and client can then use these data to guide treatment decisions according to the manual. Although some may argue that incorporating the results of assessments into treatment would change the treatment and possibly the accuracy of the assessment, it may also be argued that the generalization of a scientific method to the clinical setting requires data-driven decisions. Many empirically supported treatment manuals already include the ongoing use of instruments in implementing therapy (c.f. Beck, Rush, Shaw, & Emery, 1979).

If, for the BICID study, we were conducting our research in a real clinical setting, the brevity and clinical utility of the assessments would need to be improved while maintaining adequate reliability and validity. This may be accomplished through using the more extensive instruments before and after therapy with briefer more clinically useful measurements used on a session by session basis. At pretest and posttest, we may consider using the SCID-CV rather than the research version of the SCID to assess depression diagnosis. We may also assess pre- and postdepression and sleep severity with the 21-item BDI-II and the 19-item PSQI, respectively. On a weekly basis, we could assess depression severity with the 13-item BDI-SF, while monitoring sleep variables with the brief, more clinically useful Sleep Diary (cf. Coates et al., 1982) in which clients track variables related to time in bed and time asleep. All of these instruments are easily and quickly scored by hand and are designed to provide clinically useful information.

## Treatment

As noted earlier, the treatments used in efficacy research do not generalize well to practice. Therapists in efficacy research are often advanced clinical psychology students with extensive initial and ongoing training in the methods of a heavily structured treatment manual. Effectiveness research may enhance its generalizability by using real community therapists to conduct the interventions. These therapists may participate in training and supervision similar to what therapists in the community could actually do if they were to implement the therapy. Training may, for example, be held in two 4-hour workshops, for which participants could earn continuing education credit. Therapists could then be given the manual to use with clients who have been designated as subjects and be encouraged to phone the investigator as they have questions. In order to preserve the internal validity of the study, assessment of adherence would also be essential. The therapists could be instructed to tape their sessions with clients and forward the tapes to the investigator. The investigator would then assess the extent to which the therapists adhered to the manual. The outcome results of the therapists who adhered carefully to the manual versus those with more deviations could be examined in a model analogous to Clarke's (1995) donut model for homogeneous versus heterogeneous subjects. Therapists who adhered carefully would represent the donut hole, whereas those who more flexibly applied the manual would represent the outer ring.

## Designs

One of the major challenges facing effectiveness researchers is finding a design that balances internal and external validity. One of the most important factors in establishing internal validity is some assurance that extraneous variables, such as time, maturation, history, testing, etcetera, do not better account for your observed outcomes than your targeted intervention. Control groups are usually used to address this concern. If your treated group performs better than the control group, you can assume that it is more likely your treatment produced the effect than the extraneous variables (both the treated and control groups should be equally affected by these). Without a control group, you can never be sure that something else, like the passage of time, may not have accounted for the observed outcome. However, in practice, control groups are not used. In fact, many researchers have pointed to the fact that they may be unethical (Schwartz, Chesney, Irvine, & Keefe, 1997). Several alternatives to the no treatment control include control groups from other studies, an extended baseline, treatment-as-usual control groups, other treatment comparisons, and quasiexperimental designs.

One substitute for the use of control groups in real clinical settings involves using control group data that has already been collected in previous studies. With the plethora of studies employing RCTs over the last several decades, many control group data already exist. In this design, the outcome for a control group that closely matched the demographic and clinical features as well as the time frame would be compared to the outcome of your treatment group. The primary advantages of this design are that the ethical risks and expense of having a control group are eliminated; all participants receive the active treatment. The most glaring disadvantage is that one can never be sure that the control group is representative of the targeted population. Given that most RCTs used very homogeneous samples, it may be exceptionally difficult to find a control group that matches the clinical or demographic characteristics of a more heterogeneous effectiveness treatment sample.

Another alternative is to have individuals serve as their own control by collecting extended baseline data on a sample that will later participate in your intervention. This type of model works best in a setting such a staff-model health maintenance organization (HMO), where regular health and mental health data are routinely collected on all beneficiaries. Thus, data regarding mental health will be available at the outset of the study and will not need to be collected after the study has begun. If, for example, an individual who has been depressed without relief for 2 years significantly improves in the course of your 2-month intervention, you may assume with some certainty that the intervention contributed to this improvement. Distinct advantages to this model include the fact that you know your control group is similar to the sample (because they are the same people). The long baseline also helps control for some threats to internal validity such as history and maturation. The primary downside to this model is that it may be difficult to find a site to conduct research that has systematically collected such data. In such cases, a satisfactory alternative may be to establish a retrospective baseline based on client's self-report with an instrument such as the Longitudinal Interval Follow-Up Evaluation (LIFE; Keller et al., 1987) designed to assess the longitudinal course of Axis I disorders. Other disadvantages involve the difficulty in assessing the impact of the treatment on episodic disorders, such as Major Depressive Disorder, Recurrent.

Because one of the goals of effectiveness research is to assess relative superiority of new treatments over current methods, treatment-as-usual (TAU) control groups have recently increased in popularity (Clarke, 1995). In this model, the treatment group receives the novel intervention and the control group receives treatment as it would usually be given. This model has at least two important advantages over other control group models. First, there are no ethical concerns that some portion of your sample may not be getting adequate care. Second, the question is addressed of whether the novel treatment really has any advantage over regular treatment. The primary disadvantage is that TAU varies widely and it may be difficult to assess exactly what kind of care the control group is receiving. Assessment of the interventions that comprise the TAU is essential, because it is always possible that some members in your TAU group are receiving some or all of the novel intervention. Such a study would usually require the participation of all of the TAU providers because they will typically be better equipped to describe their interventions than the clients.

A related alternative is to compare the novel intervention with an empirically supported intervention. In the case of the BICID study, BICID may be compared with an antidepressant medication called nefazadone, which has been repeatedly shown to significantly improve both depression and sleep (cf. Keller et al, 2000). This method has the ethical advantage of ensuring that all participants are receiving effective interventions. It also allows investigators to assess whether the new intervention adds anything to other effective interventions. The greatest disadvantage to this type of research is that the vast majority of studies comparing two effective interventions have found no difference between the two conditions. Although anecdotal reports and occasional predictive measures suggest that the interventions are differentially effective for different clients, there is little robust evidence to support these claims.

A quasiexperimental design involving naturally occurring groups may also be used as an alternative to the RCT. This design uses two similar groups in similar settings and does not randomize people to conditions. If you wanted to test the BICID treatment in college students, you may administer the intervention to all people in one dorm complaining of depression and sleep problems, whereas those in another dorm meeting the same description would simply complete assessments. The most significant concerns about quasiexperimental models are ethical because one group does not receive treatment. There is also uncertainty about actual similarity of the groups.

Perhaps the simplest alternative is to verify effectiveness using a series of single-subject studies (see chap. 7, this volume). Depending on the degree of control in the hand of the research, such designs may be considered true experiments or quasiexperiments. For the BICID study, a practical and ethical option may be to begin with some single case studies. This would provide the opportunity to verify that the treatment can be implemented as planned while gaining an indication of its effectiveness. Later, if results appear promising, resource intensive efficacy studies could be conducted, followed by further effectiveness studies as needed.

### Addressing Effectiveness Questions

One of the major obstacles to bridging the gap between research and practice is that the questions of interest to academicians may not be those of interest to clients, clinicians, or policymakers. In order for research to generalize to practice, the questions addressed must hold some practical interest for those using it. Newman and Tejeda (1996) outlined four foci for conducting applicable clinical research: (1) efficacy and effectiveness research in assessing cost effectiveness, (2) differential effectiveness of different interventions with different clients, (3) behavioral outcome data, and (4) dissemination of findings to all the stakeholders in clinical care. Each of these areas will now be addressed.

*Cost Effectiveness.* Cost effectiveness is one of the most powerful underlying forces in developing policies at the macrolevel and making treatment decisions at the microlevel. Regardless of an intervention's effectiveness, it is of very little worth if it cannot be conducted within cost constraints. Take substance abuse treatment, for example; although lifetime institutionalization of substance abusers would probably increase abstinence and reduce relapse more effectively than other interventions, the cost would be prohibitive. Despite frequent calls for these data, little is known.

Assessment of cost effectiveness is more complex than it may immediately appear. Although a detailed description of cost-effectiveness analysis is beyond the scope of this chapter, some of the variables to be considered are discussed here. At the most basic level, cost effectiveness involves the interaction between

TABLE 13.3

Hypothetical Cost-Effectiveness Data for Four Depressed Clients

---

*Group Therapy Cost*
- In-session hours: 12 two-hour group sessions = 24
- Out-of-session hours: 4 hours to set up the group + 6 hours to follow-up on no shows + 12 hours total for paperwork and preparation = 22
- Revenue: $40/client/session × 12 sessions × 4 clients = $1920
- Amount paid to therapist per hour: $41.74
- Number of therapist hours used (in-session hours + out-session hours): 46

*Individual Therapy Cost*
- In-session hours: 4 clients × 12 one-hour individual sessions = 48
- Out-of-session hours: 1 hour to set up initial appointments + 3 hours to follow-up on no shows + 8 hours total for paperwork and preparation = 12
- Revenue: $80/client/session × 12 sessions × 4 clients = $3840
- Amount paid to therapist per hour: $64.00
- Number of therapist hours used (in-session hours + out-session hours): 60

---

*Note:* The amounts paid the therapists for individual and group therapy are based on a national managed care company's (Mental Health Network, 2001) maximum allowable charge for Ph.D. licensed psychologists in Portland, OR. The amounts of out-of-session hours are estimated based on the first author's (P. T.) clinical experience in conducting individual and group therapy.

the treatment cost and the treatment outcome. Antonuccio, Thomas, & Danton (1997) pointed out that although cost of treatment includes the most obvious components of cost per unit (e.g., sessions) multiplied by the number of units used, one must also consider the amount of time that treatment takes a client away from work, home, or community service. A service that is cheap but very time consuming may not be more cost effective for an individual who has to take significant time out of work to participate. Similarly, the cost of treatment involves cost to the therapist, agency, managed care organization, or insurance company, as well. The amount of time spent arranging appointments, preparing for sessions, completing paperwork, and following up on no-shows may significantly affect the cost effectiveness of therapy. In group therapy, for example, sessions are usually longer (2 hours as opposed to 1 hour individual), insurance payments are usually less, and more out-of-session time is used per in-session hour than for individual therapy. Group therapy may result in unintended costs for both the provider and the client.

If for the BICID study, we compared group and individual applications of the interventions to assess cost effectiveness, we would need to evaluate the base cost, number of hours used by the therapists, and number of hours used by the client, as well as attrition and effectiveness. Review the following hypothetical data in Table 13.3 for four clients in individual or group BICID therapy to see how the initial cost figures may be misleading. At first blush, it appears that group therapy takes up half the provider's time (24 hours) than individual therapy does (48 hours) for four clients participating in 12 sessions of therapy. However, when one considers that the therapist may spend four times the amount of time setting up the group, twice the amount of time following up on no-shows, and $\frac{1}{3}$ more time preparing for the group, the hours saved dwindles to less than 25%. The amount of money saved also decreases from 50% to 35%. Although these 25% timesavings and 35% cost savings may be enough to claim that group therapy is cheaper than individual therapy, those savings may be further diminished if recovery is lower, or attrition or relapse is higher in the group than in individual therapy.

For clients who are employed, another pertinent factor is the cost to the client in terms of hours and fees. Clients who earn $20 an hour, lose $40 in wages each time they attend group; whereas, they lose only $20 when they attend individual therapy. The wages lost combined with amount spent for therapy, in this case would be $80 for group and $100 for individual therapy. Consumers who thought they were saving 50% by attending group may actually be saving much less.

***Differential Effectiveness.***   Clinicians are faced with daily decisions about how to treat individual clients. Efficacy research has provided information about how treatment packages work with large groups of clients, but has provided information of limited utility about how different interventions work with different clients. Group design comparisons with homogeneous populations have typically found that competing treatment conditions do not produce group differences (cf. Elkin et al., 1989); however, some efficacy research has begun to address some questions of differential effectiveness. Much of this research has aimed to identify differential response to ESTs. For depression, for example, severity (Brent et al., 1999; Hirschfeld et al., 1998), chronicity (Mynors-Wallis, & Gath, 1997), perfectionism (Blatt, 1995) comorbid Axis I disorders (Brent et al., 1999), and comorbid Axis II disorders or traits (Hirschfeld et al., 1998; Shea et al., 1990) have predicted poorer response to treatment. Although these findings may alert a clinician to factors that may require different, longer, or more intense interventions, information on how to best treat these intractable cases is slim.

Some research has also attempted to address the question of which interventions work best for which clients. One of the most comprehensive attempts to identify differential effectiveness has been the National Institute of Mental Health's (NIMH) Treatment of Depression Collaborative Research Program (TDCRP) multisite RCT (Elkin et al., 1989). In this study, 250 subjects were randomly assigned to CBT, interpersonal therapy (IPT), medication only (imipramine), or a medication placebo. Although the investigators found that overall there was no difference between the active treatment conditions for a reduction in depression severity, they did find that different subjects responded differently to different interventions (Elkin, Gibbons, Shea, & Shaw,

1996; Elkin et al, 1989). The most severely depressed clients most effectively improved their depression in the medication only and IPT conditions (Elkin et al., 1989). Those with the less social dysfunction did best in IPT; those with less severe dysfunctional beliefs did best in CBT (Sotsky et al., 1991). Those with personality disorders tended to improve most in the CBT condition relative to other active conditions (Shea et al., 1990). Atypical depression features (i.e., sleeping more, eating more, hypersensitive to interpersonal events) led to inferior response in the medication condition (Stewart, Garfinkel, Nunes, Donovan, & Klein, 1998).

Although these findings offer a brief sampling of important attempts to identify predictors of differential responses to different treatments, they leave many unanswered questions for clinicians. Although they may provide some clues about how to choose among interventions for homogeneous clients, they provide little information for how to choose interventions for clients with multiple problems. Even with homogeneous clients, these findings are of limited clinical utility. First, these findings provide few clues about which of the predictors are most important in choosing a treatment direction. Second, multiple instruments are often used across studies to define these predictors. Such instruments are usually neither feasible nor available for average clinicians in defining these predictors. Little is known about how less formal methods for defining these predictors compare to standardized assessment. Third, a related problem is that even when clinicians can duplicate the assessments, these studies provide inadequate information about how to actually use the scores on these instruments. How does one decide, for example, whether someone is adequately severe to warrant encouragement for medication over CBT? Finally, even with adequate measurement, a statistically significant amount of variance accounted for by any predictor often does not exceed 20% to 30%. This leaves a huge number of potentially important variables that are unaccounted.

Many researchers have suggested that a significant proportion of the variance unaccounted for by specific therapy procedures and client variables is contained within the therapeutic relationship and client expectations (see review by Prochaska & Norcross, 1999). These findings point to an inherent problem in attempting to generalize findings from an RCT to a real clinical setting. In a RCT, participating subjects have agreed to let someone else decide what therapy they will receive. In real clinical settings, clients and clinicians decide reciprocally how to proceed in therapy. This decision-making process may involve some combination of client beliefs about what will be helpful and clinician beliefs and expertise. This decision-making process may, in fact, be very important to the client's expectations and the therapeutic relationship. Recent evidence suggests that clients who feel the therapy is a "good fit" will be more likely to stay in therapy and have better therapeutic relationship (Elkin et al., 1999). The role of client and therapist choice making in therapy has been relatively untapped in efficacy research.

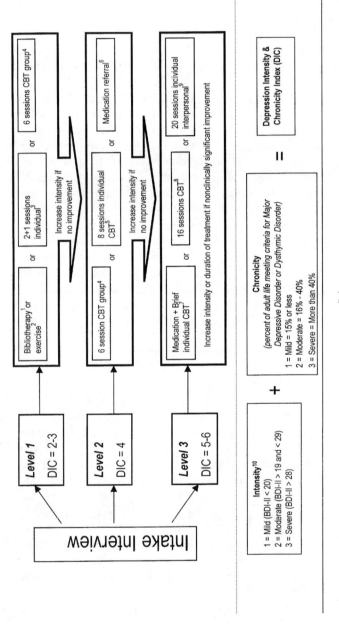

FIG. 13.2.  Example of a potential step-care model for intervening with depression.

**Intensity[10]**

1 = Mild (BDI-II < 20)
2 = Moderate (BDI-II > 19 and < 29)
3 = Severe (BDI-II > 28)

**+**

**Chronicity**
(percent of adult life meeting criteria for Major
Depressive Disorder or Dysthymic Disorder)

1 = Mild = 15% or less
2 = Moderate = 16% - 40%
3 = Severe = More than 40%

**=**

**Depression Intensity &
Chronicity Index (DIC)**

References

1   Smith, Floyd, Scogin, & Jamison (1997)
2   Ossip-Klein, Doyne, Bowman, Osborne,
     McDougall-Wilson, & Neimeyer (1989)
3   Barkham, Shapiro, Hardy,& Rees (1999)
4   Peterson & Halstead (1998)
5   Shapiro et al. (1995)

6   Sotsky et al. (1991)
7   Thase & Friedman (1999)
8   Shapiro et al. (1995)
9   Sotsky et al. (1991)
10   Beck et al. (1996)

---

Intake Interview

**Level 1**
DIC = 2-3

Bibliotherapy[1] or exercise[2]   or   2+1 sessions individual[3]   or   6 sessions CBT group[4]

Increase intensity if no improvement

**Level 2**
DIC = 4

6 session CBT group[5]   or   8 sessions individual CBT[5]   or   Medication referral[6]

Increase intensity if no improvement

**Level 3**
DIC = 5-6

Medication + Brief individual CBT[7]   or   16 sessions CBT[8]   or   20 sessions individual interpersonal[9]

Increase intensity or duration of treatment if nonclinically significant improvement

In order for differential effectiveness research to be maximally usable, both the designs and content of these studies should reflect the needs of clients, clinicians, payers, and policymakers. A number of researchers have proposed that decision-making algorithms may be more helpful, in the long run, than inflexible treatment manuals (cf. Chorpita et al., 1998; Clarke, 1995). An example of such a model for care that addresses the needs of all stakeholders is the *step-care model*. This model posits that the most ethical, cost-effective way to make treatment decisions is to begin treatment with the least intrusive intervention likely to have a positive impact (Davison, 2000); the intensity of treatment is only increased when the less intrusive level is inadequately effective. Instead of random assignment to conditions followed by analyses of predictors of differential success, assignment to treatment is made based on relevant clinical factors. Initial treatment intensity level is determined by the client's level on a robust, easily assessed predictor of differential effectiveness from RCTs such as severity or chronicity. Within each level, the clinician and client may either collaboratively choose among similarly intensive interventions or use less robust predictors to decide on treatment directions. See Fig. 13.2 for an example of how this might look for treatment of depressed mood as a primary problem. In theory, this treatment model combines the client's need for fast, effective care with the clinician's need for guidance about how to make treatment decisions with the payer and the policymaker's need for cost effectiveness. Although clinical and cost effectiveness of the step-care models have been investigated in the medical literature for problems such as hypertension (M. B. Sobell & L. C. Sobell, 2000), step-care models have received little theoretical or research attention in the psychological literature.

There are a variety of possibilities for effectiveness research on step-care models. The most comprehensive (and expensive) of these may involve random assignment of clients with a primary presenting problem of depressed mood to one of three conditions: (1) *step care + choice* (assignment to level based on severity and chronicity; assignment to specific intervention within level based on client choice; see Figure 13.2); (2) *step care + predictor* (assignment to level based on severity and chronicity; assignment to specific intervention based on an algorithm using secondary predictors such as stage of change, strengths, marital satisfaction, etc.); (3) TAU. Less comprehensive models may involve limiting samples to one or two levels of severity/chronicity and assigning to choice and predictor conditions, or including all levels of severity but having only one treatment at each level. Both clinical effectiveness and cost effectiveness would be carefully assessed for each condition.

*Behavioral Outcomes.* The latter point in the preceding discussion highlights an essential issue in effectiveness research; the outcome variables need to be relevant to the involved stakeholders. Of particular concern is how to best measure outcome for the client. Efficacy research has relied primarily on self-report of psychological symptoms as the primary outcome measure. The assumption has been that if the client reports they are feeling and functioning better, they must have made significant improvement. Although these measures are relatively cheap and easy, they may not adequately reflect other important aspects of the client's functioning (Strupp, 1996). A client who is feeling significantly less depressed after treatment but remains unemployed, living in a shelter, and unable to make child-support payments may not have made meaningful change. In order to truly understand the effectiveness of interventions, a better understanding is needed of how treatment affects salient behavioral measures such as familial functioning, occupational functioning, and future use of medical and psychological services. This will likely require a shift in data analyses, data content, and data-collection methods.

A recent innovation for increasing the clinical meaningfulness of research findings has involved analyzing the extent to which clients make clinically significant change. In a seminal article, Jacobson and Revenstrof (1988) outlined the problems with aiming for statistically significant change alone. They note that even though change may be reliable, it may not be meaningful. If a smoking cessation intervention reliably reduces the average daily cigarette consumption from 3 packs daily to $2\frac{3}{4}$ packs daily for a large sample, it is likely, that a statistically significant pretest to posttest change could be demonstrated. Yet, one might wonder whether these smokers have actually made any clinically meaningful change. They still act, feel, and have health problems more like smokers than nonsmokers. Jacobson and Revenstrof (1988) noted that unless clients are becoming more like the nonclinical population than the clinical population, they have not made clinically significant change (see chap. 12 for a more detailed discussion of clinically significant change). It appears, that at a minimum, effectiveness research should address not only whether clients improve their symptoms, but whether they improve to the extent that they are more like nondistressed clients.

A close cousin to the concept of *clinical significance* is the concept of *behavioral significance*. That is, is the client behaving more like a client from a clinical or nonclinical population? Areas of particular relevance to all stakeholders include familial and occupational functioning as well as health care usage. A significant body of research indicates that poor familial functioning leads to a more chronic course of psychological disturbance (Durbin, Klein, & Schwartz, 2000) and more rapid relapse after successful treatment (Brent et al., 1999). Similarly, poor mental health in one family member may also be related to more mental health concerns of other members (Durbin et al., 2000). Further, psychological disturbance is related to reduced occupational functioning and unemployment (Murphy & Athanasou, 1999). These variables all interact to synergistically affect the clients, payers, and policymakers. Clients' quality of life is affected. Payers are often employers who want the client maximally effective at work. Policymakers are concerned about client's ability to pay and their use of future services. Adequate assessment of these variables may involve the client's self-report of occupational and familial functioning as well as auxiliary sources such as employers and spouses or parents. Health records may also be used to assess the cost offset of psychological interventions. Aside from the expense and time involved in such a multimethod–multisource assessment, the greatest limitation is the inherent breach of client confidentiality. Such a study would always require the client's written consent to involve employers, family members, and health records in the assessment process.

***Dissemination of Findings to All Stakeholders.*** Even perfectly generalizable studies are worth little unless the findings reach the pertinent stakeholders. Unfortunately researchers have a tendency to talk primarily to other researchers (Newman & Tejeda, 1996). Although many of these gaps will be breached as the generalizability of research increases, care should be taken to ensure that findings are adequately disseminated. Perhaps the best way to increase the readership of clinicians and policymakers is to have them involved in the needs assessment from the start of the project (Goldfried & Wolfe, 1996). They may be involved as consultants in developing pertinent questions, providers for implementation, or even funders (Castonguay, Schut, Constantino, & Halperin, 1999). They may also provide valuable information on how findings may be disseminated to others involved in health care. In many cases, offering services through trainings and workshops is another excellent way to disseminate research findings. More traditional routes of conference presentations and publications may also be good sources of dissemination provided that these sources are used by the relevant stakeholders.

## When Do You Do Effectiveness Research?

Although both efficacy and effectiveness research have important roles in improving the quality of psychological interventions, it is not entirely clear what type of research should be done, and when. Traditionally, effectiveness research has been conceptualized as the final test of a treatment already demonstrated to be efficacious in a series of RCTs (Chambless & Hollon, 1998). This sentiment is mirrored in the standard model proposed by the National Cancer Institute for efficacy and effectiveness research, which includes five orderly phases (Hoagwood et al., 1995). The first phase consists of hypothesis development based on previous research. The second phase focuses on the development of research methods through the rigorous validation of all instruments. The third phase is designed to test the hypotheses developed in the first phase with well-controlled methods developed in the second phase. The first application to the real heterogenous clinical populations occurs in the fourth phase, and the in the fifth and final phase, policy changes are implemented based on efficacy and effectiveness findings. Hoagwood and colleagues (1995) noted that, although thorough, this process is also cumbersome, expensive, and often not feasible. They propose a more flexible model in which both effectiveness and efficacy research inform one another.

An alternative to first establishing efficacy before conducting effectiveness research is to reverse the order. Instead, interventions may first be tested in real clinical settings with heterogenous clients. If these interventions are acceptable to clinicians and clients, effective, and feasible, then they may be subjected to more rigorous efficacy research to refine interventions or increase information about differential effectiveness. An intervention that is clumsy, unacceptable to clinicians or clients, or ineffective probably does not warrant further expensive efficacy research. Findings of the efficacy studies may then again be tested in the community. Another alternative is to conduct effectiveness and efficacy research simultaneously through conducting research in real clinical settings with both heterogeneous and homogeneous samples as described by Clarke (1995) in the donut model.

To best assess the efficacy and effectiveness of the BICID intervention, a combination of efficacy and effectiveness interventions may be warranted. A possible long-range research strategy is outlined in Table 13.4. Because BICID's combination of interventions is novel and has no research into its feasibility or effectiveness, some low-cost, low-investment, single-subject designs may provide enough information about the acceptability and unique effectiveness of BICID to decide whether a more time-intensive, expensive research endeavor is warranted. If the single-subject designs suggest that BICID may offer advantages over the behavioral treatment for depression alone, especially for relieving symptoms of insomnia, then the second step may involve a small-scale effectiveness study. In this effectiveness study, a wide range of clinic clients with complaints of depression and insomnia may be randomly assigned to one of the three interventions with the primary goals of assessing feasibility, overall effectiveness, and cost effectiveness. If the smaller scale effectiveness study yields promising results, then the groundwork is begun for a larger scale efficacy study. The earlier single-subject design and effectiveness studies could provide pilot data for a research grant to use an RCT to evaluate the differential effectiveness of the treatments, any unique effects of the depression and insomnia interventions (mode-specific effects), and predictors of outcome in each treatment condition. Although not included in Table 13.4, a final step may be to test the results of the RCT in a broad band community study.

TABLE 13.4

Hypothetical Long-Range Research Plan for BICID

| Research Plan | Primary Goals (see below) | | | | | |
|---|---|---|---|---|---|---|
| | Feasibility | Overall Effectiveness | Differential Effectiveness | Mode Specific Effects | Predictors | Cost Effectiveness |
| 1. Multiple baseline single subject design<br>• Subjects: People who complain of both depression and sleep difficulties<br>  • Dependent Variables:<br>    • Depression level (self-report, assessed each session)<br>    • Sleep efficiency (Time in bed/time asleep) (self-report, assessed each session)<br>  • Independent Variables: Three 8-session treatments:<br>    • BICIDdepression: 4 sessions BD + 4 sessions BI<br>    • BICIDinsomnia: 4 sessions BI + 4 sessions BD<br>    • Depression Only: 8 sessions BD | X | | | X | | |
| 2. Small scale (N = 75; 25 in each group) randomized effectiveness study using "donut model" (Clarke, 1995)<br>• Subjects: Outpatient clinic clients who complain of both depression and sleep difficulties (including the "pure cases" meeting criteria only for MDD and Primary Insomnia)<br>  • Dependent Variables: depression and sleep diagnoses and severity.<br>    • Structured diagnostic interview at beginning & end of therapy.<br>    • Self-report instruments weekly.<br>  • Independent Variables: Three 8-session treatments:<br>    • BICIDdepression: 4 sessions BD + 4 sessions BI<br>    • BICIDinsomnia: 4 sessions BI + 4 sessions BD<br>    • Depression Only: 8 sessions BD | X | X | | | | X |

(Continued)

TABLE 13.4
(Contiuned)

| | | Primary Goals (see below) | | | | |
|---|---|---|---|---|---|---|
| Research Plan | Feasibility | Overall Effectiveness | Differential Effectiveness | Mode Specific Effects | Predictors | Cost Effectiveness |
| 3. Larger scale RCT (N = 300; 100 in each group) with long-term follow-up (1, 3, and 5 years)<br>• Subjects: Pure depression/insomnia cases. Other comorbid or subthreshold subjects would be excluded.<br>• Dependent Variables: depression and sleep diagnoses and severity.<br>  • Structured diagnostic interview at beginning & end of therapy.<br>  • Self-report instruments weekly.<br>• Independent Variables: Three 8-session treatments:<br>  • BICIDdepression: 4 sessions BD + 4 sessions BI<br>  • BICIDinsomnia: 4 sessions BI + 4 sessions BD<br>  • Depression Only: 8 sessions BDX | | X | X | X | X | |

*Note:* BD = Behavioral treatment for depression (behavioral activation, activity scheduling, increasing pleasurable and mastery activities), BI = Behavioral treatment for insomnia

Primary goals are defined as follows:

F. Treatment feasibility

O. Overall effectiveness of interventions

D. Differential effectiveness of interventions

M. Mode-specific effects (e.g. extent to which treatment variables differentially affect sleep and depression)

P. Predictors of outcome to different interventions

C. Cost effectiveness

## SUMMARY

Therapy outcome research shifted trends dramatically in the last century. It began with loosely controlled assessments of treatment outcome as it is actually done and moved though tightly controlled randomized efficacy studies onto effectiveness research that (ideally) both marries real-world concerns and experimental control.

Our goal in this book is for the reader to gain the knowledge and understanding necessary to critique, comprehend, and incorporate research into their own professional activities, as well as to encourage readers to actively participate in research. With time, we expect that both efficacy and effectiveness studies will become part of the fabric of professional psychology. In the future, when critiquing research, we must not only attend to the technical adequacy of a study, but also the intent of the authors. Recognition that effectiveness studies can add to our fund of knowledge and enrich both the science and practice of psychology has important implications for clinicians. Prior to the these developments, few practitioners had opportunity or incentive to participate in research. Today the technology exists or is being created to allow any clinicians who wish to take on the mantle of being a local clinical scientist to participate in clinical research while effectively serving their clients.

## REFERENCES

Addis, M. E., & Wade, W. A., & Hatgis, C. (1999). Barriers to dissemination of evidence-based practices: Addressing practitioners' concerns about manual-based psychotherapies. *Clinical Psychology: Science and Practice, 6*, 4309–441.

Ahava, G. W., Iannone, C., Brebstein, L., & Schirling, J. (1998). Is the Beck Depression Inventory reliable over time? An evaluation of multiple test-retest reliability in a nonclinical college student sample. *Journal of Personality Assessment, 70*(20), 222–231.

Antonuccio, D. L., Thomas, M., & Danton, W. G. (1997). A cost-effectiveness analysis of cognitive behavior therapy and fluoxetine (prozac) in the treatment of depression. *Behavior Therapy, 28*(2), 187–210.

Barkham, M., Shapiro, D. A., Hardy, G. E., & Rees, A. (1999). Psychotherapy in two-plus-one sessions: Outcomes of a randomized controlled trial of cognitive-behavioral and psychodynamic-interpersonal therapy for subsyndromal depression. *Journal of Consulting & Clinical Psychology, 67*(2), 201–211.

Barlow, D. H., Esler, J. L., Vitali, & A. E. (1998). Psychosocial treatments for panic disorders, phobias, and generalized anxiety disorder. In P. E. Nathan and J. M. Gorman (Eds.), *A guide to treatments that work* (pp. 288–318). New York: Oxford Press.

Beck, A. T., & Beck, R. W. (1972). Screening depressed patients in family practice: A rapid technique. *Postgraduate Medicine, 52*, 81–85.

Beck, A. T., Rush, A. J., Shaw, B. F., & Emery, G. (1979). *Cognitive therapy of depression.* New York: Guilford Press.

Beck, A. T., Steer, R. A., & Brown, G. K. (1996). *Beck Depression Inventory: Second Edition.* San Antonio, TX: The Psychological Corporation.

Blatt, S. J. (1995). The destructiveness of perfectionism: Implications for the treatment of depression. *American Psychologist, 50*(12), 1003–1020.

Brent, D. A., Kolko, D. J., Birmaher, B., Baugher, M., & Bridge, J. (1999). A clinical trial for adolescent depression: Predictors of additional treatment in the acute and follow-up phases of the trial. *Journal of the American Academy of Child and Adolescent Psychiatry, 38*(3), 263–271.

Breslau, N., Roth, T., Rosenthal, L., & Andreski, P. (1996). Sleep disturbance and psychiatric disorders: A longitudinal epidemiological study of young adults. *Biological Psychiatry, 39*(6), 411–418.

Buysse, D. J., Reynolds, C. F., Monk, T. H., Berman S. R., & Kupfer, D. J. (1989). The Pittsburgh Sleep Quality Index: A new instrument for psychiatric practice and research. *Psychiatry Research, 28*, 193–213.

Campbell, D. T., & Stanley, J. C. (1963). *Experimental and quasi-experimental designs for research.* Chicago: Rand McNally.

Castonguay, L. G., Schut, A. J., Constantino, M. J., & Halperin, G. S. (1999). Assessing the role of treatment manuals: Have they become necessary but nonsufficient ingredients of change? *Clinical Psychology: Science and Practice, 6*(4), 449–455.

Chambless, D. L., & Hollon, S. D. (1998). Defining empirically supported therapies. *Journal of Consulting & Clinical Psychology, 66*(1), 7–18.

Chorpita, B. F., Barlow, D. H., Albano, A. M., & Daleiden, E. L. (1998). Methodological strategies in child clinical trials: Advancing the efficacy and effectiveness of psychosocial treatments. *Journal of Abnormal Child Psychology, 26*(1), 7–16.

Clarke, G. N. (1995). Improving the transition from basic efficacy research to effectiveness studies: Methodological issues and procedures. *Journal of Consulting & Clinical Psychology, 63*(5), 718–725.

Coates, T. J., Killen, J. D., George, J., Silverman, S., Marchini, E., & Thoresen, C. E. (1982). Estimating sleep parameters: A multi-trait–multi-method analysis. *Journal of Consulting and Clinical Psychology, 50*, 345–352.

Cook, T. D., Campbell, D. T., & Peracchio, L. (1990). Quasi experimentation. In M. D. Dunnette, & L. M. Hough (Eds.), *Handbook of industrial and organizational psychology* (Vol. 1, 2nd Ed., pp. 491–576). Palo Alto, CA: Consulting Psychologists Press, Inc.

Craighead, W. E., Craighead, L. W., & Ilardi, S. S. (1998). Psychosocial treatments for major depressive disorder. In P. E. Nathan and J. M. Gorman (Eds.), *A guide to treatments that work* (pp. 226–239). New York: Oxford Press.

Davison, G. C. (2000). Stepped care: Doing more with less? *Journal of Consulting & Clinical Psychology, 68*(4), 580–585.

Derogatis, L. R. (1993a). *BSI: The Brief Symptom Inventory.* Minneapolis, MN: National Computer Systems.

Derogatis, L. R. (1993b). *BSI bibliography.* Minneapolis, MN: National Computer Systems.

Division 12 Task Force (1995). Training in and dissemination of empirically validated psychological treatments: Report and recommendations. *The Clinical Psychologist, 48*, 3–23.

Durbin, C. E., Klein, D. N., & Schwartz, J. E. (2000). Predicting the $2^{1}/_{2}$ year outcome of dysthymic disorder: The roles of childhood adversity and family history of psychopathology. *Journal of Consulting and Clinical Psychology, 68*(1), 57–63.

Elkin, I., Gibbons, R. D., Shea, M. T., & Shaw, B. F. (1996). Science is not a trial (but it can sometimes be a tribulation). *Journal of Consulting and Clinical Psychology, 64*(1), 92–103.

Elkin, I., Shea, M. T., Watkins, J. T., Imber, S. D., Sotsky, S. M., Collins, J. F., Glass, D. R., Pilkonis, P. A., Leber, W. R., Docherty, J. P., Fiester, S. J., & Parloff, M. B. (1989). National Institute of Mental Health Treatment of Depression Collaborative Research Program: General effectiveness of treatments. *Archives of General Psychiatry, 46*, 971–982.

Elkin, I., Yamaguchi, J. L., Arnkoff, D. B., Glass, C. R., Sotsky, S. M., & Krupnick, J. L. (1999). "Patient-treatment fit" and early engagement in therapy. *Psychotherapy Research, 9*(4), 437–451.

Eysenck, H. J. (1952). The effects of psychotherapy: An evaluation. *Journal of Consulting Psychology, 16,* 319–324.

First, M. B., Spitzer, R. L., Gibbon, M., & Williams, J. B. W. (1997a). *Structured Clinical Interview for DSM-IV Axis I Disorders, Research Version, Non-patient Edition (SCID-I/NP).* New York: Biometrics Research, New York State Psychiatric Institute, 1997.

First, M. B., Spitzer, R. L., Gibbon, M., & Williams, J. B. W. (1997b). *Users guide for the Structured Clinical Interview for DSM-IV Axis I Disorders—Clinician Version (SCID-CV).* Washington, DC: American Psychiatric Press.

Frances (1994). Psychotherapy research and practice: A response to Wolfe. *Journal of Psychotherapy Integration, 4,* 278–279.

Goldfried, M. R., & Wolfe, B. E. (1996). Psychotherapy practice and research: Repairing a strained relationship. *American Psychologist, 51,* 1007–1016.

Haberfellner, E. M. (2000). Recruitment of depressive patients for a controlled clinical trial in a psychiatric practice. *Pharmacopsychiatry, 33*(4), 142–144.

Hirschfeld, R. M. A., Russell, J. M., Delgado, P. L., Fawcett, J., Friedman, R. A., Harrison, W. M., Koran, L. M., Miller, I. W., Thase, M. E., Howland, R. H., Connolly, M. A., & Miceli, R. J. (1998). Predictors of response to acute treatment of chronic and double depression with sertraline or imipramine. *Journal of Clinical Psychiatry, 59*(12), 669–675.

Hoagwood, K., Hibbs, E., Brent, D., & Jensen, P. (1995). Introduction to the special section: Efficacy and effectiveness in studies of child and adolescent psychotherapy. *Journal of Consulting & Clinical Psychology, 63*(5), 683–687.

Hofmann, S. G., Barlow, D. H., Papp, L. A., Detweiler, M. F., Ray, S. E., Shear, M. K., Woods, S. W., & Gorman, J. M. (1998). Pretreatment attrition in a comparative treatment outcome study on panic disorder. *American Journal of Psychiatry, 155*(1), 43–47.

Howard, K. I., Kopta, S. M., Krause, M. S., & Orlinsky, D. E. (1986). The dose-effect relationship in psychotherapy. *American Psychologist, 41*(2), 159–164.

Humphreys, K., & Weisner, C. (2000). Use of exclusion criteria in selecting research subjects and its effect on the generalizability of alcohol treatment outcome studies. *American Journal of Psychiatry, 157*(4), 588–594.

Jacobson, N. S., & Christensen, A. (1996). Studying the effectiveness of psychotherapy: How well can clinical trials do the job? *American Psychologist, 51*(10), 1031–1039.

Jacobson, N. S., Dobson, K., Truax, P., Addis, M. E., Doerner, K., Gollan, J. K., Gortner, E., & Prince, S. E. (1996). A component analysis of cognitive-behavioral treatment for depression. *Journal of Consulting & Clinical Psychology, 64*(2), 295–304.

Jacobson, N. S., & Revenstrof, D. (1988). Statistics for assessing the clinical significance of psychotherapy techniques: Issues, problems, and new developments. *Behavioral Assessment, 10*(2), 133–145.

Keller, M. B., Lavori, P. W., Friedman, B., Nielson, E., Endicott, J., McDonald-Scott, P., & Andreasen, N. C. (1987). The Longitudinal Interval Follow-Up Evaluation: A comprehensive method for assessing outcome in prospective longitudinal studies. *Archives of General Psychiatry, 44,* 540–548.

Keller, M. B., McCullough, J. P., Klein, D. N., Arnow, B., Dunner, D. L., Gelenberg, A. J. Markowitz, J. C., Nemeroff, C. B., Russell, J. M., Thase, M. E., Trivedi, M. H., & Zajecka, J. (2000). A comparison of nefazodone, the cognitive behavioral-analysis system of psychotherapy, and their combination for the treatment of chronic depression. *New England Journal of Medicine, 342*(20), 1462–1470.

Kendall, P. C., & Chu, B. C. (2000). Retrospective self-reports of therapist flexibility in a manual-based treatment for youths with anxiety disorders. *Journal of Clinical Child Psychology, 29*(2), 209–220.

Luborsky, L., Diguer, L., Seligman, D. A., Rosenthal, R., Krause, E. D., Johnson, S., Halperin, G., Bishop, M., Berman, J. S., & Schweizer, E. (1999). The researcher's own therapy allegiances: A "wild card" in comparisons of treatment efficacy. *Clinical Psychology: Science & Practice, 6*(1), 95–106.

Luborksy, L., Singer, B., & Luborsky, L. (1975). Comparative studies of psychotherapies: Is it true that "Everyone has won and all must have prizes"? *Archives of General Psychitary, 32*, 995–1008.

Matt, G. E., & Navarro, A. M. (1997). What meta-analyses have and have not taught us about psychotherapy effects: A review and future directions. *Clinical Psychology Review, 17*(1), 1–32.

McRoberts, C., Burlingame, G. M., & Hoag, M. J. (1998). Comparative efficacy of individual and group psychotherapy: A meta-analytic perspective. *Group Dynamics, 2*(2). 101–117.

Mitchell, J. E., Maki, D. D., Adson, D. W., Ruskin, B. S., & Crow, S. (1997). The selectivity of inclusion and exclusion criteria in bulimia nervosa treatment studies. *International Journal of Eating Disorders, 22*(3), 243–252.

Morin, C. M., Culbert, J. P., & Schwartz, S. M. (1994). Nonpharmacological interventions for insomnia: A meta-analysis of treatment efficacy. *American Journal of Psychiatry, 151*(8), 1172–1180.

Murphy, G. C., & Athanasou, J. A. (1999). The effect of unemployment on mental health. *Journal of Occupational & Organizational Psychology, 72*(1), 83–99.

Mynors-Wallis, L., & Gath, D. (1997). Predictors of treatment outcome for major depression in primary care. *Psychological Medicine, 27*(3), 731–736.

Nathan, P. E. (2000). The Boulder Model: A dream deferred—or lost? *American Psychologist, 55*, 250–252.

Nathan, P. E., & Gorman, J. M. (1998). *A guide to treatments that work.* New York: Oxford University Press.

Newman, F. L., & Tejeda, M. J. (1996). The need for research that is designed to support decisions in the delivery of mental health services. *American Psychologist, 51*, 1040–1049.

Norenzayan, A., & Schwarz, N. (1999). Telling what they want to know: Participants tailor causal attributions to researchers' interests. *European Journal of Social Psychology, 29*(8), 1011–1020.

Ohayon, M. M., Shapiro, C. M., & Kennedy, S. H. (2000). Differentiating DSM-IV anxiety and depressive disorders in the general population: Comorbidity and treatment consequences. *Canadian Journal of Psychiatry, 45*(2), 166–172.

Ossip-Klein, D. J., Doyne, E. J., Bowman, E. D., Osborn, K. M., McDougall-Wilson, I. B., & Neimeyer, R. A. (1989). Effects of running or weight lifting on self-concept in clinically depressed women. *Journal of Consulting & Clinical Psychology, 57*(1), 158–161.

Oxman, T. E. (1997). Editorial: New paradigms for understanding the identification and treatment of depression in primary care. *General Hospital Psychiatry, 19*(2), 79–81.

Parloff, M. B. (1979). Can psychotherapy research guide the policymaker? A little knowledge may be a dangerous thing. *American Psychologist, 34*, 296–306.

Perlis, M. L., Giles, D. E., Buysse, D. J., Tu, X., & Kupfer, D. J. (1997). Self-reported sleep disturbance as a prodromal symptom in recurrent depression. *Journal of Affective Disorders, 42*(2-3), 209–212.

Peterson, A. L., & Halstead, T. S. (1998). Group cognitive behavior therapy for depression in a community setting: A clinical replication series. *Behavior Therapy, 29*(1), 3–18.

Prochaska, J. O., & Norcross, J. C. (1999). *Systems of Psychotherapy: A transtheoretical analysis.* Pacific Grove, CA: Brooks/Cole.

Schneider, L. S., Olin, J. T., Lyness, S . A., & Chui, H. C. (1997). Eligibility of Alzheimer's disease clinic patients for clinical trials. *Journal of the American Geriatrics Society, 45*(8), 923–928.

Schwartz, C. E., Chesney, M. A., Irvine, J., & Keefe, F. J. (1997). The control group dilemma in clinical research: Applications for psychosocial and behavioral medicine trials. *Psychosomatic Medicine, 59*(4), 362–371.

Seligman, M. E. P. (1995). The effectiveness of psychotherapy: The Consumer Reports study. *American Psychologist, 50*(12), 965–974.

Shapiro, D. A., Rees, A., Barkham, M. & Hardy, G. (1995). Effects of treatment duration and severity of depression on the maintenance of gains after cognitive-behavioral and psychodynamic-interpersonal psychotherapy. *Journal of Consulting & Clinical Psychology, 63*(3), 378–387.

Sharpe, J. P., & Gilbert, D. G. (1998). Effects of repeated administration of the Beck Depression Inventory and other measures of negative mood states. *Personality and Individual Differences, 24*(4), 457–463.

Shea, M. T., Pilkonis, P. A., Beckahm, E., Collins, J. F., Elkin, I., Sotsky, S. M., & Docherty, J. P. (1990). Personality disorders and treatment outcome in the NIMH Treatment of Depression Collaborative Research Program. *American Journal of Psychiatry, 147*(6), 711–718.

Smith, N. M., Floyd, M. R., Scogin, R., & Jamison, C. S. (1997). Three-year follow-up of bibliotherapy for depression. *Journal of Consulting & Clinical Psychology, 65*(2), 324–327.

Smith, M. L., & Glass, G. V. (1977). Meta-analysis of psychotherapy outcome studies. *American Psychologist, 32*, 752–760.

Sobell, M. B., & Sobell, L. C. (2000). Stepped care as a heuristic approach to the treatment of alcohol problems. *Journal of Consulting & Clinical Psychology, 68*(4), 573–579.

Sotsky, S. M., Glass, D. R., Shea, M. T., Pilkonis, P. A., Collins, J. F., Elkin, E., Watkins, J. T., Imber, S. D., Leber, W. R., & Moyer, J. (1991). Patient predictors of response to psychotherapy and pharmacotherapy: Findings in the NIMH Treatment of Depression Collaborative Research Program. *American Journal of Psychiatry, 148*(8), 997–1008.

Stewart, J. W., Garfinkel, R., Nunes, E. V., Donovan, S., & Klein, D. F. (1998). Atypical features and treatment response in the National Institute of Mental Health Treatment of Depression Collaborative Research Program. *Journal of Clinical Psychopharmacology, 18*(6), 429–434.

Street, L. L., Niederehe, G., & Lebowitz, B. D. (2000). Toward greater public health relevance for psychotherapeutic intervention research: An NIMH Workshop Report. *Clinical Psychology: Science and Practice, 7*(2), 127–137.

Stricker, G. (2000). The relationship between efficacy and effectiveness. *Prevention and Treatment, 3*, np.

Strupp, H. H. (1996). The tripartite model and the Consumer Reports Study. *American Psychologist, 51*, 1017–1024.

Thase, M. E., & Friedman, E. S. (1999). Is psychotherapy an effective treatment for melancholia and other severe depressive states? *Journal of Affective Disorders, 54*(1-2), 1–19.

Ware, J. E., Kosinski, M., & Keller, S. D. (1995). *SF-12: How to score the SF-12 physical and mental health summary scales* (2nd Edition). Boston: Health Institute, New England Medical Center.

Ware, J. E., Snow, K. K., Kosinski, M., & Gandek, B. (1993). *SF-36 Health Survey: Manual and interpretation guide.* Boston: Nimrod.

Weisz, J. R., Weiss, B., Han, S. S., Granger, D. A., & Morton, T. (1995). Effects of psychotherapy with children and adolescents revisited: A meta-analysis of treatment outcome studies. *Psychological Bulletin, 117*(3), 450–468.

# 14

# Research in Private Practice

Ricks Warren
*The Anxiety Disorders Clinic, Lake Oswego, Oregon
and Pacific University*

Jay C. Thomas
*Pacific University, Portland, Oregon*

During the senior author's 20 years of being a psychologist in private practice, he can count on one hand how many fellow psychologists conduct research in their practices. These notable few are almost all colleagues he has met through membership in the Association for Advancement of Behavior Therapy (AABT). Behavioral, cognitive and cognitive-behavior therapists (CBT) all are committed to the value of using research findings on what the most effective treatments are for specific clients problems. As noted elsewhere in this volume, empirically supported treatments (ESTs) are being designated and strongly recommended by cognitive–behaviorally oriented professionals, as well as by some professionals of eclectic and other theoretical orientations.

While most CBT therapists are dedicated consumers of this type of research, very few private practitioners of any theoretical persuasion are conductors of research. This state of affairs has been discussed frequently in the literature ever since the Boulder Model was created at the Boulder Conference in 1948. Hayes, Barlow, and Nelson-Gray (1999) provided a good discussion of this ever-evolving issue. For our present purposes, however, the scientist-practitioner continues to be a rare breed.

In this respect, the senior author stays current on the state of the art treatments (ESTs) and incorporates them in his clinical practice. But he and his colleagues also conduct research in that practice as well. In 1985, Ricks Warren and a colleague started a private clinic for the treatment of anxiety disorders. Presently, the Anxiety Disorders Clinic has grown to include eight independent practitioners, including four psychologists, one licensed professional counselor, one licensed clinical social worker, and a psychiatric nurse practitioner. The majority of our staff were once psychological residents or practicum students who stayed on as permanent staff. All staff members recognize the value in this enterprise, and have been very generous in contributing to our ongoing research.

To give you a feel for the kinds of research we do in our private practice clinic, we provide a few examples. The main research involves collecting treatment outcome data on our clients. We have collected data on panic disorder (Strand & Warren, 2001; Warren, 1995, 1996; Warren & Thomas, 1997), obsessive compulsive disorder (OCD; Warren, & Thomas, 2001), social phobia (McRitchie, 1998) and posttraumatic stress disorder (PTSD; Christiansen, 2001). Later in this chapter, we describe in detail an example from our ongoing panic disorder research. In addition to outcome research, we have also explored determinants of agoraphobic avoidance (Warren, Zgourides, & Jones, 1989), measurement of irrational beliefs (Warren & Zgourides, 1989), catastrophic cognitions about body sensations (Warren, Zgourides, & Englert, 1990), measurement of beliefs about obsessions (Warren & McCaffery, 1996), normative (Warren, Zgourides, & Monto, 1993), reliability, and validity data on the self-report version of the Yale–Brown Obsessive-Compulsive Scale (Y-BOCS; Warren, Zgourides, Monto, & Felker, 1994), use of a portable radio headset as an aid in the treatment of paruresis (Zgourides, Warren, & Englert, 1990), and stage of change and anxiety disorder treatment outcome (McDonald & Warren, 2001).

What are the benefits of a scientist–practitioner conducting research in his private practice for the last 20 years? First of all, posing research hypotheses and testing them out satisfies intellectual curiosity. Second, Warren has found he enjoys feeling a part of the scientific community, particularly with AABT colleagues, but also locally. Third, he really is interested in whether treatments are really helping clients and whether they are helping them to the degree reported in the anxiety disorder treatment literature. Relatedly, it is important when potential clients ask what our success rate is for a particular condition, (e.g., panic disorder), and they can actually be handed this information, not only according to what efficacy studies have shown, but what has been obtained right here in our local clinic. Fourth, in the age of managed care, it is important to have data to support the idea that we can successfully treat certain kinds of disorders. Fifth, we have found that one's professional and clinic reputation in the community is enhanced because of outcome research. This also increases the referral rate. Sixth, as an adjunct professor who teaches the cognitive–behavior therapy course in a clinical psychology program, The senior author believes that it is important to be able to model what he advocates: that is, the local clinical scientist (Trierweiler & Stricker, 1998).

One more benefit needs to be mentioned. Because of the senior author's interest in the assessment of beliefs related to OCD and a long history of taking workshops at AABT meetings over the years, he was very fortunate to be invited to attend an international meeting of 26 OCD clinical researchers at

Smith College in Northampton, Massachusetts in the summer of 1996. Led by Gail Steketee and Randy Frost, the group (Obsessive Compulsive Cognitions Working Group), fondly known as OCCWG, set about the task of creating two self-report measures of OCD-related beliefs. As the sole private practice clinician in the group, he was able to contribute to the group's mission by asking colleagues to join in asking clients to complete a packet of questionnaires designed to assess reliability and validity of what have come to be called the Obsessive Beliefs Questionnaire and the Interpretation of Intrusion Inventory. The thrilling history of this movement is described in detail in Obsessive Compulsive Cognitions Working Group (1997). In order to continue refining these measures, he was again quite fortunate to join the OCCWG in Padua and Venice, Italy in the fall of 1997. A meeting was arranged to coincide with the Congress of European Association for Behavioural & Cognitive Therapies, and because he had been collecting outcome data on OCD clients, he was asked to share data in a symposium (Sookman, Yaryura-Tobias, & Warren, 1997). Thus, a research based, private practice has led to international recognition, the opportunity to work with outstanding psychologists from around the world, and, of course, making a contribution to the state of knowledge about OCD.

Are there costs to conducting research in private practice? Yes, there definitely are, which is part of the reason that scientist practitioners are scarce. What are some of the costs? Probably the main cost is the time taken from seeing clients and the corresponding loss of income, although as more computer programs continue to evolve, private practice research can be conducted much more efficiently than Warren has been able to conduct in the past. Also, if one collects outcome data, rather than exploring a variety of other research domains, less time will be taken. In addition, practice research networks, such as the one now operating in Pennsylvania (Borkovec, Echemendia, Ragusea, & Ruiz, 2001) may become more widely available in the near future. Also, there are examples where health maintenance organizations (HMOs) are funding clinician time to receive training in administering and evaluating ESTs.

Although conducting an empirically oriented practice can be a great low-key marketing activity, the time spent on research could be spent on more direct forms of practice building, networking, and other activities that lead directly to practice income. However, in the long run, no other activity would have produced the same reputation for the clinic and simultaneously shown that the clients of this clinic show systematic improvement.

## DESIGNING AN EMPIRICALLY ORIENTED PRACTICE

If you wish to have an empirically oriented practice, this, of course, means that you value knowing how effective you are being with your clients, and that you believe that effectiveness needs to be assessed in ways in addition to your personal impression and the report of your clients. If you want to have associates that also participate in collecting outcome data, it is important to select colleagues who also are empirically oriented and willing to devote some of their time and energy to the research enterprise. At our clinic, the following is stated in our brochure: "The Anxiety Disorders Clinic is committed to the goal of using treatment techniques that have been empirically evaluated and shown to be effective in the treatment of anxiety disorders." In this way, we are publicly committing ourselves to the empirical enterprise to primary care physicians, other healthcare providers, and to consumers. We also mail out a newsletter two or three times a year. This gives us a regular opportunity to present relevant research findings from our practice as well as from the literature, and continues to convey to our colleagues that we operate and empirically oriented practice. It also appears to generate referrals from primary care physicians and other healthcare providers.

Clement (1996) published an article entitled "Evaluation in Private Practice," in *Clinical Psychology: Science and Practice*, in which he discussed the issue of the scarcity of true scientist–practitioners and how he has been evaluating his own practice throughout his entire private practice career. Clement's article was followed by several other articles that responded to his model both with applauds and suggestions for alternative approaches. We recommend that you read this series as you contemplate development of your own empirically oriented practice. In addition, the summer, 2001 issue of *Clinical Psychology: Science and Practice* has an up-to-date series of articles on conducting research in routine clinical practice.

## CHOOSING OUTCOME MEASURES FOR A PRIVATE PRACTICE

The second edition of *The Scientist Practioner: Research and Accountability in the Age of Managed Care* (Hayes et al.,1999) has been recently released, and we highly recommend this book. It discusses the nuts and bolts of how to conduct meaningful research in the clinical setting, and it gives good reasons why this is a good idea. For example, private practice research can improve treatment, provide accountability, and enhance clinical science. As Hayes et al. (1999) discussed it is useful to use a variety of different measures as well as types of measures on a pre-, during, and postresearch basis.

To illustrate how we chose the particular measures that we routinely use, we focus on our panic control treatment (PCT). Measures used include the following self-report measures: the Fear Questionnaire (FQ; Marks & Mathews, 1979), Mobility Inventory (MI; Chambless, Caputo, Jasin, Gracely, & Williams, 1985), Body Sensations Questionnaire (BSQ; Chambless, Caputo, Bright, & Gallagher, 1984), Agoraphobic Cognitions Questionnaire (ACQ; Chambless et al., 1984), Anxiety Sensitivity Index (ASI; Reiss, Peterson, Gursky, & McNally, 1986), Beck Depression Inventory II (BDI-II; Beck,

Steer, & Brown, 1996), Penn State Worry Questionnaire (PSQ; Meyer, Miller, Metzger, & Borkovec, 1990), and the State-Trait Anxiety Inventory–Trait Anxiety Subscale (STAI; Spielberger, Gorsuch, & Lushene, 1970). We also use self-monitoring measures, including the Panic Attack Record, the Daily Mood Record, and the Weekly Progress Record (a graph of panic attack frequency and average anxiety level), which are contained in Barlow & Craske (2000). See Warren (1995) for a detailed illustration of the use of these measures in a case study and Antony, Orsillo, and Roemer (2001) for a handbook of empirically based measures of anxiety disorders.

As Hayes et al. (1999) recommended, we use the self-report measures on a pre, post, and follow-up basis, and throughout treatment. Self-monitoring allows the therapist and client to observe immediate symptom presentations and ongoing progress (or lack thereof). For example the Panic Attack Records require that clients note thoughts, physical sensations, and possible triggers for the attacks, thus continuing to increase awareness of an individual's idiosyncratic patterns. The weekly progress record shows ongoing progress, complete with significant trends as well as the ups and downs of symptoms. This information is quite valuable in reinforcing client progress, illustrating that occasional increases in symptoms do not last forever, and affording the opportunity to adjust aspects of treatment according to client data. One of our associates at The Anxiety Disorders Clinic, Dr. Vijay Shankar, routinely assigns daily data collection as an ongoing homework assignment.

> The information that is collected is dependent on the diagnoses and needs of the patient. The specific data items to be collected are based on discussions with the patient on what is most salient for the patient's condition and is usually part of the discussion that takes place during the first treatment session. For example, for generalized anxiety disorder, one patient might be more concerned about the number of hours spent in anxiety episodes whereas another patient might be more concerned about the intensity of episodes. (V. Shankar, personal communication, August 7, 2001)

Dr. Shankar enters his patients' data into his laptop computer at the beginning of the session and shows patients a graph of their scores. He argues that this process is extremely useful for keeping track of patient progress and modifying therapeutic procedures when appropriate. This approach is consistent to assessment procedures used by Persons (2001) and colleagues in their evidenced-based practice at the San Francisco Bay Area Center for Cognitive Therapy.

There are several reasons why we chose the aforementioned measures to use in our private practice research. First, we wanted to use measures that had evidence of good reliability and validity. Second, we wanted to use measures that were previously employed in randomized controlled trials (RCTs) conducted at clinical research centers around the world, so that we could compare client characteristics and treatment outcome. Third, we wanted measures that were brief and quickly scorable, so that client and therapist time were conserved.

Finally, we wanted measures for which norms were available for clinical and nonclinical populations. This final characteristic allows us to determine the severity of the client's condition, and importantly to evaluate clinical significance of treatment effects. That is, we can determine whether at the end of treatment our clients look more like people with panic disorder or nonclinical individuals (normals).

Although the examples just mentioned pertain to the assessment of panic disorder, we follow the same plan when treating each of the other anxiety disorders. Fortunately, excellent self-report measures meeting the criteria suggested are available for these disorders, and most of the commercially available treatment manuals also include copies of the appropriate self-report and self-monitoring measures.

## Goal Attainment Scaling as an Alternative

The Anxiety Disorders Clinic has one advantage for doing research in that it specializes in treating a particular family of psychological disorders. Other clinics or agencies may see a much broader spectrum of client issues. In those situations it may not seem possible to identify a standard battery of instruments to use for outcome studies and it may be difficult to accumulate sufficient numbers of cases of any particular type to perform such a study. There are alternatives that such a practice can employ, goal attainment scaling (GAS; Kiresuk, Smith, & Cardillo, 1994) is one such method. GAS consists of identifying critical goals for each client; typically, between three and five goals are identified. The goals are set around what can be reasonably accomplished within the time and resources at hand. They are descriptive so that it can easily be determined whether the goal has been met. The reasonable expectation is scored 0. A similar goal statement representing achieving somewhat more than expected is developed and scored as a 1 and a statement for much more than expected is scored as a 2. A statement indicating achieving somewhat less than expected is scored −1 and one for much less than expected is scored −2. Table 14.1 presents an example from Kiresuk et al. (1994) for a mental health client. Other clients would probably have different goals and certainly different levels within goals. Goal statements need to be written according to rules set out in Kiresuk et al. (1994). These are illustrated by a simple checklist given in their book:

1. Has only one variable been included per scale?
2. Have all possibilities been considered?
3. Has the cell for any level been left blank?
4. Do any levels overlap?
5. Are there any gaps between levels?
6. Have any abbreviations or special terms been used? (Kiresuk et al., 1994, p. 19).

TABLE 14.1
Example Goal Attainment Scales for a Mental Health Client

| Level of Attainment | Scale 1: Career Planning | Scale 2: Control of Anger | Scale 3: Self-Esteem |
|---|---|---|---|
| Much less than expected: −2 | Has not chosen any preferred fields | Less than 25% of time | Generally negative regard (feels worthless) |
| Somewhat less than expected: −1 | One or more fields chosen but no planning | At least 25% of time | More negative features than positive |
| Expected level of outcome: 0 | Selected one or more fields with plans for achieving at least one | Controlled anger at least 50% of time in last 2 weeks (self report) | Feels his positive and negative features are about equal |
| Somewhat more than expected: +1 | Has followed through with plan (interview, etc.) | At least 65% of time | More positive features than negative |
| Much more than expected: +2 | Acquired job in selected field | At least 85% of time | Generally positive regard for self |
| Comments | | | |

*Note:* From Kiresuk, Smith, & Cardillo (1994). Reprinted with permission from Lawrence Erlbaum Associates.

GAS has a unique property as an evaluation technique in that it allows for idiographic measurement and normative comparisons. Each client's progress is considered against goals designed explicitly for him or her. This is what would make the method useful in a general practice or a community mental health setting. At the same time, some straightforward methods have been developed to allow the combining of results from many clients to permit outcome evaluation of the clinic, agency, or practice's overall success. Kiresuk et al. (1994) provided conversion tables and simple formulae for calculating a $T$ score for each client. Research in a number of locations has found that when GAS is properly developed, the $T$ score $M$ and $SD$ will be very close to the theoretical 50 and 10, respectively. Clement (1996) recommended the practice of routinely using GAS for private practice clients to allow each clinician or counselor to evaluate the success of his or her services.

## Clinical Global Impression Scales

The Clinical Global Impression of Severity (CGI-S) and the Clinical Global Impression of Improvement (CGI-I) scales (Guy, 1976) are frequently used as primary outcome measures in many pharmacological and psychosocial treatment studies. The CGI-S is a clinician rating of severity on 7-point scales from 1 (normal, *not at all ill*) to 7 (*extremely ill*). The CGI-I is a clinician rating of improvement, ranging from 1 (*very much improved*) to 7 (*very much worse*). The CGI scales are routinely used as primary outcome measures of medication treatments, and it was recently included in the assessment battery used in a multisite randomized controlled comparison of panic control treatment, imipramine, or their combination for panic disorder. Zaider, Heimberg, Schneier, and Liebowitz (2001) found that both CGI ratings were positively correlated with both self-report and clinician administered measures of social anxiety, depression, impairment, and quality of life. McDonald and Warren, (2001), exploring stage of change and anxiety disorder treatment outcome at our anxiety disorders clinic, also found the CGI rating useful. Although a more comprehensive assessment is preferable, the CGI ratings are among the least time-consuming measures available and might be beneficial for private practitioners' initial foray into the world of outcome assessment.

### Clinical Replication Series as an Integral Part of Treatment

A requirement of science is that findings be replicated in multiple settings. Although major outcome studies are usually performed in universities or other specialized research settings, it is important that the degree to which the results can be generalized and replicated in practice be established. As Hayes et al. (1999) wrote:

> It is, in fact, the unique ability of practitioners to observe extent of effect, successes, failures, and interactions that makes them the focal point in the process of intensive local observation as well as, in the last analysis, full-fledged partners in the scientific process. If properly developed, this process could be the way in which practitioners fulfill the role of scientist–practitioner so long envisioned in our training centers. . . . clinical replication is a process wherein practitioners using a clearly defined set of procedures (a "treatment") intervene with a series of cases that have a well specified and measured problem regularly encountered in applied settings. In the course of this series, the practitioner observes and records successes and failures, analyzing where possible, the reasons for these individual variations (or intersubject variability). This process embodies all of the functions if intensive local observation, as Cronbach (1975) described it, and takes advantage of the strength of practitioners, specifically their observational skills, in the most important context of all: the treatment setting. (p. 238)

Hayes et al. (1999) offered a number of useful guidelines for conducting clinical replication series research, which are quite suitable for the private practice setting. These guidelines include the following:

1. The ideal progression of research is to conduct clinical replication series to assess generalizability of findings subsequent to efficacy research;
2. Selection and characteristics of patients should be clearly described;

3. Intervention procedures and the manner in which they are implemented should be clearly described;
4. Measures should be brief, practical, and realistic for a busy practice setting, and
5. Attempts should be made to account for factors associated with differential responses to treatment, particularly failures and limited success.

As we noted in the beginning of this chapter, as far as we know, hardly anyone conducts research in private practice and publishes his or her results. A notable exception, however is Jacqueline Persons. Indeed, Persons, Bostrom, & Bertagnolli (1999), recently published an article entitled, "Results of Randomized Controlled Trials of Cognitive Therapy for Depression Generalize to Private Practice." In this article, the authors compared outcomes and clinical characteristics of 45 depressed patients treated in private practice with those treated in two RCTs. As an excellent model for conducting clinical replication series in private practice and for assessing the adherence to the five guidelines of Hayes et al. (1999), we discuss Persons et al. (1999).

A multitude of RCTs have tested the efficacy of cognitive therapy for unipolar depression, so testing the generalizability to a service setting, in this case private practice, is a crucial next step in the research process. Patients were consecutive, routine, private practice referrals. Sixty-nine percent met DSM-IIIR criteria for major depression, 7% met criteria for bipolar disorder, and 14% reported a Beck Depression Inventory (BDI; Beck, Ward, Mendelson, Mock, & Erbaugh, 1961) score of 14 or more but did not meet full criterion for major depression. Patients with current substance abuse, medical problems, comorbid disorders, and concurrent therapies (e.g., self-help groups, group therapy, 12-step groups) were included in the study. The authors also specified five selection criteria used to include these private practice patients in the study, for example, a BDI score of 14 or more; a minimum of three BDI scores had to be recorded in the clinical chart. Intervention procedures and the manner in which they were delivered were also clearly specified. For example, the authors noted that the standard CBT protocol (Beck et al., 1979) was modified in certain ways: (a) interventions were based on an individualized case formulation, rather than carried out in a standard order; (b) additional therapy sessions focused on comorbid problems when they were deemed to be a priority; (c) decisions about whether patients should be referred for concomitant pharmacotherapy were made based on clinical response; and (d) treatment was open-ended. Persons was the therapist for all of the patients.

The BDI was the outcome measure used in this study, and a specified cutoff score was used to determine clinically significant and reliable change. Finally, Persons et al. (1999) explored possible predictors of treatment outcome. Of the demographic, comorbidity, and treatment variables examined, only pretreatment BDI scores predicted posttreatment BDI scores. Clinical significance of outcomes was comparable to those obtained in RCTs. In summary, Persons et al. (1999) provided an exemplary model for conducting clinical case series research in a private practice, and how effectiveness research can extend the findings obtained in efficacy studies.

## ILLUSTRATION OF A PRIVATE PRACTICE SETTING STUDY: TREATMENT OF PANIC DISORDER

We illustrate research in a private practice setting by examining a study we conducted on effectiveness of CBT treatment for panic disorder at The Anxiety Disorders Clinic (Warren & Thomas, 1998). Panic disorder with or without agoraphobia occurs in 5% to 8% of the population of the United States, that is, between 12 and 20 million people at some time during their lifetime (Barlow & Craske, 2000). It has been well documented that panic disorder is associated with considerable social and health consequences, including substance abuse, impairments in marital, social, and occupational functioning, and frequent use of medical care and psychotropic medications (Barlow & Craske, 2000; Markowitz, Weissman, Quellette, Lish, & Klerman, 1989).

### Methods

Participants were 50 clients of The Anxiety Disorders Clinic in Lake Oswego, Oregon were either self-referred, or referred by their health care provider, their insurance company or managed care company, other mental health care providers, other community agencies, or by family or friends. In short, clients came to our clinic by the usual routes and were not solicited for research purposes. Participants met DSM-III-R or DSM-IV criteria for either panic disorder with or without agoraphobia. There were no exclusionary criteria such as presence of comorbidity or current medication usage. While these confounds make inference of causality very difficult in an efficacy study, comorbidity and medication usage are common within the clinical setting. We rely on the prior efficacy studies to have demonstrated the causality of the treatment. But in our effectiveness study, we hope to generalize the extent of response to the general, private clinic setting.

### Measures

In addition to a diagnostic interview based on DSM-III-R or DSM-IV criteria, participants were given the self-report questionnaires, described previously in this chapter, to complete at home between the first and second session. Also, the self-monitoring procedures contained in the client treatment manual were carried out throughout the course of treatment.

## Procedures

Clients included in this case series were seen at the clinic from the spring of 1993 through the fall of 1997. As the director of the clinic, Warren received the initial contact calls from the prospective clients and referred them to an appropriate clinic therapist. This determination was made after (a) talking with clients on the phone about their symptoms; (b) listening to a brief history of symptoms; (c) any preferences they had for a male or female therapist; (d) whether or not they wanted to use their insurance, and other financial considerations; (e) availability of particular therapist; and (f) Warren's initial judgment of the complexity of the case, and his initial impressions as to the client's apparent interpersonal style (i.e., did they seem like they might be particularly difficult to get along with). Warren usually asked clients whether they would prefer that the therapist contact them or would they prefer to call the therapist.

## Treatment

All clients received panic control treatment (PCT) and were provided with the manual, *Mastery of Your Anxiety and Panic* (MAP; Barlow & Craske, 1989) and, when it became available, *Mastery of Your Anxiety and Panic II* (MAP-II; Barlow & Craske, 1994). The MAP manuals include education about panic disorder, self-monitoring procedures, cognitive restructuring, diaphragm breathing training, interoceptive exposure to feared bodily sensations, and in vivo exposure to feared and/or avoided activities and places. All treatment was administered on an individual basis. Although all clients systematically followed the manual procedures, it was left to the therapist's discretion as to how quickly or slowly to move through the manual, or whether to address additional clinical problems that were present or arose during treatment. The general approach involved moving to the next chapter only when the previous one appeared to be reasonably mastered. Therapists covered the material in the session and the client read the material and performed the homework activity assignments between sessions. The length of sessions was typically about 50 min.

Some clients were on medications (typically selective serotonin reuptake inhibitors (SSRIs; or high potency benzodiazepines) when they began treatment, some began taking medications during treatment, and others came off medications during treatment. When feasible, our preferred approach was to assist patients in tapering off medications in coordination with the progression through PCT, so that the interoceptive exposure procedures and skills could be applied to physical and mental aspects of drug discontinuation.

## Therapists

Warren was the therapist for the first 23 consecutive PCT clients who came to the clinic from 1993 through 1995. Although he had been treating panic disorder clients using cognitive behavior therapy, including the 1989 version of the MAP manual, prior to 1993, he had not kept systematic data on the treatment of these clients. In 1993, he completed PCT certification provided by Barlow and Craske (1994). This training included intensive didactic instruction and telephone supervision of actual cases. The 27 subsequent clients included in this series were treated by Warren ($n = 9$), a psychiatric nurse practitioner ($n = 8$), a licensed professional counselor ($n = 9$), or a psychology resident ($n = 1$). Of the 50 clients, 40 completed the manualized treatment; 10 dropped out.

Warren then trained other therapists to administer PCT, using the MAP manual and weekly supervision sessions. However weekly supervision was not solely focused on PCT cases, but dealt with other cases presented by the therapists. As therapists appeared to themselves and Warren as more proficient and confident in delivery of PCT, supervision was decreased.

## Procedure

Each client completed a number of instruments prior to beginning therapy: the FQ, with four subscales (agoraphobia, blood/injury, social phobia, and total score), the WQ, the MI, with three scores (accompanied, alone, and panic frequency), the ACQ, BSQ, the Trait Anxiety scale from the STAI, and the BDI. The same data were collected at the end of the study and at two follow-up points, short term (5 to 16 months) and long term (22 to 45 months). Not all clients provided data at one or both follow-up points so there were only eight or nine clients for the long-term follow-up, depending on the scale.

## Results

*Demographic Characteristics.* There were 36 females and 14 males in the total sample ($n = 50$). Clients' ages ranged from 18 to 59 ($M = 34.4$, $SD = 8.9$). Duration of client's problems ranged from 4 months to 216 months ($M = 62.55$ months, $SD = 61.3$ months). Half of the clients experienced the problem for between 12 to 84 months. Twenty-nine clients were married, 11 were single, 8 were divorced or separated, and one was widowed. Comorbidity data were available for 36 clients, and 50% had comorbid conditions. Forty clients (80%) completed treatment and 10 (20%) did not. Clients received a *M* of 13.7 hrs of therapy ($SD = 6.13$), with a minimum of three hrs, maximum of 33 hrs and median of 12.8 hrs. One therapist saw clients for a $M$ of 12.7 hrs, two of the others saw the clients for about 15 hrs, but the difference was not significant. Preliminary analyses indicated that there were some small differences between the clients assigned to therapists on pretest measures. Most notably, Warren's clients scored somewhat lower (more functional) on the Mobility Inventory's Alone scale than did the clients seen by the other therapists. Analyses of covariance (ANCOVA), controlling for pretest scores and hours of treatment, did not find any differences between therapists in posttest scores.

Since there appeared to be minimal therapist effects at this point, we continued our analyses on change on the scores from the various instruments using repeated measures ANOVAs with preplanned comparisons. The comparisons were between pretests and posttests, to determine if clients changed following treatment, and between posttest and follow up. The second set of comparisons allowed us to judge whether clients retained gains made during therapy. Results of these analyses indicated that, for every scale, the clients changed significantly in the direction of improvement from pretest to posttest. In no cases was there any observable change from posttest to short-term follow up. Looking at the long-term follow up (recall there were only eight and nine clients from whom we collected this data), we found a slight, but significant, rebound in the WQ from posttest and a continued decline in the MI-Alone scale.

Each of the measures utilized in this study had been extensively employed in earlier studies and there were established norms for clinical and nonclinical groups. Prior research had established definitions for high end state functioning (HESF). Clients who met the HESF criteria were considered to be functioning as well as nonclinical adults. We used HESF instead of clinical significance because these definitions were already established in the panic treatment literature (e.g., Brown & Barlow, 1995). There were two established HESF criteria employed in this study. The first was that the client be panic free and score a 2 or less on the FQ debilitation scale. The second, and more rigorous criterion, was to meet criterion one plus achieve normal range scores on seven of eight measures.

For these HESF analyses, we concentrated on the pretest, posttest, and short-term follow-up data because the numbers were so small for the long-term follow up. The results of these analyses are shown in Table 14.2.

Additional analyses established that about half of those who attain HESF at the completion of treatment will retain that status at follow up.

This study relied on normative controls, rather than attempting to put some clients in a control group in which they received either no treatment or a placebo. Although a randomized control group is needed for establishing that the treatment caused the changes observed in the clients, such a procedure is neither ethical nor practical in a private clinic. We do not worry too much about causality issues in this study for two reasons. First, prior controlled research established that the PCT program does reduce panic (e.g., Barlow, Gorman,

TABLE 14.2
Results of High End State Functioning Analyses

| HESF Definition | | Pretest | Posttest | Follow Up |
|---|---|---|---|---|
| 1. No panic attacks and 2 or less on FQ debility scale. | | | | |
| | Total N | 46 | 36 | 28 |
| | Number meeting HESF criterion. | 0 | 23 | 14 |
| | Percent meeting HESF criterion. | 0% | 64% | 50% |
| 2. Meet criterion 1 plus achieve normal range scores on 7 of 8 measures. | | | | |
| | Total N | 46 | 36 | 28 |
| | Number meeting HESF criterion. | 0 | 15 | 13 |
| | Percent meeting HESF criterion. | 0% | 42% | 46% |

Shear, & Woods, 2000), and in fact is considered the first-line, nondrug treatment for panic disorder (American Psychiatric Association, 1998). Our concern was to determine that the treatment worked in the private clinic environment. Second, the primary threats to internal validity of this study arising from lack of a control group are regression to the mean, maturation, and history. Pretest scores represent extremes that, under a regression effect, would be expected to be less extreme on retest. However, the fact that the clients had suffered from panic disorder symptoms for many months or years prior to treatment argues against that effect having a major influence on the results. Similarly, if a maturation effect were operating, clients should show a change at roughly the same time after symptom onset. The wide variation in symptom duration indicates that the results are not due to a simple maturation process in which a disorder dissipates after a few months. Because clients were treated for, at most, a few months each over a span of 4 years, this indicates that a historical event did not account for the data. Thus, we feel reasonably assured that the effects that were observed were actually due to the PCT and not some other factor.

Overall, our study showed that panic disordered clients treated at The Anxiety Disorders Clinic showed substantial improvement in their symptoms. About half of the clients became indistinguishable from a nonclinical population; almost all of the clients who completed the therapy were functioning better than when they started. The results duplicate in many ways the results obtained in randomized clinical trials and demonstrate that the local clinic can achieve results similar to those found in major efficacy studies (Warren & Thomas, 1999). It was also important to be able to show that after a relatively few hours spent in treatment (the longest was 33 session hrs), a condition that has typically had a severe impact on the client's quality of life for many months or years could be alleviated or even disappear altogether.

## SUMMARY

The importance of the positive reactions we received reflect the current emphasis on the importance of effectiveness research within the clinical research field, is in part due to the fact that we cannot assume that results of efficacy studies are generalizable to private practice. As an illustration, Hayes et al. (1995) reported that for the multisite PCT study (Barlow et al., 2000), fully 80% of patients meeting criteria for panic disorder with mild agoraphobic avoidance were excluded from the study, due to such factors as having more than mild agorapobic avoidance and unwillingness to potentially be randomized to a nonpreferred treatment (i.e., imimipramine, PCT, or placebo). This, of course, raises significant questions as to how representative study patients are to those who seek treatment in real-world settings. Our PCT for panic disorder effectiveness study just described appears to make an important contribution in suggesting that a particular treatment, empirically supported by RCT efficacy studies, is transportable to private practice patients who often have comorbid disorders.

It is our impression that there has never before been as much recognition of the importance of research on the effectiveness of treatments administered in real-world settings. As Borkovec, Echemendia, Ragusea, & Ruiz (2001) recently reported, the National Institute of Mental Health plans to increase funding for research conducted in routine clinical settings (Foxhole, 2000). In addition, a new journal (*Clinical Case Studies*) focuses on clinical effectiveness. In addition, a number of excellent sources of measures useful in private practice are currently available for anxiety disorders (Antony et al., 2001), depression (Nezu, Ronan, Meadows, & McClure, 2000), and many other clinical problems (e.g., Corcoran & Fischer, 1994).

If a greater number of private practitioners are going to make forays into the world of research, new incentives for such endeavors are essential. Borkovec et al. (2001), based on their experience with the Practice Research Network in Pennsylvania, recommend that clinicians be given continuing education credits for time spent in clinical research and that funding agencies compensate them at their hourly fee for time spent in clinical research related activities. Also, clients will need incentives to complete assessments, particularly at the end of therapy and for any follow-up research conducted by mail. Both the therapists sharing results of the assessments in a way that is meaningful to clients and actual monetary compensation will be important to elicit client cooperation.

We would also suggest that, in addition to journals geared to private practitioners as already mentioned, the traditional academic research journals such as *Behavior Therapy Research and Practice* and *Journal of Consulting and Clinical Psychology* have a section devoted to effectiveness research conducted in private practice and community mental health settings. The Clinical Replication Series section of *Behavior Therapy* is a good model. Other ideas for incentives include state psychological associations offering dues-free annual memberships and free continuing education workshops for participation in private practice research (J. L. Deffenbacher, personal communication, July 19, 2001). National organizations, such as the APA, the AABT, the Anxiety Disorders Association of America (ADAA), and the Obsessive–Compulsive Foundation often acknowledge at their annual meetings which members have published private practice research.

In summary, with the development of instruments and research techniques useful in private practice, along with several outlets for publication of results, there are many opportunities for the empirically oriented practitioner. Being in private practice is an excellent place to do research.

## REFERENCES

American Psychiatric Association (1998). Practice guidelines for the treatment of patients with panic disorder. *American Journal of Psychiatry, 155*(May suppl.), 1–34.

Antony, M. M., Orsillo, S. M., & Roemer, L. (Eds.). (2001). *Practitioner's guide to empirically based measures of anxiety.* New York: Kluwer Academic/Plenum.

Barlow, D. H., & Craske, M. G. (1989). *Mastery of your anxiety and panic.* Albany, NY: Graywind.

Barlow, D. H., & Craske, M. G. (1994). *Mastery of your anxiety and panic—II.* San Antonio, TX: Graywind/Psychological Corporation.

Barlow, D. H., & Craske, M. G. (2000). *Mastery of your anxiety and panic—III.* San Antonio, TX: Graywind/Psychological Corporation.

Barlow, D. H., Gorman, J. M., Shear, M. K., & Woods, S. W. (2000). Cognitive-behavioral therapy, imipramine, or their combination for panic disorder: A randomized controlled trial. *JAMA, 283*(19), 2529–2536.

Beck, A. T., Steer, R. A., & Brown, G. K. (1996). Beck Depression Inventory, Second Edition, Manual. San Antonio, TX: The Psychological Corporation.

Beck, A. T., Ward, C. H., Mendelson, M., Mock, J., & Erbaugh, J. (1961). An inventory for measuring depression. *Archives of General Psychiatry, 41,* 561–571.

Beck, A. T., Rush, A. J., Shaw, B. F., & Emery, G. (1979). *Cognitive therapy of depression.* New York: Guilford Press.

Borkovec, T. K., Echemendia, R. J., Ragusea, S. A., & Ruiz, M. (2001). The Pennsylvania Practice Research Network and future possibilities for clinically meaningful and scientifically rigorous psychotherapy effectiveness research. *Clinical Psychology: Science and Practice, 8*(2), 155–167.

Brown, T. A., & Barlow, D. H. (1995). Long-term outcome in cognitive–behavioral treatment of panic disorder: Clinical predictors and alternative strategies for assessment. *Journal of Consulting and Clinical Psychology, 63,* 754–765.

Chambless, D. L., Caputo, G. C., Bright, P., & Gallagher, R. (1984). Assessment of "fear of fear" in agoraphobics: The Body Sensations Questionnaire and the Agoraphobic Cognitions Questionnaire. *Journal of Consulting and Clinical Psychology, 52,* 1090–1097.

Chambless, D. L., Caputo, G. C., Jasin, S. E., Gracely, E. J., & Williams, C. (1985). The Mobility Inventory for Agoraphobia. *Behaviour Research and Therapy, 23,* 35–44.

Christiansen, L. R. (2001). *Effectiveness of cognitive processing therapy in treating posttraumatic stress disorder in a private practice setting.* Unpublished doctoral dissertation, Pacific University, Forest Grove, Oregon.

Clement, P. (1996). Evaluation in private practice. *Clinical Psychology: Science and Practice, 3,* 146–159.

Corcoran, K., & Fischer, J. (1994). *Measures for clinical practice: A sourcebook* (Vol. 1 and Vol. 2). New York: Free Press.

Cronbach, L. J. (1975). Beyond the two disciplines of scientific psychology. *American Psychologist, 30*, 116–127.

Foxhall, K. (2000). Research for the real world. *APA Monitor, 31*, 28–36.

Guy W. (Ed.). (1976). *ECDEU assessment for psychopharmacology*. (Rev. ed.). Rockville, MD: NIMH Publications.

Hayes, S. C., Barlow, D. H., & Nelson-Gray, R. O. (1999). *The scientist practitioner: Research and accountability in the age of managed care* (2nd ed.). Boston: Allyn & Bacon.

Kiresuk, T. J., Smith, A., & Cardillo, J. E. (1994). *Goal attainment scaling: Applications, theory, and measurement.* Hillsdale, NJ: Lawrence Erlbaum Associations.

Markowitz, J. S., Weissman, M. M., Quellette, R., Lish, J. D., & Klerman, G. L. (1989). Quality of life in panic disorder. *Archives of General Psychiatry, 46*, 984–992.

Marks, I. M., & Mathews, A. M., (1979). Brief standard self-rating for phobic patients. *Behaviour Research and Therapy, 17*, 263–267.

McDonald, T., & Warren, R. (2001, July). *An investigation of the relationship between stage of change and outcome in the treatment of anxiety disorders.* Poster session presented at the World Congress of Behavioral and Cognitive Therapies, Vancouver, BC.

McRitchie, M. (1998*). Social phobia: A case study analysis of exportability for a cognitive-behavioral intervention in the clinical setting.* Unpublished master's thesis, Pacific University, Forest Grove, Oregon.

Meyer, T. J., Miller, M. L., Metzger, R. L., & Borkovec, T. D. (1990). Development and validation of the Penn State Worry Questionnaire. *Behaviour Research and Therapy, 28*, 487–495.

Nezu, A. M., Ronan, G. F., Meadows, E. A., & McClure, K. S. (Eds.). (2000). *Practitioner's guide to empirically based measures of depression.* New York: Kluwer Academic/Plenum Publishers.

Obsessive Compulsive Cognitions Working Group (OCCWG/1997). Cognitive assessment of obsessive-compulsive disorder. *Behavior Research and Therapy, 35*, 667–681.

Persons, J. B. (2001). Conducting effectiveness studies in the context of evidence-based clinical practice. *Clinical Psychology: Science and Practice, 8*(2), 168–172.

Persons, J. B., Bostrom, A., & Bertagnolli, A. (1999). Results of randomized controlled trials of cognitive therapy for depression generalized to private practice. *Cognitive Therapy and Research, 23*, 535–548.

Reiss, S., Peterson, R. A., Gursky, D. M., & McNally, R. J. (1986). Anxiety sensitivity, anxiety frequency and the prediction of fearfulness. *Behaviour Research and Therapy, 24*, 1–8.

Sookman, D., Yaryura-Tobias, J., & Warren R. (1997, September). *Issues in the integration of drug and cognitive behavioural treatments for obsessive-compulsive disorder: A clinical roundtable.* Symposium conducted at the XXVII Congress of the European Association for Behavioural & Cognitive Therapies, Venice, Italy.

Spielberger, C. D., Gorsuch, R. L., & Lushene, R. E. (1970). *Manual for the State-Trait Anxiety Inventory.* Palo Alto, CA: Consulting Psychologists Press.

Strand, J., & Warren, R. (2001, July). *Long-term outcome of panic control treatment administered in a private practice setting.* Poster session presented at the World Congress of Behavioral and Cognitive Therapies, Vancouver, BC.

Trierweiler, S., & Stricker, G. (1998). *The scientific practice of professional psychology.* New York: Plenum Press.

Warren, R. (1995). Panic control treatment of panic disorder with agoraphobia and comorbid major depression: A private practice case. *Journal of Cognitive Psychotherapy: An International Quarterly, 9*, 123–134

Warren, R. (1996). *Is panic control treatment effective in a private practice setting? A clinical case series.* Poster session presented at the Banff International Conference on Behavioral Science, Banff, Canada.

Warren, R., & McCaffery, (1996, March). *The inventory of beliefs related to obsessions: Criterion-related and convergent validity.* Poster session presented at the annual meeting of the Anxiety Disorders Association of America, Orlando, FL.

Warren, R., & Thomas, J. C. (1997, November). Is panic control treatment effective in a private practice setting? Symposium conducted at the annual meeting of the Association for Advancement of Behavior Therapy, Miami, FL.

Warren, R., & Thomas, J. C. (1999). Randomized controlled trials are relevant to routine clinical practice. *ADAA Reporter, 10*(1), 1, 17, 19, 21.

Warren, R., & Thomas, J. C. (2001). Cognitive-behavior therapy of obsessive-compulsive disorder in private practice: An effectiveness study. *Journal of Anxiety Disorders, 15*, 277–285.

Warren, R., & Zgourides, G. (1989). Further validity and normative data for the Malouff and Schutte Belief Scale. *Journal of Rational-Emotive and Cognitive-Behavior Therapy, 1*, 167–172.

Warren, R., Zgourides, G., & Englert, M. (1990). Relationships between catastrophic cognitions and body sensations in anxiety disordered, mixed diagnosis and normal subjects. *Behaviour Research and Therapy, 28*, 355–357.

Warren, R., Zgourides, G., & Jones, A. (1989). Cognitive bias and irrational belief as predictors of avoidance. *Behaviour Research and Therapy, 27*, 181–188.

Warren, R., Zgourides, G., & Monto, M. (1993). Self-report versions of the Yale–Brown Obsessive Compulsive Scale: An assessment of a sample of normals. *Psychological Reports, 73*, 574.

Warren, R., Zgourides, G., Monto, M., & Felker, J. (1994, March). *Further assessment of the reliability and validity of the self-report Yale–Brown Obsessive-Compulsive Scale.* Poster session presented at the annual meeting of the Anxiety Disorders Association of America, Santa Monica, CA.

Zaider, T. I., Heimberg, R. G., Schneier, F. R., & Liebowitz, M. R. (2001, March). *Evaluation of the Clinical Global Impression Scale among individuals with social anxiety disorder.* Poster session presented at the annual meeting of the Anxiety Disorders Association of America, Atlanta, GA.

Zgourides, G., Warren, R., & Englert, M. (1990). Uso of a portable radio headset in the treatment of paruresis: Two clinical cases. *Phobia practice and Research Journal, 3*, 43–44.

# 15

# Research with Children

Mark D. Rapport
*University of Central Florida*

Robert Randall
Gail N. Shore
Kyong-Mee Chung
*University of Hawaii*

This chapter describes and explains research methodology and research design relevant to children and how this knowledge is applied in practical settings for practical knowledge. *Research methodology* refers to the myriad principles, practices, and procedures that direct research, whereas *research design* refers to the organized plan that is used to examine the questions of interest. Both methodology and design represent important knowledge that guide the planning, implementation, and analysis of a research project, but are valuable tools only to those who have successfully formulated a research idea.

## FORMULATING RESEARCH IDEAS

Formulating an initial research idea is relatively painless for some, whereas for others, it represents an arduous process. It requires a certain degree of creativity and the ability to translate potentially interesting ideas or general hypotheses into concrete form so that they may be studied.

Ideas result from multiple sources. Some materialize from working in a particular setting (e.g., schools, mental health centers) or with a particular population (e.g., children with Attention-Deficit/Hyperactivity Disorder [ADHD]). Others result from simple curiosity about a phenomenon, personal experience (e.g., being the child of an alcoholic parent or dysfunctional marriage), discussions with mentors, or by reviewing a particular area of research and thinking about possible relationships and/or causes between and among variables in nature. Exposure to (e.g., clinical practica) and visiting a variety of settings is also a pragmatic means by which to formulate ideas that may be appropriate for study. Doing so permits direct observation of a wide range of problems encountered by children and the myriad environmental factors that mediate, moderate, and influence their behavior. Observing children in these settings can serve to stimulate creative ideas ranging from program and systems evaluation to individual (behavioral, psychopharmacological) and curricula interventions.

Operationalizing or measuring various constructs (e.g., self-concept, fearfulness) represents another avenue that may stimulate research ideas. In these cases, investigators develop particular types of instruments or scales or examine the psychometric properties (validity, reliability) of existing instruments, frequently as a precondition for future research. For example, an investigator may seek to develop or validate a measure of self-concept in children to enable further studies that examine whether self-concept is associated with particular attributes in children.

The foregoing examples are by no means exhaustive. There are infinite ways in which research ideas emerge, based on everyday experiences, stereotypic notions about behavior, cultural lore, or by focusing on a problem area of particular interest to the researcher.

## OVERVIEW

Issues relevant to conducting research with children are discussed initially in the chapter to provide readers with a working understanding of how development (maturation), measurement, confidentiality, and gaining access to educational settings influences selection of appropriate research methods and designs. An array of research methods and designs is subsequently presented and discussed to provide practical examples of the types of questions researchers ask about children, and how differing methods and designs are used to answer these questions. Studies that examine individual children (single-subject designs), differences between groups (group designs), relationships among variables (correlation), and behavior over time (longitudinal) are highlighted.

## ISSUES AND CONSIDERATIONS IN CHILD RESEARCH

### Developmental Considerations

Evaluation of treatment interventions and investigations of maladaptive behaviors are intriguing but complicated areas to research owing to a host of developmental factors. These factors play an important role in understanding maladaptive behavior, how behavior evolves over time, and whether intervention is warranted at particular ages or for particular problems. For example, many behaviors associated with or mistaken as maladjustment and emotional disturbance are relatively common during childhood. Estimated prevalence rates based on parent report indicate that fears and worries (43%), temper tantrums (80%), overactivity (49%), bedwetting (17%), restlessness (30%), and nail biting (27%) occur frequently in 6- to 12-year-old children (Lapouse & Monk, 1958), but do not necessarily portend later psychological dysfunction. In a similar vein, most children exhibit "stranger anxiety" around 8 months of age that mirrors their ability to discriminate a familiar face from an unfamiliar face. Separation anxiety becomes evident shortly after stranger anxiety begins, and is characterized by distress and an inability to be readily comforted by others in the absence of the child's parents or primary care providers. This is a normal response pattern in very young children, whereas excessive anxiety concerning separation from major attachment figures in later years accompanied by other behaviors (e.g., reluctance to attend school, unrealistic worry that an untoward calamitous event will separate the child from his parents, somatic complaints, excessive distress on separating from parents, social withdrawal) may signal the onset of a clinical disorder. Oppositional behavior is similarly viewed as a normal phase in the development of the 18- to 36-month-old child but considered maladaptive in later years if persistent and accompanied by other behavior problems.

Other problem behaviors show clear developmental trends and are not considered maladaptive until late childhood. Lying and destructiveness are common exemplars. An estimated 50% of boys (or higher) and girls engage in lying by age 6 according to their parents. Frequency of lying decreases to approximately 25% and 13% by age 7 in boys and girls, respectively, and continues to follow a downward trend as a function of increasing age in most children. Destructive behavior shows a similar developmental trend, peaking at 3 and 5 years of age in girls and boys, respectively, with a clear downward trend for both genders through age 13 (MacFarlane, Allen, & Honzik, 1954).

Other classes of maladaptive behavior may remain stable over time but change with respect to typography or form. An example of this phenomenon is the way in which children manifest aggression. Threatening, pushing, and shoving in young children may evolve into verbal and physical assault over time (Patterson, 1982). An assessment battery designed to evaluate the occurrence of or effects of treatment on a particular type or class of behavior problem may thus have to include different instruments to account for the way in which behavior evolves over time.

The foregoing examples inform us that many problematic behaviors in childhood will diminish or remit over the course of normal development and may not be appropriate or high priorities for intervention. They also suggest a clear need for understanding base rates of different behavior problems in children and how these rates change over the course of development. Failure to appreciate and control for these variables may inadvertently result in attributing change to treatment rather than maturation or other historical events.

Other developmental factors that merit consideration include evaluating the appropriateness of measures, instruments, and interviews with respect to children's abilities and background characteristics. Systematically reviewing published studies (in high-quality, peer-review journals) that deal with the phenomenon in question is a strategy commonly used by researchers to obtain examples of instruments and measures (see Table 15.1 for a listing of child-oriented journals). Age and gender norms are available for many instruments and rating scales, and these are customarily preferred over those without published norms. Others provide this information but have limited or no established psychometric properties (i.e., reliability, validity) and are thus of limited use unless the purpose of the study is to establish these metrics. Studies that involve or plan to investigate specific ethnic and/or cultural factors in children must additionally consider whether available instruments are appropriate for the selected population. Finally, the use of clinical interviews, verbally administered assessment instruments, and those that require a particular degree of cognitive sophistication require careful consideration owing to the range and developing nature of children's abilities.

## Measurement Issues

Conducting research with children requires broad knowledge of measurement issues related to maturation, selection of dependent measures, and the degree to which informants (parents, teachers, observers) agree with one another when providing information about children's behavior. This is due to several factors. Children's behavior is qualitatively different from that of adults and thus requires a completely different approach with respect to measurement and observation (i.e., attempts to extrapolate adult measures for use in child research by changing wording, modifying administration procedures, and making other adjustments usually fails). Childhood behavior problems are rarely characterized by isolated symptoms. Rather, they entail a broad range of emotional, behavioral, and social difficulties that arise in multiple situations such as at home, at school, and with peers. Multiproblem and multisituation assessment and analysis are thus nearly always required. Finally, children's rapidly emerging and changing verbal and cognitive abilities require careful consideration for research studies in which they are asked questions about themselves, others, and internal (e.g., mood/affect, anxiety) or external states (e.g., self-ratings of externalizing behavior problems such as hyperactivity or peer relationships). This consideration is complicated by extant research demonstrating differences among raters (e.g., parents, teachers, and trained observers), across settings (e.g., home and school), and for different types of behavior problems as now discussed.

TABLE 15.1
Child Oriented Journals Related to Assessment, Measurement, Treatment
Outcome, Broad and Narrow Spectrum Issues

| Journal | Publisher |
| --- | --- |
| *Focus on treatment outcome* | |
| Behavior Modification | Sage Publications, Inc. |
| Child Behavior Therapy | Haworth Press |
| Journal of Applied Behavior Analysis | Society for the Experimental Analysis of Behavior |
| *Focus on School Settings/Issues* | |
| Journal of Educational Psychology | American Psychology Association |
| Journal of Learning Disabilities | Donald Hammill/Pro*Ed |
| Journal of School Psychology | Pergamon Press |
| School Psychology Review | National Association of School Psychologists |
| *Focus on developmental factors* | |
| Child Development | Blackwell Press |
| Developmental Psychology | American Psychology Association |
| Development and Psychopathology | Cambridge University Press |
| Journal of Applied Developmental Psychology | Ablex Publishing Corporation/ Elsevier Science |
| *Focus on assessment/measurement issues* | |
| Behavioral Assessment | Pergamon Press |
| Journal of Educational Measurement | National Council on Measurement in Education |
| Journal of Psychopathology and Behavioral Assessment | Kluwer Academic/Plenum Press |
| Psychological Assessment: A Journal of Consulting and Clinical Psychology | American Psychological Association |
| *Broad-spectrum topics related to child psychopathology* | |
| Clinical Psychology Review | Pergamon Press |
| Journal of the American Academy of Child & Adolescent Psychiatry | Lippincott Williams & Wilkins |
| Journal of Abnormal Child Psychology | Kluwer Academic/Plenum Press |
| Journal of Child Psychology and Psychiatry | Cambridge University Press |
| Journal of Clinical Child Psychology | Lawrence Erlbaum Associates |
| Journal of Pediatric Psychology | Oxford University Press |
| *Narrow-spectrum topics related to child psychopathology* | |
| Journal of Developmental and Behavioral Pediatrics | Lippincott Williams & Wilkins |
| Journal of Autism and Developmental Disorders | Kluwer Academic/Plenum Press |

***Informant Ratings of Children's Behavior.*** Ratings scales are the most
commonly used and cost effective means to obtain information about children's
behavior. Standardized scales are available that provide broad (e.g., internalizing, externalizing behavior problems[1]) and narrow indices (e.g., measures of

---

[1]Internalizing and externalizing behavior problems reflect a distinction between fearful, inhibited,
overcontrolled behavior, and aggressive, antisocial, undercontrolled behavior.

particular clinical disorders or states such as depression) of behavior, as well as for particular constructs (e.g., self-esteem, perceived competence) and other types of functioning (e.g., classroom performance, adaptive behavior, peer perceptions). Incorporating rating scales in research necessitates examination of (a) the scale's psychometric properties (i.e., does the instrument provide valid and reliable information with respect to what it purports to measure?); (b) general knowledge concerning the degree to which different informants can be counted on to provide valid information about a child's behavior; and (c) factors that influence informant ratings.

Extant research examining the degree to which raters agree concerning the presence of behavior problems reveals several, relatively consistent trends. In general, informants who interact with the child in the same environment (e.g., parents) tend to show better agreement in their reports of behavior than those (e.g., parents vs. teachers vs. mental health workers) who interact with the child in different environments (Achenbach, McConaughy, & Howell, 1987). Agreement by parents, however, is less than ideal as highlighted in a recent meta-analytic review (Duhig, Renk, Epstein, & Phares, 2000). Correspondence between mother and father ratings of children's behavior problems varied depending on the category of problem behaviors examined. For example, $M$ correspondence between parents for internalizing behavior problems was .45 as opposed to .63 and .70 for externalizing and total behavior problem scores, respectively—perhaps because externalizing behavior problems are easier to judge and/or more consistent across situations or settings (Achenbach et al., 1987; Walker & Bracken, 1996). Although a correlation of .45 is considered a "moderate" level of agreement between raters, it nevertheless indicates that only 20% ($.45^2$) of the variability in one parent's ratings can be explained (predicted) by the variability of the other parent's ratings. Higher correspondence between parents was reported for adolescents than for younger children when examining both internalizing and externalizing behavior problems, and the family's socioeconomic status appears to exert small but significant effects on parent ratings.

Others report similar differences in levels of agreement for clinical and nonclinical samples, better agreement when rating young children compared with adolescents, more variable rates of agreement for particular types of behavior problems, and poor correspondence between child self-ratings and adult ratings of their behavior (Achenbach et al., 1987).

The foregoing summary indicates that parents and teachers can be relied on to provide reasonably reliable ratings of children's behavior in the context in which they observe children for broad indices such as internalizing and externalizing behavior problems. Diminished correspondence between informants is evidenced, however, for ratings of more discrete types of behavior problems, when informant ratings are based on different settings, and when comparing children's own ratings to those of adults. Investigators need to consider these issues when selecting from the panoply of behavior rating scales, instruments, and other forms of data collection such as direct observation.

Selection of appropriate instruments to use in a study depends on what the investigator wishes to measure (e.g., broad classes or types of behavior as opposed to well-defined, more discrete incidences of behavior such as motor activity), how often measurement takes place (e.g., preassessment, postassessment, in contrast to ongoing assessment), the willingness of others to serve as informants (e.g., parents, teachers, or children), and a variety of other factors such as cost and time constraints. Consultation of specialty texts on child assessment is advised for those interested in reviewing the broad range of instruments and techniques available (e.g., see Mash & Terdal, 1997, Ollendick & Hersen, 1993).

***Interview Measures of Children's Behavior.*** Interviewing children, observing their behaviors in different settings, measuring their abilities (e.g., intelligence, scholastic achievement, cognitive functioning), and obtaining performance indices are common methods for obtaining study data.

Structured and semistructured clinical interviews have gained popularity in recent years and are used primarily for establishing clinical diagnoses. Children meeting diagnostic criteria are subsequently compared to a normal peer group, a group of children with some other diagnosis, or simply identified to examine factors associated with the disorder or the effects of treatment. Clinical and semistructured interviews usually employ more questioning than do structured interviews. As a result, they frequently yield more information relevant to differential diagnosis. In either case, the use of and time required for both types of interviews is easily justified for both clinical training and diagnostic decision-making purposes. Clinicians should be aware, however, of both the individual and collective shortcomings inherent to interviews (see Edelbrock & Costello, 1984).

Numerous interviews are available and most can be administered to children as young as 8 years of age. The more common practice, however, is to interview the child's parent or caregiver. Commonly used structured and semistructured interviews are listed in Table 15.2.

***Observational Measures of Children's Behavior.*** Behavioral observation is a time-consuming but potentially more valuable approach for obtaining detailed information about children and the environments in which they learn, play, and interact with others. It refers to a process in which human observers record motor, verbal, and interactive behaviors of other humans, using carefully defined operational criteria as opposed to evaluative judgments (e.g., rating scales) or mechanically activated devises (e.g., movement monitors,

TABLE 15.2
Structured and Semistructured Interviews for Use With Children
and Their Caregivers

|  | *Time Required* | *Source* |
|---|---|---|
| *Structured interviews* | | |
| Diagnostic Interview for Children and Adolescents (DICA) | 60 to 90 minutes | Herjanic & Campbell (1977) |
| Diagnostic Interview Schedule for Children (DISC) | 60 to 90 minutes | Costello, Edelbrock, Kalas, Kessler, & Klaric (1984) |
| *Semistructured interviews* | | |
| Children's Assessment Schedule (CAS) | 45 to 120 minutes | Hodges, McKnew, Cytryn, Stern, & Klein (1982) |
| Kiddie-SADS (K-SADS) | 45 to 120 minutes | Chambers et al. (1985) |
| Interview Schedule for Children (ISC) | 45 to 120 minutes | Kovacs (1982) |

*Note:* All instruments have acceptable psychometric properties.

physiological monitoring). As such, many consider it the *sine qua non* of child assessment. An advantage of using behavioral observations is that the technique is virtually unrestricted with respect to context. Observations can be conducted in naturalistic settings (e.g., to record classroom, playground, or bus riding behavior), analogue settings (e.g., a room furnished to resemble a classroom), or child clinics (e.g., to assess memory function and corresponding changes in behavior, or to record parent–child interactions).

A wide variety of observational coding schemas is published and easily extracted for research purposes. Some permit coding of a wide range of behaviors (e.g., parent–child interactions, general classroom deportment) and are best suited for particular settings (e.g., home or classroom observations). Others were developed to permit highly refined and detailed observation, recording, and measurement of more discrete types of behavior (e.g., gross motor activity). Assessing agreement between observers (interobserver reliability) is nearly always required for research studies and involves pretraining on the selected coding schema and arranging for multiple observers to code the targeted behaviors simultaneously while in the setting or based on taped recordings. Detailed information concerning how to select particular stimuli, responses, specific recording techniques, operationalize particular types, forms and classes of behavior, and calculate interobserver reliability is readily available in classic texts on child behavior assessment (e.g., Kazdin, 1989; Ollendick & Hersen, 1993).

## Informed Consent and Confidentiality

Knowledge of regulatory statutes, the role and function of institutional review boards (IRBs), and general procedures for insuring and obtaining informed consent are essential for conducting research with children. Detailed information concerning procedures and regulatory statutes related to studies involving children can be obtained from the Department of Health and Human Services (DHHS) Website (http://ohrp.osophs.dhhs. gov/polasur.htm). These regulations provide the minimum standards for protecting human subjects, particularly under the subpart D section, which includes detailed information concerning the involvement of children in research.

Regulations require the assent of the child or minor and the permission or consent of the parent(s) or legally authorized guardian when children are involved in research. *Assent* means a child's affirmative agreement to participate in research. The standard for assent is the ability to understand, to some degree, the purpose of the research and what will happen if one participates in it.

*Permission* refers to the consent or agreement of parent(s) or guardian to the participation of their child or ward in research. There are two forms of parental consent. *Passive* parental consent is a procedure that requires parents to respond only if they do not want their child to participate in a research project. *Active* parental consent requires the parent to return a signed consent form indicating whether or not they are willing to allow their child to participate. The latter method is recommended, although many researchers prefer the passive consent procedure because of the higher response rate typically achieved. As a general rule for research involving minimal risk, it is sufficient to obtain informed consent from one parent.

Informed consent consists of three primary elements: knowledge, volition, and competency. Parents or guardians of children must be knowledgeable about all aspects of a study, which includes a thorough description of the facts, plausible risks, and potential sources of discomfort associated with an experimental study that may affect their decision to permit their child to participate. This information must be presented to the child's parents or legal guardians in an understandable fashion, followed by an opportunity for them to ask questions or clarify any issues that might not be thoroughly understood.

*Volition* refers to the process in which participants (or in the case of minor children, their parents or guardians) agree to participate in a study free of coercion or threat. Subjects (or in the case of minor children, their guardians) must be able to decline or withdraw from participating at any time preceding or during an experiment without penalty, and should be informed of this provision (i.e., participation must be entirely voluntary).

Ensuring competency in child research typically entails the parents' or guardians' ability to render an educated decision and give consent for their

TABLE 15.3
Components of Informed Consent Forms

| Section of the Form | Purpose and Contents |
|---|---|
| *Overview* | Presentation of the goals of the study, why this is conducted, who is responsible for the study and its execution. |
| *Description of procedures* | Clarification of the experimental conditions, assessment procedures, requirements of the subjects. |
| *Risks and inconveniences* | Statement of any physical and psychological risks and an estimate of their likelihood. Inconveniences and demands to be placed on the subjects (e.g., how many sessions, requests to do any thing, contact at home). |
| *Benefits* | A statement of what the subjects can reasonably hope to gain from participation, including psychological, physical, and monetary benefits. |
| *Costs and economic considerations* | Charges to the subjects (e.g., in treatment) and payment (e.g., for participation or completing various forms). |
| *Confidentiality* | Assurances that the information is confidential and will only be seen by people who need to do so for the purposes of research (e.g., scoring and data analysis), procedures to assure confidentiality (e.g., removal of names from forms, storage of data). Also, caveats are included here if it is possible that sensitive information (e.g., psychiatric information, criminal activity) can be subpoenaed. |
| *Alternative treatments* | In an intervention study, alternatives available to the client before or during participation are outlined. |
| *Voluntary participation* | A statement that the subject is willing to participate and can say *no* now or later without penalty of any kind. |
| *Questions and further information* | A statement that the subject is encouraged to ask questions at any time and can contact an individual (or individuals) (listed by name and phone number) available for such contacts. |
| *Signature lines* | A place for the subject as well as the experimenter to sign. |

*Note:* From A. E. Kazdin, *Research Design in Clinical Psychology,* Third Edition. Copyright 1998 by Allyn & Bacon. Reprinted/adapted by permission.

child to participate based on thorough knowledge and understanding of the study.

A consent form signed by the parents or guardians of children indicates their willingness to have their child participate in the study based on an informed decision. These forms traditionally undergo formal review by an institutional review board (IRB) or agency committee that evaluates the research proposal, consent procedures, and the form itself. Consent forms vary by design, but must contain a thorough description of the study, inherent and potential risks and benefits, procedures, and issues concerning confidentiality and how the study data may be used. Components of an informed consent form are detailed in Table 15.3.

IRBs serve to assess the risk, possible benefits, and associated discomforts associated with a research project. All research proposals must be submitted to an appropriate IRB for consideration and formally approved prior to beginning a project. University based projects will typically be reviewed by the institution's IRB panel and additional approvals may need to be obtained by other agency boards (e.g., hospitals, school systems, NIMH) depending on the selection of participants and whether the project is funded or sponsored by private or federal agencies.

## Child Research Settings

*General Dimensions.*   A research study may be conducted in a laboratory (e.g., clinic, university laboratory, hospital) or an applied setting (e.g., school, home). The advantage of most laboratory settings is that they typically allow for maximal control over the experiment. Their most apparent disadvantage is that the nature of the setting is usually quite different than most real-life situations, which calls into question the generality of results. The advantage of applied settings is that they frequently represent real-life situations or environments, which allows for greater generality of results. Their most obvious disadvantage is that they usually afford less control than a laboratory setting. Typically, one thinks of true experimental and quasiexperimental designs as taking place in a laboratory setting and observational designs as taking place in an applied setting (see upcoming Group Comparison Methods). This is due to the fact that in true and quasiexperimental designs, the researcher attempts to exert a high degree of control, whereas in observational designs, the researcher does not exert any control. It is important to note, however, that true or quasiexperiments can in fact be conducted in applied settings and observational studies can occur in a laboratory setting. Single-case research designs are used in both settings.

*Gaining Access to Educational Settings.*   Conducting research in the school involves striking a balance between maintaining the requisite degree of scientific rigor, on one hand, and respecting the mission and structure of the educational setting on the other hand. Research protocols must be planned such that disruption of school or classroom routine is minimized. The investigator must be mindful that in the educational setting, classes (as opposed to individuals) are frequently the units of analysis. For protocols involving individual administration, pulling a child from some class periods (e.g., recreational reading) may be less disruptive than others (e.g., small-group science activity) for the class as a whole and the child in particular. Moreover, schools may be especially protective of certain groups of students, such as children with developmental disabilities or behavioral/emotional problems. Thus, conducting research in educational settings requires careful planning and organization in order to maintain scientific rigor and accommodate the structure of the school. The ensuing discussion is particularly relevant for group studies in which a large sample of participants is required.

Gaining access to participants (subjects) is a necessary first step for most research projects, and schools are a logical source for recruitment for studies involving children. The choice of school depends on a number of factors, which vary in degree of relevance based on the focus of the investigation (Petosa & Goodman, 1991). Among the factors to consider are the socioeconomic status of the community served by the school and the ethnic distribution of the school's population of students. For investigations involving multiple groups, the number of students enrolled in the school becomes an important consideration, in light of the power needs of the study's design to detect group differences.

Prior to contacting schools, the investigator must prepare to address any questions or concerns that may be forthcoming. Petosa and Goodman (1991) outlined five phases of decision-making that school officials undergo, and discuss them in relation to decisions surrounding research proposals. In the *legitimacy phase*, the credibility of the investigator and the relevance of the study are of central concern. Representatives of the research project who contact the school should be prepared to address questions concerning the expertise and affiliation of the chief investigator, source of funding for the project, and the project's relevance for the education and welfare of children or community at large. In the second, *information-seeking phase*, the concerns of school officials involve the impact of the project on the day-to-day operation of the school. The investigator should consider the timing of the data collection with the school's schedule in mind. For example, the weeks preceding the winter holiday break and the end of the school year are best avoided as they are often hectic for school personnel. Similarly, the month of April is best avoided as it tends to be dedicated to standardized achievement testing. During the information-seeking phase, school officials will also want to know the specific requirements of the project in order to gauge its impact on the school's mission and function. The investigator should be prepared to address questions pertaining to the measures to be administered, the amount of class time required for participation in the project, the costs of participation accruing to the school (e.g., the extent of involvement of school staff), and the resources that will be available to the school (e.g., teacher training and curricular materials). During this phase, school officials will also be aware of any potential controversy that may arise from any measures to be used or procedures to be implemented. In the ensuing *expression of limitations phase*, education officials are likely to express concerns over idiosyncratic situational factors that may pose obstacles to the school's participation in the project. The resourceful

TABLE 15.4

Research Checklist for School-Based Personnel

---

1. Has a clearly defined *problem statement* been provided for review?
2. Has a copy of the *data collection instrument* been promised by the researcher?
   a. What is the *reading level* of the instrument? (*readability index*)?
   b. Will the instrument obtain *consistent results* over time? (*reliability*)?
   c. Does the instrument measure what it purports to measure? (*validity*)?
   d. Has the instrument been *field tested*?
3. How was the school *selected* to participate in the study?
   a. Was it part of a *random or convenient* selection process?
   b. Has the investigator followed a specific district protocol for proposal review? (*research review panel, school board, superintendent only, etc.*)
4. What students comprise the *sample* for the study?
   a. Will students be randomly selected *individually or by classroom*?
   b. What is the *size, grade level, gender, ability level, etc.* of students to be selected?
5. How will the data be *collected* for analysis?
   a. Who will *administer* the data collection instrument?
   b. Who will *collect* the completed instruments for analysis?
   c. How is *informed consent* obtained?
   d. What provisions are proposed to maintain *anonymity and/or confidentiality* of data collected?
   e. Are there plans for longitudinal *data collection*?
6. How will the results be *shared* with the school district and community?
7. Should results so indicate, what *commitment* has the researcher made for *follow-up program development*?
8. What can be done to *develop and maintain* mutually beneficial relationships?

---

*Note:* From "Recommendations for obtaining cooperation to conduct school-based research," by R. S. Olds and C. W. Symons, 1990, *Journal of School Health, 60*, p. 97. Copyright 1990 by American School Health Association, Kert, Ohio. Reprinted with permission.

*Source:* Olds & Symons, C. W. (1990). Reprinted with permission from author.

investigator should prepare to address concerns over issues of "fit" between the study's requirements and the school's structure, without undermining the integrity of the research project. If the investigator is successful, all parties enter the *engagement phase* of mutual problem solving, in which various ways of increasing the feasibility of the study are considered, such as finding the optimal dates and times, and allocating physical space for data collection. In the final *commitment phase*, all parties make specific plans for the school's participation in the research project. A checklist of questions that school personnel may raise in considering research proposals is shown in Table 15.4. Investigators must be prepared to address questions of this nature when approaching schools.

Gaining access to research participants involves a steplike progression to enhance the likelihood of a proposal's acceptance by educational institutions (Olds & Symons, 1990). Prior to contacting schools, it behooves the investigator to obtain endorsements from related agencies and the district superintendent of education as this smoothes the way to the engagement phase of decision making for the school principal. Subsequent contact with the principal should first be handled formally through an individually addressed cover letter that briefly explains the importance and nature of the study and mentions the endorsements received, followed by a telephone call approximately 1 week later to secure an appointment for a meeting. At the meeting, a copy of measures to be administered should be provided for the principal's perusal. Olds and Symons (1990) recommended presenting a *data collection participation* form for the principal's signature to secure the school's commitment. The initial contact with the school should be made far enough in advance to allow the school time to block the dates set aside for the data collection in its master calendar and to disseminate the information to parents and school staff. At least one week prior to the agreed-on date for data collection, a follow-up reminder to the school should be made by telephone. At that time, information concerning any changes in the school's normal schedule or routine—such as assemblies or field trips—made subsequent to the meeting with the principal should be solicited.

The foregoing information and sequence of steps pertains primarily to schoolwide or classroom studies, but is also applicable to conducting single-case research. Because single-case research impacts a classroom rather than a school, the key contact becomes the teacher, and as a courtesy, the principal, rather than the district superintendent. The decision-making process on the part of school personnel remains the same, however, and the investigator should follow the same suggestions for proactive planning and organization.

Additional considerations are warranted once project personnel are in the school to facilitate school support and cooperation. Gaining and maintaining the support of school personnel depends on the behavior and professionalism of research associates. These individuals need to be visible but unobtrusive, professional in appearance and demeanor, friendly and polite without exception, and respectful of school policies, procedures, and personnel. Research associates must be mindful of the school's mission to educate children in a safe environment, and from the outset, solicit information from school staff about such routine procedures as signing in and out on entering and leaving the campus, or whether identifying badges must be worn. Most importantly, researchers should adhere to the original contract as agreed to by the school principal, and refrain from such deviations as adding measures, collecting data on other dates, and attempting to deliver any intervention not previously agreed on.

Although the research design and methodology are of prime concern to the investigator, respect for the mission and structure of the educational setting is equally important. Demonstrating respect by minimizing disruption of daily operations increases the likelihood that the research proposal will be approved, and ensures that the data collection process will run as smoothly as possible. Moreover, following through with promised benefits after the data has been collected represents an investment in the future as the school may be amenable to participation in future research projects.

## RESEARCH METHODS

### Selection of Dependent Measures and Relationship Among Variables

Selection of measures will depend on the specific research question posed as well as the level of understanding one wishes to accomplish with respect to the phenomenon studied. For example, research may focus on (a) examining *correlates* or relationships between or among variables without consideration of time sequence or causality; (b) identifying *risk factors* or characteristics that precede and increase the likelihood of some event, outcome, or behavior pattern that may be modifiable, or *marker variables* that are not modifiable or have no effect on the outcome if modified; or (c) establishing *causal factors* wherein one variable precedes and influences some other variable. Studying variables (*moderators*) that influence the direction, magnitude, and nature of a relationship between or among variables represent important avenues for clinical research, particularly when *protective factors* (a special case of moderator variables) can be identified that reduce the likelihood of an undesirable outcome. If causal relationships have already been reasonably well established in the literature, research may focus on explaining the process or mechanism by which the process evolves (*mediator variables* such as psychological or biological mechanisms). Other measures will be more appropriate for questions concerning *treatment outcome* or *prevention* in children (for a detailed discussion, see Kazdin, 1999).

In summary, a correlational relationship represents the most basic level of understanding between or among variables. A deeper level of understanding is achieved if it can be determined that one or more variables preceded the occurrence of other variables in time. To establish causal linkage, the existence of a correlation and an ordered time relationship must be complemented by (a) a clear demonstration that the relationship is not due to other influences, (b) showing that the effects are consistent across different samples from the same population, and (c) providing a valid explanation concerning the mechanisms and processes through which the causal variables operate and are related to outcome variables. Moderator variables are examined when the researcher suspects that the relationship among two or more variables may differ because of the influence of some other variable. For example, if the relationship between acting-out behavior and attention deficit hyperactivity disorder (ADHD) is different for boys than for girls, gender may be considered a *moderator variable*. There are many potential moderating variables that may be important to examine in research with children, such as age, gender, ethnicity, height, weight, and motivation. A *mediator variable*, in contrast, is a variable that intercedes between one variable and another and reflects an indirect effect of one variable on another. For example, in a study discussed later (Rapport, Scanlon, & Denney, 1999) the relationship between attentional problems and scholastic achievement is mediated by children's classroom performance and cognitive function.

The foregoing summary suggests that researchers consider the level of understanding they wish to achieve with respect to their research topic before selecting particular measures. Selection of measures will depend on a host of factors (e.g., availability of instruments or instrumentation, time constraints, costs) and can include (a) self-report inventories, (b) behavior rating scales completed by others, (c) physiological instrumentation, (d) existing or newly defined categories of behavior that can be reliably rated by trained observers, (e) performance measures obtained through computerized assessment (e.g., continuous performance tasks) or (f) hard copies (e.g., school work), and data previously collected (e.g., archival absentee or grade failure rates recorded by a school).

As a general rule of thumb, try to incorporate multiple indices of behavior that have reasonably sound psychometric characteristics (particularly validity and test–retest reliability). That is, select instruments, indices, or observations that provide measures of both the specific behaviors of interest as well as other potentially related areas of functioning. Doing so demonstrates that identified behavior problems or changes in behavior are not confined to a particular type of instrument or recording procedure and permits measurement of corresponding improvement in other domains related to the child's functioning. For example, designing a treatment outcome study to improve a child's academic performance in the classroom may result in corresponding improvement in the child's attention and classroom behavior. In such cases, it would be desirable to use teacher rating scales coupled with direct observational recording procedures that measure domains other than just academic performance to document the broader spectrum of treatment gains related to the independent variable.

## Participant Demographics

After formulating a research question and establishing a basic design, an initial step is to consider how best to define and describe the population of interest. Review recent journal articles in credible journals to gain an understanding of how others have accomplished this task. For example, most research studies dealing with children contain basic sociodemographic information such as children's age and grade (*M* and *SD*), estimated level of intelligence, family socioeconomic status, gender, and ethnicity. This information is also included for other participants (e.g., parents) when relevant to the study (e.g., if studying mothers' attitudes toward medication compliance in their children). Detailed information is also included relevant to identifying, categorizing, or describing the population of interest. This may involve a clear description of how a diagnosis is ascertained (e.g., by means of structured or semistructured clinical interviews combined with using rating scale cutoff scores), how a group is identified (e.g., a discrepancy formula for defining learning disability), or simply detailing the characteristics of a select group of children (e.g., children already placed in a special education classroom). Studies of specific clinical groups (e.g., ADHD, childhood depression), learning problems (e.g., academic deficits), or maladaptive behavior (e.g., peer aggression) may require measures different from those used to evaluate change due to intervention. For example, structured or semistructured clinical interviews complemented by specific rating scales are traditionally used to define, classify, or describe children with a particular clinical disorder (i.e., serve as grouping variables), whereas other instruments, observations or ratings may be used to measure change associated with intervention (i.e., serve as dependent variables).

## RESEARCH DESIGNS

### Single-Subject Research Designs

*Single-case research designs* are valuable methodological tools that can be used to evaluate many different types of research questions involving individuals and groups. Consider some of the important scientific discoveries during the past two centuries, such as penicillin (Sir Alexander Fleming, 1922), the electric motor (Michael Faraday, 1883), and the telephone (Alexander Graham Bell, 1887), or more recently, highly functional or entertaining inventions such as Velcro©, duct tape, post-it notes, and frizbees. Each evolved serendipitously or through single-case research methodology. The list is no less impressive for the field of psychology. Single-case research was the principle paradigm in Wurdt's (1832–1920) investigations of sensation and perception, Ebbinghaus's (1850–1909) studies of human memory, Pavlov's (1849–1936) classic experiments in respondent conditioning, and B.F. Skinner's (1904–1990) research in operant conditioning. These designs are particularly relevant to understanding children and the environments in which they live where changes in everyday life may be of greater importance than obtaining a statistically significant change between groups (i.e., greater clinical relevance). Experimentation at the level of the individual case study may also provide greater insights with respect to understanding therapeutic change.

In contrast to the heavy reliance on established psychometric techniques and instruments required by between-group research, single-case methodology begins with identifying the focus of investigation (i.e., designating target behaviors) and proceeds to selecting potential strategies of assessment. When deciding on target behaviors, try to select observable behaviors and environmental events as opposed to covert behaviors such as thoughts, ideas, or hypothetical constructs such as anxiety and self-concept. This will facilitate objective measurement and agreement between observers. Definitions should be written with absolute clarity to avoid ambiguity, and the boundaries of the defined target behavior must be clearly specified to eliminate the need for inference concerning whether a particular behavior qualifies as an occurrence or nonoccurrence. On the surface, this may appear to be an easy task, but consider a situation in which classroom attentiveness ("on-task" in educational parlance) is selected as the target behavior. If a child is gazing up at the ceiling while working on a math assignment, should this be recorded as *off-task* or *inattentive* behavior? Perhaps the child was thinking about the problem at hand or performing mental arithmetic. Is the child permitted to ask a peer for assistance when working on a problem or permitted to get up and sharpen a pencil during an academic work period? Does a momentary glance away from one's work count as off-task, and if not, how long can a child look away from the assignment before the behavior is recorded as *inattention*? These and other definitional boundary parameters must be decided and agreed on, and preferably subjected to extensive pilot testing, prior to beginning formal observation and data collection. Once established, clear definitions of target behaviors will permit reliable baseline data to be recorded, and in turn, serve as the traditional yardstick by which change is measured.

**Assessing Behavior.**    Assessment of behavior can be accomplished in many different ways and will depend on what is being assessed and which method of recording best suits the needs of the researcher. The most commonly used methods of assessment include using frequency measures, classifying responses into discrete categories, counting the number of children or events, and measuring behavior based on discrete units of time.

*Frequency counts* should be used when dealing with discrete behaviors that require a relatively constant amount of time to perform. The first criterion enables observers to know when a designated behavior begins and ends, whereas the second permits recorded behavior to be treated as similar units for purposes of comparison. Consider the situation in which a researcher records the frequency with which a child speaks out of turn in a classroom. The child may blurt out an answer on one occasion, whereas on another, may turn and talk with a peer for 10 min or longer. Clearly, the two incidents are not comparable and an alternative assessment method such as time interval recording should be considered. For situations in which frequency measures are taken for different periods of time (e.g., 20 min on day one and 40 min on day two), calculate the frequency per min or response rate by dividing the frequency of responses by the number of minutes observed each day. This metric, frequency per min or response rate, will yield data that is comparable for different durations of observation.

*Discrete categorization* is used in situations in which behavior is best defined by categorical assignment such as *appropriate–not appropriate* (e.g., social interactions between children), *complete–not complete* (e.g., classroom assignments), or discrete behaviors that form a functional response chain such as bus riding (e.g., boarding the bus, riding the bus, getting off the bus, walking to the school's front door) and getting dressed in the morning (e.g., each article of clothing would count as a discrete behavior), or correlated but unrelated behavior chains (e.g., performing household chores).

*Counting children* is frequently used to assess the effectiveness of an intervention program. Examples include counting the number of children who perform a designated target behavior while on a school field trip, or calculating the percentage of children who complete their daily academic assignments in a third-grade classroom each morning (see Rapport & Bostow, 1976). Group-oriented and individual contingencies can subsequently be initiated to reinforce daily academic assignment completion rates, for example, by scheduling in-class free time if at least 80% of the class meets the established criterion or for children who independently complete the assigned work.

*Interval recording* is used in situations in which the researcher wishes to obtain a representative sample of a target behavior during particular times of the day. Common examples of appropriate child behaviors include staying in one's seat during an academic work period, appropriate talking with peers, and paying attention. A block of time (e.g., a 30-min daily or every other day observation period) is divided into a series of shorter intervals (e.g., 15 s observation blocks followed by 5 s recording blocks) and the target behavior is recorded as occurring or not occurring during each 15 s observation interval. The foregoing example would yield 3 observation blocks per min and a total of 90 intervals of recorded behavior per day. Variations of the interval recording method are common (e.g., time sampling) and might involve brief observations of a target behavior throughout the day rather than being confined to a single block of time.

Recording *duration* is another time-based method for observing behavior and is more appropriate for recording behaviors that are continuous rather than discrete acts. Common examples include observing ongoing social interactions between or among children or the total time required to complete an academic assignment. In these cases, the total duration or amount of time that the behavior is performed serves as the dependent variable. An interesting but infrequently used variation of the duration method involves recording elapsed time before a particular behavior is performed (i.e., response latency). An example is to record how long a child takes to perform a particular behavior or chain of behaviors following adult instruction. Contingencies could subsequently be established based on the child's complying with requests within an increasingly shorter period of time over several days or weeks.

*Research Designs.* The essence of single-subject research lies in its ability to demonstrate experimental control of an independent variable (IV) over one or more dependent variables (DV) by means of shrewd design and graphical illustration. Although statistical procedures exist that can be used to assess outcome effects associated with single-subject case studies, the more traditional means of demonstrating experimental control is to provide a compelling visual (graphical) illustration that even a "doubting Thomas" would acknowledge as evidence. To convince the scientific audience, the IV is introduced using a variety of design options such that its effects on the DV are systematically produced, reproduced, and/or eliminated as in a carefully choreographed play.

One of the most widely applied and potent designs available—an ABAB or reversal design—demonstrates experimental control by producing and eliminating an effect repeatedly over time. Reliable baseline data (A phase) of some observable behavior (e.g., children's attention) or outcome measure (e.g., teacher ratings of classroom deportment) is initially recorded until a clear and stable pattern of behavior is shown. The IV is introduced in the ensuing B phase. Changes in behavior or performance should be evidenced immediately or shortly thereafter, with stability demonstrated over a sufficient number of sessions or days to rule out alternative explanations for the results, such as novelty effects.

The initial impact or influence of the IV is demonstrated after completing the AB portion of the design, but one or more repetitions of both design phases (baseline and intervention) is required to rule out alternative explanations for the change. One essentially shows that a changed level and perhaps pattern of behavior occurs sequentially following the introduction of an IV, and that the behavior returns to preintervention levels (second baseline) on its removal. Repeating this pattern of behavior over time provides a compelling demonstration of experimental control and argues against other possible explanations that may account for the effect such as maturation or unexplained environmental phenomena. Unfortunately, the reversal design has limited applicability owing to its inherent characteristic of necessitating that behavior be changed then reverted to pre-change levels. There are many situations in

which reverting to an initial baseline level is unacceptable and perhaps unethical (e.g., self-injurious behavior in a young child) or undesirable (e.g.,
permitting a child to become overly aggressive or disrupt a classroom after decreasing this behavior). Alternative design options must be considered under
these circumstances.

A widely used alternative is the *multiple baseline design*, wherein the IV
is systematically introduced for select behaviors, individuals, or times in a
sequential manner such that changes in behavior occur only after the IV is
introduced. Experimental control is accomplished by demonstrating that behavior remains relatively stable and unchanged until the IV is introduced, and
changes in a more or less predictable fashion thereafter.

The applicability of the multiple baseline design in experimental research
is extremely broad and limited primarily by the researcher's creativity. Consider the following example that involves an $8\frac{1}{2}$-year-old boy diagnosed with
*spina bifida*—a congenital anomaly marked by defective closure of the bony
encasement of the spinal cord that frequently involves gait and orthopedic difficulties including fine and gross motor control. Despite weekly occupational
therapy to improve fine and gross motor coordination of his left hand, the child
evidenced no clear improvement during the preceding year. Extant literature
suggested that improved fine motor functioning would not necessarily spill
over to improved gross motor functioning, so initial treatment efforts focused
on the former in the context of a multiple baseline across behaviors (fine and
gross motor coordination) design (see Fig. 15.1).

Treatment consisted of continuing once weekly physical therapy and then
adding a home-based, motivational and practice component to the program.
The latter required the child to engage in a variety of fine and gross motor
activities for 30 min daily (fine motor activities during the first 28 weeks;
gross motor activities during the second 28 weeks) and provided incentives
(e.g., access to special toys and activities based on total points earned) for
completing daily activities. The results of the intervention and multiple baseline
components of the design are depicted in Fig. 15.1.

Intervention was limited to treating only the child's left hand, which enabled
the untreated and otherwise normal right hand to be used as an additional
control in the study by demonstrating the degree of change expected in fine
and gross motor coordination as a function of repeated weekly testing (practice
effects) and maturation. Notice that little or no improvement on standardized
measures of fine (upper three graphs) and gross (bottom two graphs) motor
coordination were evidence during the clinic therapy phase. Also note that
the ongoing clinical therapy served as the initial baseline phase for the design
(i.e., baseline data can reflect a starting point for comparison purposes as
opposed to a true base rate of occurrence for some behavior). Gradual but
steady gains in fine motor coordination were evidenced following the addition

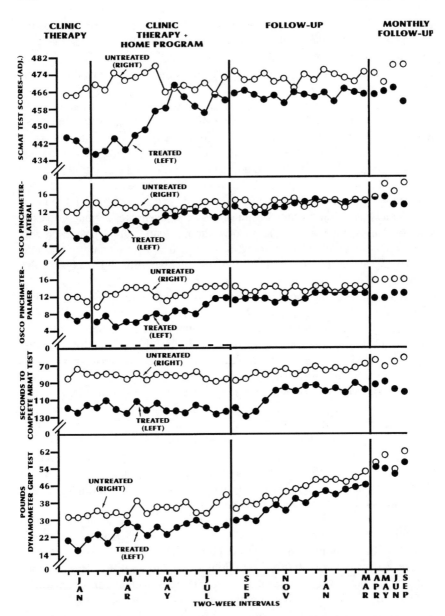

FIG. 15.1. Test performance measured at 2-week intervals for the child's treated (left) and untreated (right) hand. Southern California Motor Accuracy Test (SCMAT) is a measure of fine motor coordination and dexterity; OSCO Pinchmeter provides lateral and palmer measures of finer strength; Minnesota Rate of Manipulation Test (MRMT – Placing subtest) provides a measure of hand speed and dexterity; Dynamometer Grip Test measures hand strength. Upward movement on the ordinate represents improvement for all measures. Source: Reprinted with permission from Rapport & Bailey (1985).

of the home-based program (see upward trend in data for first three measures in Fig. 15.1), whereas gross motor coordination remained at baseline levels, except on the dynamometer grip test (see bottom graph), where the treated (left) and untreated (right) hands both showed some improvement as a function of repeated practice and testing. Experimental control is illustrated by the multiple baseline "lag" component of the design, drawn as a vertical dashed line beginning at the top of the figure and proceeding downward through the first three graphs, then over horizontally between the third and fourth graphs, and finally straight down through the remaining two graphs. By examining the data points on both sides of the vertical line, one can readily determine how long the baseline phase was lagged and whether baseline data remained relatively stable until the IV was introduced.

Elements of different single-subject research designs can also be combined to meet the specific needs of the researcher. Consider the following example in which three primary experimental conditions were compared (baseline—regular school routine, phamacotherapy at 3 levels—5 mg, 10 mg, and 15 mg, and attentional training) using an ABACBC reversal design with a multiple baseline across academic subjects component. The child's baseline rate of attention and completion of academic work was compared with three levels (5 mg, 10 mg, 15 mg) of psychostimulant medication (Ritalin①) and a second baseline phase. The most successful medication level (15 mg) was subsequently contrasted with attentional training in the ensuing three phases. Note the multiple baseline lag following the second baseline phase (upper graph in Fig. 15.2), wherein additional experimental control is demonstrated by an immediate change in behavior and performance only after initiating the attentional training treatment component.

Additional single-subject design options (e.g., changing-criterion design, multiple-treatment designs) and detailed information concerning their application with children are available (see Kazdin, 1989).

### Overview of Group Comparison Methods

Despite the numerous benefits associated with single-subject design methodology, the fact remains that an overwhelming majority of studies in psychology involve the comparison of groups, not individuals. Group designs may be used in a variety of contexts, and can normally be classified into one of three types: true-experimental designs, quasiexperimental designs, and observational designs.

In *true-experimental designs*, (also referred to as randomized controlled clinical trials or simply clinical trials), the researcher attempts to maintain complete control over the experiment by manipulating one or more IVs and measuring its effect(s) on one or more DVs. An effort is made to hold constant or control for other possible influences (i.e., extraneous or nuisance

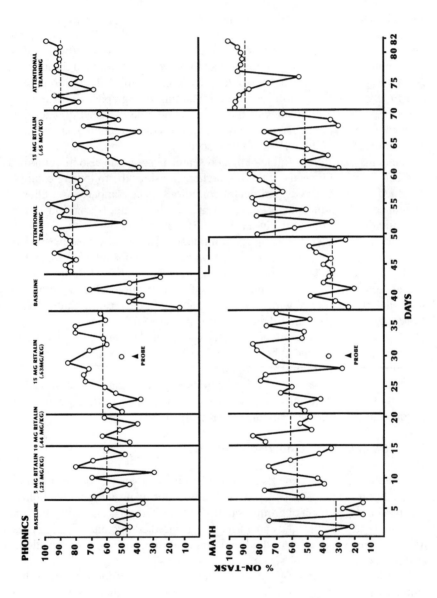

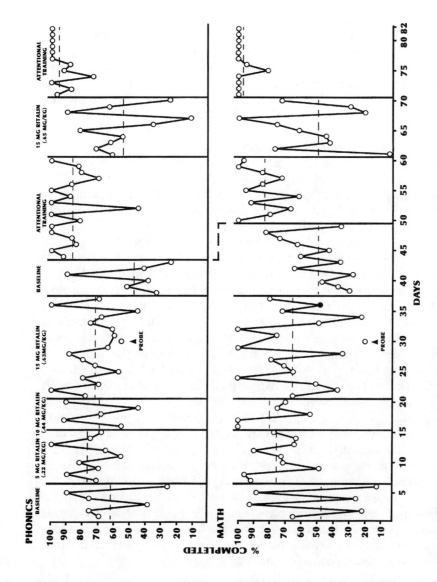

FIG. 15.2. *M* percentage of intervals of daily on-task behavior (top graph) and percentage of problems completed during two morning academic assignment periods (bottom graph). Individual *M*s for each condition are indicated by dashed lines. The datum indicated as "probe" represents a no-medication day and was not computed in the *M*. Source: From Rapport, Murphy, & Bailey (1982). Reprinted with permission.

variables) throughout the study. Only through the use of well-controlled, true experimental designs can a causal relationship between two or more variables be unequivocally proven.

A *quasiexperimental design* emulates a true experimental design but includes one or more independent variables that cannot be manipulated by the researcher (often referred to as *quasiindependent variables*). These designs are used to study variables that cannot be directly manipulated (e.g., gender, medical condition, classroom placement), and are limited in that causal inferences are difficult to discern. For example, if a significant difference is found between boys and girls for some dependent variable, the significant difference can be reported but not the cause (e.g., biological, environmental, genetic) for the difference.

In other situations, researchers simply measure variables as they occur naturally in the environment using an *observational design* (also referred to as correlational or non-experimental designs). The terms *independent variable* and *dependent variable* (which imply manipulation and measurement by the experimenter) are replaced with the terms *predictor* and *criterion variable*, respectively, and reflect the fact that all of the variables are measured, not manipulated. Because variables are measured and not manipulated, a causal relationship between two or more variables cannot be proven. Most observational studies are conducted to show that a relationship exists between two or more variables or to predict certain variables (criterion variables) from other variables (predictor variables). Although observational studies do not allow for a causal relationship to be unequivocally proven, certain statistical methods such as structural equation modeling (SEM) allow causal relationships to be tested in order to determine whether or not they fit the data. The limitation to such methods, however, is that even if a particular postulated causal relationship fits the data it does not rule out the possibility that other causal models may fit the data equally well.

Group designs may be conducted as cross-sectional designs or longitudinal designs. *Cross-sectional designs* are designs in which the measurement of the dependent variable(s) is conducted over a relatively short period of time, analogous to taking a snapshot. At one extreme, a cross-sectional design may involve simply measuring participants during one brief session, as is the case with many between-subject designs. At the other extreme, a cross-sectional design may involve measuring participants over a period of weeks or even months, as is the case with many within-subject designs. In contrast, *longitudinal designs* involve measuring participants repeatedly over an extended (i.e., years or even decades) period of time.

Cross-sectional and longitudinal designs are used to obtain different types of information. Cross-sectional designs are best used for answering questions concerning how a treatment works at a particular point in time, whereas longitudinal designs are better suited for answering questions about developmental change. Elements of both designs are occasionally combined in research with children, for example, by testing groups of different age children and retesting each group several years later.

## Sampling

Sampling is of primary importance for all types of group designs. There are two classes of samples, *probability* and *nonprobability* samples. Probability samples are samples in which every member of the population has a known probability of being selected for inclusion in the sample, whereas nonprobability samples are samples in which the probability of being selected for inclusion is unknown.

Four well-known types of probability samples are simple random samples, stratified random samples, systematic samples, and cluster samples. A *simple random sample* is a sample in which every member of the population has an equal probability of being selected, whereas a *stratified random sample* is a random sample in which the proportion of certain characteristics in the population, (e.g., race, ethnicity, culture, gender, age, education, income, socioeconomic status [SES]) are matched in the sample. For example, if gender was considered important to a study and the population under study consisted of 58% women and 42% men, then the sample would reflect these same proportions. Samples may also be stratified simultaneously on several different characteristics. For the sample to be a stratified random sample, sampling would be random within each characteristic considered important to the study.

A *systematic sample* is a sample that is selected in a nonrandom fashion. For example, if 10% of the population were to be included in the sample, then every tenth individual would be chosen for inclusion.

A *cluster sample* is a sample in which clusters (groups) are randomly selected rather than individuals. For example, if researchers were interested in sampling grade school children, they would start with a list of grade schools and randomly select which schools to include. Within each school, they could include all of the students, randomly select students for inclusion, or randomly select additional clusters (e.g., grade levels).

The most commonly used types of nonprobability samples include the *convenience sample*, the *stratified convenience sample*, and the *snowball sample*. A convenience sample is a sample of participants that are convenient for the researcher to obtain (e.g., college undergraduates, hospital patients, children that posses the characteristic under investigation). A stratified convenience sample is exactly the same as a stratified random sample, except that the participants are selected for convenience, not randomly. A snowball sample is a sample that is created by having the initial participants (e.g., children's parents) suggest additional possible participants, these additional participants suggest additional possible participants, and so on. Because researchers do not typically have access to the entire population they wish to study, most studies use nonprobability samples.

An important issue concerning samples is determining how many participants should be included in the sample. The main issue concerning sample size is that you want enough participants in order to have a powerful test, but not more than you need as this can be costly and time consuming. *Power* refers to the probability of finding a significant treatment effect when one truly exists (probability of rejecting a false null hypothesis). Power can be increased by setting alpha equal to .05 rather than .01, increasing the size of the treatment effect (increasing the between-condition, or group variation), or reducing the error (reducing the within-condition, or group variation). One method of reducing the within-condition variation (error) is to increase the number of participants. As sample size increases, within-group variation (error) decreases. It is generally thought that the minimum acceptable level of power is 80%. This means that if there truly is a treatment effect, then your statistical test has an 80% probability of finding that treatment effect (rejecting the null hypothesis). Before an experiment is conducted, one should do a power analysis in order to determine how many subjects are needed to achieve (at least) 80% power. Conducting a power analysis requires the researcher to make several educated guesses concerning the data (e.g., size of treatment effect and the population *SD*). It should be noted that a certain amount of controversy exists concerning hypothesis testing, partially due to the fact that with a large enough sample, even trivial treatment effects may be significant. For this reason, researchers should specify the minimum interesting treatment effect (i.e., the minimum effect that would be of interest) to be found with 80% power before conducting a power analysis.

### Experimental Designs

A *true experimental design* is a design in which the researcher manipulates one or more independent variables and measures one or more dependent variables. The researcher chooses what independent variables to manipulate, how they are manipulated (e.g., which levels to include), and what dependent variables to measure, based on the nature of the research question. For example, a researcher might be interested in determining what type of therapy works best for children with school phobia. Therefore, the research question has determined that the IV is "type of therapy" and the DV is "school phobia." Now, the researcher must decide whether any other independent or dependent variables should be included in the study and operationally define the IVs and the DVs. *Operationally defining* IVs refers to deciding what the levels should consist of, whereas *operationally defining* DVs refers to deciding exactly how to measure them. For example, the researcher needs to decide what levels of therapy to include (e.g., behavior therapy, cognitive therapy, cognitive behavior therapy), whether or not to include a control group (condition), and how to measure school phobia. In the context of a *between-subject design*, a control group is a randomly assigned group that receives either no experimental treatment or a substitute for the experimental treatment. In the context of a *within-subject design*, a control condition is a condition (administered to all participants) in which either no experimental treatment or a substitute for the experimental treatment is administered. Control conditions (groups) are sometimes needed to control for nonspecific treatment effects.

*Nonspecific treatment effects* refer to any effects brought about by the experiment besides the treatment, such as being aware of what the experiment is about, contact with the experimenter, and discussing the experiment with other people. *Nonspecific treatment effects* are basically extraneous (nuisance) variables related to participants' perceptions concerning the experiment. Related to nonspecific treatment effects are *placebo effects*, in which participants improve simply because they believe that they are receiving treatment. If a control condition (group) is included, it is important that there are no other differences between the control condition and the experimental conditions except for an absence or substitute for the experimental treatment, as any other differences would introduce extraneous (nuisance) variables. Control conditions are only necessary when there is concern that nonspecific treatment effects may have an effect on the results. Nonspecific treatment effects are only possible if the participants' perceptions about the experiment can have an effect on the results. There are many situations in which participants' perceptions cannot have an effect on the results. For example, if a researcher is interested in studying what type of teaching method works best for teaching mathematics to third grade children, a control condition consisting of teaching no mathematics would be benighted.

A *quasiexperimental design* is a design that is set up to emulate a true experimental design but includes one or more independent variables that cannot be manipulated by the researcher (often referred to as *quasiindependent variables*). The inability to manipulate certain variables may be due to the fact that they are participant characteristics that are impossible to manipulate such as gender, ethnicity, height, and weight, or clinical diagnoses such as ADHD or learning disorder. Another reason for the inability to manipulate certain variables may be due to ethical reasons such as substance abuse, smoking, exposure to harmful toxins, and cancer. The limitation to quasiexperimental designs is the inability to express a causal relationship for quasiindependent variables.

There are three main classes of experimental designs: the between-subject design, the within-subject design, and the mixed-subject design, each with multiple variations possible.

## Between-Subject Designs

The *between-subject design* is a design in which participants are randomly assigned to different treatment groups (levels of the IV) and each treatment group receives a different experimental condition. For example, in a single-factor experiment (an experiment with only one IV) examining two methods for teaching mathematics to third grade children (Technique 1 and Technique 2), half of the students would be randomly assigned to receive Technique 1 and half to receive Technique 2. IVs are often denoted by capital letters and the levels of the IVs denoted by lower case letters with subscripts. For example, $a_1$ is Technique 1, and $a_2$ is Technique 2. This design could be diagramed as:

| Technique 1 $a_1$ | Technique 2 $a_2$ |
|---|---|
| $\frac{1}{2}$ participants | $\frac{1}{2}$ participants |

In a factorial experiment (an experiment with more than one IV) examining different methods for teaching mathematics to third grade children (Technique 1 and Technique 2) and the mode of presentation (teacher vs. computer), $\frac{1}{4}$ of the students would be randomly assigned to receive Technique 1 via computer, $\frac{1}{4}$ to receive Technique 1 via teacher, $\frac{1}{4}$ to receive Technique 2 via computer, and $\frac{1}{4}$ to receive Technique 2 via teacher. This design could be diagramed as:

| | Technique 1 $a_1$ | Technique 2 $a_2$ |
|---|---|---|
| Teacher $b_1$ | $\frac{1}{4}$ participants | $\frac{1}{4}$ participants |
| Computer $b_2$ | $\frac{1}{4}$ participants | $\frac{1}{4}$ participants |

Advantages of the between-subject design as compared to the within-subject design include no carryover effects and no order or sequence effects. Disadvantages of the between-subject design include the fact that many more participants are required than for the within-subject design and the between-subject design yields less power than the within-subject design.

Ideally, there are an equal number of participants in each of the different treatment groups and assignment to the different treatment groups is random. Random assignment to treatment conditions simply means that each and every participant has an equal probability of being assigned to any given treatment group. Both ideals, equal number of participants per treatment group and random assignment to treatment groups, may not be possible for a given study. In the case of an equal number of participants per treatment group, the total number of participants may not be equally divisible among the various treatment groups or some participants may drop out of the study or miss the day that data are collected. In the case of random assignment of participants to the different treatment groups, this may not be possible. As in the aforementioned example concerning methods of teaching reading, it might be difficult to randomly assign half of each class to receive a different teaching method. The teacher could not very well teach half of her class at a time, and even if she could, this would introduce the confound of which method she taught first. Both problems (unequal sample size and nonrandom assignment) can frequently be handled statistically. It is important, however, to take into account both unequal sample size and nonrandom assignment when analyzing data (i.e., one should not ignore them and analyze the data as if there was equal sample size and random assignment).

Another important issue is the loss of participants from the experiment. If the loss of participants is random (e.g., roughly an equal number of participants dropped out of each of the experimental groups), then there is no problem and certain statistical techniques may be used to correct the situation. If, however, the loss of participants is not random, but due to some aspect of particular treatment conditions (e.g., almost every participant who dropped out was in one particular treatment condition), then nothing can be done to salvage the experiment.

As an additional note, the problems associated with randomly assigning some children within a given classroom to receive one level of the IV (treatment) and other children from the same classroom to receive other level(s) of the IV is not uncommon to research conducted in school settings (or even clinic or hospital settings). For example, it may not be possible for the teacher to teach some students in her class using one teaching method and the other students in her class using a different teaching method. When it is not possible to randomly assign children from the same class to different levels of the independent variable, an alternative is that different classrooms are randomly assigned to the different levels of the IV. This type of design is called a *hierarchical design* and requires special analysis. In a hierarchical design, the levels of at least one IV are nested under the levels of another IV and the remaining IVs are fully crossed. For example, if each level of IV 2 (e.g., classrooms) appears with only one level of IV 1 (e.g., teaching method), then IV 2 is said to be nested under IV 1. In the cited example examining two different methods for teaching mathematics to third grade children, two third grade classes could be randomly assigned to receive Technique 1, and two third grade classes could be randomly assigned to receive Technique 2. The design for this model may be diagramed as:

|  | Technique 1 $a_1$ |
|---|---|
| Classroom 1 $b_1$ |  |
| Classroom 2 $b_2$ |  |

|  | Technique 2 $a_2$ |
|---|---|
| Classroom 3 $b_3$ |  |
| Classroom 4 $b_3$ |  |

The separate tables for Technique 1 ($a_1$) and Technique 2 ($a_2$) indicate that the model is not fully crossed, classrooms ($b_1$, $b_2$, $b_3$, and $b_4$) are nested under techniques ($a_1$ and $a_2$). In this experiment, the IV classroom ($b_1$, $b_2$, $b_3$, $b_4$) is an extraneous (nuisance) variable. It is included in the design and analysis because it might have an effect on the DV and including it allows its effects to be isolated. If a hierarchical design is used, it is incorrect to analyze the data as if students were randomly assigned to each level of the IV (e.g., teaching method). There are additional complications that may arise when employing a hierarchical design, for example, when the levels of the nested variable (classroom) cannot be randomly assigned to the levels of the variable it is nested under (teaching method). Hierarchical designs are considered balanced if they satisfy two criteria. First, there must be an equal number of participants in each treatment combination (e.g., students in each class for each teaching method). Second, there must be an equal number of levels of the nested variable under each level of the other IV (e.g., two classes under each level of treatment method). If these criteria are not satisfied then the model is considered unbalanced and more complicated to analyze than balanced designs.

## Within-Subject Designs

The *within-subject design* is a design in which every participant receives every treatment condition (levels of the IVs). In the cited, single-factor experiment on teaching techniques, every participant would receive Technique A and Technique B. In the factorial experiment involving teaching technique and mode of presentation, every participant would receive Technique A via computer, Technique A via teacher, Technique B via computer, and Technique B via teacher. A within-subject design may have children participating in the different levels of the independent variable simultaneously, or children may complete one level of the independent variable before participating in the next level. When participants must complete one level of the independent variable before participating in the next level, it is commonly referred to as a *crossover design.*

Within-subject designs present some special problems including *carryover effects*, order effects, and sequence effects. Because participants receive every treatment condition, the effects of one treatment condition may carry over to the next treatment condition. For example, if you are comparing different methods of teaching children to read, once the children receive one method (and learn to read) they are irreversibly changed. The order in which the treatment conditions are presented to the participants may also have an effect on the results. Finally, the sequence in which the treatment conditions are presented may have an effect. For example, in a study of perceived heaviness of objects, whether someone lifted a 10-pound object and then a 20-pound object, or lifted a 20-pound object and then a 10-pound object would have an effect on the perceived heaviness of each object. Order and sequence effects may sound similar; however, *order effects* refer to the ordinal position that the condition is presented in (e.g., first, second, third, etc.). *Sequence effects*, in contrast, have to do with which treatment follows which other treatment. As an example, consider the two sequences ABC and CBA. In both sequences, B has the same ordinal position (second), however, in the first case, B follows A and in the second case, B follows C; therefore, the sequence is different. All of these problems (carryover effects, order effects, sequence effects) may frequently be controlled for using counterbalancing procedures.

*Counterbalancing* means that participants are exposed to the different treatment conditions in different orders. Ideally, one or more participants could be exposed to every possible order of treatment conditions. This is not possible with more than a few treatment conditions as the number of possible orders increases rapidly (number of possible orders is equal to $n!$). When the number of possible orders is too great, then only a subset may be used. One method of obtaining a subset of the possible orders of treatment conditions is to simply randomly select a subset of the possible orders. This may pose a problem, however, in that if the order or the sequence of treatment conditions has an effect on the dependent variable, random selection of treatment orders does not control for these effects.

Another method that not only controls for the order effect of treatment conditions, but also allows for the order effect to be analyzed separately, is the *Latin Square design.* The Latin Square design has as many orders represented as there are treatment conditions. Therefore, if there were three treatment conditions, three orders would be represented, if there were four treatment conditions, four orders would be represented. A Latin-square design involves creating an $n \times n$ matrix (where $n$ is the number of treatment conditions). For example, if there were four treatment condition the following $4 \times 4$ matrix would be created:

| A | B | C | D |
|---|---|---|---|
| B | C | D | A |
| C | D | A | B |
| D | A | B | C |

Next, a random selection is made for which treatment level corresponds to which letter. For example, if it was randomly determined that A = Level 3, B = Level 1, C = Level 4, and D = Level 2, then the matrix would become:

| Level 3 | Level 1 | Level 4 | Level 2 |
|---------|---------|---------|---------|
| Level 1 | Level 4 | Level 2 | Level 3 |
| Level 4 | Level 2 | Level 3 | Level 1 |
| Level 2 | Level 3 | Level 1 | Level 4 |

The Latin-square design ensures that every treatment condition appears in every possible order (first, second, third, etc). Therefore, if the order that participants experience the different treatment conditions has an effect on the DV, the Latin-square design will "cancel out" that effect. The Latin-square design also allows for the comparison of the different treatment orders (by including order as another IV) to determine whether there is a significant difference between the different orders. As already mentioned, in some situations, order and sequence may have an effect on the DVs. The *balanced Latin-square design* controls for the effects of order and sequence effects and allows these differences to be compared. An example of a balanced Latin-square design is:

| A | B | C | D |
|---|---|---|---|
| B | D | A | C |
| C | A | D | B |
| D | C | B | A |

Again, a random selection is made for which treatment level corresponds to which letter. For example, if it was randomly determined that A = Level 3,

B = Level 1, C = Level 4, and D = Level 2, then the matrix would become:

| Level 3 | Level 1 | Level 4 | Level 2 |
| Level 1 | Level 2 | Level 3 | Level 4 |
| Level 4 | Level 3 | Level 2 | Level 1 |
| Level 2 | Level 4 | Level 1 | Level 3 |

The balanced Latin-square design ensures that treatment condition appears in every possible order (first, second, third, etc) and that each treatment condition is preceded and followed by every other treatment condition exactly once (e.g., Level 1 is preceded once by Level 2, Level 3, and Level 4). Therefore, if the order or the sequence that the treatment conditions are presented has an effect on the DV, the balanced Latin-square design will cancel out these effects. The balanced Latin-square design also allows for the comparison of the different treatment orders and sequences (taken together, not separately) to determine whether there is a significant difference between them.

## Mixed-Subject Designs

The *mixed-subject design* is a design in which one or more independent variables are between-subject variables (e.g., different participants randomly assigned to different levels of the IVs) and one or more IVs are within-subject variables (e.g., all participants receive all levels of the IVs). For example, in the aforementioned experiment involving teaching technique and mode of presentation, every participant might receive Technique A and Technique B (teaching technique is a within-subject variable), and half of the subjects would be presented by a computer and half of the subjects would be presented by a teacher (mode of presentation is a between-subject variable). All of the issues discussed concerning between-subject designs and within-subject designs apply to mixed-subject designs.

## Extraneous Variables

A major advantage of true experimental designed experiments is that they are the only method that allows causal relationships among variables to be proven, which includes ruling out outside or extraneous influences. Thus, it is important to use a design in which nothing else differs between the experimental groups except for the experimental conditions (levels of the IV). Any other differences besides the treatment conditions (called *extraneous* or *nuisance variables*) can call into question the causal inference.

Extraneous variables can sometimes affect all treatment conditions equally, either weakening or strengthening their effects. For example, in the cited study comparing teaching technique and mode of presentation for school children, if the treatment conditions were administered immediately following recess, it is possible that participants would be too wound up to pay attention, thus weakening the effects of all of the treatment conditions. When an extraneous variable varies systematically with the different treatment conditions, it is referred to as a *confounding variable* and poses an even greater danger to the interpretation of the results. When a confounding variable is present, any changes in the DV cannot be attributed to the treatment condition with absolute certainty. Using our teacher study example, if everyone receiving Technique A via teacher had one teacher and everyone receiving Technique B via teacher had a different teacher, it could not be determined whether the different technique or the different teacher was responsible for any differences found in the DV. Thus, it is important to keep everything constrained equally across the different treatment levels except for the treatment itself. This is not always possible, especially when conducting research in school and clinic settings. It does not necessarily invalidate the study to have extraneous or confounding variables present; however, it does limit the degree of causality that you can attribute to your treatment conditions.

### Correlational Designs

In observational designs, the researcher simply measures variables as they occur naturally in the environment, which in turn, limits the degree that causality can be proven. Many observational studies, however, are conducted to examine whether a relationship exists between two or more variables or to predict certain variables (criterion variables) from other variables (predictor variables). Observational studies may also be conducted by actually observing behavior and recording predictor and criterion variables. For example, a researcher could observe children in the classroom and record the number of times children raise their hands to answer questions and the amount of praise they received from the teacher. Alternatively, observational studies may rely on self-report methods such as teacher or parent questionnaires that measure the variables of interest. Observational studies may also be conducted by obtaining ratings about children by people who know them such as parents, teachers, or peers, or use combinations of these techniques.

### Longitudinal Designs

*Longitudinal designs* involve measuring participants repeatedly over an extended period of time, perhaps years or even decades. Cross-sectional designs and longitudinal designs are ways of obtaining different types of information.

Cross-sectional designs are best used for answering questions concerning how a treatment works at one point in time. Longitudinal designs are best used for answering questions concerning developmental change. For this reason, they can be especially informative when studying children because of the rapid developmental changes. Cross-sectional designs may be set up to assess different age groups simultaneously (e.g., children at ages 2, 6, 10, 14, 18), which would answer questions concerning possible age differences. However, it is possible that differences may exist between children of different age groups at a single point in time because they have different histories (*cohort effects*). Therefore, the children that are 2 years of age at the same point in time as other children that are 14 years of age, might not display the same characteristics when they become 14 years of age. Longitudinal designs involve examining the long-term effects of some event or intervention. An additional advantage to longitudinal designs is that because information is collected with measures repeated at multiple time periods, error variance is reduced, often allowing for the detection of small behavior changes. Additionally participants are compared to themselves at different points in time. Disadvantages of longitudinal designs are mostly tied to the length of time required and inherent cost associated with the study. Because the data are collected over long periods of time, procedures and measures may become outdated and new procedures and measures may be developed. This leads to a major quandary; should the outdated procedures and/or measures be continued so that differences may be compared across time, or should the new procedures and/or measures be adopted because they are better? One possible solution is to continue using the old procedures and/or measures to ensure accurate comparison and to adopt new procedures and/or measures as they are developed. Participant attrition is also a major problem with longitudinal designs because it is quite possible that the group that remains at the end of the study is not representative of those who dropped out along the way. Additionally, participant attrition increases the probability of a Type II error (failing to find a treatment effect when one exists) and decreases the generality of the results. Another problem is the potential confound between the effects of personal age and the effects of historical period (e.g., children growing up during a particular decade may be exposed to environmental or other events such as war to which younger cohorts are not exposed).

## Example of a Cross-Sectional, Longitudinal Design

Rapport et al. (1999) conducted a cross-sectional, longitudinal study to examine the relationship between attention deficit behaviors and later scholastic achievement in children based on an conceptual model postulated by Fergusson, Horwood, and Lynskey (1993). They also sought to determine whether behavioral and cognitive pathways mediate the relationship between early attention deficit behaviors and later scholastic achievement; 325 children between 7 and 16 years of age participated in the study.

Attention deficit behaviors were measured as a manifest (observed) variable (called ADHD in the model) derived from the attention scale raw scores of the Child Behavior Checklist (CBCL). Conduct problems were measured as a latent variable (called CD in the model) based on delinquency and aggressive raw scale scores of the CBCL. Intelligence was measured as a manifest variable (called IQ in the model) derived from the composite score on the Kaufman Brief Intelligence Test (K-BIT). Classroom performance was measured as a latent variable based on the academic success, academic productivity, and academic efficiency scores of the Academic Performance Rating Scale (APRS). Vigilance was measured as a higher order latent variable based on errors scores from two distinct models of a continuous performance task (CPT). Memory was measured as a latent variable and derived by averaging children's percentage accuracy scores on the Paired Associate Learning Task (PAL-T)—a task that requires children to learn arbitrary associations between letter bigrams (e.g., "GJ") and single numerical digits (e.g., "3"). Long-term scholastic achievement was measured as a latent variable and derived from the total reading, math, and language scale scores of the Stanford Achievement Test (SAT) 3 years and 4 years after children were initially tested at the clinic.

Structural equation modeling (SEM) was used to examine the hypothesized relationships among attention deficit behaviors, intelligence, and later scholastic achievement in children, and whether behavioral and cognitive variables mediate this relationship. A direct causal relationship was postulated between ADHD and scholastic achievement, between CD and scholastic achievement, and between IQ and scholastic achievement. The numbers presented in the pathways (e.g., $-.26$ between ADHD and scholastic achievement) are standardized path coefficients and indicate the degree of change in one variable that are associated with change in another variable expressed in $SD$ units (e.g., a 1 $SD$ unit of change in ADHD ratings is associated with a $-.26$ change in children's later scholastic achievement, which implies that increased ADHD behavior is associated with decreased scholastic achievement later in life). The asterisk next to each path coefficient indicates that the path coefficient was significant. As shown in Fig. 15.3, all path coefficients were significant, except for the direct relationship of CD on scholastic achievement. Thus, ADHD has a direct causal influence on scholastic achievement and IQ has a direct causal influence on scholastic achievement. These results replicate the direct causal relationship between ADHD and scholastic achievement initially proposed by Fergusson et al. (1993).

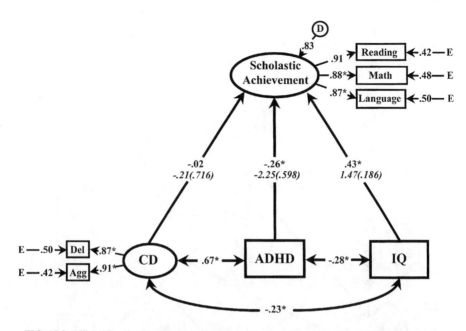

FIG. 15.3.   Fitted Replication Model depicting the relationship among CD, ADHD, IQ, and later scholastic achievement. Rectangles and ovals represent manifest (measured) and latent variables, respectively. Double-headed arrows represent nondirectional correlations and associated coefficients. Single-headed arrows between CD, ADHD, IQ and scholastic achievement represent regression pathways and associated standardized coefficients. Unstandardized values and standard errors (in brackets) are shown in italics immediately below the standardized coefficients. Single-headed arrows between latent constructs (CD, scholastic achievement) and measured variables represent confirmatory factor analysis paths and associated factor loadings. $E$ = measurement error. $D$ = disturbance term value and indicates error in the prediction of the latent variable. $*p < .05$. Comparative Fit Index (CFI) = .98.

The nature of the causal relationship of ADHD on scholastic achievement was subsequently evaluated in a second SEM (see Fig. 15.4), in which Rapport et al. (1999) hypothesized that the relationship was due to dual pathways—a behavioral pathway involving classroom performance and a cognitive pathway involving vigilance and memory. As shown in Fig. 15.4, the entire causal influence of ADHD on later scholastic achievement can be explained through the indirect effect through classroom performance (behavioral pathway) and through vigilance and memory (cognitive pathway). These results help explain the conceptual model proposed by Fergusson et al. (1993) by demonstrating that the causal relation between ADHD and later scholastic achievement is completely mediated by behavioral and cognitive factors.

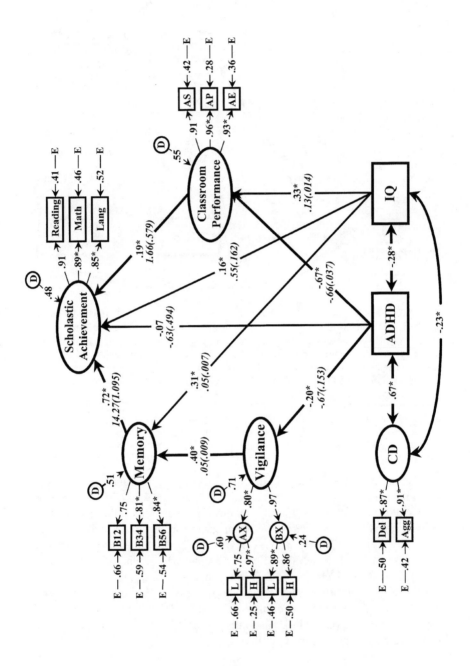

## SUMMARY

Conducting research with children is similar in many respects to studies involving adults. Both require creative thought, a thorough review, and comprehension of extant literature, an understanding of research design and methodology, careful selection of dependent measures, and knowledge of consent procedures. Studies that involve children, however, impose unique and frequently additional demands on the researcher. A broad understanding of basic developmental phenomena is required. Important differences exist concerning the selection and administration of measures appropriate for children of different ages, with particular features, from different backgrounds and with varying levels of cognitive ability. Consent forms require careful crafting because children often have little understanding of the nature of the experiment, are more vulnerable, and may react emotionally to particular questionnaires or experimental procedures imposed on them. And, gaining access to child settings (particularly schools) requires careful planning complemented by a high degree of comity, diplomacy, and flexibility. Interacting with children, appreciating the underlying heuristic function of a project, and contributing to the developing knowledge base about children, however, more than compensates for the additional demands.

---

FIG. 15.4.    Fitted Dual Pathway Model depicting the relationships among CD, ADHD, IQ, and later scholastic achievement and the mediating influence of cognitive (vigilance, memory) and behavioral (classroom performance) variables. Rectangles and ovals represent manifest (measured) and latent variables, respectively. Double-headed arrows represent nondirectional correlations and associated coefficients. Single-headed arrows between CD, ADHD, IQ and mediating cognitive (vigilance, memory) and behavioral (classroom performance) variables and later scholastic achievement represent regression pathways and associated standardized coefficients. Presented in italics below each standardized coefficient are their respective unstandardized values with standard errors in parentheses. Single-headed arrows between latent constructs (CD, scholastic achievement, vigilance, memory, classroom performance) and measured variables represent confirmatory factor analysis paths and associated factor loadings. $E$ = measurement error. $D$ = disturbance term value and indicates error in the prediction of the latent variable. $*p < .05$. Comparative fit index (CFI) $= .94$. Measurement of memory was derived using combined two-block trials (B12, B34, B56) from the PAL-T. Measurement of vigilance was derived using two versions of the CPT (AX, BX) with each version administered under low (L) and high (H) target density conditions. Measurement of classroom performance was derived from three subscales of the APRS (AS = academic success; AP = academic productivity; AE = academic efficiency). Measurement of scholastic achievement was derived from three composite indices of the SAT (reading, math, and language).

# REFERENCES

Achenbach, T. M., McConaughy, S. H., & Howell, C. T. (1987). Child/adolescent behavioral and emotional problems. Implications of cross-informant correlations for situational specificity. *Psychological Bulletin, 101*, 213–232.

Chambers, W. J., Puig-Antich, J., Hirsch, M., Paez, P., Ambrosini, P. J., Tabrizi, A., & Davies, M. (1985). The assessment of affective disorders in children and adolescents by a semi-structured interview. *Archives of General Psychiatry, 42*, 696–702.

Costello, A., Edelbrock, C., Kalas, R., Kessler, R., Kessler, M., & Klaric, S. (1984). *NIMH Diagnostic Interview Schedule for Children (DISC)*. Rockville, MD: National Institute of Mental Health.

Duhig, A. M., Renk, K., Epstein, M. K., & Phares, V. (2000). Interparental agreement on internalizing, externalizing, and total behavior problems: A meta-analysis. *Clinical Psychology Science and Practice, 7*, 435–453.

Edelbrook, C., & Costello, A. J. (1984). Structured psychiatric interviews for children and adolescents. In G. Goldstein & M. Hersen (Eds.), *Handbook of psychological assessment* (pp. 276–290). New York: Pergamon Press.

Fergusson, D. M., Horwood, L. J., & Lynskey, M. T. (1993). The effects of conduct disorder and attention deficit in middle childhood on offending and scholastic ability at age 13. *Journal of Child Psychology and Psychiatry, 34*(6), 899–916.

Herjanic, B., & Campbell, W. (1977). Differentiating psychiatrically disturbed children on the basis of a structured interview. *Journal of Abnormal Child Psychology, 5*, 127–134.

Hodges, K., McKnew, D., Cytryn, L., Stern, L., & Klein, J. (1982). The Child Assessment Scale (CAS) diagnostic interview: A report on reliability and validity. *Journal of the American Academy of Child and Adolescent Psychiatry, 21*, 468–473.

Kazdin, A. E. (1989). *Behavior modification in applied settings* (4th ed.). Monterey, CA: Brooks/Cole Publishing Company.

Kazdin, A. E. (1998). *Research design in clinical psychology* (3rd ed.). Needham Heights, MA: Allyn & Bacon.

Kazdin, A. E. (1999). Current (lack of) status of theory in child and adolescent psychotherapy research. *Journal of Clinical Child Psychology, 28*, 533–543.

Kovacs, M. (1982). *The longitudinal study of child and adolescent psychopathology: I. The semistructured psychiatric Interview Schedule for Children (ISC)*. Unpublished manuscript, Western Psychiatric Institute.

Lapouse, R., & Monk, M. A. (1958). An epidemiological study of behavior characteristics in children. *American Journal of Public Health, 48*, 1134–1144.

MacFarlane, J. W., Allen, L., & Honzik, M. P. (1954). *A developmental study of the behavior problems of normal children between 21 months and 14 years*. Berkeley: University of California Press.

Mash, E. J., & Terdal, L. G. (1997). *Assessment of childhood disorders* (3rd ed.). New York: Guilford Press.

Olds, R. S., & Symons, C. W. (1990). Recommendations for obtaining cooperation to conduct school-based research. *Journal of School Health, 60*(3), 96–98.

Ollendick, T. H., & Hersen, M. (1993). *Handbook of child and adolescent assessment*. MA: Allyn & Bacon.

Patterson, G. R. (1982). *Coercive family process*. Eugene, Oregon: Castalia.

Petosa, R., & Goodman, R. M. (1991). Recruitment and retention of schools participating in school health research. *Journal of School Health, 61*(10), 426–429.

Rapport, M. D., & Bailey, J. S. (1985). Behavioral physical therapy and *spina bifida*: A case study. *Journal of Pediatric Psychology, 10*, 87–96.

Rapport, M. D., & Bostow, D. E. (1976). The effects of access to special activities on the performance in four categories of academic tasks with third grade students. *Journal of Applied Behavior Analysis, 9*, 372.

Rapport, M. D., Murphy, A., & Bailey, J. S. (1982). Ritalin vs. response cost in the control of hyperactive children: A within-subject comparison. *Journal of Applied Behavior Analysis, 15*, 205–216.

Rapport, M. D., Scanlan, S., & Denney, C. B. (1999). Attention-deficit/hyperactivity disorder and scholastic achievement: A model of dual developmental pathways. *Journal of Child Psychiatry and Psychology, 40*, 1169–1184.

Walker, K. C., & Bracken, B. A. (1996). Inter-parent agreement on four preschool behavior rating scales: Effects of parent and child gender. *Psychology in the Schools, 33*, 273–282.

# 16

# Research with Older Adults

Ruth O'Hara[1,3]
Anne B. Higgins[4]
James A. D'Andrea[1,2]
Quinn Kennedy[1,3]
and Dolores Gallagher-Thompson[1,2,3]

[1] *Veteran's Affairs Sierra-Pacific Mental Illness Research, Education and Clinical Center (MIRECC), Palo Alto, California*
[2] *Veteran's Affairs Palo Alto Health Care System, Palo Alto, California*
[3] *Department of Psychiatry and Behavioral Sciences, Stanford University School of Medicine, Stanford University, Stanford, California*
[4] *Kaiser Permanente Medical Group Department of Behavioral Medicine/Adult Medicine, Sacramento, California*

## ISSUES IN CONDUCTING RESEARCH WITH OLDER ADULTS

The United Nations projects that between the years 2000 and 2050, the number of individuals over 65 years of age will exceed 1.1 billion worldwide. In the United States, the aged segment of the population is growing more rapidly than any other segment. Today, over 35 million Americans are estimated to be 65 years and older and by the year 2030, older adults will represent over 20% of the population (Katzman & Fox, 1999). Not only is the older population increasing but the elderly also are living longer, and currently more than 3 million Americans are over 85 years of age. These extended longevity rates and growing numbers of older adults in our society have resulted in a significant increase in research focusing on this population.

In recent years, there has been an emphasis not only on investigating the physiological, cognitive, social, and psychological impairments that accompany advanced age, but also on identifying those factors that contribute to successful aging. Elimination of mandatory retirement for most occupations has made it possible for older adults to stay in the workplace, and changing economics has made it necessary for many to continue working. Maintaining high levels of physiological, psychological, social, and cognitive functioning has become increasingly important for older adults who want to continue to work and to lead active and fulfilling lives. Preserving function with age helps maintain aspects of living, such as personal independence, that contribute to good health and overall quality of life in older adults.

The bourgeoning population of older adults in our society will also result in a higher prevalence of age-related neurological and psychological disorders. Neurodegenerative diseases rise exponentially with increasing age, and projections from the United Nations estimate that the number of individuals with dementia in developed countries alone will increase to 36.7 million by 2050 (United Nations, 1998). Currently, there are an estimated 4 million individuals with dementia in the United States. Alzheimer's disease (AD) is the most common neurodegenerative disorder, accounting for 50% to 70% of all cases and more than 100,000 deaths annually (Evans et al., 1989). The annual cost of care of AD patients in the US is estimated at $119 billion (Katzman et al., 1999). As our older population increases, AD will likely require an even larger share of healthcare costs, work hours, and hospital and nursing home beds. Indeed, the economic, psychological and social burden of age-related neurodegenerative disorders is such that investigators stress not only the importance of finding a cure but also the necessity of intervening in the early stages of dementia to prolong functionality and extend the time before institutionalization.

In addition to neurodegenerative diseases such as AD, many older adults suffer from declines in memory and cognition that may never lead to dementia, but that none the less can influence many day-to-day activities from medication adherence to productivity in the workplace and at home. A significant amount of research aims to better understand and thus ameliorate cognitive decline with age.

The later years of the human lifespan are also accompanied by significant social changes, including loss of function on retirement, death of a spouse, the demands of living alone, economic losses, and even institutionalization. Many of these social changes and losses result in psychological disorders, such as depression. Indeed, depression is one of the most prevalent of psychiatric disorders among older adults, accounting for a significant proportion of all mental illnesses in this population.

Overall, the result of the increased population of the elderly is that medical practitioners, health service workers, clinicians, and researchers will be increasingly confronted with the challenges of counseling, treating, and conducting research on a broad range of issues and disorders specific to older adults. The cognitive and physiological decline and social changes that accompany the aging process are not only the focus of research investigations, but they also impact the very process of conducting this research. In our chapter, we identify and discuss the central issues and challenges unique to conducting research with this population. Specifically, we describe fundamental concepts, methodological issues, and practical strategies involved in conducting research with older adults. In conclusion, we provide case examples of two research investigations with older subjects.

## IMPORTANT CONCEPTUAL ISSUES CENTRAL TO CONDUCTING RESEARCH ON OLDER ADULTS

### Defining Who Are Older Adults

For many years, age 65 has traditionally denoted the beginning of old age. This practice began in late 19th-Century Germany, when Otto Von Bismarck identified 65 as the qualifying age for receiving social benefits to assist with old age. In the United States, 65 became the qualifying age for receiving Social Security benefits. The qualifying age for Social Security is being gradually raised to age 67, and many individuals argue that age 70 may represent a more appropriate marker for the beginnings of old age, given the high level of function among older adults in the 21st Century. However, other researchers suggest that the aging process begins much earlier, and they argue that to more fully observe and understand the aging process, investigations of aging must include subjects much younger than 65. Several studies of cognitive, biological, and psychological aging now include individuals as young as 50 years of age. The recognition that we must include middle-aged adults in order to capture the beginnings of the aging process, combined with increasing longevity rates, has meant that aging research can span age ranges as broad as from 50 to 100 years. Yet, it is well recognized that manifestations of the aging process will be very different in an individual of 80 years of age than in an individual of 50 years of age. Typically, researchers investigating aging consider 60 years of age to be a reasonable marker for the beginning of old age, but they stress the importance of distinguishing between the young elderly (60 to 70 years of age) and the old elderly (80 to 90 years of age and above).

### Heterogeneity of Aging and the Limitations of Chronological Age as a Maker of the Aging Process

Age effects reflect differences in biological, psychological, and social processes that occur with the aging process. However, the aging process does not occur at the same rate in all individuals. Although the effects of age are strongly associated with chronological age, the significant heterogeneity in the aging process among older adults means that chronological age is not always the most appropriate way to make conclusions as to their physiological, psychological, or cognitive status. A very healthy, cognitively active 80-year-old may be at the same stage of physiological aging as a less healthy, less active 70-year-old.

The evidence suggests that there is far greater variance among older than younger adults on a range of physiological, psychological, and cognitive measures. Cultural differences, education levels, and living arrangements also tend to be more varied among older adults than younger adults. Limitations of chronological age have long been recognized in research on children, and childhood is hallmarked by developmental stages rather than by chronological age. However, such a developmental approach has yet to be applied systematically to the aging process.

As a researcher investigating the aging process, it is important to be aware of the significant heterogeneity with respect to the aging process, such that knowledge of chronological age alone may not be a useful indicator of their physiological, psychological, or cognitive functioning.

## The Confounding of Cohort and Age Effects

*Cohort effects* refer to common experiences shared by individuals who belong to the same generation or who were born during the same specific time period. A cohort can represent a very specifically demarcated time period, for example, everyone born between 1920 and 1925, or it may apply to a more general period of time, such as the World War II generation. Oftentimes, people from different cohorts show different profiles on personality and cognitive measures due to experiences unique to their particular cohort. A comparison of young and old adults that finds younger subjects to be more competent on computers might conclude that computer competency decreases with age, when it is far more likely that this finding reflects cohort differences such that older adults have not had the same exposure to computers over their lifetime as the younger subjects. When conducting aging research, it is important to distinguish between differences due to cohort effects and those due to the aging process. Additionally, several investigators point out that individuals who are considered old can often represent two or three different generations. The result is that older adults under investigation may constitute several different cohorts and thus may have a very broad and varied range of educational, vocational, sociopolitical, and life experiences.

## Distinguishing Normal from Pathological Aging

Some of the observed heterogeneity among older adults may reflect presence of pathological aging. In the field of aging research, it is extremely important to distinguish between normal and pathological aging. Many investigators have suggested that with respect to aging, normal should imply the absence of neurological or psychiatric illness (La Rue, 1992). This is particularly important because the prevalence of neurodegenerative disorders increases with age. These disorders include Alzheimer's disease, frontal lobe dementia,

Lewy-body dementia, Parkinson's disease; cerebrovascular disorders such as vascular dementia; and more benign syndromes such as mild cognitive impairment (MCI) and age-associated cognitive decline (AACD). Indeed, a significant amount of research aims to increase our understanding of the etiology of these illnesses in order to develop appropriate treatments for them. Research with elderly adults suffering from any of these disorders poses it own unique challenges. For example, an individual suffering from dementia may not be able to fully understand the research procedures and thus may not have the ability to give informed consent. In the sections to follow, we provide feedback on these challenges and the appropriate ways to deal with them.

In addition to the obvious practical issues, there are also important methodological reasons for distinguishing between normal and pathological aging. Investigation of a population that includes both cerebrally impaired and normal elderly could significantly skew the results of a study of normal cognitive aging. Similarly, knowing whether or not an older adult is suffering from a psychiatric disorder can be very important in conducting research with this population. The most common psychiatric disorder among the elderly is depression. Depression can negatively impact cognitive performance in older adults. Thus, a study of cognition in normal aging would need to be sure that the participants were not also depressed as presence of depression could significantly confound the findings.

Some investigators suggest that normal aging should refer to healthy older adults without medical illnesses of any kind and who also are taking no medications. However, given the high prevalence of medical conditions such as diabetes and heart problems in older adults, such an approach would lead to research findings that could not easily be generalized to the aging population as a whole. This has led some investigators to distinguish between research investigating "optimal" aging and research investigating "typical or usual aging." However, there has been increased recognition that although comorbid conditions are part of "typical aging," they also significantly impact research findings in this field and they need to be taken into consideration when conducting research with older adults (La Rue, 1992).

## The Impact of Comorbidities on Research Findings

A broad of range of chronic illnesses is very prevalent among older adults, and it has been suggested that at least 80% of people over 65 years of age have at least one chronic illness (Nussbaum, 1997). Additionally, the number of chronic illnesses increases with age. Recently, there has been an increased emphasis on how such comorbidities may influence research results in both normal and pathological aging. Is a high depression score a manifestation of severe cerebrovascular disease rather than depression per se? Is a low cognitive score associated with presence of hypertension or diabetes, rather than indicating preclinical dementia? It is very important to consider the impact of any chronic illnesses in older subjects on the outcome measures you are obtaining.

Chronic illnesses may also lead to impairments in sensory and motor function. Because many tests, particularly cognitive measures, are dependent on intact sensory and motor impairment, it is important when conducting research with older adults to take this issue into consideration. As Nussbaum (1997) pointed out, illnesses such as arthritis that are common among older adults can affect those tests that require a motor component. Because it is not always possible to conduct a full medical evaluation or complete a full medical history for older subjects, one way to minimize some of these problems is to avoid those measures of cognition, for example, that are likely to be impacted by motor impairment. Investigators have developed versions of cognitive and psychological tests specifically for older adults, which minimize the involvement of motor and sensory impairments.

Because the number of chronic illnesses increase with age, it follows that older adults are also taking increased numbers of medications to treat these illnesses. These medications may also impact a range of cognitive and behavioral processes, as well as sensory and motor functions. Ideally, researchers investigating older adults should obtain a medical status and history, in addition to a list of current medications, in order to consider the impact of any comorbid conditions or medications on their outcome measures.

## METHODOLOGICAL ISSUES IN CONDUCTING RESEARCH ON OLDER ADULTS

### Design Issues

*Cross-Sectional Designs.*   Much aging research is cross-sectional in design, namely the investigation of different groups at one moment in time. In aging research, cross-sectional studies are often used to compare different age groups. The $M$ values for the different age groups are interpreted as representing what happens to subjects as they age (Kraemer, Yesavage, Taylor, & Kupfer, 2000). However, investigation of aging processes using cross-sectional designs can be problematic because any observed differences between groups may reflect cohort effects rather than the age differences. Because cross-sectional studies can confound age and cohort effects, they may actually overestimate age-related changes (La Rue, 1992). Negative age patterns tend to be less apparent in longitudinal studies than in cross-sectional studies.

*Longitudinal Designs.*   Longitudinal studies investigate the same individuals on several occasions over a specified period of time. Such studies can be as short as a few weeks or as long as several decades. Longitudinal studies provide a more accurate assessment of the rate of change with respect to a variety of aging processes, but they also have some limitations. In particular, longitudinal studies may be biased by selective attrition, particularly when being conducted with older adults. In other words, older subjects who stay in longitudinal studies may be healthier, more social, or more cognitively intact. Older adults with chronic illness or cognitive impairment may be more likely to drop out of a longitudinal study before its completion. The result is that longitudinal studies may actually underestimate age effects, and findings from longitudinal studies of aging may reflect "optimal" rather than "usual" aging.

Another difficulty with longitudinal studies is the problem of practice effects. Longitudinal studies will aim to measure the same variable at each assessment time point. A longitudinal assessment of memory function, for example, would measure memory function at each of several time points in order to assess how memory changes with age. However, any observed improvement in memory function with age simply may reflect familiarity with the testing materials and procedures rather than any absolute change in memory function per se. To help with this problem, investigators recommend that the inter-assessment intervals should be sufficiently long to minimize such practice effects, and several cognitive measures have developed alternate forms, so that although the testing procedures and format are identical, the subject is not being tested on the exact same material.

Additionally, longitudinal studies have some significant practical limitations. Due to their length, they are more time consuming and more costly than cross-sectional studies. Investigators must wait longer periods of time to test their hypotheses. However, many investigators in aging research feel that the developmental processes involved in aging are best understood through use of longitudinal designs (Kraemer et al., 2000).

### Cross-Sequential and Longitudinal Sequential Designs.

One compromise to deal with the methodological limitations of cross-sectional designs and the cost of longitudinal designs has been to combine cross-sequential and longitudinal sequential designs. A cross-sequential design conducts the same cross-sectional study at different time points but on individuals of the same age adjusted for the time point in question. For example, an investigation of cognitive performance conducted on 60- to 70-year-olds in 1990 would be repeated in 2000 on different individuals who are 70 to 80 years of age. A longitudinal sequential design conducts two or more longitudinal designs that utilize two or more cohorts. Combining cross-sequential and longitudinal sequential designs one investigates a large number of cohorts, each of which is followed longitudinally for the same duration of time. This allows one to cover a broader age range over a far shorter period of time than if one were conducting a longitudinal study alone. In a study of older aviators, Yesavage, Taylor, Mumenthaler, Noda, & O'Hara (1999) utilized this type of design, and they were able to capture data for a 20-year developmental span over a 5-year investigation. However, such designs are not entirely without their limitations, as data can still be subject to cohort effects and it is still costly to conduct this kind of investigation.

***Clinical Trials.*** In recent years, there has been a significant increase in the number of clinical trials in older adults, using either pharmacological or non-pharmacological interventions. One of the limitations with randomized clinical trials is that they typically investigate only highly selected populations. Given the significant heterogeneity among older adults, the findings from many clinical trials of elderly subjects are not always representative of the population in general, and more effectiveness studies are required to provide "real world" information. Additionally, any intervention study is highly complex, particularly if it is placebo controlled and some individuals will be randomly assigned to a placebo group and will not receive the intervention in question. The issues inherent to the conduct of clinical trials are such that it is extremely important for the researcher to make sure that the older subject is absolutely aware of all the issues and potential risks involved in participating in this kind of study.

### Recruitment and Sampling Issues

In the next section, we discuss the practical issues involved in recruiting older adults into research studies. In this section, we discuss some of the methodological issues in recruitment and sample selection.

Different recruitment strategies can result in very different subject samples. For example, older adults selected from senior centers may be more social, more active, and less isolated than older adults living alone who do not belong to a senior center. Additionally, many university based aging research programs access university alumni for recruitment purposes. Such older adults have high levels of education that is not necessarily typical for their cohort and findings based on such a sample may not generalize to the rest of their cohort. It is important for the researcher to consider the potential selection bias that may result from recruitment strategies employed in a research study, and the extent to which the sample selected can adequately be used to address the research question under investigation.

When comparing groups of older adults it is very important to make sure that these groups are as similar as possible with respect to factors, such as socioeconomic group, years of education, and living arrangements, because these factors can significantly impact a broad range of behavioral, cognitive, and psychological measures. For example, with respect to cross-sectional studies, making sure that the groups are as similar as possible in all other respects will go a long way to minimize the confound of age and cohort effects. However, given the significant heterogeneity among older adults, this is not always easy to accomplish.

When researchers conduct observational or epidemiological studies of older adults, sample bias may also be an issue. For example, epidemiological studies of post-menopausal women have found use of estrogen replacement therapy (ERT) to be associated with a decreased risk of developing AD. But several investigators have suggested that women may elect to take ERT in a non-random manner. Confounding variables, such as socio-economic status, educational level, and health practices, may contribute to the decision to take ERT, and these variables may account for some of the benefits attributed to ERT.

## Measurement Issues

All measures employed in any research study should be reliable and valid. However, assessment instruments suitable for young or middle-aged populations are not always reliable and valid for the assessment of older subjects.

One example concerns the assessment of depression, a disorder that can present very differently in older than in younger adults. Thus, measures developed to assess depression in younger adults may not be valid for older adults. Many depression assessment instruments ask about suicidal intent or one's hopefulness about the future. Although hopelessness about one's future might serve as a good indicator of depression in younger adults, older adults may simply not be hopeful about the future because they are in the latter stages of their lifespan, not because they are depressed. Additionally, somatic complaints are not always useful indicators of depression in older adults because such symptoms often accompany the normal aging process. Several measures, including the Geriatric Depression Scale, have been created specifically to assess depression in the elderly.

When choosing assessment measures, it is also important that, whenever possible, normative data be available for older adults. Comparison of performance levels with those of same-aged peers is particularly important when deciding, for example, whether the cognitive performance of an older adult is above or below what is considered normal for their age. Normative data are now available for an increasing number of cognitive, behavioral, and psychological measures. However, it is important to note that many measures do not have norms available for the whole range of ages among older adults. For example, several tests have excellent norms for age ranges 60 to 75, but do not have normative data for the very elderly, namely 75 and above (Nussbaum, 1997).

When assessing cognitive function in older adults, it is important to choose tests that are not vulnerable to ceiling or floor effects. *Ceiling effects* occur when a test is so easy that subjects can perform perfectly and the researcher obtains no variability on the measure. Similarly, *floor effects* occur when a test is too difficult and subjects perform poorly, and again there is a limited range of response, which in turn limits any interpretations based on the obtained data.

Researchers in the field of aging should aim to employ measures that have established reliability, validity, and available normative data for use with older adults. However, because the field of aging research is still in development, this kind of information is not always available and the researcher may be obliged to actually obtain such norms. In the latter part of this chapter, we present a case study, which illustrates some strategies for dealing with a lack of appropriate assessment measures for investigating the outcome of interest in older adults.

## PRACTICAL ISSUES, BARRIERS, AND STRATEGIES INVOLVED IN CONDUCTING RESEARCH WITH OLDER ADULTS

In addition to the methodological issues already outlined, researchers working with older adults need to be sensitive to a wide range of factors, which may influence, prohibit, or enhance participation in standard hospital or university based research. These factors are often similar to the practical issues faced by clinicians when trying to enlist an older adult in psychological treatment. They include (a) lack of familiarity with the research process and research environment, (b) physical, sensory, or cognitive impairments that may limit participation or informed consent, and (c) practical barriers to participation such as transportation to the research site, and (d) scheduling issues. These issues must be assessed and addressed before research participation can realistically begin (Coon, Rider, Gallagher-Thompson, & Thompson 1999; Rybarczyk et al., 1992).

In the following sections we describe the practical issues, barriers, and strategies involved in conducting research with older adults, from the initial steps of recruitment through the administration and collection of data.

### Recruiting Older Adults Into Research Studies

In many research settings, some of the common mechanisms for recruiting subjects are to advertise, either in local or national newspapers, on Internet Web sites, on radio or television, in research newsletters, or on bulletin boards within the research or university setting itself.

Although these mechanisms may elicit response from older adults, a more efficient strategy of recruiting older adults for research studies may be to approach local community agencies, senior citizens centers, and retirement communities. Approaching these groups often is advantageous compared to individual recruitment because many older adults tend to be cautious or fearful of being approached by strangers and are not likely to participate in research unless referred by a trusted source. Identifying the group leader or administrative "gatekeeper" can facilitate accessing various communities where groups of older adults reside and congregate because they are well known to the target population and are viewed as trustworthy.

Gatekeepers have heterogeneous backgrounds and may be social workers, nurses, administrators, and business leaders. Some may be employed as full- or part-time staff, or may be retired while still retaining a position of leadership by virtue of their past occupational skills, for example, a social worker employed by a senior citizen center, or a retired attorney who volunteers to serve as president of a local AARP chapter. Despite their varied backgrounds, gatekeepers often share the goals of protecting their population or membership from potential harm, respecting their privacy, and shielding them from being inconvenienced by large demands placed on their time. Thus, it is very important for researchers to develop a good relationship with the gatekeeper and to explain research study to them in detail. In addition to a detailed description of exactly what is required to participate in the research, issues such as confidentiality and anonymity in the reporting of research findings, as well as the methods for safeguarding data obtained during the research project need to be reviewed with the gatekeeper before research can begin. It is very important for the researcher to take time to answer any and all questions the gatekeeper may have. If concerns of safety and privacy are dealt with adequately, appropriately, and to the satisfaction of the gatekeeper, the researcher may be given permission to approach the older adults for recruitment into their study.

Because older adults represent a vulnerable population, researchers need to invest significant time and energy in developing a good relationship with the population or community being studied. Maintaining good relationships with the population or community being studied cannot be overemphasized. Even if a monetary incentive is offered for their participation, subject recruitment efforts will be less effective if building a relationship with the target population is overlooked. It is important to keep in mind that other researchers may have approached the particular group or population being targeted for subject recruitment multiple times in the past. The population's experience with participating in prior research studies, as well as relations between the college or university where the study is originating and the community, often have a significant impact on whether members will be willing to participate in future research. Furthermore, many gatekeepers may also be reluctant to allow their membership to participate in the research study if any potential benefits of their participation are discontinued once the data are collected.

When recruiting older adults with a specific illness, such as dementia, contacting national and local agencies (e.g., the Alzheimer's Association) can be very helpful. Because conducting research with older adults with dementia is inherently complex, it is highly recommended to develop collaborative relationships with investigators in well-recognized research programs, which specialize in conducting research with this population. These investigators will have extensive experience, resources, and expertise, and will be aware of all the challenges involved in conducting research with patients with dementia. However, one concern of researchers dealing with dementia patients is the issue of patient burden. Given the increased interest in combating neurodegenerative diseases, dementia patients are likely to receive multiple offers to participate in a broad range of studies. Clinicians are concerned that participating in too many studies can be very stressful for their dementia patients. When investigating older adults, with and without dementia, researchers should be aware of the other studies that their subject may be participating in and the impact of that involvement on the scientific and practical aspects of their study, as well as the burden on the participant.

## Familiarizing the Older Adult With the Research Process and Environment

Participation in research may be a new phenomenon for many older adults. Older adults may be reluctant to participate in a study because the research environment is unfamiliar. Additionally, the lengthy assessment sessions often associated with research can be very stressful for an older adult (Edelstein & Semenchuck, 1996). To make the older adult feel more comfortable and to increase participation, it is very important to spend some time during the recruitment process to socialize the older adult to the process of research. It is important to thoroughly explain the nature of the research, including the scientific merit and if appropriate, the clinical implications of the project. It is essential to explain in detail what will be expected of the older adult as a research participant at every stage of the project, including time commitment, risks, and follow-up requirements. Spending time at the beginning of a research contact to answer questions and dispel any misconceptions will reduce participant anxiety and enhance participation.

## Scheduling Issues and the Older Adult

Once an older adult has agreed to participate in a research investigation, the next step is to schedule an appointment for participation. To do this, the researcher must also take into account the daily living patterns and settings of the research participants before data can be collected. Subjects living in retirement communities often value their privacy and may not always be interested in being solicited or recruited for research studies. It is important to recognize that when these subjects do agree to participate, their participation is a personal invitation into their home life and personal circumstances. Therefore, the researcher should emphasize to the participant that their privacy will be maintained and the researcher's appreciativeness for their participation. In assisted living settings, where older adults live more communally and where structured activities or other events are planned, the researcher should accommodate the daily routines of the residents. Residents of assisted living centers adopt routines around scheduled activities and events where transportation is involved (e.g., going shopping) and may be reluctant to participate in research if it means missing these activities. It is often helpful to obtain the scheduled list of activities from the community director ahead of time and plan interviews and testing sessions accordingly. Getting residents to complete lengthy questionnaires or test batteries may not be possible in circumstances when residents can only spare an hour in between events, for example. Repeated visits to the facility to re-interview subjects where they left off may be necessary in order to collect data.

One of the common myths about community dwelling, older adults is that they have plenty of time on their hands, particularly because many of them are in retirement. Although older adults are likely to have more flexible schedules than younger subjects, many older adults have very active schedules and it may be difficult for them to find time when they are free to participate. Often they take more vacations than their middle-aged counterparts, and researchers may need to be very flexible about the days of the week and times that these older adults are available to facilitate research participation. In many of our studies, we have been surprised to find that many older adults prefer to participate in a study on weekends or in the evening. Whenever possible, the researcher should accommodate the schedule of the subject; however, although weekend appointments may be viable, evening participation may be more problematic. Many research protocols are subject to time-of-day effects, such that performance may be far better in the morning than in the evening. This is an important consideration when scheduling older adults because they are particularly vulnerable to the effects of fatigue. However, it is important to also remember that older adults have very flexible schedules; they may not be getting up as early in the morning, particularly if they are retired. An evening appointment may actually be the equivalent of an afternoon appointment for an older adult who is rising later in the day. It is a good idea for a researcher to inquire about the daily routine of the subject before scheduling a research appointment, particularly if they are conducting a research protocol that may be vulnerable to time-of-day effects.

**Transportation Issues**

Transportation can often be a significant barrier for many older adults to participate in research. Traditionally, research is conducted in a university setting, which can present a problem for older adults who have transportation difficulties. Universities often have limited parking, or parking that is a long distance from the research site. Directions to a university research site can be confusing or intimidating for the older adult. Other transportation concerns that may limit research participation include whether the older adult has reliable transportation or is dependent on another person for transportation; or can the older adult navigate public transportation?

In these instances, it may be more practical for the researcher to be flexible about the location of the research setting. The researcher may need to consider how to implement the research protocol within an alternative location, such as the subject's home, a nursing home, a primary care clinic, or a hospital bedside, while maintaining privacy and confidentiality (Coon et al., 1999). To increase involvement in research, it is important to be accessible and make it easy for the older adult to participate.

### Involving a Collateral

When recruiting older adults with cognitive impairment, significant physical illness, or a psychiatric disorder, it is very helpful to involve a collateral. *Collaterals* are persons who are in some way involved in the care or supervision of an older adult and who usually assist the person with activities of daily living. Family members, paid caregivers, and extended care staff may function as collaterals for elderly persons living alone in the community or in long-term care settings. Collaterals can be involved in a number of ways in the lives of elders. On one end of the continuum of involvement, collaterals can be individual family members, friends, neighbors, or local senior citizen organizations that assist an elder with specific tasks such as shopping, transportation, or paying bills. On the other end of the continuum, collaterals may be involved in the day-to-day care of the elder, such as helping the person to dress, bathe, or eat. For instance, relatives of demented elderly are often in demanding caregiving roles in which they provide care and supervision on a continuous basis.

Involvement of collaterals can be advantageous in terms of subject recruitment of older adults, especially those adults with memory or functional impairments who might otherwise not be able to give informed consent or to interface between the researcher and the subject, as occurs in outcomes evaluation studies. Depending on the setting in which the study will occur, whether in the home of an individual elder living independently in the community or in extended care settings, the researcher will need to approach collaterals in different ways.

As a general rule, the more involved the collateral is in the daily care of an elder, the more important it is to secure cooperation of the collateral in conducting the research project. The importance of building a relationship with the collateral cannot be overemphasized, as the collateral may also serve as a referral source to other caregivers or elders who may benefit from participating in the study. Building a collaborative alliance with the collateral is done by allowing extra time for rapport building and by answering their questions as to the purpose the research project. Reviewing issues such as informed consent, maintaining privacy, the benefits to the elder, or collateral participating in the research, and how the research results will be reported should be done in order to address the collateral's natural concerns for the well-being of the elder.

## Obtaining Informed Consent from Older Adults

Obtaining informed consent is a necessary and extremely important aspect of conducting research. Certain considerations should be made in obtaining informed consent with older adults, particularly those suffering from cognitive impairments. In this section, we give a brief overview of what informed consent is, and issues in obtaining informed consent with older adults and with impaired older adults.

*Informed consent* is based on a person's right to autonomy, dignity, and self-determination. It consists of three main points. The first is that the person should receive sufficient information about the research project, including risks and benefits of the research, and alternative options to make a decision regarding participation. Secondly, the participant must not be coerced either by the researcher or by others into giving consent. *Coercion* can be viewed as anything—negative or positive—that would unduly influence a person's decision, such as threats of negative consequences or the promise of rewards. Finally, individuals must demonstrate that they are competent enough to make the decision. Do they show a real understanding of the procedure, risks, and benefits? Can they appreciate the potential consequences that participation may have? Is the reasoning behind their decision rational? Clearly, competency is particularly difficult to judge in persons with significant cognitive or memory impairments. This issue is discussed in more detail toward the end of the section.

When obtaining consent from older persons, some considerations should be kept in mind. For example, because older adults tend to have vision problems, having the consent form in large type is helpful. Less concrete is the fact that the older population is the most heterogeneous in our society in terms of educational levels, health problems, cognitive abilities, and personal experiences. If possible, researchers should be aware of these individual differences before obtaining informed consent. For example, an increasingly larger proportion of the older population is nonnative English speaking. Language barriers clearly impede the ability to give the participant sufficient information. Researchers should make sure that the consent form is either translated into their language and/ or ensure that a translator (who could be a family member) is present to translate the consent form and any questions the participant may have. Similarly, differences in educational levels or occupation may have a significant impact on the older subject's ability to understand all aspects of the informed consent. The language used in an informed consent form is often, by necessity, technical, and scientific in nature. The researcher needs to take sufficient time to explain the consent form and study procedures in detail in order to ensure that the subjects are completely aware of what they are signing.

One of the most difficult circumstances in which to obtain informed consent is when older subjects have cognitive impairment, dementia, or another illness, which negatively impacts their comprehension. By far the greatest challenge is determining competency. Researchers, physicians, and legal bodies have grappled with this complex issue. The following questions have been suggested as a way to determine a participant's competency for medical research (Joynt & Greenlaw, 1993):

- What is your present physical condition?
- What is the treatment being recommended for you?
- What do you and your doctor think might happen to you if you decided to accept the treatment?
- What do you and your doctor think might happen to you if you decide not to accept the recommended treatment?
- What are the alternative treatments available and what are the probable consequences of accepting each?

Yet even the answers to these questions may not clarify a participant's level of competency. If the participant is not competent or the level of competency remains unclear, researchers can use proxies. *Proxies* are persons who have durable power of attorney, guardianship, committee of the person, or a health care proxy who can make informed consent for the impaired participant. In these cases, proxies act as they think the participant would, not as they themselves would act in the same situation. Oftentimes, proxies are family members who know the participant. Although uncommon, researchers should be aware of the potential of coercion with proxies for impaired participants. Even family members may have personal motivations that go against the participant's best interests. More likely is the problem that family members may disagree among themselves as to whether the research study is in the best interests of the participant. Another option that has been developed is called the *Ulysses contract*. Here, the mildly or moderately impaired patient gives consent for future participation in research in the case that they will be too impaired later to give informed consent. Thus, after determining that a participant is not competent, several different methods can be used to obtain informed consent.

The main goals in obtaining informed consent from impaired participants are to do so at the impaired person's optimal level of competency and to maintain their dignity. To aid their level of competency, researchers should describe the study in a quiet place where the participant is less likely to become distracted or confused by too much stimuli. Researchers also should describe the study in simple, short sentences. Several tactics can be used to help preserve the patient's dignity. For example, if it becomes apparent that the participant is unable to read the consent form, researchers can say things like, "This is a lot of information, isn't it? It basically says that ..." and the researchers should paraphrase what is on the consent form without in any way minimizing what participation in the study entails. Additionally, if a family member or other person is acting as a proxy, researchers should make sure to still include the participant in the conversation, regardless of the severity of his or her impairment.

In summary, informed consent was created out of the acknowledgment that participants have the right of autonomy, dignity, and self-determination. Researchers must obtain informed consent from participants before beginning the study. Obtaining informed consent from older participants gives rise to special issues; the most complex of which is determining competency of elderly adults with impaired comprehension to give or withhold consent.

### Issues and Strategies When Collecting Data From Older Adults

As previously discussed, many older adults have significant physical limitations or sensory impairments that may require adaptations to standard research protocols. Visual or auditory impairments are often common in later life. Fifty percent of Americans ages 65 and older are affected by some type of hearing loss (Vernon, 1989). Many older adults have a partial visual impairment, including decreases in peripheral vision, depth perception, tolerance for glare, and visual acuity. Adaptations to consider in making tests or questionnaires user-friendly to older adult populations generally focus on overcoming the barriers presented by sensory impairments. A number of practical modifications can be used to overcome these barriers.

Frequently, tests are constructed and printed using type sizes that are too small for persons with decreased visual acuity to be able to read clearly or without fatigue. In addition, multiple copies made from nonoriginal paper and pencil tests also have poor letter quality. Poor reproduction quality and small type size will fatigue older adults with poor visual acuity and may also lead to greater frustration. Therefore, when using questionnaires, a good rule of thumb is to make clear copies with large, simple type on high contrast paper. In our experience, using bold, 16-point Helvetica is adequate in the majority of cases. As a matter of course, it is often to the researcher's advantage to remind all subjects to bring their corrective lenses with them. However, there are other situations when additional modifications may be needed. In cases where low vision is present, a verbal administration may be required. In such cases, having an audiotape administered version of the questionnaire would be helpful if it is anticipated that more than a few subjects will be unable to read secondary to having low vision or language difficulties. Other modifications to paper and pencil tests include using colored paper for each test or questionnaire if multiple measures will be administered, and administering the tests under ambient light conditions. Institutional and laboratory settings often use fluorescent lighting that can make reading difficult under certain conditions and therefore these conditions should be avoided. In these cases, additional lighting from a soft-white reading bulb can supplement room lighting.

Overcoming hearing deficits in older adults is a frequent problem in both research and clinical settings. All subjects should be reminded to bring their hearing aids with spare batteries to the testing session. For subjects with memory loss, involving a collateral such as a spouse, a relative, or a nurse can greatly reduce the likelihood that the hearing aid will be forgotten. In long-term care settings, geriatric patients with memory loss and poor hearing often lose their hearing aids and may at times even accuse other patients or staff of stealing them when in fact they have simply misplaced and forgotten them. Hearing aids amplify all sounds indiscriminately so that background noises are made loud as well. Therefore, testing subjects with hearing aids should be done in places where the peripheral sounds in the room are kept to a minimum. When subjects with hearing loss do not have hearing aids, they may appear somewhat confused and unable to participate in the research process due to their inability to answer conversationally. However, this obstacle can often be overcome in older subjects by writing instructions and comments down on a piece of paper. Although this may be more labor intensive than using speech, reliable and acceptable results are often obtained using this modality.

Other issues when collecting data from older subjects include assessment sessions or interviews that are too long for the person's attention span or physical stamina. Some older adults will not be able to tolerate the time requirements for many traditional research protocols. If possible, baseline assessment sessions should be broken up into several shorter, more manageable sessions, and ample breaks should be given to prevent fatigue. As previously discussed, many older adults struggle with comorbid physical conditions, which may require frequent visits to a physician, unplanned illnesses, or a complicated medication regimen. It is not uncommon for older adults to have to cancel or reschedule appointments, or for them to have difficulty keeping appointments on a regular basis (Coon et al., 1999). This can complicate their participation in a research study, especially one with multiple longitudinal follow-up sessions to schedule. Any limitations should be thoroughly evaluated before participation in the research begins, and the impact of these limitations should be consistently revisited throughout the research process. If feasible and methodologically sound, modifications should be made to the protocol and multiple modalities should be used to present information. In summary, several issues must be taken into consideration when working with older research participants. Table 16.1 outlines several tips for working with older participants.

TABLE 16.1

Ten Recommendations for Working With Older Adults as Research Subjects

---

Socialize the older adult research subject to the research environment.

Identify, assess and address practical barriers to research participation.

Be flexible about scheduling; be willing to conduct research in alternative settings such as home, hospital, or nursing home.

Avoid fatigue. If the research protocol is extensive, schedule shorter sessions, or break the protocol down into discrete sections. Allow time for breaks.

Enhance patient understanding by presenting information clearly and slowly; reduce the use of jargon and scientific terms.

Clearly identify each component of the research protocol. Break problems down into basic components if necessary.

Carefully go over every aspect of the consent form, making sure that the subject fully understands what the research entails and what any risks and benefits may be. Make sure you allow plenty of time for questions.

Make sure that all necessary forms are in a large print in language that is easy for the subject to understand.

Use of frequent repetition and elicit feedback to make sure the research subject understands all the presented material, especially with complicated research protocols or assessments.

Encourage the use of memory aids to remind subjects of appointments and follow-up interviews. Reminder letters and calls are helpful to ensure continued participation.

---

## Avoiding Ageist Biases

The Task Force to Develop Non-Ageist Guidelines for research sponsored by the American Psychological Association Board of Social and Ethical Responsibility and the Board of Scientific Affairs suggests that researchers exercise sensitivity to potential age bias and stereotypes when conducting research with older adults. Although many researchers feel that older adults may be more sensitive to being asked about personal and, in particular, sexual issues, the task force suggests that this may simply reflect age bias on behalf of researchers, and that there is insufficient empirical data to suggest that this is in fact the case. The boards suggest that rather than avoiding sensitive topics, researchers use language and terms with which an age group may be most comfortable in order to ask sensitive questions.

The task force also points out that it is very important for the researcher to avoid patronizing or infantilizing the older research participant. One significant risk in accommodating to the cognitive, sensory and motor impairments in older adults is that all too frequently it becomes easy for the researcher to perceive older subjects as incompetent. Sensory and motor impairments, and even transient short-term memory problems, which are a normal part of the aging process, do not mean that the older subject has problems with their comprehension and intellectual abilities. Older subjects should be treated with respect and researchers should avoid condescending or childlike language when communicating with an older research participant. Additionally, researchers should not call older subjects by the first name without being first invited to do so or asking permission to do so. If the researcher is much younger than the older adult, it is important for the researcher to recognize the potential impact of this age difference on the responses and attitudes of the older participant.

## Changing the Data Collection Settings

Not all research involving older adults is conducted in traditional, university based research settings. Sometimes it is convenient for the older subject and the researcher to collect data at an adult's local senior center, or at some venue closer to the subject's home. Flexibility regarding where data can be collected has several benefits. First, older adults will likely feel less anxious and more relaxed if data are collected in an environment with which they are familiar. Second, barriers to participation caused by transportation problems can be removed by collecting data at a venue that is easier for the subject to access. However, there are important disadvantages associated with changing the research venue. Experimental research needs to be conducted in a controlled manner, so that each subject is tested in the same environment. Because it is not always feasible to collect data in the exact same setting, it is very important for the researcher to insure that the any change in environment does not result in any significant changes, which might impact the research protocol. For example, if the study is typically conducted in a quiet room, with a desk and chair, and minimal amount of extraneous stimuli, it is essential that a similar, quiet room be available when conducting the research at a local senior center. Any advantages in terms of facilitating participation need to be balanced against the methodological problems associated with changing the data collection environment.

Some studies are conducted entirely in a nonuniversity setting. Many researchers are interested in investigating older adults in specialized settings, such as geropsychiatric units, acute care settings, and extended care settings. Because the data in such investigations are collected on all subjects in the same setting, the researcher does not have to deal with the methodological issues involved when the data collection environment changes. However, conducting research with older adults in specialized environments can present its own unique challenges, and we now outline some of the issues and strategies for conducting research in the extended care setting.

## Conducting Research with Older Adults in the Extended Care Setting

Extended care settings are often the sites chosen for conducting applied research with older adults, and the collaterals involved are usually facility line staff. In extended care settings, enlisting the cooperation of staff is often required to gain access to the resident population and to implement an intervention successfully. A useful strategy in conducting applied research with staff is to adopt a consultation role. This requires that the researcher develop an appreciation of the special characteristics of the resident population, the long-term care environment, and of the dynamics of dementia. Lichtenberg (1994) highlighted four important features that successful consultants in extended care settings have when implementing effective research and intervention strategies: (a) nontoken administrative support, (b) a collaborative relationship with facility personnel, (c) expertise in behavioral therapy and familiarity with general geriatric psychiatry, and (d) regular staff meetings that focus on improving psychosocial care. Each of these will now briefly be reviewed.

*Nontoken administrative support* refers to the degree of importance given the research project by facility administrators. The psychological consultant needs the support of the administration or the research project, no matter how important or beneficial the project is perceived to be by the researcher or anyone else attempting to implement it, will be nonproductive in the long run. Nontoken administrative support is required so that there will be adequate follow-through in implementing the design and that the design be carried out properly in the researcher's absence. To be effective within the system, the researcher should either identify administrators who share his or her values and support staff that wish to implement psychosocial interventions or educate/persuade the existing administrators or staff to do so. Because line staff often do not understand the role of a research psychologist in the long-term care facility, words of introduction, presence or absence of supervisors at initial staff meetings, and the respect of supervisors will have a critical effect on the way in which the researcher's words are received by caregivers and staff.

Building a collaborative relationship with staff requires more than attending weekly meetings or didactic in-service presentations, as it removes the consultant from the position of being a partner and resource to being a manager in the eyes of line staff. As a result, such meetings end up becoming an additional demand on their time that will make it harder for them to catch up afterward with their duties. Furthermore, participation in this context will most likely consist of staff simply listening and then leaving these meetings without being encouraged to bring up and discuss the issues that are most important to them as staff members.

To set up a collaborative relationship, it is important for the researcher to develop an understanding of (a) the typical duties of the line staff, (b) the characteristics of the population they serve, (c) the kinds of problems they frequently encounter, (d) the most stressful situations they are likely to encounter and how they cope with them, and (e) the most satisfying aspects of their jobs. Also, getting to know the duties and responsibilities that are faced by a staff of different disciplines is crucial to creating a team approach to implementing the intervention.

Lichtenberg (1994) pointed out that for a research project to be carried out successfully, the staff must feel a sense of ownership of the project and that their opinions on how to implement it will be valued. Only when staff members believe that the researcher understands their jobs will they begin to trust the researcher's recommendations and implement the project.

The third factor Lichtenberg identified among effective researchers in long-term care settings is to have a good understanding of both behavioral therapy and general geriatric psychiatry. Among the most common challenges faced by line staff is the management of problem behaviors among demented elderly patients. Learning concepts of conditioning and reinforcement may not be well known by staff that nonetheless are interested in finding ways to improve their working conditions. Teaching ways of how to effectively manage behavior of patients is a key step toward securing cooperation of staff in implementing future interventions. Secondly, to communicate with staff from various disciplines, and to be taken seriously, the researcher must become familiar and knowledgeable about diagnostic categories, particularly the dementias and common neurological disorders, geriatric pharmacology, discharge procedures, prototypically used therapies, prostheses, etcetera. Only then can the applied researcher effectively interface with the system, contribute as a resource to the facility, and find interventions that will actually be used within that system, or attempt to change the system.

Finally, to involve staff in the research endeavor, Lichtenberg (1994) recommended that, if possible, the researcher participate in regular staff meetings. The focus of such meetings is to address the psychosocial concerns of the residents as well as the staff. By bringing together staff, problems can be addressed collectively and new solutions found. Furthermore, the researcher can serve as a resource to solve behavioral problems among individual patients thereby enhancing the overall credibility of the researcher and the project being implemented.

### Illustrative Example of a Research Project on Older Adults

*Case Examples.*   In order to illustrate how to implement (in actual research contexts) many of the key points made thus far in this chapter, we now will present two "case examples" of recently completed intervention projects that should concretize these points. The first was conducted in an outpatient clinical research mental health center; the second is a community-based study. By contrasting these two very different kinds of settings, we hope to inform the reader about the distinct advantages and disadvantages of each.

*Treatment of Late-Life Depression.*   In this project, our aim was to compare the effectiveness of three different treatments for depression among older adult outpatients: psychotherapy alone (it was a particular type of therapy, known as cognitive/behavioral therapy or CBT, as originally developed by Beck, Rush, Shaw, and Emery (1979), and modified for use with older adults by Gallagher-Thompson and Thompson (1996); an antidepressant medication alone (in this case it was desipramine, abbreviated DES, which was chosen because of its high safety factor [overdoses are unlikely] and low prevalence of anticholinergic side effects, such as dry mouth and constipation, which can cause poor compliance for taking the medication as directed), and finally, the combination of the two methods: CBT plus desipramine (called COMBO here, meaning that the patient received both treatments simultaneously).

When the study was first designed, several factors had to be considered before choosing the final interventions, including: What kind of psychotherapy would be most likely to be effective in older adults? Which particular antidepressant medication would be best tolerated by the majority of older persons? Should we recruit both men and women participants, or only one gender? How many participants should we enroll? What will be the key outcome measures? How many times should participants be assessed? What will be our criteria for success? (How will we determine that particular clients improved, or that one type of treatment was better than the others?)

To address these questions, besides doing a comprehensive literature review relevant to these issues, several expert consultants were retained as advisors. We consulted psychiatrists and psychologists with experience doing this kind of research with older adult patients and met with them frequently at the outset in order to get the benefit of the most current thinking in the field. This is highly recommended in the early stages because a great deal of useful information may not yet be available in the published literature. For example, several new measures existed to assess improvement in terms of expressing more positive (compared to negative) affect after treatment, as well as expressing increased quality of life. These measures were not published, but excellent preliminary data were available. Their inclusion greatly enriched the project and allowed us to think of outcomes in broader terms than simply *symptom improvement*.

The question of how many older adults had to be recruited in order to adequately test the major question—namely, which treatment (if any) would be the most effective of the three?—was more complex to address because of several issues. A key one was the length of this particular study: weekly treatment sessions were offered for 20 consecutive weeks, with periodic follow-up appointments for a full year. In addition, there was an option for patients to be crossed over from one type of treatment to another after completion of the intensive 20-week phase *if* they had not responded well to whichever "arm" of the project they had been assigned to initially. Although this was considered an "elegant" design by the consultants (and the project's principal investigators), in some respects, it was not very practical for many older adults, and it made recruitment much more difficult than the investigators had anticipated. Many older adults who called us directly, or who were referred by their primary care physician, reported that the length and complex requirements of this study were very daunting and discouraged them from signing up. When one considers what they were expected to do—namely, attend both treatment sessions and evaluation appointments regularly (plus have blood drawn periodically if they were receiving antidepressant medication) and complete multiple self-report questionnaires regarding their symptoms and other issues thought to be relevant to outcome—it is not surprising that we needed to screen about 800 older adults on the phone in order to actually enroll a total of about 125 patients. Future research in this field needs to weigh the pros and cons of length and breadth versus shorter and perhaps more focused treatment for depression (and other mental health problems). For the interested reader, results of this study can be found in Thompson, Coon, Gallagher-Thompson, Sommer, and Koin (in press).

## REDUCING DISTRESS IN HISPANIC/LATINO FAMILY CAREGIVERS OF RELATIVES WITH DEMENTIA

This project was conducted and carried out in a variety of community settings that served Hispanic older adults and their families in the San Francisco Bay area, covering a territory spanning over 100 miles. The purpose of this research program initially was to increase our understanding of what caregiving for a relative with dementia meant to a broad range of Hispanic/Latino family caregivers. This group has traditionally been understudied in caregiving research, despite the fact that it is expected to grow by over 500% in the next 20 years. Minority elders, overall, are living longer; therefore, the likelihood that they will develop some type of dementia, and that their families will become long-term caregivers, is increasing as well (Gallagher-Thompson et al., 2000).

To understand how both dementia and the caregiving process are thought about and coped with by Latino families, we were advised by our Latino health professional colleagues to first conduct a series of focus groups in Spanish, with bicultural facilitators. This information was integrated with insights from the multicultural advisory board (consisting of a variety of professionals working with Latino families in different community service programs) and led to the design of a very straightforward, relatively brief (eight sessions) small-group intervention program, which focused on two key elements: (1) education about dementia itself (which we found out is an unfamiliar, highly stigmatizing illness to most Latinos, who view it as a mental illness, not a brain disease; and (2) an opportunity to learn new methods for coping with caregiving stress: for example, learning how to challenge pessimistic thoughts about their loved one's behavioral problems. If the care-receiver keeps asking, "When is lunch?," and the caregiver feels that she must repeatedly answer (becoming frustrated at having to do this many times), she may be thinking to herself: "He is just doing this to get my goat; I can't believe he can't remember something so simple!" She can learn how to replace the inaccurate thought and negative attribution here with a different view that is more adaptive for the situation; for example, "He can't help it; it's the dementia talking. I would do best to stay calm and try to distract him, instead of continuing to answer, becoming frustrated with him and myself." At the conclusion of this 8-week program, participants reported that both elements were very helpful to them, but the program was too short. They wanted more content about dementia and more opportunities to build coping skills. So next we developed longer programs of 10 and 12 sessions; further research found that the 10-session small group program was the most cost effective. Finally, we experimented with including different content, some of which was retained and some deleted when we put together the final "package" for our recently completed clinical trial, which enrolled 110 Latino caregivers and provided treatment and follow-up to them for a 3-year period.

Note that the early work in this program did not follow a randomized clinical trial methodology, as was the case in the first example. Rather, it consisted of several feasibility studies to determine what the intervention should be, how it should be delivered (what format: group or individual?) and what cultural beliefs and attitudes might impact participation. Also, because we were working with a new population, we had to understand the many practical issues that affected both recruitment and retention for this group. For example, during the feasibility phase, we learned that we had to provide transportation to the site where the intervention program was held in order to reduce the number of absences and late arrivals. We also found that we needed to conduct the research (data collection) interviews in participants' homes, rather than require them to come to our offices, in order to get the information we needed in the least intrusive manner. Another issue was that of "elder sitting"—who would care for the demented relative while the primary caregiver attended the intervention program? When we first began, we did not build this cost into the budget, but when we were finally able to conduct a more rigorous clinical trial, this was a substantial budgetary expense (for which we were prepared, given our experience while doing the pilot or preliminary work just described). Clearly, time invested *before* the actual clinical trial was initiated was time very well spent.

The two case examples provided touch on several key issues to consider when contemplating mental health research with older adults, including:

1. The topic itself (What new question does your project address? Diagnostic concerns? Treatment options? Subgroup differences in response to treatment?);

2. The population to be served (Will your project include both men and women, or is there a legitimate reason to limit the study to one or the other gender? If you are designing a project for family caregivers, will

adult sons and daughters be included, or only aged spouses? How will ethnic and cultural diversity be represented?);

3. The setting (Will your study take place in an inpatient psychiatric facility, an outpatient mental health clinic, a nursing home, or other extended care facility? Or will it be community based, in which case you need to find sites that are willing to cooperate and host the project);

4. How will participants be recruited? Will any financial incentives be used? What about practical "barriers" to research participation, such as transportation, ease of access, bilingual/bicultural staff (if appropriate) to conduct the program, etcetera;

5. Finally, what, in detail, will the intervention program actually consist of, and how will you measure its impact?

These latter questions are, of course, key to the success of your research. For example, in the second study, the content of the intervention evolved over time, whereas content was readily available before the inception of the first study. Outcome measures for both studies relied heavily on self-reports, but also used observer ratings of symptoms. Future research would do well to also include physiological measures, such as cortisol and other indices of stress, to determine if improvement in these two different arenas (psychological and physical functioning) are highly related to one another; by working on both, we should enrich elders' lives.

## SUMMARY

In this chapter, we outlined many of the issues and challenges involved in conducting research with older adults. However, it is important for researchers to remember that many older adults are eager to participate in research projects. If researchers modify their protocols to accommodate the specific needs of older subjects, and if they are willing to invest sufficient time to communicate effectively with older subjects regarding every aspect of the study being conducted, participation in research investigations can be a very positive and rewarding experience for the elderly.

## REFERENCES

Beck, Å. T., Rush, A. J., Shaw, B., Emery, G. (1979). *Cognitive therapy of depression*. New York: Guildford Press.

Coon, D., Rider, K., Gallagher-Thompson, D., & Thompson, L. (1999). Cognitive-behavioral therapy for the treatment of late-life distress. In M. Duff (Ed.), *Handbook of counseling and psychotherapy with older adults* (pp. 487–510). New York: Wiley.

Edelstein, B., & Semenchuck, E. (1996) Interviewing older adults. In L. Carstensen, B. Edelstein, & L. Dornbrand (Eds.), *The practical handbook of clinical gerontology* (pp 153–173). Thousand Oaks, CA: Sage Publications.

Evans, D. A., Funkenstein, H. H., Albert, M. S., Scherr, P. A., Cook, N. R., Chown, M. J., Hebert, L. E., Hennekens, C. H., & Taylor, V. (1989). Prevalence of Alzheimer's disease in a community population of older persons. *Journal of American Medical Association, 262*, 2551–2556.

Gallagher-Thompson, D., Arean, P., Coon, D. W., Menendez, A., Takagi, K., Haley, W., Arguelles, T., Rubert, M., Lowenstein, D., & Szapocznik, J. (2000). Development and implementation of intervention strategies for culturally diverse caregiving populations. In R. Schulz (Ed.), *Handbook on dementia caregiving* (pp. 151–185). New York: Springer.

Gallagher-Thompson, D., & Thompson, L. W. (1996). Applying cognitive behavior therapy to the common psychological problems of later life. In S. Zarit, & B. Knight (Eds.), *Psychotherapy and aging: Effective interventions with older adults* (pp. 61–82). Washington, DC: American Psychological Association.

Joynt, R. J., & Greenlaw, J. (1993). The informed consent. In N. Canal, V. C. Hachinski, G. McKhann, & M. Franceschi (Eds.), *Guidelines for drug trials in memory disorders* (pp. 7–12). New York: Raven Press.

Katzman, R., & Fox, P. (1999). The world-wide impact of dementia. Projections of prevalence and costs. In R. Mayeaux & Y. Christen (Eds.), *Epidemiology of Alzheimer's disease: From gene prevention* (pp. 1–17). New York: Springer-Verlag.

Kraemer, H. C., Yesavage, J. A., Taylor, J. L., & Kupfer, D. (2000). How can we learn about developmental processes from cross-sectional studies, or can we? *American Journal of Psychiatry, 157*(2), 163–171.

La Rue, A. (1992). *Aging and neuropsychological assessment.* New York: Plenum.

Lichtenberg, P. (1994). *A guide to psychological practice in geriatric long-term care.* New York: Haworth Press.

Nussbaum, P. D. (1997). *Handbook of neuropsychology and aging.* New York: Plenum Press.

Rybarczyk, B., Gallagher-Thompson, D., Rodman, J., Zeiss, A., Gantz, F., & Yesavage, J. (1992). Applying cognitive-behavioral psychotherapy to the chronically ill elderly: Treatment issues and case illustration. *International Journal of Psychogeriatrics, 4*, 127–140.

Thompson, L. W., Coon, D. W., Gallagher-Thompson, D., Sommer, B. R., & Koin, D. (in press). Comparison of desipramine and cognitive/behavioral therapy in the treatment of elderly outpatients with mild to moderate dementia. *American Journal of Geriatric Psychiatry.*

United Nations. (1998). World population prospects: The 1996 revision. Washington, DC: Population division of the Department of Economic and Social Affairs of the United Nations Secretariat.

Vernon, M. (1989). Assessment of persons with hearing loss. In T. Hunt & C. Lindley (Eds.), *Testing older adults: A reference guide for geropsychological assessments.* Austin: PRO-ED.

Yesavage, J. A., Taylor, J. L., Mumenthaler, M. S., Noda, A., & O'Hara, R. (1999). Relationship of age and simulated flight performance. *Journal of the American Geriatrics Society 47*, 819–823.

# Author Index

# Subject Index

**479**